COLORADO

TERRI COOK

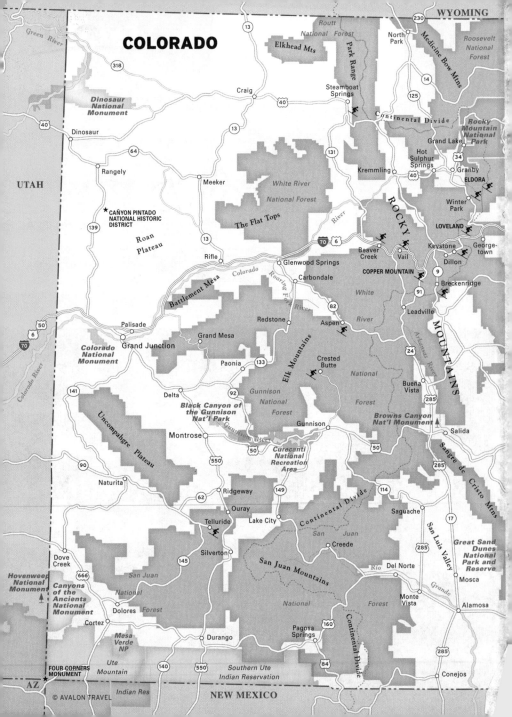

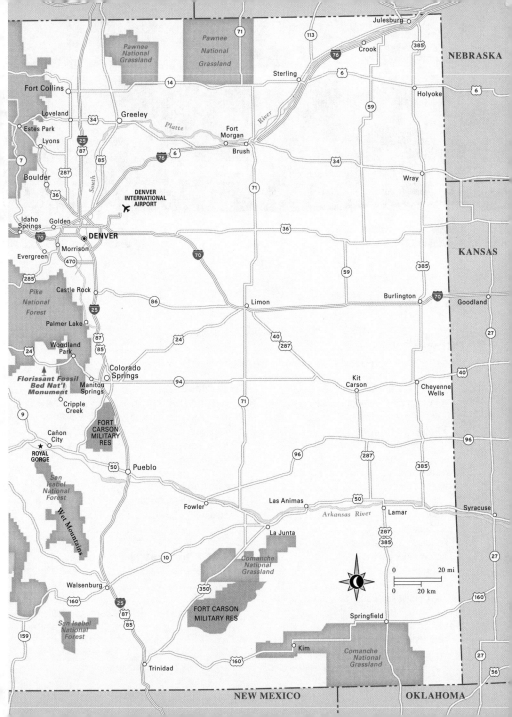

Contents

DISCOVER
Colorado

I n 1806, after weeks of trudging west across the Great Plains, Lieutenant Zebulon Pike spotted what he thought was a small cloud on the horizon. As he drew closer, a mighty snow-covered peak materialized, followed by the jagged outline of the Rocky Mountain range. Pike had never seen mountains this high. His descriptions of the peak's majesty fueled the country's imagination, imprinting the mountain—later named for him— on the public consciousness and ultimately inspiring the song *America the Beautiful*.

These lofty thoughts were on mind when I drove westward across I-70 for the first time. As the miles ticked by, I eagerly scanned the horizon. When I finally saw the majestic mountains, I too was astonished—both by how high they tower over the plains and the gleaming cities at their base. Living in Colorado, I've come to understand that the Rockies are much more than a backdrop; they are the pulse that sets the rhythm of life, dictating our relaxed pace and weekend escapes, creating our famously variable weather, and underpinning much of the economy.

Clockwise from top left: cyclists near Aspen; colorful mountain wildflowers; a marmot peeks out; golden aspen and pines in the San Juan Mountains; river runners in the Royal Gorge; Black Canyon of the Gunnison National Park.

Colorado is an environment for exploration and adventure. Relax in unspoiled nature and its primeval rhythms. Gaze at forever views of craggy, snow-capped peaks. Get goose bumps listening to the bugling of a bull elk drift through the crisp morning air. You'll want to actively experience Colorado's knee-deep powder, plunge down its frothing white-water rapids, and soak away in steaming hot springs. Delve into its unparalleled history—from the ancients who constructed Mesa Verde's pueblos to the hardy souls who pioneered its creaking ghost towns.

At the end of each adventure-filled day, savor the fresh flavors at a farm-to-table restaurant, sample some of the state's sudsy microbrews, and then slumber in a luxurious lodge or camp beneath a dark sky teeming with brilliant stars.

Each and every day, Colorado has something wonderful on tap.

Clockwise from top left: towers in Canyons of the Ancients National Monument; mountain goats on Quandary Peak; Colorado in autumn; Crested Butte Mountain Resort.

DINOSAUR
NATIONAL MONUMENT
FOSSIL BONE QUARRY

Planning Your Trip

Where to Go

Denver

The Mile High City is Colorado's cosmopolitan core. Put your finger on its pulse in the lively **Lower Downtown**. In **Larimer Square,** the city's oldest block, **colorful art galleries** and bustling bars alternate with **neighborhood eateries.** Perched high on **Capitol Hill,** the state capitol's gleaming golden dome is a beacon for **historic sites** like the mile-high marker and a mansion that once belonged to the **Unsinkable Molly Brown.** With seven professional **sports teams** and the nation's second-largest **theater** complex, there's always a show or game to catch. Above it all, to the west, is what truly sets Denver apart: the stunning backdrop of jagged, **snow-covered peaks.**

Boulder and the Northern Front Range

North of Denver, the foothills rise dramatically above a series of laid-back towns. Here **colleges, theaters,** and **brewpubs** are steps from high-tech start-ups, **ethnic restaurants,** and **eclectic shopping,** with mountain wilderness just slightly farther away. Each foothills town has its own distinct personality. Bohemian **Boulder,** home of the **University of Colorado,** thrives on its reputation as the brainiest, fittest, and foodiest city in the state. Nearby, **historic mountain towns** brimming with lore offer secluded inns, lesser-known trails, and quaint antique stores. Artsy **Fort Collins,** another active college town, is a beer and biking hub with a charming old town.

Camping is popular in Dinosaur National Monument.

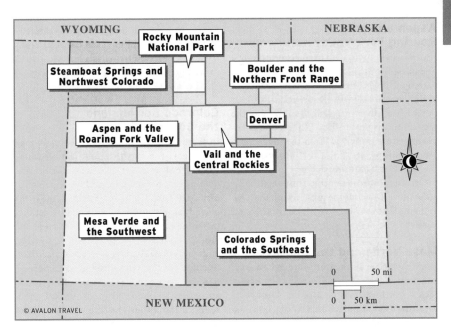

WYOMING

Rocky Mountain
National Park

NEBRASKA

Steamboat Springs and
Northwest Colorado

Boulder and the
Northern Front Range

Aspen and the
Roaring Fork Valley

Denver

Vail and the
Central Rockies

Mesa Verde and
the Southwest

Colorado Springs
and the Southeast

0   50 mi

0   50 km

NEW MEXICO

© AVALON TRAVEL

Rocky Mountain National Park

Rocky Mountain National Park encompasses
415 square miles of natural wonders. With
more than 100 sparkling alpine lakes, lush
meadows teeming with grazing elk, and a
glaciated landscape of deep valleys nestled
beneath soaring summits, the park is awe-
inspiring in its splendor—and its size. Driving
Trail Ridge Road, the park's signature scenic
drive, is the ultimate Rocky Mountain high;
its winding, hairpin curves traverse the high
tundra before crossing the lofty Continental
Divide.

Steamboat Springs and Northwest Colorado

The northwest is filled with wide-open spaces
and varied terrain. Here, some of America's
largest herds of wild horses gallop across
vast plateaus, and untamed rivers offer fantastic fly-fishing and white-water rafting.

Dinosaur National Monument preserves
some of the state's enthralling prehistoric past,
while smaller sites protect petroglyphs and
snippets of Native American and pioneer-era
history. The region's unpretentious anchor is
Steamboat Springs, where cowboy boots
and pickup trucks are standard gear, along with
downhill skis.

Vail and the Central Rockies

The center—and soul—of Colorado lies in the
knot of high mountains and deep, narrow
valleys along I-70 just west of the Continental
Divide. In winter this region is famous for
its bluebird skies, fluffy snow, and glittering
ski resorts, especially Vail. Other ski areas,
like Breckenridge, Keystone, and Copper
Mountain, serve as more down-to-earth
hubs for winter and summer recreation, from
snowshoeing into mountain huts to sailing,
biking, and hiking.

Aspen and the Roaring Fork Valley

Aspen is a **ski town** with deep historical roots. The quest for wealth in this region dates back to the mid-1800s, when prospectors began wandering up the beautiful **Roaring Fork River** in search of silver and gold. **Aspen**—and the rest of this magical valley—still retain the enduring allure of riches. From the rugged, red mountaintops, steaming **hot springs,** and **sumptuous accommodations** to a lovingly preserved **mining-era opera house,** this valley seamlessly blends the present with the past, and **small-town charm** with **sophisticated luxury.**

Mesa Verde and the Southwest

Snow-covered peaks, **aspen-studded mesas,** and earthy **sandstone plateaus** all characterize southwestern Colorado. **Ancestral Puebloan ruins** and modern tribal parks echo the area's long human occupation, while remote **mining cabins** resonate with the remnants of shattered dreams. In the north of this region, the gurgling **Gunnison River** has carved a canyon so deep and sheer that parts of it receive just minutes of sunlight each day. Upstream, friendly **Crested Butte** has a historic district so well preserved that it's called **Colorado's** "last great ski town."

Colorado Springs and the Southeast

In southeast Colorado, purple mountain majesty meets the **high desert plains** where **Pikes Peak** rises straight from the prairie, dominating the landscape and the region's history. At its base, **Colorado Springs,** the state's second-largest city, has a wealth of attractions, including the rocky fins of the **Garden of the Gods,** the **U.S. Olympic Training Center,** and the mineral waters in artsy **Manitou Springs.** To the west, adventurers come from near and far to run the river's **frothing rapids** and scale Colorado's **highest peak.** Farther south, a flat valley the size of Connecticut stretches as far as the eye can see. On its eastern edge, a field of **giant sand dunes** abuts the snow-capped **Sangre de Cristo Range,** creating one of the state's most dramatic views.

When to Go

Colorado is a year-round destination with seasonal activities that typically influence when is the best time to visit. The majority of guests arrive either during **ski season,** which runs from Thanksgiving through early April, or during the **summer.**

Winter

Ski towns such as **Aspen, Vail,** and **Steamboat Springs** are the most crowded and expensive in winter, particularly during the Thanksgiving, Christmas, Martin Luther King Jr., and Presidents Day holidays. The snow is often better, and the slopes less crowded, in **March** and **early April.** Except for Aspen, the ski towns are nearly deserted during the post-skiing "mud season" (late winter to early spring) before picking up again in July.

Spring

Spring is a wonderful time to visit with frequent flocks of migrating sandhill cranes and warm, sunny days perfect for seeing the first vibrant wildflowers. However, the **weather is notoriously fickle,** and spring often brings raging **blizzards** that can disrupt travel plans.

Longs Peak in summer

Summer

By early summer, the highest roads and **mountain passes are open,** offering unparalleled opportunities to drive **Trail Ridge Road,** view wildlife, attend **music and food festivals,** and bike, raft, and fish to your heart's content. Although the days can be hot, the humidity is low and the temperatures are comfortable at night.

Autumn

Autumn, when the mountains are carpeted with **golden aspen trees,** is my favorite season in the Centennial State. This is an ideal time to explore **Mesa Verde'**s delicate ruins, hit the trail, and bask in the sun's last warm rays at an outdoor café before Mother Nature starts her cycle anew.

The Best of Colorado

This two-week tour offers enough time to hit many of the highlights while still enjoying a few lesser-known spots. The route involves a lot of driving, but the scenery is gorgeous and diverse, and you'll still have time for hiking, wine-tasting, and visiting ancient ruins. This route divides into a northern and a southern loop. If you only have a week, you can return to Denver from Grand Junction after Day 7.

Northern Loop

Day 1

Arrive at Denver International Airport and transfer to one of the Mile High City's cozy bed-and-breakfasts. Stroll through the **Denver Botanic Gardens** or shop in bustling **Larimer Square,** the city's oldest block, before enjoying a cold craft beer at **Wynkoop Brewing Company,** Colorado's first brewpub, and a farm-to-table dinner at **The Kitchen Denver** or juicy steaks at **Elway's.**

Day 2

Head north to Boulder and hike in **Chautauqua Park** then drive up **Flagstaff Mountain** for gorgeous panoramic views. Sip a cup of tea seated at a *topchan* at the **Boulder Dushanbe Teahouse** before shopping and people-watching along the **Pearl Street Mall.** Settle into a downtown hotel and dine at **Frasca Food and Wine** or **The Med.**

the view along Trail Ridge Road

Day 3

Drive through artsy Lyons en route to **Estes Park,** the gateway to **Rocky Mountain National Park.** Look for bighorn sheep at **Sheep Lakes** and elk in **Moraine Park,** then tuck into a picnic lunch near sparkling **Bear Lake.** Take an afternoon hike followed by a casual dinner in downtown Estes Park.

Day 4

Fuel up at **Notchtop Bakery & Cafe** before re-entering the park to drive the winding hairpins along **Trail Ridge Road,** one of Colorado's most spectacular drives. Stop at the vista points, trailheads, and **Alpine Visitor Center** along the way, then spend the night at the rustic **Grand Lake Lodge,** perched high above **Grand Lake,** a year-round recreation hub on the west side.

Day 5

Head northwest to Colorado's cowboy corner, anchored by the ranching-turned-recreation town of **Steamboat Springs.** Spend the afternoon hiking or horseback riding through the **Mount Zirkel Wilderness Area** or zip-lining near **Rabbit Ears Pass.** Shop for Western wear at **F. M. Light & Sons** before savoring a classic Italian dinner at **Mambo Italiano** or **Mazzola's Italian Restaurant.**

Day 6

Get up early to visit **Dinosaur National Monument,** a three-hour drive west. Veer briefly into Utah to visit the **Dinosaur Quarry's** famous bones then drive to the **Echo Park Overlook** to see the gorgeous valley where the Yampa and Green Rivers meet. Camp in the monument or bunk down in **Craig.**

Day 7

Search for ancient pictographs in the **Cañyon Pintado National Historic District** en route to **Grand Junction.** Pedal, hike, or raft through the beautiful high-desert scenery or explore the dizzying heights of the world's largest flat-topped mountain along the **Grand Mesa Scenic and Historic Byway.** Save time for a **wine-tasting** in nearby **Palisade** before enjoying fresh farm-to-table fare at **Bin 707 Foodbar.**

the Colorado Welcome Center in Dinosaur

historical Larimer Square

Bridal Veil Falls in Telluride

Southern Loop

Day 8

After breakfast in Grand Junction at **Main Street Bagels,** visit the sandstone towers and hidden crannies of **Colorado National Monument.** View the fossil treasures at the **Dinosaur Journey Museum** before another **wine-tasting** and an overnight in or near Grand Junction.

Day 9

Head southeast to view the sheer, dark walls of **Black Canyon of the Gunnison National Park** before driving south to **Ouray.** Enjoy dinner in the historic downtown followed by a decadent dessert at **Mouse's Chocolates** and a relaxing soak in the **Ouray Hot Springs.**

Day 10

In the morning, take a jeep tour to wildflower-filled **Yankee Boy Basin,** then drive to **Telluride** and enjoy a leisurely lunch in the historic downtown. Soak up the scenery by riding the free, year-round **gondola** up to the mountain village or hiking to beautiful **Bridal Veil Falls.** Check in at the historic **Madeline Hotel,** then walk to **La Marmotte** for dinner.

Day 11

Leave early for the stunning drive through the **San Juan Mountains** and down to the sweeping sandstone landscape around **Cortez.** Visit the **Anasazi Heritage Center** before exploring the twisting chasms and ancient pueblos in **Canyons of the Ancients National Monument.** Top off your day with an icy margarita and delicious Mexican food at **Pepperhead Restaurant.**

Day 12

Spend the day exploring **Mesa Verde National Park.** Arrive early at the visitor center to snag tickets to **Balcony House** or **Cliff Palace,** then head to **Chapin Mesa** to visit the archaeological

Colorado is a top skiing and snowboarding destination, with diverse terrain, some of the nation's largest drops, and impressively long seasons. Here are some of the top resorts.

- **Arapahoe Basin:** Although it can be cold and windy, this venerable resort has some of the state's steepest and hardest runs, as well as the longest season (page 256).

- **Aspen:** With four nearby mountains to choose from and all the luxurious trappings, Aspen is a destination unto itself (page 268).

- **Beaver Creek:** Known for its luxurious ski-in, ski-out accommodations and attentive customer service, Beaver Creek is an exclusive resort with many excellent runs (page 226).

- **Copper Mountain:** The state's best laid-out mountain neatly separates skiers of varying abilities and offers reasonably priced lift tickets and less-crowded slopes (page 256).

- **Crested Butte:** Colorado's "last great ski town" offers a world-class mountain as well as a charming historic downtown to enjoy an après-ski dinner or drink (page 320).

- **Steamboat Springs:** Feet of champagne powder and superb glade skiing make Steamboat an ideal destination for intermediate and advanced skiers (page 182).

- **Telluride:** You just might spot Oprah Winfrey, Jerry Seinfeld, or another celeb as you cruise down the slopes of Colorado's most remote ski resort (page 327).

riding the chairlift

- **Vail:** The queen of glitz and glamour, Vail is also America's biggest mountain. Its 3,450 feet of vertical drop, 195 runs, 31 lifts, and great ski and board school make it a perfect choice for groups and skiers of every ability (page 216).

- **Winter Park:** Winter Park is a large, family-friendly resort that can be visited on a day trip from Denver (page 78).

museum and drive the scenic **Mesa Top Loop Road.** End your day in lively **Durango** with dinner at the **Steamworks Brewing Company.**

Day 13

Board the historic **Durango & Silverton Narrow Gauge Railroad** for an all-day outing in the heart of the rugged San Juan Mountains. While in **Silverton,** explore quaint shops and

colorful mining-era buildings before returning to Durango for a second night.

Day 14

It's a six-hour drive to Denver via U.S. 160 and U.S. 285. Stop for lunch at **Little Red Hen Bakery** in **Salida** and stretch your legs at **Red Rocks Amphitheatre.** Settle into your downtown hotel, then enjoy dinner and live music in **LoDo.**

A Taste of the Wild West

Once a sleepy outpost on the Western frontier, Colorado became a hive of activity in the late 1800s after gold was discovered in its clear, cold streams. Fortune seekers flocked here, as did gun-slinging outlaws and other colorful characters who profoundly influenced the state's history. The new arrivals laid the foundation for the state's largest cities as well as its quaint Victorian mountain towns. History buffs can explore old forts, gaze at gleaming gold, sashay into old saloons, and even wash down Old West grub with historic cocktails. Every corner of the state hosts a nugget of history, but due to the long driving distances, you're better off limiting your explorations to one or two regions at a time.

Denver

Tour the restored mansion at the **Molly Brown House Museum,** then learn about the West's African American cowboys at the **Black American West Museum & Heritage Center.** After lunch, visit the **Denver Museum of Nature and Science** to view sparkling samples of gold.

The Denver Foothills

The West lives on in the town of **Golden,** home of the **Buffalo Bill Museum and Grave** (where he may—or may not—be buried), the **Colorado Railroad Museum,** and the haunted saloon **Buffalo Rose.** Nearby **Morrison** offers a taste of the *really* Wild West—**Dinosaur Ridge,** where armored stegosaurus once roamed. Chow down at **The Fort,** a restaurant specializing in Old West food and drink, including historic cocktails.

Colorado Springs

Celebrate the skill of America's best calf ropers and bull riders at the **ProRodeo Hall of Fame and Museum of the American Cowboy,** then ride a horse through **Colorado Springs'** stunning **Garden of the Gods** or wander

Welcome to Golden.

More than Mountains

rock towers in Colorado National Monument

Colorado has a host of natural areas where you can admire some of Mother Nature's scenic wonders.

- **Black Canyon of the Gunnison National Park:** Peer over the edge of this awe-inspiring canyon in this quiet national park to gaze at the sparkling Gunnison River flowing almost half a mile below (page 315).

- **Browns Canyon National Monument:** This national monument highlights the frothing Arkansas River and its pristine canyon, a beacon for anglers, white-water rafters, photographers, and hikers (page 377).

- **Canyons of the Ancients National Monument:** This lesser-known gem harbors the nation's largest concentration of archaeological sites, as well as inspiring biking and hiking trails (page 343).

- **Colorado National Monument:** Bike, hike, or drive through this pristine wilderness of twisting canyons, sloping slickrock, and sandstone towers looming above pinyon- and juniper-dotted slopes (page 309).

- **Dinosaur National Monument:** This remote monument features the remains of Jurassic giants and a beautiful valley where two of the Colorado River's most important tributaries meet (page 199).

- **Eldorado Canyon State Park:** This beautiful canyon near Boulder boasts streamside picnicking, angling, hiking, and world-class rock climbing (page 114).

- **Garden of the Gods:** Drive or hike among the rocky fins while enjoying dramatic views of Pikes Peak far above (page 364).

- **Great Sand Dunes National Park and Preserve:** This 150,000-acre park protects the continent's tallest sand dunes, which are backdropped by towering summits of the snow-capped Sangre de Cristo Mountains (page 381).

- **Royal Gorge:** The Arkansas River has carved a mighty gorge 10 miles long and up to 1,200 feet high. Explore its depths via an excursion train or a soaring suspension bridge (page 381).

through Old Colorado City, the Territory of Colorado's first capital. Delve further into the past at the Old Colorado History Center or visit historic Bent's Old Fort National Historic Site along the mountain branch of the Santa Fe Trail, two hours southeast. Take a detour to serve some time at the Museum of Colorado Prisons in Cañon City. At night, rustle up some grub at the Colorado Mountain Brewery, located in a beautifully restored railroad roundhouse.

Steamboat Springs

Known for its Western-themed Hot Air Balloon Rodeo and Wild West Air Fest, Steamboat Springs is also the home of the Tread of Pioneers Museum, which tells the story of local outlaw Harry Tracy, who once ran with Butch Cassidy. While in town, saddle up a steed at one of the many local ranches, shop for cowboy boots at F. M. Light & Sons, ski with former Olympian Billy Kidd, and pamper yourself at the Vista Verde Guest Ranch.

Roaring Fork Valley

Discover Aspen's historical roots at the Wheeler Opera House and Wheeler Stallard Museum, both built by a department store-turned-mining entrepreneur. In summer, bike or drive to the eerie ghost town of Independence, where miners caught in the state's worst blizzard once dismantled their homes to make skis, which they used to escape. Farther north, soak in the historic hot springs in the railroad hub of Glenwood Springs.

Summer in the Rockies

Summer is prime time for those who enjoy the high country. The central Rockies—with their stunning scenery, close proximity to Denver, and outstanding year-round recreation—are the ideal place to taste the state's alpine grandeur while still leaving plenty of time for many other activities on offer. Take this trip between Memorial Day and early November, when Independence Pass is open.

Day 1

Arrive at Denver International Airport and transfer to your hotel downtown. Visit the State Capitol Building to see the city's celebrated mile-high marker, then enjoy an unforgettable view of the Rockies from City Park or the top of the Ferris wheel at Elitch Gardens before heading to LoDo for dinner.

Day 2

Drive west on I-70 into the Rocky Mountains, stopping in the colorful, mining-era town of Idaho Springs to explore the Argo Gold Mill and Museum or the Phoenix Gold Mine.

Fill up with Mountain Pie pizza at Beau Jo's before driving the spectacular Mount Evans Scenic and Historic Byway, North America's highest paved road. Settle into your hotel in Breckenridge and enjoy drinks and dinner in the charming historic downtown.

Day 3

Fortify yourself at Cuppa Joe and walk the Boreas Pass Road, or, if you're acclimated, rise with the sun and hike up Quandary Peak, one of Colorado's famous fourteeners. Next, drive over 10,662-foot Vail Pass to the town of Vail. Take a twilight stroll through the Betty Ford Alpine Gardens before relaxing over aperitifs at the Root & Flower Wine Bar and dining at Sweet Basil.

Day 4

Savor the mountain views while playing a round of golf, biking up Vail Pass, or shopping in Vail Village before eating lunch at The Little Diner. In the afternoon, drive an hour west to Glenwood Springs, stopping along

Fun in the Sun

Hikers enjoy the view from Mount Elbert.

Colorado is a mecca for summer outdoor recreation. Here are some of the best places for fun in the sun.

HIKING

Denver, Golden, and Vail all have walking trails. Intermediate options include trails in Boulder's Chautauqua Park. Rocky Mountain National Park has numerous trails—from easy strolls to backpacking a portion of the challenging Continental Divide Trail.

Climb the slopes of one of the state's fourteeners (peaks that rise above 14,000 feet in elevation). Quandary Peak, near Breckenridge, and Mount Elbert, near Leadville, are both relatively straightforward fourteeners.

BIKING

Colorado's classic routes include Flagstaff Mountain west of Boulder, Lookout Mountain in Golden, and many of the state's highest passes and pavement, including Trail Ridge Road, Vail Pass, and the Mount Evans Scenic and Historic Byway. Mountain bikers flock to Grand Junction, the start of Kokopelli's Trail, as well as Crested Butte.

WATER SPORTS

Popular areas for white-water rafting and kayaking include the Arkansas River, Clear Creek near Golden, the Colorado River by Glenwood Springs and Grand Junction, and the Yampa and Green Rivers in Dinosaur National Monument. Lake Dillon near Breckenridge, Grand Lake in Rocky Mountain National Park, and Blue Mesa Reservoir near Gunnison all offer sailing, stand-up paddle boarding, and angling.

GOLF

Lower your handicap at highly regarded courses designed by masters like Jack Nicklaus and Greg Norman, such as the Breckenridge Golf Club, the Beaver Creek Golf Club, or the Aspen Golf & Tennis Club. Near Denver, putt next to prehistoric dinosaur fossils at the Fossil Trace Golf Club.

the ghost town of Independence, high above Aspen

the way to hike up to **Hanging Lake** in gorgeous Glenwood Canyon. After exploring the downtown, walk to the **Glenwood Canyon Brewing Company** for dinner before watching the sunset while soaking in **Glenwood Hot Springs.**

Day 5

Drive south along the Roaring Fork River to **Aspen.** After checking into the **Limelight Hotel,** ride the bus up **Maroon Creek Valley** to see Colorado's most-photographed peaks— the crimson twin summits of the **Maroon Bells.** Go for a hike or return to Aspen and spend the rest of the day exploring the town's art galleries. For dinner, sample the sushi at

Matsuhisa or charcuterie and crepes at **La Creperie du Village.**

Day 6

Drive over the dizzying heights of 12,095-foot **Independence Pass,** stopping at **the Grottos** and the ghost town of **Independence.** After descending to the beautiful Arkansas River Valley, return to **Denver** via one of two routes: drive south for white-water rafting in **Browns Canyon National Monument;** or head north to historic **Leadville,** America's highest incorporated city, where colorful characters like **Horace** and **"Baby Doe" Tabor** and **Molly Brown** once struck it rich in the district's high-elevation mines.

Denver

Look for ★ to find recommended sights, activities, dining, and lodging.

Highlights

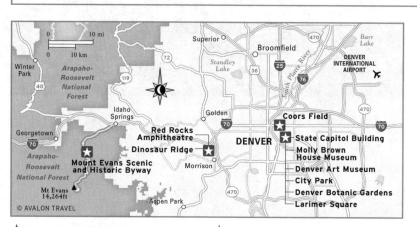

★ **State Capitol Building:** The glistening dome of Denver's most prominent landmark is plated with 200 ounces of 24-carat gold (page 30).

★ **Molly Brown House Museum:** Tour the House of Lions, the beautifully restored Victorian mansion of Denver's most famous resident (page 31).

★ **Denver Art Museum:** Its striking arrowhead-like Hamilton Building houses a massive collection of Native American art (page 32).

★ **City Park:** Denver's largest park hosts the Denver Zoo, the Denver Museum of Nature and Science, two lakes, free jazz concerts, and some of the very best views in town (page 36).

★ **Denver Botanic Gardens:** Stroll through a 24-acre urban oasis teeming with 34,000 different plants (page 37).

★ **Coors Field:** This retro purple-and-brown stadium, with its ensconcing eateries and bars, hums with energy (page 42).

★ **Larimer Square:** This spirited district bustles with colorful art galleries, exclusive boutiques, lively bars, and hip restaurants (page 47).

★ **Red Rocks Amphitheatre:** Perfect acoustics beneath this circle of stones make concerts unforgettable (page 68).

★ **Dinosaur Ridge:** Delve into Denver's prehistory with a remarkable series of dinosaur tracks, ancient ripple marks, and the first evidence of dinosaur courtship (page 68).

★ **Mount Evans Scenic and Historic Byway:** Drive the highest paved road in North America to the summit of beautiful Mount Evans, one of Colorado's 54 fourteeners (page 73).

Just as the dramatic backdrop of towering, snow-covered peaks dominates Denver's skyline, the city has strongly influenced Colorado's history and culture.

Its vibrant downtown played a key role in establishing Colorado as a state. Denver's rise to prominence began in the summer of 1858, when a party of prospectors from Oklahoma crossed the plains to reach the eastern Rockies' clear mountain streams. In early August, the group discovered gold near the spot where Cherry Creek flows into the South Platte River, the site of modern Denver's Confluence Park. Although the prospectors didn't find much gold, word of the strike spread like wildfire, sparking the Pikes Peak Gold Rush, named for a mountain that lay far to the south.

The prospectors could be forgiven for not knowing the local geography; until the mid-19th century, what is now Colorado had long been a sleepy outpost on the far-western fringes of the Kansas and Nebraska Territories. But after the Oklahomans struck gold, several groups quickly began to plat and build communities. On the east bank of Cherry Creek, General William Larimer laid out a town and named it after James Denver, the Kansas Territory Governor, in the hope of currying political favor. His town competed fiercely with neighboring Auraria in what evolved into bitter rivalry. Realizing that such animosity would ultimately harm everyone, the adversaries did a very Denver-like thing: they met on the bridge spanning Cherry Creek and resolved their dispute for the price of a barrel of whiskey.

Despite a number of booms and busts—including an attack by a Confederate Army from Texas, a devastating fire, and a major flood on Cherry Creek in 1864—Denver has remained Colorado's cultural, social, and political nerve center. After a survey discovered that one of the Capitol Building's steps is located exactly one mile above sea level, the city earned its famous nickname, the "Mile High City."

Today, Denver's river network is the basis for the city's metropolitan trail system, which makes it easy to travel between fascinating attractions, trendy restaurants, chic shopping districts, and thriving art outlets.

Previous: Downtown Denver; Sports Authority Field at Mile High. **Above:** The Capital Grille in Larimer Square.

Downtown

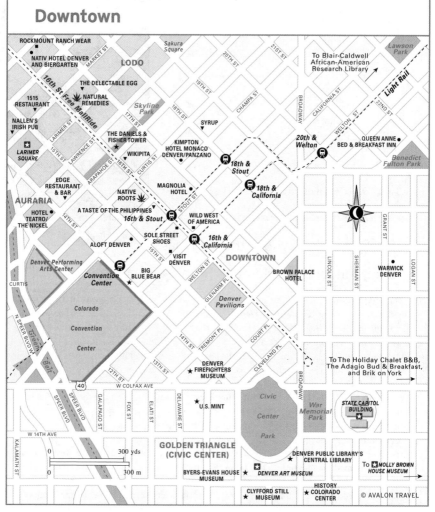

ROCKMOUNT RANCH WEAR

NATIV HOTEL DENVER AND BIERGARTEN

Sakura Square

To Blair-Caldwell African-American Research Library

LODO

Lawson Park

Light Rail

THE DELECTABLE EGG

1515 RESTAURANT

NATURAL REMEDIES

Skyline Park

NALLEN'S IRISH PUB

THE DANIELS & FISHER TOWER

SYRUP

20th & Welton

QUEEN ANNE BED & BREAKFAST INN

LARIMER SQUARE

KIMPTON HOTEL MONACO DENVER/PANZANO

WIKIPITA

18th & Stout

Benedict Fulton Park

AURARIA

EDGE RESTAURANT & BAR

NATIVE ROOTS

MAGNOLIA HOTEL

18th & California

HOTEL TEATRO/ THE NICKEL

A TASTE OF THE PHILIPPINES

16th & Stout

WILD WEST OF AMERICA

ALOFT DENVER

SOLE STREET SHOES

16th & California

Denver Performing Arts Center

VISIT DENVER

DOWNTOWN

Convention Center

BIG BLUE BEAR

BROWN PALACE HOTEL

WARWICK DENVER

CURTIS

Colorado Convention Center

Denver Pavilions

DENVER FIREFIGHTERS MUSEUM

To The Holiday Chalet B&B, The Adagio Bud & Breakfast, and Brik on York

W COLFAX AVE

U.S. MINT

Civic Center Park

War Memorial Park

STATE CAPITOL BUILDING

W 14TH AVE

0   300 yds
0   300 m

GOLDEN TRIANGLE (CIVIC CENTER)

BYERS-EVANS HOUSE MUSEUM

DENVER PUBLIC LIBRARY'S CENTRAL LIBRARY

DENVER ART MUSEUM

To MOLLY BROWN HOUSE MUSEUM

CLYFFORD STILL MUSEUM

HISTORY COLORADO CENTER

© AVALON TRAVEL

These highlights make Denver the state's cosmopolitan core and a highlight of any visit to Colorado.

PLANNING YOUR TIME

If you're planning to visit other parts of Colorado, **1-2 days** will still suffice to see the major downtown attractions, sample a couple of locally crafted beers, enjoy one of the city's innovative restaurants, and stroll along the busy 16th Street Mall.

To truly capture the city's flavor, spend at least **four days** to enjoy the LoDo nightlife, visit a few museums, watch a sports game, stroll or cycle one of the city's many paths, and take a day trip up Mount Evans. In the foothills, you can ski like a local, view ancient dinosaur tracks, or visit one of the historical Victorian mining towns.

In **winter,** the weather can be cold and icy, but it's also the time of the Christkindl Market, when Skyline Park is transformed into a quaint Bavarian village. In **summer,** the days can be hot, but the heat is usually broken by mid-afternoon thunderstorms. It's a great time to take a hike, dine outdoors, and cheer on the Rockies baseball team. Temperatures are usually mild in **spring and fall,** both great times to visit. However, occasional blizzards can still disrupt transportation during those milder seasons.

ORIENTATION

With a population of nearly three million, the Denver metro area hosts more than half of the state's population in a relatively compact area. The city is located on the western edge of the Great Plains, a short distance east of where the Rocky Mountain foothills rise sharply skyward. Locals often refer to the first wall of mountains, so clearly visible from downtown Denver, as the "Front Range." The mountains-to-plains transition runs north-south along the state's entire length, and this is where the majority of the population lives. If you remember that the mountains are to the west, it's easy to get your bearings.

Downtown Denver has a number of distinct neighborhoods. These include the lively **downtown** and Lower Downtown (**LoDo**), centered around Sports Authority Field at Mile High and Union Station; the **Highlands and Platte River Valley** includes the riverfront area near Confluence Park and the heavily Hispanic region to the northwest; the central-eastern **City Park and Environs** is home to the city's zoo, botanic gardens, nature and science museum, and its largest park. **Cherry Creek** is the city's most affluent district, and the site of a high-end mall.

West of the city, the **Denver foothills** host the cowboy town of Golden and the gorgeous Red Rocks Amphitheatre. As I-70 enters the Denver Rockies, it passes several old mining towns on its way to Denver's two closest ski areas, Winter Park and Loveland.

Sights

Denver's main attractions are located in a relatively compact area south of the South Platte River and east of Speer Boulevard, within walking distance of Union Station and Coors Field.

DOWNTOWN AND LODO
Sakura Square

Denver's "Little Tokyo" is **Sakura Square,** a small plaza located northeast of the Larimer Street/19th Street intersection in LoDo. Heavily populated by post-World War II internment-camp refugees and their offspring, this square hosts a Japanese market, restaurants, and apartments surrounding a statue of Ralph Carr, the former governor of Colorado. (Carr was the only elected official in the country who publicly apologized to the Japanese American community for their internment after they were released.) The plaza's centerpiece is the **Tri-State Denver Buddhist Temple** (1947 Lawrence St., 303/295-1844,

http://tsdbt.org, 8am-3pm daily), which offers frequent services and lectures.

Daniels & Fisher Tower

One of Denver's most distinctive landmarks is the 1910 **Daniels & Fisher Tower** (1601 Arapahoe St.), a 375-foot tower that rises above the pedestrian-friendly 16th Street Mall. When it was built next to a large department store in 1910, this tower was the highest building west of the Mississippi. Modeled after Saint Mark's bell tower in Venice's Piazza San Marco, the tower features four clocks, each 16 feet high. Although the rest of the building was knocked down in the 1970s, the tower was thankfully preserved and has been converted into an entertainment venue called Lannie's Clocktower Cabaret. Learn more about this landmark, and the people who saved it from the wrecking ball, on 90-minute walking tours of **Historic Denver**

LoDo

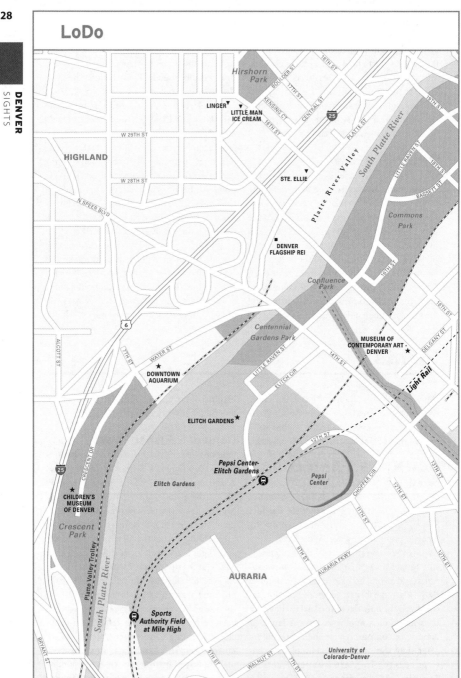

Hirshorn Park

18TH ST
17TH ST
BOULDER ST
KENSING CT
CENTRAL ST
19TH ST

LINGER ▼
▼ LITTLE MAN
ICE CREAM
18TH ST
PLATTE ST

W 29TH ST

HIGHLAND

W 28TH ST

STE. ELLIE ▼

Platte River Valley
South Platte River

LITTLE RAVEN ST
18TH ST
BASSETT ST

N SPEER BLVD

Commons Park

■ DENVER
FLAGSHIP REI

Confluence Park

16TH ST

18TH ST

Centennial Gardens Park

6

ALCOTT ST
17TH ST
WATER ST
LITTLE RAVEN ST
14TH ST
DELGANY ST

★ DOWNTOWN
AQUARIUM

MUSEUM OF
CONTEMPORARY ART -
DENVER ★

Light Rail

ELITCH GIR

ELITCH GARDENS ★

12TH ST

13TH ST

Pepsi Center-
Elitch Gardens
●

Pepsi Center

CHOPPER CIR

12TH ST

CRESCENT DR

25

Elitch Gardens

★ CHILDREN'S
MUSEUM
OF DENVER

11TH ST

12TH ST

Crescent Park

Platte Valley Trolley

5TH ST

AURARIA PKWY

AURARIA

● Sports
Authority Field
at Mile High

South Platte River

5TH ST
WALNUT ST
7TH ST

University of
Colorado-Denver

BRYANT ST

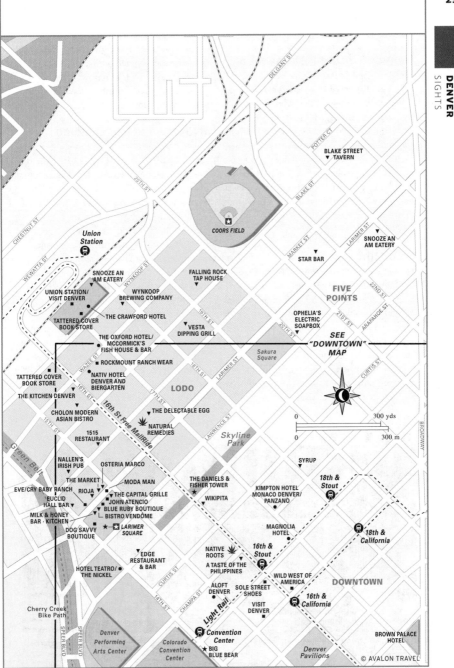

DELGANY ST

POTTER CT

BLAKE STREET ▼ TAVERN

BLAKE ST

MARKET ST

LARIMER ST

20TH ST

CHESTNUT ST

Union Station

★ COORS FIELD

SNOOZE AN AM EATERY ▼

STAR BAR ▼

WEWATTA ST

WYNKOOP ST

SNOOZE AN AM EATERY ▼

FALLING ROCK TAP HOUSE ▼

FIVE POINTS

22ND ST

UNION STATION/ VISIT DENVER

WYNKOOP BREWING COMPANY

19TH ST

OPHELIA'S ELECTRIC SOAPBOX ▼

21ST ST

ARAPAHOE ST

THE CRAWFORD HOTEL

TATTERED COVER BOOK STORE

VESTA DIPPING GRILL ▼

20TH ST

THE OXFORD HOTEL/ McCORMICK'S FISH HOUSE & BAR

SEE "DOWNTOWN" MAP

Sakura Square

CURTIS ST

ROCKMOUNT RANCH WEAR

WAZEE ST

18TH ST

LARIMER ST

TATTERED COVER BOOK STORE

NATIV HOTEL DENVER AND BIERGARTEN

17TH ST

LODO

THE KITCHEN DENVER

16TH ST

BROADWAY

CHOLON MODERN ASIAN BISTRO

16th St Free MallRide

THE DELECTABLE EGG ▼

NATURAL REMEDIES

LAWRENCE ST

1515 RESTAURANT ▼

15TH ST

Skyline Park

0   300 yds

0   300 m

Green Belt

NALLEN'S IRISH PUB ▼

OSTERIA MARCO

SYRUP ▼

THE MARKET ▼

MODA MAN

THE DANIELS & FISHER TOWER

18th & Stout

EVE/CRY BABY RANCH ▼

RIOJA ▼

THE CAPITAL GRILLE

KIMPTON HOTEL MONACO DENVER/ PANZANO

EUCLID HALL BAR ▼

JOHN ATENCIO

WIKIPITA

MILK & HONEY BAR · KITCHEN

BLUE RUBY BOUTIQUE

BISTRO VENDÔME

MAGNOLIA HOTEL

18th & California

DOG SAVVY BOUTIQUE

★ LARIMER SQUARE

EDGE RESTAURANT & BAR

NATIVE ROOTS

16th & Stout

A TASTE OF THE PHILIPPINES

CURTIS ST

HOTEL TEATRO/ THE NICKEL

WILD WEST OF AMERICA

DOWNTOWN

14TH ST

ALOFT DENVER

SOLE STREET SHOES

16th & California

Light Rail

CHAMPA ST

VISIT DENVER

Cherry Creek Bike Path

SPEER BLVD

SPEER BLVD

Denver Performing Arts Center

Colorado Convention Center

Convention Center

★ BIG BLUE BEAR

Denver Pavilions

BROWN PALACE HOTEL

© AVALON TRAVEL

Larimer Square (1420 Larimer St., 303/534-5288, www.historicdenver.org, 2pm Thurs. and Sat., $20).

Denver Firefighters Museum

The city's first firehouse now hosts the small **Denver Firefighters Museum** (1326 Tremont Pl., 303/892-1436, www.denverfirefightersmuseum.org, 10am-4pm Mon.-Sat., $7). Exhibits focus on the history of firefighting in Denver and include antique equipment such as an 1867 hand-drawn fire pumper, old lockers, and displays informing how protective clothing has evolved over time. Kids will delight in clambering aboard a fire engine, donning gear, and sliding down the old fire pole.

U.S. Mint

Denver's branch of the **U.S. Mint** (320 W. Colfax Ave., 303/405-4761, www.usmint.gov) is one of the federal government's four official places where it makes money—more than 50 million coins per day! Established in 1863 as an assay office, this facility was converted into a working mint in 1904. Today, this branch makes all denominations of circulating coins, as well as commemorative and uncirculated coin sets, and stores silver

bullion. The 45-minute **tour** (8am-3:30pm Mon.-Thurs., free) covers the steps involved in coin manufacturing and the mint's long history and ends at the gift shop, where you can purchase commemorative coins and other paraphernalia. Register online for tours far in advance, as space is limited. Weekday mornings have the most availability.

★ State Capitol Building

One of Denver's most familiar sights is the **State Capitol Building** (200 E. Colfax Ave., 303/866-2604, www.colorado.gov, tours 10am-3pm Mon.-Fri., free), whose glistening dome rises an impressive 272 feet high. Intentionally designed to mimic the U.S. Capitol, the building was constructed during the 1890s using beautiful native stone, including sparkling Yule Marble, quarried near Marble, Colorado (near Aspen), for the floors and a pink marble so rare that the entire supply, which came from the Pueblo area, was consumed in its construction.

The dome was originally made of copper, but over the years, it became so tarnished that it turned black. In 1908, officials decided to gild the copper plates with 200 ounces of 24-carat gold to commemorate the state's Gold Rush and to improve its appearance. In 2013,

the U.S. Mint

the State Capitol Building

the copper was once again replaced and regilded during a $17 million renovation. When the legislature is in session (usually mid-Jan.-mid-May), you can watch the action from the third-floor viewing area. There are also year-round tours of the building, which include a visit to the rotunda and a 99-step ascent to an observation area in the dome with panoramic views of downtown, the plains, and the Rockies. Tours start on the hour and include a visit to "Mr. Brown's Attic," an exhibit devoted to the state's early history, including the design and construction of the Capitol.

Civic Center Park

The grassy **Civic Center Park** (Colfax Ave., Bannock St., and 14th Ave.) is one of many civic improvements proposed in 1916 by Mayor Robert Speer. Today the park is the centerpiece of Denver's green spaces, with 25,000 square feet of blossoming flower beds and a restored Greek amphitheater that hosts concerts and other events, including A Taste of Colorado. The park is surrounded by cultural attractions and is such a hub of civic life that it has its own Facebook page and Twitter handle (@CivicCenterPark). You should, however, avoid walking around this area at night.

★ Molly Brown House Museum

One of Denver's most fascinating historic sites is the **Molly Brown House Museum** (1340 Pennsylvania St., 303/832-4092, www.mollybrown.org, 10am-4pm Mon.-Fri., 10am-3:30pm Sat., noon-3:30pm Sun., closed Mon. in winter, $8), the beautifully restored home of the *Titanic* survivor Margaret "Molly" Brown, who arrived in Leadville, Colorado, in 1886. After she and her husband, mining engineer J. J. Brown, struck it rich in the Little Johnny Mine, they moved to Denver. In 1894, they bought this beautiful, Queen Anne-style Capitol Hill home whose entrance was flanked by two stone lions. The home has been painstakingly restored to its circa-1910 appearance based on a series of photographs commissioned by Brown. The entryway is decorated with gold-painted Anaglypta wallpaper, a grand wooden staircase, and intricate stained glass windows. Next to the staircase, Brown's Black-a-Moor statue held a brass plate where visitors placed their cards. If the Browns were at home, the guests were entertained in the formal parlor, with its magnificent grand piano and fuzzy polar-bear rug. From the china-laden dining table to Margaret's emerald-green bedroom (where you can envision her packing for her next voyage), the museum brings alive this remarkable woman's story. After the couple eventually separated, Brown kept the home but rented it out and stayed in the Brown Palace Hotel whenever she was in town.

History Colorado Center

The **History Colorado Center** (1200 Broadway, 303/447-8679, www.historycolorado.org, 10am-5pm daily, $12) has six permanent exhibits that delve into every aspect of Colorado's fascinating history, from the

The Unsinkable Molly Brown

Just before midnight on the night of April 14, 1912, Margaret "Molly" Brown was reading a book in her cabin aboard the **RMS *Titanic*** when she felt a crash and was tossed to the floor. She donned a dressing gown and went out into the corridor. Everything seemed normal, so she returned to bed and continued reading. Shortly afterward, another passenger knocked on her door and cried, "Get your life preserver!" Brown rose, pulled on her warmest outfit, seven pairs of stockings, and a sable stole. She then strapped on her lifebelt, grabbed the blanket from the bed, and headed to the boat deck. The rest of the evening is a sad and familiar tale. On its maiden voyage from England to New York City, the world's largest passenger steamship struck an iceberg, which tore open compartments the length of a football field along the ship's side. The captain ordered the lifeboats lowered, but there weren't enough for all the passengers, and most were launched only partially full. Of the 2,223 people on board, only 710 lived, including the legendary Molly Brown. According to the book *Molly Brown: Unraveling the Myth* by Kristen Iversen, Brown shared her stockings with the other passengers and encouraged people to keep rowing to stay warm.

the former home of Molly Brown

After their lifeboat was rescued by the RMS *Carpathia,* Brown consoled other survivors and established and chaired a Survivors' Committee that raised tens of thousands of dollars to help people who had lost everything. The disaster was a pivotal event for Molly Brown; the instant celebrity vaulted the wealthy socialite into the upper echelons of society, offering an international platform to promote the causes near and dear to her heart, including a juvenile justice system, the rights of workers, and women's suffrage.

state's prehistoric inhabitants to old silver-mining towns to the history of ski jumping and its relevance to modern-day Colorado. Some of the exhibits also tackle tougher issues, like the Sand Creek Massacre and the Granada War Relocation Center, a Japanese internment camp in southeastern Colorado. The museum's signature display is the Time Machine, a 40-by-60-foot map of the state that uses screens, lasers, and other modern technology to bring Colorado's history alive.

Central Library

The Denver Public Library's 540,000-square-foot **Central Library** (10 W. 14th Ave., 720/865-1111, www.denverlibrary.org, 10am-8pm Mon.-Tues., 10am-6pm Wed.-Fri., 9am-5pm Sat., 1pm-5pm Sun., free) has a lot more

of interest to visitors than periodicals and books. It hosts a large Western history collection, 20,000 railroad photographs, and an extensive assortment of art from the American West, including a large landscape mural painted by Edward Ruscha. A smaller branch in Five Points, the **Blair-Caldwell African-American Research Library** (2401 Welton St., 720/865-2401, https://history.denverlibrary.org, noon-8pm Mon. and Wed., 10am-6pm Tues. and Thurs.-Fri., 9am-5pm Sat., free) also has a number of interesting exhibits, including one that follows the footsteps of African Americans who settled in the West.

★ Denver Art Museum

Although the **Denver Art Museum** (100 W. 14th Ave., 720/865-5000, http://

denverartmuseum.org, 10am-5pm Tues.-Thurs., 10am-8pm Fri., 10am-5pm Sat.-Sun., $10-13) was founded in 1923, it wasn't until 1971, with the completion of the castle-like North Building, that all of its collections could be displayed together. The museum is best known for its striking, geometric **Frederic C. Hamilton Building,** designed by architect Daniel Libeskind. Completed in 2006, this metallic, arrowhead-shaped building houses the contemporary, African, and Oceanic art collections. The museum typically displays more than a dozen rotating exhibits at any given time, as well as portions of its permanent collections, including an American Indian gallery whose holdings represent more than 100 North American tribes. The museum also has an extensive Western American art collection that includes *In the Enemy's Country* by Charles M. Russell, Frederic Remington's *The Cheyenne,* and *Long Jakes,* an oil painting by Charles Deas, as anchors.

Byers-Evans House Museum

The Italianate-style **Byers-Evans House Museum** (1310 Bannock St., 303/620-4933, www.historycolorado.org, 10am-4pm Mon.-Sat., 1pm-4pm Sun., $6) was built in 1883 by *Rocky Mountain News* publisher William Byers. A few years later, Byers sold the home to William G. Evans of the Denver Tramway Company. Evans' descendants lived here until 1981, when the house was donated to the Colorado Historical Society to be used as a museum. The elegant home has been restored to the 1912-1924 period and includes about 90 percent of the original furniture and household items. Guided **tours** run every 30 minutes.

Clyfford Still Museum

The **Clyfford Still Museum** (1250 Bannock St., 720/354-4880, https://clyffordstillmuseum.org, 10am-5pm Tues.-Thurs. and Sat.-Sun., 10am-8pm Fri., $10) features the iconoclastic work of one of the most important painters of the 20th century. Clyfford Still pioneered abstract expressionist art in the years following World War II. More than 3,100 paintings are displayed in a corrugated building built for this collection. The museum's paintings represent 95 percent of Still's work, making it possible to watch his art evolve from the 1920s through the 1970s.

the Denver Art Museum

The Capitol's Mile-High Marker

Although most of downtown Denver is located just below 5,280 feet in elevation, the Capitol Hill district is slightly higher because it's perched on a rocky knoll. As a result, the Capitol steps exceed this magic threshold, giving Denver its claim to mile-high fame. But exactly which step marks the mile-high elevation? On the building's west side, the words **One Mile Above Sea Level** are inscribed into the 15th step (counting from the bottom). This phrase was carved into the Colorado white granite in 1947 after several markers, including the original 1909 plaque, had been stolen. But in 1969, a survey by some engineering students from Colorado State University showed that the inscription had been placed several steps too low, so a new brass benchmark was attached to the 18th step. The situation changed again in 2013, when even more precise measurements determined that the second marker had been placed just over three feet too high. This time, a new benchmark depicting the Rocky Mountains was affixed to the 13th step. Just how long the 13th step remains the lucky one, however, remains to be seen.

HIGHLANDS AND PLATTE RIVER VALLEY

Northwest of the downtown core, these neighborhoods are centered on the South Platte and Cherry Creek Rivers, which join in the popular Confluence Park on the west edge of LoDo. The Hispanic neighborhoods to the northwest host a number of excellent restaurants and a wonderful museum dedicated to Latino art.

Museum of Contemporary Art Denver

The stated goal of the **Museum of Contemporary Art Denver** (1485 Delgany St., 303/298-7554, http://mcadenver.org, noon-7pm Tues.-Thurs., noon-9pm Fri., 10am-5pm Sat.-Sun., $8) is to "promote creative experimentation with art and ideas." This hits you with an eye-catching "bleeding heart" sculpture, *Toxic Schizophrenia,* mounted beside the museum's entrance. Everything about this museum is modern—from its sleek, glassy exterior to its thought-provoking exhibits by mostly Colorado artists. The museum's rooftop café is a great place to enjoy amazing city views along with lunch or cocktails.

Confluence Park

Confluence Park (2250 15th St.) surrounds the spot where Cherry Creek joins the South Platte River. It was here, back in 1858, that prospectors discovered gold and sparked the

Pikes Peak Gold Rush. Today the park is a playground for sunbathers, kayakers, runners, walkers, and cyclists, as well as the home of a free summer concert series on Thursday evenings.

Downtown Aquarium

The **Downtown Aquarium** (700 Water St., 303/561-4450, www.aquariumrestaurants. com, 10am-9pm Sun.-Thurs., 10am-9:30pm Fri.-Sat., $19.50) is both an aquarium and a seafood restaurant; you'll sit next to floor-to-ceiling windows surrounding a 50,000-gallon tank filled with brightly colored tropical fish. The aquarium exhibits feature marine ecosystems from around the world, a Stingray Reef touch tank, and a 4-D theater.

Elitch Gardens

A popular amusement and water park, **Elitch Gardens** (2000 Elitch Cir., 303/595-4386, www.elitchgardens.com, 10am-7pm Mon.-Thurs., 10am-10pm Fri.-Sun. in summer, $36) originally opened in 1890 as a theater and botanical garden on 16 acres of farmland in northwest Denver; it relocated to this location in 1995. The carousel took three years to carve and has been spinning kids around since 1928. Other rides include the Mind Eraser, a corkscrewing coaster that exceeds 50 miles per hour, and the Tower of Doom, which plunges riders 20 stories down at stomach-churning

Highlands and Platte River Valley

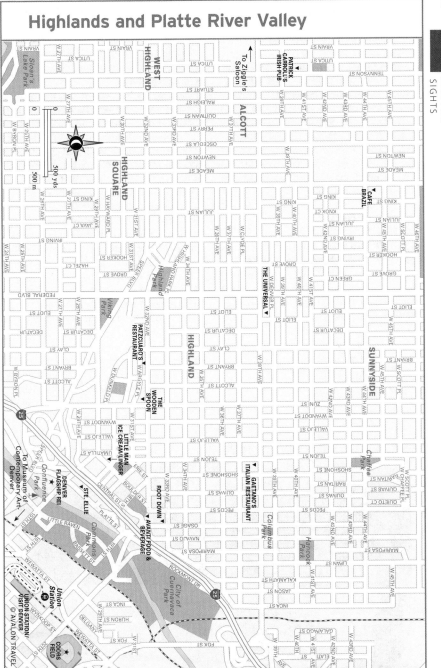

speeds up to 60 miles per hour. I much prefer the 100-foot-tall Ferris wheel, which has great views of the mountains and the city.

Children's Museum of Denver

The **Children's Museum of Denver** (2121 Children's Museum Dr., 303/433-7444, www.mychildsmuseum.org, 9am-4pm Mon.-Tues. and Thurs.-Fri., 9am-7:30pm Wed., 10am-5pm Sat.-Sun., $13) is a creative and fun-filled place where kids (and those young at heart) can leap through a waterfall, crawl through the backyard, and zip-line or spelunk through their own adventure park.

CITY PARK AND ENVIRONS

Black American West Museum & Heritage Center

Originally founded to tell the story of the West's "Black Cowboys," the **Black American West Museum & Heritage Center** (3091 California St., 720/242-7428, www.blackamericanwestmuseum.org, 10am-2pm Fri.-Sat., $8) has broadened its scope to teach about the many crucial roles filled by African Americans during our nation's westward expansion. Exhibits include the Buffalo Soldiers, black military units that played a

crucial role in settling the West; Dr. Justina Ford, Denver's first female doctor of the early 20th century; and Henry Parker, one of the first miners to discover gold in Colorado.

★ City Park

The urban, 314-acre **City Park** (17th Ave. and Colorado Blvd., www.denvergov.org) is a beautiful place to relax, picnic, and enjoy the excellent mountain views. The largest of Denver's many parks, and one of the city's oldest public spaces, it's best known for hosting the Denver Zoo and the Denver Museum of Nature and Science. City Park is also a recreation hub with the Mile High Loop, a tree-lined, walking/running path, a golf course, tennis courts, fountains, flower beds, and a lake where you can rent out kayaks and pedal boats.

DENVER ZOO

Spread across 75 acres, the **Denver Zoo** (2300 Steele St., 720/337-1400, http://denverzoo.org, 9am-5pm daily, $17) houses more than 4,000 animals from all corners of the globe. Amazingly, it began with just one animal, an orphaned black bear, which was given to the keeper of City Park in 1896. From these humble origins, the zoo grew quickly and

City Park

pioneered the use of natural-looking enclosures rather than cages to contain the animals. The enormous 10-acre Toyota Elephant Passage can host up to 12 elephants along with other creatures like Indian rhinos, clouded leopards, Malayan tapirs, and agile gibbons swinging in the trees.

DENVER MUSEUM OF NATURE AND SCIENCE

The **Denver Museum of Nature and Science** (2001 Colorado Blvd., 303/370-6000, www.dmns.org, 9am-5pm daily, $15) is filled with natural wonders, from sparkling crystals and golden nuggets found in Colorado to ancient Egyptian mummies. Displays include two fantastic permanent exhibits, **Space Odyssey,** where you can drive a space shuttle and view a Martian canyon, and **Prehistoric Journeys,** which travels through 3.5 billion years of Earth history to trace the evolution of life. Part of the exhibit is a laboratory where many of the fossils on display were prepared, including the 80-foot-long diplodocus skeleton that's locked in battle with a stegosaurus and an allosaurus. Kids love the hands-on Discovery Zone and looking for eight painted elves hidden in its dioramas (these aren't advertised; ask for information at the entrance).

★ Denver Botanic Gardens

Located just east of Cheesman Park, the **Denver Botanic Gardens** (1007 York St., 720/865-3501, www.botanicgardens.org, 9am-8pm daily, $12.50) is a lush, 24-acre urban oasis featuring the continent's largest collection of plants from cold, temperate climates. The location's 45 gardens host 34,000 different plants and include the 1986 Xeriscape Demonstration Garden, a Japanese show garden, and a peaceful water garden. A glass **Science Pyramid** hosts an interactive science exhibit that follows researchers around the globe to learn about the cold, semi-arid ecosystems known as steppes.

The Gardens offers horticulturist-led **tours** (Sat., $14) and other classes and events, including a **Summer Concert Series** (http://

concerts.botanicgardens.org). The Gardens also has two restaurants: the **Offshoots at the Gardens Café** (9am-8:30pm daily mid-May-Sept., 9am-4pm daily Oct.-mid-May, $6-8), which serves seared panini, freshly baked calzones, and soups and salads; and the **Hive Garden Bistro** (10am-8pm daily, $10-16), which has a large deck under the trees next to the Monet Pool. The menu features toasted sandwiches, a variety of fresh tacos, and salads with fresh, locally grown produce. The Offshoots café also features Denver's first publicly accessible "green" roof, which has panoramic views of Denver and its famous mountain backdrop.

GREATER DENVER
Butterfly Pavilion

The highlight of the peaceful **Butterfly Pavilion** (6252 W. 104th Ave., Westminster, 303/469-5441, www.butterflies.org, 9am-5pm daily, $11), the nation's first solo invertebrate zoo, is an enormous greenhouse that hosts a tropical forest filled with more than 1,500 fluttering butterflies. Don't leave without touching a sea cucumber and holding Rosie, the pavilion's friendly tarantula.

Forney Museum of Transportation

The **Forney Museum of Transportation** (4303 Brighton Blvd., 303/297-1113, www.forneymuseum.org, 10am-4pm Mon.-Sat., noon-4pm Sun., $11) provides a historical perspective on modern transportation with its unique collection of more than 600 vehicles, including buggies, steam locomotives, sleighs, and bikes. Highlights include Amelia Earhart's sleek, yellow 1923 Kissel "Gold Bug," a Case steam tractor, and a stylish, six-wheel 1923 Hispano Suiza Victoria Town Car that has appeared in a number of movies.

Wings Over the Rockies Air & Space Museum

Located in a 1930s-era hangar on the grounds of a former air force base, the **Wings Over the Rockies Air & Space Museum**

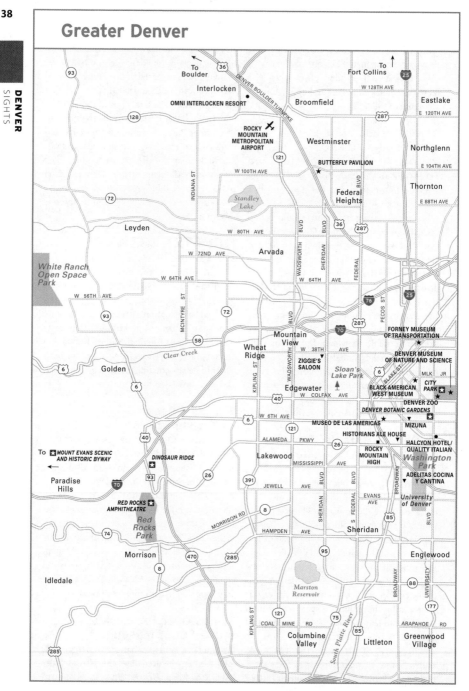

Greater Denver

To Boulder
36
93
Interlocken
DENVER BOULDER TURNPIKE
OMNI INTERLOCKEN RESORT
128

To Fort Collins
25
W 128TH AVE
Broomfield
Eastlake
287
E 120TH AVE

ROCKY MOUNTAIN METROPOLITAN AIRPORT
121
W 100TH AVE
Westminster
BUTTERFLY PAVILION
Northglenn
E 104TH AVE

72
INDIANA ST
Standley Lake
Federal Heights
BLVD
Thornton
E 88TH AVE

Leyden
W 80TH AVE
BLVD
BLVD
36
287

White Ranch Open Space Park
W 72ND AVE
Arvada
WADSWORTH
SHERIDAN
FEDERAL

W 64TH AVE
W 64TH AVE

W 56TH AVE
MCINTYRE ST
76
PECOS ST
25

93
72
BLVD
287
70
FORNEY MUSEUM OF TRANSPORTATION

58
Clear Creek
Mountain View
Wheat Ridge
WADSWORTH
W 38TH AVE
ZIGGIE'S SALOON
DENVER MUSEUM OF NATURE AND SCIENCE

6
Golden
6
KIPLING ST
Sloan's Lake Park
6
BLAKE ST
MLK JR
CITY PARK

Edgewater
40
W COLFAX AVE
BLACK AMERICAN WEST MUSEUM

DENVER ZOO
DENVER BOTANIC GARDENS

40
6
W 6TH AVE
121
MUSEO DE LAS AMERICAS
MIZUNA

ALAMEDA PKWY
HISTORIANS ALE HOUSE
26
ROCKY MOUNTAIN HIGH
HALCYON HOTEL/ QUALITY ITALIAN

To MOUNT EVANS SCENIC AND HISTORIC BYWAY
DINOSAUR RIDGE
Lakewood
MISSISSIPPI AVE
Washington Park

Paradise Hills
70
93
26
391
JEWELL AVE
BLVD
BLVD
BROADWAY
ADELITAS COCINA Y CANTINA

RED ROCKS AMPHITHEATRE
Red Rocks Park
8
SHERIDAN
S FEDERAL
EVANS AVE
University of Denver

74
MORRISON RD
HAMPDEN AVE
Sheridan
85
BLVD

Morrison
470
285
95
Englewood

Idledale
8
Marston Reservoir
BROADWAY
UNIVERSITY
88

KIPLING ST
121
COAL MINE RD
75
ARAPAHOE RD
177

285
Columbine Valley
85
South Platte River
Littleton
Greenwood Village

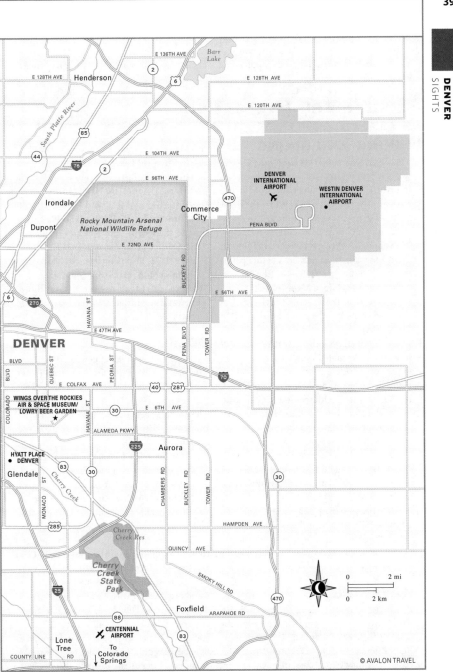

(7711 E. Academy Blvd., 303/360-5360, http://wingsmuseum.org, 10am-5pm Mon.-Sat., noon-5pm Sun., $12.50) is a highlight for space and science buffs. The museum features models of moon-landing equipment, a real moon rock, and four dozen space and aircraft, including a 1966 F-4E Phantom II jet, a 1964 F-104C Starfighter, and—for *Star Wars* fans—an X-Wing Starfighter that George Lucas used to promote his *Star Wars* Trilogy.

Sports and Recreation

HIKING AND BIKING

The **Cherry Creek Trail** (24.6 miles, www.walkridecolorado.com) is a mostly paved, multi-use path that runs from Confluence Park south through **Cherry Creek State Park** (4201 S. Parker Rd., Aurora, http://cpw.state.co.us, 303/690-1166, 5am-10pm daily). The state park also hosts two dozen additional multi-use trails and a number of other paths, including the Centennial (C-470), the Baldwin Gulch, and the Hidden Mesa Trails.

Intersecting the Cherry Creek Trail at Confluence Park is the paved **South Platte River Trail** (www.walkridecolorado.com), which follows the South Platte River about 10 miles south through downtown Denver to the suburb of Sheridan. From the intersection of Hampden Avenue and S. Santa Fe Boulevard, the trail connects with the **Bear Creek Bike Trail,** which heads 14.5 miles west to the town of Morrison in the Denver foothills.

The South Platte River Trail also extends 10 miles north to Commerce City, where it connects with the **Sand Creek Regional Greenway Trail** (64th Ave. and York St.) east for 14.6 miles to Aurora.

Confluence Kayaks (2373 15th St., 303/433-3676, http://confluencekayaks.com, 10am-8pm Mon.-Fri., 10am-6pm Sat., noon-5pm Sun.) rents easy-to-ride, cruiser- and townie-style bicycles.

KAYAKING

Paddlers congregate along the South Platte River, which flows from the reservoir in **Chatfield State Park** (11500 Roxborough Rd., Littleton, 303/791-7275, http://cpw.state.co.us, $8 all-day vehicle pass) through the city.

In addition to kayaking, you can also boat and fish in Chatfield Lake.

There are multiple access points for paddlers, including **Overland Park** (Florida Ave. and S. Platte River Dr.) and **Confluence Park** (15th St. and Platte St.) next to the REI store. Close to Confluence Park, **Confluence Kayaks** (2373 15th St., 303/433-3676, http://confluencekayaks.com, 10am-8pm Mon.-Fri., 10am-6pm Sat., noon-5pm Sun., $55 for all-day kayak) rents tubes, whitewater and inflatable kayaks, and stand-up paddleboards.

GOLF

Denver has a number of good golf courses. The par-72 **City Park Golf Course** (2500 York St., 720/865-3410, www.cityofdenvergolf.com, $27-39) is located within City Park. The 18-hole regulation course has a driving range and putting green, as well as an on-site restaurant.

Willis Case Golf Course (4999 Vrain St., 720/865-0700, www.cityofdenvergolf.com, $27-39) is located about six miles northeast of downtown with great mountain views. Facilities include a clubhouse, putting green, and on-site restaurant.

There are more golf courses in the surrounding suburbs. South of Denver is the **Fox Hollow Golf Course** (13410 W. Morrison Rd., Lakewood, 303/986-7888, www.lakewood.org, $52-76), with 27 holes on three very different nines: The Meadow, which features creekside fairways; The Links, a Scottish-style course; and The Canyon, which is dominated by a narrow gulch. The popular 18-hole par-72 championship **Foothills Golf Course** (3901

S. Carr St., Littleton, 303/409-2400, www.foot-hillsgolf.org, $41-44) is south in Littleton.

About 20 miles south, the Ridge at Castle Pines North (1414 Castle Pines Pkwy., Castle Pines, 303/688-4301, www.playtheridge.com, $82-145), was voted the Best Denver Region Course in 2015 by *Colorado Avid Golfer*.

SPECTATOR SPORTS

No matter how many "Rocktobers" local baseball fans celebrate, Denver is, and will always remain, a football town at heart. Legendary Broncos quarterback (and current General Manager) John Elway's back-to-back Super Bowl victories in 1997 and 1998 helped to ease, if not erase, the team's four, earlier, agonizing Super Bowl losses. Peyton Manning's 2015 victory, enabled by one of the league's best-ever defenses, was merely icing on the cake for this city's hungry sports fans.

Sports Authority Field at Mile High

The Denver Broncos play football at Sports Authority Field at Mile High (1701 Bryant St., 720/258-3333, www.sportsauthorityfieldatmilehigh.com, $50), an enormous, shiny, glass-and-metal stadium next to the South Platte River and I-25 on the western reaches of downtown. Seeing a game is a high-octane experience, with 76,125 orange-and-blue-clad fans tossing beach balls, making waves, and screaming bloody murder at the top of their lungs. If you don't enjoy getting drenched with beer, there is a family-friendly section where no alcohol is allowed. The weather is legendary; it can be 70 and sunny, or below zero and a blizzard, so come well prepared to sit outdoors for the duration.

Broncos tickets are extremely hard to get; it's a point of local pride that every (non-strike) home Broncos game has sold out since 1970. Season ticket holders scoop up 97 percent of the tickets; the only single-game tickets available are 2,000 half-price seats required by the law approved by Colorado voters that authorized the current stadium's funding, and a few odds-and-ends, which are usually snapped up in the first 10 minutes of online sales in early July. If you don't get any of these, your best bet is TicketExchange (www.ticketexchangebyticketmaster.co), which guarantees the tickets you buy are authentic, if much more expensive than the original price. Die-hard fans will enjoy a 90-minute, behind-the-scenes stadium tour (720/258-3888, 10am-2pm Thurs.-Sat. on the hour Sept.-May, 10am-2pm Mon.-Sat. on the hour June-Aug.,

Sports Authority Field at Mile High

$20 adults, $15 seniors and children), which visits the team mascot Thunder's stall, the players' field entrance tunnel, the posh executive suites, and the **Colorado Sports Hall of Fame Museum** (720/258-3888, www.coloradosports.org, 10am-3pm Thurs.-Sat., free), which you can also visit on your own. The city's Major League lacrosse team, the **Denver Outlaws** (www.denveroutlaws.com), also plays at the stadium.

★ Coors Field

The **Colorado Rockies** play baseball at **Coors Field** (2001 Blake St., 303/292-0200, http://colorado.rockies.mlb.com, 9am-5:30pm Mon.-Fri., 9:30am-3:30pm Sat. on non-game days, $4-70). Built in 1995, Coors Field is the anchor of the Lodo's thriving business and residential area. The beautiful stadium has a classic ambience with purple and black accents, including a row of purple seats in the upper deck that mark the mile-high elevation, making it by far the highest major league baseball park. Highlights include a Coors-operated brewery just behind the right field stands, as well as "The Rockpile," a central section of bleachers where the tickets sell for just a few dollars apiece.

On non-game days during baseball season, 70-80 minutes **tours** (303/762-5437, 10am,

noon, and 2pm Mon.-Sat. in season; noon and 2pm Mon., Wed., and Fri.-Sat. in off-season, $10 adults) offer a behind-the-scenes glimpse of the ballpark.

Pepsi Center

The 2001 and 1996 Stanley Cup champions, the **Colorado Avalanche** (http://avalanche.nhl.com), play hockey at the **Pepsi Center** (1000 Chopper Cir., 303/405-1100, http://www.pepsicenter.com; tickets 866/461-6556, www.altitudetickets.com), just south of Elitch Gardens. Also here are the **Denver Nuggets** (www.nba.com), the city's perpetually underscoring basketball team. The Pepsi Center hosts the **Colorado Mammoth** (www.coloradomammoth.com) lacrosse team, as well as frequent concerts, monster-truck rallies, and Cirque du Soleil performances.

Dick's Sporting Goods Park

Denver's Major League Soccer team, the **Colorado Rapids** (www.coloradorapids.com), plays in the shiny, new **Dick's Sporting Goods Park** (6000 Victory Way, Commerce City, 303/727-3500, www.dickssportinggoodspark.com). This is also the home of the state's pro rugby team, the **Denver Barbarians** (www.rockymountainrugby.org).

Entertainment and Events

NIGHTLIFE
Bars and Breweries

With 125 breweries and taprooms, it's hard to go anywhere in the city without finding the perfect spot for a pint of craft beer. Denver's bars and brewpubs are clustered in several hot spots, especially LoDo, the Highlands, and Cherry Creek.

DOWNTOWN AND LODO

Sandwiched between the Pepsi Center and Coors Field are nearly 90 bars and brewpubs, many of which are housed in beautifully

restored, red-brick buildings that once served as warehouses. The crowds are usually lively, especially after a Rockies, Nuggets, or Avalanche game when thousands of fans pour in to either celebrate a victory or drown their sorrows following a defeat.

Outside of Union Station, **Wynkoop Brewing Company** (1634 18th St., 303/297-2700, www.wynkoop.com, 11am-midnight Sun.-Thurs., 11am-2am Fri.-Sat.) was Colorado's first brewpub. It was started in the 1980s by four guys, including John Hickenlooper, who later went on to

Festivals and Events

With its active population, relaxed lifestyle, cultural diversity, and great (if sometimes unpredictable) weather, Denver is prime for parties and festivals. Here are some of the biggest and best:

National Western Stock Show (www.nationalwestern.com, Jan.): The world's largest stock show features livestock, horse, and trade shows, plus a professional rodeo.

St. Patrick's Day Parade (www.denver.org, Mar.): From bagpipes to shamrocks, this lively downtown Denver parade celebrates all things Irish.

Denver March Pow Wow (www.denvermarchpowwow.org, Mar.): This traditional Native American social gathering honors their heritage with workshops, intertribal and competitive dances, handmade crafts, and drumming.

Denver 420 Festival (http://denver420fest.com, Apr.): Denver's premier 420-friendly fest celebrates the cannabis culture with live music, art, and plenty of hemp products.

Cherry Blossom Festival (http://cherryblossomdenver.org, June): This festival features martial arts, drumming, and ukulele performances, along with Japanese food.

Denver PrideFest (www.glbtcolorado.org, June): Held in Civic Center Park, the two-day PrideFest includes a colorful parade, music, speeches, and lots of food and beverage stalls.

Cherry Creek Arts Festival (www.cherryarts.org, July): Collaborative murals, a kids' art station, seven performance stages, and dozens of art booths make this the nation's top outdoor arts festival.

Denver Food & Wine Festival (https://denverfoodandwine.com, Sept.): This six-day festival features more than 700 wines and spirits, plus delicious samples from more than 40 local restaurants.

Great American Beer Festival (www.greatamericanbeerfestival.com, Sept.): Visitors from around the globe flock to Denver to sample and celebrate American craft beer.

ChristKindl Market (www.denverchristkindlmarket.com, mid-Nov.-Dec. 25): Denver's Skyline Park is transformed into a German outdoor holiday market, complete with serenading musicians, food and craft booths, and hot mulled wine.

---

become Denver's mayor, then the governor of Colorado. They built a brewery and a couple of bars in an old mercantile building in what at the time was a much sketchier LoDo. Today, Wynkoop is one of the state's largest breweries and is still known for its innovative brews, which over the years have included some unusual ingredients like green chiles and gummy bears.

Denver's oldest Irish tavern, the red-doored **Nallen's Irish Pub** (1429 Market St., 303/527-0667, www.nallensdenver.com, 2pm-2am daily) serves up countless pints of dark, foamy Guinness and has special festivities, including bagpipers and Irish dancers on St. Paddy's Day. **Blake Street Tavern** (2301 Blake St., 303/675-0505, www.blakestreettavern.com, 11am-2am Mon.-Fri., 9am-2am Sat., 10am-2am Sun.) is one of Denver's best sports bars. In addition to 60 big-screen TVs where you can watch a game, it also has an underground level where you can play one yourself—shuffleboard, Skee Ball, darts, and even Pac-Man and other 1980s video games.

Located in an 1883 building that once housed Soapy Smith's Bar, **Euclid Hall Bar** (1317 14th St., 303/595-4255, euclidhall.com, 11:30am-2am Mon.-Fri., 2pm-2am Sat.-Sun.) is an "American tavern" with a large beer selection and good pub food with an international and meaty twist, including po' boys, schnitzel, and house-made sausage.

Located near Coors Field, the **Falling Rock Tap House** (1919 Blake St., 303/293-8338, http://fallingrocktaphouse.com, 11am-2am daily) is a quieter bar with a large patio and an enormous list of beers, with more than 75 on tap and 130 different kinds of bottles. The 2,200 bottles of beer lining the walls belong to Chris, who drank most of them himself. Nearby, the **Star Bar** (2137 Larimer St., 720/328-2420, www.starbardenver.com, 4pm-1:30am daily) is full of contradictions; its plain, wood-paneled exterior belies its surprisingly sophisticated cocktails, which are made with top-shelf liquors, but it also serves canned(!) wine made nearby at **The Infinite Monkey Theorem** (www.theinfinitemonkeytheorem.com) winery.

HIGHLANDS AND PLATTE RIVER VALLEY

Gaetano's Italian Restaurant (3760 Tejon St., 303/445-9852, www.gaetanositalian.com, 11am-10:30pm Mon.-Thurs., 11am-11pm Fri., 2pm-11pm Sat., 2pm-10:30pm Sun.) is known as much for its bottomless pomegranate mimosas and Sunday morning Bloody Mary bar, with garlic-infused vodka and 75 varieties of hot sauce, as for its select menu of traditional Italian dishes like spaghetti Bolognese and Clams Aglio & Olio.

If you're looking for a more upscale nightlife option, sophisticated **Ste. Ellie** (1553 Platte St., 303/477-1447, www.saintellie.com, 6pm-midnight Tues.-Thurs., 6pm-1am Fri.-Sat.) has a long, marble bar, rich leather chairs, seasonal cocktails like Pennies from Heaven (Tequila Ocho Blanco, rose hip, grapefruit, and lime), and small and large plates of deviled eggs, soba noodles, mac and cheese, and other delicious comfort foods.

Patrick Carroll's Irish Pub (3963 Tennyson St., 303/458-6666, http://patrickcarrolls.com, 11am-2am daily) has nightly specials and traditional pub fare. **Ziggie's Saloon** (4923 W. 38th St., 303/455-9930, www.ziggieslivemusic.com, 6:30pm-midnight daily), Denver's oldest blues bar, has a reputation for cheap beer and great live music most Thursday, Friday, and Saturday nights at 8pm.

CHERRY CREEK

In addition to a menu of Colorado-grown and raised food, **Historians Ale House** (24 Broadway #102, 720/479-8505, http://historiansalehouse.com, 11am-2am Mon.-Fri.,

10am-2am Sat.-Sun.) has an all-day happy hour that features a rotating brewery of the month and 40 beers on tap.

Modeled after a German *biergarten,* **Lowry Beer Garden** (7577 E. Academy Blvd., 303/366-0114, www.lowrybeergarden.com, 11am-10pm Mon.-Thurs., 11am-11pm Fri.-Sat., 11am-8pm Sun.) is a relaxed spot with a huge, 4,500-square-foot outdoor patio with communal tables plus table tennis and foosball games.

Dance Clubs

For those who like to dance the night away, Denver has some great spots to get your groove on. Dubbed the Best Dance Club in America by *Rolling Stone,* the **Beta Nightclub** (1909 Blake St., 303/383-1909, www.betanightclub.com, 9pm-2am Thurs.-Sat., 3pm-9pm Sun.) has a 72,000-watt sound system and an enormous dance floor. Downtown Denver's only country bar, the **Cowboy Lounge** (1941 Market St., 303/226-1570, www.tavernhg.com, 8pm-2am Thurs.-Sat.) looks like it belongs more in Steamboat Springs than in Denver. It emphasizes country and rock music, Stetson hats, and ladies' night drink specials.

Denver's hottest nightlife area is the **South of Colfax Nightlife District** (Colfax, Speer, and Lincoln Sts., http://coclubs.com, $15 cover). One admission gets you into seven different clubs, where you can dance to music ranging from reggae and Top 40 to R&B and hip-hop. Venues include **Milk** (1037 Broadway, 303/832-8628, 9pm-2am Wed.-Sat.), where you can enjoy live jazz and dancing on the rooftop lounge with panoramic city views; the more upscale **Club Vinyl** (1082 Broadway, 303/506-8078, 9am-2am Fri.-Sat.); and **The Church** (1160 N. Lincoln St., 303/832-2383, http://coclubs.com, 9pm-2am Fri.-Sun.), which is exactly what it sounds like—a unique dance club housed inside a former place of worship, with stained-glass windows, multiple dance floors, a rib-blasting sound system, a sushi bar, and a loyal "congregation."

Denver Marijuana Guide

When Colorado voters passed Amendment 64 in November 2012, the measure legalized marijuana and led to the rise of **cannabis tourism**. What can be confusing for tourists is that there are different sets of rules governing its purchase and use for residents and visitors. Although non-residents can legally possess up to 1 ounce, they may only buy 0.25 ounces (seven grams) in a single transaction. Once you leave the state, however, you can be prosecuted for possessing any amount.

When you visit a pot shop, be prepared to be carded; it's illegal for budtenders to serve anyone under age 21. Also be prepared to pay in cash; because marijuana is still illegal at the federal level, most pot shops can't open bank accounts. Many have ATMs right in their shop. If it's your first time, or you have only limited experience, be sure to ask lots of questions. Most pot shops sell 20 or more strains, which can have different side effects, as well as a long list of oils and edibles. Once you make your purchase, be careful to store it away from minors and to avoid consuming pot in public, which is illegal, as is driving under the influence. If you're coming from sea level, be aware that the elevation can enhance marijuana's effects. Stay hydrated and start with a low dose; the number of visitors who end up in Colorado emergency rooms for marijuana-related reasons nearly doubled after it was legalized.

Denver has the highest concentration of recreational pot shops in the state, including **Natural Remedies** (1620 Market St., 303/953-0884, http://lodosdispensary.com, 9am-7pm daily), **Rocky Mountain High** (1538 Wazee St., 303/623-7246, http://rockymountainhigh.co, 9am-7pm daily), which sells hash, edibles, extracts, and oils in addition to buds, and **Native Roots – Denver** (1555 Champa St., 303/623-1900, https://nativerootsdispensary.com, 9am-7pm daily), which has a menu of topicals (like Hash Bath), bubbles, shatter, and wax.

For up-to-date information about the locations of licensed **retail marijuana stores** (the only legal outlets), visit www.coloradopotguide.com and http://weedmaps.com.

Live Music

The best place to see a show is the **Red Rocks Amphitheatre** (18300 W. Alameda Pkwy., Morrison, 720/865-2494, http://redrocksonline.com), in the Denver foothills, where the scenery and the acoustics are both amazing. The **Pepsi Center** (1000 Chopper Cir., 303/405-1100, http://www.pepsicenter.com) and the older **Denver Coliseum** (4600 Humboldt St., 720/865-2475, www.denvercoliseum.com) also host major shows. Denver also has several mid-size venues where big names frequently play, including the 1,600-seat **Ogden Theatre** (935 E. Colfax Ave., 303/832-1874, www.ogdentheatre.com), the historic, 3,700-seat **Fillmore Auditorium** (1510 Clarkson St., 303/837-0360, www.fillmoreauditorium.org), and the art deco **Paramount Theatre** (1621 Glenarm Pl., 303/623-0106, www.paramountdenver.com).

Denver is home to a number of intimate venues and clubs as well. North of downtown is the **Grizzly Rose** (5450 N. Valley Hwy., 303/295-1330, www.grizzlyrose.com, open Tues.-Sun.), where you can learn to line-dance and enjoy up-and-coming country acts. In the Capitol Hill area, **DazzleJazz** (930 Lincoln St., 303/839-5100, http://dazzlejazz.com, 3pm-10pm Mon., 3pm-midnight Tues.-Wed., 3pm-1am Thurs. and Sat., 11am-1am Fri., 9:30am-10pm Sun.) was named the Best Jazz Club by *Westword* in 2016.

Near Sakura Square, **Ophelia's Electric Soapbox** (1215 20th St., 303/993-8023, http://opheliasdenver.com, 4pm-close Mon.-Fri., brunch 10am-2:30pm Sat.-Sun.) bills itself as a "gastro-brothel," a restaurant with a large dance floor and regular live music performances. In the Cherry Creek/Lowry area, **The Soiled Dove Underground** (7401 E. 1st Ave., 303/830-9214, www.tavernhg.com) draws mellow folk, jazz, and R&B performances.

Comedy

Denver has a surprisingly rich comedy scene headlined by **Comedy Works Denver** (1226 15th St., 303/595-3637, www.comedyworks.com), which snags local stars like John Heffron and Josh Blue (who both won NBC's *Last Comic Standing*), as well as occasional big names like Jimmy Fallon and John Oliver. The **Bovine Metropolis Theater** (1527 Champa St., 303/758-4722, www.bovinemetropolis.com) holds improv classes and hosts the Improv Hootenanny. **The Oriental Theater** (4335 W. 44th Ave., 720/420-0030, http://www.theorientaltheater.com), in the Highlands, often features local comedians on stage.

PERFORMING ARTS

The centerpiece of Denver culture and entertainment, the **Denver Performing Arts Complex** (1400 Curtis St., 720/865-4220, box office 800/641-1222, www.artscomplex.com) is one of the largest performing arts centers in the country. The four-block complex contains 10 performance spaces with more than 10,000 seats and is home to an opera house, the Boettcher Concert Hall, and the Buell Theatre. With an 80-foot-high glass room covering the venues, the complex dominates downtown

even on nights when no shows are scheduled. In addition to regular performances by the Colorado Ballet, Opera Colorado, and the Colorado Symphony Orchestra, the center features many award-winning Broadway musicals, Pulitzer Prize-winning plays, and family-friendly performances.

Housed in the Denver Performing Arts Complex, the **Denver Center Theatre Company** (14th and Curtis Sts., 800/641-1222, www.denvercenter.org) is the region's largest resident theater company. It is known for both classical and contemporary dramas, as well as a large number of world premieres. Denver has some other notable troupes and diverse venues, including **Su Teatro Cultural and Performing Arts Center** (721 Santa Fe Dr., 303/296-0219, http://suteatro.org), which highlights Latino culture. The Center hosts the annual Chicano Music Festival (July) and the **Shadow Theatre Company** (720/238-1323, http://thesourcedenver.org), which features African American theater.

Smaller venues include the **Bug Theatre Company** (3654 Navajo St., 303/477-5977, http://bugtheatre.info) and the **Buntport Theater Company** (717 Lipan St., 720/946-1388, http://buntport.com), which specialize in children's and impromptu performances.

Shopping

Denver has a fun mix of indie boutiques, innovative art galleries, and reputable chains. Prices are reasonable and the selection is excellent, especially in popular Larimer Square and the 16th Street Mall. Affluent Cherry Creek has two huge shopping areas that collectively comprise the largest, most-varied shopping district.

SHOPPING DISTRICTS
16th Street Mall

The 1.25-mile **16th Street Mall** (Wynkoop St. to Broadway) is known for its pedestrian-friendly shopping. It's easy to stroll between

the several hundred stores and restaurants; if you get tired, hop on the **MallRide** (www.rtd-denver.com, 4:59am-1:21am Mon.-Fri., 5:30am-1:21am Sat., 6:30am-1:21am Sun.), a free electric bus that stops at every block along the mall between Civic Center and Union Station.

The mall consists primarily of chain stores, especially casual clothing outlets. Scattered in between are a few more unique options. **Sole St. Shoes** (716 16th St., 303/893-5280, www.solestreetshoes.com, 10am-8pm Mon.-Sat., 10am-7pm Sun.) is a "sneaker boutique" with retro options as well as standard brands like Nike and New Balance. **Wild West of**

America (715 16th St., 303/446-8640, 9am-7pm daily) sells moccasins, key chains, and dozens of knickknacks.

★ Larimer Square

Denver's oldest and most historic block, **Larimer Square** (14th and 15th Sts. at Larimer St., www.larimersquare.com) was the first place the miners constructed buildings after they settled along the South Platte River. Most of the square's lovingly restored buildings date to the 1880s. They house a variety of shops and restaurants, making it one of Denver's most popular destinations. It's also fiercely autonomous; 20 out of the square's 23 shops are independently owned.

The **Blue Ruby Boutique** (1426 Larimer St., 720/259-0031, http://bluerubydesignboutique.com, 10am-6pm Mon.-Wed., 10am-8pm Thurs.-Sat., 11am-5pm Sun.) is a chic clothing store that features men's and women's garments from local designers as well as top New York brands. **Eve** (1413 Larimer St., 720/932-9382, www.eveinc.net, 10am-7pm Mon.-Fri., 10am-6pm Sat., noon-5pm Sun.) focuses on stylish women's clothing and accessories, including products from Papillon, Capote, and Trina Turk.

From boots and buckles to belts and bolos, **Cry Baby Ranch** (1421 Larimer St., 303/623-3979, www.crybabyranch.com, 10am-7pm Mon.-Fri., 10am-6pm Sat., noon-5pm Sun.) sells anything your inner cowgirl (or boy) might crave. **Moda Man** (1459 Larimer St., 303/862-5949, www.modaman.com, 10am-7pm Mon.-Thurs., 10am-8pm Fri.-Sat., noon-5pm Sun.) sells contemporary-casual men's clothing by top fashion designers and also specializes in custom garments.

Ever since he made his girlfriend a silver ring 40 years ago, **John Atencio** (1440 Larimer St., 303/534-4277, https://johnatencio.com, 10am-6pm Mon.-Sat.) has been designing and selling beautiful handcrafted jewelry in Colorado. His shop features a sparkling selection of beautiful rings, signature pendants, and gold and silver bracelets, crosses, and earrings.

If you have a furry friend to shop for, stop by the upscale **Dog Savvy Boutique** (1402 Larimer St., 303/623-3979, http://dogsavvy.com, 10am-7pm Mon.-Thurs., 10am-6pm Fri.-Sat., 11am-5pm Sun.) for toys, beds, and oatmeal-peanut butter doggie treats, as well as blueberry facials and other spa treatments for the puppy who has it all.

colorful Larimer Square

Cherry Creek Mall

Denver's ritziest shopping district is located about four miles southeast of Union Station, just east of the Denver Country Club and south of Speer Boulevard. In this area are two upscale shopping areas: the indoor **Cherry Creek Mall** (3000 E. 1st Ave., 303/388-3900, www.shopcherrycreek.com, 10am-9pm Mon.-Sat., 11am-6pm Sun.), Denver's largest, and the outdoor **Cherry Creek North** (299 Milwaukee St., Ste. 201, 303/394-2904, https://cherrycreeknorth.com, 10am-6pm Mon.-Sat., 11am-5pm Sun.), which has more character and correspondingly higher prices.

Cherry Creek Mall features mostly high-end chains, including Louis Vuitton, Ralph Lauren, Tiffany & Co., and Neiman Marcus, as well as an Apple Store, which is always packed. Cherry Creek North is a more spread-out shopping and restaurant district with a great selection of fun and fashionable shops, including **Little Feet** (201 University Blvd., 303/388-9535, www.littlefeetdenver.com, 10am-6pm Mon.-Sat., noon-4pm Sun.), a family-owned store that specializes in kids' shoes, **Title Nine** (160 Steele St., 303/321-4001, www.titlenine.com, 10am-6pm Mon.-Sat., noon-5pm Sun.), which features super-comfortable women's sportswear and casual clothing,

and the **Artisan Center** (2757 E. 3rd Ave., 303/333-1201, www.artisancenterdenver.com, 10am-5:30pm daily), a colorful and eclectic shop selling cards, candles, chimes, jewelry, and scarves made by mostly local artists.

DOWNTOWN AND LODO
Books and Music

On the edge of the 16th Street Mall, the **Tattered Cover Book Store** (1628 16th St., 303/436-1070, www.tatteredcover.com, 6:30am-9pm Mon.-Fri., 9am-9pm Sat., 10am-6pm Sun.), founded in 1971, is one of the best bookstores. It has remained a classic, community-oriented retailer, with regular local-author lectures and book signings, kid-friendly activities, comfy leather couches, and delicious coffee and pastries. Its floor-to-ceiling stacks feature more than 150,000 titles, with an entire room devoted to travel and maps (with an emphasis on Colorado), and the most extensive magazine selection in the state. It's one of downtown Denver's most venerable and popular institutions, with two other downtown locations: one in City Park (2526 E. Colfax Ave., 303/322-7727, 9am-9pm Mon.-Sat., 10am-6pm Sun.) and a smaller outlet in Union Station (1701 Wynkoop St., 8am-7pm Mon.-Fri., 9am-7pm Sat., 10am-5pm Sun.).

LoDo is a great place to shop and eat.

Two classic Denver shops are located near the Colorado State Capitol. **Capitol Hill Books** (300 E. Colfax Ave., 303/837-0700, http://capitolhillbooks.com, 10am-6pm Mon.-Sat., 10am-5pm Sun.) consistently ranks as Denver's top used bookstore. **Wax Trax Records** (638 E. 13th Ave., 303/831-7246, www.waxtraxrecords.com, 10am-7pm Mon.-Thurs., 10am-8pm Fri.-Sat., 11am-6pm Sun.) is a real brick-and-mortar store selling new and used vinyl records and other music-related paraphernalia.

Clothing and Accessories

The third-generation business **Rockmount Ranchwear** (1626 Wazee St., 303/629-7777, www.rockmount.com, 8am-6pm Mon.-Fri., 10am-6pm Sat., 11am-4pm Sun.) sells classic men's and women's Western clothing, including the original snap-button shirts designed by founder Jack Weil. The shop has a huge selection of hats, leather belts, cowboy boots, and fringed jackets. The well-known brand has been worn on stage and in films by the likes of Elvis Presley, Bruce Springsteen, and Tom Hanks.

HIGHLANDS AND PLATTE RIVER VALLEY
Outdoor Equipment

On the northwestern edge of downtown, perched on the bank above Confluence Park, the **Denver Flagship REI** (1416 Platte St., 303/756-3100, www.rei.com, 9am-9pm Mon.-Sat., 10am-7pm Sun.) is an adventure in shopping. The huge brick warehouse has an enormous selection from bikes and kayaks to windbreakers, gloves, and freeze-dried meals and also offers plenty of classes and clinics. The flagship store includes a climbing wall, a third-floor play area for kids, and a Starbucks with a nice deck where you can toast the hundreds of other bikers, hikers, and kayakers passing by.

Food

DOWNTOWN AND LODO
Breakfast and Cafés

Part of a small Denver-based chain, **Snooze, an A.M. Eatery** (1701 Wynkoop St., 303/825-3536, http://snoozeeatery.com, 6:30am-2:30pm daily, $7-13) is known for its friendly service, fun atmosphere, and inventive menu with treats like green eggs 'n' hamwich, pineapple upside down pancakes, and quinoa porridge as well as Violet Beauregarde and other (potent) morning cocktails. On Market Street, the **Delectable Egg** (1642 Market St., 303/572-8146, www.delectableegg.com, 6:30am-2pm Mon.-Fri., 7am-2pm Sat.-Sun., $7-10) has been a local breakfast and lunch tradition since 1982, thanks to its diverse menu with several French toast options (like peanut butter crunch), frittatas, and quiche Lorraine crêpes.

Consistently ranked as one of Denver's best breakfast spots, **Sam's No. 3** (1500 Curtis St., 303/534-1927, http://samsno3.com, 5:30am-10pm Mon.-Wed., 5:30am-11pm Thurs., 5:30am-midnight Fri., 7am-midnight Sat., 7am-10pm Sun., $7-23) is a popular diner serving up huge portions of tasty food. Choose from classic egg dishes or fluffy pancakes to smothered "Big as Your Head" two-pound breakfast burritos.

For an upscale weekend brunch, head to **Milk & Honey Bar + Kitchen** (1414 Larimer St., 303/997-7590, http://milkandhoneybarkitchen.com, 4pm-10:30pm Tues.-Sun., brunch 10:30am-2:30pm Sat.-Sun., $12-16) in Larimer Square, where you'll enjoy impeccably presented meals like jumbo blue crab toast on pumpernickel and brisket hash, plus a special brunch drinks menu. A few doors down, **The Market** (1445 Larimer St., 303/534-5140, http://themarketatlarimer.com, 6am-10pm Sun.-Thurs., 6am-11pm Fri.-Sat., $5-11) is a deli-style establishment with a mouthwatering assortment of pastries, salads, and sandwiches plus a coffee bar with a hot toddy menu to ward off those cold winter mornings.

Fresh and Local

A "community bistro" located in the historic Sugar Building, **The Kitchen Denver** (1530 16th St., 303/623-3127, http://thekitchen.com, 11am-9:30pm Sun.-Tues., 11am-10:30pm Wed.-Sat., $17-34) is a bright and spacious "garden-to-table" restaurant that sources ingredients from two dozen purveyors to create snacks, like ricotta crostini, cheese and charcuterie plates, and inspired mains, such as lamb kabobs and its signature dish, the Kitchen Bolognese. They also have a popular weekday happy hour (3pm-6pm).

American

For the best hot dog in town, head to **Biker Jim's Gourmet Dogs** (2148 Larimer St., 720/746-9355, www.bikerjimsdogs.com, 11am-10pm Sun.-Thurs., 11am-3am Fri.-Sat., $6.50). Founded by Jim Pittenger, the restaurant is known for its relaxed "biker vibe" and juicy dogs made from exotic meats, including rattlesnake, pheasant, and buffalo. Top your choice with funky toppings like cactus, curry jam, or Coca-Cola-soaked onions for a memorable meal. Biker Jim's also has a cart on the 16th Street Mall (Arapahoe St., 10am-3pm Mon.-Fri.).

Asian

The signature dish of ★ **A Taste of the Philippines** (16th St. and Champa St., www. atasteofthephilippines.com, $8-10), a food cart on the 16th Street Mall, is the chicken adobo, a simple dish of chicken braised in garlic and seasoned vinegar served over rice. Since opening her cart in 2011, owner and chef Kathy Poland, who was born in the Philippines, has been featured in numerous publications and the Food Network show *Cutthroat Kitchen*. Poland opened a second location in **Finn's Manor** (2927 Larimer St.).

Named for the largest Chinese market in Saigon, Vietnam, **CholLon Modern Asian Bistro** (1555 Blake St., 303/353-5223, www. cholon.com, 11am-close Mon.-Fri., 2pm-close Sat.-Sun., $13-37) was a 2011 James Beard finalist for the Best New Restaurant in America. It's the passion of executive chef Lon Symensma, whose colorful dishes are works of art. Main plates include fresh and flavorful combos like lobster Saigon crêpes and watermelon-tomato salad with curried ricotta and Sriracha vinaigrette.

the Bistro Vendome

French

Modeled after the Place Vendome in Paris, the chic ★ **Bistro Vendome** (1420 Larimer St., 303/825-3232, www.bistrovendome.com, 5pm-10pm Mon.-Thurs., 5pm-11pm Fri., 10am-2pm and 5pm-11pm Sat., 10am-2pm and 5pm-9pm Sun., $20-26) is widely praised as Denver's best French restaurant. Its short menu includes classic options like *poisson entier* (whole-fried fish) and hearty bouillabaisse stew made with pan-seared halibut, shrimp, mussels, clams, and potatoes.

Mediterranean

For a quick, casual bite while you're walking the mall, you can't beat the cleverly named **WikiPita** (16th St. Mall and Arapahoe St., 8:30am-6pm Mon.-Fri., noon-6pm Sat., $8), a small stall that sells fragrant gyros, falafel, and hummus rolled up with veggies and yogurt in freshly baked pitas. For more upscale Mediterranean, try ★ **Rioja** (1431 Larimer St., 303/820-2282, www.riojadenver.com, 4pm-10pm daily, $20-58). Executive chef and owner Jennifer Jasinski was named a James Beard Foundation semifinalist for Outstanding Chef in 2016. The carefully culled menu changes seasonally but typically features chef Jen's handmade pastas as well as a few seafood entrées like pan-seared barramundi.

Italian

Osteria Marco (1453 Larimer St., 303/534-5855, www.osteriamarco.com, 11am-10pm Sun.-Thurs., 11am-11pm Fri.-Sat., $10-29) bills itself as "a humble restaurant where friends gather to casually enjoy their wine with food." The informal, lower-level interior is indeed a great place to gather, although it can at times be a touch too loud. The fabulous menu includes rabbit, handcrafted pizzas with unusual ingredients like figs and goat cheese, and on Sunday nights, slow-roasted suckling pig. Located less than two blocks from Coors Field, **Racca's Pizzeria Napoletana** (2129 Larimer St., 303/296-7000, www.raccaspizzeria.com, 11am-10pm Sun.-Thurs., 11am-11pm

Fri.-Sat., $11-19) is known for its mouthwatering Neapolitan-style pizzas made by hand from imported Italian ingredients. The cozy booths, brick walls, and pizza oven make it an especially comfortable place to enjoy their signature limoncello chicken wings and meatball sliders, or to share a decadent Nutella-stuffed pizza.

The Hotel Monaco's posh restaurant, **Panzano** (909 17th St., 303/296-3525, www.panzano-denver.com, 6:30am-10pm Mon.-Fri., 8am-11pm Sat., 8am-9:30pm Sun., $26-46), has earned numerous accolades. With impeccable service, an award-winning wine list, and a diverse menu of northern Italian cuisine built around seasonal and local ingredients, Panzano is a great place for happy hour, a romantic dinner, or a post-theater splurge.

Mexican

Part of celebrity chef Richard Sandoval's restaurant empire, **Tamayo** (1400 Larimer St., 720/946-1433, www.richardsandoval.com, 11am-2pm Mon.-Fri., 10:30am-2:30pm Sat.-Sun., and 5pm-10pm Sun.-Thurs., 5pm-11pm Fri.-Sat., $13-30) features fresh Mexican fare in creative combinations like crab and shrimp enchiladas and smoked brisket tacos. The establishment has an enormous rooftop deck, a great place to sip one of the 100 tequilas.

Steakhouse

The **EDGE Restaurant & Bar** (1111 14th St., 303/389-3000, www.edgerestaurantdenver.com, 6:30am-10pm daily, $31-50) focuses on custom dry-aged steaks sourced from some of Colorado's best ranches. Following starters like Bangs Island mussels and tuna tartare, hungry diners tuck into buffalo rib eye and filet mignon or New York strip loin prepared on the pecan wood grill. The meals are served with an assortment of unusual condiments like confit garlic and brandy peppercorn.

With its lion-flanked exterior and a posh, dark-wood-paneled interior, **The Capital Grille** (1450 Larimer St., 303/539-2500, www.thecapitalgrille.com, 11am-10pm Mon.-Thurs., 11am-11pm Fri., 4:30pm-11pm Sat., 4pm-9pm Sun., $35-50) serves up some of the fanciest food in town, including fresh Maine lobster, double-cut lamb rib chops, and, of course, plenty of porterhouse and rib eye steak. The large wine cellar is overseen by master sommelier Goerge Miliotes.

Fine Dining

At the wood-and-brick-lined **Vesta Dipping Grill** (1822 Blake St., 303/296-1970, www.vestagrill.com, 5pm-10pm Sun.-Thurs., 5pm-11pm Fri.-Sat., $20-40), almost all the food comes in small bites, so you can dip it in some of the 20 different sauces, which range from fig mojo and pearl onion jam to ghost chili barbecue. You can pick two sauces or enjoy the ones already paired with an entrée, which include caramelized cauliflower and Madras grilled venison.

The **1515 Restaurant** (1515 Market St., 303/571-0011, www.1515restaurant.com, 5pm-10pm Mon.-Thurs., 11am-10pm Fri., 5pm-10pm Sat., $19-60) serves molecular gastronomy American-French cuisine. The menu is influenced by chef Gene Tang's childhood, which was spent in Hong Kong, and features Colorado steak, game, and chops. The casually elegant dining room, with the historic building's original brick walls, is complemented by light green cushioned seat backs. The restaurant's 22,000-bottle cellar has received a Wine Spectator Award of Excellence every year since 2000; the restaurant offers six- and eight-course tasting menus with or without wine pairings.

CAPITOL HILL
Fresh and Local

Consistently ranked one of Denver's top vegetarian restaurants, **City O' City** (206 E. 13th Ave., 303/831-6443, www.cityocitydenver.com, 11am-2am daily, $8-13) is a cheerful, community-oriented spot with unusual artwork and a relaxed vibe. Notable menu items include the savory waffle (topped with seasonal vegetable ragù and vegan cheese fondue), all-day breakfast sandwiches, and both small and large dinner plates, including kimchi stew and pumpkin curry pasta.

A great vegan option is cheerful **Watercourse Foods** (837 E. 17th Ave., 303/832-7313, www.watercoursefoods.com, 9am-11pm daily, $12-16), whose walls are decorated with *Watership Down*-inspired murals. Even guests who eat meat enjoy the large menu, which ranges from crispy taco salad and beet Wellington to blackened tofu Caesar wraps. Be sure to save enough room for key lime pie or a vodka-spiked espresso shake.

Repeatedly lauded as one of Colorado's top dinner establishments, **Fruition Restaurant** (1313 E. 6th Ave., 303/831-1962, www.fruitionrestaurant.com, 5pm-10pm Mon.-Sat., 5pm-9pm Sun., $25-31) is a small, contemporary-chic restaurant with short, seasonal menus designed around produce, honey, and artisanal sheep's milk cheeses produced from chef Alex Seidel's local farm. Mains include Maple Leaf Farms duck breast served with savory pistachio olive oil cake and seared diver scallops with coriander coconut curry.

American

Named for a famous '50s restaurant in Boston, **Steuben's Food Service** (523 E. 17th Ave., 303/830-1001, www.steubens.com, 11am-11pm Mon.-Thurs., 11am-midnight Fri., 10am-midnight Sat., 10am-11pm Sun., $5-20) is a casual, retro-style diner focused on classic dishes like meatloaf with gravy-draped mashed potatoes and sumptuous mac and cheese. It's also a great place for weekend brunch or an evening cocktail.

Fine Dining

Local celebrity chef Frank Bonanno considers his tiny ★ **Mizuna** (225 E. 7th Ave., 303/832-4778, www.mizunadenver.com, 5pm-10pm Tues.-Sat., $28-43) a culinary think tank. Critics agree: It is one of the top-rated restaurants in Denver. A menu of inspired French cuisine changes monthly, but often features a few fish entrées (aloe vera and coconut poached halibut), several meat options, such as dry-aged magret duck breast, and a vegetarian dish. Pair it with a glass of wine or a Stolen Dabloons cocktail, and save room for the pièce

de résistance, Chocolate Sphere—a flourless chocolate cake with Nutella mousse, sponge toffee, and Demerara cream.

CITY PARK AND ENVIRONS
Italian

The **Barolo Grill** (3030 E. 6th Ave., 303/393-1040, http://barologrilldenver.com, 5:30pm-10:30pm Tues.-Fri., 5:15pm-10:30pm Sat., $21-26) is a romantic, upscale restaurant with an extensive wine list and a chef's tasting menu ($70). À la carte items include mouthwatering northern Italian dishes like scallop- and crab-filled tortellini and European bass served with zucchini-potato *torta*. Don't leave without trying one of the house-made desserts, like strawberry granita or chocolate ganache truffles.

Southern

Get your Southern-style biscuit fix at the **Denver Biscuit Company** (3237 E. Colfax Ave., 303/377-7900, www.denbisco.com, 8am-2pm Mon.-Fri., 8am-3pm Sat.-Sun., $8-11). This popular, locally owned company has a simple menu built on big, buttery, melt-in-your-mouth biscuits. Eat 'em in sandwiches, sweet platters (such as biscuit French toast), or in savory biscuit bowls like the classic shrimp and grits.

HIGHLANDS AND PLATTE RIVER VALLEY
Breakfast and Cafés

Consistently ranked as one of Denver's top breakfast joints, ★ **The Universal** (2911 W. 38th Ave., 303/955-0815, 7am-2:30pm daily, $5-11) has a menu of Southern-inspired meals like sausage gravy-smothered biscuits, custard toast, and corn bread rancheros, with creamy grits on the side. **The Wooden Spoon** (2418 W. 32nd Ave., 303/999-0327, http://woodenspoondenver.com, 7am-2pm Tues.-Fri., 8am-2pm Sat., 8am-noon Sun., $6-11) is a quaint family-run bakery that feels like a French café. It's best known for its tantalizing pastries, including enormous cinnamon rolls and flaky, fresh-baked croissants, as well as enticing breakfast and lunch sandwiches.

Fresh and Local

Located in an old gas station, **Root Down** (1600 W. 33rd St., 303/993-4200, www.rootdowndenver.com, brunch 11am-2pm Fri. and 10am-2:30pm Sat.-Sun., dinner 5pm-10pm Sun.-Thurs., 5pm-11pm Fri.-Sat., $14-34) is all about community and the environment. It's completely wind-powered and has two on-site gardens that provide many of the fresh, organic ingredients for their dishes. Although the prices are a tad high for a casual eatery, it's a great cause, and there are less-expensive shared plates like sorrel gnocchi and Colorado lamb sliders in case the flatiron steak from Aspen Ridge or the Longs Peak rack of lamb seems a bit pricey.

Root Down's owner Justin Cucci also owns **Linger** (2030 W. 30th Ave., 303/993-3120, http://lingerdenver.com, 5:30pm-10pm Mon.-Thurs., 5:30pm-11pm Fri.-Sat., $9-24). Thanks to its location in an old mortuary building, Linger humorously bills itself as "Denver's finest Eatuary." The diverse dinner menu features dishes such as Asian ginger chili shrimp or Middle Eastern *fattoush* salad. The open dining area is often packed, especially for the weeknight happy hour (4pm-6:30pm Mon.-Fri.). There is also a special rooftop food truck menu, weather permitting.

If you follow culinary trends, head to ★ **Avanti Food & Beverage** (3200 Pecos St., 720/269-4778, http://avantifandb.com, $11-15), a collective, European-style eatery that houses seven different restaurants, each of which is testing out new ideas and menus. **Bamboo Sushi** (11am-2pm and 5pm-9pm Mon.-Wed., 11am-2pm and 5pm-10pm Thurs., 11am-10pm Fri.-Sat., 11am-9pm Sun.) serves fresh Japanese fare like traditional salmon rolls and tuna *nigiri*. **Bixo Mexiterranean Bites'** (11am-10pm Sun.-Thurs., 11am-midnight Fri.-Sat.) intriguingly named tapas include albacore crudo in cricket crust and mallard duck magret mole. Communal areas include a large rooftop deck where you can chat with friends while sipping a cocktail from one of the two bars.

Brazilian

Family-run **Café Brazil** (4408 Lowell Blvd., 303/480-1877, www.cafebrazildenver.com, 5pm-10pm Tues.-Sat., $16-22) is known for its flowing rum and authentic South American cuisine. The colorful café is popular with locals and visitors alike, who enjoy steaming bowls of *feijoada completa,* a black bean and meat stew that is Brazil's national dish. Enjoy your meal with a mojito or other rum cocktail.

Mexican

Decorated with black-and-white photos of sombrero-toting hombres, **Taqueria Patzcuaro** (2616 W. 32nd Ave., 303/455-4389, www.patzcuaros.com, 11am-9pm Mon.-Sat., 11am-8pm Sun., $10-16) is an atmospheric taqueria with a dozen casual indoor tables and a private outdoor seating area. In addition to a good selection of tequilas, top-shelf margaritas, and beer, the menu features piping-hot plates of seafood, tacos, and enchiladas smothered with red or green chile sauce and melted cheese.

Dessert

No visit to Denver is complete without a stop at ★ **Little Man Ice Cream** (2620 16th St., 303/455-3811, www.littlemanicecream.com, 10am-1am daily). Inspired by the Coney Island hot dog-shaped stands, Little Man is housed in a 28-foot-tall, 14,000-pound cream can. Smiling employees in vintage uniforms serve heaping waffle cones of cinnabun, toffee coffee, and fluffernutter ice cream, as well as thick shakes and ice cream sammies, along with hot fudge, sprinkles, and other decadent toppings.

CHERRY CREEK
Breakfast and Cafés

Syrup (300 Josephine St., 720/945-1111, http://syruprestaurant.com, 7am-2pm Mon.-Fri., 7:30am-2pm Sat.-Sun., $9-14) is one of three locations owned by Milwaukee native Tim Doherty. After he tired of late nights as a barman, Doherty opened this contemporary pancake house. It can be hard to choose from so many great breakfast options—from classic omelets and Benedicts to old-school pancakes or sweet up-starts like Nutella-stuffed French toast and baked apple pie pancakes.

Avanti Food & Beverage

Asian

Although it only has a few tables, **Sushi Tazu** (300 Fillmore St., 303/320-1672, 11:30am-2:30pm and 4:30pm-10pm Mon.-Thurs., 11:30am-2:30pm and 4:30pm-10:30pm Fri., 11:30am-10:30pm Sat., $10-30) is known for its consistently fresh sushi. From the long counter, watch the chefs at work preparing beef soba and other traditional noodle dishes, as well as melt-in-your-mouth tempura and tasty octopus, abalone, and other nigiri.

Mexican

Adelitas Cocina Y Cantina (1294 Broadway, 303/778-1294, www.adelitasdenver.com, 11am-11pm Mon.-Thurs., 11am-midnight Fri., 10am-midnight Sat., 10am-11pm Sun., $9-15) is known for its margaritas, but also has great traditional Mexican food from the state of Michoacán. Choose from a variety of tasty tacos, veggie and mole-draped enchiladas, and sizzling fajitas.

Steakhouse

Cherry Creek's best upscale restaurant is ★ **Elway's** (2500 E. 1st Ave., 303/399-5353, www.elways.com, 11am-10pm Mon.-Thurs., 11am-11pm Fri.-Sat., 11am-9pm Sun., $17-56), named after co-founder and Denver Broncos quarterback. The elegant steakhouse's beautifully appointed dining room feels relaxed yet upscale, with understated decor, muted lighting, and white tablecloths. The extensive menu features "fresh fish and cold water crustaceans," as well as prime, hand-cut steaks and classic entrées such as roasted chicken or prime beef enchiladas. It's worth taking a look at the dessert menu for decadent treats like their strawberry-topped cheesecake and classic Ding Dongs.

Accommodations

DOWNTOWN AND LODO
$150-250

Located near the Convention Center, the **Warwick Denver** (1776 Grant St., 303/861-2000, http://warwickhotels.com, $189-250) has generously sized rooms and suites with a mix of classic and contemporary decor. Amenities include a nice gym with floor-to-ceiling windows and stunning views, same-day laundry and dry cleaning service, and complimentary cruiser bikes.

On the eastern edge of the downtown, the ★ **Queen Anne Bed & Breakfast Inn** (2147 Tremont Pl., 303/296-6666, www.queenannebnb.com, $155-230) is an eco-friendly establishment with four "local artist" suites and nine bright and colorful rooms. Some rooms overlook the peaceful garden, where the owners grow more than 100 varieties of fruits, herbs, and vegetables. It's a great place to lounge with coffee in the morning before the organic breakfast is served.

In the heart of LoDo, the hip **NATIV Hotel** Denver (1612 Wazee St., 720/485-6450, www.nativhotels.com, $175) is a colorful and charismatic hotel with a brightly painted mural covering one exterior wall and bright rooms with white bedspreads and bold accents. Some of the suites have rooftop patios. The hotel also has a café that serves organic coffee and teas, a retro lounge with a bustling dance floor, and the **Biergarten** (720/485-6450, 11am-midnight daily, $10-24), a casual restaurant with self-serve taps and an eclectic menu.

The **Aloft Denver** (800 15th St., 303/623-3063, www.aloftdenverdowntown.com, $229) looks like a piece of modern art, with its strikingly angular roof and a high-ceilinged, industrial-chic lobby decorated with contemporary art and brassy throw pillows. The sparsely furnished rooms include one king or two queen beds, an ergonomic work station, high-speed Wi-Fi, flat-screen TVs, and mini-fridges. You can't beat the location just a block from the Convention Center and the 16th Street Mall.

From the attentive staff, to the ornate and intricately painted lobby ceiling, the experience at the **Kimpton Hotel Monaco Denver** (1717 Champa St., 303/296-1717, www.monaco-denver.com, $179-404) is memorable. The upscale rooms are playfully decorated with geometric patterns and brightly colored accents. Standard rooms have oversized working areas and a choice of bed configurations; larger rooms and suites are also available. Amenities range from a fitness center to unusual perks like yoga mats in every room.

Over $250

Located in one of Denver's most significant landmarks, **The Crawford Hotel** (Union Station, 1701 Wynkoop St., 720/460-3700, www.thecrawfordhotel.com, $280-376) features three floors of unique rooms. Each room represents a different era of the station's history—from the art-deco Pullman Room to the Victorian Classic to the upstairs Loft Rooms with 14-foot ceilings, original beams, and brick walls. Bathrooms vary, with amenities ranging from freestanding claw-foot tubs to modern rain showers.

★ **The Oxford Hotel** (1600 17th St., 303/628-5400, www.theoxfordhotel.com,

$240-336) is a LoDo property filled with historic charm. Prominent guests such as the Dalai Lama and Hillary Clinton have stayed in the classically designed rooms, which feature upgraded beds as well as timeless touches like antique headboards, full drapery, and claw-foot tubs. Luxury amenities include a full-service spa and fitness center, a martini bar, and the in-house **McCormick's Fish House & Bar** (6:30am-10pm Sun.-Thurs., 6:30am-11pm Fri.-Sat., $15-35).

With both comfort and historical charm, ★ **Hotel Teatro** (1100 14th St., 303/228-1100, www.hotelteatro.com, $259) provides nice views and an excellent location just steps from Larimer Square and the performing arts complex. The 110 rooms and suites feature lofty, 12-foot ceilings, in-room coffee makers, thick Simmons Beautyrest mattresses, and plush terrycloth robes. In addition to **The Study**, a relaxed coffee lounge lined with floor-to-ceiling bookcases, the hotel has an upscale restaurant, **The Nickel** (720/889-2128, www.thenickeldenver.com, 11am-2:30pm and 5pm-10pm Sun.-Thurs., 11am-11pm Fri.-Sat.), named for the fare once collected from customers who rode the streetcars when this building served as the Denver Tramway.

the Oxford Hotel

The **Magnolia Hotel** (818 17th St., 303/607-9000, www.magnoliahotels.com, $269-299) has been restored to reflect its original appearance as the historical American National Bank Building. The large boutique property features 297 stylish rooms with either two queens bed or one king-sized bed and oversize baths with a choice of tub or a walk-in shower. Large windows give each room a bright and spacious appearance. Another plus is its great central location just steps from the 16th Street Mall.

The city's most luxurious accommodations in 1892, the ★ **Brown Palace Hotel** (321 17th St., 303/297-3111, www.brown-palace.com, $269-615) remains a venerable downtown institution. At the time it was built, the $2 million hotel sold its guest rooms for $3-5 per night. Although the prices have since increased, many things have not changed, including the 26 stone medallions carved with images of Colorado wildlife on the building's exterior and the eight-story atrium with cast-iron railings and ornate grillwork panels (two of which were mysteriously installed upside down and remain that way today). The renovated guest rooms sport a modern Victorian look; rooms come with queen- or king-size beds, and suites are named for famous guests, including Presidents Roosevelt, Eisenhower, and Reagan. The popular Beatles Suite includes framed records and a custom jukebox. The hotel has an on-site spa and several dining options, including a tavern with a classic pub vibe and an upscale restaurant.

CAPITOL HILL
$150-250
The ★ **Capitol Hill Mansion Bed and Breakfast Inn** (1207 Pennsylvania St., 303/839-5221, www.capitolhillmansion.com, $164-249) offers eight rooms and suites, each named after a Colorado wildflower. The most luxurious is the Elk Thistle Suite, which has a cozy sitting room with a gas fireplace and views of the State Capitol and the Rockies. Amenities vary by room and can include balconies and whirlpool tubs. Guests enjoy a delicious, home-cooked breakfast.

Over $250
A beautiful bed-and-breakfast, the **Patterson Inn** (420 E. 11th Ave., 303/955-5142, www.pattersoninn.com, $241-315) features nine upscale suites housed in a late-1800s mansion in the historic Capitol Hill district. Each suite has a private bath and is uniquely decorated to reflect a theme, such as the Gusteau, whose whitewashed furnishings evoke the romance of Paris. Guests enjoy a wraparound porch, secluded decks, and a hot, made-from-scratch breakfast each morning.

CITY PARK AND ENVIRONS
$150-250
A historic bed-and-breakfast, the **Holiday Chalet Bed & Breakfast** (1820 E. Colfax Ave., 303/437-8245, www.theholidaychalet. com, $149-238) is located in an 1896 Victorian brownstone in Denver's Wyman district. Once a boarding house for women, the chalet now has 10 guest rooms, all with private baths; eight rooms include kitchenettes. Guests can enjoy a cup of tea served in china designed by the inn's original owner, garden s'mores on the weekend, and an in-house massage.

Over $250
Not far from City Park, **The Adagio Bud & Breakfast** (1430 Race St., 303/870-0903, www.budandbfast.com, $299-399) is an intimate, 420-friendly establishment with six colorful suites in a large 1880 mansion.

CHERRY CREEK
With few exceptions, most of the hotels near Cherry Creek are luxurious chains, with correspondingly high prices.

$150-250
The 194-room **Hyatt Place Denver/Cherry Creek** (4150 E. Mississippi Ave., Glendale, http://denvercherrycreek.place.hyatt.com, $195) is in a central location, although it's

most convenient to have a rental car if you plan to stay here. The spacious, contemporary rooms feature corner sofas, free Wi-Fi, and 42-inch HDTVs. Rate includes a breakfast bar.

One of the area's few boutique hotels, ★ **The Inn at Cherry Creek** (233 Clayton St., 303/377-8577, http://innatcherrycreek. com, $169-199) bills itself as the place "where friendly meets sophisticated." Each of the 35 rooms feature large desks and free Wi-Fi; some rooms have fireplaces. The building is within walking distance of the Cherry Creek Mall, the Cherry Creek bike path, and the Colorado Convention Center.

Over $250

Cherry Creek's most luxurious lodging is the 196-room **JW Marriott Denver/Cherry Creek** (150 Clayton Lane, 303/316-2700, www.jwmarriottdenver.com, $342-409). Immaculate guest rooms feature super-comfortable beds, and many have unobstructed mountain views. Amenities include a spacious, contemporary lobby decorated with works by Colorado-based artists, a well-appointed fitness center, and an award-winning restaurant, **Second Home** (6:30am-2pm and 5pm-10pm Mon.-Thurs., 6:30am-2pm and

5pm-11pm Fri., 7am-2pm and 5pm-11pm Sat., 7am-2pm and 5pm-10pm Sun., $14-26). The hotel also offers small, personalized touches, like a local jogging map for people (like me) who always manage to get lost during their morning jog.

The **Halcyon Hotel Cherry Creek** (245 Columbine St., 844/442-5296, www.halcyonhotelcherrycreek.com, $299-399) features thoughtfully decorated rooms with Enseo entertainment systems and in-room libraries. Amenities include a rooftop pool and bar, a lobby espresso stand, and a "gear garage" with cruiser bikes, Vespa scooters, and longboards to launch you on your next adventure. The hotel also has two restaurants.

GREATER DENVER

About 18 miles northwest of downtown, the **Omni Interlocken Resort** (500 Interlocken Blvd., Broomfield, 303/438-6600, www.omnihotels.com, $249) is an enormous hotel complex off of Highway 36. The contemporary resort features a luxurious spa, a 27-hole championship golf course, two heated outdoor pools, and 390 guest rooms, many of which have amazing views of the Flatirons and snow-capped Front Range.

Transportation and Services

AIR

Located about 25 miles east of the downtown, **Denver International Airport** (DEN, 8500 Peña Blvd., 303/342-2000, http://www.flydenver.com) is the city's primary commercial airport. Serviced by 20 airlines, including all major American airlines, DIA is a hub for United, Southwest, and Great Lakes Airlines and is Colorado's primary location from which to connect to flights to other cities in Colorado, including the mountain resorts.

There are three concourses: A, B, and C. Arrivals at Concourse A can either walk to the main Jeppesen Terminal or take the concourse train; arrivals at the other two concourses

must take the concourse train. The Jeppesen Terminal is divided into two sides: east and west (facing the mountains). After exiting the concourse train, take the escalator up to Level 5 to get to the baggage claims, which are located on both the east and west sides.

Airport Transportation

The **RTD University of Colorado A-Line** train (303/299-6000, www.rtd-denver.com, $9 one-way) takes 37 minutes to travel between the airport and downtown Denver's Union Station (1701 Wynkoop St.), the main transportation hub. Most trains run every 15 minutes. Service at Union Station starts at 3:15am and the last train leaves the airport at about 1:25am. The RTD A-Line train picks up at the **Transit Center,** located on the south side of the main terminal. (Exit the terminal and take an escalator down to the Center.) Train tickets are available for purchase from the kiosks.

Several hotels offer shuttle service from the airport (pick up is from Level 5, Island 3). Shuttles usually visit both east and west side terminal locations before departing. In addition, many shuttle services operate between the airport and other metro mountain destinations.

Taxis pick up and drop off from Level 5, Island 1. Fares to most metro locations are meter-based, but some destinations have flat, one-way rates from the airport to Denver ($88.57), the Denver Tech Center ($61.57), Broomfield and Louisville destinations ($70.57, Yellow Cab only), and Boulder ($88.57).

CAR

Denver is located just south of the intersection of two major interstates. **I-70** runs east-west and is the main route from the airport into the city. **I-25** runs north-south from Wyoming to New Mexico.

To reach downtown Denver from Denver International Airport, drive west on Peña Boulevard. After 11 miles, merge onto I-70 west and follow this about 9 miles to Exit 274 toward Colorado Springs. Exit here and stay left at the fork, following signs for I-25 South. Merge onto I-25 south-bound. Exit 212C leads to 20th Street, the northeastern boundary of Lower Downtown (LoDo), while Exit 212 leads to Speer Boulevard, located southwest of LoDo. The drive between the airport and downtown typically takes half an hour, depending upon traffic.

Car Rental

All of the major car rental companies have depots at or near the airport, including **Avis** (800/352-7900, www.avis.com), **Hertz** (800/654-4173, www.hertz.com), and **Thrifty** (800/847-4389, www.thrifty.com). Most require you to first visit their desk on Level 5, then ride a shuttle a short distance to the depot. Shuttles pick up and drop off from Level 5, Island 4, outside doors 505-513 on the east side and 504-512 on the west side.

Denver also has several car share companies, including **eGo** (1536 Wynkoop St., #101, 303/720-1185, http://carshare.org), with locations for vehicle pick-up.

TRAIN

Amtrak (800/872-7245, www.amtrak.com) offers daily service to Denver along the California Zephyr route. Tickets are available online or in person at Union Station (1701 Wynkoop St.). Amtrak also has seasonal weekend service from Union Station to Winter Park Resort.

BUS

The **Regional Transportation District** (RTD, www.rtd-denver.com, $2.60-9.00) operates a network of buses and light-rail trains that transports passengers throughout Denver and connects with regional buses to Boulder and Fort Collins. The Union Station (1701 Wynkoop St.) concourse serves 16 bus routes, including the four Flatirons Flyer routes to Boulder and the free MetroRide and 16th Street MallRide.

Greyhound (www.greyhound.com) and the Colorado Department of Transportation's **Bustang** (800/900-3011, www.codot.gov) offer regional service between Union Station (1701 Wynkoop St.) and locations such as Colorado Springs, Vail, Glenwood Springs, and Grand Junction.

BIKE

Denver B Cycle (https://denver.bcycle.com, $9 for 24 hours) has several bike rental stations, including one station at 1425 North Ogden Street, about half a mile east of the State Capitol. Helmets are not included.

TAXI

Taxis are convenient for short trips, especially downtown. Local companies include

Yellow Cab (303/777-777, http://www.denveryellowcab.com), Metro Taxi (303/333-3333, www.metrotaxidenver.com), and Union Taxi Cooperative (303/922-2222, http://www.uniontaxidenver.net).

SERVICES

Visitor Information

Visit Denver (303/892-1112, www.denver.org) operates several Tourist Information Centers (TICs). The Denver International Airport TIC (8500 Peña Blvd., 303/317-0629, 8am-5pm Mon.-Sat.) is located on the northeast corner of Level 5, the same floor where passengers exit the concourse trains. Denver's Downtown TIC (1575 California St., 303/892-1505, 9am-6pm Mon.-Fri., 9am-5pm Sat., 10:30am-2:30pm Sun. May-Oct., 9am-5pm Mon.-Fri., 9am-2pm Sat., 10am-2pm Sun. Nov.-Apr.) has interactive screens to help you plan your time in town and also sells RTD passes. If you're in Denver for a convention, you can also obtain information at the Colorado Convention Center TIC (700 14th St., 303/228-8000, hours vary). There is also a Tourist Information Desk at Union Station (1701 Wynkoop St., 9am-6pm Mon.-Sat., 10am-2pm Sun.).

Media and Communications

The Denver Post (www.denverpost.com), the city's main daily newspaper, is a good source of information about local news, sports, and events. The Westword is an alternative, weekly paper. Denver's best-known radio news stations are KOA (850 AM), KHOW (630 AM), KVOD (90.1 FM), the local public radio station, and the Spanish language station KNRV (1150 AM).

There are two post offices in downtown Denver, one branch at 951 20th Street (303/296-2071, 8:30am-6pm Mon.-Fri., 9am-6pm Sat.) and a second located at 450 West 14th Avenue (303/571-0796, 9am-5pm Mon.-Fri., 9:30am-12:30pm Sat.). There is also a small branch located on the west side of Level 6 of Denver International Airport's main terminal building.

Many Denver-area locations of interest to visitors have free Wi-Fi, including Denver International Airport, the Denver Botanic Gardens, the Tattered Cover Book Stores, and many restaurants. All branches of the Denver Public Library also offer free Wi-Fi as well as public Internet workstations, from which you can print documents.

Medical

Denver has a number of excellent hospitals, including the University of Colorado Hospital (12605 E. 16th Ave., Aurora, 720/848-0000, www.uchealth.org), St. Anthony Central (11600 W. 2nd Pl., Lakewood, 720/321-0000, www.stanthonyhosp.org), Denver Health (777 Bannock St., 303/436-6000, www.denverhealth.org), and Presbyterian/St. Luke's Medical Center (1719 E. 19th Ave., 303/839-6000, http://pslmc.com). The Children's Hospital Colorado (www.childrenscolorado.org) also has several metro-area locations, including a large campus in Aurora (13123 E. 16th Ave., Aurora, 720/777-1234).

Downtown Denver has a number of urgent care facilities, including one operated by Concentra (1730 Blake St., 303/296-2273, www.concentra.com, 8am-6pm Mon.-Fri.). Located south of downtown is Guardian Urgent Care Center (1 Broadway, Bldg. A, Ste. 100, 303/455-6345, http://guardianurgentcare.com, 8am-7pm Mon.-Fri., 8am-5pm Sat.-Sun.).

Denver Foothills

West of Denver, the Rocky Mountains rise dramatically from the flat and featureless plains. What first appears to be a "wall" of mountains gradually resolves itself into a foreground of forested foothills, deep canyons, and steeply tilted layers of reddish rocks, all of which are overshadowed by the prominent, snow-capped summits of Mount Evans, Grays Peak, and Torreys Peak, which rise above 14,000 feet in elevation.

Denver's foothills are absolutely packed with interesting attractions. Visit Buffalo Bill's gravesite, perched high on a mountain above the western-themed town of Golden. Head to Morrison for a performance at the stunning open-air Red Rocks Amphitheatre, Colorado's most famous music venue. Explore historic mines where you can try your luck panning for gold. The foothills are also home to small, colorful towns, whose superb

restaurants, quaint shops, and craft brewpubs are easy to explore by foot. Recreational opportunities abound, including hiking and cycling, snowboarding and downhill skiing at Winter Park and Loveland, white-water rafting, and golf.

GOLDEN

Founded during the Pikes Peak gold rush, the small town of Golden, located at the mouth of beautiful Clear Creek, has harnessed its excellent historical (and prehistoric) attractions to become a prime destination focused on Western heritage. This is exemplified by the town's motto, "Where the West Lives," which is prominently displayed on a large wooden arch that spans the main downtown thoroughfare, along with the words, "Howdy Folks! Welcome to Golden." In addition to hosting Buffalo Bill's gravesite, Golden is best

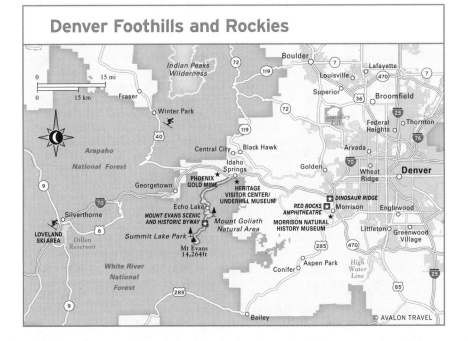

Denver Foothills and Rockies

known as the home of the Colorado School of Mines and the enormous MillerCoors Brewery. Golden sits in the shadow of Lookout Mountain, located just west of town, a favorite hang gliding launch and the site of a beautiful nature preserve.

Sights

The downtown is clustered around the half dozen blocks of Washington Avenue that lie south of Clear Creek. Once you find a parking spot, this lively downtown, which is filled with small, indie shops and student-oriented restaurants housed in carefully restored 19th-century buildings, is a fun place to explore on foot, even if you only have a short time to visit.

The **Clear Creek History Park** (1020 11th St., 303/278-3557, www.goldenhistory. org, 6am-10pm daily, free) offers a glimpse into pioneer history via a collection of original ranch buildings built in 1878. People interested in crafts will also enjoy the cozy **Rocky Mountain Quilt Museum** (1213 Washington Ave., 303/277-0377, www. rmqm.org, 10am-4pm Mon.-Sat., 11am-4pm Sun., $6).

MILLERCOORS BREWERY

The **MillerCoors Brewery** (13th and Ford St., 303/277-2233, www.millercoors.com, tours 10am-4pm Mon.-Sat., noon-4pm Sun. June-mid-Aug., 10am-4pm Thurs.-Mon., noon-4pm Sun. mid-Aug.-May, free) began operations in 1873, when Adolph Coors set up a brewery on the banks of picturesque Clear Creek. Today the facility produces 13 million barrels of beer annually, making it the largest single-site brewery in the world. A 30-minute educational **tour** highlights the malting, brewing, and bottling processes. This is followed by a visit to the refrigerated "Fresh Beer Room," where you can taste a cold sample and sit on ice-cube benches. Tours are free but require a ticket to board a bus to the facility. No backpacks are allowed and lockers are not available; visitors under age 18 must be accompanied by an adult.

BUFFALO BILL MUSEUM AND GRAVE

Perched high on a mountain above Golden, the **Buffalo Bill Museum and Grave** (987 ½ Lookout Mountain Rd., 303/526-0744, www. buffalobill.org, 9am-5pm daily May-Oct., 9am-5pm Tues.-Sun. Nov.-Apr., $5) is the final resting site of William Frederick "Buffalo Bill" Cody, the buffalo-hunter-turned-showman who was buried atop Lookout Mountain following his death in 1917. Photos, recordings, and artifacts help chronicle the adventurous life and lasting legacy of this beloved icon of the American West. Visitors will see the Stetson hat worn by Buffalo Bill at his last performance, several of Cody's firearms, and a peace pipe that belonged to Sitting Bill.

COLORADO SCHOOL OF MINES GEOLOGY MUSEUM

Located on the southwestern edge of downtown, the Colorado School of Mines has a wonderful **Geology Museum** (1310 Maple St., 303/273-3815, www.mines.edu, 9am-4pm Mon.-Sat., 1pm-4pm Sun., free). Begun in 1874, this museum features 50,000 sparkling specimens of gemstones, minerals, fossils, and other artifacts, including a piece of the moon collected by Apollo 17 astronauts.

On the edge of campus, the 1.5-mile (round-trip) **Triceratops Trail** (1400 Jones Rd., www.dinoridge.org, free) follows a short path with interpretive signs that highlight four types of dinosaur tracks, excellent palm frond prints, and even ancient raindrop impressions!

THE BRADFORD WASHBURN AMERICAN MOUNTAINEERING MUSEUM

The nation's one and only museum dedicated to the history of mountaineering, **The Bradford Washburn America Mountaineering Museum** (710 10th St., 303/996-2747, www.mountaineeringmuseum. org, 10am-4pm Mon.-Tues. and Thurs.-Fri., 10am-6pm Wed., noon-5pm Sat., $5) has engaging displays of old climbing gear, photos,

Golden

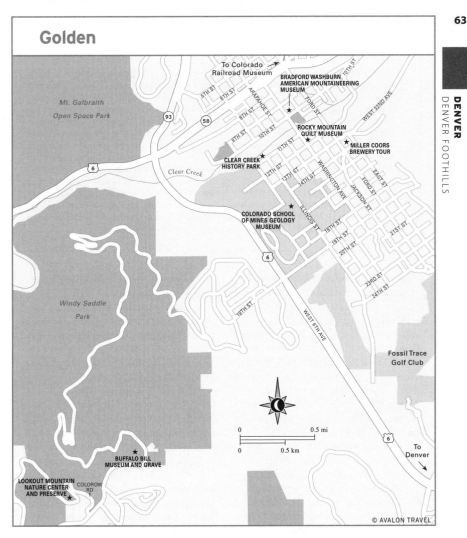

© AVALON TRAVEL

outfits, and artifacts from early Himalayan and other mountaineering expeditions, as well as stunning photography from more recent adventures.

COLORADO RAILROAD MUSEUM

"Lose track of time" is the motto of the **Colorado Railroad Museum** (17155 W. 44th Ave., 303/279-4591, http://coloradorailroadmuseum.org, 9am-5pm daily, $4). The museum features more than 100 steam and diesel locomotives, passenger cars, and red cabooses, as well as a roundhouse restoration facility and an operating train model.

LOOKOUT MOUNTAIN NATURE CENTER AND PRESERVE

The **Lariat Loop National Scenic Byway** (www.lariatloop.org) is a 40-mile byway that links Golden with the towns of Morrison and Evergreen. Along the way, the drive passes a number of interesting sights and

Buffalo Bill's Grave

When William Frederick "Buffalo Bill" Cody died in January 1917, the ground was reportedly too frozen to bury him, so his funeral and the accompanying procession of tens of thousands of mourners were postponed until early June. Meanwhile, according to some theories, several of Cody's friends snuck into the mortuary, swapped his body with someone else's, bribed the mortuary to make him look more like Cody, and buried his actual remains on Cedar Mountain just outside of Cody, Wyoming, the town that he helped found and that still carries his name. The citizens of Cody had always expected that Buffalo Bill would be buried there. Some folks blame Harry Tammen, publisher of *The Denver Post*, for bribing Cody's wife, Louisa, to bury him on Lookout Mountain. Others claim that Buffalo Bill had always wanted to be buried there. The controversy simmered for decades until 1948, when things became so heated that members of Cody, Wyoming's, American Legion post offered a $10,000 reward for the return of Cody's body. This led Denver, which took the threat seriously, to call out the Colorado National Guard to protect the grave, which in the 1920s had been reinforced with 20 tons of concrete. Regardless of where Buffalo Bill is actually buried, this controversy is certainly the stuff of legends.

beautiful foothills scenery. One of the highlights is the **Boettcher Mansion** (900 Colorow Rd., 720/497-7630, http://jeffco.us/boettcher-mansion, 8am-4pm Mon.-Fri., free), located within the **Lookout Mountain Nature Center and Preserve** (910 Colorow Rd., 720/497-7600, http://jeffco.us, 10am-4pm Tues.-Sun., free). Built in 1908 as a private summer home for wealthy Denver entrepreneur Charles Boettcher, it has been used by several of Colorado's governors since 1960.

From downtown Golden, follow Washington Avenue south to 19th Street. Continue west on 19th Street, which becomes Lookout Mountain Road after crossing U.S. 6. Wind your way up Lookout Mountain for about six miles to the junction with Colorow Road. Turn right onto Colorow Road, which leads to the nature center.

Sports and Recreation
HIKING AND BIKING

Clear Creek winds its way through Golden paralleled by the paved **Clear Creek Trail** (http://jeffco.us), which runs about 20 miles from Golden to the city of Thornton. It's a great spot for walking or cycling, as well as kayaking in the creek. Access the path

downtown near the Golden Visitor Center (1010 Washington Ave.).

The road up **Lookout Mountain** is a popular and challenging bike ride; simply head west on 19th Street from its intersection with 6th Avenue and pedal hard until you reach the top in about six miles. There are also multiple hiking trailheads along the road.

A few miles northwest of Golden, the 12,000-acre **Golden Gate Canyon State Park** (92 Crawford Gulch Rd., 303/582-3707, http://cpw.state.co.us, $7 per vehicle) has 36 miles of hiking trails, about half of which are also open to mountain bikes. It's also a great spot for picnicking, camping, and watching for wildlife, including the startlingly black Abert's squirrels, which thrive in the park's beautiful ponderosa pine forests. To get there from downtown Golden, drive west to the junction with Highway 93 and continue north for one mile to Golden Gate Canyon Road. Turn left (west) and follow the road 13 miles to the park.

The twin flat-topped mesas rising north and south of town are North and South Table Mountains, respectively. Protected by their hard lava caps, formed about 64 million years ago from a nearby volcano that has since eroded away, both mountains have been preserved as part of the extensive Jefferson County Open Space system. Of the two, **North Table Mountain Park** (http://jeffco.us, free) is the better option, with more access points and 15 miles of biking and hiking trails, including a 3.2-mile loop with great views of downtown Denver that begins at the trailhead on the park's western edge. It follows the obvious road up to the junction with the North Table Loop Trail. I prefer to head left to stroll through the grassy meadows for about 0.8 mile before turning right onto the Mesa Top Trail, which climbs up the mesa's steep edge. The rest of the route follows the mesa's gentle top along the 0.9-mile Tilting Mesa Trail before reaching a junction with the North Table Mountain Loop. Turn right to descend the path back to your car.

To reach the trailhead from downtown Golden, follow Washington Avenue west to Highway 93. Turn right to head north on Highway 93 for about two miles to a signed access road to the trailhead on the east (right) side of the road.

Peak Cycles Bike Shop (1224 Washington Ave., 303/216-1616, www.bikeparts.com 10am-6pm Mon.-Fri., 10am-5pm Sat., $30-40 for 4 hours) has road, mountain bike, and townie rentals.

RAFTING

Clear Creek Rafting (800/353-9901, http://clearcreekrafting.com, $50-160) offers guided white-water rafting trips on Clear Creek beginning in May. Later in the summer, if water levels are too low, the same firm also offers white-water trips on the Arkansas River. Difficulty levels range from a family-friendly beginner trip to expert (Class V).

GOLF

Just south of Golden, the award-winning **Fossil Trace Golf Club** (3050 Illinois St., 303/277-8750, www.fossiltrace.com, $80-90 for 18 holes) offers Colorado's most unique golf experience: putting next to prehistoric fossils. Sculpted out of an old clay quarry, the course has a variety of historic mementos, including a half-ton shovel and a three-quarter-ton dragline bucket. But on the 12th hole, which *Golf Digest* has rated as one of the 18 "most fun holes" in America, there are a series of sandstone pillars resting in the fairway and, along the left side, a long sandstone wall with the fossils of palm fronds and triceratops tracks embedded in it. The Fossil Trace Clubhouse has some interesting fossil displays, including the cast of a triceratops skull found nearby.

DENVER
DENVER FOOTHILLS

North Table Mountain above Golden

Entertainment and Events

Golden has a number of fun places to kick back and have a drink or two. Most are located within blocks of Washington Avenue, the town's main drag, and have outdoor seating to take advantage of the balmy summer evenings. The most historic is the **Buffalo Rose** (1119 Washington Ave., 303/278-6800, http://buffalorose.net, 11am-2am daily). In the 1870s, this was a hotel and restaurant serving thirsty customers traveling on Wells Fargo stagecoaches. Guests were U.S. generals, as well as shadier characters who got into shootouts with the sheriff. After a snakebite or Buffalo Rose-a-rita (or two), you just may see the ghosts of the several men killed during these battles, who reportedly still haunt the place today.

The **Barrels & Bottles Brewery** (600 12th St., #160, 720/328-3643, www.barrelsbottles. com, 11am-10pm Mon.-Sat., 11am-8pm Sun.) has 20 craft beers on tap and serves wine slushies with a menu of cheese platters, baguettes, and other tapas. In operation since 1961, **Ace Hi Tavern** (1216 Washington Ave., 303/279-9043, http://ace-hi-tavern.com, 7am-2am Mon.-Sat., 8am-2am Sun.) is best known for its twice-daily, college-student happy hours (7am-11am and 3pm-7pm Mon.-Fri.).

Golden's signature event is **Buffalo Bill Days** (www.buffalobilldays.com, late-July, free), an annual celebration that began in the 1940s as a trail ride up Lookout Mountain to Buffalo Bill's grave. It has since grown into three days of parades, car shows, golf tournaments, and live entertainment. The town also turns out en masse for the **Olde Golden Christmas** (www.oldegoldenchristmas.com, Dec., free), held the three Saturdays prior to Christmas. The event features caroling, bands, a parade, and a celebratory candlelight walk.

Shopping

To add some Western wear to your wardrobe, sashay over to **The Silver Horse** (1114 Washington Ave., 303/279-6313, 9am-7pm Mon.-Sat., 10am-7pm Sun.), which specializes in women's boots, belts, clothes, and hats, as well as turquoise-and-silver Native American jewelry. A few steps away, **Baby Doe's** (1116 Washington Ave., 303/279-8100, www.baby-doesclothing.com, 10am-5pm Mon. and Sat., 10am-6pm Tues.-Fri., noon-4pm Sun.) features comfy, casual clothing and a great selection of accessories, including Boulder-made Wallaroo hats and half a dozen brands of distinctive bags and purses. For a perfect souvenir, stop by **Golden Goods** (1201 Washington Ave., 303/216-2123, 10am-8pm daily) for T-shirts, mugs, and large sign-holding bear statues.

Food

Named for a natural foothills feature on the way up to Lookout Mountain, the cozy **Windy Saddle Café** (1110 Washington Ave., 303/279-1905, http://windysaddle.com, 7am-6pm daily, $6-10) has great lattes and other hot drinks, toasted breakfast croissant sandwiches, and a large selection of sandwiches, like the hummus-and-veggie roundup wrap. Housed in a beautifully restored brick building with some of the old plaster still intact, this is a comfortable spot to catch up on email or chat with family and friends.

For dinner, my kids will only eat at one Golden restaurant: **Woody's Wood-Fired Pizza** (1305 Washington Ave., 303/277-0443, www.woodysgolden.com, 11am-midnight daily, $12 for all-you-can-eat buffet), best known for its large all-you-can-eat, all-day pizza and salad buffet. With a large bar and 16 TVs, Woody's is a casual place to watch a game while munching away. There's almost always a wait to get in, so it's a good idea to get here early.

For delicious Lebanese and Mediterranean food, head to **Ali Baba Grill** (109 N. Ruby Dr., 303/279-2228, www.alibabagrill.com, 11am-9pm daily, $12-18), which serves up generous platters of kabobs, gyros, and falafel.

The more upscale **Indulge Bistro & Wine Bar** (1299 Washington Ave., 303/277-9991, www.indulgewinebar.com, 11am-10pm Mon.-Thurs. and Sun., 11am-midnight Fri.-Sat., $11-32) offers half a dozen different wine flights, a good selection of vintages sold by the glass or bottle, and an extensive menu of Colorado-beef burgers, sandwiches, fresh salads, and steaming soups.

Accommodations

Although it's housed in a plain-looking brick building, **The Golden Hotel** (800 11th St., 303/800-5045, www.thegoldenhotel.com, $289) is an immaculate, upscale mountain lodge with beautifully decorated rooms in an ideal location along Clear Creek at the edge of the lively downtown. A few blocks away, smack in the center of town, the distinctive, adobe-style **Table Mountain Inn** (1310 Washington Ave., 303/277-9898, www.tablemountaininn.com, $229) has a comfy lobby with brown leather sofas and colorful Southwestern decor. The inn offers six types of rooms and suites, half of which have nice foothills views, and has a good Mexican restaurant. Both hotels are pet-friendly.

Transportation and Services

Golden is located 15 miles west of Denver. From Denver, head west on West Colfax Avenue to its junction with U.S. 6. Follow U.S. 6 west to 19th Street and turn right here. Drive east to Washington Avenue; turn left on Washington Avenue and take it to downtown Golden.

Golden is accessible from downtown Denver via the **West "W" light-rail line** ($4 one-way fare), which drops you off at the Jefferson County Government Center/Golden Station, located about 2.5 miles from downtown Golden. If you request a transfer, you can use this to travel by RTD Bus number 16 at no additional charge, or you can taxi, walk, or bike the 6th Avenue Trail to get there. Bus 16 leaves from the Oak Station at the corner of West Colfax Avenue and Oak Street, a six-minute walk from Golden Station.

The best source of information is the **Golden Visitors Center** (1010 Washington Ave., 303/279-2282, http://visitgolden.com, 8:30am-5pm Mon.-Fri., 10am-4pm Sat.), conveniently located on the main road at the north end of the downtown next to Clear Creek.

MORRISON

The little town of Morrison (http://town.morrison.co.us) has just 432 residents and sits nestled in a stunning valley tucked behind the dramatic first line of Rocky Mountain foothills known as the "hogback." The small downtown is a fun place to explore, with a

Red Rocks Amphitheatre

number of good restaurants and amazing scenery that feels a world apart from the big city suburbs just a few miles away. Out of all proportion to its size, Morrison has two major attractions: Red Rocks Amphitheatre, the renowned outdoor concert venue, and Dinosaur Ridge, with famous dinosaur fossil localities.

Sights

★ RED ROCKS AMPHITHEATRE

Red Rocks Park hosts the famous **Red Rocks Amphitheatre** (18300 W. Alameda Pkwy., 720/865-2494, http://redrocksonline. com, sunrise-sunset daily, hours vary on concert days, free), Colorado's iconic outdoor concert venue that regularly attracts top music stars from around the world. Big-name acts like The Beatles, Bruce Springsteen, R.E.M., Peter Gabriel, The Fray, Coldplay, and The Grateful Dead have all performed here.

The nearly 900-acre park has a **visitor center** (7am-7pm daily Apr.-Oct., 8am-4pm daily Nov.-Mar.) with displays about the venue's musical history and the amazing geologic events that created this remarkable amphitheater. You can see the fossilized fragments of a 40-foot-long sea serpent and flying reptiles, view dinosaur tracks, and get up-close looks of the amphitheater's two main rock slabs, Ship Rock and Creation Rock, which are both about 300 feet tall. The center also has information about hiking in the park, exercising on the amphitheater's storied steps, and summer Saturday yoga sessions.

To learn more about Colorado's impressive musical legacy, stop by the **Colorado Music Hall of Fame** at the park's **Trading Post** (17900 Trading Post Rd., 303/697-6910, http://cmhof.org, 9am-4pm daily, $6). A series of exhibits focus on musical stars with connections to the state, and there are displays of historical artifacts.

★ DINOSAUR RIDGE

Located atop the first ridge of the foothills west of Denver, **Dinosaur Ridge** (16831 W. Alameda Pkwy., 303/697-3466, www.dinoridge.org, 9am-5pm Mon.-Sat., 10am-5pm

Sun. May-Oct., 9am-4pm Mon.-Sat., 10am-4pm Sun. Nov.-Apr., $6 for guided shuttle tour) is one of the world's most famous fossil localities. Some of the best-known giants were first discovered here, including the bus-sized, armored stegosaurus, the Colorado state fossil; the huge carnivore allosaurus; and the long-necked, plant-eating apatosaurus (formerly called brontosaurus), which at 33-38 tons was one of the largest land animals that ever lived.

The site has two visitor facilities. The main **Visitor Center** (16831 W. Alameda Pkwy., Morrison, 303/697-3466, www.dinoridge.org, 9am-5pm Mon.-Sat., 10am-5pm Sun. in summer, $2) is on the east side of the ridge; the smaller **Discovery Center** (17681 W. Alameda Pkwy., Golden, 303/697-3466, www.dinoridge.org, 9am-5pm Mon.-Sat., noon-5pm Sun. in summer, $2) is on the west. Both have small displays about the dinosaur species that once roamed here as well as the area's geologic history. The 40-minute narrated **shuttle bus tours** (hourly 10am-4pm May-Oct., 10am-3pm Nov.-Apr., $6) begin at the east-side Visitor Center and travel across the ridge.

The highlight of any visit is walking the paved **Dinosaur Ridge Trail** (1.5-mile one way) between the two visitor centers. From the west-side Discovery Center, interpretive signs point out many interesting natural features, such as the **Dinosaur Bone Quarry,** where a jumble of dark-brown dinosaur bones are encased in a block of buff-colored sandstone, and the **Jurassic Time Bronto Bulges,** an impressive set of tracks left by a 30-ton, long-necked dinosaur.

Near the crest of the ridge is a younger rock unit from the Cretaceous Period, when very different dinosaurs roamed the region. As you descend, you'll pass amazing ripple marks and the impressions of several mangroves. Located just uphill is the ridge's main attraction: the **Dinosaur Tracks,** a huge, tilted sandstone slab crisscrossed with more than 330 dinosaur footprints.

To reach the main Visitor Center from

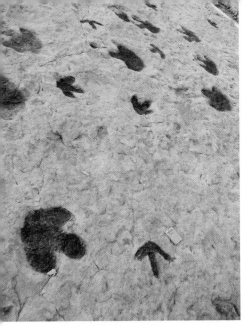
ancient tracks on Dinosaur Ridge

Denver, follow U.S. 6 west to West Alameda Parkway. Take the exit onto I-70 West toward Grand Junction. In 0.9 mile, take Exit 260 to merge onto Highway 470 East toward Colorado Springs. In 2.1 miles, take the Alameda Parkway exit. Turn right onto West Alameda Parkway and follow it 0.1 mile to the Visitor Center.

MORRISON NATURAL HISTORY MUSEUM
Just south of downtown, the small **Morrison Natural History Museum** (501 Hwy. 8, 303/697-1873, www.mnhm.org, 10am-4pm daily, $8) has interesting, hands-on exhibits about the area's amazing fossil finds. Expert guides lead **tours** of the museum (10:15am, 12:15pm, and 2:15pm daily), or visitors can wander on their own. Exhibits include the Time Garden, which explores Morrison's distinctive setting; a working lab where you can watch staff and volunteers searching for and preparing fossils; and a Jurassic Garden, where you can learn more about Jurassic

giants like the armored, plant-eating stegosaurus and the fierce, carnivorous allosaurus.

Entertainment and Events
Located in a pretty 1870s cottage with a beautiful garden, **Flights Wine Café** (116 Stone St., 303/697-0492, http://flightswinecafe.com, 4pm-4pm Tues.-Thurs., 4pm-10pm Fri., 2pm-10pm Sat., 2pm-7pm Sun.) has a selection of more than 100 wines, as well as a tapas-style menu of cold and hot plates. Freshly cooked dishes include smoked salmon and feta-stuffed petite grilled peppers. The **Morrison Holiday Bar** (403 Bear Creek Ave., 303/697-5658, www.morrisonholidaybar.com, 10am-2am daily) is a fun, sensory-overloading sports bar filled with big-screen TVs, foosball tables, darts, and video games. It is best known for its daily live music and drink specials.

Nicknamed Thunder Mountain, the **Bandimere Speedway** (3051 S. Rooney Rd., 303/697-6001, www.bandimere.com, hours and prices vary) is a 0.25-mile drag strip just outside of Morrison. The speedway hosts a series of races; the best known is the National Hot Rod Association's **Mopar Mile-High Nationals** ($47-63), held each July.

Accommodations and Food
Morrison has a couple of intimate bed-and-breakfasts located just minutes from Red Rocks. The **Arrowhead Manor Inn** (9284 Hwy. 285, 303/738-8454, http://arrowhead-manor.com, $150-540) houses six beautifully decorated rooms and one suite. Rooms have fireplaces, private travertine-tiled bathrooms with jetted tubs, and surround-sound movie systems. This 420-friendly hotel also has a large deck with beautiful mountain views. Housed in a brick mansion built in 1864, the **Cliff House Lodge** (121 Stone St., 303/697-9732, http://cliffhouselodge.net, $190-700) has seven cottages, each decorated with a different theme. Stone Street is a "rock-n-roll cottage" decorated with paintings by Red Rocks resident artist Scramble Campbell. Most of the cottages have hot tubs and outdoor seating

The Bone Wars

It was in 1877 when Arthur Lakes, a professor at the Colorado School of Mines, first spotted an enormous vertebra in a chunk of sandstone on a ridge near Golden. His discovery grabbed the attention of two of the nation's top paleontologists, Edward Cope of Philadelphia's Academy of Natural Sciences and Othniel Marsh at Yale University. The two became bitter competitors and bore one another such ill will that they spied on each other's excavations, stole the other's fossils, and tried to sabotage each other's reputations. The rivalry, known as the **Bone Wars,** became so acrimonious that Marsh destroyed one of his quarries to prevent Cope from benefitting from it, and Cope, upon his death, left his skull to science with the expectation that once measured, his (presumably) larger brain would prove that his intelligence was superior to Marsh's. Because the bones that Lakes discovered on what today is known as **Dinosaur Ridge** were the largest ever found, the two rivals immediately shifted their attention to the Denver area. Although both paleontologists made some sloppy mistakes in their rush to one-up each other (Marsh, for example, placed the wrong skull on the torso of an apatosaurus, a mistake that wasn't corrected for more than a century), the duo unearthed and preserved many important fossils that firmly established the Denver area as one of the world's leading paleontology research sites. Studies of these and other, more recent finds have kept the area at the forefront of dinosaur research, while conservation efforts have (so far) protected many irreplaceable sites from Denver's rapidly expanding suburbs.

areas. Prices at both facilities are highest on concert nights.

Located two miles south of Red Rocks Amphitheatre, **The Fort** (19192 Hwy. 8, 303/697-4771, http://thefort.com, 5:30pm-10pm Mon.-Fri., 5pm-10pm Sat.-Sun., $24-56) is one of the area's most unique dining experiences. Made of more than 80,000 mud and straw bricks, this huge adobe building is modeled after Bent's Old Fort, an 1840s adobe trading post built along the Santa Fe Trail. Built by the Arnold family, The Fort was originally going to be their home, but after construction costs exceeded their budget, the family decided to turn the bottom floor into a trading post and restaurant specializing in food and drink of the early West, including dishes that the early pioneers, Spanish traders, and native tribes

ate. The restaurant's signature dishes are meat—buffalo, quail, elk, and choice cuts of Colorado-raised beef—and the most popular menu item is The Fort's Game Plate, which includes an elk chop, a Buffalo sirloin medallion, and grilled teriyaki quail. The Fort also serves authentic cocktails whose recipes date back 170 years, including the 1840 Hailstorm Premiere Julep—a mix of bourbon or scotch with mint, sugar, and ice—the first cocktail ever served at Bent's Fort.

Transportation and Services

To reach Morrison from Denver, drive west on U.S. 6 to its junction with South Kipling Street. Turn left and follow Kipling south to the junction with Morrison Road. Turn right and follow Morrison Road about five miles west to downtown Morrison.

The Denver Rockies

IDAHO SPRINGS

Idaho Springs lies in the deep Clear Creek valley at the toe of mighty Mount Evans, the most prominent peak behind Denver's skyline. Founded during the Pikes Peak Gold Rush, Idaho Springs was the site of both the Argo Tunnel, which accessed nearly all of the mines between Clear Creek and Central City, as well as the location of some hot springs. Following the collapse of silver, however, the town's population plummeted. Fortunately, the route soon became an important stop for travelers crossing the Rockies west of Denver, and it remains a colorful destination along I-70.

Sights

A number of attractions in Idaho Springs (http://visitidahospringscolorado.com) celebrate the town's mining heritage, but it is also an enjoyable place to stop and simply amble along Clear Creek and the historic downtown, especially the group of colorfully painted wooden Victorian buildings along Miner Street, located just north of I-70.

HERITAGE VISITOR CENTER

A good first stop is the **Heritage Visitor Center** (2060 Miner St., 303/567-4382, http://visitidahospringscolorado.com, 9am-5pm daily in summer, free), which has a small museum where you can learn more about the town's mining heritage and history, including when and how gold was discovered in Idaho Springs and what its impact has been.

ARGO GOLD MILL AND MUSEUM

The **Argo Gold Mill and Museum** (2350 Riverside Dr., 303/567-2421, http://historicargotours.com, 9:30am-5pm daily May-mid-Sept., $16) are located at one end of the 4.5-mile-long Argo Tunnel. The tunnel was completed in 1910 to access and ventilate the many mines riddling the mountains between Idaho Springs and Central City, including the Double Eagle gold mine, an important source of the rich gold ore processed by the Argo Mill. Tours begin with a live demonstration of the rock drilling techniques used at the time, followed by a mine tour and a guided walk through the mill. This mill processed

the Argo Gold Mill and Museum

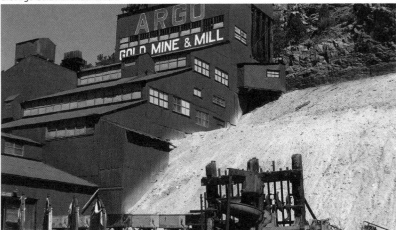

Beau Jo's 14er Challenge

If you've been in Colorado for a few days, chances are you've already heard about our obsession with climbing "fourteeners," the state's 54 peaks over 14,000 feet in elevation. Shortly after opening in 1973, Beau Jo's, the homegrown pizza chain famous for its Colorado-style, thick-crust pizzas, created its own fourteener challenge. But instead of traipsing up a peak, this one involves conquering a different type of fourteener: a massive, 14-pound grand Sicilian pizza. Beau Jo's chefs begin with an extra-thick 16-inch crust, pile it high with pounds of sausage, pepperoni, hamburger, onions, mushrooms, and peppers, and then smother it with pounds of cheese before baking it to perfection. The challenge, if you choose to accept it, is for two people to eat the entire pie in one hour during one sitting. If you manage to succeed (and only three teams have in the last 42 years), you get the $80 pizza for free, T-shirts, a $100 gift card, and your proud photo displayed on the restaurant wall. If you fail, your photo is hung instead on the "wall of shame" and (even worse) you have to pay the bill.

more than $100 million of gold during a period when the prices ranged $18-35 per ounce. Today, that price is north of $1,300! Following the tour, you can try your own luck panning for gold.

PHOENIX GOLD MINE

Tours of the working **Phoenix Gold Mine** (800 Trail Creek Rd., 303/567-0422, www. phoenixmine.com, 10am-6pm daily, $10) are led by two seasoned miners, Al and Dave Mosch, members of what claims to be Colorado's oldest continuous gold-mining family. After visiting the underground mining shafts and viewing old mining equipment, the hour-long tour visits the Resurrection Vein, a fracture in the mine wall filled with rich gold ore. After your tour, you can try panning for gold in the adjacent stream and keep any flakes that you find.

UNDERHILL MUSEUM

The **Underhill Museum** (1416 Miner St., 303/567-4709, http://historicidahosprings. com, 11am-5pm Sat.-Sun., free) offers a peek at life in Idaho Springs in the early 1900s. Housed in the former home of mining engineer James Underhill and his wife, Lucy, the museum collection includes turn-of-the-20th-century photographs, furnishings, and mining equipment.

INDIAN HOT SPRINGS RESORT

The historic **Indian Hot Springs Resort** (302 Soda Creek Rd., 303/989-6666, www. indianhotsprings.com, 9am-10pm daily, $17-19) offers numerous ways to relax in mineral-rich waters, including geothermal caves with walk-in hot tubs, outdoor whirlpool tubs, private indoor baths, and a family-friendly swimming pool surrounded by tropical gardens beneath a large, glass dome. Since its construction in 1869, the complex has hosted many famous visitors, including Baby Doe Tabor, the Vanderbilts, the Roosevelts, John Denver, and Clint Eastwood.

Food

Smokin Yard's BBQ (2736 Colorado Blvd., 303/567-9273, http://smokinyards.com, 11am-9pm Sun.-Thurs., 11am-10pm Fri.-Sat., $6-27) serves up "real southern BBQ," including sliced beef brisket and smoked chicken, as well as hotlinks, burnt ends, and other spicy delights by the pound. You can sit inside, at the bar, or on the patio next to Clear Creek. One of Idaho Spring's most popular restaurants is **Beau Jo's** (1517 Miner St., 303/567-4376, www.beaujos.com, 11am-9:30pm Sun.-Thurs., 11am-10pm Fri.-Sat., $10-12), a small Colorado chain best known for its Mountain Pie pizza—the crust is so thick they serve honey to squirt on it like bread.

The menu also includes calzones, Beaughetti (spaghetti served in a garlic bread bowl), and a large salad bar situated in an old-fashioned bathtub. Beau Jo's is also the home of the legendary 14er pizza-eating challenge.

Transportation and Services

From Denver, I-70 west leads directly to Idaho Springs in 32 miles; take Exits 241 or 240. In good conditions, the trip to Idaho Springs should take under an hour, but it can take substantially longer during rush hour and/or inclement weather.

Greyhound (www.greyhound.com, $15 one-way) offers service several times daily from downtown Denver's Union Station (1701 Wynkoop St.) to the Idaho Springs station (2712 Colorado Blvd.).

★ Mount Evans Scenic and Historic Byway

One of the highlights of any summer visit to the Denver foothills is driving or biking the **Mount Evans Scenic and Historic Byway** (Hwy. 5, www.fs.usda.gov, May-Oct.), the highest paved road in North America. From its start at about 7,500 feet elevation near Idaho

Springs, this "road to the sky" climbs nearly 7,000 vertical feet in just 28 miles, passing several ecosystems along the way—large stands of aspen, dense evergreen forest, and treeless, windblown tundra bursting with wildflowers.

The road is typically open Memorial Day through September, weather permitting. Check with the Arapahoe Forest Service's **Clear Creek Ranger District** (2060 Miner St., 303/567-4382, www.fs.usda.gov) or CDOT (www.cotrip.org) before planning the drive.

ECHO LAKE

From Idaho Springs, access the byway by taking I-70 west to Exit 240. The byway follows Highway 103 south along Chicago Creek, passing the Black Eagle mill site and several beautiful picnic areas before reaching the **Echo Lake** fee station ($10) and **campground** (www.recreation.gov, June-Sept., $17) at 10,600 feet in 15 miles.

MOUNT GOLIATH NATURAL AREA

From Echo Lake, the byway follows **Mountain Evans Road** (Hwy. 5) south, passing the 160-acre **Mount Goliath Natural Area** (www.fs.usda.gov). Mount Goliath was

Mount Evans Scenic and Historic Byway

set aside to protect one of the Rockies' northernmost groves of beautiful bristlecone pines, trees that range 700-1,600 years old. The **Dos Chappell Nature Center** (10am-5pm daily in summer) at 11,540 feet has a number of exhibits about these remarkable trees and the construction of the Mount Evans Road. The natural area also has a few trails, including the 0.25-mile **Bristlecone Loop,** which passes some of these trees, and the moderate, 1.5-mile (one-way) **M. Walter Pesman Trail,** which starts behind the nature center.

SUMMIT LAKE PARK

From the Mount Goliath Natural Area, the Mount Evans Byway continues to climb south on Highway 5, passing Lincoln Lake and two thirteeners—Rogers Peak and Mount Warren—on the way to **Summit Lake Park** (Hwy. 5, 303/567-2901, https://denvermountainparks.wordpress.com, $5 fee payable at Echo Lake), at 12,830 feet. Nestled in a cirque below Mount Evans, this glistening gem is the byway's most accessible alpine lake. It's located a few hundred feet from the Summit Lake parking area and is a great place to stop for wildflower photos and to search for mountains goats, which are often spotted in the area. Be sure to walk the 0.25-mile (one-way) trail to see the spectacular view from the Chicago Lake Basin Overlook. Vault toilets are available at the park.

SUMMIT OF MOUNT EVANS

From Summit Lake, you can either hike the remaining 1,475 vertical feet to the summit via the 1.75-mile (one-way) **Summit Lake Trail,** or drive the impressive maze of switchbacks up to the **Summit of Mount Evans Interpretive Site,** where it's just a few minutes' walk to the actual 14,264-foot summit, marked by an official bronze plaque embedded in the coarse rock. From the top, you're treated to some of the best views in Colorado, including Mount Bierstadt and Grays and Torreys Peaks to the west— the two highest points on the Continental Divide—and the spectacular Front Range to

the east. Picnic tables and vault toilets are available at the site.

GEORGETOWN

Located 12 miles west of Idaho Springs, Georgetown (www.georgetowncolorado.com) has a small population of just over 1,000 residents and a number of interesting attractions, including a popular historic narrow-gauge railroad ride.

Sights
GEORGETOWN LOOP HISTORIC RAILROAD

At the time of its completion in 1884, the four-mile stretch of the three-foot narrow-gauge railroad that runs between Georgetown and Silver Plume was considered an engineering marvel due to the area's extreme terrain. To reduce the average grade to 3 percent, which could be managed by most steam engines, the engineers had to devise a special series of hairpin turns, four bridges, and a 30-degree horseshoe bend between the two towns. After years of restoration work, the **Georgetown Loop Historic Railroad** (Loop Dr., Georgetown, 888/456-6777, http://georgetownlooprr.com, May-Dec., $26-35 round-trip) once again transports passengers between these two historic mining towns along this infamous track. The trip lasts 1.25 hours through beautiful forested scenery and crosses the evocatively named Devil's Gate High Bridge.

HAMILL HOUSE MUSEUM

Originally built as a modest country home, the **Hamill House Museum** (305 Argentine St., 303/569-2840, www.historicgeorgetown. org, 10am-4pm Tues.-Sun. in summer, $7) was later significantly expanded by silver baron William Arthur Hamill. Strolling through this historic home on a self-guided tour gives you a great sense of how well the wealthy lived in the late 19th century; you'll see Hamill's opulent tastes extended to gas lighting, bay windows, and even central heating (a luxury at the time). In addition to the main house, you can visit a number of

Central City and Black Hawk

Central City

Located north of Idaho Springs, the twin towns of **Central City** and **Black Hawk** both have "rich" histories that began in 1859, when a prospector named John Gregory discovered a large deposit of gold in a narrow canyon between the future townsites. Following more gold strikes, nearly 10,000 people arrived, but as the veins were exhausted, many left, and the area gradually fell on hard times, dropping to a combined population of a few hundred in the 1950s. With the once-grandiose Victorian buildings rapidly deteriorating, there seemed little hope to revive these historical treasures until 1991, when Coloradans passed a citizen's amendment allowing limited-stakes gambling in both towns, as well as in **Cripple Creek,** another historic mining town west of Colorado Springs.

With this change, many millions of dollars flooded in, money that was used to build fancy casinos, luxurious hotels, and other tourist amenities, but also to restore many of the towns' beautiful historic buildings. Although both Central City and Black Hawk feel rather touristy, the measure definitely served its purpose of revitalizing these towns. If you decide to visit, take the time to catch a show at the beautiful **Central City Opera House** (124 Eureka St., 303/292-6700, https://centralcityopera.org, hours and prices vary), built in 1878 by the citizens of Central City (mostly Cornish and Welsh miners) who wanted a musical venue worthy of the town's growing status as "the richest square mile on earth." Buffalo Bill performed one of his routines here, as did P.T. Barnum's circus. Today this legendary building is the concert venue for the **Central City Opera Company,** which presents several different musicals here each summer, usually early July-early August.

The **Gilpin County History Museum** (2228 E. High St., 303/582-5283, www.gilpinhistory. org, 10am-4pm Tues.-Sat. late May-early Sept., $6) is a former schoolhouse with displays about local history, including the century-old **Mountain Submarine,** whose designer, Rufus Owen, tried to sail in nearby Missouri Lake in 1898. Like many gambles, Owen's did not pay off, and the sub sank and sat on the bottom of the lake until 1944, when it was raised and placed on display.

outbuildings, including the carriage house, a summer kitchen, and a six-seat privy.

HOTEL DE PARIS MUSEUM

Louis Dupuy, a French miner-turned-hotelier, converted this mining-boom property into one of Colorado's fanciest hotels, now the **Hotel de Paris Museum** (409 6th Ave., 303/569-2311, www.hoteldeparismuseum.org, 10am-5pm Mon.-Sat., noon-5pm Sun. in summer, reduced hours in winter, $7). Half-hour, docent-led tours visit the elegant dining room, where the tables were set with the finest linens and imported Haviland china, and the sophisticated hotel rooms, featuring indoor plumbing and a complete set of Encyclopedia Britannica.

Events

Since 1976, a group named **Our Gang 4 Wheelers** (http://ourgangiceracing.com, Jan.-Feb.) has hosted car races each winter on the frozen surface of Georgetown Lake, a small lake sandwiched between I-70 and Georgetown. The races occur on six consecutive weekends and include a street division (regular cars), a "pro street" division (cars with special tires), and a division for off-road vehicles. Visitors are welcome to watch—and participate.

Food

The **Dusty Rose Tea Room** (614 Rose St., 303/569-3100, https://dustyrosetearoom.com, 11:30am-5pm Wed.-Sun., $10-12) is located in a yellow mid-1870s Italianate building that has housed a hotel and restaurant since 1877. Today, it's the home of a miniatures shop and this tearoom. It's a great place to relax over a cup of tea or enjoy a "historic combo" of deviled eggs and a black walnut cookie. They also serve afternoon and Victorian high teas. In the center of town on the banks of Clear Creek, **A Whistle Stop Café** (1400 Argentine St., 303/569-5053, 7am-3pm Mon.-Thurs., 7am-7pm Fri.-Sun., $6-10) serves up large portions of pancakes, cheese-stuffed omelets, pulled-pork sandwiches, and hand-breaded chicken fried steak.

the Georgetown Loop Historic Railroad

Transportation and Services

Georgetown is 12 miles west of Idaho Springs via I-70. From Denver, take I-70 west for 45 miles to Exit 228.

Guanella Pass Scenic and Historic Byway

For a quick taste of the Rocky Mountains, drive the beautiful, 22-mile **Guanella Pass Scenic and Historic Byway** (www.fs.usda.gov, free). The paved route between Georgetown on I-70 and the town of Grant on U.S. 285 takes only an hour to drive, but offers great photo-ops, especially the far-ranging vistas from 11,669-foot Guanella Pass, which has great views of two fourteeners, Mount Evans and Mount Bierstadt. It's common to see mule deer and sure-footed bighorn sheep cavorting in this area. Although it's dependent upon the weather, this paved road is typically open from late May through early November.

To get to the pass from Georgetown's informative **Gateway Visitor Center** (1491 Argentine St., 303/569-2405, www.

Loveland Ski Area

Loveland Ski Area

Although the big-ticket resorts like Vail and Winter Park receive all of the attention, locals swear by **Loveland Ski Area** (I-70, Exit 216, 800/736-3754, http://skiloveland.com, 9am-4pm Mon.-Fri., 8:30am-4pm Sat.-Sun., $45-65), a snowboarding and ski area located right on the Continental Divide about 13 miles west of Georgetown and just 1.5 miles east of the **Eisenhower Tunnel** on I-70. With a base elevation of 10,800 feet (more than two miles above sea level) and an average of 422 inches of snow per year, more than any of the state's major resorts, Loveland is usually able to open as early as October, close as late as June, and keep their deep base through spring warm-ups that devastate the larger resorts. Add to this more affordable ticket prices, convenient parking, inexpensive food at the lodge, and some of the least-crowded slopes in the area, and you can see why Loveland is king among die-hard locals.

Loveland is divided into two base areas, **Loveland Valley,** a separate area for beginners, and **Loveland Basin,** which is known for its advanced and expert mogul runs like **Cat's Meow** and **Zoom.** Before you clip in, however, be warned: Loveland is not for the faint of heart. Because much of the terrain is above tree line, gale-force winds, subzero temperatures, and blowing snow are fairly regular here. But for locals, these conditions just add to the adventure.

georgetowntrust.org, 9am-5pm daily), turn right to head south on Argentine Street, which turns into Brownell Street. About 0.7 mile from the visitor center, turn left onto 6th Street, then right onto Rose Street. At the junction with 2nd Street, turn left onto the Guanella Pass Road and follow it 10.5 miles to the 11,669-foot pass.

WINTER PARK

Winter Park's fabulous terrain, spread across three very different mountains, and its proximity to Denver make it one of Colorado's most beloved resorts. Consistently ranked in the top 10 ski resorts in the nation, Winter Park had rather humble beginnings. In 1937, after the construction of the Moffat railroad tunnel through the Continental Divide finally connected Denver with the West Slope, the U.S. Forest Service built a ski jump and a few trails near the railroad portal. A couple of years later, the nearby mountain officially opened as the Winter Park Ski Area. Despite having just one J-bar tow, the "ski area" racked up more than 10,500 skier days, and the numbers climbed rapidly from there.

Winter Park Resort

In addition to skiing and snowboarding in winter, **Winter Park Resort** (85 Parsenn Rd., 970/726-1564, www.winterparkresort.com, 9am-4pm Mon.-Fri., 8:30am-4pm Sat.-Sun. mid-Nov.-mid-Apr., $144) also offers snow tubing and ski bike tours, snowcat tours, and snowshoe tours. Summer activities include a giant bungee, a climbing wall, a putting course, and Colorado's longest alpine slide. You can pick two for $30 or buy an all-day pass for $47 (if you book at least 48 hours in advance).

DOWNHILL SKIING
AND SNOWBOARDING

With 3,081 skiable acres, 143 trails, and 25 lifts, Winter Park Resort is one of the biggest and best ski areas in the state. Winter Park has some of the most consistent snow, averaging about 350 inches (that's more than 29 feet!) per year. If Mother Nature doesn't cooperate, the resort has enough snowmaking equipment to blanket 27 trails—enough to guarantee that the resort will open around Thanksgiving each year. With terrain suitable for all abilities and levels, it's a great area for beginners and families with a mixture of skills. Winter Park also has an extra blue/black difficulty rating to cover advanced intermediate terrain, so it's also a good choice for skiers growing into advanced (black) terrain.

Spread across three mountains, Winter Park is divided into seven territories, each with its own character. **Mary Jane** is infamous for its advanced and expert mogul runs, while **Winter Park,** the original mountain, has a nice mix of difficulty levels and is easily accessed from the resort's main base area.

Start your day at the **Winter Park Base Area,** which has the greatest concentration of beginner (green) runs, many of which are clustered around the Gemini Express and Olympia Express lifts. To avoid long lines, more experienced skiers should head immediately to the Zephyr Express lift to enjoy classic runs, including Cranmer, a blue, the blue/black Bradley's Bash, and the black-diamond Mulligan's Mile. Intermediate skiers will enjoy **Vasquez Ridge** and the more adventurous high-alpine **Parsenn Bowl,** which is not usually groomed.

Advanced and expert skiers like to test their mettle on **Outhouse,** which has the reputation of being Winter Park's hardest run. Outhouse conveniently leads to Mary Jane,

Winter Park in summer

which is heaven on earth for boarders and skiers who delight in steep bump runs.

Winter Park also has six **Terrain Parks** with more than 80 features, including an 18-foot superpipe. The largest park, Dark Territory, has the most technical jibs, jumps, and rails and requires a special pass to enter. To get the pass, which is valid for the entire season, freeriders need to watch a video and sign an extra liability form.

LESSONS AND RENTALS

Winter Park is known for its excellent disabled skiers program and its **Ski + Ride School** (800/729-7907, www.winterparkresort.com, from $199 for full-day kid's lesson), which offers both group and private lessons for every ability level. You can rent boards and skis at **Winter Park Resort Rentals** (800/979-0328, www.winterparkresort.com, $36 for an all-day board or ski package), which has several base-area locations and offers discounts up to 25 percent for bookings made at least 48 hours in advance.

BIKING

The resort's marquee summer attraction is **Trestle Bike Park** (970/726-1564, http://trestlebikepark.com, 9:30am-5pm daily June-Sept., $140 for all-day bike rental and lift ticket), which has about 50 trails of varying difficulty levels accessed by the Zephyr Express lift. The resort also offers lessons, guided tours, and rentals.

Entertainment and Events

Winter Park nightlife is generally limited to après-ski drinks and appetizers in hotels and bars. Good slope-side options include the contemporary **Moffat Station Micro Brew & Restaurant** (Winter Park Mountain Lodge, 81699 U.S. 40, 970/726-4211, http://winterparkhotel.com, 4pm-10pm daily) and the **Vertical Bistro & Tap** (130 Parry Peak Way, 970/363-7053, http://verticalbistro.com, 11am-9pm Sun.-Thurs., 11am-11pm Fri.-Sat.), located just a few steps from the Zephyr Express lift.

In the town of Winter Park, younger crowds usually follow the "See ya at the pub" bumper stickers to the **Winter Park Pub** (78260 U.S. 40, 970/726-4929, 11am-2am Mon.-Sat., 11am-midnight Sun.), which has good happy hour deals and live music on the weekends during ski season. **The Peak Bistro & Brewery** (78491 U.S. 40, 970/726-7951, 11am-2am daily) has a great selection of craft beers and burgers, paninis, and pizzas in case you have the munchies.

Food and Accommodations

WINTER PARK RESORT

The resort's most upscale accommodations can be found at the **Zephyr Mountain Lodge** (201 Zephyr Way, 970/726-8400, www.zephyrlodge.com, $284 for a 1-bed condo). The property features 1-, 2-, and 3-bedroom units in two buildings; the "riverside" lodge and the "slope-side" lodge, a ski-in/ski-out property, are located just 110 feet from the central Zephyr Express lift. Most units have private decks with great views, gas fireplaces, and fully equipped kitchens, and all have access to a modern fitness room, on-site gear storage, and four steaming outdoor hot tubs.

Located at the resort entrance next to the Cabriolet Gondola, the **Vintage Hotel** (100 Winter Park Dr., 970/726-8801, www.winterparkresort.com, $199-239) is another popular place to stay. Although its rooms are pretty plain, it's in a good location with quick access to the slopes, a dry sauna, and an outdoor hot tub and heated pool. Kids also love the video arcade.

In the heart of Winter Park's base village, **Lime** (135 Parry Peak Way, 970/726-5463, http://eatatlime.com, 11am-10pm daily, $11-30) is known for its great 3pm-6pm happy hours, which feature $3 house margaritas, as well as an extensive menu of fresh Mexican fare, including sweet corn tamales and scorpions—butterflied shrimp with spicy jalapeños and chipotle cheese.

Located at 10,700 feet atop the mountain and accessed by lift, **The Lodge at Sunspot** (160 Sunspot Way, 970/726-1446, www.winterparkresort.com, 11am-2pm daily in winter and summer, plus 6pm-close Fri.-Sat. in winter, $25 for lunch ticket and chairlift ride in summer) has stunning views of the Fraser Valley and the snow-capped peaks on the Continental Divide. The summer lunch menu typically includes a small selection of sandwiches that you can enjoy on the outdoor patio, while in winter, you can eat at an upscale food court or enjoy formal, sit-down service. The Sunspot also has several unique weekend dining options during the ski season, including a five-course meal and romantic fireside fondue.

DOWNTOWN WINTER PARK

A few miles from the resort, the good-value **Valley Hi Motel** (79025 U.S. 40, 970/726-4171, www.winterparkresort.com, $120-140) has 14 basic rooms that are clean and comfortable in a convenient, central location right off of U.S. 40. The **Trailhead Inn** (78572 U.S. 40, 970/726-8843, http://trailheadinn.com, $99-129) has 40 remodeled rooms that are excellent value. On-site amenities include a pool and hot tub.

There are many good, casual dining options in the town of Winter Park. One is **Hernando's Pizza Pub** (78199 U.S. 40, 970/726-5409, http://hernandospizzapub.com, 4pm-10pm daily in high season, $7-11), a local institution since 1967 that is best known for its traditional and Roma-style pizzas and an initial bet that led to tens of thousands of decorated dollar bills affixed to its ceiling and walls. **Deno's Mountain Bistro** (78911 U.S. 40, 970/726-5332, www.denoswp.com, 11:30am-close daily, $11-38) is an "upscale casual" restaurant housed in an early-1900s building that once served as a stagecoach stop

before being converted into a restaurant a few decades later. The Greek and Italian menu includes unusual small plates, like Greek lamb sliders, large burgers and juicy steaks, seafood, and a long wine list worthy of a Wine Spectator's Award of Excellence.

Transportation and Services

From Denver, take I-70 west for 40 miles to U.S. 40 and Exit 232. Follow U.S. 40 north for 24 miles, crossing over **Berthoud Pass.** Winter Park Resort is located just west of the highway. In good conditions, the 65-mile trip should take about 1.5 hours, but it can take substantially longer during rush hour and/or inclement weather, especially over the pass. In winter, check road conditions and chain laws online at the Colorado Department of Transportation (www.cotrip.org).

The most convenient parking is in the **Village Garage** ($22 per day) in the main Winter Park Resort base area. Free parking is also available at the walk-in/walk-out North Bench Lot (accessed from the resort's north entrance), as well as several lots serviced by Park-N-Ride shuttles, including Lots F and G. For snow and weather conditions at Winter Park Resort, call 303/572-7669.

Rally Bus (http://rallybus.net) offers limited bus service to Winter Park from various points in the Denver metro area; since the dates and times can change, check the website for up-to-date details.

The resort has a ski patrol for slope-side emergencies as well as the **East Grand Community Clinic and Emergency Center** (145 Parsenn Rd., 970/726-4299, www.denverhealth.org, 9:30am-6pm daily in winter) in the base area.

Boulder and the Northern Front Range

Look for ★ to find recommended sights, activities, dining, and lodging.

Highlights

★ **Pearl Street Mall:** Boulder's heart lies in this lively pedestrian mall, home to some of the best restaurants, bars, galleries, and shops in the state (page 87).

★ **Chautauqua:** This historic complex at the base of the Flatirons offers an idyllic spot to enjoy the stunning views (page 89).

★ **Bolder Boulder:** Summer starts with this footrace when more than 50,000 people run, walk, and race wheelchairs 10 kilometers through town (page 100).

★ **Boulder Dushanbe Teahouse:** This handcrafted Persian teahouse is a stunning work of art, as well as a restaurant (page 107).

★ **Eldorado Canyon State Park:** This spectacular canyon offers a variety of hikes, picnic spots, panoramic views, and rock climbing (page 114).

★ **Brainard Lake:** Nestled in a glacier-carved valley close to the Continental Divide, this sparkling alpine lake is a great place to spot wildlife and enjoy year-round recreation (page 119).

★ **Gold Hill Inn:** Savor a gourmet meal in this historic dining hall in the hamlet of Gold Hill, where prospectors struck it rich in 1859 (page 120).

★ **New Belgium Brewing:** Sign up for a tour around this hip brewery's environmentally friendly facility and sample its Belgian-style beer (page 126).

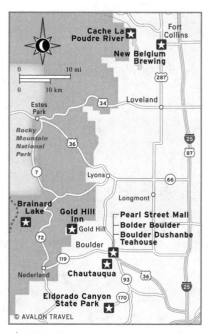

★ **Cache La Poudre River:** This Wild and Scenic River alternates between quiet fishing holes and frothing white-water rapids, with plentiful wildlife in between (page 128).

N orth of Denver, the Front Range foothills rise dramatically above a string of laid-back towns.

The scenery is spectacular, the recreation is endless, and the climate is ideal, with more than 300 days of sunshine a year. Colleges, concerts, and brewpubs sit steps away from high-tech start-ups. Ethnic restaurants, eclectic shopping, and mountain wilderness lie slightly farther away.

Each town has its own distinct personality. Bohemian Boulder, home of the University of Colorado and several federal research labs, thrives on its reputation as the brainiest, fittest, and foodiest city around. Its eye-popping backdrop of pointed rock fins and snow-capped summits attracts a liberal, affluent, and environmentally conscious crowd who enthusiastically embrace all the town has to offer—organic food at the local farmers market, farm-to-table restaurants, Buddhist meditation centers, distinguished lectures, and a vibrant performing arts scene.

One hour north, lively Fort Collins is an active college town and a beer and biking hub. Its charming Old Town Square "hops" with microbreweries and art deco buildings housing trendy boutiques, cafés, and confectioneries. Close to town, Horsetooth Reservoir draws anglers, paddlers, mountain bikers, and hikers. For a break from the college towns and their fast-paced fun, head up into the foothills, where historic mountain towns brimming with lore offer secluded inns, lesser-known trails, and funky antique stores.

PLANNING YOUR TIME

Boulder is ideal for a **three-day getaway;** it also makes a convenient base for a week-long exploration of the northern foothills. Crowds descend in **summer,** especially on holiday weekends like Memorial Day when the Boulder Creek Festival and the Bolder Boulder are held. There are fewer students, and the Pearl Street buskers, theatrical and musical performances, and outdoor dining are in full swing. Summer is the sporting and festival season, when Boulder hosts the Ironman, tiny Lyons hosts several prominent music festivals, and Fort Collins bursts with "bikes, beer, and bemusement" during the Tour de Fat and other fun-filled festivities.

Winter, when most travelers are here to ski, can be windy and snowy—or warm and sunny—or anywhere in between. You'll find

Previous: Boulder's spectacular mountain backdrop; Boulder's Royal Arch. **Above:** bikes in front of New Belgium Brewery.

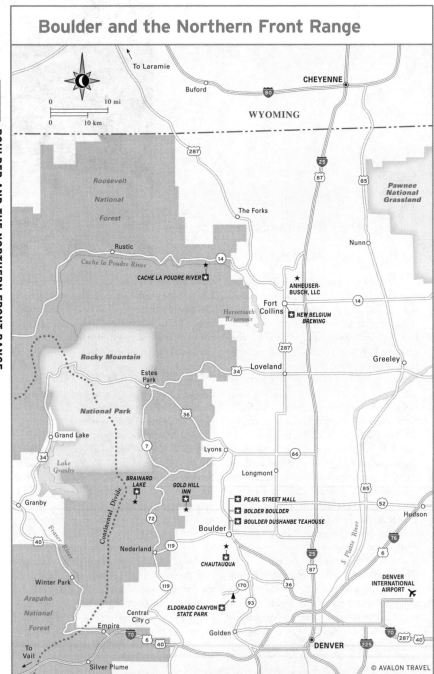

Boulder and the Northern Front Range

To Laramie

Buford

CHEYENNE

80

WYOMING

0   10 mi

0   10 km

287

25

87

85

Roosevelt

National

Forest

The Forks

Pawnee
National
Grassland

Rustic

Nunn

Cache la Poudre River

14

CACHE LA POUDRE RIVER

ANHEUSER-
BUSCH, LLC

Fort
Collins

14

Horsetooth
Reservoir

NEW BELGIUM
BREWING

Rocky Mountain

287

Estes
Park

Loveland

34

Greeley

National Park

36

Grand Lake

7

Lyons

66

34

Lake
Granby

Granby

BRAINARD
LAKE

GOLD HILL
INN

Longmont

85

52

Hudson

72

PEARL STREET MALL

BOLDER BOULDER

BOULDER DUSHANBE TEAHOUSE

Fraser River

Boulder

76

Continental Divide

Nederland

119

CHAUTAUQUA

25

6

87

S Platte River

Winter Park

40

119

170

36

DENVER
INTERNATIONAL
AIRPORT

Arapaho

National

Forest

Central
City

ELDORADO CANYON
STATE PARK

93

Empire

70

6

40

Golden

DENVER

70

287

40

To
Vail

Silver Plume

225

© AVALON TRAVEL

the northern Front Range calmer and the weather more moderate during the shoulder seasons. In **spring,** gentle rains (and the occasional blizzard) bring emerald-green grass, wildflowers, and thousands of tulips along the downtown mall. For hiking, visit in **autumn,** when the weather is most stable. September and October are an ideal time—warm, sunny days follow crisp nights and the aspen and cottonwoods slowly turn to gold.

Boulder

Boulder is a half-hour drive northwest of Denver on U.S. 36, or, thanks to the convenient regional transportation network, an easy hour-long RTD bus ride from Denver International Airport or Union Station in downtown Denver. Once in Boulder, you can explore much of town by foot, bus, or bike, although it's easiest to get to Chautauqua Park and other foothills sights by car. The town core forms a rectangle with foothills to the west, the University of Colorado (CU) campus to the south, Pearl Street to the north, and the Twenty Ninth Street Mall to the east.

SIGHTS
University of Colorado
OLD MAIN

In 1872, after the territorial legislature provided funds to establish the University of Colorado, there was a competition between Cañon City and Boulder to host it. After Boulder was selected, Cañon City's consolation prize was the new Colorado State Prison. Perhaps sensing they got the better deal, Boulder citizens joined forces to raise $15,000 to help construct Old Main, CU's first building, on land donated by several well-to-do citizens. Completed in 1876, the distinctive, Gothic-style brick building topped with two towers housed the president and the custodian as well as classrooms, labs, and a library. From these humble beginnings, CU-Boulder has grown into a tier-one research university with many globally and nationally ranked departments, five Nobel laureates, and 30,000 students.

Refurbished in the early 1980s, Old Main today includes a small chapel and the **CU Heritage Center** (Old Main Building, 1600 Pleasant St., 303/492-6329, http://cuheritage. org, 10am-4pm Mon.-Sat., free), whose exhibits relay the history of the university's flagship campus. Of special interest are the exhibits about alumni Glen Miller, who spent three semesters on campus before pawning his trombone for a ticket to Los Angeles, and the Space Exploration Gallery. The only university to have sent instruments to every planet in our solar system (plus Pluto), CU is often called the "University of the Universe." The exhibit includes a moon rock collected by Apollo 15 astronauts as well as artifacts and equipment used by some of the 20 astronaut alums, who include Scott Carpenter, Jack Swigert, and Ellison Onizuka, one of the astronauts aboard the Space Shuttle Challenger when it exploded.

Old Main is located on the north side of the **Norlin Quadrangle,** a large, grassy lawn surrounded by towering trees where students love to lounge on warm, sunny days. This is the heart of the main campus, which has repeatedly been named as one of the country's most beautiful. This is largely due to the uniform "Tuscan vernacular" style of its buildings, inspired by architect Charles Klauder's visit to Florence, Siena, and other Italian hilltop towns. Characterized by sandstone walls, white trim, and the distinctive, red-tiled roofs, this unique style takes advantage of local stone quarried north of town to create a campus that blends congruously with its spectacular mountain backdrop.

Boulder

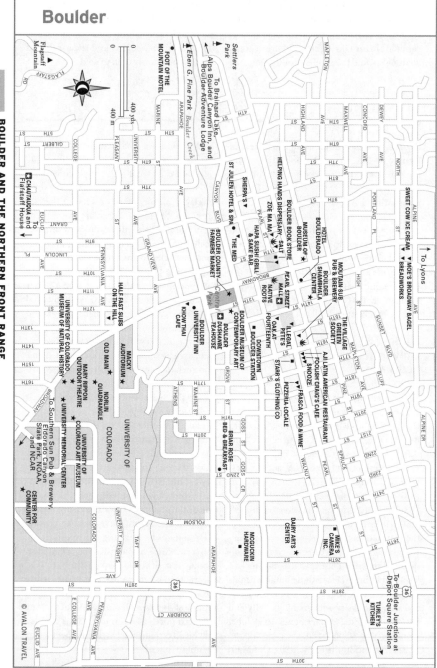

Flagstaff Mountain

Settlers Park

Eben G. Fine Park

FOOT OF THE MOUNTAIN MOTEL

To Brainard Lake, Alps Boulder Canyon Inn, and Boulder Adventure Lodge

Boulder Creek

CHAUTAUQUA and Flatstaff House

To Southern Sun Pub & Brewery, Eldorado Canyon State Park, NOAA, and NCAR

SHERPA'S

ST JULIEN HOTEL & SPA

BOULDER COUNTY FARMERS MARKET

HELPING HANDS DISPENSARY

ZOE MA MA

HAPA SUSHI GRILL & SAKE BAR

BOULDER BOOK STORE

SALT

THE MED

MUSEUM OF BOULDER

HOTEL BOULDERADO

MOUTAIN SUB PUB & BREWERY

BOULDER SHAMBHALA CENTER

PEARL STREET MALL

NATIVE ROOTS

Central Park

BOULDER MUSEUM OF CONTEMPORARY ART

BOULDER DUSHANBE TEAHOUSE

KHOW THAI CAFE

BOULDER UNIVERSITY INN

HALF FAST SUBS ON THE HILL

OLD MAIN

MACKY AUDITORIUM

NORLIN QUADRANGLE

MARY RIPPON OUTDOOR THEATRE

UNIVERSITY OF COLORADO MUSEUM OF NATURAL HISTORY

UNIVERSITY OF COLORADO ART MUSEUM

UNIVERSITY MEMORIAL CENTER

UNIVERSITY OF COLORADO

CENTER FOR COMMUNITY

DOWNTOWN BOULDER STATION

OAK AT FOURTEENTH

ILLEGAL PETE'S

STARR'S CLOTHING CO

PIZZERIA LOCALE

FRASCA FOOD & WINE

SNOOZE

FOOLISH CRAIG'S CAFE

AJI LATIN AMERICAN RESTAURANT

THE VILLAGE GREEN SOCIETY

BRIAR ROSE BED & BREAKFAST

DAIRY ARTS CENTER

MCGUCKIN HARDWARE

MIKE'S CAMERA INC.

TURLEY'S KITCHEN

To Boulder Junction at Depot Square Station

SWEET COW ICE CREAM

MOE'S BROADWAY BAGEL

BREADWORKS

To Lyons

MAPLETON

HIGHLAND AVE

MAXWELL AVE

CONCORD AVE

DEWEY AVE

NORTH

PORTLAND PL

ALPINE

HIGH ST

MAPLETON AVE

PINE ST

SPRUCE ST

PEARL ST

WALNUT

GOSS

GOSS CR

BLUFF ST

SUNSET BLVD

ALPINE DR

4TH ST

5TH ST

6TH ST

7TH ST

8TH ST

9TH ST

10TH ST

11TH ST

12TH ST

13TH ST

14TH ST

15TH ST

16TH ST

17TH ST

18TH ST

19TH ST

20TH ST

21ST ST

22ND ST

23RD ST

24TH ST

26TH ST

28TH ST

30TH ST

CANYON BLVD

ARAPAHOE

BROADWAY

GRAND VIEW AVE

GROVE ST

ATHENS ST

MARINE ST

FOLSOM ST

UNIVERSITY AVE

COLORADO

UNIVERSITY HEIGHTS

TAFT DR

COLORADO AVE

PENNSYLVANIA AVE

E COLLEGE AVE

EUCLID AVE

COURTRY CT

ARAPAHOE

GRANT ST

LINCOLN PL

PENNSYLVANIA AVE

EUCLID AVE

PLEASANT ST

UNIVERSITY AVE

GILBERT ST

COLLEGE

MARINE

ARAPAHOE

FLAGSTAFF RD

5TH ST

FLAGSTAFF RD

UNIVERSITY OF COLORADO

400 yds

400 m

© AVALON TRAVEL

THE QUAD

The Quad includes several buildings of interest to visitors, including the Neo-Gothic **Macky Auditorium** (1595 Pleasant St., 303/492-8423, www.colorado.edu/macky, 9am-5pm Mon.-Fri.), named for a Boulder gold-rush settler-turned-banker who in 1907 bequeathed the university $300,000 (while leaving his daughter nothing). The 2,052-seat concert hall hosts big-name speakers and musical performances year-round as well as the engaging **Conference on World Affairs** (Apr.). South of the Quad, the **University Memorial Center** (1669 Euclid Ave., 303/492-6161, www.colorado.edu/umc, hours vary by season) has a pretty outdoor fountain plaza where kids love to splash in the summer, as well as eateries, cafés, a bowling alley, and a bookstore that are open to the public. Southeast of the UMC, the **Center for Community** (C4C, 2249 Willard Loop Dr., 303/492-6541, www.colorado.edu/centerforcommunity, 7am-8pm Mon.-Fri., 10am-8pm Sat.-Sun.) has an award-winning food court with 10 "micro-restaurants" that serve everything from Persian to Italian food.

MUSEUMS

The **CU Art Museum** (1085 18th St., 303/492-8300, www.colorado.edu/cuartmuseum, 11am-5pm Mon., Wed., and Fri.-Sat., 11am-7pm Tues. and Thurs., free) highlights artwork in diverse mediums covering more than 10,000 years of human history. On the campus's western edge, the **CU Museum of Natural History** (1030 Broadway St., 303/492-6892, http://cumuseum.colorado.edu, 9am-5pm Mon.-Fri., 9am-4pm Sat., 10am-4pm Sun., free) houses more than four million natural artifacts—including the state's biggest collection of bee specimens—and offers interesting programs and well-curated exhibits, including a permanent one on how fossils provide clues to the past.

FISKE PLANETARIUM

On the south side of campus, the renovated **Fiske Planetarium** (2414 Regent Dr., 303/492-5002, http://fiske.colorado.edu, 9am-5pm Mon.-Fri.) has a new, high-definition IMAX-sized screen and a state-of-the-art Megastar projector for its 360-degree star shows, movies, lectures, and popular late-night laser shows, as well as several free exhibits in the lobby. On a clear Friday night, you can catch Fiske's evening star show, then walk next door to the **Sommers-Bausch Observatory** (http://outreach.colorado.edu) for a free stargazing session using their 16- to 24-inch telescopes and the world's largest star wheel. Weather permitting, the sessions begin at 8pm during the school year and 9pm in summer.

UNIVERSITY HILL

CU's social hub is **University Hill,** the student-centered district west of campus with a compact collection of offbeat indie shops, cafés, bars, and restaurants covering several blocks between University and College Avenues. Although the establishments frequently change, a few have persevered, including the historic 1926 **Fox Theatre,** a popular live music venue, and **The Sink,** a classic college pizza joint with autographs, newspaper clippings, and cartoons of illustrious customers like President Obama, as well as their most famous employee, Robert Redford, who swabbed the floors while working here as a student in 1955.

★ Pearl Street Mall

Boulder's social hub is the **Pearl Street Mall** (Pearl St. between 11th and 15th Sts., www.boulderdowntown.com). Wandering the four, brick-paved, pedestrian blocks decorated with fountains and flowers is a highlight of Boulder. Visitors and locals browse Boulder Bookstore, Art Mart, Peppercorn; families flock to see the Balloon Man and the pop-jet fountain; and students (along with high-tech execs) linger at the many coffee shops.

Summer evenings are when Pearl Street truly bustles; chatting couples wander hand-in-hand, al fresco dining venues overflow with hungry patrons, and bars and brewpubs fill up. Entertainment ranges from outdoor movies and Boulder Theater shows to street performers who juggle fire, sing and dance, and keep the crowds laughing. Hopefully you'll have a chance to see Ibashi-i, the Caribbean contortionist, or David Rosdeitcher, Boulder's mighty "Zip Code Man," who has memorized more than 40,000 postal codes and uses this knowledge to entertain the large crowds that gather to test him.

The blocks surrounding the mall are home to dozens of historic buildings, including a Queen Anne-style home at 1619 Pine Street, where scenes from the TV sitcom *Mork and Mindy* were filmed. An impromptu memorial sprang up here in 2014 after the untimely death of Robin Williams, who played the loveable alien from Ork. A slew of late-19th- and early-20th-century buildings that once housed saloons and other venues have been preserved in the **Downtown Boulder Historic District;** the pricey homes in the **Mapleton Historic District** to the northwest include the 1865 Squires House (1019 Spruce St.), Boulder's oldest home.

Museum of Boulder

The **Museum of Boulder** (2205 Broadway St., 303/449-3464, http://boulderhistory.org, by appt. only, $6) was founded in 1944 by the then-publisher of the *Boulder Daily Camera,* A. A. "Gov." Paddock. A new building in 2017 will have more space to display the thousands of artifacts donated by Boulder-area citizens over the past six decades, including a horse-drawn sleigh and carriage, historic microscopes and chemistry sets, and artifacts related to Chief Niwot, leader of the local Arapaho tribe who was fatally wounded at the tragic Sand Creek Massacre.

Boulder Shambhala Center

The **Boulder Shambhala Center** (1345 Spruce St., 303/444-0190, http://boulder. shambhala.org, noon-6pm Mon.-Fri., 9am-noon Sun.) is a meditation and retreat center based on Buddhism's contemplative teachings. Established in 1973 by a Tibetan Buddhist master, the center offers weekly drop-in meditation sessions, classes, and retreats. People of all faiths are welcome.

Boulder Museum of Contemporary Art

The renovated **Boulder Museum of Contemporary Art** (1750 13th St., 303/443-2122, http://bmoca.org, 11am-5pm Tues.-Sun., $1) features three rotating exhibits by

Tulips bloom along Pearl Street in spring.

Pearl Street

The land on which Boulder is built was initially part of a winter camp for the nomadic Southern Arapaho tribe. But after gold was discovered in the foothills in 1859, "Boulder City" was quickly founded as a supply town for the miners working their claims. Caucasian settlers established the first permanent camp in **Settlers Park** at the mouth of Boulder Canyon, where striking red rock fins provided shelter for their tents. The settlers quickly divided up the land along Boulder Creek, selling the lots for $1,000 apiece, and established a commercial district along the newly platted Pearl Street.

Through the decades, Boulder morphed from a remote territorial outpost into a thriving city, and the Pearl Street district evolved as well. The original dirt road was full of ruts whenever it rained or snowed, so in 1891, the city installed a horse-drawn streetcar along its length, followed 10 years later by electric streetcars. In 1917, after automobiles had become the norm, Pearl was the first street in Boulder to be paved, and the earliest to sport a streetlight. After World War II, however, the district's fortunes faded as the historic buildings deteriorated and the populace began to shop on the outskirts of town. To revitalize the district, the city closed four blocks to traffic in 1976, and the citizens taxed themselves to pay for architectural improvements. This brilliant strategy resulted in today's Pearl Street Mall, which has, in the words of one of its designers, Richard Foy, transitioned from a commercial artery to Boulder's "cultural heart and soul."

nationally and internationally renowned artists in a historic 1906 red-brick warehouse. It's adjacent to Central Park, a grassy area with a concrete bunker-like band shell, and the beautiful Boulder Dushanbe Teahouse.

Boulder County Farmers Market

USA Today has ranked the **Boulder County Farmers Market** (13th St. between Canyon and Arapaho Sts., 303/910-2236, www.bcfm.org, 8am-2pm Sat. Apr.-Nov., plus 4pm-8pm Wed. May-Sept.) as the best in the country. What started as a few tables of produce in the mid-1980s is now the town's pride and joy, a colorful jumble of more than 150 stalls selling organic produce picked that morning, locally made wine, honey, gluten-free bread, and cheeses, as well as jewelry, plants, and pottery. With the spectacular Flatirons backdrop, live music, and food carts peddling locally churned ice cream, fresh falafel, and *pupusas,* the farmers market is Boulder at its best.

★ Chautauqua

Tucked beneath the third Flatiron (counting from the right), the Colorado Chautauqua has an intriguing history. The 40-acre National

Historic Landmark was originally built as a summer school for Texas teachers as part of the Chautauqua adult education movement that spread across the nation in the late 19th and early 20th centuries. Although the teachers were housed in tents the first summer, the complex quickly grew to include 98 quaint cottages, many of which visitors can still rent today. One of only four such groups to operate continuously since the movement's heyday in the 1920s, the nonprofit **Colorado Chautauqua Association** (303/442-3282, www.chautauqua.com) offers artistic performances, scholarly lectures, and films, just as it did when the so-called Texado Park opened in 1898. Many of these events are held in the Chautauqua Auditorium, a large wooden structure with great acoustics that was hastily erected for the original Fourth of July opening. A large, green lawn on the complex's northern side is a favorite local summer hangout and picnic spot, despite the ongoing challenge of finding a convenient parking spot.

On the complex's western edge is the jewel of Boulder's extensive open-space system, gorgeous **Chautauqua Park** (900 Baseline Rd., www.bouldercolorado.gov), where grassy meadows dotted with spring wildflowers rise

How The Flatirons Formed

To the west, the Flatirons loom high above Boulder. How exactly these distinctive rock formations got their name is unknown, but locals like to speculate that it comes from their resemblance to pointy clothes irons. Thanks to the detective work of geologists at CU, we do know that these 300-million-year-old reddish rocks were shed off an older mountain chain that stood in nearly the same spot. Piece by piece, swift mountain streams carted away this ancient range, depositing the sand and stones in cone-shaped piles along the mountain front. Over time, these sediments were buried and compacted into the dense, hard rock visible today. Originally deposited in nearly horizontal layers, the Flatirons were tilted into place when tremendous forces associated with the modern Rockies' uplift removed the overlying sediment and tipped these layers down to the east, creating Boulder's signature backdrop.

to meet the serrated Flatirons. Toward the south, the rocky fins blend into the slopes of Bear Peak, Boulder's highest summit, and the distinctive Devil's Thumb, while to the north, Flagstaff Mountain and the foothills near the town of Lyons tower above the plains.

Chautauqua is located at the base of the foothills on Boulder's western edge. From downtown, it's an easy drive south on Broadway Street, then just over a mile west on Baseline Road. It's best to go early in the morning to find a parking spot.

Flagstaff Mountain

West of Chautauqua Park, Baseline Road

climbs a series of impressive switchbacks to ascend **Flagstaff Mountain** (Flagstaff Rd., https://bouldercolorado.gov), a gem in Boulder's extensive Open Space and Mountain Parks. **Panorama Point,** the first parking area on the right, and the **Sunrise Amphitheater** at the summit offer incredible views of the city, including straight-as-an-arrow Baseline Road—so named because it follows the 40th parallel north. The Denver skyline, NCAR's geometric architecture, the red-roofed CU campus, Pearl Street, and the reservoirs, towns, and pancake-flat plains stretch to the east. The mountain is famous for the iconic **Flagstaff House** (1138 Flagstaff

Boulder's Flatirons from the Mesa Trail

Rd., 303/442-4640, www.flagstaffhouse. com), one of Colorado's best restaurants, which is celebrated for its stunning views, its 16,000-bottle wine cellar, and its exceptional food and service.

National Center for Atmospheric Research

On the city's southwestern fringe is the **National Center for Atmospheric Research** (NCAR, 1850 Table Mesa Dr., 303/497-1000, http://ncar.ucar.edu, 8am-5pm Mon.-Fri., 9am-4pm Sat.-Sun. and holidays, free), one of Boulder's three federal labs, which conducts cutting-edge atmospheric research (and explores its human implications) using some of the nation's fastest supercomputers. Built in a spectacular (and at the time, controversial) setting, high on a flat-topped mesa at the western end of Table Mesa Drive, this blocky, concrete complex was designed to look like part of the landscape by the famous architect I. M. Pei, whose plans were inspired by the Mesa Verde cliff dwellings. Tours and exhibits in the lobby let you feel a cloud, steer a hurricane, examine the sun, and learn more about the research happening here. You can also visit two galleries that highlight the connection between art and science, eat in the cafeteria, and walk the easy, outdoor Weather Trail, where signs describe phenomena like mountain wave clouds, climate zones, and cold fronts. The Earth System Research Lab at the **National Oceanic & Atmospheric Administration** (NOAA, 325 Broadway St., 303/497-4091, www.esrl.noaa.gov/outreach/ tours) also offers free public tours (with proper ID) on Tuesdays at 1pm.

Celestial Seasonings

Back in 1969, a group of young entrepreneurs led by hippie Mo Siegel began to pick wild herbs in the mountains, then dry, blend, and hand-sew them into muslin bags to sell in local health-food stores. Based originally in a barn, this enterprise quickly grew into **Celestial Seasonings** (4600 Sleepytime Dr., 303/581-1266, www.celestialseasonings. com, tours 10am-4pm Mon.-Sat., 11am-3pm Sun., free), North America's largest specialty-tea manufacturer, which today sells more than 1.6 billion tea bags per year. Now operated by the Hain Celestial Group, the company makes around 100 varieties of tea using ingredients carefully sourced from more than 35 countries. With 2.1 million visitors a year, the facility is one of the area's most popular attractions.

Celestial Seasonings' tea shop

At its headquarters northeast of Boulder, Celestial Seasonings offers behind-the-scenes tours that show how their tea is transformed from the raw ingredients to the packaged products. The starting point is the tasting bar, where you can sample any of the teas the company currently produces. The highlight, however, is the unique Mint Room, where the aroma is strong enough to make a grown-up cry. There is also a colorful café where you can enjoy a made-from-scratch breakfast or lunch, as well as a tea shop, which offers discounted Celestial products and collectible tea items.

Leanin' Tree Museum of Western Art

The **Leanin' Tree Museum of Western Art** (6055 Longbow Dr., 303/729-3412, www. leanintreemuseum.com, museum: 8am-6pm Mon.-Fri., 9am-5pm Sat., 10am-5pm Sun., tours: 9am, 10am, 1pm, and 2pm Mon.-Fri., free) has one of the country's biggest private collections of Western art. It was assembled by Ed Trumble, founder and chairman of Leanin' Tree, publisher of fine-art greeting cards. When Ed and his partner, Bob Lorenz, began their business with just four designs in 1949, they were so strapped for cash that they traded their artwork for free advertising. The response was overwhelming, but their first-year profits were almost completely wiped out after the printer misspelled Christmas. The company now offers a selection of 3,000 cards and ships more than 30 million per year, all from this modest-looking facility. On weekdays, visitors can tour the plant to see how flat sheets of paper are transformed into greeting cards. Ed's search for original artwork for his cards led to friendships with many artists whose paintings and sculptures are featured in the museum and sculpture garden, which are open seven days a week.

SPORTS AND RECREATION

With more than 300 days of sunshine a year, both flat and steep terrain, a large network of hiking trails and biking paths, and

world-class rock climbing and training facilities, it's no wonder that *Outside* magazine has named Boulder America's top sports town. In addition to the many professional athletes who train and live here, Boulder is a community whose residents embrace an active lifestyle. It's not unusual to see people running at night with headlamps or biking through the snow. But you don't need to be an avid athlete to enjoy the diverse recreation the area has to offer.

Hiking

The Boulder area has more than 250 miles of hiking trails to explore. Almost any road west into the foothills will eventually lead to a trailhead; green areas in and around the city offer flatter walks and stellar mountain views. Don't forget to pack sunscreen, water, and extra clothing before you head out.

The **City of Boulder Open Space and Mountain Parks** (303/441-3440, www.osmp. org, @boulderosmp) organizes nature hikes and many outdoor programs, offers trail maps and safety tips, and provides up-to-date information on dog regulations, seasonal wildlife restrictions, and trail closures. The **Boulder County Parks and Open Space** (5201 Saint Vrain Rd., Longmont, 303/678-6200, www.bouldercounty.org, @BoCo_trails) offers the same information for county-owned properties.

In downtown Boulder, the paved, 5.5-mile-long **Boulder Creek Path** meanders through the center of town, following Boulder Creek's every twist and turn from Eben G. Fine Park at the head of Boulder Canyon to the Stazzio Ballfields near 55th Street in the east. Strolling this artery is one of the best ways to get a feel for the town. It can easily be accessed almost anywhere along its length, including near the band shell in Central Park. On the northwest side of **Chautauqua Park** (900 Baseline Rd.), a great 3.2-mile loop follows the Gregory Canyon Trail as it ascends to Realization Point, then heads south on the Ranger Trail. After veering east on the Greenman Trail, complete the loop via the Saddle Rock Trail.

Boulder's Open Space

Intrinsic to Boulder's appeal is the city's 45,000 acres of open space. With 5.3 million visits per year—more than all of Colorado's national parks combined—the land acquisition program is arguably the most successful in the country. In addition to preserving native plants, sheltering local wildlife, and providing recreation, the land serves as a crucial buffer between the city and encroaching development. The story of how locals fought to preserve this open space, and how they continue to tax themselves to expand it, is integral to Boulder's identity.

The story begins after World War II, when Boulder was a small, backwoods town. But after the city's population doubled between 1950 and 1960, many locals became concerned about urban sprawl. In 1959, a few CU faculty and staff got together to brainstorm what could be done to keep the bulldozers at bay. Their strategy was brilliant; in the foothills, they mapped a north-south "Blue Line" at 5,750 feet elevation, above which, according to their plan, no city water could be delivered. After obtaining enough signatures to put their initiative on the ballot, the group embarked upon a spirited campaign to pass it. Their efforts paid off when voters overwhelmingly approved the amendment, which remains in effect today.

Aware the Blue Line would only protect the foothills, the group founded PLAN-Boulder, a grassroots organization whose mission is to preserve green spaces in and around the city. The group's first success came in 1962, when voters passed a bond issue to buy the Enchanted Mesa property south of Chautauqua. To acquire more land, the group realized they would need a permanent funding source. Their advocacy and foresight again paid off in 1967, when Boulder became the nation's first city to approve a sales tax to buy and maintain open space. With continued strong support from voters, the city's **Open Space and Mountain Parks** program has spent about $200 million to acquire more than 400 properties to date.

MESA TRAIL

The crown jewel of Boulder's extensive trail system is the 7.3-mile-long **Mesa Trail,** a north-south route that parallels the base of the Flatirons. The trail offers gorgeous views, plus a peek at some of the damage wrought by the devastating September 2013 floods. This trail is not a loop, so you'll either need to hike it round-trip, plan a shuttle, or hike one section at a time. I prefer to start at the **South Mesa Trailhead** (4111 Eldorado Springs Dr.), where parking is a bit easier to find. Head north toward its end at Chautauqua Park (900 Baseline Rd.).

To get to the South Mesa Trailhead, head south on Broadway Street to its junction with Highway 170. Turn right and follow this road about 1.5 miles to the parking area on the right. From the South Mesa Trailhead, the route climbs steadily through the grasslands up to the mesa top, then undulates through lush forests humming with birds and other wildlife like the black Abert's squirrel, which only lives in Southwestern ponderosa pine forests. Side trails along the way include the **Fern Canyon Trail** (2.8 miles one-way), a classic uphill hike that ascends Bear Peak, Boulder's highest summit. The trail ends on an exposed, craggy summit with panoramic views from the high peaks to the plains. From the top, either retrace your steps down Fern Canyon or descend the longer and more moderate **West Ridge Trail** on Bear Peak's western side, where ghostly stumps left from a 2012 wildfire still loom above the path. After 2 miles, the West Ridge joins up with the **Bear Canyon Trail,** which intersects the Mesa Trail about 0.5 mile north.

As the Mesa Trail nears its end at the ranger cottage at **Chautauqua Park** (900 Baseline Rd.), more trails branch off. Favorites include the Enchanted Mesa Trail and the steep Royal Arch Trail, which climbs up to a beautiful natural arch with amazing views of the city.

NORTH OF BOULDER

North Boulder also has many good hiking options, including the easy, 1.5-mile loop around

Wonderland Lake Park (4201 N. Broadway St.), where birds of prey, waterfowl, and coyote are often spotted. North of town, the Foothills Trailhead is accessed by heading north on Broadway Street to its junction with U.S. 36 (locally called 28th Street), then turning left (north) onto U.S. 36 for a few hundred feet to a parking area on the right side of the road. From here, the **Foothills Trail** leads uphill to the 1.8-mile Hogback Ridge Loop, which wanders through ponderosa pines past several springs, with great views all around. Three miles north of the Foothills Trailhead, on the west side of U.S. 36, a mellow four-mile hike begins at the **Interim Joder Trailhead** and follows a wide, gravel road through a former Arabian horse ranch up to a view toward Left Hand Canyon.

SOUTH OF BOULDER

Four miles south of town, the **Flatirons Vista Trailhead** (3363 Hwy. 93) accesses the 3.5-mile **Flatirons Vista Trail,** a flat multi-use loop with killer views of the Flatirons and several options for lengthening your route. More great hiking can be accessed from the **Marshall Mesa Trailhead** (5258 Eldorado Springs Dr.); head south on Broadway to its junction with Highway 170, then turn left and then immediately right into the large parking area. From here you can walk the Marshall Valley-Marshall Mesa-Coal Seam Trails, a nice 2.5-mile loop. For an eight-mile hiking loop, head west on the Coal Seam Trail to the Highway 93 underpass. Follow the Community Ditch Trail to the Doudy Draw Trail to Flatirons Vista North. Complete the loop by crossing Highway 93 to the Greenbelt Plateau Trail, which returns you back to the Coal Seam Trail and your vehicle.

Road Biking

The canyons and mountains west of Broadway offer road bikers many excellent choices; any of the bike shops in town can offer suggestions and advice, and **University Bicycles** (839 Pearl St., 303/444-4196, http://ubikes. com, 10am-7pm Mon.-Fri., 10am-6pm Sat.,

10am-5pm Sun.) rents road as well as mountain, snow, kid, and town bikes. A great place to meet up with other cyclists is the Uptown **Amante Coffee** (4580 Broadway St., 303/448-9999, www.amantecoffee.com, 5:45am-7pm daily), next to **Boulder Cycle Sport** (4580 Broadway St., 303/444-2453, www.bouldercyclesport.com, 10am-6pm Mon.-Fri., 10am-5pm Sat., 10am-4pm Sun., $50 per day), which also rents road and mountain bicycles.

NORTH OF BOULDER

About six miles north of Boulder, **Lefthand Canyon Drive** is one of Boulder's most popular (and gentle) canyon rides. From its junction with U.S. 36 just north of The Greenbriar Inn (8735 Foothills Hwy.), the quiet, shady road climbs gradually for eight miles along Lefthand Creek to tiny Jamestown, which was almost completely leveled during the September 2013 floods. A more challenging ride with a 3,500-foot elevation gain starts in the same place but turns left after five miles to begin the climb up to the hippy enclave of Ward. At 15 miles from the start, the gradient increases painfully for the last mile and a half. Luckily, you can rest and refuel at the tiny **Ward General Store** (62 Utica St., 303/459-1010, hours vary) before speeding back down to the start.

WEST OF BOULDER

For a challenging and beautiful canyon ride easily accessed from town, head four blocks north of Pearl Street, then turn west on tree-lined Mapleton Avenue, which leads past some of Boulder's oldest homes to **Sunshine Canyon.** This steep (up to a 23 percent grade) paved ride ends where the road turns to dirt just past Bald Mountain Scenic Area, which has picnic tables and a short, picturesque hike.

Thanks to the tremendous views and the satisfaction of completing a difficult climb, **Flagstaff Mountain** (4 miles, one-way) is my favorite ride. The climb begins on Broadway Street at its junction with Baseline Road, 1.6 miles south of Pearl Street. The first 1.3 miles is a steady, uphill ride west to Chautauqua Park where the road really kicks up. Keep cranking the pedals past Panorama Point, a fantastic overlook, and the entrance to the Flagstaff House Restaurant, where the gradient eases noticeably; you'll get a few breathers between the winding switchbacks. After 3.5 miles, turn right onto the half-mile spur road to the Sunrise Amphitheater, which is a great place to drink some water and enjoy the views of the plains.

SOUTH OF BOULDER

For a shorter climb with amazing Flatirons views, try the road up to the **National Center for Atmospheric Research** (1850 Table Mesa Dr.). To access this climb, follow Broadway Street south from Pearl Street for 3 miles, then turn right up Table Mesa Drive and head west for 1.2 miles. From the gate at the start of the open space, the road climbs almost 500 feet over the next 1.1 miles. If you can do three laps up NCAR, you're ready for Flagstaff!

Mountain Biking
NORTH OF BOULDER

Two beginner trails offer nice views of the northern foothills and plains. From the Boulder Valley Ranch Trailhead, the **Eagle Trail** climbs only 400 feet in about three miles, with one short but steep section that reaches a 15 percent grade. After 1.6 miles, the 1.1-mile **Sage Trail** branches off to the north. Where it rejoins the Eagle Trail, turn right to return to the trailhead or left to extend your ride to the **Boulder Reservoir** (5565 N. 51st St.). To get here, head north on Broadway Street to its junction with U.S. 36 (locally called 28th Street). Turn left (north) onto U.S. 36 and continue north for one mile. Turn right onto Longhorn Road and follow this east for one mile to the trailhead.

WEST OF BOULDER

For great foothills rides through the ponderosa pine trees, head to the **Betasso Preserve** (377 Betasso Rd., Thurs.-Fri. and Sun.-Tues.

only). The most popular rides are the moderate 7.5-mile **Benjamin Loop** and the more challenging 6-mile **Betasso-Canyon Loop.** To reach the preserve, follow Broadway Street south from Pearl Street for three blocks, then turn right onto Canyon Boulevard. Follow Canyon Boulevard west for 4.3 miles and turn right onto Sugarloaf Mountain Road, then right again onto Betasso Road. Parking lots appear in about one mile.

SOUTH OF BOULDER

South of town are two flatter rides. The **Marshall Mesa Trailhead** (5258 Eldorado Springs Dr.) is accessed by heading south on Broadway to its junction with Highway 170, then turning left and immediately right into a large parking area. This is the start of the Dirty Bismark Route, a fun 15-mile dirt loop with great views and 1,500 feet of climbing. The **Doudy Draw Trailhead** provides access to the 10.4-mile Doudy Draw Double Lollipop Loop, as well as the 22-mile-long Super Loop, which combines the best of the foothills and the flats. To get here, head south on Broadway Street to the junction with Highway 170. Turn right and follow Highway 170 1.5 miles to the parking area on the left.

Water Sports

Anglers try their luck in **Walden and Sawhill Ponds** (75th St., one mile north of Valmont Dr.), a group of ponds that contains both smallmouth and largemouth bass. The habitat is also a great place to watch for wildlife, including beaver, muskrat, and hundreds of birds. For information about guided fishing trips, equipment, river reports, and expert advice, stop by **Rocky Mountain Anglers** (1904 Arapahoe Ave., 303/447-2400, http://rockymtanglers.com, 7am-7pm Mon.-Fri., 7am-6pm Sat., 8am-4pm Sun.).

During spring runoff, Boulder Creek is popular with white-water kayakers. At the western end of town, near the mouth of Boulder Canyon, is a 0.5-mile-long Class II **Boulder Kayak Playpark** (Eben G. Fine Park, 101 Arapahoe Ave.) that starts with an exciting six-foot drop into a large pool. The **Boulder Outdoor Center** (2525 Arapahoe Ave. #E4-228, 303/444-8420, http://boc123.com) is the best source for local boating information.

On summer afternoons after the water levels have dropped, Boulder Creek is a popular spot for tubing; flop into a blown-up inner tube and float down the creek. Tubes are available at the **Conoco Station** (1201 Arapahoe Ave., 303/442-6293, 7am-9pm Mon.-Sat., 8am-8pm Sun., $15) one block north of the creek. Rent singles or doubles from the **Whitewater Tube Co.** (3600 Arapahoe Ave., 720/239-2179, www.whitewatertubing.com, 10am-6pm daily May-Labor Day, $16-21), which also offers shuttles.

The best outdoor swim spot is **Boulder Reservoir** (5565 North 51st St., 303/441-3461, www.boulderrez.org). The 700-acre complex is a popular summer hangout and a recreation hotspot, with sailboating, canoeing, waterskiing, and fishing. The picnic area has tables, a grill, horseshoes, and a volleyball court, while the dirt path around the lake is a favorite running and cycling spot.

inner tubing down Boulder Creek

Golf

The county has two courses, the **Flatirons Golf Course** (5706 Arapahoe Ave., 303/442-7851, www.flatironsgolf.com, $34-39), which is operated by the City of Boulder, and the **Indian Peaks Golf Course** (2300 Indian Peaks Trail, Lafayette, 303/900-4657, www.indianpeaksgolf.com, $45), located about 10 miles east in Lafayette. Both are 18-hole courses with wonderful views.

Skiing

When there's enough snow, the open space trails are great for snowshoeing and cross-country skiing. Between November and March, as conditions allow, the nonprofit **Boulder Nordic Club** (http://bouldernordic.org) grooms trails in **North Boulder Park** (9th St. and Cedar Ave.). **Crystal Ski Shop** (1933 28th St., 303/449-7669, http://

www.crystalskishop.com, 7am-8pm daily) rents snowshoes and telemark and alpine skiing gear.

Spectator Sports

An NCAA Division I school, CU began competing in the Pac-12 conference in 2011. Of the university's 17 varsity sports, the traditionally most competitive teams are men's and women's cross country and, of course, skiing. The Buffs' basketball teams play in the **Coors Events Center** (950 Regent Dr.). The team has rebounded (the men appeared in several recent NCAA tournaments), but the sport that gets the most attention is football. Despite the Buffs' record, hopeful fans still pack the renovated **Folsom Field** (2400 Colorado Ave.) to cheer on their team and watch Ralphie V, the university's live buffalo, stampede around the field before each game, trailed by her team of handlers. Call or check online for tickets (303/492-8337, www.cubuffs.com).

ENTERTAINMENT AND EVENTS

Nightlife

After a day of hard work (and even harder workouts), Boulderites enjoy a lively nightlife. Boulder's population always seems ready to quit work a little early, and with the sizeable number of students, the nightlife in Boulder stretches from happy hour 'til the buffaloes come home. Boulder's clubs and bars are concentrated in two clusters: downtown and the Hill by CU, but there are also taverns and breweries around town.

DOWNTOWN

Pearl Street and surrounds offer the highest concentration of bars, breweries, and clubs. For a summer sundown drink, head to the fabulous rooftop decks at **West End Tavern** (926 Pearl St., 303/444-3535, www.thewestendtavern.com, 11:30am-10pm Sun.-Wed., 11:30am-midnight Thurs., 11:30am-1am Fri.-Sat.), which has 25 craft beers on tap, or the **Rio Grande Mexican Restaurant** (1101 Walnut St., 303/444-3690, www.riograndemexican.com, 11am-11pm daily), for a rainbow of margarita choices. The **Lazy Dog Sports Bar and Grill** (1346 Pearl St., 303/440-3355, www.thelazydog.com, 11am-9pm Sun.-Mon., 11am-10pm Tues.-Sat.) has Boulder's largest full-service rooftop deck.

For happy hour deals, try the **Bitter Bar** (835 Walnut St., 303/442-3050, www.thebitterbar.com, 5pm-1am daily), a hip lounge with a creative cocktail menu with fun names like Pillow Talk and Corpse Reviver No. 2 and 5pm-8pm weekday specials. **Japango** (1136 Pearl St., 303/938-0330, www.boulderjapango.com, 11am-10pm Sun.-Thurs., 11am-midnight Fri.-Sat.) has a daily afternoon happy hour that includes hot sake and Sapporo Draft to sip on their outdoor Pearl Street patio. **Conor O'Neill's Irish Pub and Restaurant** (1922 13th St., 303/449-1922, www.conoroneills.com, 11am-2am Mon.-Fri., 10am-2am Sat.-Sun.) is a traditional Irish pub serving up plenty of stout and live music and daily 3pm-7pm happy hour food and drink specials.

Frequented mostly by CU students, the **Walrus Saloon** (1911 11th St., 303/443-9902, http://boulderwalrus.com, 4pm-2am Mon.-Sat., 7pm-2am Sun.) is a dark dive with pool tables, pinball machines, and other games. It's known more for its drink specials, loud music, and free peanuts than its food (feel free to throw the shells on the floor, everyone else does!). **Pearl Street Pub & Cellar** (1108 Pearl St., 303/939-9900, noon-2am daily) is a small and low-key spot with bar games, a jukebox, and live music most evenings, plus a 21st birthday tradition of kissing the buffalo head. The **Sundown Saloon** (1136 Pearl St., 303/449-4987, 3pm-2am daily) is another favorite college student haunt, with cheap beer, $1 kamikaze shots, and plenty of pool tables, foosball, and darts.

Formerly the iconic Catacombs Bar, the more upscale **License No. 1** (2115 13th St., 303/443-0486, http://license1boulderado.com, 5pm-midnight daily) still holds Boulder's first legal liquor license. Located in the basement of the Hotel Boulderado, the bar features an upgraded cocktail menu, including the old-fashioned, made with the hotel's own Buffalo Trace Bourbon.

THE HILL

Up on the Hill next to CU, **The Sink** (1165 13th St., 303/444-7465, http://thesink.com, 11am-2am daily) is a true Boulder institution, with walls covered with retro artwork and ceilings full of celebrity and other scribbled signatures dating back decades. In addition to serving up heavily topped pizza and "the best darn burger in Boulder," the city's oldest bar and restaurant is legendary for its daily themed happy hours.

A block away, **Half Fast Subs** (1215 13th St., 303/449-0404, www.halffastsubs.com, 10:30am-11pm Mon.-Wed., 10:30am-1am Thurs.-Fri., 11am-1am Sat., 11am-10pm Sun.) has an outdoor patio where you can sip Megaritas and Strong Islands from Cousin Paul's

Killer Drink Menu. A couple blocks north, the inconspicuous **No Name Bar** (1325 Broadway St., 4pm-1am daily) truly has no name, but it does have live music and a good selection of craft beer and infused tequilas.

About 1.5 miles southeast of the Hill, the **Dark Horse** (2922 Baseline Rd., 303/442-8162, http://darkhorsebar.com, 11am-2am daily), established in 1975, has a dark interior filled with bizarre antiques and old movie props. If you've had enough organic, local food, come here for some greasy wings and burgers. It's a great place to watch a game or compete in the "world famous" trike races every Tuesday at 10pm, when beer-toting contestants ride on three wheels 'round and 'round the bar.

Breweries

Boulder's 20 breweries are scattered all across town, so have a fun night or two following part of the visitor bureau's **Boulder Beer Trail** (www.bouldercoloradousa.com). In the downtown are two perennial favorites: **Walnut Brewery** (1123 Walnut St., 303/447-1345, www.walnutbrewery.com, 11am-11pm Sun.-Thurs., 11am-midnight Fri.-Sat.), Boulder's "original brewpub," best known for its award-winning Old Elk brown ale and its specialty dark beers; and **Mountain Sun Pub & Brewery** (1535 Pearl St., 303/546-0886, www.mountainsunpub.com, 11:30am-1am Mon.-Sat., noon-1am Sun.), a more laid-back spot with delicious food and a large selection of house and seasonal ales, including my favorite, the not-too-sweet Blackberry Wheat, and the popular Isadore Java porter.

A 10-minute drive east of downtown, **Boulder Beer Company** (2880 Wilderness Pl., 303/444-8448, http://boulderbeer.com, 11am-10pm Mon.-Fri., noon-10pm Sat.; tours 2pm Mon.-Fri., 2pm and 4pm Sat., free) is Colorado's oldest microbrewery, founded in an old goat shed in 1979 by two CU profs. Today, it's a state-of-the-art facility with free behind-the-scenes tours. In addition to oak-aged Oatmeal Stout and Mojo Risin' beers, the pub offers a full menu, including Boulder

porter milkshakes for dessert. **Sanitas Brewing** (3550 Frontier Ave. #A, 303/442-4130, www.sanitasbrewing.com, 3pm-10pm Mon.-Fri., noon-10pm Sat., noon-8pm Sun.), named for another summit in Boulder's spectacular backdrop, has a large outdoor patio with Flatirons views and bocce ball, as well as an industrial-chic taproom with a great selection of IPAs and fruity farmhouse ales.

Much farther east, but well worth the trip, is the popular **Avery Brewing Company** (4910 Nautilus Ct., 303/440-4324, www.avery-brewing.com, 3pm-11pm Mon., 11am-11pm Tues.-Sun.), which offers daily guided tours that you can reserve online, plus an award-winning dining menu and a rotating selection of unusual beers like Mayan Goddess—a stout with chiles, vanilla, and cinnamon—and Chai Brown, an American brown brewed with local, fair-trade chai.

Live Music

Boulder's best-known live-music venue is **The Fox Theatre** (1135 13th St., 720/645-2467, http://foxtheatre.com). Originally built on the Hill as a movie theater in 1926, the building was converted into a funky concert hall in 1991. The 625-seat venue is known for its great sound, as well as its diverse calendar of indie hip-hop, up-and-coming acts, great local musicians, and renowned national acts. The historic **Boulder Theater** (2032 14th St., 303/786-7030, www.bouldertheater.com), housed in a 1906 art-deco opera building just steps from Pearl Street, offers 250 events a year from headline speakers and film festivals to performances by well-known names like Lyle Lovett and the local hit band Big Head Todd and the Monsters.

Performing Arts

The modern **Dairy Arts Center** (2590 Walnut St., 303/440-7826, http://thedairy. org) houses Boulder's largest art center in a renovated dairy plant, with a cinema, theater, galleries—and musical and theatrical performances—all under one roof. The residents include the **Boulder Ensemble Theater**

Company (303/351-2382, www.betc.org) and **Boulder Ballet** (303/443-0028, www.boulderballet.org), the county's premier professional dance company, which offers shows throughout the year, including The Nutcracker, performed each Thanksgiving weekend at CU's **Macky Auditorium** (1595 Pleasant Ave., 303/492-8423, www.colorado.edu/macky).

The **Boulder Philharmonic Orchestra** (2590 Walnut St., 303/449-1343 ext. 108, www.boulderphil.org), which also performs regularly at Macky Auditorium, is one of several of the city's acclaimed orchestral groups, along with the **Boulder Chamber Orchestra** (4735 Walnut St. #F, 303/583-1278, www.boulderchamberorchestra.com) and the **Boulder Symphony Orchestra** (970/577-1550, http://bouldersymphony.org). CU's **College of Music** (18th St., 303/492-6352, www.colorado.edu/music) hosts more than 400 jazz, classical, opera, and other performances a year, most of which are free and open to the public. **BDT Stage** (5501 Arapahoe Ave., 303/449-6000, www.bdtstage.com), formerly the Boulder Dinner Theatre, offers performances of recent and classic musical productions along with a small selection of entrées for dinner.

Festivals and Events

Boulder's summer is bookended by two major events, the Memorial Day weekend **Boulder Creek Festival** (303/449-3137, www.bouldercreekfestival.com, free) and the Labor Day weekend **Hometown Festival** (www.boulderdowntown.com, free). Both feature rides for young kids, live music performances in the downtown band shell, a food court and beer garden, and hundreds of arts and crafts and other vendors spread across Central Park and along the Boulder Creek Path.

The acclaimed **Colorado Shakespeare Festival** (303/492-8008, www.coloradoshakes.org, June-Aug., $35-65) performs in CU's Mary Rippon Theatre (1030 Broadway St.), an open-air amphitheater on the western side of campus. The **Colorado Music Festival** (303/440-7666, www.comusic.org, late June-early Aug., $12-51) is a series of classical and chamber performances held each summer at the Chautauqua Auditorium (900 Baseline Rd.). It features both traditional and contemporary artists in instrumental and vocal performances as well as a patriotic family concert around the Fourth of July. The popular downtown **Boulder Craft Beer Fest** (303/449-3774, www.boulderdowntown.com, mid-Aug., $40) features samples

the Boulder Theater

from the county's best breweries along with live music and food.

Major sporting events include the **Ironman** (www.ironman.com, Aug.) triathlon and the **Buffalo Bicycle Classic** (www.buffalobicycleclassic.com, Sept.), which features seven organized road-bike rides ranging 35-100 miles in length. The **Boulder Backroads Marathon** (http://flatironsrunningevents.com, Sept.) encompasses a 26.2-mile race route on quiet back roads.

★ BOLDER BOULDER

What started in 1979 as a few hundred people running through the streets of Boulder has since grown into the largest foot race in the United States, and one of the largest in the world. Held each Memorial Day, the **Bolder Boulder** (550 Central Ave. #110, 303/444-7223, www.bolderboulder.com, $55-85, register in advance) begins near the Twenty Ninth Street Mall and winds 10 kilometers through town, ending at CU's Folsom Field. The organizers divide the 50,000-plus participants into 100 waves so that runners, joggers, and walkers can go at their own tempo and avoid tripping over each other. The wheelchairs head out first at breakneck speeds, followed by the first 30 waves—the serious runners who must

qualify for these spots with previous finish times of less than 68 minutes.

Next come about 70 more waves, with the walkers leaving last. The more relaxed participants in these slower-paced groups dress up in crazy costumes and enjoy the party atmosphere, including dozens of live bands scattered along the route and enthusiastic crowds cheering and doing crazy stunts like spraying participants with hoses and tossing them marshmallows. The event ends at CU's packed stadium, where beneath the Flatirons, the crowds applaud each finisher as they cross the line. After the course cutoff time, the atmosphere is electric as everyone cheers on the professional international team races and watches one of the nation's largest Memorial Day tributes.

SHOPPING

Boulder is known for its eclectic mix of funky boutiques, indie bookstores, local art galleries, and notable chains. The prices are reasonable and the selection is excellent, especially in the downtown area around Pearl Street, which is lined with trendy clothing and jewelry shops, specialty food stores, cool kiosk carts, and outdoor clothing chains. Just 1.5 miles east is the Twenty Ninth Street Mall, an open-air

the Colorado Shakespeare Festival on the CU campus

retail center filled with upscale chains and practical stores, as well as yoga and fitness studios. If you buy too much to carry home, **Pak Mail** (2525 Arapahoe Ave., 303/444-0831, www.pakmailboulder.com, 8:30am-6pm Mon.-Fri., 10am-4pm Sat.) can pick things up from your hotel and safely ship them.

Downtown
CLOTHING AND ACCESSORIES
Get the casual, comfy Boulder look at **Starr's Clothing Company** (1630 Pearl St., 303/442-3056, www.starrsclothingco.com, 10am-7pm Mon.-Sat., 11am-6pm Sun.), which first opened in 1914. The friendly boutique specializes in jeans, with labels including Levi's, Lucky Brand, and Tommy Bahama, as well as other casual men's and women's clothing. **Chelsea** (1646 Pearl St., 303/447-3760, www.chelseabella.com, 10am-6pm Mon.-Sat., noon-5pm Sun.) offers an assortment of contemporary clothing, stylish accessories, and gifts from dozens of designers from A to Z, including Amanda Stringer, Mia & Moss, Suss, and Zeal.

Two Sole Sisters (1703 Pearl St., 303/442-0404, www.twosolesisters.com, 10am-6pm Mon.-Sat., noon-5pm Sun.) is named for the two sisters who founded this local indie store. The shabby-chic boutique sells fun and funky handbags and jewelry, and lots of stylish shoes from high-heeled sandals to all-weather boots. **Common Era** (1500 Pearl St., 303/444-1799, http://mycommonera.com, 11am-6pm Mon.-Sat., 11am-5pm Sun.) is an affordable "big city" clothing and accessory store started by Debra Mazur in 1999, whose time—and merchandise—is focused not on the calendar era, but on the here and now. Mazur's passion is evident in the store and its devoted clientele. The store mostly sells clothing like colored jeans and sequined tops and shoes from manufacturers that specialize in small runs, which makes for an unusual and constantly changing inventory. Mazur and the staff also make much of their own jewelry and carry colorful accessories from other local artists, too.

Weekends (1200 Pearl St., 303/444-4231, http://weekendsboulder.com, 10am-7pm Mon.-Sat., 11am-6pm Sun.) is one of Pearl Street's largest retailers. The shop has a large selection of casual men's and women's shoes and clothing from brands like Frye Shoes, Shinola, and Rebecca Taylor. Weekends also specializes in denim clothing from fashion-forward designers like rag & bone, J Brand, and KATO'—as well as custom tailoring. On the more casual side, **Goldmine Vintage** (1123 Pearl St., 303/447-0065, www.goldminevintage.com, 11am-8pm Mon.-Thurs., 11am-9pm Fri.-Sat., 11am-7pm Sun.) is a retro thrift store overflowing with vintage and contemporary clothing, jewelry, shoes, and even records. **Where the Buffalo Roam** (1320 Pearl St., 303/938-1424, 10am-6pm daily) is a souvenir shop that specializes in T-shirts and CU apparel, while right next door, **Alpaca Connection** (1326 Pearl St., 303/447-2047, www.thealpacaconnection.com, 11am-6pm daily), founded by a CU grad more than 25 years ago, sells wool sweaters and other Peruvian clothing.

Walking in the door of **Gypsy Jewelry** (820 Pearl St., 303/442-4500, 10am-6pm Mon.-Sat., 11am-5pm Sun.) is like stepping into a rainbow. The vibrant, family-run store overflows with stacks of colorful silk scarves, funky jewelry, and home furniture and decor imported from Southeast Asia. **The Little Jewel** (1225 Pearl St., 303/443-3353, www.thelittlejewelco.com, 10am-6pm Mon.-Sat., 12:30pm-5pm Sun.), a family-owned shop, and **Hurdle's Jewelry** (1402 Pearl St., 303/443-1084, www.hurdlesjewelry.com, 10am-5:30pm Mon.-Sat.) are both venerable Pearl Street vendors with large selections of custom and designer fine jewelry.

For practical footwear, my favorite shoe store is the **Pedestrian Shops** (1425 Pearl St., 303/449-5260, www.comfortableshoes.com, 10am-7pm Mon.-Sat., 11am-7pm Sun.), which specializes in comfortable shoes, clogs, and sandals, including, of course, Birkenstocks. Founded by three friends from Boulder, **Crocs** (1129 Pearl St., 303/442-4261, www.crocs.com, 10am-8pm Mon.-Thurs., 10am-9pm Fri.-Sat.,

11am-7pm Sun.) have become an international sensation, with huge sales spikes after well-known names like George W. Bush and the young British Prince George were spotted wearing them. The Pearl Street store has all the latest styles, from fuzz-filled winter models to kids' splash boots and women's ballet wedges. A second location is in the Village (2525 Arapahoe Ave.).

Changes in Latitude (2525 Arapahoe Ave., 303/786-8406, www.cil.com, 10am-6pm Mon.-Sat., noon-5pm, Sun.) is a self-declared "one-of-a-kind traveler boutique" with everything from travel-friendly clothing to pillows and luggage.

BOOKSTORES

Boulder has several excellent bookstores. My personal favorite is **Boulder Book Store** (1107 Pearl St., 303/447-2074, www.boulder-bookstore.net, 10am-10pm Mon.-Sat., 10am-8pm Sun.), a local landmark since 1973. It's nearly impossible to go inside the crammed store without finding a recent release or used classic that you must read. Three stories are divided into helpful sections, which include separate children's and teens areas, travel guides, local reads, and lots of periodicals. For topo maps and local guidebooks, try **Boulder Map Gallery** (607 S. Broadway St., 303/444-1406, http://bouldermapgallery.com, 10am-6pm Mon.-Fri., 10am-4pm Sat.).

To get into the New Age spirit, visit the **Lighthouse Bookstore** (1201 Pearl St., 303/939-8355, 10am-6pm Mon.-Sat., 11am-6pm Sun.), which specializes in metaphysical, spiritual, and Magick books as well as runes and tarot cards.

The **Beat Book Shop** (1200 Pearl St., 303/444-7111, 3pm-8pm Sun.-Mon., 1pm-9pm Tues.-Thurs., 1pm-10pm Fri.-Sat.) is only open in the afternoons, but if you're here at the right time, it's a fun place to browse for unusual books and records. On the mall's eastern end, **Trident Booksellers and Café** (940 Pearl St., 303/443-3133, www.tridentcafe.com, 6:30am-11pm Mon.-Sat., 7am-11pm Sun.) has been a local Zen hangout since 1980, selling coffee

plus new and collectible books focused on philosophy, religion, metaphysics, and history.

ART GALLERIES AND SHOPS

One of the best places to pick up an affordable gift or a Colorado souvenir is **Artmart** (1326 Pearl St., 303/443-8248, www.artmart-gifts.com, 11am-8pm Mon.-Thurs., 10am-9pm Fri.-Sun.), which features the work of more than 300 artists, many of whom are local. Much of their inventory is Boulder- and Colorado-centric, including vintage-looking plaques and innovative word picture frames, as well as handmade jewelry, wall signs, and other decor. A block away, **Art Source International** (1237 Pearl St., 303/444-4080, www.rare-maps.com, 10am-6pm Mon.-Sat., 11am-6pm Sun.) specializes in antique maps, globes, and vintage posters.

One of the oldest artist-owned cooperatives in the United States, **Boulder Arts & Crafts Gallery** (1421 Pearl St., 303/443-3683, http://boulderartsandcrafts.com, 10am-6pm Mon.-Sat., 11am-5pm Sun.) is a bright and cheerful shop filled with beautiful displays of artwork in many mediums—ceramics, fiber, wood, glass, and paint—plus photography and jewelry. This is a great place for a splurge if you want to take home a special memory of your trip to Colorado. Pearl Street also hosts a number of traditional fine art galleries, each with its own distinct style. **Art + Soul Gallery** (1615 Pearl St., 303/544-5803, www.artandsoulboulder.com, 11am-6pm Mon.-Sat., 11am-5pm Sun.) highlights contemporary creativity in its fine art and diverse selection of designer jewelry. The **15th Street Gallery** (1708 15th St., 303/447-2841, http://15thstreetgalleryboulder.com, 10am-5:30pm Tues.-Fri., 10am-5pm Sat.) is a swanky contemporary gallery showcasing work by established artists in a wide range of mediums, including etchings, woodcuts, sculpture, and acrylic and oil paintings. **Earthwood Gallery** (1412 Pearl St., 303/444-3838, www.earth-woodgalleries.com, 10am-6pm Mon.-Thurs., 10am-7pm Fri.-Sat., 10am-5pm Sun.) emphasizes beautiful American art and has striking

displays that are fun to browse, including colorful blown, fused, and stained glass.

HOME AND GIFT

Don't leave town without visiting **Peppercorn** (1235 Pearl St., 303/449-5847, www.peppercorn.com, 10am-6pm Mon.-Thurs. and Sat., 10am-7pm Fri., 11am-5pm Sun.), Boulder's premier housewares store, which has been located on the mall for more than 35 years. Its crowded aisles feature a potpourri of kitchen, bath, and home merchandise, including an impressive selection of cookbooks, kitchen gadgets, dishes, and candles and gourmet foodstuff galore. "Spice up your life" is the theme at **Bayleaf on Pearl** (1222 Pearl St., 720/565-2477, 10am-6pm Mon.-Sat., 10am-5pm Sun.), which sells high-end housewares, cookbooks, unusual gifts, and lots of heavily scented aromatherapy candles. Half a block north of the mall, the fragrant shop **Savory Spice** (2041 Broadway St., 303/444-0668, www.savoryspiceshop.com, 10am-6pm Mon.-Sat., 11am-5pm Sun.) offers real spices for all your cooking needs. **Bliss** (1643 Pearl St., 303/443-0355, www.blissboulder.com, 9am-7pm Mon.-Sat., 10am-6pm Sun.) is a locally owned boutique with a stylish and quirky selection of vases, pillows, furniture, and baby items, plus lots of cards, journals, and other paper goods.

KIDS AND PETS

Adults and kids both love to visit **Into the Wind** (1408 Pearl St., 303/449-5356, http://intothewind.com, 10am-6pm daily). Established more than 35 years ago as a kite store, it carries both classic and new toys, games and joke gifts, decorative wind kites, and hundreds of traditional and stunt kites perfect for trying out during one of Boulder's frequent wind storms. Not every city has a cat and dog boutique, so if you have a furry friend, you'll want to stop by **Farfel's Farm** (906 Pearl St., 303/443-7711, www.farfels.com, 10am-6pm Mon.-Sat., 11am-5pm Sun.) for a large and luxurious selection of leashes, collars, food, toys, and Boulder-made pet treats. **Nest** (2525 Arapahoe Ave., 720/524-7676, http://

nestchildrensboutique.com, 9am-6pm Mon.-Sat., 11am-5pm Sun.) is a fun, upscale kids clothing store for newborns through age six.

SWEET TREATS

Just walking into **Piece, Love & Chocolate** (805 Pearl St., 303/449-4804, http://pieceloveandchocolate.com, 8am-6pm Mon.-Thurs., 8am-9pm Fri., 9am-9pm Sat., 10:30am-6pm Sun.) on the eastern edge of the mall will make your mouth water. This chocolate boutique sources their sumptuous sweets from all over the world. They offer in-store baking and pairing classes, as well as a tempting daily selection of 50 different flavors of in-house truffles and chocolates, including several cordials featuring local beers and wines. Best of all, they have a small café and seating area where you can savor their signature hot sipping chocolate, a mocha-chocolate Molten Jolt, or a decadent white chocolate chai.

If you're in the mood for ice cream, try **Fior di Latte** (1433 Pearl St., 720/269-4117, http://fiordilattegelato.com, noon-9pm Mon.-Thurs., noon-11pm Fri., 11am-11pm Sat., 11am-9pm Sun.), whose creamy gelato is made from scratch daily, or find the **Glacier Homemade Ice Cream** cart (1400 Pearl St., 303/440-6542, www.glaciericecream.com) near the mall's eastern end to try some innovative ice cream flavors.

Twenty Ninth Street Mall

Twenty Ninth Street Mall (1710 29th St., 303/444-0722, www.twentyninthstreet.com, 10am-8pm Mon.-Sat., 11am-6pm Sun.) is the most recent reincarnation of the old Crossroads Mall, which closed in 2004. This upscale version, while lacking the character and vivacity of Pearl Street, hosts a diverse assortment of stores, including Macy's, Anthropologie, Nordstrom's, Trader Joe's, and an always-crowded Apple Store, as well as a movie theater and—being Boulder—the swanky Colorado Athletic Club. Restaurants include a diverse selection of casual and upscale food, from BJ's Restaurant & Brewhouse and Chipotle to the Garbanzo Mediterranean Grill.

Boulder Marijuana Guide

It's no surprise that this counter-culture college town has a high concentration of recreational dispensaries. The rules stipulate that people age 21 and over can, with a valid ID, possess up to six plants or one ounce of pot; anything more and they're considered a business and must therefore hold several special licenses. The only exception is for medical marijuana patients, who may possess up to two ounces. Out-of-state visitors, however, are limited to 0.25 ounce. The city charges a voter-approved 3.5 percent sales and use tax in addition to the current 8.845 percent tax. Driving under the influence of pot is illegal, and users are still required to follow Boulder's strict no-smoking laws.

A variety of websites, including www.coloradopotguide.com and http://weedmaps.com, are helpful for up-to-date information about the locations of licensed retail marijuana stores, which are the only legal outlets. The greatest concentration of dispensaries is located downtown, including **Native Roots** (1146 Pearl St., 720/726-5126, http://nativerootsboulder.com, 9am-7pm daily), which offers indica, sativa, and hybrid strains, a large selection of edibles like organic fruity hearts and Cheeba Chews, and drinks like CWD Stoned Cold Lemonade. The **Helping Hands Dispensary** (1021 Pearl St., 720/476-6186, http://helpinghandsdispensary.com, 9am-6:45pm Mon.-Fri., 10am-6:45pm Sat.-Sun.) sells seeds, growing equipment, and dozens of Colorado strains with amusing names like Big Bubba Diesel and Jamaican Voodoo. One block north of Pearl Street, **The Village Green Society** (2043 16th St., 720/389-5726, www.vgsboulder.com, 9am-7pm daily) has "budtenders" on hand who can help you select just the right bud, edible, or therapeutic CBD (cannabidiol) product to lessen pain or treat conditions like arthritis, epilepsy, and anxiety disorders.

FOOD

Dining is one of Boulder's many great pleasures. The city offers a disproportionately large variety of cuisines and high-quality establishments. Most Boulderites enjoy taking advantage of this diversity, as well as the abundance of fresh, local, and organic ingredients creatively combined by local chefs. Pearl Street offers the highest concentration of options, including many award-winning restaurants, but it's worth exploring away from the city center to discover some of Boulder's other culinary gems.

Downtown
BREAKFAST AND CAFÉS
Sure, ★ **Snooze** (1617 Pearl St., 303/225-7344, http://snoozeeatery.com, 7am-3pm daily, $7-13) is a small chain based in Denver, but its eclectic atmosphere, friendly service, and unusual twists on breakfast classics really stand out. Founded by two brothers who believe that a good breakfast "marks the beginning of a new day," this eatery not only

serves up delicious food, it also works hard to sustain the Earth and give back to the local community. You can customize your food, like huevos rancheros topped with meat or veggies, or enjoy two half-orders of your favorite benedicts if you can't choose. If you prefer your food sweet, try the incredible mascarpone-stuffed and caramel-topped OMG! French toast. Farther west on Pearl Street, **Foolish Craig's** (1611 Pearl St., 303/247-9383, www.foolishcraigs.com, 8am-9:30pm Mon.-Sat., 8am-9pm Sun., $7-11) serves three meals a day but is best known for its crêpes with funny names like The Homer (D'oh!), which is stuffed with Mediterranean veggies and topped with sour cream, the Fahgeddaboudit (Think Brooklyn), and the visitor/hangover favorite, The Altitude Adjustment.

FRESH AND LOCAL
When the historic Tom's Tavern, a 40-year fixture on Pearl Street, closed in 2007 after its iconic owner died, local chef Bradford Heap

knew he'd have some big shoes (and empty stomachs) to fill. Happily, since its opening in 2009, ★ **SALT** (1047 Pearl St., 303/444-7258, http://saltthebistro.com, 11am-9pm Sun.-Thurs., 11am-10pm Fri.-Sat., $15-30), Heap's farm-to-table concept, has created quite a buzz. Named for the mineral's simplicity, which is echoed in the vibrant yellow and brick decor, the restaurant features straightforward and elegantly displayed dishes featuring fresh, local produce and natural meats sourced from local farmers and ranchers. The menu changes with the seasons but may include dishes like butternut squash risotto or Colorado trout topped with a mixture of beans, olives, turnips, tomatillo sauce, and parsley.

Oak at Fourteenth (1400 Pearl St., 303/444-3622, http://oakatfourteenth.com, 11:30am-10pm Mon.-Wed., 11:30am-midnight Thurs.-Sat., 2:30pm-10pm Sun., $5-30) features seasonal, local produce. Chef Steven Redzikowski, a semifinalist multiple times in the annual James Beard Foundation Awards, has created a menu of New American cuisine centered around the contemporary restaurant's one-of-a-kind, oak-fired oven and grill and Colorado's abundant produce. Although the long row of windows lining the room can make you feel as if you're in a fishbowl and the dining room is often loud, the service is impeccable and the food draws rave reviews. The diners, who are mostly young professionals, can choose between small, tapas-style plates with delicacies like grilled Gullo octopus and roasted kale toast or larger entrées like roasted free range chicken. The Oak is also well known for its unique libations, including concoctions like Red Zephyr, a colorful combo of Dimmi, Contratto Rosso, raspberry, lime, and egg white.

ASIAN

A few blocks south of Pearl Street, **Khow Thai** (1600 Broadway St., 303/447-0273, http://khow-thai.com, 11am-9:45pm Mon.-Thurs., 11am-10pm Fri., 5pm-10pm Sat., 5pm-9:45pm Sun., $11-15) is a small, no-frills establishment that looks like a cafeteria but smells heavenly when you walk in the door. Their peanut-topped pad Thai with shrimp or veggies is perfectly spiced, and the piquant green papaya salad, with lime juice and fish sauce, is a great break from traditional green salads.

Tiny **Zoe Ma Ma** (2010 10th St., 303/545-6262, www.zoemama.com, 11am-10pm Sun.-Thurs., 11am-11pm Fri.-Sat., $7-13) features a simple menu of street food inspired by the owner's mother's cooking. Its best-selling *za jiang mian* (a pork noodle dish) was featured on the Food Network's *Cheap Eats*. The long outdoor booth and cafeteria-style tables are always overflowing.

A bit more upscale is **Hapa Sushi** (1117 Pearl St., 303/473-4730, http://hapasushi.com, 11am-10pm Sun.-Wed., 11am-midnight Thurs.-Sat., $9-20), whose name is derived from a Hawaiian word meaning a harmonious blend of American and Asian cultures. The food is a similar combination of traditional Japanese cooking and outside, creative influences. The menu features a variety of sushi rolls—beginner, intermediate, and original—and a large selection of nigiri, as well as good vegetarian and vegan options and several types of sake.

Located just a block south of the mall, ★ **Sherpa's** (825 Walnut St., 303/440-7151, 11am-3pm and 5pm-9:30pm Sun.-Wed., 11am-3pm and 5pm-10pm Thurs.-Sat., $9-21) has Boulder's best Nepalese and Tibetan food, made from authentic recipes by chef Jangbu Sherpa, who has summited Mt. Everest an astounding 10 times without using supplemental oxygen. Located in an old house with one of Boulder's best outdoor seating areas, the restaurant is divided into many small rooms and has an overall relaxed atmosphere, with photos of Himalayan peaks tacked to the walls. The menu includes Himalayan staples like *dal baht* and Tibetan *momos* (steamed or fried dumplings with veggies or meat) and spicy yak sherpa stew. After a long hike, add an order of freshly baked naan bread and a cold pint for a very satisfying meal.

ITALIAN

Pizzeria Locale (1730 Pearl St., 303/442-3003, http://localeboulder.com, 11:30am-10pm Mon.-Thurs., 11:30am-10:30pm Fri.-Sat., 11:30am-9pm Sun., $9-18), a casual establishment specializing in Napoletana-style pizza, is the product of an odd partnership between the owners of Frasca's, one of Boulder's most upscale establishments, and the healthy fast-casual chain Chipotle Mexican Grill. The centerpiece of the stark, white-tiled interior is a special 1,000°F oven, which cooks the 48-hour, cold-rise dough in less than two minutes and endows the modest space with the Old World scents of roasted tomato and freshly baked bread. For a classic option, enjoy the mouthwatering margherita pizza. Gluten-free options, simple salads, and a good selection of wine, beer, and cocktails are also available.

A multiple-year semifinalist in the Outstanding Restaurant category of the prestigious James Beard Awards, **Frasca Food & Wine** (1738 Pearl St., 303/442-6966, www.frascafoodandwine.com, 5:30pm-9:30pm Mon.-Thurs., 5:30pm-10:30pm Fri., 5pm-10:30pm Sat., $50-105) features northern Italian food from the Friuli-Venezia Giulia region made with local ingredients

and paired with top-flight wines. The name comes from an Italian word for informal gatherings, places where people share a meal and a bottle of wine. Frasca's wine list boasts more than 200 varieties. The menu offers both à la carte and five-course Friulano tasting dinners paired with an optional wine flight ($95) by master sommelier Bobby Stuckey and chef Lachlan Mackinnon-Patterson. On Monday nights, the duo offers special wine dinners consisting of a four-plate menu and a guest wine pairing ($45). Reservations are accepted up to two months in advance.

MEDITERRANEAN

The Mediterranean Restaurant, locally called ★ **The Med** (1002 Walnut St., 303/444-5335, www.themedboulder.com, 11am-10pm Mon.-Thurs., 11am-11pm Fri.-Sat., 11am-9pm Sun., $8-30), is a local favorite so popular that several years ago the owners doubled their space by expanding into the building next door. That hasn't done much to alleviate the sometimes-noisy crowds who flock to the restaurant for its large selection of tapas, excellent Mediterranean-inspired entrées, wood-fired pizzas, and one of Boulder's liveliest happy hours.

Sherpa's

★ **BOULDER DUSHANBE TEAHOUSE**

Back in 1982, two Boulderites decided to do something positive about the strained Soviet-U.S. relations. The pair organized a local group to educate themselves about Soviet culture and began lobbying officials in the Soviet Union to establish a sister city. Unable to penetrate the Soviet red tape, the group finally chose Dushanbe, the current capital of Tajikistan, and persistently pursued officials there, sending messages via CU scientists who were authorized to conduct fieldwork behind the Iron Curtain. Their persistence finally paid off in 1987, when the mayor of Dushanbe visited Boulder, cementing the relationship and promising that as a gesture of friendship, his city would present the citizens of Boulder with a traditional Tajik teahouse.

Following years of debate in Boulder about where to erect the teahouse and how to pay for its installation, the **Boulder Dushanbe Teahouse** (1770 13th St., 303/442-4993, http://boulderteahouse.com, 8am-9pm daily, $13-22), the only Persian-style teahouse in the Western Hemisphere, was finally erected next to Central Park. Crafted entirely by hand, the building is a work of art created by more than 40 Tajik artisans using traditional Persian designs that feature gardens and water. The teahouse is built around a central fish pool encircled by copper sculptures of seven maidens who were the subjects of a popular 12th-century poem. The brightly painted wooden beams and recessed ceiling panels are a plot of vibrant flowers, entangled vines, and colorful geometric designs, while hand-embossed wooden pillars, carved from trees hand-selected from Russia's Lake Baikal area, support the ceiling.

On the side walls, delicate white-plaster panels frame mirrors, while traditional Tajik furniture, including low, painted tables and chairs, and *topchans*—traditional platforms with low tables encircled by cushions—fill the interior along with regular tables and chairs. The exterior is graced with eight ceramic panels with Tree of Life motifs whose

the Boulder Dushanbe Teahouse

MEXICAN AND LATIN AMERICAN

On the eastern end of the Pearl Street Mall, **Illegal Pete's** (1447 Pearl St., 303/440-3955, http://illegalpetes.com, 7am-midnight Mon.-Wed., 7am-2:30am Thurs.-Fri., 9am-2:30am Sat., 9am-midnight Sun., $6-8), a small local chain, serves up big, all-natural Mission-style burritos overflowing with toppings to the hungry masses as well as a limited breakfast menu. There is a second location on the Hill (1124 13th St., 303/444-3055, 11am-midnight Sun.-Wed., 11am-2:30am Thurs.-Sat.), and both locations feature daily 3pm-8pm happy hours. **Aji Latin American Restaurant** (1601 Pearl St., 303/442-3464, http://ajirestaurant.com, 11:30am-9pm Mon.-Thurs., 11:30am-10pm Fri., 10am-10pm Sat., 10am-9pm Sun., $14-36) has a meat-heavy menu featuring *churrasco,* South American-style barbeque ($21-32), a meal that includes salad, traditional baked cheese rolls, your choice of meat, sides like cowboy beans or toasted coconut rice, and spicy sauces such as cumin chipotle dijon.

pieces were sculpted, cut up, fired, and shipped to Boulder, where they were carefully reassembled. Visitors and locals both love to relax here and scan the artwork while sipping a cup of fragrant, house-made chai or one of the dozens of loose-leaf teas. The teahouse is also a full-service restaurant with reasonable prices in what definitely feels like a more upscale environment. The menu has an international focus and varies by season; sample entrées include Persian chickpea *kufteh* and spicy Indonesian peanut noodles. The afternoon tea, with a three-tiered tray filled with sweet and savory pastries, tea sandwiches, sweets, and fresh fruit, is also a fun way to celebrate on vacation. Reservations are required for afternoon tea and recommended for dinner.

South of Downtown

If you're out on the trails south of the University of Colorado campus or are searching for a moderately priced meal at a popular local establishment, these places located within a few miles of downtown are worth the drive or Skip bus ride to get there.

BREAKFAST AND CAFÉS

The **South Side Walnut Café** (673 S. Broadway St., 720/304-8118, www.walnut-cafe.com, 7am-3:30pm daily, $7-10) is the southern spinoff of the popular **Walnut Café** (3073 Walnut St., 303/447-2315, 7am-3:30pm daily) just east of the Twenty Ninth Street Mall. Although both locations can get crowded and a bit noisy, they're worth the visit for their diverse menu of breakfast and lunch options, including so-called "Boulder fare"—delicious combos like the eggless Boulder scramble with tofu, veggies, and cheese, or the Bowl O'Granola— that pokes fun at the populace's gluten-free, vegan love affair. Other tasty options include meaty sandwiches like Philly steak and BLTs. Top it off with a slice of fresh-baked pie, the house specialty, and a locally brewed Bhakti chai.

BREWPUBS

The ★ **Southern Sun Pub & Brewery** (627 S. Broadway St., 303/543-0886, www.mountainsunpub.com, 4pm-1am Mon., 11:30am-1am Tues.-Sun., $6-12) is the southern cousin of the downtown **Mountain Sun Pub & Brewery** (1535 Pearl St., 303/546-0886, 11:30am-1am Mon.-Sat., noon-1am Sun.), both of which feature a simple menu of fresh sandwiches, salads, and burgers made from vegetarian-fed, steroid-free Colorado beef. Try the basil blue cheese-burger with fresh, house-made fries, or the vegetarian portobello boom boom sandwich washed down with a foaming pint of Annapurna Amber. Despite its many tables and long, wooden bar, the Southern Sun is usually packed and noisy; so when a restaurant closed downstairs, the owners expanded into that space, creating **Under the Sun** (627 S. Broadway St., 303/927-6921, 5pm-midnight Mon.-Fri., 9am-midnight Sat.-Sun. $11-17), a more contemporary-looking pub that's also extremely popular. On the weekend, this restaurant serves a limited but innovative breakfast menu, which includes the corny hash skillet, with corned beef, potatoes, sauerkraut, eggs, and cheese topped by Thousand Island dressing, and my kids' favorite Captain's French Toast, made with Captain Crunch-coated challah bread. The breakfast and dinner menus feature 10 different wood-fired pizzas, including the must-try fig and prosciutto. Before you order, however, be aware that none of the Suns accept credit cards.

Located a couple miles east of downtown in a chic-industrial warehouse building, **FATE Brewing Company** (1600 38th St., 303/449-3283, http://fatebrewingcompany.com, 11am-10pm Mon.-Fri., 10am-10pm Sat.-Sun., $11-22) is Boulder's first "brew-bistro." Despite the large interior, the bar and booths usually fill up quickly—perhaps because it takes so long to decide which brew to try from the house and rotating guest taps. If you can't pick just one, try the core beer flight, which lets you sample their five staple Belgian-style beers, including my favorite, the banana-scented hoppy Parcae pale ale. There are plenty of choices for food, as well, from pub plates of caramelized sweet potatoes and kale Caesar salads to entrées like roasted mushroom ramen.

INDIAN

Boulder's best Indian restaurant is **Tandoori Grill** (619 S. Broadway St., 303/543-7339, http://tandoorigrillboulder. com, 11:30am-2:30pm and 5pm-9:30pm Mon.-Thurs., 5pm-10pm Fri.-Sat., 5pm-9pm Sun., $10-17), a quieter option with large, padded booths, a family-oriented clientele, and a wonderful, spicy scent. During lunch, the restaurant features an all-you-can-eat buffet. In the evening, the lengthy menu includes innovative dishes like eye-watering chili shrimp along with traditional favorites like tandoori chicken and *bengan bartha* eggplant, my favorite Friday night take-out dish.

ITALIAN

Strangely situated in a strip mall near CU's towering Williams Village dorms, ★ **Carelli's of Boulder** (645 30th St., 303/938-9300, www.carellis.com, 11am-11pm Mon.-Fri., 4pm-11pm Sat., $10-30) offers traditional northern and southern Italian food in a comfortable, wood-paneled interior dominated by a cozy, open metal fireplace and a swanky, backlit bar. Despite the proximity to campus, the restaurant is a favorite of young and middle-aged professionals who enjoy the happy hour deals and, in summer, the outdoor seating. With white linen tablecloths, a long wine list, and excellent service, the restaurant always feels like a special treat when my husband and I escape for a romantic date night. In addition to a good selection of antipasti and salads, the lengthy menu features *secondi piatti* like mussels *carciofi* and basil-topped artisanal margherita pizza, plus a good variety of fresh-baked calzones and fancy sandwiches like arugula-covered smoked salmon panini.

UPSCALE

If you're here to celebrate a special event or in the mood for a splurge, the ★ **Flagstaff House** (1138 Flagstaff Rd., 303/442-4640, www. flagstaffhouse.com, 6pm-10pm Sun.-Fri., 5pm-10pm Sat., $38-74) high on Flagstaff Mountain is *the* place to do it, even though there is no public transport. Originally built as a summer cabin in 1929, the building has been expanded and updated through the years to create what is arguably Boulder's most memorable dining experience. The floor-to-ceiling picture windows and outdoor terraces offer unparalleled views of the surrounding foothills and the sparkling city lights, while the gleaming mahogany bar and crackling fireplace make an ideal winter retreat. The restaurant is best known for its extensive cellar of 16,000 bottles of wine and its coveted Wine Spectator Grand Award, of which only 81 have been awarded worldwide. The food is French-American, with main courses ranging from pan-roasted filet mignon to mushroom-filled poached New Zealand John Dory. The restaurant has a business-casual dress code and does not accept checks.

DESSERT

The south Boulder **Sweet Cow Ice Cream** (669 S. Broadway St., 303/494-4269, www. sweetcowicecream.com, noon-9pm Sun.-Thurs., noon-10pm Fri.-Sat.) is the perfect spot for a sweet post-hike treat. This six-store local chain has another family-friendly shop in north Boulder (2628 Broadway St., 303/447-3269), which is open the same hours. Both feature a sparsely decorated interior with a long counter and stools and a tempting selection of 24 wonderful flavors, 15 of which rotate regularly. The ice cream is made from locally sourced ingredients and includes some imaginative concoctions, like peanut butter brownie, malted milk ball, and the Halloween favorite Trick or Treat. Cool tip: The hot fudge sundaes are to die for!

North of Downtown

North of downtown Boulder, there are many establishments well worth the trip to get here. Those on Broadway Street are accessible via the Skip bus, whereas others are more easily accessible by car.

BREAKFAST AND CAFÉS

At its three family-friendly Boulder locations, **Moe's Broadway Bagel** (2650 Broadway St., 303/444-3252, www.moesbagel.com, 5:30am-5pm daily, $3-8) serves more than 20 flavors of chewy, fresh-baked bagels topped with plain, garlic herb, and other cream cheeses. In the same plaza, **Breadworks** (2644 Broadway St., 303/444-5667, 7am-7pm Mon.-Fri., 7am-6pm Sat.-Sun., $7-14) is a sunny bakery and café featuring organic artisan bread and a large selection of fresh soups, grab-and-go sandwiches, pizza, and design-your-own salads. Although it closes too early for my dinnertime, it's a great place to head for lunch or a sweet afternoon pastry.

For a healthy and delicious breakfast or lunch, follow the locals to **Tangerine** (2777 Iris Ave., 303/443-2333, http://tangerineboulder.com, 7am-2:30pm daily, $6-14) for a menu inspired by simple Mediterranean flavors. The name comes from a teaching by the Buddha that inspired chef/proprietor Alec Schuler, an avid biker, skier, and qigong practitioner. With comfortable booths and tangerine-colored highlights, the chic and sunny interior is as appealing as the food, which frequently features seasonal Colorado farm products. My daughter raves about (but never lets me share) the large portion of BLR pancakes (blueberry, lemon, and ricotta pancakes topped with blueberry sauce), while I enjoy the unusual eggs on salad, a lighter dish with two sunny-side eggs and charred asparagus over fresh, lemon-dressed salad.

FRESH AND LOCAL

Owned by the same chef as Tangerine, **Arugula Bar e Ristorante** (2785 Iris Ave., 303/443-5100, http://arugularistorante.com,

5pm-9pm Sun.-Tues., 11:30am-2:30pm and 5pm-9pm Wed.-Thurs., 11:30am-2:30pm and 5pm-10pm Fri., 5pm-10pm Sat., $20-34) is a more upscale concept. Its spacious yet intimate sunlit interior is decorated with unique corkscrew artwork and antique wine implements, and in summer, the flower basket-lined outdoor patio is a wonderful place to enjoy a mint martini or a glass of sparkling wine from the carefully selected list. For dinner, your table can order a five-course tasting menu or try the house-marinated mixed olives followed by seared Pacific albacore tuna.

★ **Turley's Kitchen** (2805 Pearl St., 303/442-2800, www.turleysrestaurant.com, 6:30am-9pm Mon.-Fri., 7am-9pm Sat.-Sun., $11-19), located a mile east of the Pearl Street Mall, is one of Boulder's hidden gems where friendly staff have been serving up heaping portions of all-natural food since 1977. As you enter the red-brick building, you're greeted by the enticing scent of cinnamon-spice tea and a colorful chalkboard listing the day's locally grown organic ingredients. The snug booths and spacious outdoor patio fill quickly on the weekend. Breakfast, served all day, includes thick fruit smoothies, gluten-free pumpkin waffles, and cage-free egg concoctions like green eggs and (antibiotic-free) ham. For dinner, try the juicy buffalo meatloaf, pesto-stuffed chicken, or flaky veggie potpie. If you still have enough room, top it off with the decadent, gluten-free chocolate torte.

ASIAN

A few blocks north of Pearl, **Chez Thuy** (2655 28th St., 303/442-1700, www.chezthuy.com, 11am-10pm Mon.-Sat., 4pm-10pm Sun., winter hours may vary, $7-30) has, despite its less-than-ideal location, served an enormous and consistently good menu of Vietnamese, Chinese, Thai, and Chinese food since 1993. If you're in northeast Boulder, it's definitely worth settling into one of the maroon-colored booths for their lunchtime pho (traditional Vietnamese noodle soup) or the fresh pineapple stir-fry, five-spice duck, or cashew tofu for dinner. Wash it down with a watermelon boba and, for dessert, a velvety Thuy coffee float.

ACCOMMODATIONS

Although Boulder has some great places to stay overnight, none are cheap. Prices spike around big CU events, like graduation and football games, as well as during summer. Rates are often lower in winter, despite being prime ski season. While there is no camping available within the Boulder city limits, there are several options within an hour's drive along the Peak-to-Peak Highway.

$100-150

While the rustic, red-trimmed log cabins at the family run **Foot of the Mountain Motel** (200 W. Arapahoe Ave., 303/442-5688, www. footofthemountainmotel.com, $122-181) are pretty basic and dark, they are also clean, comfortable, and positioned in an ideal location along Boulder Creek, with tubing, hiking, and biking right outside the door and within walking distance of Pearl Street.

$150-250

The renovated **Boulder University Inn** (1632 Broadway St., 303/417-1700, www. boulderuniversityinn.com, $239-269) is ideally situated between CU and the downtown, just steps from Boulder Creek. Although some guests complain of noise, especially from rooms closest to Broadway, it's a comfortable stop for travelers, with flat-screen TVs and all the other expected amenities. Nine blocks east of the Pearl Street Mall, the ★ **Briar Rose Bed & Breakfast** (2151 Arapahoe Ave., 303/442-3007, www.briarrosebb.com, $179-234) is a cozy bed-and-breakfast with 10 rooms in a house built in the 1880s. Operated by a Zen monk, the inn feels like a home, with private gardens, a wood-burning fireplace, and tea trays with shortbread butter cookies on demand. Best of all is the delicious organic breakfast, which includes ripe fruit, sweet

breads, an egg dish with toast, plus freshly brewed coffee and loose-leaf teas.

Up Boulder Canyon, the boutique **Alps Boulder Canyon Inn** (38619 Boulder Canyon Dr., 303/444-5445, www.alpsinn. com, $159-235) has 12 distinct guest rooms, all with private bathrooms and cozy working fireplaces. In addition to complimentary beverages, afternoon tea with homemade cookies, and evening desserts, the inn serves fantastic breakfasts that usually include fresh-baked scones with homemade lemon curd, fresh-squeezed juices, their own house-blended coffee, and seasonally inspired entrées. Up Fourmile Canyon just a couple miles from downtown, the **Boulder Adventure Lodge** (A-Lodge, 91 Fourmile Canyon Dr., 303/444-0882, http://a-lodge. com, $169) is a welcome new addition to the Boulder area. The hostel-hotel has a wide variety of rooms ranging from Boulder's only bunkroom ($59) to standard queens and spacious suites. In addition to an outdoor patio, pool, and hot tub, the lodge has a slacklining park and quick access to the Boulder Creek Path and Fourmile Creek. The focus here is adventure, so the lodge has a free weekend shuttle to Eldora Mountain Resort and partners with local guide services to offer memorable experiences like cliff camping and ascending mighty Long's Peak.

Over $250

Just south of the Pearl Street Mall, the luxurious, 201-room **St Julien Hotel & Spa** (900 Walnut St., 720/406-9696, http://stjulien.com, $290-371) has plush, pillow-top beds, oversized bathrooms with soaking tubs, and stunning views of Boulder's beautiful mountain backdrop from some of the more expensive rooms. The hotel also has an upscale restaurant, Jill's, and a bar, and sponsors fun events like Saturday afternoon tea, when hot or iced tea and champagne cocktails are served alongside dainty tea sandwiches and scones. The hotel also offers popular holiday gingerbread teas, where kids don chef hats and aprons to decorate cookies alongside the hotel's culinary team.

The landmark ★ **Hotel Boulderado** (2115 13th St., 303/442-4344, www.boulderado.com, $279-319) is housed in a five-story, historic brick building with bright-green awnings just a two-minute walk from Pearl Street. Local business people raised the funds to build it as the city's first upscale hotel, which opened on Near Year's Day in 1909. Since then, many well-known guests have stayed in the stylish Victorian rooms, including conservationist Enos Mills, Helen Keller, Louis Armstrong, and Robert Frost. Of special note is the lobby's stunning stained-glass ceiling, which was restored in the late 1970s after the original Italian glass was destroyed during a particularly heavy late-season snowstorm in 1959.

Just one block from Pearl Street, The **Bradley Boulder Inn** (2040 16th St., 303/545-5200, www.thebradleyboulder.com, $245-270) is a refined bed-and-breakfast with 12 stylish rooms with a variety of amenities from baths with jetted tubs to balconies with mountain views. The cozy sitting room features a large stone fireplace surrounded by plush chairs, which "feels like a wealthy aunt's home" according to *Every Day with Rachael Ray*. With a wine-and-cheese hour each evening, a home-cooked breakfast, and nearby health-club privileges, you'll want to visit your long-lost relative for a very long time. Kids under 14 are not allowed, and second-floor access is by stairs only.

★ **The Colorado Chautauqua Association** (900 Baseline Rd., 303/952-1611, www.chautauqua.com, $190-275) rents out some of its 99 historic cottages nestled beneath the Flatirons at the edge of gorgeous Chautauqua Park on Baseline Road. Quaint (and sometimes a bit run-down) cottages are available in studio, 1-, 2-, and 3-bedroom configurations, all with fully equipped kitchens, screened-in porches, and front door access to many of Boulder's best hiking trails. During the busy summer season, a minimum four-night stay is required, but there are also

two lodges, one of which has apartment-style rooms available for nightly rentals from mid-June through August.

TRANSPORTATION AND SERVICES
Air
Denver International Airport (DEN, 8500 Peña Blvd., 303/342-2000, www.flydenver.com) is the most convenient airport to get to Boulder. Locally owned **Green Ride** (303/997-0238, http://greenrideboulder.com) and **SuperShuttle** (800/258-3826, www.supershuttle.com) offers door-to-door service. The **Regional Transportation District** (RTD, www.rtd-denver.com) offers efficient and less-expensive service on the AB route to several locations in Boulder.

Car
To reach Boulder from downtown Denver, merge onto I-70 west for 4 miles, then continue west on I-270 for 6.5 miles to U.S. 36 west to Boulder. This 30-mile trip takes about an hour, but can take substantially longer during rush hour and/or inclement weather. If you decide to rent a car in Boulder, Enterprise, Avis, and Hertz have depots within a few miles of downtown.

Bus
The **Regional Transportation District** (RTD, www.rtd-denver.com, $2.60-13 one-way) operates a network of buses throughout the city and connects with regional buses to Denver, Nederland, and Fort Collins. The excellent local service features brightly painted buses with fun names like **Hop,** which runs between CU, downtown, and Twenty Ninth Street Mall; **Skip,** which runs along Broadway Street; and **Jump,** which runs east-west along Arapahoe Avenue. Visit **Go Boulder** (http://bouldercolorado.gov/goboulder) for maps and information.

Purchase tickets at one of the two RTD hubs: the downtown **RTD Bus Station** (1800 14th St., 303/299-6000, 7am-6:30pm Mon.-Fri.) or the **Boulder Junction at Depot**

Square Station (3175 Pearl Pkwy., 303/299-6000, 7am-6:30pm Mon.-Fri.). Many Safeway and King Soopers stores also sell 10-packs of single-fare passes, or you can pay on the bus with exact change.

Bike

The **Boulder B Cycle** (303/532-4412, http://boulder.bcycle.com, $8 for 24 hours) offers a year-round 24/7 bike rental program; helmets are not included.

Tours

Many downtown tours are available. **Banjo Billy Bus Tours** (720/938-8885, www.banjobilly.com, $15-23) recount local legends and ghost lore in a school bus-turned-hillbilly shack. **Historic Boulder** (1123 Spruce St., 303/444-5192, www.historicboulder.org, 9am-5pm Mon.-Fri., $20) and **Boulder Walking Tours** (720/243-1376, http://boulderwalkingtours.com, $20) both offer guided history strolls. **Local Table Tours** (303/909-5747, www.localtabletours.com, $30-75) leads coffee and pastry, cocktail, and market-to-table trips. **Boulder Brew Tours** (303/522-3236, http://boulderbrewtours.com, $32) organizes a sequence of microbrewery visits.

Services

VISITOR INFORMATION

The **Boulder Convention & Visitors Bureau** (2440 Pearl St., 303/442-2911, www.bouldercoloradousa.com) offers visitor brochures at two information kiosks, one at the Davidson Mesa Overlook a few miles southeast of Boulder on U.S. 36 and a second on Pearl Street between 13th and 14th Streets. The **City of Boulder** (303/441-3388, http://bouldercolorado.gov) offers logistical information about how to get around and enjoy Boulder. The most convenient place to find outdoor info is at **Boulder Open Space**

and **Mountain Parks** (http://osmp.org). Obtain maps, brochures, and information at the **Chautauqua Ranger Cottage** (900 Baseline Rd., 303/441-3440, 9am-4pm Mon.-Fri., 8am-6pm Sat.-Sun. May-Sept., shorter hours Oct.-Apr.).

MEDIA AND COMMUNICATIONS

Boulder's downtown **post office** (1905 15th St., 303/938-3704, 8:30am-5:30pm Mon.-Fri., 10am-2pm Sat.) is conveniently located a few blocks southeast of the Pearl Street Mall.

The *Boulder Daily Camera* (www.dailycamera.com) is Boulder's daily paper, which publishes listings of daily events. The *Colorado Daily* (www.coloradodaily.com) focuses on CU, but also includes local news stories. The *Boulder Weekly* (www.boulderweekly.com) has a strong environmental focus and also covers local events. The student-run *CU Independent* (http://cuindependent.com) covers campus and local news.

Boulder's best-known radio station, **KBCO** (97.3 FM), is now a corporate-owned entity that operates out of Denver. Their "World Class Rock" format features a mixture of pop, classic rock, blues, folk, and reggae music. The community-oriented **KGNU** (88.5 FM) features more local news and musicians.

MEDICAL

The city's main hospitals are **Boulder Community Health** (4747 Arapahoe Ave., 303/415-7000, www.bch.org) and **Boulder Medical Center** (2750 Broadway St., 303/440-3000, and 4750 Arapahoe Ave., Ste. 200, 303/938-4700, www.bouldermedicalcenter.com). Urgent care facilities include **Rocky Mountain Urgent Care** (4800 Baseline Rd. #106, 303/499-4800, www.rockymountainurgentcare.com, 8am-7pm Mon.-Fri., 9am-4pm Sat.-Sun.) and **Concentra Urgent Care** (3300 28th St., 303/541-9090, www.concentra.com, 8am-6pm Mon.-Fri.).

Vicinity of Boulder

Just south of Boulder is Eldorado Canyon State Park, a narrow abyss carved through the flank of the Rockies by the gurgling South Boulder Creek. To the west lie a series of historic towns built around old gold-mining camps, a small ski resort, and the spectacular backdrop of the Indian Peaks, a remote and rugged wilderness of deep valleys, sparkling alpine lakes, and high peaks that form the Continental Divide. To the north, Lyons is a vibrant, artsy community built around the quarrying of local stone.

★ ELDORADO CANYON STATE PARK

Eldorado Canyon State Park (9 Kneale Rd., Eldorado Springs, http://cpw.state.co.us/placestogo/parks/EldoradoCanyon, 6am-8pm daily, $8 per car) is one of the prettiest—and most popular—of Colorado's 42 state parks. Located at the end of the road just past the close-knit community of Eldorado Springs, the park is best known for its technical **rock climbing**, as well as streamside picnicking, hiking, and angling. With more than 40 picnic spots available, including many along the creek, it's a popular place for families and anglers. When the weather is mild, you can easily spot climbers crimping tiny edges on their way up the vertical sandstone cliffs. More than 500 trad routes grace the golden canyon walls, including classic multi-pitch routes like **Bastille Crack** (5.7), **Yellow Spur** (5.9), and the famous **Naked Edge** fingercrack (5.11b), a normally full-day route that a team of Colorado speedsters climbed—and descended—in less than 25 minutes.

If you'd rather keep your feet on the ground, the hiking in "Eldo" is fantastic. From the Rattlesnake Gulch Trailhead (on the left about 0.5 mile down the main dirt road), the flat **Fowler Trail** (2 miles, one-way) is a pleasant jaunt that passes directly behind the Bastille, a rock formation named for a notorious French prison. From the same trailhead, you can ascend the **Rattlesnake Gulch Trail,** a steep 3.5-mile loop that climbs more than 1,200 feet past the burned ruins of a historic hotel to views of the snow-capped Continental Divide. My favorite hike here is the **Eldorado Canyon Trail,** a seven-mile out-and-back climb up a well-graded path to patches of peaceful pines. The trail then descends to the **Walker Ranch Loop,** where you can enjoy a well-deserved lunch by a small waterfall before retracing your steps.

After your hike, climb, or afternoon nap, stop in Eldorado Springs, where natural artesian springs continuously feed the refreshing (and cold!) **Eldorado Swimming Pool** (294 Artesian Dr., 303/499-9640, www.eldoradosprings.com, 10am-6pm daily Memorial Day-Labor Day, $10 adults, $7 children). The historic site was once part of a resort in the

Eldorado Canyon State Park attracts rock climbers.

Vicinity of Boulder

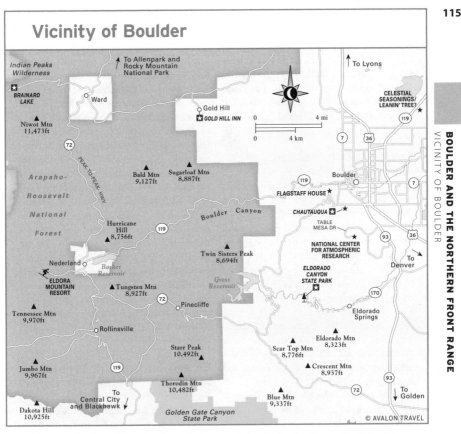

early 1900s that hosted luminaries and athletes from around the world.

There are no public transport options to Eldorado Canyon State Park. From Pearl Street in Boulder, head south on Broadway Street for 5.5 miles to the junction with Highway 170. Turn right and follow Highway 170 for three miles to the state park entrance booth.

NEDERLAND

If Boulder is on the edge of reality, then it's hard to determine what exactly that makes Nederland. Located at the head of twisting Boulder Canyon, about half an hour's drive west of Boulder, this mountain community of 1,500 people is best known for two things that more or less bracket its personality: skiing at the local Eldora Mountain Resort and

partying during the Frozen Dead Guy Days, a winter music-and-beer carnival held in honor of Nederland's most infamous resident.

Sights

The main draw to this area is recreation, but if you're interested in the town's mining history, the **Nederland Mining Museum** (200 N. Bridge St., 303/258-0567, http://nederlandhistoricalsociety.org/museums.html, 10am-4pm Fri.-Sun. June-Oct., free) is worth a visit to see the tools of the trade, like the operational Bucyrus 50B steam shovel that's on display, and to get a better sense of what the miners' lives were like while they struggled to make a living here. The local historical society also operates the 1907 **Gillaspie House** (Corner of Bridge and 4th Sts., 303/258-0567,

10am-4pm Fri.-Sun. June-Oct., free), which houses displays of clothing and furnishings typical of early Nederland homes. More to the kids' liking is the **Carousel of Happiness** (20 Lakeview Dr., 303/258-3457, www.carouselofhappiness.org, seasonally open 11am-6pm Thurs.-Mon., $1), a restored 1910 Looff carousel whose 56 hand-carved animals still revolve to the tune of a 1913 Wurlitzer organ.

Sports and Recreation

Boulder's closest alpine skiing is at **Eldora Mountain Resort** (2861 Eldora Ski Rd., 303/440-8700, www.eldora.com, 9am-4pm daily Nov.-Apr. weather permitting, $89), located up Boulder Canyon, 21 miles west of town. It's a favorite spot for families and locals tired of dealing with the I-70 ski traffic. With 300 inches of snow per year, 50 miles of terrain, and runs up to 3 miles long, there's enough intermediate and advanced terrain for a fun day or two on the slopes. My favorite runs include La Belle, Jolly Jug, and Windmill, which are all blues, and Corona, a fun black diamond. My son, who's a much better skier than I am, also likes West Ridge, a steep and challenging double black.

From Boulder, Eldora Mountain Resort is a 45-minute drive up a winding canyon road.

From Pearl Street, head south on Broadway to Canyon Boulevard (Hwy. 119). Turn west and drive 15 miles to Nederland. At the town's only traffic circle, take the third exit to continue on Highway 119. After 0.6 mile, turn right onto Eldora Road and continue 1.5 miles. At the junction with Shelf Road, veer left for three miles to the resort parking lot.

A great place to hike is **Caribou Ranch** (144 County Rd. 126, Nederland, www.bouldercounty.org), a Boulder County Open Space parcel located two miles west of Nederland on Highway 72. The combined **DeLonde Trail** and **Blue Bird Loop** offer a mellow, 4.2-mile outing through quaking aspen, ponderosa pines, and Douglas fir trees. Along the way, the route passes an access road to the old Blue Bird Mine complex, including an old bunkhouse, and later, the historic DeLonde ranch house and barn. In the 1970s, this was a professional music studio where rock-and-roll legends like the Beach Boys, Supertramp, Michael Jackson, and John Lennon came to record their next hit songs.

Entertainment and Events

Held in early March each year, **Frozen Dead Guy Days** (http://frozendeadguydays.org, Mar., $10) is a fun tribute to Grandpa Bredo

South Boulder Creek

Morstoel, a native Norwegian who lies cryogenically frozen in a Tuff shed on the edge of town. After he died of heart disease in Norway in 1989, Grandpa Bredo's family packed his corpse on dry ice and shipped it to a cryonics facility in California. After four years in liquid nitrogen, his body was sent to relatives who happened to live in Nederland. After his relatives returned to Norway, local Bo Shaffer applied for—and accepted—one of the world's strangest jobs: packing Bredo's shed with dry ice once every month to keep him at a cool -60°F.

This unique tale is the inspiration for the festival that celebrates the end of winter. For three days, most of the town closes down and people from near and far join in zany contests like coffin races, frozen T-shirt contests, and the frozen salmon toss. Thirty bands play live music in heated tents, the beer flows fast, and local breweries, distilleries, and food vendors peddle everything from bacon to Frozen Dead Guy ice cream, a custom **Glacier Ice Cream** blend of blue ice cream with crushed cookies and gummy worms.

Less strange festivals include the **High Peaks Art Festival** (http://highpeaksartfestival.com, late June, free), the **Miners' Days** (http://nederlandhistoricalsociety.org, dates vary, free) and **Hotrods and Classics in the High Country** (www.hotrodhotline.com, July) celebrations, the **NedFest** (www.nedfest.org, Aug., $135 for 3 days) music festival, and the kite-flying **Windfest** (Guercio Field 151 East St., Sept., free).

Shopping

You don't need to be a geologist to love **Nature's Own** (5 E. First St., 303/258-3557, http://naturesown.com, 10am-5pm daily), Nederland's little rock shop, which sells science toys, sparkling crystals, fossils, and beautiful stone jewelry. **The Alpaca Store and More** (30 W. Boulder St., 303/258-1400, 10am-5pm daily) features gloves, hats, jackets, socks, and warm, comfy sweaters—perfect if you're on your way up to ski at Eldora.

Food and Accommodations

Nederland is more popular as a day trip than an overnight destination. If you're prepared to camp, the **Boulder Ranger District** (303/541-2500 or 877/444-6777, www.fs.usda.gov, $19) of the Arapaho-Roosevelt National Forest has seven campgrounds, including the **Kelly Dahl** (Hwy. 119), four miles south of Nederland, and the popular **Pawnee Campground,** in the Brainard Lake Recreation Area.

Among Nederland's assortment of restaurants, the **Very Nice Brewing Company** (20 Lakeview Dr. #112, 303/258-3770, www.verynicebrewing.com, noon-9pm Wed.-Sat., noon-8pm Sun., $10-15) stands out. This laid-back spot brews up small batches of six regular beers, including Steffie's Heffe and Fuggly & Brown (named after Fuggles, a citrusy hop), and serves tasty pizzas, chips and salsa, and pub fare. Dogs are welcome.

Transportation and Services

From Boulder, head south on Broadway to Canyon Boulevard (Hwy. 119). Turn west and drive 15 miles to Nederland. If you don't have a vehicle, **RTD**'s convenient "N" bus (303/299-6000, www.rtd-denver.com, $4.50 one-way) departs regularly from Boulder's downtown bus station (1800 14th St., 303/299-6000, 7am-6:30pm Mon.-Fri.). Not all buses go as far as Eldora, so check the schedule.

The **Nederland Chamber of Commerce** (2 W. 1st St., 303/258-3936, hours and days vary seasonally) staffs a visitor center and is the main source of information about local events.

INDIAN PEAKS WILDERNESS

Part of the vast Arapaho and Roosevelt National Forest, the 76,700-acre **Indian Peaks Wilderness** (www.fs.usda.gov) is one of the most popular wilderness areas in the country. With elevations ranging 8,300 feet to more than 13,500 feet, this rugged, mountainous terrain offers extensive hiking and recreational opportunities. The area is divided

Peak-to-Peak Highway

quaking aspen along the Peak-to-Peak Highway

Of the many scenic mountain roads in Colorado, one of the most famous is the Peak-to-Peak Highway. Running 55 miles from Longs Peak in the north to Mount Evans in the south, Colorado's oldest scenic byway offers some of the most stunning views the Front Range has to offer. Jagged peaks and their rugged, bowl-shaped cirques, where glaciers once lay, are front and center as you drive (or bike) at a leisurely pace through evergreen forests and sunlit groves of quaking aspen stretching between a string of pretty mountain communities.

In addition to the bookend towns of Estes Park and Idaho Springs, the Peak-to-Peak has several access points from the plains. The most popular is via **Boulder Canyon** to the small town of **Nederland,** established in the 1850s as a trading post between European settlers and native Utes.

Along the way, the road winds past old mining tailings and several quaint communities, including tiny **Allenspark,** named for Alonzo Allen, a miner from Wisconsin who built a cabin here, **Ward,** an isolated community of self-described recluses or misfits, and, to the south, the mining-turned-gambling towns of **Blackhawk** and **Central City.**

Along its length, the Peak-to-Peak also accesses some of the region's best recreation. In summer and early autumn, **Brainard Lake** and the **Fourth of July Trailhead** offer world-class hiking, angling, wildlife spotting, and more tremendous views. In winter, you can cross-country ski into **Brainard Lake** or snowshoe through sunny glades in the serene **Peaceful Valley.** North of Ward, **Camp Dick,** a Civilian Conservation Corps-built camp along the Middle St. Vrain Creek, offers fantastic fly-fishing, while the nearby **Buchanan Pass** and **Sourdough Trails** are ideal for hiking and mountain biking. If you can, visit during the week, especially during the modern gold rush—the busy September leaf-peeping season.

into 17 zones; separate camping permits for the peak season (June 1-Sept. 15) must be obtained from the **Boulder Ranger Station** (2140 Yarmouth Ave., 303/541-2500, www.fs.usda.gov, $5 reservation).

The **Hessie Trailhead** (www.fs.usda.gov), just west of the town of Eldora, accesses a number of alpine lakes, including **Lost Lake** (3 miles round-trip) and **Woodland Lake** (5 miles round-trip). Parking at the trailhead is limited, so take the **Hessie shuttle service** (Nederland RTD Park-n-Ride, 300 Jackson St., free) during the peak season.

North of the town of Eldora, the **Fourth of July Trailhead** is accessed via a rough dirt road. This is a very popular start to several great treks, including the **Arapaho Pass Trail** (4 miles round-trip), one of the state's best wildflower hikes. The trail passes **Diamond Lake** and the **Fourth of July Mine** before intersecting the **Arapaho Glacier Trail,** a great hike with views of one of the Rockies' southernmost glaciers. From the junction, the Arapaho Pass Trail continues west along an old road for another 1.2 miles to the pass, offering great views of the Continental Divide.

★ Brainard Lake

Nestled in a glacier-carved valley surrounded by pristine forest with craggy, snow-capped peaks as its backdrop, sparkling **Brainard Lake** looks like a quintessential Rocky Mountain postcard. One of the main access points to the Indian Peaks Wilderness Area, the popular **Brainard Lake Recreation Area** (Boulder Ranger District, 303/541-2500, www.fs.usda.gov, June-Oct., $10 for 3 days, cash or check only) offers backcountry skiing and snowshoeing (from the main

road) in winter, leaf-peeping in autumn, and backpacking, hiking, picnicking, and angling in late spring and summer. Brainard is also a great spot to search for wildlife, especially moose, who love to hang out in the valley surrounding the lake.

Brainard Lake lies at the junction of two valleys, both of which offer great hiking to a series of lakes. The western valley leads first to **Long Lake,** which you can circle on the **Jean Lunnings Trail** for an easy 2.75-mile loop. If you continue west for another, steeper mile, the path leads to beautiful **Lake Isabelle** (4.5 miles round-trip). If the weather holds, you can carry on to **Pawnee Pass** (9 miles round-trip) to see plenty of colorful wildflowers and more amazing views.

The northern river valley leads to the summit of **Mount Audubon,** one of the area's best hikes. After veering off the Beaver Creek Trail, the **Mount Audubon Trail** climbs above tree line to the bald, exposed summit, about 3.7 miles (and 3,000 vertical feet) from the trailhead. The panoramic views from the high peaks to the plains are worth every sweaty step!

Brainard Lake is located 15 miles north of Nederland. From the town's only traffic circle, at the junction with Highway 119 and Bridge

a frozen alpine lake beneath Mt. Toll in the Indian Peaks

Street, head west on Highway 72, the Peak-to-Peak Highway, for about 12 miles, then turn left onto the signed Brainard Lake Road and follow this to its end in 3 miles. If the gate on this road is closed, park in the large lot by the fee station.

GOLD HILL

In the 1850s, Colorado was a sleepy outpost on the far-western fringe of the Nebraska and Kansas territories. Things changed quickly when, in January 1859, a prospector found nuggets of gold in the bed of Clear Creek at the future location of Idaho Springs. Just a week later, the motherlode source of this gold was discovered in Gold Hill in the foothills above the future site of Boulder. The Pikes Peak Gold Rush was on! Tens of thousands of Euro-Americans, infected with gold fever, flocked to the area, purportedly crying, "Pikes Peak or bust!" (despite the fact that the gold was found far from that well-known landmark).

Gold Hill remained an important mining camp through much of the 19th century, reaching a peak population close to 1,500. After the gold ran out, however, the town's population dropped precipitously. Today, Gold Hill is a small cluster of mostly ramshackle cottages with a population hovering

around 200. Although the last four miles of the road are dirt, it's well worth the trip to see the cute two-room schoolhouse built in 1873, the General Store, which has been for sale for years, the row of antique shops along the main street, and the after-effects of a severe 2010 wildfire.

★ Gold Hill Inn

The Gold Hill Inn (401 Main St., 303/443-6461, www.goldhillinn.com, seatings 6pm-8:30pm Wed.-Sat., 5pm-7:30pm Sun. May-Oct., plus 6pm-8:30pm Mon. in summer, 6pm-8:30pm Fri.-Sat. Nov.-mid-Dec., $28-36) is a highlight of the foothills and a quintessential Colorado experience. Housed in a historic log cabin built in 1924, the restaurant serves a six-course, set-price meal in a quaint and comfortable setting. *Gourmet Magazine* has dubbed it "one of the best restaurant values in America." Walking through the door into the spacious front lounge, you're immediately enveloped by the warm, wooden atmosphere. On cool nights, there's a crackling fire surrounded by comfy chairs just steps from the gleaming bar. At the entrance to the enormous dining room, stands a chalkboard with the day's handwritten menu. This typically includes your choice of an appetizer

Brainard Lake

followed by a hot or cold soup and thick slabs of homemade bread, a salad, and a difficult choice between several tantalizing entrées. It's important to pace yourself, so that you're not completely stuffed by the time the tray of decadent desserts, like sour-cream apple pie, comes around, followed by a fruit and specialty cheese tray. You're never rushed and are free to linger, sip your glass of wine or coffee beneath the open wooden beams, and soak up the remarkable atmosphere. Reservations are a must; call ahead for vegetarian, vegan, or other special diet requests.

From Pearl Street in Boulder, head north on Broadway for three blocks, then turn left onto Mapleton Avenue. Continue on for 10 miles west up Sunshine Canyon Drive. In about 30 minutes, Sunshine Canyon Drive becomes Main Street in Gold Hill.

LYONS

Sited at the confluence of two tributaries of the South Platte River beneath crimson- and tan-colored cliffs, pretty Lyons is a vibrant town best known for its two annual music festivals. The town is in the perfect location for travelers heading into the foothills. Just west of town, there's a major fork between U.S. 36, which winds northward up the Little Thompson Canyon toward Estes Park, and Highway 7, which heads west along South St. Vrain Creek toward the Peak-to-Peak Highway. Sadly, the devastating 500-year flood in September 2013 hit Lyons especially hard, but the community has proven resilient and is still, to this day, rebuilding.

Sights

Once the winter grounds for native Ute, Arapaho, and other tribes, this area was overrun with Euro-Americans after gold was discovered in the nearby foothills. The town of Lyons was founded in 1881 after Edward S. Lyon, who hailed from Connecticut, took notice of the excellent conditions for farming and the nearby cliffs of red sandstone, which, he realized, could easily be quarried. The legacy of 280 million-year-old sand dunes deposited in a desert the size of the modern Sahara, the Lyons sandstone is a strong, clean-breaking rock ideal for use as flagstone. It has been used throughout the region, including to create the distinctive look of Boulder's University of Colorado campus, as well as many local historic buildings like the town's 1881 schoolhouse, now the **Lyons Redstone Museum** (340 High St., 303/823-5271, www. lyonsredstonemuseum.com, 9:30am-4:30pm Mon.-Sat., 12:30pm-4:30pm Sun. May-Sept., donation requested), as well as many modern-day porches and patios.

Sports and Recreation

Just outside of Lyons are two large Boulder County Open Space parcels (www.boulder-county.org) that offer excellent hiking and mountain biking—just watch out for rattle-snakes. East of town and north of Highway 66, **Rabbit Mountain** has several trails, including the easy **Indian Mesa Trail** (4.4 miles round-trip), which ends abruptly at the park's northern border. One of my favorites is the moderate **Eagle Wind Loop** (4 miles). From the trailhead, the route climbs up the mountain for 0.5 mile, then heads south through mixed-grass prairie to the edge of the mesa. Along the ensuing lollipop loop, you're treated to views of the high peaks to the west and the prairie stretching to the east. In addition to cottontails, you may spot elk, chattering black-tailed prairie dogs, mule deer, and coyotes. Black bears and bobcats have also been spotted here. The mesa edge is a great place for bird-watching; look for western meadow-larks, mountain bluebirds, and golden eagles, known to nest in or visit the area. Both trails are open to hikers, equestrians, and mountain bikers.

Just west of town, on the north side of Highway 7, **Hall Ranch** has five great hiking trails, three of which are also open to mountain bikers. This open space parcel samples many environments—sandstone bluffs, rolling grasslands, and smooth granite boulders tucked among ponderosa pine and juniper trees. For a longer hike, try the 9.5-mile-long

Loveland, the Sweetheart City

the serrated spikes of the Devil's Backbone

Back in 1946, Elmer Ivers, the postmaster of Loveland, Colorado, came up with a sweetheart of an idea: to share the city's romantic name with the rest of the world by stamping Valentine's cards with a special Cupid label and re-mailing them. Since the inauguration of this program in February of 1947, Loveland—now globally known as the Sweetheart City—has re-mailed millions of valentines to every state and more than 110 countries. It's not uncommon for the valentines that pass through Loveland to be from celebrities, athletes, mothers, troops—and even the president of the Unites States. To send your loved one a special message, pre-address and stamp the valentine, place it in a bigger envelope, and mail it to: Postmaster, Attn: Valentine Re-mailing, 446 E. 29th St., Loveland, CO 80538-9998. When your card arrives in Loveland, one of 60 volunteers will hand-stamp it with that year's special Valentine verse and send it on to your loved ones.

Originally a farming town along the Colorado Central Railroad, Loveland has developed into an industrial and ranching hub. If you find yourself in the Sweetheart City, save enough time to explore the 2,200-acre **Devil's Backbone Open Space** (www.co.larimer.co.us), a beautiful parcel of preserved land seven miles west of town featuring a rugged hogback of rock poking out of the plains. Its 2.5-mile **Wild Loop,** which is open to both pedestrians and bikes, most closely follows the devil's vertebrae. You can easily extend this trek by adding on the **Hunter** and/or **Laughing Horse Loops.** Top off your visit with a lovable treat at the **Dairy Delite** (3080 W. Eisenhower Blvd., 970/667-2111, 11am-7pm daily).

combination that begins from the paved upper parking lot on the **Bitterbrush Trail,** which wanders beneath blocky sandstone bluffs before climbing steeply through gray granite boulders. About two miles from the trailhead, you break out of the trees near a large colony of noisy prairie dogs and are treated to beautiful views into the North St. Vrain River Canyon. Continue down the slope to the junction with the **Nelson Loop Trail,** best followed along its southern fork so that you can walk past the old 1918 Nelson Ranch House. From here, bikers must return along the loop, but hikers have the option of taking the **Nighthawk Trail** back to their cars. I often spot mule deer along this peaceful trail, which also has views of some of the peaks in Rocky Mountain National Park.

Events

Lyons is best known for its summer music festivals, which are held on a 20-acre complex called **Planet Bluegrass** (500 W. Main St., 303/823-0848, tickets: 800/624-2422, www.bluegrass.com). These include **RockyGrass** (July) and **Rocky Mountain Folks Festival** (Aug.), the final and largest event, featuring big names like The Decemberists. Tickets ($65-155) and camping passes ($35-220) for the multi-day festivals sell out months in advance, but you might be able to score tickets to some smaller, single-day concerts.

Food and Accommodations

There are plenty of chains in nearby Longmont, just nine miles to the east, but big-box names just do not fit into Lyons' indie culture. In town, pretty and family-owned **Stone Mountain Lodge and Cabins** (18055 N. St. Vrain Dr., 303/823-6091, http://stonemountainlodge.com, $119-245) has cozy cabins in a peaceful setting along the creek.

For handcrafted beer, pub grub, and local character, stop by **Oskar Blues Grill & Brew** (303 Main St., 303/823-6685, www.oskarblues.com, 11am-9pm daily, $10-24). Enjoy the tie-dye decorations, live music, including blues, and the self-proclaimed best wings in Colorado. Nosh on spicy Cajun fare and sip great beers like the strong Old Chub Scottish Ale. **Lyons Fork** (450 Main St., 303/823-5014, www.lyonsfork.com, 5pm-9pm Mon.-Thurs., 9am-2pm and 5pm-9pm Fri.-Sun., $14-25) is a contemporary, family-run restaurant. This is a great spot for fresh food, especially the Parmesan-topped truffle fries and icy-cold margaritas. The restaurant locally sources many of their ingredients, which are creatively combined into dishes like fried chicken mole and pasta primavera Alfredo.

Transportation and Services

Lyons is located about 16 miles north of Boulder, a 20 minutes' drive. From Pearl Street head north on Broadway. At the junction with U.S. 36 (locally called 28th Street), turn left and follow U.S. 36 north for 14 miles to Lyons. If you don't have a vehicle, you can get there via RTD's route Y bus (303/299-6000, www.rtd-denver.com, 7am-6:30pm Mon.-Fri., $4.50 one-way), which departs six times per day from Boulder's downtown 14th Street bus station (1800 14th St.).

Although not geared toward tourists, the **Lyons Area Chamber of Commerce** (www.lyons-colorado.com) and the **Town of Lyons** (www.townoflyons.com) website have some helpful information about the town, including its history. More practical information for visitors can be found on the **Planet Bluegrass** (www.bluegrass.com) site, although this is, of course, focused on the summer concert series.

Fort Collins

Fort Collins is a thriving, medium-sized city noted for being the home of Colorado State University, a beautiful, historic downtown, an ideal climate and abundant recreation, and—first and foremost—for being Colorado's craft beer capital.

Fort Collins was founded in 1864 as a military encampment along the Cache La Poudre River to protect travelers along the Colorado branch of the Overland Trail that had been routed through the region. After a flood damaged the camp a few years later, the commander moved the outpost a few miles downstream, to a higher piece of land next to the current Old Town. With its rich soils and plenty of water available, Fort Collins quickly grew into a prosperous farming community, which incorporated in 1873.

Split by railroad tracks early in its history, Fort Collins is now divided by U.S. 287 (locally called College Ave.), which runs north-south through town. The Cache La Poudre

Fort Collins

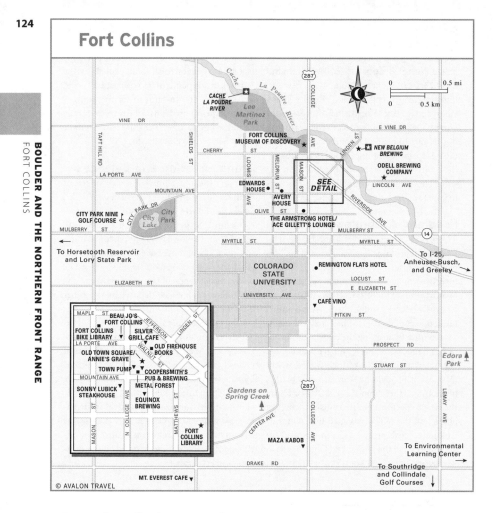

CACHE LA POUDRE RIVER

Lee Martinez Park

VINE DR

TAFT HILL RD

SHIELDS ST

CHERRY ST

FORT COLLINS MUSEUM OF DISCOVERY

COLLEGE AVE

E VINE DR

LINDEN ST

NEW BELGIUM BREWING

ODELL BREWING COMPANY

LA PORTE AVE

LOOMIS AVE

MELDRUM ST

MASON ST

SEE DETAIL

LINCOLN AVE

MOUNTAIN AVE

EDWARDS HOUSE

AVERY HOUSE

RIVERSIDE AVE

CITY PARK NINE GOLF COURSE

CITY PARK DR

City Park

City Lake

OLIVE ST

THE ARMSTRONG HOTEL/ ACE GILLETT'S LOUNGE

MULBERRY ST

MULBERRY ST

14

MYRTLE ST

MYRTLE ST

To Horsetooth Reservoir and Lory State Park

COLORADO STATE UNIVERSITY

REMINGTON FLATS HOTEL

To I-25, Anheuser-Busch, and Greeley

ELIZABETH ST

LOCUST ST

E ELIZABETH ST

UNIVERSITY AVE

CAFÉ VINO

PITKIN ST

MAPLE ST

BEAU JO'S

FORT COLLINS

JEFFERSON ST

LINDEN ST

FORT COLLINS BIKE LIBRARY

SILVER GRILL CAFE

LA PORTE AVE

WALNUT ST

OLD FIREHOUSE BOOKS

PROSPECT RD

Edora Park

OLD TOWN SQUARE/ ANNIE'S GRAVE

TOWN PUMP

COOPERSMITH'S PUB & BREWING

STUART ST

LEMAY AVE

MOUNTAIN AVE

METAL FOREST

SONNY LUBICK STEAKHOUSE

1ST

N COLLEGE AVE

EQUINOX BREWING

MATTHEWS ST

Gardens on Spring Creek

287

COLLEGE AVE

MASON ST

N COLLEGE AVE

FORT COLLINS LIBRARY

CENTER AVE

MAZA KABOB

To Environmental Learning Center

DRAKE RD

To Southridge and Collindale Golf Courses

MT. EVEREST CAFE

© AVALON TRAVEL

287

La Poudre River

Cache

COLLEGE

0   0.5 mi

0   0.5 km

River is a focus of local recreation and an important source of water for the parched plains. Once in town, it's easy to use bikes and buses to navigate the main areas of interest, including the buzzing 32,00-student Colorado State University campus and the lovingly preserved shopping and dining district in the historic Old Town.

SIGHTS

On the northern edge of town, the **Fort Collins Museum of Discovery** (408 Mason Ct., 970/221-6738, http://fcmod.org,

10am-5pm Tues.-Sun., 10am-8pm Thurs., $9.50) is a fun, hands-on learning center that houses a combined history museum and science center to create a state-of-the-art facility that explores the science and history of northern Colorado. Facilities include a digital dome theater for astronomy and other shows, a music garage, kids' science classrooms, and rotating exhibits like the current one about the devastating 2015 High Park Wildfire.

About six miles southeast of Old Town, CSU's **Environmental Learning Center**

Walt Disney's Inspiration

When Fort Collins-born artist Harper Goff tried to buy a model train at a specialty shop in London in 1951, another man was interested in purchasing the same engine. That customer turned out to be Walt Disney, who asked Harper what he did for a living. When Harper, more than a little startled, stammered that he was an artist, Disney—who wound up buying the train—asked him to stop by and talk with him. Little did Harper know how much this chance encounter would change his life—and immortalize his birthplace as the archetypal American town.

Old Town Square

Harper went on to work for Disney, first creating the storyboards and the submarine design for the Oscar-winning movie *20,000 Leagues Under the Sea*. He also worked closely with Disney to "imagineer" the plans for the Jungle Cruise and the conceptual design of Disneyland, including Main Street U.S.A., the nostalgic, turn-of-the-20th-century heart of an American town visible as guests first enter the park.

When Harper showed Disney photos from Fort Collins' Old Town, Disney loved the look and incorporated many of the stone buildings' features into his plans. These include the distinctive dome of the now-demolished 1887 Larimer County Courthouse, which inspired the dome on Disney's City Hall, as well as buildings along the **Miller Block** of Linden Street and the tower and archways in the old red-brick Fort Collins Firehouse, now the Walnut Street home of **Old Firehouse Books,** which became the model for Disney's fire station. In addition, the corner entrance to the building that still stands on the corner of Walnut and Linden Streets (the former Poudre Valley Bank) served as the source of inspiration for the entrance to the Disneyland Emporium shops.

(2400 S. County Rd. 9, 970/491-1661, www.csuelc.org, sunrise-sunset daily, free) helps connect people with nature at its 212-acre facility, located along the Cache La Poudre River. In addition to a short self-guided nature trail and picnic pavilion, the center offers many school, scouting, and summer camp programs for area kids. The organization also runs the **Rocky Mountain Raptor Program** (720B E. Vine Dr., 970/484-7756, www.rmrp.org), which rehabilitates and releases hundreds of injured and orphaned birds each year.

Old Town Square

During the 1870s, buildings began to spring up on the old fort site. Then (as now), the **Old Town Square** was the city's heart and soul,

with a general store, post office, school, and even a small hotel. Today, Old Town is both a national and a local historic district that's distinguished by its unusual fish-bone street pattern, with minor streets feeding into a main thoroughfare. The district is located in the northeastern part of town, in a triangle bounded by U.S. 287 to the west, Walnut Street to the north, and East Mountain Avenue to the south.

Several of the beautiful old buildings have been preserved and are currently being used for retail space and apartments, including the **Lacourt Hotel** (232 Pine St.), the **Candy Kitchen** (255 Linden St.), and the **Linden Hotel** (250 Walnut St.). Step back in time by visiting the restored 1879 **Avery House** (328 W. Mountain Ave., 970/221-0533, http://

poudrelandmarks.org, tours 1pm-4pm Sat.-Sun., free), the family home of surveyor Franklin Avery. A talented man who designed the city's wide streets, Avery founded the First National Bank and helped develop irrigation canals and other agricultural water projects. Members of the Avery family lived in this sandstone house until 1962.

For a self-guided tour of other historic Old Square and downtown sites, visit the **Poudre Landmarks Foundation** (http://poudre-landmarks.org) or take a walking tour with **Fort Collins Tours** (www.fortcollinstours.com).

Just outside of Old Town Square, visit the poignant **grave of Annie** (136 Laporte Ave.), Fort Collins' inspiring dog that locals fought so hard to keep. The story so inspired local artist Dawn Weimar that she cast 35 bronze statues of the hero. One of these now stands in front of the main **Fort Collins Library** (201 Peterson St.).

a colorful alley in downtown Fort Collins

Brewery Tours

Despite the fact that Fort Collins was dry until 1969, the city is now so well known for beer brewing that it's often called the Napa Valley of beer. Fort Collins currently has 20 breweries, which collectively account for 70 percent of the craft beer produced in the state. Each brewery has its own distinct personality. Visiting one (or several) is a highlight of Fort Collins, as are the fun-filled summer beer festivals.

★ NEW BELGIUM BREWING

Many of Fort Collins' breweries are located within the historic downtown district, including the industry-leading **New Belguim Brewing** (500 Linden St., 970/221-0524, www.newbelgium.com, tours 11:30am-4:30pm daily, tasting room 11am-8pm daily), a craft brewery inspired by one of the co-founders' experiences biking across Belgium (with his fat-tire bike) and sampling that country's amazing beer. When he returned to the United States, Jeff Lebesch began to brew beer in his cellar. From these humble but inspired beginnings emerged what is now America's fourth-largest craft brewery.

The free, 90-minute tours of the facility are very popular, so it's best to book ahead online, which you can do up to two months in advance. You don't need to be 21 to tour the facility, although you do need to be of age, of course, to actually taste the beer. The tour includes a visit to the enormous, multifloor fermentation tanks, a look at the employee bar, and plenty of entertaining tales about the company's history, its unique corporate philosophy, and its deep commitment to sustainability, which even extends to employee parking: The greener the mode of transport, the higher parking priority an employee receives.

Outside of the impressive canning facility, in the so-called Liquid Center, visitors can taste Fat Tire Amber Ale, New Belgium's flagship beer and one of the first brewed by Lebesch after he returned home from Europe. In addition to a selection of seasonal

Annie the Dog

Back in the 1930s, when Fort Collins was just a small railroad hub, a worker found a scruffy-looking dog wandering around the tracks. In spite of the company's strict no-dogs rule, he brought her back to the Colorado & Southern Depot, where she quickly became the town's ambassador. With the arrival of every train, Annie—as she was known—would dash outside, warmly wag, and run to the disembarking newcomers for petting. After World War II, when soldiers returning home from the war would drop to their knees, overcome with emotion, she would run up and lick away their tears, according to local legend. After she died in 1948, railroad employees buried her in the yard with a special gravestone that read, From C and S Men to Annie Our Dog, 1934-1948. When the depot was later renovated and the construction threatened the grave, there was a hue and cry from the local citizens, who cherished the easy-going friendliness that she embodied. These traits also typify Fort Collins' personality, which despite its rapid growth over the last 20 years remains a laid-back and friendly place to visit.

brews, you can also taste some of the other year-round beers, including the unfiltered Snapshot Wheat Beer, the intensely hoppy Ranger IPA, and Glutiny, the tongue-in-cheek label for their smooth, gluten-reduced golden and pale ales.

ODELL BREWING COMPANY

Fort Collins' second-oldest brewery, **Odell Brewing Company** (800 E. Lincoln Ave., 970/498-9070, www.odellbrewing.com, tours noon-3pm daily, taproom 11am-6pm Sun.-Tues., 11am-7pm Wed.-Sat.), offers four free tours of its facility per day. Spots can be reserved online up to 24 hours in advance, and participants must be at least 12 years old. It's amazing to see all of the equipment involved in their brewing process, from the 125-barrel brew house that was custom-built in Germany, to the mill where the barley is crushed, to the gleaming fermenters where the alcohol is produced. Odell is also well known for its leadership in sustainability, as well as its flagship brews, including the light, unfiltered Easy Street Wheat and the 90 Shilling Ale—a copper-colored amber named for a special Scottish tax imposed on the country's highest-quality beers. As you'll discover firsthand in the taproom, Odell also has a reputation for innovation and experiments like using wooden barrels to age some of its beer.

ANHEUSER-BUSCH

An interesting contrast to the microbrewery tours is a visit to the huge **Anheuser-Busch** facility (2351 Busch Dr., 970/490-4691, www.budweisertours.com, tours 10am-4pm daily, Biergarten 10am-7:30pm Mon.-Sat., 10am-5:30pm Sun.), which opened in 1988 and distributes beer across the Southwest. This is one of six locations around the country where you can tour the St. Louis-based company's breweries, and the only home of the famous Budweiser Clydesdales. If they're not jetting around the country, you can even have your photo taken with them.

SPORTS AND RECREATION
Horsetooth Reservoir

Fort Collins has an unusual diversity of water-related sports. Many are centered around the 6.25-mile-long **Horsetooth Reservoir** (County Rd. 38E, the western extension of Harmony Rd., 970/498-7000, www.co.larimer.co.us/parks/horsetooth.cfm, $6-7), located west of town. The 1,900-acre reservoir is named for a distinctive rock formation in the foothills looming over the water. The lake has four ramps for boating and offers good angling for walleye, trout, and smallmouth bass. The reservoir has two camping areas: **South Bay** on the southern end and **Inlet Bay** in the southwest. Campsites at both facilities, as well as the **boat-in campsites** (970/679-4570, www.co.larimer.co.us) on the western side, can be reserved online up to 180 days in advance.

Along the north shore in Santanka Cove, rent stand-up paddleboards from **Mountain′ SUP** (970/480-7867, www.mountainsup.com). With two locations, **St. Peter's Fly Shop** (202 Remington St., 970/498-8968; 2008 E. Harmony Rd., 970/377-3785, www.stpetes.com) offers plenty of guided trips throughout the region, plus gear, river reports, and advice for anglers in the area.

★ Cache La Poudre River

From its headwaters among the rugged peaks on the northern side of Rocky Mountain National Park, the beautiful **Cache La Poudre River** flows northward through its namesake wilderness, then quickly descends through the narrow, 40-mile-long **Poudre Canyon.** The river emerges from the Front Range foothills a few miles northwest of downtown Fort Collins. From there, the river flows eastward across the plains to Greeley before merging with the larger South Platte River.

The river's unusual French name, which locals shorten to just "The Poo-der," translates into English as "hide the powder." This purportedly stems from an incident in the early 1800s when roaming French-Canadian fur traders were caught out in a sudden mountain snowstorm. To lighten their load, they stashed large amounts of gunpowder (*poudre* in French) in a hiding place (a cache) along the banks of a river—hence the moniker Cache la Poudre River.

The river comprises the core of the National Park Service's **Cache La Poudre River National Heritage Area** (www.nps.gov), which celebrates the river's important contributions to the development of water delivery systems and Western water law.

The sparkling river is infamous for its devastating floods, including the one in 1864 that destroyed the original military outpost. It's best known, however, for having Colorado's only Wild and Scenic River designation for its unspoiled beauty and abundant recreation. The sparkling stream is a favorite fishing spot for trout and a destination for white-water rafting and kayaking. Depending upon the flows, the boating season can stretch from May to August. The Cache La Poudre has a good variety of runs, ranging from intermediate (Class III) to expert (Class V) rapids.

A number of Fort Collins-based

the Cache La Poudre River

companies offer half- to multi-day kayaking and rafting trips, including **Rocky Mountain Adventures** (1117 N. U.S. 287, 970/493-4005, www.shoprma.com), **Mountain Whitewater Descents** (1329 N. U.S. 287, 970/419-0917, www.raftmwd.com), and **A1 Wildwater** (2801 N. Shields St., 970/224-3379, www.a1wildwater.com). Rocky Mountain Adventures and A1 also offer trips on other northern Colorado rivers, including the North Platte, Clear Creek, and the Upper Colorado.

Hiking and Biking

The area around Horsetooth Reservoir has some excellent trails of varying difficulty levels, including a dozen in **Lory State Park** (708 Lodgepole Dr., Bellvue, 970/493-1623, http://cpw.state.co.us, visitor center 8:30am-4pm daily, $7 per car). The park has short, kid-friendly hikes; moderate walks with great lake views, like the **Timber-Kimmons-West Valley** loop (4 miles); and a challenging climb up to a summit along **Arthur's Rock Trail** (1.7 miles one-way). Eight of the park's trails are also open to mountain bikes, which range from the easy **Shoreline Trail** (1 mile one-way) to the snaking switchbacks along the **Howard Trail** (2.1 miles one-way). The park also offers technical rock climbing on granite, volleyball at the Timber Group picnic area, and easy-to-advanced horseback riding.

Lory State Park adjoins **Horsetooth Mountain Open Space**, whose 29 miles of trails are another big draw for area hikers and bikers. The **Blue Sky Trail** begins at the open space's southern edge and is especially popular with mountain bikers. From the trailhead, the route heads south for more than six miles, crossing two other Larimer County Open Space parcels before its terminus in the **Devil's Backbone Open Space** at U.S. 34, just west of the town of Loveland.

The City of Fort Collins manages a number of beautiful natural areas, including the **Bobcat Ridge Natural Area** (10184 County Rd. 32C, www.fcgov.com), whose **Valley Loop Trail** (4 miles) passes a historic cabin.

Far north of the city (near the Wyoming border), the wonderful 18,000-acre **Soapstone Prairie Natural Area** (www.fcgov.com) is a remote and gorgeous parcel known for its wildlife, including elk, fox, mule deer, and birds, as well as the **Lindenmeier Archaeological Site,** whose record of human occupation dates back 12,000 years.

Golf

Fort Collins operates two 18-hole courses, one at **Southridge** (5750 S. Lemay Ave., 970/416-2828, www.fcgov.com, $35-38) and a second at **Collindale** (1441 E. Horsetooth Rd., 970/221-6651, www.fcgov.com, $35-38), plus a 9-hole course, **City Park Nine** (411 S. Bryan Ave., 970/221-6650, www.fcgov.com, $16-19). As a bonus, if you visit in winter and the greens are clear of snow, you can tee off for free.

Spectator Sports

The **Colorado State University Rams** (www.csurams.com) are increasingly competitive in the NCAA Division I Mountain West Conference. The Rams play in **Hughes Stadium** (location under construction, 800/491-7267), except for the September game against Boulder's CU Buffs. This huge in-state rivalry is played on the more neutral turf at Denver's Sports Authority Field at Mile High Stadium.

ENTERTAINMENT AND EVENTS
Nightlife

Much of Fort Collins' nightlife is centered around Old Town Square and the city's many microbreweries. Especially popular are **Equinox Brewing** (133 Remington St., 970/484-1368, www.equinoxbrewing.com, noon-8pm Mon., noon-9pm Tues.-Thurs., noon-10pm Fri., 11am-10pm Sat., noon-7pm Sun.), located a few blocks south of Old Town Square, and **Coopersmith's Pub & Brewing** (5 Old Town Square, 970/498-0483, http://coopersmithspub.com, 11am-11pm Sun.-Thurs., 11am-midnight Fri.-Sat.), a popular hangout for college students with a tempting beer list, a large outdoor seating area, and a long and diverse menu.

Fort Collins' oldest bar, **Town Pump** (124 N. College Ave., 970/493-4404, www.townpump1909.com, 3pm-12:30am Mon.-Thurs., 3pm-1am Fri., noon-1am Sat., noon-12:30am Sun.), was founded in 1909. Its tiny interior is a great place to soak up a bit of the city's history and try some great local beer.

Live Music

Located beneath the historic Armstrong Hotel, **Ace Gillett's** bar (239 S. College Ave., 970/449-4797, https://acegilletts.com, 4pm-late Sun.-Tues., 4pm-2am Wed.-Sat.) is a large and classy spot to unwind, enjoy a hand-mixed martini, and listen to live jazz. For more live music, head up the Poudre Canyon Highway to the Mish, the local name for the **Mishawaka Amphitheatre** (13714 Poudre Canyon Hwy., Bellvue, 970/482-4420, www.themishawaka.com), a legendary live-music venue, plus bar and restaurant, located in the Poudre Canyon.

Festivals and Events

Fort Collins hosts several festivals throughout the summer season. Especially big draws are the **Colorado Brewers' Festival** (http://downtownfortcollins.com, late June, $25 for tasting package), which brings about 20,000 people to downtown; the **Bohemian Nights at NewWestFest**, (www.bohemiannights.org, Aug., free), which draws 100,000 people to listen to Coloradoan and other musicians; and the **Tour de Fat** (www.newbelgium.com, early Sept., by donation), the "bikes, beer, and bemusement" celebration that includes a bike parade and lots of flowing taps.

SHOPPING

Fort Collins has two main shopping districts that offer very different experiences. **Old Town Square** is filled with cute, local boutiques like **The Metal Forest** (1 Old Town Square #107, 970/407-1677, www.metalforest.com, 10:30am-5:30pm Mon.-Sat.), which specializes in unique metal art and funky home

accessories. **Trimble Court Artisans** (118 Trimble Ct., 970/221-0051, www.trimblecourt.com, 10am-6pm Mon.-Thurs. and Sat., 10am-8pm Fri., 11am-5pm Sun.) is an arts and crafts coop featuring the masterpieces of more than 50 Colorado artists who take turns running the shop as part of their agreement.

Founded in 1991 by a woman from Colorado and a man who attended elementary school on the Navajo Reservation, **Santa Fe Craftsman** (118 N. College Ave., 970/224-1415, http://santafecraftsman.com, 10am-7pm Mon.-Fri., 10am-6pm Sat., noon-5pm Sun.) sells Southwestern- and Native American-inspired jewelry, pottery, fetishes, and other unusual gifts. For those young at heart, the **Science Toy Magic** (11 Old Town Square #119, 970/484-2377, 10am-6pm Wed.-Sat.) is filled with great games and gifts, like boomerangs, laser games, and digeridoos.

The **Foothills Mall** (215 E. Foothills Pkwy., 970/226-5555, http://shopfoothills.com, 10am-8pm Mon.-Thurs., 10am-9pm Fri.-Sat., 11am-6pm Sun.) on the southeastern side of town is anchored by a movie theater and a Macy's.

FOOD

For breakfast, go to **La Creperie & Bakery of Fort Collins** (2722 S. College Ave., 970/224-2640, www.fortcollinscreperiebakery.com, 7:30am-2:30pm Tues.-Sat., 7:30am-2pm Sun., $7-14), the city's only French bakery. They serve a mouthwatering selection of pastries and flaky croissants, plus delicious pancake crêpes and savory stuffed buckwheat galettes, as well as a buttery croissant French toast. The **Silver Grill Café** (218 Walnut St., 970/484-4656, www.silvergrill.com, 7am-2pm daily, $6-12) is a local diner best known for its giant, gooey cinnamon rolls that are baked fresh daily. The oldest restaurant in northern Colorado, it's been serving up breakfast and lunch since 1933. With cozy booths and large windows looking out over the Old Town, it's a great spot to sip some Joe and fill up with breakfast tacos, chicken fried steak and eggs, or veggie huevos rancheros, before heading out on a long hike or ride.

For a quick, counter-service eatery with delicious Afghan food, try **Maza Kabob** (2427 S. College Ave., 970/484-6292, www.mazakabob.com, 11am-9pm Mon.-Thurs., 11am-10pm Fri.-Sat., 3pm-9pm Sun., $4-14). The place is often packed with students, who know how to find great value. The chicken kabobs are juicy and tender, and the Burrani eggplant dish is perfectly spiced. Be sure to order a side of JonAma (yogurt salad) or chewy naan, and top it off with a creamy rice pudding. Fort Collins' best Nepalese and Tibetan food can be found at the **Mt. Everest Café** (1113 W. Drake Rd., 970/223-8212, http://mteverestcafe.com, 11am-2:30pm and 5pm-9pm daily, $11-17). The all-you-can-eat daily buffets draw a large college crowd, but you can also order lunch and dinner dishes à la carte, like large bowls of *thukpa* Tibetan noodle soup or lamb coconut curry.

After a long day outdoors, my family's favorite restaurant is **Beau Jo's** (205 N. College Ave., 970/498-8898, www.beaujos.com, 11am-9pm Sun.-Thurs., 11am-9:30pm Fri.-Sat., $10-25). Located in the downtown in a modern, red-brick building, this small, local chain is known for its Colorado-style pizza, particularly the Mountain Pies, whose thick crust has a hand-rolled edge that tastes like bread, which you can smother with the accompanying honey. The all-you-can-eat salad bar has lots of fresh choices artfully arranged in ice-filled bathtubs.

The versatile **Café Vino** (1200 S. College Ave., 970/212-3388, http://cafevino.com, 7am-midnight daily, $8-17) is a coffee shop by day and a wine bar by night. Its diverse, European-inspired menu features buttery pastries and fresh, seasonal salads, as well as thin-crust pizzas. For dinner, the café serves small plates of tapas like goat cheese-stuffed peppadews or full entrées like the unusual gorgonzola pear ravioli, along with a choice of 200 wines and 20 craft beers on tap. The **Sonny Lubick Steakhouse** (115 S. College Ave., 970/484-9200, www.sonnylubicksteakhouse.com,

4pm-10pm Mon.-Thurs., 4pm-midnight Fri.-Sat., 4pm-9pm Sun., $25-49) is more upscale, with an extensive list of mostly American wines and, of course, thick, juicy steaks. These include the signature, slow-roasted prime rib of beef, which is offered in three different sizes, as well as a New York strip. They also offer a limited happy-hour selection (4pm-7pm Mon.-Fri., 4pm-close Sun.).

ACCOMMODATIONS

Fort Collins has some unique, locally owned accommodations. The bright-green boutique **Remington Flats Hotel** (813 Remington St., 970/699-1189, www.remingtonflats.com, $199) is in a great downtown location within walking distance of many restaurants and microbreweries. Renovated in 2015, the four large and pet-friendly studios have a funky and bright decor, plus amenities that include on-site laundry and free, high-speed Wi-Fi. **The Armstrong Hotel** (259 S. College Ave., 970/484-3883, http://thearmstronghotel. com, $189-219) is one of three historic hotels downtown—and the only one still operating today. Its 45 rooms and suites come in both modern and vintage decor and have en suite bathrooms.

A few blocks west of Old Town Square, the beautiful bed-and-breakfast **Edwards House** (402 W. Mountain Ave., 970/493-9191, http:// edwardshouse.com, $175-225) is located in a renovated 1904 Victorian house that has seven rooms plus one suite, each named for someone who played an important role in Fort Collins' history. The Auntie Stone room is named in honor of Elizabeth "Auntie" Stone, the first Euro-American to settle in town. Stone operated a mess hall and boarding house; the room named for her features a queen-sized bed with luxurious linens, a gas fireplace, and antique keys on the wall.

If you'd rather sleep under the stars, there are more than 50 campgrounds in the 1.5-million-acre **Arapaho-Roosevelt National Forest and Pawnee National Grassland** (2150 Centre Ave. #E, 970/295-6600, www. fs.usda.gov).

Greeley and the Pawnee National Grassland

the Pawnee National Grassland

Greeley is a Colorado college town, but given its position on the Great Plains, it has a distinctly rural and agrarian character. The city of nearly 100,000 is the gateway to the **Pawnee National Grassland** (www.fs.usda.gov), almost 200,000 acres of windswept plains that are internationally renowned for bird-watching. More than 250 species have been observed here, including many birds of prey and the Colorado state bird, the lark bunting. The grassland also hosts many species unique to the high plains, including the burrowing owl and the mountain plover. While you explore around the namesake Pawnee Buttes, you may stumble across arrowheads and fossils, but be sure to leave them undisturbed.

If all that exploring makes you hungry, return to Greeley for a meal at the relaxed **Kenny's Steakhouse** (3502 W. 10th St., 970/395-0100, www.kennysteakhouse.com, 11am-9pm Mon.-Sat.), which reportedly has the town's best burgers.

TRANSPORTATION AND SERVICES

Car

Fort Collins is located 70 miles (1.25 hours' drive) northwest of Denver. From Denver International Airport, drive west for 10 miles on Peña Boulevard to E-470 North, a toll road. Drive 18 miles to Exit 47, where you merge onto I-25 North. Follow I-25 North for 42 miles to Exit 269B, then turn left onto Highway 14, which leads into town.

From Pearl Street in Boulder, head north on Broadway to the junction with U.S. 36. Turn left and head north on U.S. 36 to the junction with Highway 66. Turn right here and follow this road east to the junction with U.S. 287. Turn left and follow U.S. 287 north to Fort Collins.

Enterprise (www.enterprise.com) and Hertz (www.hertz.com) have car rental depots east of downtown Fort Collins near Highway 14. Avis has a depot on U.S. 287 north of downtown.

Bus and Shuttle

Both **Green Ride** (970/226-5533, www.greenrideco.com) and **SuperShuttle** (800/258-3826, www.supershuttle.com) offer door-to-door service. There are no buses that go from Denver International Airport directly to Fort Collins; you can first catch the **Regional Transportation District** (RTD, www.rtd-denver.com) AB bus to Boulder, followed by the FLEX bus to Fort Collins, but the journey will take close to five hours. Fortunately, transportation in and around Fort Collins is much more efficient; check **Transfort** (970/221-6620, www.ridetransfort.com) for details.

Bike

If you'd like to get around town on two wheels and avoid the downtown and campus parking hassles, reserve and pick up a bike at the **Bike Library** (250 N. Mason St., 970/419-1050, www.fcbikelibrary.org, hours vary Apr.-mid-Dec.).

Services

The **Fort Collins Convention and Visitors Bureau** (19 Old Town Square #137, 970/232-3840, www.visitftcollins.com, 8:30am-5pm Mon.-Fri., 11am-5pm Sat.-Sun.) has a very helpful website. The **City of Fort Collins** (300 LaPorte Ave., 970/221-6878, www.fcgov.com, #FCTrails on Twitter) has information about the city's natural areas, including nature programs and updates on trail conditions and closures. The local newspaper is *The Coloradoan* (www.coloradoan.com), whose ad-heavy website contains some information about local dining. **KRFC** (88.9 FM, www.krfcfm.org) is the community radio station; programming includes plenty of locally oriented segments like a Bikes and Beer show, plus a weekly Support Local Culture show focused on the county's artists.

The city's main hospital is **Poudre Valley Hospital** (1024 S. Lemay Ave., 970/495-7000, www.uchealth.org); urgent care facilities include **Concentra Urgent Care** (620 S. Lemay Ave., 970/221-5811, www.concentra.com, 7am-7pm Mon.-Fri., 9am-1pm Sat.) and the **Associates in Family Medicine** (3519 Richmond Dr., 970/204-0300, www.afmfc.com, 8am-8pm daily).

Rocky Mountain National Park

This 265,000-acre park guards a dramatic and wild landscape that is by far Colorado's best-known and most popular attraction.

Exiting the narrow, winding canyons that lead from the Front Range up to Rocky Mountain National Park, you abruptly emerge into a beautiful valley. In the space of a few heartbeats, you quickly realize that behind this vale is an even more remarkable scene: a backdrop of sheer cliffs and soaring peaks so large and majestic that the first sight takes your breath away. In the early 20th century, the grandeur of this scenery and the abundance of wildlife inspired conservationists to protect it before the National Park System even existed.

Rocky is a land of simplicity—a place of regular cycles of sunshine and seasons—as well as stark contrasts and sweeping change. Once covered by thick glaciers that sculpted the pointy peaks and ground out the wide valleys, the park lands are still evolving today, shaped by the slow forces of snow, rain, and wind, as well as more dramatic events like natural floods and a 1982 dam failure.

From the lowest valley to the flat top of 14,259-foot-high Longs Peak, the enormous changes in elevation within the park create a mosaic of interconnected ecosystems where numerous plants and animals thrive. Some wildlife remains here year-round, whereas other animals move to lower elevations or migrate south to avoid the long winters. While the west winds howl and a thick blanket of snow drapes the land, you can still drive to Bear Lake, whose azure waters are even more stunning against the backdrop of evergreen forest and freshly fallen snow. Each spring, the cycle of life begins anew as the sun climbs higher in the sky, the birds return, the meadows turn green, and mule deer and other mammals give birth. Summer heralds the opening of Trail Ridge Road, the park's signature scenic drive, a winding ribbon of hairpin bends, each with a new vista of snow-capped peaks and windswept alpine tundra.

Take time here to enjoy the fresh scent of pine after an afternoon thunderstorm, to nap on a smooth, sun-kissed rock, and to listen to the poignant, spine-tingling bugle of a 700-pound elk. You'll be glad you did.

Previous: view from Trail Ridge Road; bighorn sheep. **Above:** waterfall on the west side.

Look for ★ to find recommended sights, activities, dining, and lodging.

Highlights

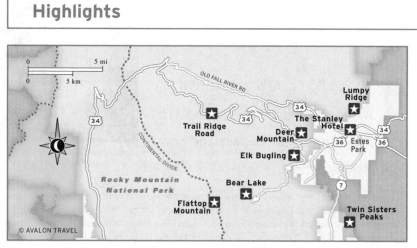

★ **The Stanley Hotel:** This grand, turn-of-the-20th-century hotel is famous as the inspiration for Stephen King's horror tale *The Shining*—and for its ghostly guests (page 139).

★ **Trail Ridge Road:** Cross North America's backbone while driving to dizzying heights along this paved, top-of-the-world road (page 146).

★ **Elk Bugling:** Listen to the eerie mating call of a graceful brown bull elk echoing through the still morning air (page 149).

★ **Bear Lake:** Enjoy the scenery and a stroll around this glistening, turquoise-blue lake (page 150).

★ **Lumpy Ridge:** These sheer granite cliffs beckon hikers, rock climbers, and photographers who strive to capture the perfect image of the Twin Owls (page 152).

★ **Deer Mountain:** This straightforward trail on the park's east side makes a great first summit hike (page 156).

★ **Flattop Mountain:** A historic trail up to the Continental Divide offers phenomenal views (page 156).

★ **Twin Sisters Peaks:** Scout for picas and marmots on this scramble to two summits, the highest of which is 11,428 feet (page 158).

Rocky Mountain National Park

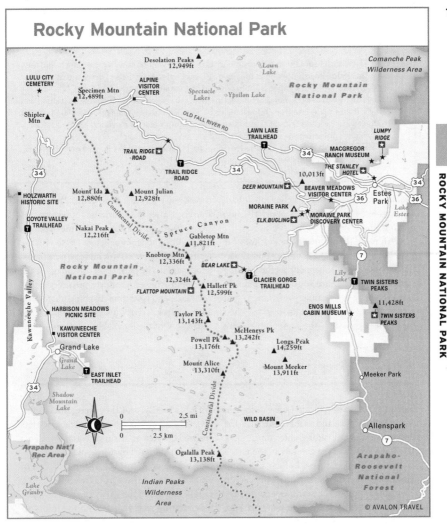

PLANNING YOUR TIME

Rocky Mountain National Park (970/586-1206, www.nps.gov/romo, $20 per vehicle) is separated by the Continental Divide into east and west sides. These sides are only connected when **Trail Ridge Road** is open (Memorial Day–mid-Oct.). From mid-October through Memorial Day, **Estes Park** offers the main driving access. In late spring, after hardworking crews have scraped 30 feet or more of snow

off the pavement, U.S. 34 reopens, connecting both halves of the park.

The park's **east side** is open year-round and hosts most of the iconic attractions. Estes Park, with its much larger selection of lodging, shopping, and dining options, makes a more convenient base. The quieter **west side,** just north of the gateway town of Grand Lake, is worth a visit to immerse yourself in nature and enjoy plentiful recreation with fewer

If You Have...

ONE DAY: Visit Bear Lake and stroll around its turquoise waters, enjoy a picnic lunch, and then drive Trail Ridge Road, lingering at the Alpine Visitor Center, Many Parks Curve, and other stops for short hikes, wildlife sightings, photo ops, and phenomenal panoramic views.

A WEEKEND: Add a morning hike up the Twin Sisters Peaks or to Wild Basin's rushing waterfalls, then stop in Estes for a refreshing lunch and a visit to the Stanley Hotel before heading to Horseshoe Park and Sheep Lakes to search for bighorn sheep and grazing elk silhouetted in the twilight's golden glow.

THREE OR MORE DAYS: Add a long day hike like the route to Sky Pond, a horseback ride, or a rock climb on Lumpy Ridge.

people. Grand Lake makes a convenient base for summer recreation, especially fishing, boating, and hiking.

With more than four million visitors per year, Rocky is one of the country's busiest national parks; if you're here during the bustling **summer** season, brace yourself and plan accordingly. Try to schedule your time so that you're on the trails close to sunrise, when they're less crowded, the temperatures are cooler, and wildlife is more frequently spotted. Evenings, after the afternoon thunderstorms have passed, are another great time to search for wildlife and enjoy a picnic. Try to visit the western side or Estes Park midday, when most people are in the park. Take advantage of the free shuttle buses whenever possible so that you can spend your time snapping photos and gazing at the scenery instead of at the traffic during one of the inevitable "elk jams."

Estes Park

Bustling Estes Park is located a few miles east of the national park and its main entrance, the Beaver Meadows Visitor Center on U.S. 36. The town serves as the gateway to the park's east side with easy access to Bear Lake and Moraine Park. Estes Park is small and easy to navigate, although the summer and holiday traffic often gridlock the town's small streets, and parking is usually at a premium. Most of the attractions are clustered in the walkable downtown, centered around the junction between U.S. 34 and U.S. 36, where the bulk of the restaurants and accommodations are located. Additional options stretch along both roads up to the very edge of the national park.

The wide, flat intermontane valley was initially the summer home of the Arapaho tribe, whose members once trapped eagles on Longs Peak to collect their feathers. In 1863, Joel Estes, a native of Missouri, settled here with his family, and they were quickly followed by other homesteaders. These settlers realized the great tourism potential of the area and built cabins to house intrepid travelers exploring the area. In 1872, the fourth Earl of Dunraven moved here from Ireland and tried to take control of the valley to use it as a private hunting reserve. After failing in his attempt, the earl opened the area's first resort, setting the stage for Estes Park's current role as a tourism hub.

SIGHTS
Estes Park Museum
The small **Estes Park Museum** (200 Fourth St., 970/586-6256, http://estesparkmuseum-friends.org, 10am-5pm Mon.-Sat., 1pm-5pm Sun. May-Oct., 10am-5pm Fri.-Sat., 1pm-5pm Sun. Nov.-Apr., free) has programs and displays that narrate the history of Estes Park,

Estes Park

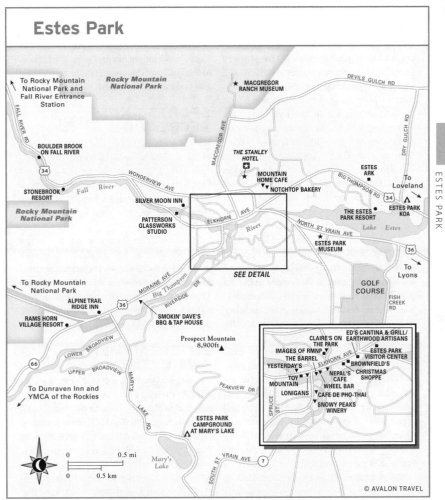

To Rocky Mountain National Park and Fall River Entrance Station

FALL RIVER RD

Rocky Mountain National Park

DEVILS GULCH RD

★ MACGREGOR RANCH MUSEUM

DRY GULCH RD

MACGREGOR AVE

BOULDER BROOK ON FALL RIVER

34

STONEBROOK RESORT *Fall River*

WONDERVIEW AVE

SILVER MOON INN ■

PATTERSON GLASSWORKS STUDIO

ELKHORN AVE

THE STANLEY HOTEL

MOUNTAIN HOME CAFE ★
▼▼ NOTCHTOP BAKERY

ESTES ARK ■

BIG THOMPSON RD

To Loveland

34

ESTES PARK KOA ●

Lake *Estes*

THE ESTES PARK RESORT ●

NORTH ST VRAIN AVE

★ ESTES PARK MUSEUM

36

To Lyons

River

SEE DETAIL

Rocky Mountain National Park

To Rocky Mountain National Park

ALPINE TRAIL RIDGE INN ●

RAMS HORN VILLAGE RESORT ●

MORAINE AVE

Big Thompson

RIVERSIDE DR

36

SMOKIN' DAVE'S BBQ & TAP HOUSE

GOLF COURSE

FISH CREEK RD

BROADVIEW

LOWER BROADVIEW

66

UPPER BROADVIEW

MARY'S LAKE RD

Prospect Mountain 8,900ft ▲

PEAKVIEW DR

To Dunraven Inn and YMCA of the Rockies

ESTES PARK CAMPGROUND ▲ AT MARY'S LAKE

SPRUCE ST

CLAIRE'S ON THE PARK
IMAGES OF RMNP ●▼
THE BARREL ▼
YESTERDAY'S ▼

TOY ■ ▼
MOUNTAIN
LONIGANS ▼

ED'S CANTINA & GRILL/ EARTHWOOD ARTISANS ■

ELKHORN AVE

ESTES PARK ■ VISITOR CENTER

BROWNFIELD'S ■

NEPAL'S CAFE ▼
WHEEL BAR ▼
CAFE DE PHO-THAI ▼
SNOWY PEAKS WINERY ▼

CHRISTMAS SHOPPE ■

0   0.5 mi
0   0.5 km

Mary's Lake

SOUTH ST VRAIN AVE

7

© AVALON TRAVEL

ROCKY MOUNTAIN NATIONAL PARK
ESTES PARK

from the formation of the modern landscape during the last Ice Age to the present. The property includes two historical buildings: a 1908 cabin furnished from that era and the old National Park Service headquarters.

Macgregor Ranch Museum

At the base of Lumpy Ridge on the north side of Estes Park, the **MacGregor Ranch Museum** (180 MacGregor La., 970/586-3749, www.macgregorranch.org, 10am-4pm Tues.-Sat. late May-late Aug., $5) provides an

intimate glimpse of what life was like for early homesteaders in the region. The MacGregor family settled this property in the 1870s. Today, visitors can take a guided tour of their 1896 ranch house, with original furnishings, as well as clothing, diaries, and historic photos. The outbuildings, including a blacksmith shop and root cellar, can be explored on their own.

★ The Stanley Hotel

As you drive into Estes Park, you can't help

but notice the enormous, gleaming white building with the bright red roof perched high on a hill in front of the dramatic granite outcrops of Lumpy Ridge. This is **The Stanley Hotel** (333 Wonderview Ave., 800/976-1377, www.stanleyhotel.com, $329-419), the most distinctive building in Estes Park and one of the oldest. It was built in 1909 by F. O. Stanley, who, along with his twin, was the co-owner of the company that built the famous Stanley Steamers. After being diagnosed with tuberculosis at the age of 54, Stanley moved to Estes Park to take advantage of its fresh air and copious sunshine. During the course of his first summer here, Stanley's health rebounded and he purchased some property with the intent of returning every summer. But Stanley and his wife, Flora, craved the more refined accommodations and social scene they were used to on the East Coast. They decided to build a grand colonial revival-style hotel with innovations like electricity throughout the building. Completion of the original 48-room Stanley Hotel in 1909 spurred the local economy, as did Stanley's efforts to improve and pave the roads from the Front Range up to Estes Park.

Today, the 140-room hotel is known for its amazing views from every window and for hosting horror writer Stephen King and serving as the inspiration for the terrifying Overlook Hotel in his best-selling novel *The Shining*. Reputedly one of the nation's most active sites for paranormal activity, the hotel is infamous for its ghostly guests, including Stanley and his wife, Flora, who apparently enjoys playing her antique piano in the middle of the night.

TOURS

Take a **Night Ghost Tour** (970/577-4111, $28) through the hotel's most haunted areas. To learn more about its history, architecture, and famous (live) guests, sign up for **The Stanley Tour** (970/577-4111, $23). The hotel also offers an evening of mystery with a master **magician** (970/577-4111, Sat. evenings in summer, $25). Show any tour, restaurant, or hotel reservation to avoid the $10 parking fee.

Each spring, the hotel sponsors the four-day **Stanley Film Festival** (www.stanleyfilmfest.com, Apr.), a ghoulish mixture of classic and modern horror flicks, workshops, and a student film competition. Buy tickets and book accommodations well in advance.

SPORTS AND RECREATION

Kirk's Flyshop (230 E. Elkhorn Ave., 970/577-0790, www.kirksflyshop.com, 7am-7pm daily, $10 per day for fly rod and reel) has all the fishing gear you'll need. They also lead many classes and a variety of fishing trips, including raft, horseback, and llama pack expeditions.

In winter, rent sleds at either the **Estes Park Mountain Shop** (2050 Thompson Ave., 970/586-6548, www.estesparkmountainshop.com, 8am-9pm daily, $5 per day) or **The Warming House** (790 Moraine Ave., 970/586-2995, www.warminghouse.com, 9am-5pm daily, $5 per day).

ENTERTAINMENT AND EVENTS

Although Estes Park is better known for its wildlife than its nightlife, the town has several decent pubs and bars. **Lonigans** (110 W. Elkhorn Ave., 970/586-4346, www.lonigans.com, 11am-2am daily), which bills itself as "the local's town pub," has regular open stage and karaoke nights, plenty of Irish and local beer, and a typical pub menu. **The Barrel** (116 E. Elkhorn Ave., 970/616-2090, www.thebarrel.beer, 11am-11pm Mon.-Sat., 11am-9pm Sun. May-Oct.) is an outdoor beer garden with 60 taps that rotate through a great selection of cider, mead, and craft beer.

In the center of downtown, the **Wheel Bar** (132 E. Elkhorn Ave., 970/586-9381, www.thewheelbar.com, 10am-2am daily), an Estes Park institution since 1945, serves up plenty of local atmosphere along with its cocktails and bar food. If you enjoy wine, stop by the **Snowy Peaks Winery** (292 Moraine Ave., 970/586-2099, www.snowypeakswinery.com, 11am-5pm Mon.-Thurs., 11am-6pm Fri.-Sun.) for a taste of their current vintages, made locally from handpicked, Colorado-grown grapes. Previous vintages of the Élevé, a Rhône-style red blend, and the cabernet sauvignon have won medals in the state's prestigious Governors Cup competition.

SHOPPING

Downtown Estes Park has plenty of shopping options, especially along Elkhorn Avenue, the town's main street, and the blocks immediately adjacent to it. If you're searching for artwork inspired by the national park, **Images of Rocky Mountain National Park** (203 Park La., 970/586-4352, http://imagesofrmnp.com, 10am-5pm Mon.-Thurs., 10am-6pm Fri.-Sat.) features more than 200 stunning photographs by Erik Stensland, a local who frequently hikes into the wilderness long before sunrise to capture these images. Downtown Estes also has two nice glasswork shops where you can watch demos and purchase unique and color glassware, the **Patterson Glassworks Studio & Gallery** (323 W. Elkhorn Ave., 970/586-8619, www.glassworksofestespark.com, 10am-4pm daily) and **Mountain Blown Glass** (101-A W. Elkhorn Ave., 970/577-0880, www.mountainblownglass.net, 10am-5pm daily).

Earthwood Artisans (141 E. Elkhorn Ave., 970/586-2151, www.earthwoodgalleries.com, 10am-5pm daily) has a large selection of handmade jewelry, stained glass, wind chimes, and pottery made by American artists. If the Christmas spirit lingers in your heart year-round, the **Christmas Shoppe** (332 E. Elkhorn Ave., 970/586-2882, www.thechristmasshops.com, 10am-5pm Sun.-Thurs., 10am-6pm Fri.-Sat.) is the best place in town to splurge on decorations, including moose and bugling elk tree ornaments. For T-shirts, souvenir patches, calendars, and outdoor gear, stop by **Brownfield's** (350 E. Elkhorn Ave., 970/586-3275, www.shopbrownfields.com, 10am-7pm Mon.-Sat., 1pm-7pm Sun.). Kids will love both **Toy Mountain** (160 W. Elkhorn Ave., 970/586-3552, http://toy-mtn.com, 10am-5pm daily) and **Estes Ark** (521 Lone Pine Dr., 970/586-6483, www.estesark.

com, 9am-7pm Fri.-Mon., 9:30am-6pm Tues.-Thurs.), which specializes in talking teddies, stuffed versions of the wildlife you hope to see in the park, slot cars, and many other fun gizmos.

FOOD

For a filling, pre-hike breakfast, head to the low-key **Mountain Home Café** (457 E. Wonderview Ave., 970/586-6624, http://mountainhomecafe.com, 6:30am-3pm Mon.-Sat., 6:30am-2:30pm Sun., $7-14), well known locally for its buttermilk pancakes, enormous three-egg omelets, and skillet potatoes piled high with eggs, cheese, and other delicious toppings. The ★ **Notchtop Bakery & Cafe** (459 E. Wonderview Ave., 970/586-0272, http://www.thenotchtop.com, 7am-3pm daily, $6-12) is a great place to stop for organic, direct-trade coffee and a freshly baked croissant or to order off the extensive breakfast and lunch menus. The bakery uses only naturally grown ingredients to whip up amazing plates of Rocky Mountain trout and eggs, veggie wraps, and Rueben sandwiches. Half-orders are available for many breakfast dishes.

Claire's on the Park (225 Park La., 970/586-9564, www.clairesonthepark.net, 7:30am-8pm daily, $16-21) serves meals with an emphasis on fresh and seasonal ingredients. The patio is a great place to relax and enjoy crab cake Benedict, a New Orleans-style muffuletta, or a Santa Fe salad. If you enjoy spicy food, stop by the small **Nepal's Café** (184 E. Elkhorn Ave., 970/577-7035, 11am-9pm daily, $9-14), whose pre-meal *papadum*, extensive lunch buffet, *momo* (dumplings), and curries are the perfect way to end a long day of hiking or horseback riding in the park. For Thai or Vietnamese food, try **Café de Pho-Thai** (225 W. Riverside Dr., 970/577-0682, www.cafedephothai.com, 11am-9pm daily, $10-15) for authentic noodle soup, papaya salad, and peanut-topped pad Thai.

For BBQ and cold craft beer, head straight to **Smokin' Dave's BBQ & Taphouse** (820 Moraine Ave., 970/577-7427, www.smokindavesq.com, 11am-8pm daily, $12-25), a friendly place that serves up large, meaty meals like the Big Kahuna Belly Buster, pecan-crusted trout, and surprisingly good salads, accompanied by a wide selection of BBQ sauces. On the east end of the main street, ★ **Ed's Cantina & Grill** (390 E. Elkhorn Ave., 970/586-2919, http://edscantina.com, 11am-9pm Mon.-Thurs., 11am-9:30pm Fri.-Sat., $9-15) is a locally owned climber's hangout with Grateful Dead-themed paintings and an inspired menu of fresh Mexican dishes, like bison enchiladas, sizzling veggie fajitas, and fish tacos, along with a long list of *blanco, reposado,* and *anejo* tequilas and frosty margaritas (try the avocado).

For a more upscale meal, try the **Dunraven Inn** (2470 Hwy. 66, 970/586-6409, www.dunraveninn.com, 4pm-9pm daily, $16-33). Located a few miles southwest of town, the inn has an extensive wine selection and freshly made Italian favorites, like meatballs and spaghetti, standard steak and seafood dishes, and some unusual combos like baked lobster ziti. If you have enough room, top off your meal with espresso-drenched tiramisu. Reservations are recommended, and kids are welcome (and have their own great selection to choose from).

Estes also has plenty of places to satisfy your family's sweet cravings, including my daughter's favorite, **Laura's Fine Candy** (129 E. Elkhorn Ave., 970/586-4004, www.pioneercandy.com, 10am-10pm daily), which is well known for its creamy fudge, candy-studded caramel apples, and gourmet popcorn. My son prefers the Dutch chocolate ice cream in a chocolate-chip waffle cone at **Yesterday's Ice Cream Shoppe** (191 W. Elkhorn Ave., 970/586-8624, www.yesterdaysicecream.com, 11am-9pm Tues.-Sat., noon-8pm Sun.).

ACCOMMODATIONS
$150-200

Tucked into the forest a few miles from Estes, the **Estes Park Center/YMCA of the Rockies** (2515 Tunnel Rd., 888/613-9622, http://ymcarockies.org, $119-389) is a large and beautifully maintained complex with multiple lodges and cabins that can accommodate any group size. Basic lodge rooms ($139-179) accommodate 5-6 people with two queen beds plus a futon or bunk; most have full en suite bathrooms. Cabins and vacation homes ($149-464) vary in size with 2-4 bedrooms, full kitchens, and fireplaces; each has a private bath. YMCA members obtain a small discount off the standard prices.

Located along Fall River just a five-minute walk from downtown, the **Silver Moon Inn** (175 Spruce Dr., 970/586-6006, http://silvermooninn.com, $185-290) has renovated king and two-queen rooms, as well as two suites, one with two bedrooms and another with three bedrooms and a full kitchen. There's a gas fire pit by the creek, where there are free s'mores each night, as well as a pool, hot tubs, and free continental breakfast each morning.

Along U.S. 36 just outside of the national park, the **Alpine Trail Ridge Inn** (927 Moraine Ave., 800/233-5023, www.alpinetrailridgeinn.com, late Apr.-mid-Oct., $135-220) gets consistently great reviews for its great location, friendly owners, heated outdoor pool, free Wi-Fi, and on-site restaurant. Western-style rooms are clean and comfortable with gleaming wood trim, colorful accents, and a choice of queen or double beds; several two-bedroom family units sleep 6 (some with full kitchens).

Estes has many additional lodges and hotels strung along the narrow strip between Fall River and U.S. 34, which leads to the park's Fall River entrance. The adults-only ★ **Stonebrook Resort** (1710 Fall River Rd., 970/586-4629, www.stonebrookresort.com, $145-245) has more than a dozen beautiful cottages, cabins, and suites, including several adjacent to the river. While most are intended for two people, several will house up to four. Some feature perks like private riverside hot tubs, an in-room whirlpool tub, and a gas fireplace. There is no on-site food service, but all units have small kitchens. You can hike from here straight into the park.

Over $200

Just off of U.S. 36 next to the Beaver Meadows entrance, the ★ **Rams Horn Village Resort** (1565 Hwy. 66, 800/229-4676, www.luxuryestesparkcabins.com, $279-414) is my favorite place to stay. The completely furnished cabins feel like a home away from home, with high-quality beds and sleeper sofas, 600-count sheets, fully equipped kitchens, picnic tables, and private decks. Each cabin can sleep 2-6 people, and you can't beat the location.

After tiring of the corporate rat race, Kimberly and Christopher Campbell decided to purchase a business in the mountains. In 2008, they chose a beautiful property, the 19-suite **Boulder Brook on Fall River** (1900 Fall River Rd., 970/586-0910, www.boulderbrook.com, $230-260), which they have lovingly maintained ever since. Boulder Brook is a great place to relax and enjoy wildlife sightings from the resort's tall picture windows and private decks, as well as fishing in the creek. The adults-only spa suites have fireplaces and private, two-person jetted tubs.

History buffs and horror flick fans will enjoy staying at **The Stanley Hotel** (333 Wonderview Ave., 800/976-1377, www.stanleyhotel.com, $329-499), the stately white hotel with gorgeous views that served as inspiration for the terrifying Overlook Hotel in Stephen King's best-seller *The Shining*. The hotel has a large array of rooms and suites that vary from the classic queen or king rooms in the main 1909 building to upscale condominiums with 1-3 bedrooms, fully equipped kitchens, stunning views, and even a garage. Of special note are five haunted rooms, including the suite where Stephen King stayed, as well as the *Ghost Hunters'* favorite room, which can only be booked by phone.

For an elegant retreat, try **The Estes Park Resort** (1700 Big Thompson Ave., 855/377-3778, www.theestesparkresort.com, $229-569), located next to the small marina on beautiful Lakes Estes. It's located slightly east of Estes Park; during high season, guests can take a city shuttle to access the downtown and the national park. Accommodations include comfortable double queen and king rooms with pillow-top mattresses, free Wi-Fi, and mini fridges, as well as several types of suites that can sleep up to six people. On-site amenities include a spa and an elegant restaurant with tremendous views.

CAMPING

If the sites in the national park are full, Estes Park and its environs have several options for sleeping out. The kid-friendly **Jellystone Park of Estes** (5495 U.S. 36, 970/586-4230, www.jellystoneofestes.com, May-Oct., $38-60) has a pool, mini-golf course, tent and full hook-up sites, plus cabins that can sleep up to 12. **Estes Park KOA** (2051 Big Thompson Ave., 800/562-1887, http://koa.com, May-mid-Oct., $40-65) has tent and RV sites with hookups, cabins (no bath), and cottages that sleep 4-6, in addition to a pet park, playground, free Wi-Fi, a dump station, and a snack bar. Farther from town, the **Estes Park Campground at Mary's Lake** (2120 Mary's Lake Rd., 970/577-1026, www.evrpd.com, mid-May-early Oct., $30-45) is located a stone's throw from Mary's Lake, where you can fish and look for wildlife.

TRANSPORTATION AND SERVICES

Car

To reach Estes Park from Denver, take I-25 north to U.S. 36 West, following signs for Boulder. Continue west on U.S. 36 for about 32 miles. At the junction with U.S. 34, turn left to remain on U.S. 36 (called Moraine Ave.), which passes through Estes Park before arriving at the Beaver Meadows Entrance Station. In good weather and traffic conditions, this trip typically takes about two hours.

From the east, there are two other routes that lead to Estes Park. From Loveland, U.S. 34 winds east along the Big Thompson River to Lake Estes, then continues west through Estes Park to the Fall River Entrance Station. A third route branches off from U.S. 36 at the town of Lyons to follow Highway 7 west then north up the South and Middle St. Vrain Canyons to the tiny town of Allenspark. From here, Highway 7 heads north, passing the Longs Peak and Wild Basin parcels of the national park, before rejoining U.S. 36 in Estes Park.

Shuttle

Estes Park Shuttle (1805 Cherokee Dr., 970/586-5151, www.estesparkshuttle.com, $45 one-way DIA to Estes Park) offers year-round, scheduled, door-to-door service from the Denver airport to all Estes Park venues. With advance reservations, the company will also pick up passengers at the Denver Amtrak and Greyhound stations, as well as limited locations in Lyons, Boulder, and Longmont.

Within Estes Park, **shuttle buses** (www.colorado.gov, from 9am daily late June-mid-Sept., free) operate five different color-coded routes, all of which begin at the **Estes Park Visitor Center** (500 Big Thompson Ave., 800/443-7837, www.visitestespark.com, 9am-5pm Mon.-Sat., 10am-4pm Sun.) and offer access to most of the local hotels, campgrounds, and other outlying facilities.

At the Estes Park Visitor Center, the national park's **Hiker Shuttle Route** (www.nps.gov, 7:30am-8pm daily late June-mid-Sept., 7:30am-8pm Sat.-Sun. mid-Sept.-mid-Oct., free) runs to the large **Park & Ride** on Bear Lake Road, with one stop at the Beaver Meadows Visitor Center on the way.

Services

For maps, brochures, travel advice, free Wi-Fi, and guest computers, head to the **Estes Park Visitor Center** (500 Big Thompson Ave., 800/443-7837, www.visitestespark.com, 9am-5pm Mon.-Sat., 10am-4pm Sun.) near the U.S. 34 and U.S. 36 junction. In addition to picnic tables and a bookstore, the center also has free parking; in the summer you can gratefully ditch your vehicle and hop on one of the park's convenient and free shuttles.

For medical care, head to the **Estes Park Medical Center** (555 Prospect Ave., 970/586-2317, www.epmedcenter.com), which has a 24-hour emergency department. Local urgent care facilities include **Timberline Urgent Care** (131 Stanley Ave., 970/586-2343, www.urgentcare.com, 8am-5pm Mon.-Fri., 9am-1pm Sat.).

East Side

The park's eastern half, located just west of the gateway town of Estes Park, is open year-round and hosts most of the iconic attractions, including glistening Bear Lake, Moraine Park's elk-filled meadows, graceful Wild Basin waterfalls, and the towering, 14,259-foot flat-topped summit of Longs Peak. The bustling east side of Rocky Mountain National Park (www.nps.gov/romo, 970/586-1206) has two main entrances: the **Fall River Entrance Station** via U.S. 34 and the main **Beaver Meadows Entrance Station** on U.S. 36.

FALL RIVER AREA

Located just east of the Fall River Entrance Station is the **Fall River Visitor Center**

(U.S. 34, 5 miles west of Estes Park, 970/586-1206, www.nps.gov, 9am-4pm Fri.-Sat. mid-May, 9am-5pm daily late May-mid-Oct.; limited hours Nov.-Dec.). View a short film, collect brochures and maps, investigate kid-friendly exhibits, shop at the bookstore, and ask questions of the knowledgeable staff and volunteers.

Sheep Lakes and Horseshoe Park

Just two miles west of the Fall River Visitor Center, the **Sheep Lakes,** nestled in the large surrounding valley called **Horseshoe Park,** are the best place to look for the graceful **bighorn sheep,** the nimble symbol of this wildlife-rich national park. The largest wild sheep on the continent, the rams typically stand three feet at the shoulder, can weigh more than 300 pounds, and sport large, curling horns. Females are about half this size and have smaller horns that curve to a distinct point. Thanks to their sharp hearing, keen sense of smell, and widely spaced eyes, which allow a wide field of vision, bighorns can sense danger from far away, giving them ample time to escape using their special hooves and sticky soles to catch themselves on rocky ledges after what looks (to humans) like death-defying jumps.

Unlike elk, bighorn sheep overwinter at high elevations and descend to the montane valleys in late spring, when they visit Sheep Lakes to graze on the lush grass and eat the surrounding soil to replenish themselves with minerals not available at higher elevations. Because crossing the highway stresses the animals out and reduces their ability to fight disease, the park service created a **Bighorn Crossing Zone** in Horseshoe Park, where stop sign-toting rangers control automobile traffic to allow the sheep to move more peacefully in and out of the meadow, while also providing great photo ops for visitors caught in the "sheep jam."

Although the movements of any wildlife are difficult to predict, the sheep are typically in this area between 9am and 3pm, and sightings can range from lone individuals to groups of up to 60. Given that the park's bighorn population nearly died out due to hunting, habitat destruction, and disease, these numbers are remarkable. From a low of about 150 sheep in the 1950s, the population has more than doubled.

To get to Sheep Lakes from the Fall River Entrance Station, continue west on U.S. 34 for about 1.75 miles.

Alluvial Fan

Just past Sheep Lakes, Old Fall River Road branches off of U.S. 34 toward Endovalley. In stark contrast to the tens of thousands of years that it took glaciers to sculpt the park's large, U-shaped valleys, the prominent, treeless scar on the northern flank of Horseshoe Park was created in just a few hours when, on July 15, 1982, the Lawn Lake Dam collapsed, sending 129 million gallons of water racing down Roaring River and knocking down every tree in its path. After this wall of water reached flat Horseshoe Park, it slowed dramatically and dropped the boulders it was carrying, creating a distinct cone of sand, gravel, and boulders called an **alluvial fan.** It's visible from the Alluvial Fan Parking Area on the Endovalley Road. From here, the floodwaters raced toward Estes Park, tragically killing three campers and then inundating the town beneath with up to six feet of water, causing $31 million in damage. You can see some of the devastation firsthand by strolling the **Alluvial Fan Trail** (0.15 mile one-way), which was rebuilt after the 2013 flood wiped out the original path.

To get to the alluvial fan from the Fall River Entrance Station, continue west on U.S. 34 for two miles to the junction with Old Fall River Road. Turn right onto Old Fall River Road and continue about a mile to the signed parking area on the right.

Old Fall River Road

Old Fall River Road (July-Oct., closed in winter) is one of the park's signature scenic drives. Built between 1913 and 1920, the road follows a trail long used by Native Americans who traversed this area in search of game. Although the dirt surface is frequently graded and accessible to regular passenger vehicles, it's intended as a leisurely scenic drive, with a **15-mile-per-hour** speed limit, no guardrails, and 16 switchbacks so tight that some early motorists had to do a series of back-and-forth turns to get around the curves. Because it's too narrow and winding for cars to safely pass, the **11-mile route** is a **one-way drive.**

From U.S. 34, at the bend between Sheep Lakes and Horseshoe Park, the road heads northwest from the Endovalley to the Alpine Visitor Center on Trail Ridge Road. After leaving the valley, the road climbs steadily through thick evergreen forest. About a mile from its start, there's a short excursion from a small pullout on the left side down a stone pathway to **Chasm Falls.** From this stop, the road continues beneath the looming bulk of 12,454-foot Mount Chapin. After passing **Willow Park,** where you can often spot elk, Old Fall River Road crosses into the treeless alpine tundra. Near the crest at **Fall River Pass,** the road contours around the **Fall River Cirque,** a giant cookie bite that a glacier sculpted out of the hard rock, before joining Trail Ridge Road at the Alpine Visitor Center.

★ TRAIL RIDGE ROAD

Trail Ridge Road (U.S. 34, May-mid-Oct.), the 48-mile paved road between Estes Park and Grand Lake, is the only road that crosses Rocky Mountain National Park. The country's highest continuous paved road, Trail Ridge tops out at an impressive 12,183 feet. Although there are great views all along the route, the best are from the 11-mile section above tree line, where you are surrounded by windswept tundra stretching in every direction towards snow-capped peaks, dramatic steep-walled cirques, and deep valleys. This so-called Trail to the Sky offers some of the

continent's easiest access to the fragile tundra, where the growing season can last for as few as 40 days per year.

Trail Ridge Road was built between 1926 and 1932 to replace Old Fall River Road, which was too steep and narrow for drivers to easily navigate and too shady to provide early summer access. Thanks to its ridge-top location, Trail Ridge has less snow accumulation and more sunshine, attributes that allow the park service to open it much earlier—usually by Memorial Day weekend—and to keep it open until mid-October. Each year in mid-May, two veteran road crews, one on each side of the park, begin the painstaking and dangerous job of removing the 30 feet of snow that typically cover the road and whose layers often linger along the side until late June. Even after the crews meet, the park service sometimes needs to temporarily close the road, especially to avoid dangerous black ice.

Once Trail Ridge is open, driving it is an awe-inspiring adventure with stunning views that Horace Albright, a former director of the National Park Service, described as "the whole sweep of the Rockies before you in all directions." From the lush, montane forests and fertile lowlands at either end, the road quickly climbs up to the tundra, a harsh environment

Trail Ridge Road

The Continental Divide

Rocky Mountain National Park is separated by a line of rocky peaks that collectively comprise part of North America's **Continental Divide.** This divide is a major separation of water drainages: water flowing down the east side of the divide eventually runs into the Atlantic Ocean; on the west side, the water ultimately enters the Pacific. The Continental Divide snakes across the entire North American continent, from the Canadian wilderness to the Panama Canal, and frequently coincides with some of the highest points in the 3,000-mile Rocky Mountain chain. Since the divide usually runs along some of the tallest and most rugged alpine ridges and peaks, it's rare to have a road that crosses it. Where one does, there is usually a sign to celebrate the crossing, and these are popular photo ops for people who like to be in two places at once.

the Continental Divide on Trail Ridge Road

where fierce winds, strong ultraviolet light, and intense cold greatly limit the plants and animals found here. Yet for a few precious weeks each summer, the tundra is home to carpets of dozens of different types of tiny wildflowers, glistening alpine lakes, and migratory and resident wildlife, which you can often spot from your car.

Fortunately for drivers, there are many pullouts along the way, which are safe places to stop and snap photos and enjoy the forever views. From east to west, great viewpoints include **Hidden Valley,** where you can often spot chipmunks, **Many Parks Curve,** the highest point to which the eastern side of Trail Ridge is plowed in winter, and **Rainbow Curve,** where you can see the flat Great Plains stretching far to the east. Farther west along the road, you can learn more about the tundra at the **Tundra World Nature Trail,** an easy half-hour walk from the **Rock Cut.** Two miles west of the road's highest point, which is unmarked, the **Alpine Visitor Center** awaits.

Continuing west on Trail Ridge Road, you cross the **Continental Divide** at 10,758-foot

Milner Pass and have stunning views into the upper Colorado River Valley from the aptly named **Farview Curve,** a short distance above the gate that closes the road in winter.

Alpine Visitor Center

Located at 11,796 feet in elevation, the **Alpine Visitor Center** (Trail Ridge Rd., 970/586-1222, www.nps.gov, 10:30am-4:30pm daily late May-mid-Oct.) feels like it's perched on top of the world. Originally built in 1935, the center has been renovated several times, most recently in 2001. The building has a low profile and distinctive roof reinforced with large beams to withstand the fierce winds and crushing weight of dozens of feet of snow that can cover the structure in the winter. The center's back windows and deck have one of the best views in Colorado, a panorama looking down Fall River Canyon toward Longs Peak and Estes Park far below.

The center has a few informative exhibits about the tundra, staff that can answer questions and help in case of an emergency, and restrooms (although it does not always have

Rocky's Ecosystems

a herd of elk

Rocky Mountain National Park is one of the nation's highest national parks, with elevations stretching 7,800-14,000 feet above sea level. It encompasses three separate biological communities known as ecosystems. Each is a system where plants and animals interact with each other and their physical environment.

The **montane** ecosystem is found below 9,000 feet and is the most diverse. It includes wildflower-filled meadows, ponderosa pine forests, and groves of quaking aspen near the park's visitor centers. Most of Rocky's wildlife, including elk, bighorn sheep, mule deer, and moose, spend at least part of the year here.

The **sub-alpine** ecosystem lies 9,000-11,400 feet in elevation and experiences longer, colder winters. It's characterized by spruce-fir forests with lots of brushy undergrowth and, at higher elevations, stunted trees. Many birds, including ravens, downy and hairy woodpeckers, and Steller's jays, can be seen here, along with long-eared snowshoe hares and roaming black bears, bobcats, and mountain lions.

Above 11,400 feet is the fragile **alpine** ecosystem, a wild and windy place with no trees to protect the animals. Tiny wildflowers like baby-blue alpine forget-me-nots cling close to the ground, while camouflaged ptarmigans, squeaky hamster-like picas, and yellow-bellied marmots scurry all around.

running water). Next door is the park's only café, where you can also buy souvenirs.

BEAVER MEADOWS AREA
Beaver Meadows Visitor Center

Three miles west of Estes Park, the **Beaver Meadows Visitor Center** (U.S. 36, 970/586-1206, www.nps.gov, 8am-5pm daily in summer, 8am-4:30pm daily in winter) is the park's primary access point. In addition to an information desk, bookstore, and nature exhibits, the center houses one of the park's two **Backcountry Permit Offices** (970/586-1242), where you can gather information and obtain backcountry camping permits ($26 per reservation) on a space-available basis. Beginning in mid-April, this visitor center also offers a variety of **ranger-led programs** tuned to the seasons, including bird and other wildlife walks, evening educational programs, and the popular Bear Necessities talk, which covers Rocky's black bears and how to help save them.

Moraine Park

The large meadow west of the Beaver Meadows Entrance Station on U.S. 36 is **Moraine Park,** one of the best places to spot wildlife, especially **elk.** Its name is a combination of the term "park," which is widely used in the western U.S. to describe a wide, flat valley tucked between mountain ranges, and "moraine," which is the pile of debris left behind by a glacier as it begins to melt away. Moraine Park stretches from **Bear Lake Road** to **Deer Ridge Junction,** where U.S. 36 and U.S. 34 meet. You can obtain great views of the meadow from both roads, as well as from the two side roads that pierce the meadow's eastern side to access several trailheads, picnic areas, and the **Moraine Park Stables.**

Moraine Park Discovery Center

On Bear Lake Road (0.5 mile south of the junction with U.S. 36), the park operates the seasonal **Moraine Park Discovery Center** (Bear Lake Rd., 970/586-1242, www.nps. gov, 9am-4:30pm daily late May-mid-Oct.). Housed in a historic log and stone building, this center has a natural history exhibit describing how Rocky's distinctive landscape formed, a half-mile nature trail, and a gift shop and bookstore.

Wildlife-Watching

Moraine Park is a great place to spot yellow sage buttercups, purple mountain iris, and other colorful wildflowers in spring, as well as North American **elk,** who typically graze in this meadow in the spring and again in fall, when they descend from the tundra to breed. It's fortunate that visitors today can still see these graceful, brown animals with dark manes and tan rumps. Hunting once so severely depleted their numbers that by the start of the 20th century there were only a few hundred left in Colorado. In 1914, about 50 elk captured in Montana were released around Estes Park, and the species has made a dramatic comeback; the state now hosts about 260,000, the largest population in any U.S. state. There are now so many that the national park has begun to quietly cull the herd.

★ ELK BUGLING

Hearing the eerie sounds of 1,100-pound bull elks echoing through the air is a quintessential Rocky Mountain experience, especially in the early morning, when the crowds are minimal and the rising rays cast a magical glow across the vibrant autumn landscape. Elk are social animals who migrate in groups of up to several hundred cows, calves, and young bulls, roaming large distances to follow their favorite foods, which include fresh wildflowers, grass, and tender willow buds. Older bulls linger in small groups or remain alone until the fall breeding season, which typically occurs **mid-September to mid-October.** During this time, anxious males round up their harems and bugle, issuing a loud and peculiar noise that begins at a deep, resonant sound, then rises to a high-pitched squeal, before ending in a series of grunts.

The bugles contain very different information, according to recent research by University of Northern Colorado researcher Jennifer Clarke. Some bugles tell the cows that they're straying too far away; others warn nearby bulls that they're too close and the bugler is ready and willing to protect his mating rights. With so many elk congregated together, the calls often overlap, and the echoes seem to reverberate across the landscape. Occasionally, a renegade bull will challenge one of the larger, antlered males. Such competition is mostly in the form of strutting and displays of antlers rather than actual fighting, but two bulls will occasionally get into a tussle that can result in broken antlers. Fortunately, these drop each winter and regrow during the spring at rates of up to an inch per day.

Elk typically bugle between dusk and

dawn, the best times for visitors to both see and hear the rutting ritual. **Dusk** is the most popular time, so the roads around **Moraine** and **Horsehoe Parks** and **Upper Beaver Meadows** are typically very crowded. To avoid the masses, try these same areas at dawn, as well as the Kawuneeche Valley on the west side. In the summer, you still have a great chance of seeing elk, especially along Trail Ridge Road, but they won't be rutting. Always exercise caution around elk (and all other wildlife); never approach a wild animal and do not wander into the meadows during the mating season. Watch and listen from a safe distance (at least 25-100 feet) for your own and the wildlife's safety.

BEAR LAKE AREA

From its junction with U.S. 36 just west of the Beaver Meadows Entrance Station, the paved Bear Lake Road climbs nine miles through the forest before ending at beautiful **Bear Lake,** one of the park's well-known destinations. Along the way, the road passes a large **Park & Ride,** from which you can catch any of the free seasonal shuttles, including the orange line to Bear Lake, where the parking lot is almost always full. The road also passes the **Glacier Basin Campground** and several picnic areas and trailheads, including those at **Sprague Lake.**

★ Bear Lake

The shimmering, cobalt-blue waters of **Bear Lake** are nestled beneath the soaring summit of Hallett Peak, with many other impressive mountains, including Longs Peak, rising to the south and east. The stunning view of Longs Peak from the lake's northern shore is so iconic that the scene is the one displayed on the back of the Colorado state quarter.

The basin in which Bear Lake sits was scooped out by glaciers that repeatedly flowed down the Glacier Creek valley during the last Ice Age. After the final glacier melted away about 12,000 years ago, the bowl naturally filled with water to create today's sparkling gem. You can obtain a nice view of the lake by walking a short distance north of the parking area, but the best way to experience its beauty is by strolling the undulating, 0.5-mile-long **walking path** around it. From the shore, you'll enjoy great views of Longs and other towering peaks and get a good look at the mix of spruce, lodgepole pine, and fir trees typical of the park's moist sub-alpine ecosystem. There are also some nice stands of aspen, opportunistic organisms that took root here

a bugling bull elk

Bear Lake

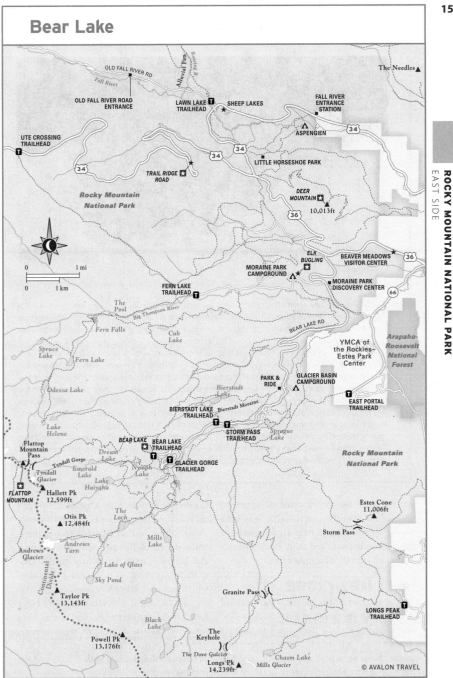

Above the Tree Line

krummholz

As you explore Colorado's Rocky Mountains, you'll undoubtedly hear the term **tree line,** a biological term for the edge of the habitat above which trees are unable to grow. Their extent is limited by the extremely cold temperatures, which drop sharply with increasing elevation. In places like Colorado where the air holds little moisture, this so-called **lapse rate** is 5.4°F per 1,000 feet in elevation gain. This means that the temperature outside Rocky's Alpine Visitor Center, at 11,796 feet in elevation, is typically about 23°F cooler than the temperature in downtown Estes Park (which is why Trail Ridge visitors should always bring extra layers). The lapse rate has important biological implications because there is a point beyond which trees cannot tolerate the harsh climate. Depending upon which direction the slope is facing and other local conditions, tree line in Colorado typically occurs between 11,000 and 12,000 feet. As you climb, the trees become increasingly shorter until an abrupt "last stand" of trees, which are typically stunted, forming gnarly, matted bushes called **krummholz** (the German word for twisted wood). Beyond tree line lies the windswept tundra, where few living things can survive year-round due to the inhospitable weather, intense sunlight, lack of nutrients, and the extremely short growing season.

after a big forest fire (caused by campers) burned much of the area in 1900. Bear Lake is also a great place to begin more extended hikes as well as relax and enjoy a delicious picnic along with the stunning views.

★ LUMPY RIDGE

In the portion of the national park east of U.S. 34 and due north of Estes Park, a dramatic line of rocky cliffs known as **Lumpy Ridge** rises high above the town. The name comes from its bumpy appearance, which is typical of how Mother Nature breaks down the coarse granite rock. One of the ridge's most distinctive features is the **Twin Owls,** a rock formation that, from the proper angle, really does look like two owls perched on a slab known as the **Roosting Ramp.** Due to its topography, no roads cross the ridge, which is a well-known destination for hiking and technical rock climbing. The ridge is accessed from a trailhead on Devils Gulch Road, a continuation of MacGregor Avenue, which heads north from the stretch of U.S. 34 between the junction with U.S. 36 and the national park.

LONGS PEAK AND WILD BASIN

Lily Lake

Located at the toe of the Twin Sisters Peaks, Lily Lake is one of Rocky's most accessible alpine lakes. Lying just feet from Highway 7 about six miles south of Estes Park, this turquoise lake is a popular place to picnic and stroll along the shoreline, much like Enos Mills once did from his nearby cabin. The 0.8-mile-long, wheelchair-accessible trail is completely flat, making it an excellent outing for families and visitors not yet acclimated to the elevation.

Enos Mills Cabin Museum

When Enos Mills was 14 years old, he hitch-hiked from his family's farm to Kansas City, where he worked at a bakery until he'd earned enough to pay for his train fare to Denver. After arriving in Estes Park in 1884, Mills saw Longs Peak for the first time and fell in love with it. After his cousin led him to the summit in 1885, he began to guide people up the mountain, ultimately climbing the peak more than 60 times. Although he'd leave Estes Park in the winter to work other jobs and to travel, Mills consistently returned. Over the course of a couple of years, he built a simple homestead cabin in a wildflower-filled meadow with a stunning view of The Diamond on the east face of Longs Peak.

After a chance meeting with John Muir in California, who encouraged him to write about his travels and to pursue his interests in nature and conservation, Mills began to advocate for wilderness preservation. He started to publish his writings in prestigious magazines and ultimately wrote 20 books. From 1909 until his death in 1922, Mills gave public talks around the country to generate support for conserving large areas of land. The culmination of his work came in 1915, when Congress created Rocky Mountain National Park.

With advance reservations, you can visit the Enos Mills Cabin Museum (6760 Hwy. 7, 970/586-4706, www.enosmills.com, tours by appointment, $20) to learn more about the fascinating "Father of Rocky Mountain National Park" during an hour-long tour led by one of his descendants. Housed in the wooden cabin built by Mills in 1885, the small museum has old photographs, letters, and other artifacts that help visitors appreciate the achievements of this accomplished naturalist. The highlights are the gorgeous scenery and the opportunity to learn about the family's history from one of Mill's relatives.

EAST SIDE

ROCKY MOUNTAIN NATIONAL PARK

the Twin Owls on Lumpy Ridge

Longs Peak

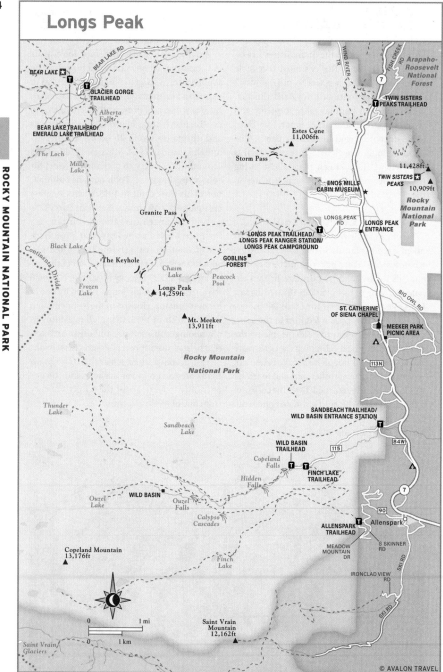

BEAR LAKE RD

BEAR LAKE

GLACIER GORGE
TRAILHEAD

Alberta
Falls

BEAR LAKE TRAILHEAD/
EMERALD LAKE TRAILHEAD

The Loch

Mills
Lake

Black Lake

The Keyhole

Granite Pass

Continental Divide

Frozen
Lake

Chasm
Lake

Longs Peak
14,259ft

Mt. Meeker
13,911ft

WIND RIVER TR

FISH CREEK RD

Arapaho-
Roosevelt
National
Forest

TWIN SISTERS
PEAKS TRAILHEAD

Estes Cone
11,006ft

Storm Pass

ENOS MILLS
CABIN MUSEUM

LONGS PEAK
RD

11,428ft

TWIN SISTERS
PEAKS   10,909ft

Rocky
Mountain
National
Park

LONGS PEAK
ENTRANCE

LONGS PEAK TRAILHEAD/
LONGS PEAK RANGER STATION/
LONGS PEAK CAMPGROUND

GOBLINS
FOREST

Peacock
Pool

BIG OWL RD

ST. CATHERINE
OF SIENA CHAPEL

MEEKER PARK
PICNIC AREA

Rocky Mountain

National Park

113N

Thunder
Lake

Sandbeach
Lake

SANDBEACH TRAILHEAD/
WILD BASIN ENTRANCE STATION

WILD BASIN
TRAILHEAD

84W

115

Copeland
Falls

FINCH LAKE
TRAILHEAD

Hidden
Falls

7

Ouzel
Lake

WILD BASIN

Ouzel
Falls

Calypso
Cascades

90

ALLENSPARK
TRAILHEAD

Allenspark

Copeland Mountain
13,176ft

Finch
Lake

MEADOW
MOUNTAIN
DR

S SKINNER
RD

SKI RD

IRONCLAD VIEW
RD

0   1 mi

0   1 km

Saint Vrain
Mountain
12,162ft

SKI RD

Saint Vrain
Glaciers

© AVALON TRAVEL

Longs Peak

The 14,259-foot **Longs Peak** is unique in many respects. It's the highest and most distinctive peak in Rocky Mountain National Park, the northernmost fourteener (a peak over 14,000 feet) in the Rockies, and it's the prominent peak featured on the Colorado state quarter. Along with its flat-topped summit, Longs' east face, which features a vertical, 1,000-foot, diamond-shaped wall called The Diamond, comprises one of the most iconic sights in Rocky Mountain National Park.

The mountain is named for Stephen Harriman Long, a major who in 1920 was reportedly the first U.S. government official to spot it. Members of John Wesley Powell's first survey expedition successfully ascended it in 1868. Because the mountain is so distinctive, Longs Peak is a very popular (but also very difficult) challenge for mountaineers and technical rock climbers, with about 30,000 people attempting to climb it each year.

The **Longs Peak trailhead** and **campground** (tents only) are located south of Estes Park at the end of a short spur road that leaves Highway 7 nine miles south of town.

Wild Basin

Tucked into the park's southeastern corner, beautiful **Wild Basin** is one of my favorite places in Rocky Mountain National Park. Its series of waterfalls and gorgeous wildflowers, including vivid clusters of delicate Colorado blue columbine (Colorado's state flower), make it a prime destination. Because of it outlying location, the crowds are often smaller than in the main park. Wild Basin is primarily a hiking destination, but **Lower Copeland Falls** lies just 0.3 mile from the Wild Basin trailhead, making it accessible to most visitors.

To reach Wild Basin from Estes Park, drive south on Highway 7 for 12.5 miles to the junction with Wild Basin Road. Turn right (west) onto this road. After 0.4 mile, turn right and follow the narrow gravel road for 2 miles to the trailhead.

RECREATION
Hiking

Hiking is the main recreational activity within Rocky Mountain National Park. With 355 miles of trails crisscrossing every region, hikes span a wide range of difficulty levels,

The Diamond on Longs Peak

lengths, elevations, and destinations, which range from lofty summits to roaring waterfalls. No matter which you choose, each one is a journey through the incredible landscape that comprises the nation's 10th national park.

Elevations within the park range from 7,500 feet to more than 14,000 feet and the weather changes quickly. It's important to properly acclimate before you hike; watch for symptoms of altitude sickness and take appropriate safety precautions. Before you hit the trail, check with a ranger or the backcountry office about the conditions, and obtain a map and detailed route description.

LAWN LAKE

A great path for exploring some of the extensive wilderness in the park's northeastern corner is the moderate **Lawn Lake Trail** (6.2 miles one-way). After departing from the Lawn Lake Trailhead on the Endovalley Road just west of its junction with U.S. 34, this trail follows the path of the Roaring River, providing good views of the devastation wrought here by the 1982 failure of the Lawn Lake Dam, en route to Lawn and Crystal Lakes. Additional (natural) flooding in 2013 took out a couple of bridges on this trail. While there are logs that you can cross, the route may be impassable when the water is high; check with the backcountry office or a ranger before you head out.

★ DEER MOUNTAIN

Although climbing a peak takes both physical and mental endurance, the thrill of standing on the summit, drinking in the panoramic, top-of-the-world views, is an incomparable experience. Fortunately, you don't need to be a technical rock climber to enjoy these rewards; Rocky Mountain National Park has several great peaks that acclimated and reasonably fit individuals can ascend. One of these is 10,013-foot **Deer Mountain** (3 miles one-way), whose modest 1,083-foot elevation gain on a straightforward trail makes it a great first summit and one that is usually accessible by late spring.

The trail begins at Deer Ridge Junction (U.S. 34 and U.S. 36), about three miles west of the Beaver Meadows Entrance Station. The route begins in a beautiful ponderosa pine forest, then crosses mostly open terrain, where there are great views of the steep and often-snow-covered Mummy Range. The route switchbacks up the mountain's western slopes before flattening out. At the junction about three miles from the trailhead, turn right to make the final climb to the summit, where there are fabulous views of Estes Park, Longs Peak, and the summits along the Continental Divide.

FERN LAKE

The **Fern Lake Trail** (3.8 miles one-way) follows an easy route along a creek through a deep and shady valley. From the trailhead to The Pool, a popular picnic and fishing spot, is a distance of 1.7 miles. From this point, the trail steadily climbs two miles past several pretty waterfalls along a fern-draped path to beautiful Fern Lake, nestled beneath the Little Matterhorn. You can either retrace your steps or create a nice loop by combining this route with the **Cub Lake Trail.** Both trails begin from their namesake trailheads on a spur road that branches off from Bear Lake Road, just south of its junction with U.S. 36.

BEAR LAKE

Bear Lake is the start of many fabulous walks, most of which follow a string of gorgeous, deep-blue lakes. The easy, 0.5-mile stroll around the shoreline suits most visitors. Hardier hikers can use the Emerald Lake Trailhead to follow the **Bear Lake Trail** to spritely Nymph Lake (0.5 mile one-way), then to celestial Dream Lake (1.1 miles one-way, 425 feet), and sparkling Lake Haiyaha (2.1 miles one-way). Alternatively, above Nymph Lake you can branch off to the west to reach Emerald Lake (1.8 miles one-way).

★ FLATTOP MOUNTAIN

The **Flattop Mountain Trail** (4.4 miles one-way) ascends 12,324-foot Flattop Mountain,

Bear Lake

National Scenic Trails, both of which head into the park's western half and end in the vicinity of Grand Lake Village. The sweeping summit views include the Never Summer and Mummy Ranges, the distinctive Notchtop Peak to the north, and Hallett Peak, the prominent peak to the south, which requires another 0.75 mile and 400 feet to climb.

GLACIER GORGE

From the **Glacier Gorge Trailhead,** located a few switchbacks east of Bear Lake, there are several more amazing trails, including the short hike to the 30-foot-tall **Alberta Falls** (0.8 mile one-way). From here you can continue on to a couple of alpine lakes. At the junction with the North Longs Peak Trail about 1.6 miles from the trailhead, turn right. Half a mile later, at the Mills Junction, turn left (east) and continue to **Mills Lake** (2.8 miles one-way, 750 feet) and **Black Lake** (5 miles one-way).

If you turn instead right at the Mills Junction to follow the **Loch Vale Trail,** this leads past a series of waterfalls and lakes to **Sky Pond** (4.9 miles one-way), one of my favorite places in the park due to its remoteness, its stunning backdrop, and its crystal-clear waters. Some scrambling is required to get there.

LUMPY RIDGE

One of the best moderate trails in the park is the classic route to **Gem Lake** (1.6 miles one-way) on Lumpy Ridge. This route climbs steadily from the **Lumpy Ridge Trailhead** through evergreen forest and sparkling ancient granite, which ice, wind, and rain have sculpted over millions of years into the ridge's distinctive knobs. At the junction with the Black Canyon Trail about half a mile from the trailhead, veer to the right (east) to head toward the lake. This section has many aspen trees, making it a great place to visit in early autumn when the leaves slowly turn to gold. About 1.5 miles from the trailhead, after ascending several small switchbacks, you'll reach a distinctive rock formation creatively

located right on the Continental Divide. This historic route begins at the **Bear Lake Trailhead** at the very end of Bear Lake Road (9 miles west of the U.S. 36 turnoff). From the trailhead, turn right onto the Bear Lake Loop Trail, then right again onto the Flattop Mountain Trail, where it crosses through a stand of quaking aspen and climbs a steep pile of debris left behind by a glacier.

At the junction about half a mile from the trailhead, turn left to continue west for another half mile to another junction. From here, turn left to follow the Flattop Mountain Trail up the mountain's steep eastern slopes. About 1.75 miles from the trailhead, the **Dream Lake Overlook** is a scenic spot to rest, with great views of Longs Peak. At about 2.4 miles, the trail passes tree line, and about 3 miles from the trailhead, the **Emerald Lake Overlook** has great views of the lake and Hallett Peak. About a mile farther, and just below the summit, the gradient lessens. The trail ends at the junction with the **North Inlet** and **Tonahutu Creek/Continental Divide** called Paul Bunyan's Boot (note the hole in the "sole"). From here, the final climb up to Gem Lake is steep, but the views along the way of Longs Peak, Mount Meeker, and Estes Park are well worth the effort. There are great places to rest along the lake, including several rocky outcrops and a small, sandy beach ideal for a well-deserved picnic.

★ TWIN SISTERS PEAKS

The adventure of hiking up the **Twin Sisters Peaks** (3.7 miles one-way) is one that you'll never forget. It's a Goldilocks peak—it's just the right amount of distance and vertical gain to make it memorable but still achievable for most acclimated and fit individuals. The views of Estes Park, the national park, and the Great Plains from the top are breathtaking. The trail begins at a trailhead reached by driving 6.3 miles south of Estes Park on Highway 7. Across the highway from (and just past) Lily Lake, turn left (east) and drive up the good gravel road for about half a mile to where it dead-ends at the trailhead; park along the road.

The first mile of the trail leads through the forest to a huge landslide that cut loose following the rain that fell in the area in September 2013. The landslide destroyed a short section of the trail and almost took out the buildings far below. Follow the well-trodden path, which is marked with stacks of rocks (cairns), across the landslide and continue on the path that climbs a series of switchbacks before rejoining the original trail about 1.6 miles from the trailhead. From here, the trail is easy to follow, with great views of Longs Peak the higher you climb. After reaching tree line at about 11,000 feet, the trail angles across a long, straight slope through granite slabs shattered by frost. This is the best area on the trail to look for squeaking picas and chirping marmots. About 3.25 miles from the start, the trail reaches the saddle between the Twin Sisters Peaks. From here, cairns mark the scramble to each summit, the highest of which is the 11,428-foot eastern peak. From the saddle and both summits, there are stunning, 360-degree views from the Continental Divide and Longs Peak to the vast Great Plains stretching far to the east.

near the top of the Twin Sisters

LONGS PEAK

The most famous ascent in Rocky Mountain National Park is the challenging **Keyhole Route** (8 miles one-way), which ascends 14,259-foot Longs Peak, the park's tallest and most distinctive mountain. During the summer when conditions allow, thousands of people attempt this difficult summit. The trail climbs nearly 5,000 vertical feet and involves scrambling, steep drop-offs, and extreme exposure to the highly changeable alpine weather. A pre-dawn start is essential, as is a detailed route description, a map, and appropriate safety gear. Consult the park service (www.nps.gov) for more extensive information, including a list of FAQs, and be certain to check with a ranger about the conditions before you start. The Longs Peak trailhead and campground are located south of Estes Park at the end of a short spur road that leaves Highway 7 nine miles south of town.

WILD BASIN

This area in the southeastern corner of the park is one of the best places to see waterfalls gushing in late spring through mid-summer and to search for wildflowers, especially the gorgeous purple-and-white columbine. The **Wild Basin Trailhead** accesses an extensive system of trails. One of the best routes for day hikers follows a string of waterfalls, beginning with **Copeland Falls** (0.3 mile one-way), then leading past an unnamed waterfall to the 200-foot-long **Calypso Cascades** (1.8 miles one-way) and 40-foot-high **Ouzel Falls** (2.7 miles one-way), named for a small bird that dives into water in search of food.

For a longer hike, continue up the trail to the next junction. The left (west) branch leads to **Ouzel Lake** (4.9 miles one-way) and eventually to pretty **Bluebird Lake** (6 miles one-way). The right (north) branch climbs to another junction, where you can turn left to reach **Thunder Lake** (6.8 miles one-way) or right to **Lion Lake No. 1** (7 miles one-way).

To reach Wild Basin from Estes Park, drive south on Highway 7 for 12.5 miles to the junction with Wild Basin Road. Turn right (west)

onto this road. After 0.4 mile, turn right into the national park and follow the narrow gravel road for 2 miles to the trailhead. Due to the presence of black bears in the area, day visitors must store all food, drinks, and toiletries in their trunks and close and lock the windows and doors. Overnight visitors must use the food storage lockers provided at the trailhead.

Backpacking

Rocky Mountain National Park has many backpacking options ranging from single-night stays to demanding, multi-day routes across the Continental Divide. Many of the day hikes can be extended overnight, such as the hike to **Fern Lake** (3.8 miles one-way), which leaves from Fern Lake Trailhead (at the end of the spur road near the start of Bear Lake Rd.).

Backcountry camping permits can be requested in advance in person (970/586-1242, www.pay.gov, $26 per reservation) or by stopping at the **Backcountry Permit Offices** (Beaver Meadows Visitor Center, http://rockymountainnationalpark.com), where you can obtain information and camping permits.

Rock Climbing

Rocky Mountain National Park is well known for its world-class rock climbing and mountaineering. These traditions started here in the late 1800s and include snow and ice routes, bouldering, and traditional (trad) and big-wall climbing. Because of this long history, trad climbing is the norm; participants are not allowed to place new bolts or create new holds.

The park's most famous multi-pitch technical route ascends **The Diamond,** the sheer, diamond-shaped alpine wall on Longs Peak's upper-east face. **Lumpy Ridge**'s granite walls feature almost 400 trad routes, including such classics as the 4-pitch Batman and Robin, the 4-pitch J Crack, and the challenging 2-pitch Finger Lickin' Good. The **Colorado Mountain School** (341 Moraine Ave., Estes Park, 970/586-4677, http://coloradomountainschool.com) is the state's largest guiding service and offers classes and guided rock climbing, ice, and mountaineering trips in Estes Park and beyond.

Horseback Riding

A fun way to experience the park's spectacular scenery and large network of trails is from the back of a trotting horse. There are two stables within the national park: **Moraine Park Stable** (549 Fern Lake Rd., 970/586-2327, www.sombrero.com, $55 for a 2-hour ride) and **Glacier Creek Stable** (on a spur road off of Bear Lake Rd., 9 miles south of U.S. 36, 970/586-3244, www.sombrero.com, $55 for a 2-hour ride). Both offer more than a dozen rides daily. The ride to Beaver Meadows from Moraine Park (2 hours) is open to ages two and older. The ride from Glacier Creek Stable (10 hours one-way) crosses the Continental Divide on the way to Grand Lake; return transport is provided. This full-day trip must be reserved well in advance.

Fishing

Sport fishing is popular both within the park and in the surrounding area's many lakes and streams. Four trout species—brook, brown, rainbow, and cutthroat—are found within the park, and suckers also reside in some of the lakes and streams. Two great locations for catch-and-release fishing are **Fern Lake** and **Lawn Lake,** both of which host native greenback cutthroat trout. A valid Colorado fishing license is required for everyone age 16 years and older.

The park stocks some of the native species to help restore their numbers. Rangers strictly enforce the possession limits and other regulations, which are detailed online (www.nps.gov).

Winter Sports

SLEDDING

Once a downhill ski area within the park, **Hidden Valley** (Trail Ridge. Rd., 10am-4pm daily in winter) has been redeveloped into a fun, do-it-yourself sledding and tubing hill complete with picnic tables, a warming hut (weekends and holidays), and (bonus!) year-round flush toilets. To reach

this snow play area from Estes Park, follow U.S. 36 west to the Beaver Meadows Entrance Station and continue north to U.S. 34. Take Trail Ridge Road west to the Hidden Valley parking lot.

CROSS-COUNTRY SKIING AND SNOWSHOEING

Many of the park's summer hiking trails make excellent snowshoeing and backcountry ski trails in winter, including a couple of short recreational trails that leave from **Hidden Valley.**

In winter, the park service offers several ranger-led snowshoeing and cross-country ski programs, including beginner **Snowshoe Walks** (www.nps.gov, Jan.-Mar., free), as well as snowshoeing and skiing programs on the west side. Although the programs are free, advance reservations are required.

If you're heading out on your own, be sure to check on the current conditions at one of the visitor centers and obtain an update from the **Colorado Avalanche Information Center** (http://avalanche.state.co.us).

FOOD

The **Trail Ridge Store** (Trail Ridge Rd., 10am-4:30pm daily in summer, $6-15) is the only place in the park where you can grab food or snacks. The combination café-gift shop is located next to the Alpine Visitor Center on Trail Ridge Road. While it's a handy place to stop for drinks, you're better off packing a lunch to enjoy at one of the many lovely picnic tables throughout the park.

CAMPING

There is no lodging available within Rocky Mountain National Park; camping is the only overnight option. It's very popular, and only a small number of sites are available, so make **reservations** (877/444-6777, www.recreation.gov) well in advance; reservations open up on December 1 for the following year. The park's east side has several choices; three campgrounds accept reservations.

The **Moraine Park Campground** (244

sites, Bear Lake Rd., www.recreation.gov, year-round, $18-26) sits tucked beneath a stand of ponderosa pines about 2.5 miles south of the Beaver Meadows Entrance Station. Sites accommodate tents and RVs (40 ft. max.) and facilities include vault and flush toilets, drinking water, a dump station, and access to both the park shuttle and the Estes Park hiker shuttle. In winter, toilets and drinking water are not available and sites are first-come, first-served.

Sites for tents and RVs (35 ft. max.) may be reserved at **Glacier Basin Campground** (150 sites, Bear Lake Rd., www.recreation.gov, June-Sept., $26), about six miles south of the Beaver Meadows Entrance Station. Facilities include drinking water, flush toilets, and food storage lockers, and there is a park shuttle stop nearby. Tent-only group sites ($4 per person) are also available.

The **Aspenglen Campground** (53 sites, U.S. 34, www.recreation.gov, late May-late Sept., $26) is located near the Fall River Visitor Center. Campsite reservations can be made for tents and RVs (30 ft. max.). Facilities include drinking water, flush toilets, and food storage lockers.

Located nine miles south of Estes Park just west of Highway 7, the **Longs Peak Campground** (26 sites, www.recreation.gov, first-come, first-served, June-Sept., $26) is the best place to stay if you're planning on an early start to climb Longs Peak. Sites are tent-only; vault toilets are available.

Backcountry Camping

To camp in the backcountry, you must obtain a permit. Permits are available in advance or on a space-available basis from one of the **Backcountry Permit Offices** (Beaver Creek Visitor Center, 970/586-1242, www.nps.gov/romo, $26 per reservation).

During the winter and early spring, you can self-register at the Wild Basin or Beaver Meadows Entrance Stations, the Longs Peak Ranger Station, and the Dunraven Trailhead. From June through September, campers are limited to a maximum of seven nights. The rest of the year the limit is 14 nights, with no more than 21 nights allowed per year.

TRANSPORTATION AND SERVICES

Car

In Estes Park, U.S. 36 (locally called Moraine Avenue) continues east to the Beaver Meadows Entrance Station in four miles. From Beaver Meadows, U.S. 36 continues west then north, passing Bear Lake Road to the south (which connects to Moraine Park and Bear Lake). At the Deer Mountain Junction, the road splits: Trail Ridge Road heads west, while U.S. 34 continues north to meet Old Fall River Road before veering west to the Fall River Visitor Center.

The Fall River Visitor Center on U.S. 34 offers convenient access to both Trail Ridge and Fall River Roads (open seasonally). In summer, Trail Ridge Road usually opens by Memorial Day weekend and remains open until mid-October. For the status of Trail Ridge Road, call 970/586-1222.

Shuttles

Both the town of Estes Park and the national park run summer shuttles, all of which are free, cut down on traffic and emissions within the park, and avoid the considerable hassle of trying to find a parking spot when all of the lots are filled, which happens nearly every summer day.

From the **Estes Park Visitor Center** (500 Big Thompson Ave., 800/443-7837, www.visitestespark.com, 9am-5pm Mon.-Sat., 10am-4pm Sun.), the national park's **Hiker Shuttle Route** (www.nps.gov, 7:30am-8pm daily late June-mid-Sept., 7:30am-8pm Sat.-Sun. mid-Sept.-mid-Oct., free) runs to the large **Park & Ride** (Bear Lake Rd.), with one stop at the Beaver Meadows Visitor Center on the way.

The national park has two additional shuttle bus routes. The orange **Bear Lake Route** (www.nps.gov, 7am-7pm daily, early May-mid-Oct.) runs every 10-15 minutes between the Park & Ride on Bear Lake Road and the end of the road at Bear Lake, with stops at the Bierstadt Lake Trailhead and Glacier Gorge Trailhead en route.

The green **Moraine Park Route** (www. nps.gov, 7am-7pm daily, late May-mid-Oct.) runs every half hour between the Park &

Ride on Bear Lake Road and the Fern Lake bus stop, with stops at Sprague Lake/Glacier Creek Livery, Hollowell Park, Tuxedo Park, Moraine Park Discovery Center, Moraine Park Campground (C Loop), and the Cub Lake Trailhead en route.

West Side

Away from the crowds in the park's eastern half and much farther removed from the Front Range cities, the western side of Rocky Mountain National Park is perceptibly quieter, even though its scenery is just as spectacular. If you're searching for wide-open views, star-filled skies, easy access to less-congested trails, wandering moose and other wildlife, and a fascinating glimpse into the lives of the hardy souls who once settled in this region, be sure to take a day or more to explore Rocky Mountain National Park's more wild western side.

The main entrance to the west side is through **Trail Ridge Road** (open May-mid-Oct.). To the south is the **Grand Lake Entrance Station** (U.S. 34), located just north of the town of Grand Lake.

KAWUNEECHE VALLEY
Trail Ridge Road

Descending the western side of **Trail Ridge Road,** you're treated to spectacular views of snow-capped peaks, the upper Colorado River Valley, lush meadows, dense pine forests, and glimpses of the shimmering blue waters of Grand and several other lakes far below. Although you can't drive into the remote Never Summer Range, which is part of a 21,000-acre wilderness area, there are great views of its craggy peaks during the descent, particularly from **Farview Curve,** a large pullout just above the seasonal closure gate and due east of the heavenly peaks. The range's name is loosely based on the translation of the native Arapaho name of Ni-chebe-chii, Never No Summer.

mining cabin at Holzwarth Historic Site

The Never Summer Range

the Never Summer Range from Trail Ridge Road

In the park's northwestern corner is a remote range of 17 peaks known as the Never Summer Range. Formed primarily by massive outpourings of volcanic rocks between about 25 and 30 million years ago and much more recently carved by glaciers, this range is one of the most rugged in the park, as well as one of the most isolated. No roads lead into the Never Summers, but for intrepid visitors, there are a handful of trails that explore the deep valleys and lofty peaks with ethereal names like Mount Cumulus, Mount Nimbus, and Mount Stratus. The network includes the Red Mountain Trail, from which you can take a spur to the Lake of the Clouds, a turquoise lake nestled beneath 12,797-foot Mount Cirrus; the Baker Gulch Trail, which accesses the Grand Ditch Trail that parallels part of a water diversion project that diverts up to 40 percent of the runoff from the Never Summers to the eastern plains; and the Bowen Gulch Trail, one segment of the 3,100-mile Continental Divide Trail that runs between Canada and Mexico.

Holzwarth Historic Site

The Holzwarth Historic Site (U.S. 36, mid-June-Labor Day) is the site homesteaded by German immigrant John Holzwarth Sr. after he unexpectedly lost his job as a saloon keeper in Denver when prohibition began in 1917. The spectacular setting and fabulous location adjacent to the national park quickly attracted visitors to the area. The family built a guest ranch, which John named the Holzwarth Trout Lodge, and for $2 a day guests could ride horses, fish, and hunt on the property. From the parking area, walk a short, smooth trail that crosses the Colorado River before looping through the historic buildings, a series of rustic, hand-hewn wooden cabins. Now empty, these buildings once housed the guests as well as a kitchen where John's wife, Sofia, prepared their meals.

Before John died, he sold the ranch to The Nature Conservancy to protect it in perpetuity. In 1975, this land was added to Rocky Mountain National Park, which has preserved the ranch to educate visitors about this aspect of Colorado history. Although the buildings are only open to visitors from mid-June through Labor Day, you can walk around the site any time of year. Next to the trailhead parking lot is an old miner's cabin, now empty.

Kawuneeche Valley

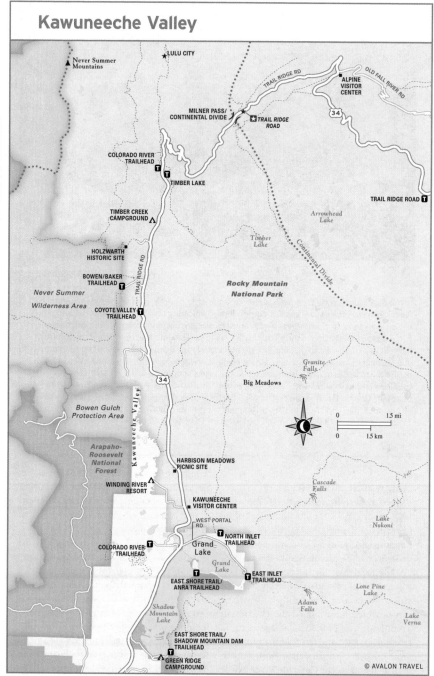

Never Summer
Mountains

★ LULU CITY

TRAIL RIDGE RD

OLD FALL RIVER RD

ALPINE
VISITOR
CENTER

MILNER PASS/
CONTINENTAL DIVIDE

34

★ TRAIL RIDGE
ROAD

COLORADO RIVER
TRAILHEAD 🅣

🅣 TIMBER LAKE

TRAIL RIDGE ROAD 🅣

TIMBER CREEK
CAMPGROUND ⛺

Arrowhead
Lake

Timber
Lake

Continental Divide

HOLZWARTH
HISTORIC SITE

TRAIL RIDGE RD

BOWEN/BAKER
TRAILHEAD 🅣

Never Summer
Wilderness Area

Rocky Mountain
National Park

COYOTE VALLEY 🅣
TRAILHEAD

Granite
Falls

34

Big Meadows

0   1.5 mi

0   1.5 km

Bowen Gulch
Protection Area

Kawuneeche Valley

Arapaho-
Roosevelt
National
Forest

HARBISON MEADOWS
PICNIC SITE

Cascade
Falls

WINDING RIVER ⛺
RESORT

■ KAWUNEECHE
VISITOR CENTER

Lake
Nokoni

WEST PORTAL
RD

🅣 NORTH INLET
TRAILHEAD

COLORADO RIVER 🅣
TRAILHEAD

Grand
Lake

Grand
Lake

🅣 EAST INLET
TRAILHEAD

🅣
EAST SHORE TRAIL/
ANRA TRAILHEAD

Adams
Falls

Lone Pine
Lake

Shadow
Mountain
Lake

Lake
Verna

EAST SHORE TRAIL/
SHADOW MOUNTAIN DAM
TRAILHEAD

🅣
GREEN RIDGE
CAMPGROUND

© AVALON TRAVEL

West Side Wildlife

Moose are plentiful on the park's west side.

The west side of Trail Ridge Road is a great place to spot wildlife, especially **moose,** the largest members of the deer family. Adults usually stand 6-7 feet tall at the shoulder, and large bulls can weigh up to 1,500 pounds and sport branching antlers up to 5 feet across and weighing 75 pounds. After mating season ends, the males drop their antlers to conserve energy throughout the long winter. The antlers begin to grow again in spring, taking up to five months to develop, and they usually grow back larger every year. Females bear their calves during the summer and are extremely protective of their young. Moose eat stems, buds, leaves, and bark, and their favorite snacks are aquatic plants (which are high in sodium and protein), along with willow and aspen bark. Since moose eat up to 70 pounds of food per day, they are usually found in wetland areas grazing on willows and tender plants.

As you drive along the **Kawuneeche Valley** (the native name for the upper Colorado River Valley, which translates as Valley of the Coyote), look across the marshy valley for munching moose, as well as the coyotes for whom the valley is named, plus elk and mule deer. Beavers are often observed at the **Beaver Ponds** on the west side of the road a few tenths of a mile past the **Timber Lake Trailhead.** Although sightings are quite rare, mountain lions can also sometimes be spotted in the valley, especially at dawn.

Peer into it to appreciate how simply miners lived at the beginning of the 20th century.

Holzwarth Historic Site is located off U.S. 34 less than 1 mile south of the Timber Creek Campground and 7.4 miles north of the Grand Lake Entrance Station.

Harbison Meadows

Harbison Meadows is the former site of two more homesteads belonging to sisters Annie and Kitty Harbison, who along with their family migrated here from Kansas in the late 1800s. Today, the empty grass meadows are a beautiful spot to enjoy a picnic lunch and watch for wildlife.

The picnic area is located off U.S. 34, about a mile north of the Kawuneeche Visitor Center.

Kawuneeche Visitor Center

The west side of Rocky Mountain National Park has just one entrance, which leads to the

Kawuneeche Visitor Center (16018 U.S. 34, Grand Lake, 970/627-3471, www.nps.gov, 8am-5pm daily in summer, 8am-4:30pm daily in winter, $20 per vehicle for a 1-day pass, $30 per vehicle for a 7-day pass). Stop here to orient yourself with displays about the Colorado River, maps, and a 20-minute film about the park. You can also reserve backcountry campsites.

RECREATION
Hiking

Rocky's west side has plenty of trails to explore, including several options well off the beaten path. Most day hikes can be extended into multi-day backpacks using the many beautiful backcountry camping sites scattered across the area. In winter, these trails are open to cross-country skiers and snowshoers; check at the Kawuneeche Visitor Center and the Colorado Avalanche Information Center (http://avalanche.state.co.us) for updates before you head out.

COLORADO RIVER TRAIL TO LULU CITY

From the Colorado River Trailhead just north of Trail Ridge Road's western seasonal closure gate, the easy Colorado River Trail (3.7 miles one-way) wanders through Shipler Park at the base of the Never Summer Range to Lulu City. This mining town was built in 1879 and, at its peak, had about 200 residents. After it was deserted, the wood was pilfered and reused at other settlements. Only the foundations from a couple of cabins remain.

North of Lulu City, the trail climbs about 1.5 miles past several small waterfalls to Little Yellowstone, so named due to its slight resemblance to the Grand Canyon of the Yellowstone in Yellowstone National Park. To extend your hike, continue north to La Poudre Pass and the headwaters of the Colorado River; here another trail leads to Specimen Mountain and eventually to Milner Pass on Trail Ridge Road. Alternatively, you can branch off to the west to reach the Grand Ditch and 11,331-foot Thunder Pass.

TIMBER LAKE

The Timber Lake Trail (4.6 miles one-way) climbs about 2,000 feet through the forest to an open basin and the chilly blue waters of Timber Lake, located beneath the nearly 13,000-foot summit of Mount Ida. The trailhead is located near the seasonal closure gate, just before the lowest hairpin curve on Trail Ridge Road.

PARIKA LAKE

About 1.5 miles south of the Holzwarth Historic Site, the Bowen/Baker Trailhead is the start of a strenuous day hike to Parika Lake (5.4 miles one-way), which climbs about 2,500 feet. The route crosses the river, then wanders for about a mile through the forest to the boundary of the Never Summer Wilderness. At the Y-junction, veer right toward Baker Gulch. The trail continues to climb through dense forest and open meadows (look for moose) before veering west to pretty Parika Lake.

For a great backpacking route, loop back to the trailhead by following the ridge to the south. Head east along the Continental Divide/Bowen Gulch Trail before taking a connector back to Backer Gulch.

COYOTE VALLEY

For a great sunset stroll with a good chance of spotting wildlife, drive to the Coyote Valley Trailhead. A one-mile, wheelchair-accessible trail crosses the river just 10 miles downstream of its origin. The trail meanders through the beautiful Kawuneeche Valley next to prime moose and elk habitat. River otter can also be spotted here, as can beaver, deer, coyotes, and several species of birds of prey, including golden eagles and fish-loving osprey. To extend your outing, bring a picnic dinner to enjoy at the wooden tables.

NORTH INLET TRAIL

North of Grand Lake, the North Inlet Trail offers several great hiking options. The closest destinations are the gushing Cascade

Falls (3.4 miles one-way) and the Big Pool, a swimming hole 4.8 miles from the trailhead. Other day hikes or backpacking trips include the amazing route over the Continental Divide to **Flattop Mountain** (12 miles one-way) and **Bear Lake** (17 miles one-way) on the east side. Alternatively, you can branch off onto the steeper **Lake Nanita Trail** (10.9 miles one-way), which leads to the park's largest lake, shimmering Lake Nanita.

To reach the trailhead from Grand Lake Village, head north on Hancock Road. At the junction with the West Portal Road, continue straight (uphill) on Road 663 to its end at the trailhead.

EAST INLET TRAIL

On Grand Lake's east side, the **East Inlet Trail** leads to pretty **Adams Falls.** Located just 0.3 mile from the trailhead, this short stroll showcases a pretty cascade of water tumbling down the final, steep pitch before mixing with the smooth waters of Grand Lake. For more of a workout, follow the trail to **Lone Pine Lake** (5.5 miles one-way), **Lake Verna** (6.9 miles one-way), **Spirit Lake** (8 miles one-way), and **Boulder-Grand Pass** (9.5 miles one-way).

To get to the trailhead from Grand Lake Village, head north on Garfield Street to its junction with West Portal Road. Turn right and continue down this road for about a mile, following the signs for Adams Falls. The trailhead parking area is on the left.

Backpacking

On the west side of the park, the **East Inlet Trailhead** (at the end of the only road leading to the east side of Grand Lake Village) leads to **Lake Verna** (13.8 miles one-way), passing **Lone Pine Lake** (11 miles round-trip) en route. From the nearby **North Inlet Trailhead,** located at the end of a spur that branches off from the same road, you can hike up and over the Continental Divide along the North Inlet Trail to Flattop Mountain, then follow the Flattop Mountain Trail to Bear Lake.

Fishing

The clear, rushing **Colorado River** is a great place for fly-fishing, especially for brown and cutthroat trout that like to lurk beneath overhanging banks and within the deep pools. Because the river is so close to its origin, it's usually pretty shallow and easy to wade through. There are a number of good access points along lower Trail Ridge Road, including the **Coyote Valley Trailhead,** the **Holzwarth Historic Site,** and several unnamed pullouts. The closest place to obtain a fishing license is in Grand Lake.

CAMPING

The only campground in the park's west half is **Timber Creek** (98 sites, www.recreation.gov, first-come, first-served, late May-early Nov., $26 per site), located just west of U.S. 34, about 10 miles north of Grand Lake. Sites accommodate tents and RVs (30 ft. max.), but services are limited to flush toilets and drinking water; generators are allowed (7:30am-10am and 4pm-8:30pm daily). Due to the pine beetle infestation, there is little shade.

To camp in the backcountry, obtain a permit in advance or on a space-available basis from the **Backcountry Permit Office** (Kawuneechee Visitor Center, 970/586-1242, www.nps.gov/romo, $26 per reservation).

TRANSPORTATION

Trail Ridge Road (U.S. 34, open May-mid-Oct.) is the only road into the park's west side. In summer, Trail Ridge Road is accessible from the east side at the junction of U.S. 34 and U.S. 36. In winter, the road closes and the west side must be accessed through the Grand Lake Entrance Station.

From Denver, follow I-70 west for about 29 miles to U.S. 40 (Exit 232). Follow U.S. 40 west for about 47 miles to the junction with U.S. 34, just north of Granby. Turn right onto U.S. 34 and drive 16 miles to the Grand Lake Entrance Station.

There is no public transport or shuttle service to the west side of Rocky Mountain National Park.

Grand Lake

West of the Continental Divide, Grand County stretches across a large and sparsely populated region replete with recreational opportunities. Of the county's roughly 1.2 million acres, 68 percent is owned by the federal government, including portions of Rocky Mountain National Park, several reservoirs and wildlife areas, and sections of the Arapaho-Roosevelt, Medicine Bow-Routt, and White River National Forests.

These abundant public lands feature a great diversity of terrain, from high mountain summits to deep river gorges and large lakes where boating and fishing are huge draws. This area is drained by dozens of streams, all of which flow into the upper Colorado River as it starts its grand journey to the sea.

The county hosts more than 600 miles of marked trails, 1,000 miles of rivers, 1,000 acres of alpine lakes, and 11,000 acres of reservoirs. Thanks to these merits, as well as the relatively quick access to Denver, Grand County is a serene part of the state where you can still easily escape for a day or a week to enjoy the abundant recreation, plentiful wildlife, small, friendly towns, and beautiful scenery.

SIGHTS

Located along the shores of Colorado's largest natural lake, the community of Grand Lake Village is the region's largest tourist hub and a great base for boating, fishing, and snowmobiling, as well as forays into the national forests and the western side of Rocky Mountain National Park.

A rustic two-story log cabin built in 1892, the **Kauffmann House Museum** (407 Pitkin St., 970/627-9644, http://grandcountyhistory.org, 11am-5pm daily Memorial Day-Aug., weekends in Sept., $5) served as a hotel until 1946. The region's only remaining 19th-century log hotel, the property is listed on the National Register of Historic Places.

Take a peek at the parlor: The original wallpaper has been reproduced except for one small portion, where the original wall, covered with 1893 newspapers and tin cans covering up the cracks, has been left exposed.

SPORTS AND RECREATION
Water Sports

The 568-acre **Grand Lake** is the state's deepest and largest natural lake. Located near the headwaters of the Colorado River, the shimmering, cobalt-blue lake fills a glacial valley dammed by debris unceremoniously dumped by the last glacier to cover this area before it began to melt away about 12,000 years ago. Once called Spirit Lake by the Ute, who avoided it because they believed spirits dwelled within its chilly waters, Grand Lake is fed by clear mountain streams tumbling out of Rocky Mountain National Park, which surrounds the lake on three sides.

A great place to start is **The Beach at Grand Lake** (between Hancock and Ellsworth Sts., 970/627-3435, www.townofgrandlake.com, dawn-dusk daily, free), part of the town's Lakefront Park. You can swim, picnic, fish, and lounge on the tiny sand beach, but the most popular outing is to paddle around the lake, which takes about two hours at a leisurely pace. You can also explore farther afield by paddling or boating right through the narrow channel connecting Grand with Shadow Mountain Lake, the larger reservoir directly west of Grand Lake.

EQUIPMENT RENTALS AND TOURS

In the heart of Grand Lake Village, **Rocky Mountain Outfitters** (900 Grand Ave., 970/798-8021, www.rkymtnoutfitters.com, 7am-6pm Mon.-Fri., 6:30am-6pm Sat.-Sun.) sells bait and tackle, rents fly-fishing equipment, and offers guided fishing trips year-round. The **Headwaters Marina** (the beach at Grand Lake, 970/627-5031, www.townof-grandlake.com/headwaters-marina, 10am-5pm Mon.-Thurs., 9am-5pm Fri.-Sun. late May-early Sept.) rents fishing, pedal, and pontoon boats by the hour ($25-115) and also offers scenic lake tours (10:30am, noon, and 2pm daily, $20), as well as one-hour sunset cruises (6pm Tues.-Wed. and Fri.-Sat., $20). Next door, the **Kayak Shack** (1030 Lake Ave., 970/531-6334, www.mountainpaddlers.com, 8am-6pm daily late May-early Sept., $20-40 per hour) rents out tandem, solo, and junior-sized kayaks. Just to the east, **Grand Lake Marina** (Grand Lake waterfront, 970/627-9273, www.glmarina.com, 8am-5pm daily Memorial Day-mid June; 8am-7pm daily mid-June-Labor Day, $22-28 per hour for a kayak) rents out party, pontoon, and speed boats, as well as kayaks, canoes, and stand up paddle-boards by the hour or the day.

On the western shore of Shadow Mountain Lake, the **Trail Ridge Marina** (12634 U.S. 34, 970/627-3586, www.trailridgemarina.com, 9am-6pm daily May-Oct., $45-50 for 2 hours of kayaking) rents stand up paddle-boards, one- and two-person kayaks, and several types of boats. The lake is stocked with brown and other types of trout.

Horseback Riding

A great way to enjoy Grand County's wide-open spaces is by horseback. **Winding River Resort** (970/627-3215, www.windingriver-resort.com, late May-late Sept., $45-65) has one- and two-hour trail rides four times per day in summer, as well as pony and hay rides. In winter, the resort offers sleigh rides and also rents out snowmobiles. To get here from Grand Lake Village, head north on U.S. 34 for 1.5 miles. Across from the national park visitor center, turn left and follow Road 491 for 1.5 miles to the resort.

Golf

Designed by Dick Phelps, the city-operated **Grand Lake Golf Course** (1415 County Rd. 48, 970/627-8008, www.grandlakerecreation.com, $60-70 mid-June-Labor Day, $40-55

mid-May-mid-June and Labor Day-close) is surrounded by native trees and has great views of the high peaks in Rocky Mountain National Park. It's not unusual to have deer, fox, chipmunks, and even moose or elk watch you play a round.

Winter Sports

Grand Lake is also a center for winter recreation, particularly snowmobiling and ice fishing. Be sure to check with the Colorado Avalanche Information Center (http://avalanche.state.co.us) for updates before you head out.

CROSS-COUNTRY SKIING AND SNOWSHOEING

Grand County's ample public lands offer access to many miles of backcountry trails, some of which are groomed. The **Grand Lake Nordic Center** (1415 County Rd. 48, 970/627-8008, www.grandlakeski.com, 9am-4pm daily in season, $16 day pass, $16 per day ski rental) features 35 kilometers of groomed trails, equipment rentals, lessons, and guided snowshoe hikes on beginner to advanced terrain. Once per month, the center also offers full moon skis, after which you enjoy a roaring bonfire and steaming hot chocolate.

SNOWMOBILING

The self-dubbed Snowmobiling Capital of Colorado, Grand Lake Village leaves its streets snow-packed in winter so that snowmobilers can ride right through town on their way to the region's thousand-mile network of trails. If you don't have your own machine, you can rent one at **Lone Eagle Lodge** (712 Grand Ave., 970/627-3310, www.loneeaglelodge.com/wp, $110 per hour for 1 passenger) or **On the Trail Rentals** (1447 County Rd. 491, 970/627-0171, www.onthetrailrentals.com, $110-180 for 2 hours), from which you can directly access 130 miles of trails in Arapaho-Roosevelt National Forest.

Grand Adventures (304 W. Portal Rd., 970/726-9247, https://grandadventures.com, $105-150 for 2 hours) offers two-, four-, and eight-hour rentals and is a good source of information about local routes. If you're a beginner or prefer to ride in a group, Grand Adventures also offers several types of tours from its locations in Beaver Village (79309 U.S. 40, Winter Park) and Fraser Valley (566 County Rd. 721). These include a two-hour Continental Divide Adventure ($115-175 for 1-2 people), which follows a historic railroad route up to 11,676-foot Rollins Pass, and a more advanced two-hour Trailblazer tour ($105-165 for 1-2 people).

Good sources of information include the nonprofit **Grand Lake Trail Groomers** (www.grandlaketrailgroomers.com), which maintains more than 80 miles of snowmobile trails in and around Grand Lake Village, and the **Colorado Snowmobile Association** (www.coloradosledcity.com).

ICE FISHING
Since fish don't hibernate, there's no reason to let a little cold stop you from catching one of Grand County's trophy trout. You can rent ice rods, shelters, and augers from **Rocky Mountain Outfitters** (900 Grand Ave., 970/798-8021, www.rkymtnoutfitters.com, 7am-6pm Mon.-Fri., 6:30am-6pm Sat.-Sun.), which also offers ice fishing setups and year-round guided fishing trips.

ENTERTAINMENT
Surprising given the town's population of 450 people, Grand Lake is home to what the *Denver Post* called "Colorado's premier summer musical company." At the **Rocky Mountain Repertory Theatre** (800 Grand Ave., 970/627-3421, www.rockymountain-rep.com, box office 10am-4pm Mon.-Thurs., 10am-1pm Fri., $35-45), more than 1,200 actors audition each year for the honor of performing in one of the rotating series of Broadway musicals produced in the state-of-the-art venue. Starting in mid-June, performances run throughout summer and have included hit shows such as *The Addams Family, Rock of Ages,* and Disney's *The Little Mermaid*.

SHOPPING
Jackstraw Mountain Gallery (1030 Grand Ave., 970/627-8111, www.jackstrawgallery.com, 10:30am-5:30pm daily) showcases the work of pastel artist (and interior designer) Marjorie Cranston, who uses the space as a studio as well as a shop, where she sells her beautiful drawings of quintessential Rocky Mountain scenery, plus some neat furniture and accessories. For the young at heart, the **Quacker Gift Shop** (1034 Grand Ave., 970/798-8014, www.quackergiftshop.com, 10:30am-5pm Mon.-Fri., 10:30am-6pm Sat., 11am-4pm Sun.) is a rubber duckie superstore that is "the most quacktacular place on Earth." Where else can you buy a snowboarder or day spa rubber duckie? **Cascades of the Rockies** (928 Grand Ave., 970/627-8166, https://grandlakebookstore.com, 11am-5pm daily), Grand County's only bookstore, specializes in adventure, Colorado-related, and kids' books.

Cabin Quilts & Stitches (908 Grand Ave., 970/627-3810, www.cabinquiltsnstitches.com, 10am-5pm Sun.-Fri., 10am-6pm Sat.) has more than 1,700 bolts of fabric and other crafty items, as well as tasteful gifts, "by the lake" home and kitchen accessories, and a few baby items. Across the street, **Never Summer Mountain Products** (919 Grand Ave., 970/627-3642, www.neversummermtn.com, 9am-5:30pm daily in summer, call for spring, winter, and fall hours) has all the hiking and camping gear, outdoor clothing and footwear, and sporting equipment you'll need to get ready for your next adventure. They also rent cross-country skis, snowshoes, strollers, and bear canisters.

Grand Lake Village has plenty of spots to satisfy your sweet tooth, including **Grand Lake Chocolates** (918 Grand Ave., 970/627-9494, 11am-9pm Mon.-Wed., 11am-10pm Thurs.-Fri. and Sun., 11am-11pm Sat.) and **Polly's Sweet Shop** (1106 Grand Ave., hours vary).

FOOD
For a delicious cup of morning joe or a post-hike chocolate espresso drink, stop by the

Colorado River Headwaters Scenic and Historic Byway

The headwaters of the Colorado River begin on the park's west side.

Designated in 2005, the 69-mile-long Colorado River Headwaters Scenic and Historic Byway visits the source of what is arguably the American West's most important river because it provides water and power to about 40 million people across the Southwest. Although the Colorado River is most commonly linked with the Grand Canyon and the southwestern desert, it begins as a clear mountain stream at 10,184-foot La Poudre Pass on the northern boundary of Rocky Mountain National Park. From this lofty origin, the river begins its epic 1,440-mile journey through seven states and northern Mexico, where it joins the sea in the Gulf of California. Even though the headwaters are in Colorado and the state is the source of more than half of the river's water, Colorado has rights to less than one-quarter of its flow. The remainder continues downhill to thirsty cites and fertile fields in Arizona, California, and northern Mexico.

From its start at the **Grand Lake Visitors Center** on U.S. 34, this byway, which takes a couple of hours to drive, drops 1,700 feet along the Colorado's uppermost course. Heading south from Grand Lake, the byway passes three beautiful lakes nestled in the shadow of the high Rockies before reaching the old railroad town of **Granby,** where the route veers onto U.S. 40. The byway continues to parallel the river past open grasslands and scattered ranches to the hamlet of **Hot Sulphur Springs,** once a winter campground for native Utes, who used the springs for healing purposes. From here, the road leads to **Kremmling,** where the route briefly heads south on Highway 9 before veering west onto Trough Road (Road 1), a former wagon trail that leads to **State Bridge,** an old stagecoach stop and the site of Colorado's first grant to build a public bridge. Although it's passable year-round, this byway is most frequently visited during the warmer summer months. The stretch from Kremmling to State Bridge is a good gravel road, but not recommended for buses or large RVs, and there are only limited services available in this area.

family-owned **Back Forty Coffee & Tea Company** (1141 Grand Ave., 573/513-6779, www.backfortycoffee.com, 8am-5pm daily), where the owners contribute all of the net profit to the fight against epilepsy. When you

walk in the door of the **Blue Water Bakery** (928 Grand Ave., 970/627-5416, http://bluewaterbakery.com, 6am-5pm daily, $6-9), the first thing you see (and smell) is a large glass case filled with flaky pastries. With a few outdoor tables, lots of nooks tucked between the cheerful yellow walls, and the lowest prices in town, the bakery is also a great place to stop by for breakfast (try the stuffed French toast) or lunch, when the bakery serves a large selection of hot and cold sandwiches and crispy salads.

For filling breakfast, lunch, and brunch options, try the popular ★ **Fat Cat Café** (916 Grand Ave., 970/627-0900, 7am-11am Mon., 7am-2pm Wed.-Fri., 7am-1pm Sat.-Sun., $8-15), where Miss Sally has been serving up filling breakfasts and homemade pie since 2006. On the weekends, there's a buffet that includes soup, salad, potatoes, fruit, eggs, meat, and a dozen types of pie. Weekdays, there are separate breakfast (7am-11am) and lunch menus featuring everything from stuffed three-egg omelets to a juicy French dip.

For some local color, mosey on over to the **Sagebrush BBQ & Grill** (1101 Grand Ave., 970/627-1404, www.sagebrushbbq.com, 7am-9pm daily, $9-33), which has two entrances—one for the restaurant and one for the bar, which you enter through a set of original, swinging jail doors made in the 1880s. Despite a Western atmosphere that's so relaxed that you can throw your peanut shells on the floor, the restaurant has a large and diverse menu of delicious food that goes well beyond traditional BBQ. Although it's best known for its ribs, steaks, burgers, and sausage platters, there are several fish and pasta dishes as well as vegetarian and gluten-free options. Sagebrush also offers a full breakfast menu (7am-11am daily) and a hiker's brown bag lunch.

The best pizza at 8,437 feet elevation can be had at **Grand Pizza** (1131 Grand Ave., 970/627-8390, www.grand-pizza.com, 11:30am-7pm Wed.-Thurs. and Sun., 11:30am-8pm Fri.-Sat., $10-15), where you can choose from 34 toppings and several pizza sauces, from traditional red to creamy garlic. Other options include sandwiches, salads, or spaghetti and meatballs. If you're a fan of spice, be sure to douse your food with their peppery Moose Juice hot sauce.

With floral print chairs, wooden accents, and only a few tables, the ★ **O A Bistro** (928 Grand Ave., 970/627-5080, http://o-abistro. com, noon-3pm and 5:30pm-8pm Fri., 8am-11am, noon-3pm, and 5:30pm-8pm Sat., 8am-11am and noon-3pm Sun., $16-30) is Grand Lake Village's most upscale option. In addition to delicious breakfasts, the bistro has a wine bar/café where you can order small plates like garlic shrimp or Mediterranean bruschetta and choose from their extensive list of wines, which are all available by the bottle or the glass. Each weekend, the tiny dining room also features a limited selection of entrées, available as part of a two-course meal or a very reasonably priced two-hour, six-course feast with wine pairing.

ACCOMMODATIONS

Accommodations in Grand Lake are limited, so it's best to book ahead in May through September, by far the region's busiest season.

My top choice is the ★ **Grand Lake Lodge** (15500 U.S. 34, 970/627-3967, www. grandlakelodge.com, May-Sept., $150-155), a rustic mountain lodge with stunning views best enjoyed from one of the large porch swings. Perched on a mountainside above Grand Lake, and nearly encircled by the national park, this lodge has rented out rooms and cabins since 1920 (Henry Ford stayed here in 1927). A large reception area features an enormous circular fireplace surrounded by cozy chairs and mounted animal heads. The historic dining room, with its glossy wooden beams and dangling antler chandeliers, serves three meals daily, including a hot and cold breakfast buffet. The lodge also has laundry facilities and a recreation room. Guests can hike, ride horses, and play volleyball on the grounds, as well as swim in the heated pool. The lodge can be a little tricky to find. Descending Trail Ridge Road (U.S. 34) heading west, you'll pass the Kawuneeche Visitor Center. At the next curve, look for a small brown and white sign to the lodge; turn left onto a dirt road, which leads directly to the lodge.

Built in 2000, the family-owned **Gateway Inn** (200 W. Portal Rd., 970/627-2400, www.

gatewayinn.com, $145-195) has hotel-style rooms with two queen beds, a romantic canopy king room, and several spotless cabins (some with kitchens for long-term stays). No two rooms are alike, and if no one has booked the fancier rooms (with fireplaces and balconies), the owners will upgrade you for free. The large porch has great mountain views, cushy chairs, and fire pits; it's a great place to watch the stars pop out of the inky black sky. A spacious lounge hosts a free happy hour (4pm-6pm daily). No pets are allowed.

The **Western Riviera** (419 Garfield St., 970/627-3580, www.westernriv.com, $150-240) offers the town's only lakeside accommodations, including basic hotel rooms as well as cabins, some of which have great views of the lake. All are within steps of downtown.

Two miles south of town, the cozy **Black Bear Lodge** (12255 U.S. 34, 970/627-3654, http://blackbeargrandlake.com, $90-145) has 17 clean and cozy rooms, several of which can sleep up to six people; two rooms are pet-friendly. Amenities include a coffee maker, microwave, and flat-screen TV. A two-night minimum is required on summer and holiday weekends.

CAMPING

If you prefer to sleep out under the stars, the **Elk Creek Campground & RV Park** (143 County Rd. 48, 970/627-8502, www.elkcreek-camp.com, May 15-Oct 15, $29 per tent site) has graded, gravel RV and walk-in tent sites, as well as a tipi that can sleep up to eight people. Basic cabins can sleep up to five people, but you must bring your own bedding. To get here from Grand Village, head north on U.S. 34 for 0.4 mile, then turn left onto County Road 48 and follow this for 0.2 mile to the campground.

Three miles northwest of Grand Lake, the **Winding River Resort** (1447 County Rd. 491, 970/627-3215, www.windingriverresort.com, $35 per tent site) has tent and RV sites with full hookups, horse runs, cabins (bring your own linens, $60-75), and clean, comfortable lodge rooms ($110-135) with queen beds,

microwaves, mini fridges, and private baths. The resort also offers five cabins ($180-275) with full kitchens and baths that can accommodate up to 10 people (bring your own toiletries). To get here from Grand Lake Village, drive west on U.S. 34 for 1.5 miles. Across from the Kawuneeche Visitor Center, turn left onto Road 491 and follow this for 1.5 miles to the resort.

TRANSPORTATION AND SERVICES
Car

To reach Grand Lake from Denver, take I-70 west for 40 miles to U.S. 40 (Exit 232). Continue straight on U.S. 40 west for 47 miles to the junction with U.S. 34, just north of Granby. Turn right onto U.S. 34 and continue north for 15 miles to Grand Lake.

From Estes Park, **Trail Ridge Road** (U.S. 34, open May-mid-Oct.) is the only road into the park's west side. From the Alpine Visitor Center, it is 22 miles south on U.S. 34 to Grand Lake.

Services

The friendly staff at the **Grand Lake Visitor Center** (U.S. 34 and West Portal Rd., 970/627-3402, 10am-4pm daily in summer, 10am-4pm Mon.-Fri. in winter) help orient you and offer plenty of insider tips. Both the local chamber of commerce (http://grandlakechamber.com) and Grand County (www.visitgrandcounty.com) have helpful websites.

The closest medical care is in Granby, 15 miles to the southwest, where the **Middle Park Medical Center** (1000 Granby Park Dr. S., 970/887-5800, www.mpmc.org) operates a small facility, which includes emergency care.

ARAPAHO NATIONAL RECREATION AREA
Lake Granby

Just south of Shadow Mountain Lake, the much larger Lake Granby, the state's third-largest body of water, is a reservoir created as part of the Colorado-Big Thompson Project, an enormous water diversion scheme that sends water from the west side of the Rockies to the thirsty cities east of the divide. The centerpiece of the **Arapaho National Recreation Area** (www.fs.usda.gov), Lake Granby has two boat ramps (Sunset Point and Stillwater) and several campgrounds. A very popular fishing spot, the 7,000-acre lake is regularly stocked with trophy rainbow trout and kokanee salmon. Several marinas include **Indian Peaks Marina** (6862 U.S. 34, Granby, 970/887-3456, www.indianpeaksmarina.com, 8am-5pm Mon.-Thurs. and 8am-6pm Fri.-Sun. mid-May-mid-Oct., closed Wed. mid-Sept.-mid-Oct., $120-140 for 2-hr pontoon boat rental), which rents out slips, pontoon and speed boats, and unsinkable, James Bond-like Craig Cats (2-seat catamarans). The marina also has a bait and tackle shop as well as a small restaurant.

Hiking

Just east of Lake Granby's toe, tiny **Monarch Lake** is a peaceful spot with a 3.9-mile trail that circumnavigates its pristine shoreline. This easy trail begins at the lake's northwestern corner, where it's best to first head south on the **Arapaho Pass Trail,** which crosses a small dam with spectacular views of the towering Indian Peaks to the east. The trail bends east to follow the lake's southern shore to the junction with the **High Lonesome Trail.** This undulating path wanders about a mile through the trees, providing tantalizing glimpses of the lake, where you often spot people fishing for brook, brown, rainbow, and cutthroat trout, as well as moose who frequent this area. At the next junction, turn left (west) on the **Cascade Creek Trail,** which continues west through the shady lodgepole pine forest

before dropping down to the lake's northern shore and returning you all too soon to the trailhead. To get to the trailhead from Granby, follow U.S. 34 north for about six miles to the Arapaho Bay Road (Road 6). Turn right (east) and follow this good dirt road 10 miles to its end in a large parking lot.

The same trailhead offers many longer and more challenging hikes. By continuing on the Arapaho Pass Trail, you can hike to the 11,906-foot **Arapaho Pass** and **Junco Lake** (9.5 and 9.6 miles one-way from the trailhead, respectively), as well as to **Devils Thumb Park** (21 miles one-way from the trailhead). If you head left at the trailhead to follow the **Cascade Trail** along Monarch Lake's northern shore, you'll reach **Cascade Falls** (4.4 miles one-way), beautiful **Crater Lake** (7.3 miles one-way), and the Continental Divide at 12,542-foot **Pawnee Pass** (8.7 miles one-way).

Camping

If you don't mind the lack of electricity, there are half a dozen campgrounds within the Arapaho National Recreation Area (www.fs.usda.gov). The first-come, first-served **Sunset Point Campground** (1.5 miles east of U.S. 34 on County Rd. 6, late May-late Sept., $22) is located next to a boat ramp on the southeast end of Lake Granby. The campground has vault toilets and drinking water. The **Big Rock Campground** (www.recreation.gov, mid-May-mid-Oct., $19 per site), located at the end of the Arapaho Bay Road next to Monarch Lake, has plenty of hiking and fishing right outside your flap. A national recreation area fee ($5 per day) is required in addition to payment for each campsite.

Steamboat Springs and Northwest Colorado

Highlights

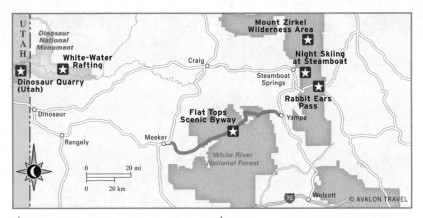

★ **Night Skiing at Steamboat:** Steamboat Ski Resort is one of the few places where you can swish down the slopes beneath the light of countless sparkling stars (page 183).

★ **Rabbit Ears Pass:** Straddle the Continental Divide atop this high mountain pass (page 183).

★ **Mount Zirkel Wilderness Area:** Escape to a simpler life of sun and sky in one of the state's most beautiful wilderness areas (page 187).

★ **Dinosaur Quarry:** This remote monument offers an irresistible mix of history, scenery, and recreation (page 200).

★ **White-Water Rafting:** Explore northwestern Colorado's tight, twisting Green and Yampa River canyons from the bottom up (page 204).

★ **Flat Tops Scenic Byway:** Get off the beaten path along this unpaved adventure through the forested Flat Top Mountains (page 207).

Stretching west of the Front Range, Colorado's "cowboy corner" is a remote and varied region of fertile forests, broad valleys, and immense expanses of windswept, arid land where herds of horses roam free.

Over vast sweeps of time, glaciers, wind, and rain have carved this landscape into an enchanting series of rugged mountaintops, towering sandstone cliffs, and wide, flat plateaus. This lengthy history has endowed the region with abundant recreation and many fascinating sights, including thousands of prehistoric petroglyphs, the deep and narrow canyons of the Yampa and Green Rivers, and the fossilized bones of giant dinosaurs.

The region's anchor is the ranching-turned-ski town of Steamboat Springs. Called Ski Town, USA®, for the many athletes it has sent to the Winter Olympics, this relaxed town of 12,000 is internationally renowned for its ski resort and celebrated Champagne Powder® snow. Aside from Steamboat, there are a few other year-round communities— small, scattered ranching towns like Craig, Meeker, and Yampa. Isolated in the winter, these communities blossom with wildflowers

in early summer, when adventurous visitors seek out the region's vast network of trails, untamed rivers teeming with trout, and acre upon acre of untouched wilderness. Between these towns are beautiful picnic spots, countless fishing holes, several small museums, and lonely outposts where some of the West's last outlaws once hid.

Whether you're searching for thrilling white-water rafting, new cowboy boots, or a sense of adventure in an undiscovered country, there's nowhere else like the northwestern corner of Colorado.

PLANNING YOUR TIME

In **winter,** Steamboat Springs is a destination in itself, and few people wander far from the powder-covered slopes. In **summer,** visitors use the town as a base from which to explore the state's vast northwestern corner. Set aside at least a **few days** to see some of the area's sparkling lakes, panoramic vistas,

---

Previous: northwestern Colorado; the Yampa River. **Above:** welcome sign for town of Dinosaur.

Steamboat Springs and Northwest Colorado

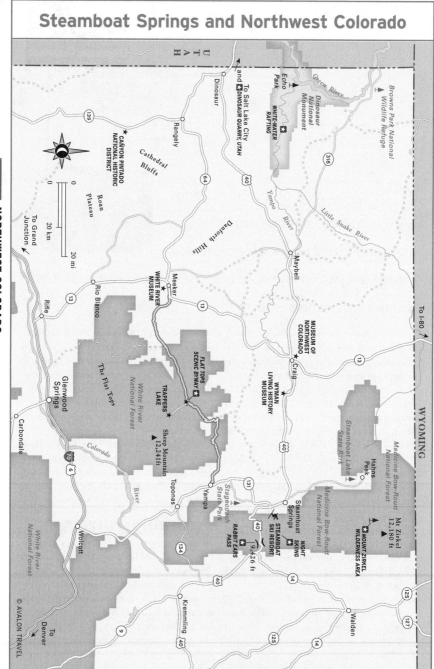

© AVALON TRAVEL

ancient dinosaur fossils, and carefully carved petroglyphs. To include rafting, hiking, angling, or any of the region's many other recreational activities, plan on **one week** in the area. If you can push your visit back to **late**

summer or **early autumn,** you'll miss some of the crowds and you'll have an opportunity to see Mother Nature's stunning fall foliage before snow once again drapes Steamboat's storied ski slopes.

Steamboat Springs

In 1913, Norwegian Carl Howelsen arrived in Steamboat Springs following a seven-year stint with the Barnum & Bailey Circus, where the "Flying Norseman" wowed crowds by skiing down a 100-foot slide greased with Vaseline, soaring over the backs of two circus elephants, and landing on a stage 75 feet away. Within a year of stepping off the train in Steamboat, Howelsen built a ski jump and introduced this virtually unheard-of sport to his adopted hometown, forever changing the community.

The Norseman's legacy endures today at Howelsen Hill, the small ski area he developed near downtown Steamboat. The town has sent an impressive 89 athletes to the Winter Olympics, including 14 to the 2014 games in Sochi, Russia—a larger delegation than many small countries. This success is due in large

part to the continuation of the youth training club that Howelsen organized, as well as the sport's growing popularity through fun festivities like the Winter Carnival, which the Norseman also started. Held in early February, this event embodies Steamboat's independent, fun-loving spirit with zany stunts like skiers jumping through hoops of fire, Olympic athletes flipping through the air, and a torchlight parade of LED-lit skiers gracefully turning down the Howelsen Hill slopes, followed by one of the country's largest fireworks displays.

The Winter Carnival is just one of many fun events regularly held in Steamboat. But it's also a great town to just visit, to ski some runs or ride a horse, relax in a hot spring, browse for Western wear along the historic main street, and simply linger over a cup of

NORTHWEST COLORADO
STEAMBOAT SPRINGS

downtown Steamboat Springs

coffee or a glass of wine in one of the town's noteworthy restaurants.

SIGHTS

Steamboat Springs is small and easy to navigate. Most of the attractions are in the historic downtown, which is centered on U.S. 40 (locally called Lincoln Avenue).

Museums

Housed in a 1901 Queen Anne-style Victorian home, the **Tread of Pioneers Museum** (800 Oak St., 970/879-2214, www.treadofpioneers. org, 11am-5pm Tues.-Sat., $5) has a number of interesting exhibits about the local history, including the Native Americans who enjoyed the area's thermal waters, the first pioneers who settled here, the evolution of skiing in the town, and the story of Harry Tracy, the local outlaw who once ran with Butch Cassidy. The museum also sponsors guided, weekly **Olympic heritage walking tours** (www. steamboatchamber.com, free), which visit Howelsen Hill, North America's largest natural ski-jumping complex, in winter, as well as summer downtown historical walking tours.

Located in a historic bank building built in 1905, the **Steamboat Art Museum** (801 Lincoln Ave., 970/870-1755, www.steamboatartmuseum.org, 11am-6pm Tues.-Sat., free) opened in 2005 with a mission of preserving and presenting northwestern Colorado art. In addition to seasonally rotating exhibits, the facility hosts regular workshops and a weeklong paint-out in June, when the wildflowers are blooming.

Hot Springs

In the early 1800s, trappers exploring the Yampa River Valley heard what they thought was the sound of a chugging steamboat engine. To their surprise, they discovered the noise was instead coming from a gurgling geyser that periodically shot jets of water up to 14 feet into the air. Although the spring gave the town its catchy name, it ceased to chug after crews damaged it while blasting out the railroad bed in 1909. You can still visit

Steamboat Spring (south side of the Yampa River northeast of the ball field) and six other historic springs following the do-it-yourself Springs of Steamboat Springs (www.treadofpioneers.org) walking tour available at the visitor center.

To enjoy a relaxing hot springs soak, visit the **Old Town Hot Springs** (136 Lincoln Ave., 970/879-1828, www.oldtownhotsprings. org, 5:30am-10pm Mon.-Fri., 7am-9pm Sat., 8am-9pm Sun., $18 per day), a modern aquatics and fitness center offering classes, childcare, massages, lap and hot pools, as well as kid-friendly fun like a floating obstacle course and 230-foot waterslides.

In the mountains seven miles northeast of town, **Strawberry Park Hot Springs** (44200 County Rd. 36, 970/879-0342, http:// strawberryhotsprings.com, 10am-10:30pm Sun.-Thurs., 10am-midnight Fri.-Sat., $15) is a more rustic facility featuring a series of 101-105°F pools in a natural environment along Hot Springs Creek; changing areas, picnic tables, and sparse cabins are available. The springs become clothing-optional after sunset (18 years and older only). To get here from downtown, head north on 7th Street. Turn right on Missouri Avenue, then turn left on North Park Road. After bending to the right, North Park turns into County Road 36. The last two miles to the hot springs are unpaved; in November-May, drivers without chains or a four-wheel drive vehicle can be ticketed, not to mention seriously stuck. Fortunately, **Sweet Pea Tours** (970/879-5820, http://sweetpeatours.com, $45 includes admission) provides year-round transport to the springs.

SPORTS AND RECREATION

While snowboarding and downhill skiing are Steamboat's biggest winter draws, the area also has great snowshoeing and cross-country skiing, particularly on nearby Rabbit Ears Pass. In summer, visitors choose from mellow hikes, horseback riding, and cycling to more adrenaline-packed adventures like floating in a hot air balloon or streaking down a zip line.

Steamboat Springs

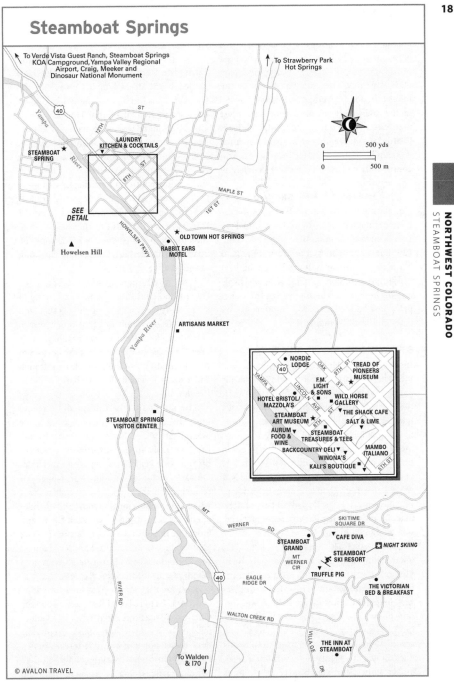

To Verde Vista Guest Ranch, Steamboat Springs KOA Campground, Yampa Valley Regional Airport, Craig, Meeker and Dinosaur National Monument

To Strawberry Park Hot Springs

40

Yampa

ST

7TH

12TH

LAUNDRY KITCHEN & COCKTAILS

STEAMBOAT SPRING

River

8TH ST

MAPLE ST

1ST ST

SEE DETAIL

HOWELSEN PKWY

OLD TOWN HOT SPRINGS

Howelsen Hill

RABBIT EARS MOTEL

0   500 yds

0   500 m

Yampa River

ARTISANS MARKET

NORDIC LODGE

40

TREAD OF PIONEERS MUSEUM

OAK ST

9TH ST

YAMPA ST

LINCOLN AVE

F.M. LIGHT & SONS

HOTEL BRISTOL/ MAZZOLA'S

WILD HORSE GALLERY

STEAMBOAT ART MUSEUM

8TH ST

THE SHACK CAFE

SALT & LIME

STEAMBOAT SPRINGS VISITOR CENTER

AURUM FOOD & WINE

STEAMBOAT TREASURES & TEES

BACKCOUNTRY DELI

WINONA'S

MAMBO ITALIANO

KALI'S BOUTIQUE

5TH ST

MT

WERNER   RD

SKI TIME SQUARE DR

CAFE DIVA

STEAMBOAT GRAND

MT WERNER CIR

STEAMBOAT SKI RESORT

NIGHT SKIING

40

EAGLE RIDGE DR

TRUFFLE PIG

RIVER RD

THE VICTORIAN BED & BREAKFAST

WALTON CREEK RD

VILLA GE

THE INN AT STEAMBOAT

To Walden & I70

DR

© AVALON TRAVEL

NORTHWEST COLORADO

STEAMBOAT SPRINGS

182

Downhill Skiing
and Snowboarding

Steamboat is best known for its snow, which is so smooth and light that the trademarked term Champagne Powder™ was coined here. Day after day, the fluffy flakes coat the mountain, for an average annual total of 350 inches, making it one of the state's snowiest mountains—and one of the most fun places to ride or ski. Steamboat is also known for its friendly, cowboy-hatted employees, who consistently go out of their way to be friendly and helpful.

The **Howelsen Hill Ski Area** (845 Howelsen Pkwy., 970/879-8499, www.steamboatsprings.net, 1pm-6pm Tues. and Fri., 1pm-8pm Wed.-Thurs., 10am-4pm Sat.-Sun., $25) has a handful each of green, blue, and black runs, plus the nation's largest natural ski-jumping complex. This local area also offers night skiing, which is worth the ticket price just to watch the ski jumpers flying through the chilly night air.

STEAMBOAT SKI RESORT

Inspired by Carl Howelsen's soaring success, locals began searching for terrain suitable for a much larger ski area. After World War II, they settled on Storm Mountain, located just a few miles south of Steamboat's historic downtown. Despite their lack of capital and equipment—one rancher bet founder Jim Temple a case of whiskey that he would fail—the resort opened in 1958 with one Poma lift. Clearly it wound up being a good long-term investment; in 2006, Intrawest, a Canadian corporation that also owns Winter Park, purchased the resort for $265 million.

Steamboat Ski Resort (970/879-6111, www.steamboat.com, late Nov.-early Apr., $160 full-day lift ticket) is a great area for intermediate and advanced boarders and skiers who love good snow, glade skiing, and terrain parks. The resort boasts a thigh-burning 3,668-foot vertical drop and 2,965 skiable acres. Although this is smaller than Vail's Back Bowls, it's plenty of terrain for a week on the slopes, and Steamboat's much lower

base elevation (6,900 feet) makes the altitude adjustment easier here than at many of Colorado's other resorts.

The resort has three peaks: **Storm** and **Sunshine Peaks,** as well as **Mt. Werner,** named for the local Olympic alpine skier who tragically died in an avalanche while filming a movie in Switzerland. The base area is Gondola Square, where the main gondola delivers you to the mid-mountain Thunderhead Lodge, from which you can access most of the resort. During busy weekends, however, the gondola is often a bottleneck, with waits that can exceed an hour. A locals' trick is to walk a little farther north and catch the Christie Peak Express lift, then ski down to the Thunderhead Express, which delivers you up to the Thunderhead Lodge—the same spot as the gondola.

With just 14 percent of Steamboat's 165 trails rated beginner (green), and many of these being cat tracks (windy roads that tend to be long, flat, and not that much fun to ski), Steamboat is not known as a beginner's area. The best of the lot are at the bottom of the mountain off of the short Bashor, Rough Rider, and—just upslope of the base area—the Preview lifts.

The abundance of intermediate (blue) and advanced (black) runs are what make Steamboat special. For a large concentration of blues, head to the Sunshine Express lift on Sunshine Peak to try the Western classics Quickdraw, Flintlock, and High Noon. For some great black runs, head to Storm Peak, which is infamous for whiteouts and its wide-open mogul fields on Storm Peak North and Storm Peak South. Great glade runs include Closets and Shadows off the Sundown Express lift, Twilight off the Sunshine Express, and Fetcher Glade off the Pony Express.

Steamboat is also a great area for snowboarders. Expert freeriders rave about the Christmas Tree Bowl and neighboring Chutes on the north side of Storm Peak. Freestylers have their choice of multiple terrain parks, ranging from the entry-level Lil' Rodeo, which features small boxes, jumps, and

NORTHWEST COLORADO
STEAMBOAT SPRINGS

rollers, as well as the Mini-Mav half-pipe, the little sister of the 450-foot-long, 18-foot-high Mavericks superpipe in the Mavericks Terrain Park, which also has jumps up to 70 feet high, plus the usual jibs, rails, and something called "log jobs." In between is the intermediate-level Rabbit Ears Park, accessible from the Main Drag Trail off the Christie Peak Express.

★ NIGHT SKIING

Steamboat Ski Resort is known for its **night skiing** (5:30pm-8:30pm Thurs.-Mon. mid-Dec.-late Feb., 6pm-9pm late Feb.-late Mar., $39), a treat only offered by one other major resort in the state. Night skiing is a very different experience, not least because of the totally different mood on the mountain. At night, crowds are a nonissue, and while you ride the Christie Peak Express up the mountain, it's dark, silent, and cold. When you reach the top, however, the brilliant floodlights are dazzling, especially through your goggles, which create some groovy patterns and colors. Once you hop off the lift, you can choose between several black and blue trails, including Sitz, See Me, and Vogue, as well as one green, Stampede, accessible from the intermediate unloading area. All of the runs are groomed, and the visibility is comparable to a cloudy day, but the experience is quite different because of the shadows and the stillness. Best of all, there are no lift lines, even on a holiday weekend, and there's an upbeat, celebratory mood. If the skies are clear, you're also treated to the beautiful alpenglow followed by brilliant starlight; if it's snowing, you have the powder almost to yourself, plus the fun of catching snowflakes on your tongue.

LESSONS AND RENTALS

Since he retired from World Cup skiing, Olympic gold medalist Billy Kidd (not Billy the Kid) has directed the **Steamboat Ski & Snowboard School** (800/299-5017, www. steamboat.com, $234 for a full-day clinic including lift ticket), which offers group and private boarding and skiing lessons for ages six and up, as well as the highly acclaimed Billy

Kidd Performance Center, whose camps provide video analysis and personalized instruction for aspiring athletes. Even if you don't sign up for a lesson, you can ski down the mountain with the icon as part of his free 1pm clinic, which begins at the top of the Why Not Trail (near the top of the gondola). Although Kidd now wears a helmet instead of his signature Stetson hat, he's still entertaining and full of great stories and tips.

With five locations, including one at the main Gondola Square, **Steamboat Ski & Sport** (970/871-5358 or 800/859-9959, www. steamboat.com, $39-62 per day for an all-day board or ski package) is a convenient one-stop shop for all of your equipment needs. Book online at least a week in advance to save a few bucks.

Cross-Country Skiing and Snowshoeing

Steamboat boasts some excellent Nordic skiing. The **Steamboat Ski Touring Center** (1230 Steamboat Blvd., 970/879-8180, www. steamboatnordiccenter.com, 9am-5pm daily, $20 for all-day trail pass) has groomed trails for classic and skate skiing as well as separate snowshoeing trails along Fish Creek. Rentals and lessons are available, as are backcountry skiing and snowshoeing tours. The **Haymaker Nordic Center** (34855 E. U.S. 40, 970/879-9444, www.steamboatnordic-center.com, 9am-4pm daily, $20 for all-day trail pass) has eight kilometers of trails, all of which are rated easy, plus rentals. Pets can share in the fun here on Sundays, Mondays, and Thursdays.

The **Howelsen Hill Nordic Center** (845 Howelsen Pkwy., 970/871-7084, www.steam-boatsprings.net, $14 for all-day trail pass) has 21 kilometers of trails, the majority of which are rated expert level. The complex also has a tubing hill and an alpine slide.

★ Rabbit Ears Pass

Rabbit Ears Pass is a forested alpine area and recreation mecca a 20-minute drive southeast of Steamboat Springs. This high alpine plateau stretches seven miles along U.S. 40 between the 9,401-foot West Summit and the slightly higher crest, the 9,426-foot East Summit. Named for the prominent bunny-eared peak to the north, this pass straddles the Continental Divide, separating the Pacific-draining Yampa River from the Atlantic-bound North Platte River.

Thanks to its lofty position, Rabbit Ears provides some of the easiest access to the **Continental Divide Trail,** including a popular 16-mile biking and hiking segment that stretches north from Dumont Lake (north of the eastern summit on Road 315) to Buffalo Pass, 15 miles northeast of Steamboat Springs. Also accessible from the eastern summit is a beautiful and gentle trail up **Rabbit Ears Peak** (6 miles round-trip), where you can get an up-close look at the bunny ears—remnants of a series of volcanoes that belched lava and ash across this part of Colorado about 30 million years ago.

To get here from Steamboat Springs, follow U.S. 40 for 19 miles southeast, then turn left at the sign for Dumont Lake and follow Forest Road 315 for 1 mile to a historic marker. Turn left onto Forest Road 311 and, if your vehicle has enough clearance, drive another 0.25 mile to the junction with Forest Road 291.

Park here and follow Road 311 to the base of the peak.

Many other great trails branch off from U.S. 40 (accessible in summer to hikers, bikers, and equestrians, in winter to snowshoers, cross-country skiers, and snowmobilers), and the pass's west, middle, and east sno-parks provide easy winter parking. For something more ambitious, try cycling up the pass from Steamboat Springs—an especially amazing ride in September when the quaking aspen are turning gold. You can also fly over the treetops near the base of the pass with **Steamboat Zipline Adventures** (970/879-6500, www.steamboat.com, $125 includes round-trip transport).

Fat Biking

Fat biking (also called snow biking) involves riding through the snow on a bike with fat tires. It's a great workout and a fun way to get around while the flakes are still falling. Fat biking is offered at several local trail networks, including **Lake Catamount** (29554 County Rd. 18, 970/871-6667, http://steamboatxcski.com, 9am-4pm daily, $20 for all-day trail pass), a private golf club that allows public fat biking, snowshoeing, and skiing on its groomed paths. Dogs are allowed on two

volcanic peaks above Rabbit Ears Pass near Steamboat Springs

routes (Mon.-Thurs.) and lessons and rentals ($25 for fat bike, $20 for skis) are available. The **Howelsen Hill Nordic Center** (845 Howelsen Pkwy., 970/871-7084, www.steamboatsprings.net, $14 for an all-day pass) allows fat biking during limited hours. Rentals are available at **Ski Haus** (1457 Pine Grove Rd., 844/878-0385, http://skihaussteamboat.com, $30 per day).

Snowmobiling

Snowmobile tours are an increasingly popular way to explore the beautiful Routt National Forest. **Steamboat Snowmobile Tours** (31749 Forest Rd. 302, 970/879-6500, www.steamboatsnowmobile.com, 8am-10pm daily in winter, $129-329) offers two-hour to full-day tours for riders of all ability levels on Rabbit Ears Pass. The price includes shuttle service from your lodging to a mountain cabin, where you receive basic instruction and your gear before roaring off to explore winding paths through the snow-covered trees and open meadows with beautiful views. You can also combine a two-hour ride with dinner on a Sunset or Moonlight Dinner Tour.

High Mountain Snowmobile Tours (Seedhouse Rd., Clark, 970/879-9073, www.steamboatsnowmobile.com, 8am-10pm daily in winter, $129-329) is geared for higher ability levels. Tours begin about 24 miles northeast of town in the Elk Valley River. **Hahn's Peak Roadhouse** (60880 County Rd. 129, 970/879-4404, http://hahnspeakroadhouse.com, 7:30am-9pm daily, tours $105, rentals $195-225 for 4 hours), about 26 miles north of Steamboat Springs, offers two-hour guided snowmobile tours three times daily and rents snowmobiles. The roadhouse is a center for many additional winter activities, including sleigh rides, winter horseback riding, and ice fishing.

Dog Sledding

Drive your own team of Alaskan huskies along a beautiful 12.5-mile backcountry trail with **Grizzle-T Dog & Sled Works** (970/870-1782, www.steamboatdogsledding.com, $160 includes transport). Owned and operated by Kris Hoffman, an Iditarod musher who now breeds huskies for the Alaskan race, the emphasis is on learning how to drive your own team, but you can also come along for a ride.

Ice Climbing

If you've ever dreamed of hacking your way up a 200-foot-high frozen waterfall, **Rocky Mountain Ventures** (865 Weiss Cir. #776798, 970/870-8440, http://steamboatclimbing.com, $250 for 4 hours) will guide you through the experience. The price includes gear and transportation to Fish Creek Falls.

Hiking and Biking

Steamboat Springs has registered the name Bike Town USA® and actively encourages cycling. Most trails are multi-use, which means they're open to hikers, mountain bikers, and sometimes equestrians. The town's *Bike Guide* is available for free at the Visitor Center.

Steamboat Springs maintains 55 miles of trails in the area, including the paved 7.5-mile, multi-use **Yampa River Core Trail,** which runs along the river on the town's western edge. The trail passes many great picnic spots and parks along the way, including the **Yampa River Botanic Garden** (Trafalger Dr., 970/846-5172, www.yampariverbotanicpark.org, sunrise-sunset May-Oct., free) with six acres of peaceful ponds, sculptures, flower gardens, and native trees.

The second of Steamboat's three major trail systems is the **Spring Creek Trail** (Amethyst and East Maple Sts.), a 5.2-mile route accessed from a parking area; follow 4th Street northwest from downtown. The trail follows County Road 34 for 0.5 mile north to Spring Creek Park, then continues up the canyon, climbing along the creek to Dry Lake Campground. The town's third major trail system is the extensive network of multi-use trails on **Emerald Mountain** above Howelsen Hill. There are 24 miles of single and double tracks with great names like Root Canal and Lane of Pain. These are most easily accessed by crossing the Yampa River on the 5th Street Bridge, then turning right and following the road as it bends west and ends at the Howelsen Hill parking lots.

Steamboat Ski & Bike (442 Lincoln Ave., 970/879-9144, www.steamboatskiandbike. com, 9am-7pm Mon.-Sat., 9am-6pm Sun., $17-80 per day) rents a wide variety of bikes in summer as well as skis in winter.

STEAMBOAT SKI RESORT

During the summer, many of the **Steamboat Ski Resort** (970/879-6111, www.steamboat. com) trails are open to hikers and mountain bikers. The **Thunderhead Hiking Trail** (3.8 miles one-way) offers two great options. If you're acclimated, hike the 2,180 vertical feet to the top of the gondola and either hike back down or ride the gondola down for free (10am-4pm daily in summer). Alternatively, you can ride the gondola up ($23) and hike back down the slope. Bikes are not allowed on this trail, so it's a great option for families.

Mountain bikers can buy an all-day **Bike Access Pass** (10am-4pm Mon.-Sat., 9:30am-4pm Sun. mid-June-late Aug., 10am-4pm Fri.-Sun. early Sept.-late Sept., $39), which allows cyclists to bring their bikes up on the gondola to Thunderhead Lodge. Here you can explore more than 50 miles of downhill trails, as well as freeride terrain suitable for all ability levels, including gnarly sounding features like step down rollers, 10-foot wooden ladder step downs, and table-top dirt jumps.

STAGECOACH STATE PARK

In **Stagecoach State Park** (25500 County Rd. 14, Oak Creek, 970/736-2436, http://cpw. state.co.us, 6am-10pm daily, $7 day pass), the **Elk Run Trail** (4.5 miles one-way) is a great place for spotting wildlife. This wide gravel trail begins at the reservoir's southwestern tip and heads east. After the trail crosses the dam, you can either retrace your route or complete the "Grand Traverse" around the lake by continuing west on County Road 18 to the one-mile **Overlook Trail,** which wraps around the reservoir's north side to the mile-long **Lakeside Trail,** which joins up with County

Road 14 (once an old stagecoach route) and then County Road 16 to complete the loop.

From downtown, travel east on U.S. 40, then south on Highway 131 for five miles to County Road 14. Turn left and follow County Road 14 south for six miles to the park entrance. Pay the entry fee and continue south on County Road 14 to its junction with County Road 16. Turn left and park in the trailhead lot on the left.

STEAMBOAT LAKE STATE PARK

North of town, **Steamboat Lake State Park** (61105 County Rd. 129, Clark, 970/879-7019, http://cpw.state.co.us, $7 day pass) has several short, family-friendly strolls, including the **Poverty Bar Trail** (1.1 miles), which displays the area's gold mining history and connects to the extensive system of trails in the Routt National Forest. The most popular trail is the **Tombstone Nature Trail** (1.1 miles), a short and gentle walk with views of the lake interspersed with natural history displays. To reach the park from downtown Steamboat Springs, drive west on U.S. 40 to County Road 129 (Elk River Rd.). Turn north on County Road 129 and continue for 25 miles. Both trails begin at the Visitor Center, visible on the left.

MEDICINE BOW-ROUTT NATIONAL FOREST

The **Medicine Bow-Routt National Forest** (www.fs.usda.gov) encompasses more than 2.2 million acres stretching from the area around Steamboat Springs to southern Wyoming. The local **Hahns Peak/Bears Ears Ranger District** (925 Weiss Dr., 970/870-2299, www. fs.usda.gov, 8am-5pm Mon.-Fri.) is a great resource for information on the more than 80 maintained trails in the vicinity of Steamboat Springs.

One of the most popular trails is the short stroll to the 200-foot-high **Fish Creek Falls,** one of Colorado's prettiest waterfalls. There are great views of the gushing water from an overlook at the end of a wheelchair-accessible path a short walk from the parking lot. Or, follow the slightly longer dirt trail that descends

The Continental Divide Trail

Running along the backbone of the Rockies from Canada to Mexico, the **Continental Divide Trail** (http://continentaldividetrail.org) is one of the world's greatest long-distance trails. One-third of the hiking "triple crown," which also includes the Appalachian and Pacific Crest Trails, this route is the highest, most remote, and most challenging of all of America's National Scenic Trails, as well as one of the largest conservation efforts in American history. Because the route, which passes through five Western states, is currently only about 70 percent complete, through-hikers must still bushwhack through, or walk around, the incomplete sections.

Based just outside of Denver, the nonprofit **Continental Divide Trail Coalition** (http://continentaldividetrail.org), in partnership with federal land management agencies and tens of thousands of volunteers, is advocating for and working to complete the trail, which has been a dream since 1968, when the National Trails System Act was passed. Since few people can muster the 6-7 months of vacation time necessary to hike the entire route, most visitors experience shorter portions of the trail, which is marked as CDT on most Colorado maps.

Highlights of the 800 miles that cross through Colorado include the alpine tundra of the La Garita, Weminuche, and South San Juan Wilderness Areas, where the trail remains above 11,000 feet for almost 70 miles; the summit of 14,270-foot-high Grays Peak, the Continental Divide Trail's highest point; the 30 miles through Rocky Mountain National Park; and the gorgeous 21-mile stretch through the Mount Zirkel Wilderness between the **Buffalo Pass** and the **North Lake Trailheads,** a fantastic backpacking adventure easily accessible from Steamboat Springs.

to the falls' base and crosses an old bridge, where you're treated to a different perspective—and some refreshing spray—from this local landmark.

After crossing the creek, this path, officially known as the **Fish Creek National Recreation Trail** (#1102), continues another five miles to beautiful Long Lake, passing Upper Fish Creek Falls along the way. Just before Long Lake, the route intersects the **Mountain View Trail** (#1032), a popular biking and hiking route that leads to Storm Peak in the Steamboat Ski Area. Just east of the lake, the Fish Creek Falls Trail ends at the Continental Divide Trail (#1101). To visit the falls, follow Lincoln Avenue west to 3rd Street. Turn right (north) here and right again onto Fish Creek Falls Road. Follow this road for four miles to the parking area ($5 per vehicle).

★ **MOUNT ZIRKEL WILDERNESS AREA**
Tucked into the heart of Routt National Forest are 160,308 untrammeled acres of azure alpine lakes, lofty, snow-capped peaks, and pristine pine and spruce woodlands. The **Mount Zirkel Wilderness Area** (Medicine Bow-Routt National Forest, 307/745-2300, www.fs.usda.gov), and its highest peak, are both named for Ferdinand Zirkel, a German geologist who participated in the United States' 1867-1872 40th Parallel Survey. The Zirkel Wilderness Area straddles the Continental Divide and encompasses some of Colorado's highest and most rugged country, with 15 peaks exceeding 12,000 feet in elevation, as well as 70 alpine lakes. Despite the network of more than 150 miles of trails, lacing up your boots and heading into this remote and rugged landscape feels almost as adventurous today as it did for the region's earliest explorers.

The area's wonderful trails include the moderate **Gilpin Lake Trail** (#1161, 5.7 miles one-way), a gorgeous hike through dense conifer forest to one of the area's most popular destinations, Gilpin Lake, named for Colorado Territory's first governor. The trail has beautiful views of the jagged Sawtooth Range and offers the option of completing a great hiking or equestrian loop called the Zirkel Circle.

From the Slavonia Trailhead, walk 0.25 mile from the parking lot to where the trail forks; the left branch (#1161) heads toward Gilpin Lake. You will enter the wilderness area after 1.6 miles, and will reach the lake about 4 miles from the trailhead. After soaking up the amazing views across the 29-acre, cobalt-blue lake, either retrace your steps or complete the 11-mile **Zirkel Circle** by continuing up the trail and crossing the 9,840-foot saddle between Gilpin and Gold Creeks. Descend to the junction with the Gold Creek Trail (#1150), then turn right onto the trail, which leads back to the Slavonia Trailhead.

From the same trailhead, you can hike directly to **Gold Creek Lake** (#1150). Follow the right fork 0.25 mile from the parking lot. From the junction, reach the pretty, eight-acre lake in about three miles (one-way). It's a beautiful walk along the creek through shady fir and lodgepole pine forest, and you pass several small waterfalls en route. Another great option from the Slavonia Trailhead is the **Mica Basin Trail** (#1162). Begin this route by following the Gilpin Lake Trail, then branch off to the left onto Trail #1162 just after entering the wilderness area. From here, it's a steep 2.7-mile climb up to Mica Lake, above which tower Big Agnes and Little Agnes Mountains.

To get here from Steamboat Springs, head west on U.S. 40 for two miles, then turn right on County Road 129 (Elk River Rd.) and follow County Road 129 north about 18 miles to Forest Service Road 400 (Seedhouse Rd.). Turn right and follow Forest Service Road 400 east for 11 miles to the trailhead parking area.

Horseback Riding

Steamboat Springs is surrounded by ranches, and many offer trail rides from one hour to several days. One great option is **Saddleback Ranch** (37350 County Rd. 179, 970/879-3711, www.saddlebackranch.net, $55 for one hour), an 8,000-acre, fourth-generation working cattle ranch located about 17 miles southwest of town. Nestled in a valley below scenic Saddle Mountain, the ranch is a great place to explore on horseback via a one- or two-hour trail ride, a morning cattle drive, or a wagon or horseback dinner ride. In winter, Saddleback Ranch offers two-hour horseback rides as well as sleigh rides, tubing, and snowmobile tours.

Located 20 miles north in the community of Clark, **Del's Triangle 3 Ranch** (55675 County Rd. 62, Clark, 970/879-3495, https://steamboathorses.com, $55 for one hour) has been outfitting and riding horses through the

one of the amazing views along the Zirkel Circle

Wild and Wonderful North Park

In far northern Colorado, encircled by tall mountain ranges, is a wide, flat, and sparsely populated valley called **North Park**. The northernmost of three high-elevation, intermontane valleys in central Colorado, North Park encompasses roughly a million acres of land, about two-thirds of which are public. The park sits at an average elevation of about 8,800 feet and is a wonderful place to enjoy nature at its finest.

Inhabited long ago by Native Americans, and later by trappers and mountain men, the valley's windswept grasslands, sagebrush-dotted hills, and dense aspen groves support an impressive wildlife population, including an estimated 10,000 elk, along with antelope, deer, big horn sheep, black bears, and moose. Roughly 600 moose roam the park, which has been dubbed the Moose Viewing Capital of Colorado. Although these creatures can be spotted almost anywhere in the valley (including in its largest town, **Walden**), the best place to spot them is along the valley's eastern edge.

Walden in the North Park valley

Located near one of the valley's early logging camps, the 71,000-acre State Forest State Park has a **Moose Visitor Center** (56750 Hwy. 14, Walden, 970/723-8366, http://cpw.state.co.us, 9am-5pm daily, $7 day pass), where you can obtain maps and up-to-date information, and learn more about these wild creatures.

Fishing and birding are also huge draws to the park; **Lake John, Walden Reservoir,** and the **North Platte River** support large beaver and fish populations. In spring and fall, huge flocks of waterfowl migrate through the region. Look for these and other birds at the 23,000-acre **Arapaho National Wildlife Refuge** (County Rd. 32, Walden, www.fws.gov, 7am-3pm Mon.-Fri. year-round), where you can explore the Moose-Goose Nature Trail, follow an Auto Tour, search for shorebirds, and—after a beautiful sunset—gaze at the incredibly brilliant stars.

To reach the Walden area from Steamboat Springs, follow U.S. 40 south for about 24 miles to County Road 14 east. Turn left (east) onto County Road 14 and continue 32 miles north to the town of Walden.

Mount Zirkel Wilderness for more than 50 years. Trail rides follow narrow elk and deer paths and range in length from one hour to one day. The **Elk River Guest Ranch** (29840 County Rd. 64, Clark, 970/879-1946, www. elkrivergr.com, $59 for one hour) is a dude ranch located nearby on land homesteaded in 1902. It was once used as a summer camp for miners; now it offers rides through aspen and pine forests and open meadows overflowing with wildflowers.

Water Sports

One of the few white-water rafting companies based in Steamboat Springs, **Blue Sky West** (970/871-4260, blueskywestrafting.com, $75-98) tailors its trips to your preferences and current river flows. Early in the season (usually May-June), they run half-day trips on the Elk River, while later in the summer, trips usually head to the Colorado River.

Inner tubing through Steamboat Springs on the Yampa River is a popular summer activity. **Bucking Rainbow Outfitters** (730 Lincoln Ave., 970/879-8747, www.buckingrainbow.com, 10am-3:30pm daily, $18 includes shuttle and gear) and **Backdoor Sports** (841 Yampa St., 970/879-6249, http:// backdoorsports.com, 10am-4pm daily, $19 includes shuttle and gear) can rent you the gear you'll need and help organize a shuttle. Shoes and life jackets are required at higher flows. **Steamboat Lake State Park** (61105 County Rd. 129, Clark, 970/879-7019, http://steamboatlakemarina.com, $7 day pass) has a marina where you can fish, boat, water-ski, and swim at The Dutch Hill beach. **Stagecoach State Park** (25500 County Rd. 14, Oak Creek, 970/736-2436, http://cpw.state.co.us, 6am-10pm daily, $7 day pass) is centered around an 820-acre reservoir known for its great fishing, especially fast-growing rainbow trout. The marina rents non-motorized watercraft, including kayaks, canoes, and stand up paddleboards. Swimming is allowed in the designated area at the marina.

Golf
The Sheraton Steamboat Resort's **Rollingstone Ranch Golf Club** (1230 Steamboat Blvd., 970/879-1391, www.rollingstoneranchgolf.com, $119-159) is an 18-hole, par-72 championship course designed by Robert Trent Jones II. It's known for its stunning views, aspen- and pine-framed fairways, and water hazards, including beautiful Fish Creek, which flows through six of the holes. The **Haymaker Golf Course** (34855 U.S. 40 E., 970/870-1846, www.haymakergolf.com, $84-129 including cart) is an 18-hole, Audubon International-certified course owned by the city with nice valley views.

ENTERTAINMENT AND EVENTS
Nightlife
As you make your way off the slopes, a great place to head to is the **T-Bar** (2045 Ski Time Square Dr., 970/879-6652, 11am-9pm daily), the closest thing the resort has to a dive bar. Located near the base of the Christie III lift, this ski-patrol trailer-turned-watering hole has mostly outdoor seating and plenty of cold beer, as well as surprisingly good food (try the chorizo mac and cheese). A popular ski patrol hangout is the family-owned **Gondola Pub and Grill** (2305 Mt. Werner Cir., 970/879-4448, www.gondolapubandgrill.com,

8am-6pm daily in winter, 11am-5pm daily in summer), known for its happy hour (3pm-6pm) as well as its "powder clause"—if the 5am snow report says the mid-mountain has received more than six inches of snow, Bloody Marys are half-price until 11am. Whether it's actually easier to ski powder after a Bloody Mary is the subject of heated debate.

One of Billy Kidd's favorite haunts, the **Slopeside Grill** (1855 Ski Time Square Dr., 970/879-2916, http://slopesidegrill.com, 11am-midnight daily) has been named Steamboat's best après-ski spot by *Outside* magazine. It's known for its burgers, wood-fired pizza, and "the Beach," a large outdoor seating area where the restaurant sets up an enormous ice bar each spring.

The locally owned and operated **Mahogany Ridge Brewery & Grill** (435 Lincoln Ave., 970/879-3773, www.mahoganyridgesteamboat.com, 4pm-close daily) is a great place to hang out and sip a foamy brew. Consistently voted one of Steamboat's best bars, Mahogany has a great happy hour and the town's best late-night food. Don't leave town without trying the amber Alpenglow or the creamy, citrus-flavored Powder Clause. Sports fans will love the **Tap House** (729 Lincoln Ave., 970/879-2431, http://thetaphouse.com, 11am-2am Mon.-Fri., 10am-2am Sat.-Sun.), which has 50 HD TVs (try counting them), comfy booths, and 20 Colorado beers on tap.

Located next to the Yampa River, **Sunpie's Bistro** (735 Yampa Ave., 970/870-3360, noon-2am Mon.-Sat., 11am-2am Sun.) is one of the town's best late-night hangouts, especially in summer, when the cramped indoor seating expands outdoors to the river bank. Opened by a couple from Louisiana, Sunpie's retains its Big Easy appeal, including powerful hurricanes and filling po'boy sandwiches.

Downtown Steamboat's best place to catch live music (and dance the night away) is **Schmiggity's** (821 Lincoln Ave., 970/879-4100, http://schmiggitys.com, 7pm-2am daily, $10), which features a wide variety of shows from funk to "bad ass bass," as well as two-step dancing on Tuesday and karaoke every Wednesday night.

Festivals and Events

In keeping with its laid-back character and fun-loving spirit, Steamboat has a busy year-round calendar of festivities. Howelsen's **Winter Carnival** (Feb., $10 admission) is a five-day, mid-winter fest that includes plenty of ski jumping and parades of kids on skis (and adults on shovels) pulled down the main drag by horses. The spectacular Saturday night torchlight procession down Howelsen Hill always ends with the Lighted Man, whose battery-powered suit weighs 70 pounds.

Summer events include the **Steamboat Marathon** (Routt County Courthouse, 522 Lincoln Ave., June, $75-95), which, despite the altitude, is a great qualifying run since most of the course is downhill. The longstanding **Hot Air Balloon Rodeo** (Bald Eagle Lake, 35565 S. U.S. 40, mid-July, free) is a colorful mix of hot air balloon launches and unique balloon rodeo events. The **Steamboat All Arts Festival** (locations vary, mid-Aug.) features literary, visual, dance, and even culinary arts, as well as a juried art show; many of the events are free.

Over Labor Day, acrobatic air shows are the centerpiece of Steamboat's **Wild West Air Fest** (Sept., $10 per day), which includes vintage aircraft and car displays, plus a chili-cooking contest and a bull-riding event. The summer winds down with **Oktoberwest** (downtown and Steamboat Mountain Village, mid-Sept., free), a relaxing weekend of Rocky Mountain beer, musical entertainment, and great food at the ski resort.

SHOPPING

Shopping in Steamboat is concentrated in two areas: the ski resort's base village and the lively downtown, which has more innovative and affordable options. One highlight is **F. M. Light & Sons** (830 Lincoln Ave., 970/879-1822, http://fmlight.com, 8:30am-10pm Mon.-Sat., 9am-9pm Sun.), a Western wear shop founded in 1905 by Frank M. Light, his wife, Carrie, and their seven children after they moved here from Ohio to alleviate Frank's severe asthma. Within days of arriving, Light noticed the lack of a men's clothing store in town, and seven months later, he opened this shop, with the first day's receipts totaling $11.50, according to the store's website. Light survived the Great Depression by creating a mobile store on wheels, and he's also the one who crafted the captivating black and yellow

the Hot Air Balloon Rodeo

192

signs you saw driving into town. Now run by the family's fifth generation, the shop is a fun place to look for cowboy hats, flannel shirts, jeans, boots, and trinkets like sling shots, as well as take a photo of Lightning, the fiberglass horse that has faithfully stood outside the door since 1949.

Steamboat Treasures & Tees (743 Lincoln Ave., 970/879-1107, 10am-8pm daily) is the place to head for Colorado T-shirts and inexpensive trinkets like alien sunglasses. For more upscale clothing from designers such as BCBG, Desigual, and Qi, women should head to **Kali's Boutique** (525 Lincoln Ave., 970/870-6658, 10am-6pm Mon.-Sat., 11am-5pm Sun.), which has a good selection of accessories.

The **Artisans Market** (626 S. Lincoln Ave., 970/879-7512, www.steamboatartisansmarket.com, 11am-6pm daily) is a colorful and cluttered co-op featuring a fun and eclectic mix of antiques, toys, purses, pottery, photographs, and jewelry crafted by more than 150 Colorado artists. A few blocks away, the larger and more upscale **Steamboat Art Company** (903 Lincoln Ave., 970/879-3383, www.steamboat-art.com, 10am-8pm) has artfully arranged displays of cheerful home decor, locally made ceramics, glassware, clothing, and custom furniture.

Steamboat's main street has several nice art galleries, including the **Wild Horse Gallery** (802 Lincoln Ave., 970/879-5515, www.wildhorsegallery.com, 11am-6pm Tues.-Sat.), which features "fine contemporary realism" by local and nationally renowned artists, including drawings, etchings, jewelry, blown glass, and limited edition canvas prints. **Closer to the Sun Gallery** (635 Lincoln Ave., 970/879-1904, http://closertothesungallery.com, 11am-7pm Tues.-Sat.) bills itself as a small, refined gallery that showcases the work of the two co-owners, Johannah Hall and Jonathan Barrett, and many other artists in traditional and unusual mediums such as hand-cut paper and paper castings.

Steamboat Springs' only bookstore is **Off the Beaten Path** (68 9th St., 970/879-6830,

a historical plaque outside F. M. Light & Sons

www.steamboatbooks.com, 8am-6pm Mon.-Tues., 8am-8pm Wed.-Sat., 9am-6pm Sun. in winter, 8am-8pm Mon.-Sat., 9am-6pm Sun. in summer, reduced hours in spring and fall), located west of Lincoln Avenue. In addition to a large selection of travel guides, maps, New Age and kids' books (and a treehouse reading space), this great indie store has a nice café and sponsors many local events, including poetry readings, wine and sign parties, and concerts.

FOOD
Breakfast and Cafés
With all that fresh air and exercise, don't feel one bit guilty eating at ★ **Winona's** (617 Lincoln Ave., 970/879-2483, http://winonassteamboat.com, 7am-3pm daily, $7-14), even if you indulge in one of their enormous frosted cinnamon rolls, which have been featured in both *Bon Appetit* and *Gourmet* magazines. The wood-paneled restaurant is crammed full of tables packed with happy patrons scarfing down oversized portions of

home-cooked specialties like the bacon, spinach and crab Benedict topped with creamy Hollandaise sauce, cinnamon French toast made from their famous cinnamon-roll dough, or the long list of egg-stravaganza dishes like Greek omelets and tofu scramble that are well worth the usual wait to be seated. Definitely come hungry.

A popular downtown breakfast and lunch spot is The Shack Café (740 Lincoln Ave., 970/879-9975, 6am-2pm daily, $6-15), a diner-style establishment with a long wooden bar lined with green swivel stools. The café serves up generous portions of breakfast favorites like fluffy pancakes or biscuits and gravy, plus an extensive list of hot sandwiches.

Casual

For a quick grab-n-go sandwich, head to Backcountry Delicatessen (635 Lincoln Ave., 970/879-3617, http://backcountry-deli.com, 7am-5pm daily, $5-10), the original seed of what's blossomed into a five-store Colorado chain. Choose from one of the dozen specialty sandwiches, like the Backcountry Cuban, or build your own. It's located in the same mini-plaza as Skull Creek Greek (635 Lincoln Ave., 970/879-1339, www.skullcreekgreek.com, 11am-close daily, $5-7), an amazingly affordable eatery whose signature dish is the melt-in-your-mouth roasted lamb pita sandwich, served with thick and creamy tzatziki yogurt sauce. Their falafel is just as delicious, especially when followed by gooey baklava.

Salt & Lime (628 Lincoln Ave., 970/871-6277, www.suckalime.com, 11am-11pm daily, $10-15) is not your typical Mexican restaurant. With its chic-industrial white interior and updated menu classics, like potato-filled chile rellenos, mix-and-match tacos, and quirky side dishes like cauliflower hash, this restaurant introduces a fresh and flavorful twist on south-of-the-border food. Kids love the chips and salsa and the chicken *tinga* tacos, as well as the pop rock floater. It's also an inviting place for adults to stop by for a shot (or flight) of tequila.

Steamboat has two great Italian restaurants, both of which often have a wait. Modern Mambo Italiano (521 Lincoln Ave., 970/870-0500, www.mambos.com, 4pm-close daily, $10-26) has a great outdoor deck and even better food; just walking by and catching the delicious scent is enough to turn your feet toward the door. The piping-hot, personal-size pizzas and traditional spaghetti and meatballs will keep the kids happy while adults enjoy more contemporary dishes like an arugula and fennel salad or fava bean *agnolotti*. Mazzola's Italian Restaurant (917 Lincoln Ave., 970/879-2405, www.mazzolas.com, 5pm-10pm daily, $13-25) has a darker interior in the basement beneath the Hotel Bristol, but features equally delicious food, including homemade lobster tortellini, garlic-laced Alfredo pasta, and the Colorado-inspired, cheese-smothered bison lasagna.

Upscale

In the northeast corner of town, Laundry Kitchen & Cocktails (127 11th St., 970/870-0681, www.thelaundryrestaurant.com, 4:30pm-11pm Wed.-Sun., small plates $7-15) is a cozy brick-and-wood gastro-pub located in a historic building that once housed the Steamboat Laundry. Dinner here is a series of small charcuterie and smoked cheese plates, as well as seasonal dishes like hash, a satisfying combination of roasted Brussels sprouts mixed with bacon, goat cheese, and crispy onions. Ask the staff for pairing recommendations from the long wine list.

Perched on the bank above the Yampa River, Aurum Food & Wine (811 Yampa St., 970/879-9500, www.aurumsteamboat.com, 5pm-10pm daily, $28-55) has an inviting deck with gas fireplaces so that you can enjoy year-round views of Howelsen Hill across the running water. Executive chef Patrick Funk's new American cuisine highlights the seasonal flavors of local ingredients combined in innovative ways like buttermilk-marinated quail, served with garlic mash, Tabasco velouté, and other vegetables. Try to save enough room to try one of the tempting desserts, like the chocolate pot au crème served with sea salt caramel mousse and 23K Gold Flake. Live acoustic music (6pm-8pm Tues.-Sat.) is an added bonus.

At the ski resort, the business-casual **Café Diva** (Torian Plum Plaza, 1855 Ski Times Square Dr., 970/871-0508, www.cafediva.com, 5:30pm-close daily, $23-45), located close to the Steamboat Grand, first opened as a wine bar but has since expanded to include an intimate dining room that blends antique accents with a colorful, modern ambiance. Executive chef Kate Van Rensselaer Rench creates four seasonal menus per year; each focuses on family-farmed produce and locally sourced meats, like elk tenderloin, and sustainably harvested seafood such as seared diver scallops. The café has many vegetarian and gluten-free options, and a long wine list highlights Californian and French producers.

Located a few steps from the gondola, the **Truffle Pig** (2250 Après Ski Way, 970/879-7470, www.trufflepigrestaurant.com, 11:30am-10pm daily in winter, $19-45) has a warm and welcoming atmosphere. The blazing fire pit on the outdoor deck is a nice place to enjoy a light lunch or drinks and "squealin' good" appetizers (along with the great views). While the emphasis is on seafood and meat, the dinner menu also includes daily pasta dishes (try the rich lobster mac and cheese), a few vegetarian plates, and fresh salads.

ACCOMMODATIONS

The largest concentration of accommodations is around the ski resort's base area. Rates tend to rise the closer you get to the slopes and during the winter holidays. If you're willing to drive a bit farther, there are some cheaper (though not as upscale) options a few miles away. In summer, camping in the Routt National Forest is a great option to keep costs down.

$100-150

You can't miss the motel with the vintage pink bunny sign as you drive into town. Although a bit dated, the locally owned **Rabbit Ears Motel** (201 Lincoln Ave., 800/828-7702, www.rabbitearsmotel.com, $149-179) is centrally located, within walking distance of the downtown, and across the street from the Old Town Hot Springs. Rooms are small but clean and have everything a budget traveler needs, including a fridge. The staff is very friendly and helpful. It's about three miles from the motel to the gondola; two lines of the free city bus stop just a block away.

Right in the heart of downtown, the **Hotel Bristol** (917 Lincoln Ave., 800/851-0872, www.steamboathotelbristol.com, $129-169) is a historical property with 18 guest rooms. Built in 1948 by the local police chief, the distinctive blue building is adorned with colorful flowers in summer and festive lights in winter. The cozy lobby has a library, comfy couches, and a fireplace. While the rooms are small, they are attractively decorated with photographs of cowboys, overstuffed buffalo pillows, and other Western-themed decor. As with most historic properties, the hotel has thin walls, and most rooms have a shower but no tub.

$150-250

In a great location within easy walking distance of downtown, the comfortable ★ **Nordic Lodge** (1036 Lincoln Ave., 800/364-0331, www.nordiclodgeofsteamboat.com, $149-179) is one of Steamboat's best values. Each bright and spotlessly clean room is equipped with a small fridge and microwave, and the most recently remodeled bathrooms have granite countertops. Rooms range in size from one queen or king to two-bed and two-bedroom suites. Owned and operated by a friendly, local family, the hotel has a free shuttle to the ski resort, an extended continental breakfast, free Wi-Fi, and a large indoor hot tub. Pets are welcome for a fee ($20 per pet per night).

Over $250

The Inn at Steamboat (3070 Columbine Dr., 970/879-2600, www.innatsteamboat.com, $263-319) is an attractive

the Hotel Bristol

European-style boutique hotel located just four blocks from the gondola. If that's too far to clomp in ski boots, the inn offers a complimentary winter shuttle service to and from the base area, as well as free ski and bike storage. The outdoor hot tub and pool (heated year-round) are nice perks, as is the better-than-average continental breakfast (7am-10am daily). Some rooms have nice unobstructed views of the Yampa Valley; those on the top floor are the quietest.

If you feel like splurging, click your heels together to head to **The Victorian Bed & Breakfast** (2405 Ski Trail Lane, 970/879-7781, http://victoriansteamboat.com, $240-375), a lovingly maintained building originally built in Kansas in 1881, then dismantled into five pieces and transported 650 miles to Steamboat in 1991. In its new location below the gondola and within walking distance to the base area, The Victorian has transformed into a unique and luxurious bed-and-breakfast. Rent one of the five elegant suites or guest rooms, or rent out the entire house (sleeps 14) for a special event. Amenities include a theater room, pool table, delicious breakfast, complimentary happy hour, and a whirlpool hot tub on the deck with stunning views that remind you you're not in Kansas anymore.

Located a few minutes' walk from the gondola, the enormous, seven-story **Steamboat Grand** (2300 Mt. Werner Cir., 970/871-5500, http://steamboatgrand.com, $269-368) has 328 guest rooms, including standard king or double queen rooms, one-, two-, and three-bedroom condos, and eight luxurious penthouses. Rooms have a view of either Mount Werner or the Yampa Valley; on-site amenities include a nice fitness center, the Grand Spa, hot tubs, and an outdoor pool (heated year-round). The resort also offers slopeside board and ski storage, free shuttles downtown, and several dining options.

For a respite from your hectic life, escape to the **Vista Verde Guest Ranch** (58000 Cowboy Way, Clark, 800/526-7433, www.vistaverde.com, $565-600 per night all-inclusive), a luxury dude ranch 25 miles north of Steamboat Springs in the community of Clark. Guests rave about the experience, including the well-appointed accommodations, top-notch service, and scrumptious food. The myriad activities range from cooking classes to horseback riding and yoga.

Camping

Northwest of town, the **Steamboat Springs KOA Campground** (3603 Lincoln Ave., 800/562-7782, https://koa.com, 2-night minimum, $35-185) has wide gravel pads and hookups for RVs, grassy tent sites, and basic cabins with both private and shared bathrooms.

In the Medicine Bow-Routt National Forest, **Dry Lake** (Buffalo Pass Rd., www.fs.usda.gov, mid-June-late Oct., $10 per site) has eight sites available on a first-come, first-served basis. There are vault toilets, but no running water. From Steamboat Springs, drive 4 miles north on Routt County Road 36, then continue 3.6 miles east on Buffalo Pass Road.

TRANSPORTATION AND SERVICES

Air

Denver International Airport (DEN, 8500 Peña Blvd., 303/342-2000, http://www.flydenver.com) is the closest major airport to Steamboat Springs. The smaller **Yampa Valley Regional Airport** (HDN, 11005 RCR 51A, Hayden, 970/276-5000, www.yampavalleyregionalairport.com) offers direct summer flights from Denver, Houston, and Dallas/Fort Worth, and nonstop service from 10 major cities, including Atlanta, Chicago, New York, Houston, and Los Angeles, during ski season.

If you're focusing solely on Steamboat Springs, it may make sense to fly directly into the Yampa Valley Regional Airport (HDN), a 30-minute drive west. To reach Steamboat from the Yampa Valley airport, follow U.S. 40 east for about 26 miles. If you'd rather take advantage of the lower fares into Denver, the drive from the Front Range takes just four hours in good weather.

Car

Steamboat Springs is located along U.S. 40, the major east-west road through the region. West of town, U.S. 40 leads to Craig and, close to the border with Utah, the tiny settlement of Dinosaur, the gateway to Dinosaur National Monument. East of Steamboat, U.S. 40 climbs Rabbit Ears Pass before dropping toward Kremmling, from where Highway 9 leads south to Silverthorne and I-70. On the east side of Rabbit Ears Pass, Highway 14 branches off of U.S. 40 to head north across North Park and eventually reaches the Front Range near the town of Fort Collins.

To reach Steamboat Springs from Denver, drive west on I-70 for about 78 miles to Exit 205 for Silverthorne and Dillon. From this exit, turn right onto Highway 9 north for approximately 40 miles to the town of Kremmling. Turn left onto U.S. 40 and continue 50 miles west to Steamboat Springs.

The 156-mile drive takes about four hours, although it can take substantially longer during rush hour and/or inclement weather.

Avis, Budget, and Hertz have depots at the Yampa Valley Regional Airport. In town, **Cook Chevrolet** (970/701-4769) and **Steamboat Motor Rentals** (970/879-8880) offer a variety of rental cars.

Parking

During ski season, two free and convenient places to park are both accessed from U.S. 40. Driving north on U.S. 40 toward the resort, turn right after Walton Creek Road, then left onto Pine Grove Road. Continuing north, you'll arrive at **The Meadows Lot;** a free shuttle transports visitors to the base area. Or, after Walton Creek Road, turn right onto Bangtail Way; this leads to the **Wildhorse Lot.** It's a short walk from the Wildhorse Gondola, which quickly delivers you to the base area. The resort also operates several pay lots near the base area, although these often fill on weekends.

Shuttle and Bus

Several shuttle services provide transport to Steamboat Springs from both airports. **Go Alpine** (970/879-2800, www.goalpine.com, $93 one-way from DIA, $39 one-way from HDN) offers scheduled service several times daily to in-town locations. **Storm Mountain Express** (877/844-8787, www.stormmountainexpress.com, $38 one-way) offers shared shuttles from the Yampa Valley airport to Steamboat. **Greyhound** (www.greyhound.com, $23-50 one-way) provides service from downtown Denver to Steamboat Springs, although the ride can take quite a bit longer than a shuttle.

Steamboat's **bus system** (970/879-3717, http://steamboatsprings.net, year-round, free) shuttles people between the ski resort, downtown, and most lodgings. Six lines circulate about every 20 minutes. Service is reduced outside of the main ski season (early Dec.-mid-Apr.).

Services

VISITOR INFORMATION

The **Steamboat Springs Visitor Center** (125 Anglers Dr., 970/879-0880, www.steamboatchamber.com, 8am-5pm Mon.-Fri., 10am-3pm Sat. in winter, 8am-5pm Mon.-Fri., 10am-3pm Sat.-Sun. in summer, reduced hours in spring and fall) is located just west of U.S. 40 (across from McDonald's) between the ski resort and the historic downtown. Stop by for friendly help with reservations, information, free Wi-Fi, maps, and brochures.

For ski information, contact **Steamboat Ski Resort** (970/879-6111 and 877/783-2628, snow reports 970/879-7300, www.steamboat.com).

MEDIA AND COMMUNICATIONS

The *Steamboat Pilot & Today* (www.steamboattoday.com) features local news, sports, and events. KMFU Steamboat Springs (104.1 FM), the town's solar-powered adult rock station, KBCR country radio (96.9 FM), and KUNC (88.5 FM) all have a strong, community-oriented focus.

The **post office** (200 Lincoln Ave., 970/870-3001, 8:30am-5pm Mon.-Fri., 9am-noon Sat.) is located on the north side of the main street on the south side of town.

The **Bud Werner Memorial Library** (1289 Lincoln Ave., 970/879-0240, www.steamboatlibrary.org, 9am-8pm Mon.-Thurs., 9am-6pm Fri., 9am-5pm Sat., 10am-5pm Sun.) has free public Internet workstations and wireless Internet access.

MEDICAL

The **Yampa Valley Medical Center** (1024 Central Park Dr., 970/879-1322, www.yvmc.org) serves the entire valley. **Steamboat Medical** (1475 Pine Grove Rd. #102, 970/879-0203, www.steamboatmedical.com, 8am-7pm Mon.-Fri., 9am-2pm Sat., 9am-noon Sun.) offers urgent care seven days a week. The resort also has a ski patrol for slopeside emergencies.

197

NORTHWEST COLORADO
THE NORTHWEST CORNER

The Northwest Corner

You don't need to travel very far west from Steamboat Springs' ski slopes to feel as though you've stepped onto a different planet. Instead of snowy peaks and sparkling alpine lakes, the northwestern corner is distinguished by a more arid environment, where flat-topped mesas in subtle brown are dissected by deep valleys where native cutthroat trout swim through swiftly flowing streams. Pockets of forest carpet the higher mesa tops, including dense stands crowning the Flat Tops Wilderness Area, a beautiful destination for anglers and backcountry explorers who yearn for an escape. Crisscrossing the region are several larger rivers, hubs for angling, camping, and white-water rafting, particularly in and around Dinosaur National Monument, the 329-square-mile wonderland of cliffs, canyons, and dinosaur fossils that comprises the northwestern corner's crown jewel.

CRAIG

This flat, dusty town of about 9,000 is best known as the location of a 1,300-megawatt, coal-fired power plant that brings an estimated $428 million economic benefit to the region. There are a few attractions in town that are worth a quick stop, and it's the most convenient base for white-water rafting trips on the Green and Yampa Rivers.

Sights
MUSEUM OF NORTHWEST COLORADO

Housed in a 90-year-old armory building, the **Museum of Northwest Colorado** (590 Yampa Ave., 970/824-6360, www.museumnwco.org, 9am-5pm Mon.-Fri., 10am-4pm Sat., free) would be like any other local history museum if it weren't for the cowboy and gunfighter collection on the top floor. One of the largest collections of cowboy gear on public display, the exhibit includes more than 1,000 Wild West artifacts—guns, chaps, saddles, and spurs, to name just a few.

WYMAN LIVING HISTORY MUSEUM

Four miles east of Craig, the **Wyman Living History Museum** (94350 U.S. 40, 970/824-6346, www.wymanmuseum.com, 10am-4pm Mon.-Fri., 11am-4pm Sat.-Sun., closed Wed. in winter, free) is a hodgepodge of antique cars; chainsaws; a complete collection of Colorado license plates; a relocated barn built in 1920 by the father of Lou Wyman, the museum's founder; and Junior, the Wyman family's resident elk.

Sports and Recreation

Angling in the many local lakes, streams, and rivers is by far the area's most popular outdoor activity. The Yampa River has two main sections: The upper stretch from Steamboat to Craig is noted for brown and rainbow trout and pike, while the lower stretch from Craig to the Utah border boasts more warm-water species like catfish and smallmouth bass. **Yampa River State Park** (6185 U.S. 40, Hayden, 970/276-2061, http://cpw.state.co.us, 8:30am-4:30pm Mon.-Fri., weekends as staffing allows, $7 day pass) has 13 public access sites for fishing and boating, as well as a mile-long nature trail with an observation deck for bird-watching.

Northeast of Craig, 900-acre **Elkhead Reservoir** (Lower Elkhead Rd., Hayden, 970/276-2061, http://cpw.state.co.us, 6:30am-8:30pm daily in summer, dawn-dusk in winter, $7 day pass) has plenty of smallmouth bass, crappie, catfish, and trout. The **Freeman Reservoir** (http://www.craigchamber.com), 21 miles north of Craig, is known for its cutthroat trout. From Craig, drive north on Road 13 for about 12 miles, then turn right onto Road 11. Continue 10 miles to the reservoir.

For more information, contact the **Moffatt County Visitor Center/Sportsman Information Center** (360 E. Victory Way, 970/824-5689, http://visitmoffatcounty.com, 9am-5pm Mon.-Fri.). **M.J.K. Sales and Feed** (2315 W. 1st St., 970/824-6581, www.acehardware.com, 7am-6pm Mon.-Sat., 9am-5pm Sun.) sells fishing and hunting licenses as well as bait, tackle, and other sporting goods.

Festivals and Events

Craig's annual summer kickoff is the **Grand Olde West Days** (www.grandoldewestdays.com, May), a Memorial Day weekend of heel-kickin' fun, including live music, Iron Man (and Iron Woman) Ranch Bronc Riding, a draft horse and mule show, and a Sunday afternoon rodeo. The **Craig Sheep Wagon Days** (http://visitmoffatcounty.com, Sept.) highlight the region's long history of sheep ranching with a weekend of sheep-shearing, sheep dog demos, a hay maze, and antique tractor pulls.

Food and Accommodations

Craig has a number of chain hotels, as well as a few local establishments whose quality is not on par with most Steamboat Springs accommodations. A better option is the family-run **Elk Run Inn** (627 W. Victory Way, 970/826-4444, www.elkruninn.com, $69-77), located in the center of town. The larger-than-average rooms are named in honor of local wildlife and include handy kitchenettes. Be sure to request a non-smoking room if you don't smoke.

For pizza or pasta, head to **Carelli's Italian Restaurant** (465 Yampa Ave., 970/824-6868, www.carellispizza.com, 11am-9:30pm Tues.-Sat., $12-18), a small, informal restaurant whose snowboard decor belies its menu of great New York-style pizza, extensive salad selection, and authentic Italian suppers.

Sure, ★ **Fiesta Jalisco** (410 Ranney St., 970/826-0500, http://fiestajalisco.net, 11am-10pm daily, $10-14) is part of a Colorado chain, but it's still the best Mexican food in northwestern Colorado. The menu includes traditional combination platters, several *platos de gringos* (like hamburgers), and a surprising number of healthy options. There is also a large selection of appetizers perfect

Browns Park National Wildlife Refuge

A great place for bird-watching is the 12,150-acre **Browns Park National Wildlife Refuge** (1318 Hwy. 318, Maybell, 970/365-3613, www.fws.gov), located along the Green River close to where it flows into Utah. The refuge protects crucial riparian habitat that nourishes thousands of migrating songbirds like the Wilson's warbler and the lazuli bunting on their stopovers between their northern breeding grounds. Songbirds like the tiny black-chinned hummingbird nest here, and moose and river otter raise their young in the same setting. The refuge also conserves wetlands, grasslands, and shrub lands, home to many bird species, including several ducks and pinyon jays, as well as large mammals like antelope, elk, and bighorn sheep.

The area has long been used by Native Americans, including members of the Comanche and Navajo tribes. Both the Dominguez-Escalante and the Lewis and Clark Expeditions passed through this region. Later, the area's remoteness attracted rustlers, thieves, and outlaws, including Robert Leroy Parker, who reportedly got his infamous nickname, Butch Cassidy, while working for a nearby rancher.

The refuge is a 1.5-hour drive from Craig. Head west on U.S. 40 (locally called Victory Way) and drive 31 miles to the junction with County Road 318 in Maybell. Turn right onto County Road 318 and head north for 59 miles to the refuge.

for a kid's meal, not to mention a long list of frosty margaritas.

Transportation and Services

Craig is 40 miles west of Steamboat Springs on U.S. 40. It's a long trip of at least 5.5 hours, but **Greyhound** (www.greyhound.com, $35-63) does offer bus service between Craig and Denver. There is also **regional bus service** (http://steamboatsprings.net, $6 one-way) between Craig and Steamboat Springs. Buses leave the Craig Regional Facility (U.S. 40) at 5:15am and 6:15am and return from the Gondola Transit Center at 4:25pm and 5:25pm daily.

The Craig Chamber of Commerce and the **Moffatt County Visitor Center** (360 E. Victory Way, 970/824-5689, www.craig-chamber.com, 9am-5pm Mon.-Fri., 9am-1pm Sat.) share an informative visitor center on the east side of town, just south of U.S. 40.

The small **Memorial Hospital** (750 Hospital Loop, 970/824-9411, http://www.thememorialhospital.com) is Craig's only option in case of an emergency. The hospital also has an associated **medical clinic** (785 Russell St., 970/826-2400, www.thememorialhospital.com, 8am-7pm Mon.-Thurs., 8am-5pm Fri.).

DINOSAUR NATIONAL MONUMENT

Dinosaur National Monument (435/781-7700, www.nps.gov/dino, $20 vehicle) is not a place that you accidentally stumble across; it is a long drive from anywhere and this isolation, along with its diverse scenery and amazing fossil display, is a huge part of its appeal. After Earl Douglass, a paleontologist from the Carnegie Museum of Natural History in Pittsburgh, unearthed one of the world's greatest concentrations of dinosaur bones, his discovery set off a fossil-hunting frenzy across the western United States. To protect this dinosaur graveyard, President Woodrow Wilson designated the quarry and the surrounding 80 acres as a national monument. In 1938, President Franklin D. Roosevelt greatly expanded its area to include the canyons of the Yampa and Green Rivers.

Today the monument straddles many worlds, both modern and ancient. Its 210,000 acres stretch across portions of both Utah and Colorado, and its topography rises from 4,740 feet elevation along the Green River to more than 9,000 feet at the summit of Zenobia Peak. The park also spans vast periods of time, from the giant dinosaurs that roamed this land 150 million years ago to (relatively) recent tribes, gutsy explorers, and Wild West outlaws. The park's rocks preserve fossils from even older ecosystems. Geologists have used these rare and precious time capsules to reconstruct how this landscape has changed during the past 1.2 billion years, one-quarter of Earth's incredibly long history.

The famous Dinosaur Quarry, the park's raison d'être, is located on the Utah side of the border, about a 20-minute drive from tiny Dinosaur, Colorado's westernmost town. The larger and quieter Colorado side of the monument features Echo Park, the gorgeous valley where the Green and Yampa Rivers meet, as well as peaceful high-desert scenery, excellent hiking, and thrilling white-water rafting. Not far to the south, the peaceful Cañon Pintado preserves dozens of pictograph sites, where you can gaze at hand prints, painted animals, and masonry walls made by people of the Fremont culture 2,000 years ago.

sunset in Dinosaur National Monument

★ Dinosaur Quarry (Utah)

Although Douglass continued to excavate the quarry and send the best bones to Pittsburgh, he was one of the first people to suggest that some of the fossils be left in place. Dinosaur thus became the first and best-known location where dinosaur bones were left intact for public viewing. The result is the amazing Cleveland-Lloyd Dinosaur Quarry (Elmo, Utah, 435/636-3600, www.blm.gov, 10am-5pm Mon.-Sat. and noon-5pm Sun. late May-early Sept., 10am-5pm Thurs.-Sat. in spring and fall, $20 per vehicle), a 150-foot-long wall embedded with more than 1,500 dinosaur bones, including those of fierce, meat-eating predators like *allosaurus,* whose enormous mouth was filled with viciously serrated teeth; *stegosaurus,* the familiar plant-eating dinosaur (and Colorado state fossil) with the distinctive plates on its back and large spikes on the end of its tail; and *apatosaurus* and *camarasaurus,* two long-necked, plant-eating giants. The two skulls visible on the bone wall both belong to *camarasaurus,* and if you look closely, several neck bones are visible at the base of one

of these skulls. Both adult and juvenile *camarasaurus* remains have been found at Dinosaur, including one nearly whole and still-assembled juvenile that remains the most complete long-necked dinosaur skeleton ever found.

These precious fossils are embedded in lenses of sandstone surrounded by soft mudstone, deposits characteristic of lazy rivers meandering their way across swampy lowlands, much like today's Mississippi River Valley. This layer, called the Morrison Formation (in honor of the town of Morrison just west of Denver where the rocks were first studied), is present in eight Western states and is the North American continent's most abundant source of dinosaur bones. Additional fossils of plants, pollen, and animals found in the monument indicate that 150 million years ago, this real-life Jurassic Park was a warm, swampy lowland covered with ferns, horsetails, and stands of pine-like trees up to 150 feet tall, with abundant crayfish, frogs, lizards, snails, and other creatures thriving in the boggy lowlands.

Dinosaur National Monument

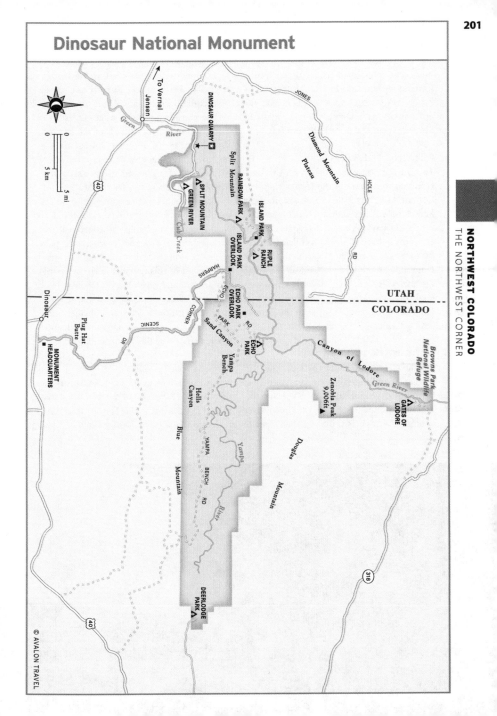

© AVALON TRAVEL

After rivers covered the dinosaur remains with sediment, they were gradually buried and, over millions of years, slowly compressed into stone. Much later, these time capsules from an ancient world were uplifted and re-exposed at the surface, where Douglass and other sharp-eyed scientists would eventually discover them and unlock their secrets.

GETTING THERE

To visit the Dinosaur Quarry on the Utah side, you must park at the **Quarry Visitor Center** (435/781-7700, 8am-5:30pm daily May-Sept., 9:30am-4pm daily Sept.-May) and take a free park service shuttle or, in winter, car caravan to the **Quarry Exhibit Hall.** To get to the Dinosaur Quarry from the town of Dinosaur, Colorado, drive west on U.S. 40 to the town of Jensen, Utah. At the junction with Highway 149, turn right and drive north on Highway 149 for seven miles to the Quarry Visitor Center.

Echo Park (Colorado)

On the Colorado side of the monument in the center of Dinosaur's canyon country is **Echo Park,** a beautiful valley where the still-untamed Yampa River joins the Green River to create the largest tributary of the Colorado River. Just below the confluence, the Green River gracefully winds around towering **Steamboat Rock,** Dinosaur's second-best-known landmark. A lush oasis in the dry desert, Echo Park is a special place to visit, picnic, hike, camp, and reflect.

There are two ways to access Echo Park. The first is by driving north from the **Canyon Visitor Center** (U.S. 40, 970/374-3000, www.nps.gov/dino, 9am-5pm daily, reduced hours off-season) along paved **Harpers Corner Road** to the **Echo Park Overlook.**

The second is by branching off onto the rough, dirt **Echo Park Road** (14 miles one-way) down to the bank of the Green River. Although most of the road is graded, the park service recommends that only high-clearance vehicles make this trip due to the steep initial descent and several dry wash crossings. The road can become impassible when wet, so check with the visitor center before heading out. A short path leads to the confluence, where you can see the Yampa's muddy brown waters mix with the clear, green waters of the dam-controlled Green.

Also located on the Echo Park Road are the **Pool Creek Petroglyphs,** an unusual display of dot designs visible above a creek on a rock face an easy stroll west of the road.

ancient handprints in Cañyon Pintado National Historic District

The Echo Park Dam Controversy

In the 1950s, the U.S. Bureau of Reclamation proposed the Colorado River Storage Project, a massive water-development scheme to store water and provide hydroelectric power and flood control for the five states in the upper portions of the Colorado River Basin—Wyoming, Utah, Arizona, New Mexico, and Colorado. The proposal entailed the construction of several massive dams, including the Flaming Gorge Dam on the Green River in Wyoming, New Mexico's Navajo Dam on the San Juan River, Glen Canyon Dam on the main stem of the Colorado River in Arizona, and several dams on the Gunnison River in Colorado. The original plan also called for a high dam in **Echo Park,** the gorgeous valley in Dinosaur National Monument where the Yampa joins the Green River. Fortunately, an alliance of river runners and environmentalists banded together to fight the construction of the 529-foot-high dam, whose reservoir would have submerged more than half of Steamboat Rock's beautiful walls.

One leader of this alliance was **David Brower,** executive director of the Sierra Club, who agreed to fight the proposal after a raft trip through the area. The Sierra Club challenged the Bureau of Reclamation's claims regarding the dam's benefits and ultimately forced a compromise that removed Echo Park Dam from the storage project plans. In return, however, Brower agreed not to oppose the construction of Glen Canyon Dam. Brower visited Glen Canyon years later, prior to its flooding by Lake Powell, and the lost beauty of Glen Canyon (which he later wrote about in his book *The Place No One Knew*) haunted Brower for the rest of his life. The compromise succeeded in preserving Echo Park, which quickly became a symbol of wilderness. The success of the fight to preserve this valley was also instrumental in the growth of America's environmental movement.

Cañyon Pintado National Historic District

Part of the **Dinosaur Diamond Scenic and Historic Byway** (www.dinosaurdiamond.org), the **Cañyon Pintado National Historic District** (970/878-3800, www.blm.gov, free) is a series of dozens of ancient pictograph sites scattered throughout the Douglas Creek Canyon south of Rangely. Most of the pictographs (painted figures) represent various occupations by the Fremont culture here (AD 0-1300), with some later designs by the Ute tribe (AD 1300-1881). There are also petroglyphs (carved or carefully pecked-out figures) visible on the canyon's beautiful buff-colored sandstone walls.

Cañyon Pintado is a BLM-managed district well off the beaten path; seven of the archaeological sites are open for public viewing. Each is easily accessible from Route 139 and includes interpretive panels describing the history of the site and the people who created the striking figures. From the north, the

18-mile-long district includes **Lookout Point** (milepost 67.6), a Fremont-created masonry room with mysterious holes drilled into the bedrock that may have been used to predict astronomical events. At milepost 56.5, a short trail leads to a viewing platform, from which you can see human figures as well as small, white birds. The southernmost stop, **Waving Hands** (milepost 53.5), is one of two short trails accessing a rock shelter decorated with both Fremont and Ute artwork; the latter is distinguishable by the drawings of horses, first introduced to the area by the Spanish in the late 1600s.

To access the canyon from the town of Dinosaur, drive south on County Road 64 to the town of Rangely. At the junction with Route 139, turn right to follow Route 139 south; look for roadside signs announcing the archaeological sites.

Sports and Recreation

Dinosaur National Monument has outstanding recreational opportunities, especially hiking and white-water rafting—two wonderful ways to immerse yourself in the monument's striking scenery.

HIKING

Harpers Corner Road is a great place for hiking. One option is the short and easy **Harpers Corner Trail** (3 miles round-trip), which leaves from the end of the road and has great views of Echo Park and the Green and Yampa canyons. If it's hot, try the **Plug Hat Butte Trail** (0.5 mile round-trip), a paved path that leaves from the Plug Hat pullout along the same road. This trail offers a peaceful stroll through piñon-juniper woodlands, where you often hear birds singing early in the morning. To access both trails, drive north on paved Harpers Corner Road from the Canyon Visitor Center.

If the conditions are right for a more challenging hike, the **Bull Canyon Trail** (3 miles round-trip) drops steeply from the Yampa Bench Road down to the Harding Hole on the Yampa River. A high-clearance, four-wheel drive vehicle is required to reach the trailhead. From the Canyon Visitor Center, drive north on Harpers Corner Road, then turn right onto Echo Park Road. Continue eight miles to the remote and rough Yampa Bench Road. Turn right and follow the road to the trailhead east of the Wagon Wheel Point Overlook.

There are many wonderful hikes on the Utah side of the border, including the moderate **Fossil Discovery Trail** (2.4 miles round-trip) and the intermediate **Desert Voices Trail** (1.5 miles round-trip), which has nice views of Split Mountain. The very short **Petroglyphs Trail** (0.2 mile round-trip) begins along Cub Creek Road and leads to some interesting petroglyphs believed to be 1,000 years old.

★ WHITE-WATER RAFTING

One of the most exciting ways to enjoy Dinosaur National Monument is from the bottom of the Green or Yampa River canyons. Successfully navigating a frothing rapid, sleeping on a sandy beach beneath countless twinkling stars, and savoring the serenity at dawn while taking the first sip of river coffee is an incomparable experience.

From their snowy origins high in the Rocky Mountains, both the Green and the Yampa Rivers lazily meander their way across sagebrush-dotted plains until they reach the outstretched edge of the Uinta Mountains, where—within the borders of the national monument—both rivers have carved

Enjoy exciting white-water action.

spectacular canyons up to 3,000 feet deep. Within their depths, turbulent white-water rapids alternate with quiet stretches where you can soak up some of the copious sunshine along with the slickrock scenery.

Enjoy a taste of river life on a one-day, family-friendly trip with a commercial outfitter on the Green River through Split Mountain Canyon. Two companies offer this trip daily departing from Utah: **Adrift Adventures** (9500 E. 6000 S., Jensen, Utah, 800/824-0150, www.adrift.com, $99) and **Don Hatch River Expeditions** (221 N. 400 E., Vernal, Utah, 800/342-8243, www.donhatchrivertrips.com, $105).

Multi-day trips through the Gates of Lodore on the Green River typically include three-, four-, and five-day options ($749-1,199). This stretch of river is fed by Wyoming's Flaming Gorge Reservoir, so it's navigable throughout the summer and features several difficult rapids with brow-raising names like Disaster Falls and Hell's Half Mile, the Green River's steepest and most difficult stretch.

Most outfitters also offer four- and five-day trips on the Yampa River ($899-1,199); trips are only available in late spring and early summer, with the last departures in mid-to-late June. The Yampa's canyon is equally spectacular; there's great side hiking, and the run includes several difficult rapids, like Teepee and Warm Springs, one of the 10 most difficult white-water rapids in the country.

Food

There aren't many dining options in the town of Dinosaur. Your best bet is a tuna melt, thick shake, or a dino-themed Espressosaurus at the **Bedrock Depot** (214 Brontosaurus Blvd., 970/374-2336, www.bedrockdepot.com, 11am-7pm Mon.-Sat., 1pm-6pm Sun., closed in winter, $6-8), which also has a gift shop stocked with mugs, T-shirts, and dino-themed paraphernalia. A local's favorite, the **Massadona Tavern & Steak House** (22926 U.S. 40, 970/374-2324, 4pm-8pm Wed.-Fri., noon-8pm Sat.-Sun., $6-10) is a friendly and clean place that serves up juicy burgers, thick steaks, and heaping portions of fish and chips.

Camping

There are no lodges within the national monument; camping is the only option to stay overnight. The park has six campgrounds, half of which are located on the Colorado side (www.nps.gov/dino, $10): **Gates of Lodore** along the Green River in the far north; **Echo Park** (tents only) near the confluence of the Green and Yampa Rivers (summer only); and **Deerlodge Park** (tents only) along the Yampa River on the park's eastern edge. All three are small, first-come, first-served sites and have water only during the summer.

The park's prettiest place to camp is on the Utah side at the **Green River Campground** (www.nps.gov/dino, early Apr.-mid-Oct., $18), located on the banks of the Green River, four miles east of the Quarry Visitor Center. Facilities here are limited to water and flush toilets; no hookups are available.

Transportation and Services

There is no public transportation to the national monument; however, **Greyhound** (www.greyhound) buses traveling between Denver and Salt Lake City stop in the town of Dinosaur. There is no shuttle service within the Colorado side of the monument. To visit the Dinosaur Quarry on the Utah side, you must park at the Quarry Visitor Center and take a free park service shuttle (or in winter, a car caravan) to the Quarry Exhibit Hall.

The **Northwest Colorado Cultural Heritage Program** (http://nwcoloradoheritagetravel.org) is a good source of information. The small **Rangely District Hospital** (225 Eagle Crest Dr., Rangely, 970/675-5011, http://www.rangelyhospital.com) is the closest option for medical care.

MEEKER

Tiny Meeker sits perched at 6,240 feet in elevation in the pretty White River Valley, surrounded by high mesas where historic ranches still run sheep and cattle drives.

The Isolated Empire

the Roan Plateau

Between the White and Colorado Rivers in far western Colorado lies the **Roan Plateau,** a large tableland rising several thousand feet above the surrounding countryside. Once dubbed the Isolated Empire due to its remoteness, this region was virtually unheard of until the 1940s, when oil was discovered near **Rangely.** The Rangely oil field is still the Rocky Mountain region's largest oil producer, and the plateau also hosts rich coal and natural gas reserves. In addition, the Roan Plateau is known for its biological diversity. A wide variety of wildlife habitats, including piñon-juniper woodlands, sagebrush, meadows, and forest, support a tremendous assortment of plants and wildlife, such as black bears, mountain lions, and some of the nation's largest herds of elk, mule deer, and wild horses. The abundance of both energy and biological resources has often pitted recreationists and environmentalists against those favoring energy development. Most of the plateau is managed by the federal Bureau of Land Management (BLM), which has the difficult task of trying to balance the desires of these different users with the many laws enacted to conserve biodiversity.

The 1971 Wild Free-Roaming Horses and Burros Act was intended to manage and protect wild horses and burros as "living symbols of the historic and pioneer spirit of the west." How to manage the Colorado herds, however, has been the subject of heated debate. In 2015, after a long court battle, the BLM conducted a helicopter roundup of an entire wild horse herd, an action fiercely opposed by many groups, including American Wild Horse Preservation. Today, Colorado has four wild horse management areas, including the Piceance/East Douglas range west of Meeker, where about 165 wild horses roam year-round in small bands. The Town of Rangely has a recommended **Wild Horse Loop** (www.rangely.com) to try to spot one of these enduring symbols of the American West.

The town is named for Nathan Meeker, a so-called "Indian agent" for the federal government who was one of a dozen people killed during a Ute uprising in what is infamously known as the 1879 Meeker Massacre. The tragic site (marked by a large sign) is located just south of Highway 64, a few miles west of town. The year following the massacre, Congress passed legislation forcing the tribe to relocate to reservations in Utah. The Army established a garrison at the site where the town is now located.

Today, the **White River Museum** (565 Park Ave., 970/878-9982, www.meekercolorado.com, 9am-5pm daily mid-Apr.-late Nov., 10am-4pm daily in winter, by donation) details the history of the uprising and massacre. Displays are located in several rough-hewn log cabins the garrison sold to the town when the Army later withdrew.

Following the Army's departure, Meeker evolved into a regional center and important stagecoach stop. President Theodore Roosevelt, who loved this region, spent time here while on a big-game hunting trip. Roosevelt once stayed in the 1896 **Meeker Hotel & Café** (560 Main St., 970/878-5255, www.meekerhotel.com, $80-125), where one of the 14 rooms is named in his honor. One of the state's oldest operating hotels, the Meeker is also known for the many hunting trophies hanging in the restored lobby, including some gigantic elk. More mounts hang on the walls of the cozy **café** (970/878-5062, 7am-8pm daily, $9-14), which is housed in a stone building originally built in 1891 for the town's post office.

The town's biggest event of the year is the **Meeker Classic Sheepdog Championship Trials** (http://meekersheepdog.com, early Sept.), which includes the traditional competition as well as community events like agility demonstrations, a lamb cook-off, and an art show.

Getting There

From Craig, drive 49 miles south on Highway 13 to Meeker. In good conditions, the trip should take less than an hour.

★ FLAT TOPS SCENIC BYWAY

The **Flat Tops Scenic Byway** (http://meekerchamber.com, summer only) is one of Colorado's hidden gems. This 82-mile scenic drive winds through green river valleys and gorgeous alpine scenery from the small town of Yampa, located 30 miles south of Steamboat Springs, to Meeker, a ranching town of 2,200. Along the way, the route skirts the northern border of the Flat Tops Wilderness Area, 235,000 acres of heavily forested plateaus dotted with glistening alpine lakes, including pristine Trappers Lake, the birthplace of America's wilderness movement.

Places of interest include the 10,343-foot **Ripple Creek Overlook,** a must-stop photo op of the White River Valley and the vast Flat

the Flat Tops Scenic Byway

Tops Wilderness; the drive along the pretty White River; trails galore, including the hike to Pagoda Lake (7.25 miles round-trip); spontaneous wildlife viewing; and the nonstop scenery in this less-visited part of Colorado.

Trappers Lake

The highlight of the scenic byway is Trappers Lake, an eight-mile detour just before the route reaches the banks of the White River. This 300-acre, sapphire-blue gem is located just inside the wilderness boundary (no motorized boats), creating a serene setting from which to enjoy the abundant sunshine and the open views of the surrounding volcanic cliffs. In 1919, Arthur Carhart, a Forest Service official, was surveying this area for a resort. He became so enthralled with the lake and its postcard panoramas that he petitioned the U.S. Forest Service for its preservation so that it could remain wild forever. The Forest Service finally recognized the Flat Tops Primitive Area in 1932; the wilderness area was formally established in 1975. Despite a large fire that scorched much of the valley in 2002,

Trappers Lake remains a very special place that's still relatively unknown.

Trappers Lake Lodge & Resort (7700 Trappers Lake Rd., 970/878-3336, www.trapperslake.com, May-Oct.) rents canoes ($25-35 per person) and rustic cabins ($70-155) and serves hearty meals (7:30am-2pm Mon., 7:30am-7:30pm Tues.-Sun.) for very reasonable prices.

Getting There

The byway is accessible by any passenger vehicle in summer. From Yampa, start west on Route 17 and follow the signed byway for 82 miles to Meeker, crossing over Dunckley Pass on Forest Road 16. Allow at least half a day to complete the drive, including the side trip to Trappers Lake.

Because the byway follows a series of roads, it's best to obtain a detailed map ahead of time. The mostly unpaved route is closed in winter between Dunckley Pass on the east and a parking lot at mile marker 31 on the west side. There is no gas en route, so fill up before you leave Yampa or Meeker. Contact the Colorado Department of Transportation (in-state 511, www.cotrip.org) for road conditions.

Vail and the
Central Rockies

Highlights

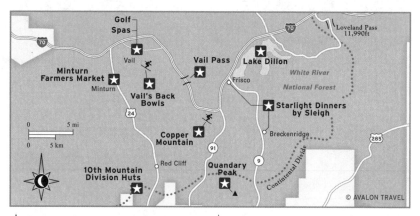

© AVALON TRAVEL

★ **Vail's Back Bowls:** The legendary 3,000 acres of wide-open slopes with stunning views on the backside of Vail Mountain are pure bliss (page 216).

★ **10th Mountain Division Huts:** A series of cozy backcountry huts provide a convenient base for year-round recreation (page 216).

★ **Vail Pass:** At 10,662 feet in elevation, this pass is a great starting point for summer bike rides and winter backcountry outings (page 219).

★ **Golf:** With a half dozen 18-hole championship courses within 40 minutes' drive, Vail is a great place to lower your handicap (pages 220, 228, 241, and 253).

★ **Spas:** Pamper yourself in one of the area's many luxurious spas, where you can unwind in a whirlpool, detoxify your skin, or enjoy a full-body massage (pages 221, 228, and 253).

★ **Minturn Farmers Market:** On summer Saturdays, tiny Minturn hosts the high country's best farmers market (page 231).

★ **Quandary Peak:** One of the most straightforward fourteener trails has a "modest" elevation gain of 3,450 feet (page 241).

★ **Starlight Dinners by Sleigh:** Glide across the snow in a horse-drawn sleigh en route to a hearty three-course dinner and musical entertainment (pages 245 and 250).

★ **Lake Dillon:** Located beneath towering, snow-capped peaks, this sapphire-blue lake is a hub of year-round recreation (page 248).

★ **Copper Mountain:** This relaxed resort has outstanding terrain that naturally separates beginners from more advanced snowboarders and skiers (page 256).

Renowned for its world-class skiing and snowboarding, Colorado's central Rockies are a popular playground for year-round recreation.

A quick glimpse at any map of Colorado is enough to recognize that the rugged Rocky Mountains are the state's most distinctive geographic feature. The north-south chain of high, craggy peaks and intervening valleys dictates the courses of rivers and roads, the rhythm of the seasons, and the outdoor lifestyles of many locals, who often arrange their schedules around mountain outings.

Colorado's ski resorts are synonymous with plentiful powder, long runs, extended seasons, and expansive resorts. The state's largest ski area, Vail Mountain, boasts 195 trails on nearly 5,300 acres of varied terrain and an average of 354 inches—29.5 *feet*—of snow per year. Celebrities like Tiger Woods and Michelle Obama have been spotted on Vail's runs, and President Gerald Ford and his wife, Betty, had strong ties to the area.

Off the slopes, the town of Vail, built as the mountain's base village in the early 1960s, perpetuates the resort's reputation for glitz and glamour, with exclusive clubs, luxury amenities, fine art galleries, and scores of award-winning restaurants. But Vail is just the start of what Colorado's central Rockies have on offer. The old gold-mining town of Breckenridge, located next to another first-rate ski resort, has a historic downtown whose main street is lined with quaint, false-fronted buildings hosting eclectic boutiques, cozy coffee shops, and a great selection of pubs and restaurants. The other central Colorado ski resorts have their own unique personalities, from lavish luxury at Beaver Creek to Arapahoe Basin's precipitously steep expert terrain.

During summer, this same area becomes a focal point of warm weather recreation, from hiking and cycling to golf, rafting, and sailing, as well as fun cultural festivals and sporting events. Small towns like Frisco, Minturn, and Leadville take their turns shining in the spotlight, sharing their fascinating histories and local traditions with all who venture there.

Previous: the valley of the Blue River; the slopes at Breckenridge Ski Resort. **Above:** ski art in Vail.

Vail and the Central Rockies

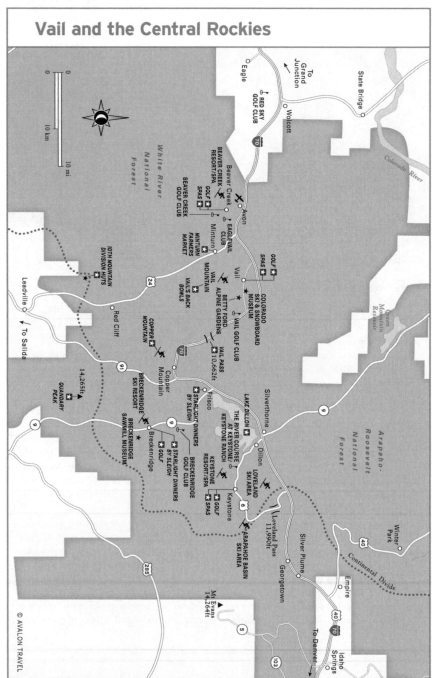

the Colorado Ski & Snowboard Museum

PLANNING YOUR TIME

Vail's busiest tourist season is winter (late Nov.-Apr.), when the entire town revolves around skiing—and various ways of relaxing afterward. Prices are highest, and the slopes the most crowded, during the major holidays, especially between Christmas and New Year's. The snow, however, is often more plentiful, and the temperatures generally warmer, in March and early April, when the resorts fill with exuberant spring breakers. Most visitors

stay for a week to thoroughly enjoy Vail's world-class slopes and to get a taste of at least one of the region's other fabulous resorts, such as Breckenridge, Copper Mountain, or Beaver Creek. If your budget allows, you can stay at a well-appointed lodge in Vail and never need a car, or you can rent a vehicle and drive between resorts from one of the less-expensive mountain towns tucked into one of the region's deep valleys.

Summer is central Colorado's second high season. Vail makes a great summer base for several days of exploration. Catch a sunrise round of golf or a bike ride up Vail Pass, followed by a bit of shopping, a facial at one of the local spas, and a heart-pounding zip-line ride. Next, settle in for a cocktail on a spacious outdoor patio and watch the afternoon thunderheads build above the peaks. Complete your perfect day with dinner at one of Vail's many award-winning restaurants, followed by live music or dancing at one of the town's upscale venues—or a simple, starlight stroll along gurgling Gore Creek.

September is a fabulous time to visit the Colorado high country. The crowds begin to thin, the peaks receive their first dustings of snow, and the quaking aspen leaves put on a gorgeous show. October-mid-November and mid-April-May are the "mud seasons"— the quietest times of year, when there are good lodging deals to be had, although recreation options are more limited and some shops and restaurants cut back their hours or even close.

Vail

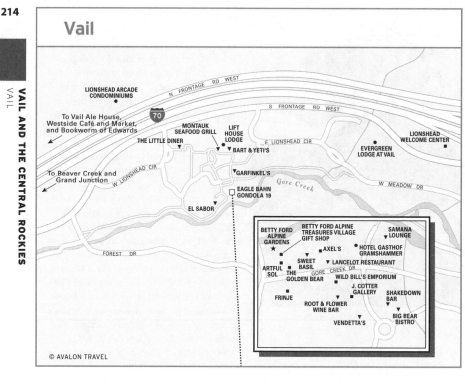

LIONSHEAD ARCADE
CONDOMINIUMS

N FRONTAGE RD WEST

S FRONTAGE RD WEST

To Vail Ale House,
Westside Café and Market,
and Bookworm of Edwards

70

MONTAUK
SEAFOOD GRILL

LIFT
HOUSE
LODGE

THE LITTLE DINER

BART & YETI'S

E LIONSHEAD CIR

LIONSHEAD
WELCOME CENTER

EVERGREEN
LODGE AT VAIL

To Beaver Creek and
Grand Junction

W LIONSHEAD CIR

GARFINKEL'S

Gore Creek

W MEADOW DR

EAGLE BAHN
GONDOLA 19

EL SABOR

FOREST DR

BETTY FORD
ALPINE
GARDENS

BETTY FORD ALPINE
TREASURES VILLAGE
GIFT SHOP

AXEL'S

SAMANA
LOUNGE

HOTEL GASTHOF
GRAMSHAMMER

ARTFUL
SOL

SWEET
BASIL

THE
GOLDEN BEAR

GORE CREEK DR

LANCELOT RESTAURANT

WILD BILL'S EMPORIUM

J. COTTER
GALLERY

FRINJE

ROOT & FLOWER
WINE BAR

VENDETTA'S

SHAKEDOWN
BAR

BIG BEAR
BISTRO

© AVALON TRAVEL

Vail

Vail is situated on the west side of Vail Pass, a major mountain pass that is sometimes impassible during winter storms. The ski resort rises above the south side of the town, which is tucked into a glacial valley so long and narrow that it requires three interstate exits: East Vail, Vail Village, and West Vail. How easy it is to get around depends upon where your accommodations are located. Places south of the interstate and in Vail Village have the most convenient access to the mountain and the thriving town center, whose heated, pedestrian-friendly streets are easy to navigate, even in winter. Vail Mountain has three base areas, Cascade, Lionshead, and Vail Villages, all of which have quick and convenient access to the slopes.

In summer, the paved Vail Recreation Path along Gore Creek links all three base areas with Vail Pass to the east and the town of Avon to the west. The valley also has an extensive bus system, and shuttle services are available between the central Rockies' major resorts. To really explore the valley, however, it's nice to have a car.

SIGHTS
Colorado Ski & Snowboard Museum
Located on the 3rd level of the Vail Village parking garage, the renovated **Colorado Ski & Snowboard Museum** (231 S. Frontage Rd., 970/476-1876, www.skimuseum.net, 10am-6pm daily in high season, 10:30am-5:30pm in off-season, by donation) commemorates the contributions that Coloradoans

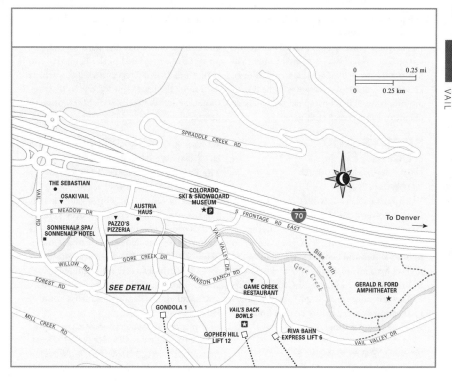

have made to the sports of skiing and snowboarding. The museum features half a dozen galleries that explore the legacy of the 10th Mountain Division, the World War II ski troopers who trained in nearby Camp Hale, as well as the history of the state's ski industry. Additional exhibits chronicle the development of Vail Mountain, showcase old gear and memorabilia from U.S. Ski Team athletes, and highlight the dramatic changes in ski gear over the decades. Weekly programs, including museum tours and walking tours of Vail Village, are also available.

Betty Ford Alpine Gardens

Gerald Ford first skied at Vail in 1968 as a congressman from Michigan. Two years later, according to the *Denver Post,* he borrowed $50,000 from his kids' life insurance policies to buy a condo at The Lodge at Vail. The so-called "first skiing president" loved to carve turns at both Vail and Beaver Creek, where he and his wife, Betty, later bought a retirement home. The press coverage during their annual visits, and his efforts to bring two Alpine World Ski Championships to the state, drew considerable attention to both resorts, helping to place them on the international map.

After Gerald retired from politics, the Fords split their time between California and Beaver Creek, where they became an important part of the community. In addition to hosting an annual forum of international and business leaders in the Vail Valley, Ford raised funds to construct the **Betty Ford Alpine Gardens** (522 S. Frontage Rd., 970/476-0103, www.bettyfordalpinegardens.org, dawn-dusk year-round, free), the highest botanical garden in the United States, to honor his wife, who loved gardening. The gardens help conserve rare and endangered alpine flowers and plants and provide a tranquil space for visitors and locals to meditate, relax, and learn more about alpine species.

The gardens are located in Ford Park, close to the Gerald R. Ford Amphitheater (530 S. Frontage Rd., 970/476-5612, www.vvf.org), an outdoor, 1,260-seat venue with beautiful mountain views that hosts a packed calendar of cultural events each summer.

SPORTS AND RECREATION

Downhill Skiing and Snowboarding

Vail's raison d'être is winter recreation; the focus revolves around Colorado's biggest ski resort, and life here moves to the rhythm of chairlifts and moguls. The runs are open to both skiers and boarders. If you're in the market for a lesson, Vail Ski & Snowboard School (586 W. Lionshead Cir., 800/475-4543, www.vail.com, $189-675 per day) offers instruction at every ability level in both private and group settings.

★ VAIL'S BACK BOWLS

Vail's Back Bowls are legendary; the seven wide-open, ungroomed basins are heaven on Earth, especially after a big snowstorm. Covering a little more than 3,000 acres, the Back Bowls are a great place for experienced skiers, many of whom challenge themselves by trying to ski all seven in a single day. Although it can feel as if it's easy to get lost in this vast area, all of the runs end at a lift, so it's difficult to go too far astray.

Strong intermediate skiers will enjoy China Bowl, where there are several steep blue runs, including Chopstix and Poppyfields. Pete's Bowl in the Blue Sky Basin is so remote that my son calls it the "back back bowl"; it also has several challenging blues.

Black skiers have their pick of dozens of fantastic runs. Forever in Sun Down Bowl is one of Vail's best. Try its 1,850 feet of thigh-burning vertical early in the day, while your legs are still fresh. Next to it is Wow, a slightly shorter classic. Locals like to link the top of Wow with the bottom of Forever for an unforgettable Wow-Ever. Other must-dos are Milt's Face and Yonder in the Sun Up Bowl and Genghis Kahn in the China Bowl. For a real adventure, head to the Far East—the Inner and Outer Mongolia Bowls, which tend to be the least crowded due to their remoteness and the Poma-style lift required to get there.

Cross-Country Skiing and Snowshoeing

The Vail Nordic Center (1778 Vail Valley Dr., 970/476-8366, www.vail.com, $17-22) offers daily rentals for winter gear, including snowshoes and cross-country skis, as well as group and private cross-country ski lessons. The Vail Nordic School (Golden Peak, 970/754-3200, www.vail.com, tours $98-141, includes gear) leads guided cross-country and snowshoe tours for all ability levels and offers telemark and cross-country ski lessons.

If you venture out on your own, the Eagle-Holy Cross Ranger District (24747 U.S. 24, Minturn, 970/827-5715, www.fs.usda.gov) of the White River National Forest has 225 miles of trails to explore. Check weather conditions with the ranger district and the Colorado Avalanche Information Center (http://avalanche.state.co.us), which has a Know Before You Go section and a sign-up for Twitter updates.

★ 10TH MOUNTAIN DIVISION HUTS

During World War II, after a group of Finnish ski troops were able to fend off a fierce attack by a much larger Soviet force, the U.S. War Department decided to form a special Army division to train U.S. troops in mountain warfare. In 1944, the unit was designated as the 10th Mountain Division and moved to Camp Hale, a training facility in White River National Forest tucked between Avon and Leadville, where 14,000 troops were trained in winter warfare, including such skills as cold-weather survival, skiing, and climbing.

Navigating Colorado's Biggest Ski Mountain

With more than 5,200 acres and 31 lifts, Vail Mountain is so large that it can be difficult to figure out where and how to start. Here are a few tips to help you maximize your time on the slopes:

- Buy lift tickets ahead of time as part of a package deal or an **Epic Pass** ($149 per day, $429 for 4 days) from Vail Resorts, which offers a substantial discount and allows you to ski at any of Vail's four Colorado resorts.

- Download Vail Resorts' free **EpicMix** app, which compares lift line times, shows your location on the trails, helps you plan an itinerary, and tracks how many vertical feet you've skied.

- Grab or download a **trail map** and **grooming report** available online (www.vail.com) or at the kiosks near the lifts and ticket windows.

- Know where to park. The **Vail Village** parking structure ($25) is a five-minute walk to Gondola One, which swiftly delivers you to Mid-Vail, from where you can access most of the mountain. The **Lionshead Village** garage ($25) has quick pedestrian access to the Eagle Bahn Gondola and Born Free lift, both of which deliver you to Eagle's Nest.

- Plan where to start skiing. From **Mid-Vail,** a great place to start is the Mountaintop lift, which accesses the intermediate caffeine-themed Expresso and Cappuccino runs. From **Eagle's Nest,** try one of the great safari-themed blues, especially Born Free, Simba, and Safari.

- Once you've warmed up, head out to the **Back Bowls,** whose lifts close earlier than those lower on the mountain, or east toward the **Northwoods** and **Highline** lifts, which access many more great blues and blacks.

- Match your ability level to the slopes. Intermediate (blue) skiers shouldn't miss the **Wildwood** lift to **Hunky Dory; The Woods** near **Game Creek** lift; or **Avanti,** a fun, long cruiser. More advanced (black) skiers will love the classic, four-mile-long **Riva Ridge, Gandy Dancer,** and **Lindsey's.** Beginner (green) skiers enjoy **Lost Boy** and **The Meadows** from the top of the **Game Creek** lift and **Tin Pants, Sourdough,** and **Boomer** from the **Sourdough** lift.

- Pace yourself! Vail is huge and at high elevation, so you'll tire more quickly than you would at sea level. Drink plenty of water and take breaks throughout the day. To help **avoid the crowds,** try taking an early (before 11am) or a late (after 1:30pm) lunch.

- Rent gear at a shop whose price includes overnight storage, such as **Vail Skibase** (610 W. Lionshead Cir., 970/476-5799, http://vailskibase.com, $23-30 day), so you don't have to lug it around.

The division experienced its first combat in Italy, where the division scaled 1,500-feet-high cliffs at night to take a peak held by German troops. Thanks in large part to their Colorado-based training, the 10th's surprise attack was successful, and the Americans were able to hold the peak through seven counterattacks and use their position to break through the German line, which ultimately opened up a path to the strategically important Po Valley.

Upon their return to the United States, many veterans of the 10th Mountain Division laid the foundations of the modern ski industry, improving gear, constructing lodges, and designing chair lifts and ski trails at many Colorado resorts, including Arapahoe Basin, Aspen, and Vail. Fritz Benedict, another 10th veteran, formed the nonprofit **10th Mountain Division Hut Association** (970/925-5775, https://olb.huts.org, $33-43), which builds and operates a group of 34 comfortable huts named in the division's honor. The network connects 350 miles of trails, offering comfortable, year-round bases for exploring the Colorado backcountry.

Reservations (970/925-5775, limited hours, www.huts.org) are accepted online or by phone. The huts are scattered across a wide region; trips vary depending upon location and time of year. A few huts are accessible by vehicles (sometimes only 4WD), others only by foot. Carefully research each hut, noting its access and facilities, before booking. The rustic cabins usually include a series of bunks with simple mattresses (but no linens), a wood stove, and basic cooking facilities, including a propane burner. For space in one of the more popular huts (especially during winter weekends), join one of the affiliated associations; members can participate in an early booking lottery each spring.

Hiking

Vail Mountain is a good place to hike, especially if you're still acclimating to the elevation. A fun and easy option starts in the Lionshead base area, where you can take the Eagle Bahn Gondola up to the **Eagle's Loop** (1 mile), a pleasant stroll with awesome views of the Mount of the Holy Cross. Grab some lunch at the Eagle's Nest, then descend the 3.2-mile **Berrypicker Trail** to either Vail Village or back to Lionshead.

Around Vail, there are plenty of great options in the 2.3-million-acre **White River National Forest** (970/827-5715, www.fs.usda.gov), including the **Eagle's Nest Wilderness,** a remote, 133,00-acre parcel that protects much of the rugged Gore Range. An easy hike is the **Upper Piney Lake Trail** (2.25 miles), which leads past the lake to a waterfall. To get here from Vail, take the North Frontage Road west to Red Sand Stone Road. Follow this to Piney River Road, which leads to the trailhead. Along the way, you'll pass the parking lot for the hike up to **Lost Lake Trail** (7.5 miles round-trip), a moderate and popular hike.

Shrine Mountain Inn, one of the 10th Mountain Division Huts

EAST VAIL

From East Vail there are several great walks, including the **Gore Creek Trail,** a beautiful hike through groves of quaking aspen and lush, wildflower-filled meadows stretching along the creek. After four miles, the trail forks. The left branch climbs 1.5 miles through dense spruce and fir trees to the alpine tundra and sparkling **Gore Lake.** The right branch climbs three more miles to **Red Buffalo Pass,** an unusual gateway to Summit County. To get here from Vail, head east on I-70 to Exit 180. Turn right at the bottom of the off-ramp and continue east on Bighorn Road for about 2.5 miles. The trailhead is on the left before you reach the campground. Parking is limited, so it's a good idea to get an early start.

The **Booth Creek Falls Trail** (2 miles one-way) climbs steeply through aspen groves, then parallels Booth Creek to the beautiful, 60-foot falls. In good weather, you can continue two more miles to Booth Lake for a total gain of 3,036 feet in elevation. To get here from

Vail, take Exit 180 off I-70, turn left and drive beneath the interstate. Turn left onto the north frontage road and drive about a mile to Booth Creek Road. Turn right onto this road and follow it to the trailhead parking area at its end.

GUIDES

Vail Resorts (970/754-8245, www.vail.com) offers guided hikes on the mountain, leaving from the Lionshead ticket office. **Walking Mountains Science Center** (www.walkingmountains.org, $30-80) has a large slate of full-day and family hikes with trained naturalists who are also certified wilderness first responders. The **Vail Nature Center** (601 Vail Valley Dr., 970/479-2291, www.walkingmountains.org, 9am-4pm Mon.-Sat. mid-June-Sept., by donation), a 1940s homestead nestled in a beautiful, wildflower-filled meadow along Gore Creek, houses a nature center and offers a series of guided hikes and other nature tours.

Biking

Vail Mountain (www.vail.com, all-day bike haul ticket $40) offers downhill mountain biking serviced by Vail's gondolas, which access 10 different trails. The mountain also has

seven "freeride" bike trails, which are more technical and require special equipment and skills. Guided biking tours are also available; check the ticket offices at the base of either gondola. **Vail Sports** (Gondola One, 244 Wall St., 970/479-0600, www.vailsports.com, 10am-5pm daily) in Vail Village rents bikes and helmets ($47 for 4 hours) and road bikes ($63 for 4 hours), and leads guided tours (daily Memorial Day-Labor Day).

★ VAIL PASS

Summiting 10,662-foot-high Vail Pass on I-70 feels like an accomplishment, even in a car. Imagine the sense of triumph after ascending it on a bike! This is Colorado's only pass with a paved bike path running the entire distance on both sides, giving you two different routes to choose from. The scenery is spectacular, the descent is fast, and the air is thin, so bring plenty of water as well as rain and wind gear. This ride is only possible in high summer **(mid-June-early Sept.)**; cyclists should be acclimated to the high elevation and must begin early in the morning.

The 12-mile, 1,550-foot ride up Vail Pass's **east side** begins from a parking lot in Frisco (west end of Main St.). A side trail at the back of the lot crosses a bridge before joining the

Shrine Pass links Vail Pass to the town of Red Cliff.

paved path that runs between Breckenridge and Copper Mountain. From this junction, follow the path west through the lush forest in Ten Mile Canyon to the Copper Mountain Conoco Station, the half-way point. At the resort's western edge, the path picks up again on the right side and continues another 4.5 miles through the valley between the east- and westbound interstate lanes. The path ends at the summit rest area, where there are tremendous views and a few interesting signs about the archaeological finds discovered here.

Vail is the typical start for the 15-mile ascent up the pass's **west side,** which is longer, steeper, and has more elevation gain (about 2,400 feet). Through most of Vail Village the path stretches on the valley's north side, so it's easy to find. Heading west, the path merges with the interstate frontage road before crossing to the south side. After a short but steep climb, the route once again becomes a paved path, which climbs (and climbs) to the top, where you pass a small lake before reaching the rest area.

In addition to road cycling, Vail Pass offers many other recreational opportunities. It's one end of the **Shrine Pass Road,** a popular summer four-wheel drive, hiking, and mountain biking route (and enjoyable winter cross-country ski route) that ends in the tiny community of Red Cliff.

Horseback Riding

Vail Stables (915 Spraddle Creek Rd., 970-476-6941, www.vailstables.com, Tues.-Sun. June-Sept., $85 for 1.5 hours) offers the area's only horseback riding, as well as pony rides, available on a walk-up basis.

★ Golf

With 17 courses within 38 miles of town, the Vail Valley is a great place to practice your swing—especially since, at this elevation, the ball travels 10 percent farther thanks to the high, thin air. Although the season is short (mid-May-Oct.), the cooler daytime temperatures, well-designed courses, and inspiring mountain scenery will make your time on the links an unforgettable experience.

The **Vail Golf Club** (1775 Sunburst Dr., 970/479-2260, www.vailrec.com, summer only, $55-90) is a highly rated, par-71 public course with some of the most affordable prices in town, especially the twilight rates ($55 after 3:30pm). Four miles west of Vail, the **EagleVail Club** (459 Eagle Dr., Avon, 970/949-5267, www.eaglevailgolfclub.com, $30-104) has both a regulation 18-hole course

golfing in Vail

and a par-3 FootGolf course ($12), where you use your feet and a soccer ball instead of a club and golf ball—a great combo for family fun.

★ Spa

One of Vail's best retreats is the **Sonnenalp Spa** (20 Vail Rd., 970/476-5656, www.sonnenalp.com, 8am-8pm daily during peak season, open year-round, $150 for 50-minute massage), which has an extensive menu of services including a deluxe caviar facial and couple's massages.

ENTERTAINMENT AND EVENTS

Nightlife

Known as the ski patrol hangout, laid-back **Vendetta's** (291 Bridge St., 970/476-5070, www.vendettasvail.com, 11am-2am daily) has one of Vail's best decks, good après-ski deals, and great pizza and other filling, late-night food. Run by a professional sommelier, the small and chic **Root & Flower Wine Bar** (225 Wall St., 970/763-5101, http://rootandflowervail.com, 3pm-close Wed.-Sun.) in the center of Vail Village features a long wine list and hand-crafted cocktails along with carefully paired appetizers. They also offer classes where you can learn how to taste wine like a pro.

One of Vail's best places for live music is the **Shakedown Bar** (304 Bridge St., 970/479-0556, www.shakedownbarvail.com, 3pm-2am Wed.-Sat., 9pm-2am Sun.-Tues.), a 160-seat music venue and bar just east of the fountain in Vail Village. Operated by guitarist Scott Rednor, who has toured with the likes of Lenny Kravitz and Blues Traveler, the intimate venue hosts both local and national acts. The New York City-style **Samana Lounge** (228 Bridge St., 970/476-3433, http://samanalounge.com, 9pm-close Tues. and Thurs.-Sun.) is a basement nightclub featuring both DJs and musical acts ranging from classic rock to funk.

In the Lifthouse Lodge in Lionshead Village, **Bart & Yeti's** (553 E. Lionshead Cir., 970/476-2754, http://bartnyetis.com, 11am-10pm daily), which is named for two local dogs, has a rustic, relaxed atmosphere and

plenty of cold beer, as well as live music at 8pm on most Fridays and Saturdays. Locally known as "Garf's," **Garfinkel's** (536 E. Lionshead Cir., 970/476-3789, https://garfsvail.com, 11am-midnight daily) is a popular sports bar full of sporting memorabilia and a large, sunny deck that's an ideal spot for a relaxing après-ski drink.

Beer lovers should head to the **Vail Ale House** (2161 N. Frontage Rd. West, 970/476-4314, www.vailalehouse.com, 11:30am-midnight Mon.-Fri., 10am-midnight Sat.-Sun.) in West Vail, where there are more than 20 craft beers on tap— as well as the Vail Valley's largest dance floor.

Festivals and Events

Although it's best known for winter sports, Vail also hosts a number of festivals and fairs in the off-season. The annual **Vail Film Fest** (www.vailfilmfestival.com, mid-Apr., $10 per show) features more than 60 films, including a number of world premieres. The **GoPro Mountain Games** (www.mountaingames.com, early June) celebrate the unusual combination of "adventure sports, music, and the mountain lifestyle," with cycling and foot races (including a mud race), stand-up paddle sprinting, and slack-lining, as well as concerts and art displays.

The **Vail Arts Festival** (www.vailartsfestival.com, late June) is a long-standing tradition where more than 80 artists display and sell their masterpieces. One of the top classical music festivals, the **Bravo! Vail** (https://bravovail.org, late June-early Aug., $28-129) is a six-week celebration that attracts more than 60,000 attendees for performances from the Philadelphia Orchestra and the New York Philharmonic. For two weeks, the **Vail International Dance Festival** (www.vvf.org, late July, $50-150) features ballet performances as well as modern shows like Dance TV, starring artists from *Dancing with the Stars* and other TV shows.

SHOPPING

Between the Vail Village and Lionshead base areas, hundreds of shops sell everything from ski helmets to jewelry and designer clothing. The area is a well-known shopping destination, and although the prices are generally quite steep, strolling around the town, searching for the perfect gift or souvenir, is a fun way to spend an afternoon or an evening.

One of the most established shops is the **Golden Bear** (Vail Village, 183 Gore Creek Dr., 970/476-4082, www.thegoldenbear.com, 10am-6pm daily), which sells jewelry handcrafted in their local studio. The shop is so well known that their bear logo has become a symbol of the Vail Valley. The town's only nonprofit store, the **Betty Ford Alpine Treasures Village Gift Shop** (183 Gore Creek Dr., 970/479-7365, 10am-6pm Sun.-Thurs., 10am-8pm Fri.-Sat.) is a surprisingly affordable boutique whose proceeds benefit the Betty Ford Alpine Gardens. The well-rounded selection includes candles, hats, scarves, and stained glass. **Wild Bill's Emporium** (225 Wall St., 970/476-5738, 10am-9pm daily) is the place to go for knickknacks like coffee mugs, cowboy hats, and pillows with pithy sayings like, "Life's too short to dance with ugly men."

Axel's (201 Gore Creek Dr., 970/497-4888, https://axelsltd.com, 10am-9pm daily) is a men's fashion store featuring classic Southwestern clothing, Stallion boots, made-to-order shirts, and a variety of handcrafted sterling-silver belt buckles (north of $1,800). For contemporary women's and girls' clothing, head to **FRINJE** (172 Gore Creek Dr., 970/476-7774, 10am-8pm daily), which features trendsetting and classic labels from Minnie Rose to Custom Ketchup.

There are a number of high-end art galleries in Vail Village, including the **J. Cotter Gallery** (234 E. Wall St., 970/476-3131, www.jcottergallery.com, 10am-8pm daily), with a selection of boldly designed, contemporary jewelry made from gold, silver, and other materials. **Artful Sol** (183 Gore Creek Dr., 970/476-1339, www.artfulsol.com, noon-9pm Mon.-Sat., noon-6pm Sun.) features eye-catching sculpture and paintings by contemporary artists like Jamsu and Shawna Moore, as well as one-of-a-kind silver jewelry.

The Vail Valley's only bookstore is **The Bookworm** (295 Main St., Edwards, 970/926-7323, www.bookwormofedwards.com, 8am-7pm Mon.-Fri., 9am-5pm Sat.-Sun.), located in the Riverwalk shopping center in the small town of Edwards, 14 miles west of Vail. The Bookworm has a strong local focus, with plenty of maps and local interest books, as well as a café serving up an enticing selection of sweet and savory crepes, salads, and smoothies.

FOOD
Breakfast and Cafés

For a steaming latte, head to **Big Bear Bistro** (297 Hanson Ranch Rd., 970/445-1007, www.bigbearbistro.com, 8am-5pm Sun.-Thurs., 8am-6pm Fri.-Sat., $5-12), which serves Lavazza coffees, thick sandwiches with Boar's Head meats on fresh-baked, organic ciabatta bread, and all-day breakfasts like the Da Vinci—smoked sockeye salmon on a warm bagel with cream cheese, tomato, onion, and capers.

Usually filled with happy repeat customers is **The Little Diner** (616 W. Lionshead Cir., 970/476-4279, http://thelittlediner.com, 7am-2pm daily, $8-13) in Lionshead Village. With almost everything on the breakfast and lunch menu made from scratch, it's like dining at your grandma's house, only a lot more modern, with a large, wooden dining bar surrounding the bustling kitchen and enormous stainless hood. Many of the ingredients are locally sourced and the prices are actually *affordable*. Don't leave Vail without trying the *pannekoeken* (soufflé-like popovers).

Casual

At the west end of the Vail Village parking structure, **Pazzo's Pizzeria** (122 E. Meadow Dr., 970/476-9026, www.pazzospizza.com, 11am-close daily, $11-15) was founded by three ski bums-turned-restaurateurs. It's a laid-back spot to stop for a bite before you jump in your car or head to the bowling alley or ice-skating rink across the street. In addition to some great pizza combos like the Cabbo Pazzo (shrimp, jalapeños, pineapple, cilantro, and garlic), they serve up cheesy baked rigatoni, big pasta dinners, and Pazzones—pizza pockets stuffed with pepperoni, mushrooms, and other fresh ingredients.

In Lionshead, the cheerful, diner-style **Westside Café and Market** (2211 N. Frontage Rd. West, 970/476-7890, www.westsidecafe.net, 7am-3pm Mon.-Wed., 7am-9:30pm Thurs.-Sun., $14-28) is usually packed with chattering patrons enjoying "authentic American comfort food." From great pre-ski plates like dirty biscuits and gravy and the world's best Benes (eggs Benedict) to black and bleu burgers and bison meatloaf, every meal is covered. There are some tempting veggie options, as well. Across the street from the Eagle Bahn Gondola and a big deck overlooking Gore Creek, **El Sabor** (660 Lionshead Pl., 970/477-4410, http://elsaborvail.com, 8am-10pm daily, $16-25) is the place to head for big portions of Latino food. The grab-and-go breakfast options are perfect if you're on your way up the slopes, and the margaritas are very popular for après-ski, especially on sunny days when you can enjoy the large deck. The *camarones del diablo*—shrimp sautéed with spicy chiles—is highly recommended, as is the mole chicken.

Upscale

With a great location in Vail Village, **Sweet Basil** (193 E. Gore Creek Dr., 970/476-0125, https://sweetbasilvail.com, 11:30am-10pm daily, $33-52) is an eco-minded establishment with an interesting menu format: The dishes showcase organic and sustainably sourced foods, from ahi ceviche to wild mushrooms and she crab soup. The nearby **Lancelot Restaurant** (201 Gore Creek Dr., 970/476-5828, www.lancelotvail.com, 5:30pm-10pm daily, $26-42) has been serving up seafood and slow-roasted prime rib since 1969. The Austrian chef features traditional favorites like wiener schnitzel as well as tender cuts of filet mignon and New York strip steaks. If

you have any room left, try the divine mudpie (with peanut butter ice cream) or the housemade apple strudel, served with a scoop of vanilla bean ice cream.

Across from the Sonnenalp in Vail Village, **Osaki Vail** (168 E. Meadow Dr., 970/476-0977, www.osakivail.com, 5:30pm-close Tues.-Sun., $12-80) serves the freshest sushi in town, along with sake and Japanese beer. Choose between hot and cold rolls or combination entrées. If you just can't decide, try the seven-course chef's tasting menu ($80). It's a small venue, so reservations are a must. In the center of Lionshead Village, **Montauk Seafood Grill** (549 E. Lionshead Cir., 970/476-2601, www.montaukseafood.com, après-ski 3pm-5pm daily, dinner 6pm-close daily, $30-65) has a long wine list to pair with its beautifully presented seafood dishes. The fish varies daily and is always fresh; choose how you'd like it prepared—seared, steamed, herb-crusted, or grilled. Reservations are recommended.

Vail's signature dining locale is the **Game Creek Restaurant** (278 Hanson Ranch Rd., 970/754-4275, www.gamecreekvail.com, 5:30pm-9pm Tues.-Sat. in winter; 5:30pm-8:30pm Thurs.-Sat., 11am-2pm Sun. in summer, $99-140), a chalet-style restaurant overlooking the Game Creek back bowl. Accessible only by snowcat in winter and hiking or four-wheel drive in summer, dining here is as much about the experience as the food—five-star cuisine served in three, four, or five-course dinners, as well as a three-course child's menu your little one will actually enjoy. Since it's a special meal, save room for one of the tempting desserts, such as beignets topped with dark chocolate sauce, caramel hazelnuts, and raspberry dust.

ACCOMMODATIONS

Most of Vail's hotels are located in the central part of town between the Vail and Lionshead Villages. Except during mud season, there are few deals to be had; expect to pay dearly, especially if the lodging is located close to the slopes. Fortunately, Vail is an easy town to navigate, with many walking paths, heated (ice-free) streets, and convenient shuttles. Less-expensive accommodations can be found in Edwards (14 miles west) or in Minturn.

In the heart of Vail Village, the 25-room **Austria Haus** (242 E. Meadow Dr., 866/921-4050, www.austriahaushotel.com, $502-949) is styled after traditional chalets in the Austrian Alps. The Haus has an amazing pool right on Gore Creek, as well as remodeled bathrooms complete with heated marble floors, gas fireplaces in the suites, and a hearty mountain breakfast with fruit, oatmeal, meats and cheeses, and fresh-baked goodies. The **Hotel Gasthof Gramshammer** (231 Gore Creek Dr., 970/476-5626, www. pepis.com, $306-815) was established in 1964 by former Austrian Olympic ski racer Pepi Gramshammer and his wife, Sheika, who hails from an old innkeeper's family. When they opened their hotel, it was the only building in this part of town; now it has one of the resort's best locations just steps from downtown and Gondola One. Options range from a beautifully appointed and sunny penthouse suite to standard rooms with two double or one king bed (these are located above the bar where there's live music until 10pm on winter nights).

A bit farther from Gondola One is **The Sebastian** (16 Vail Rd., 800/354-6908, www.thesebastianvail.com, $1,100-1,227), whose elegant rooms were remodeled in 2014. The hotel has all the perks, from ski-in valet service, hot cocoa and boot warmers, to estate-quality furnishings, limited-edition artwork, and thick duvet covers in their standard rooms (never mind the suites). Located between Vail and Lionshead Villages, the **Evergreen Lodge at Vail** (250 S. Frontage Rd. West, 800/284-8245, http://evergreenvail. com, $365-730) has half-off lodging deals if you book far in advance. Their oversized valley- and mountain-view rooms have recliner chairs, mini-fridges, and coffee makers, and the fitness center, saunas, and game room are a nice plus.

In Lionshead Village, Vail Resort Rentals

the Hotel Gasthof Gramshammer

manages the two-bed, two-bath **Lionshead Arcade Condominiums** (635 N. Frontage Rd., 800/456-8245, www.lionsheadarcade. com, $256-805), situated in a prime spot steps from the Lionshead Gondola. Covered parking and substantial discounts are available for longer stays. In the same location, the **Lift House Lodge** (555 E. Lionshead Cir., 800/654-0635, http://lifthousevail.com, $109-499) has some of Vail's most affordable accommodations: "hotel residences" (1-bed, 1-bath) that allow up to two pets ($30 per pet per night).

Colorado's biggest resort has one on-mountain lodging option at the Swiss-style **Game Creek Chalet** (970/754-7777, http://arrabelle. rockresorts.com, $1,200 per night). Tucked into the glades in Game Creek Bowl, 2,000 feet above Vail Village, this secluded four-bed, five-bath home has all the amenities—a gourmet kitchen, high-speed Wi-Fi, satellite TV, and personal concierge service—plus a steaming hot tub with one of the most amazing views in Colorado.

TRANSPORTATION AND SERVICES

Air

Denver International Airport (DEN, 8500 Peña Blvd., 303/342-2000, http://www.flydenver.com) is the closest major airport to Vail. The smaller **Eagle County Regional Airport** (EGE, 219 Eldon Wilson Rd., Gypsum, 970/328-2680, www.eaglecounty.us), a 40-minute drive west of Vail on I-70, offers nonstop service to 10 major cities, including New York, Atlanta, Chicago, Houston, and Toronto, during the ski season. Summer flights are more limited, but include service to Denver and Houston.

To reach Vail from the Eagle County Regional Airport, take the main airport road (Cooley Mesa Rd.) to U.S. 6. Turn right, heading east, and follow U.S. 6 to I-70. Merge and follow I-70 east for 35 miles to the Vail exit. It's most convenient to park in either the Vail Village or the Lionshead parking structures.

Car

Vail is located 100 miles west of Denver, and 120 miles west of Denver International Airport, on I-70. To reach Vail from Denver, follow I-70 west directly to Vail. In ideal conditions, this 120-mile trip takes two hours, but it can take substantially longer during rush hour and/or inclement weather.

Due to Vail's high real estate prices, there are no depots for major car rental companies. Avis, Dollar, and Thrifty have locations at the Eagle County Regional Airport. Enterprise and Hertz have depots in Avon, near the Beaver Creek Resort, about 13 miles west of Vail.

Shuttle and Bus

Several shuttle services provide transport to Vail from both airports, including **Colorado Mountain Express** (970/754-7433, www.coloradomountainexpress.com, year-round, $85-99 one-way from DIA, $39-49 one-way from EGE), which offers frequent shuttles to hotels, condos, and other locations in the Vail Valley as well as Summit County.

Fresh Tracks Transportation (970/453-7433, www.freshtrackstransportation.com, $45 Vail to Breckenridge) operates resort-to-resort shuttles between Vail, Beaver Creek, Copper Mountain, Keystone, Breckenridge, and Arapahoe Basin.

ECO Transit (970/328-3520, www.eaglecounty.us, $7 one-way Vail to Beaver Creek) offers service between the **Vail Transportation Center** (241 S. Frontage Rd. East) and Beaver Creek, Leadville, and other towns in Eagle County. The Colorado Department of Transportation's **Bustang** (800/900-3011, www.codot.gov, $28 one-way) has once-daily regional service between Union Station in Denver and Glenwood Springs; it also stops at the Vail Transportation Center.

Vail has a **local bus** (970/477-3456, www.vailgov.com, year-round, free) that shuttles people to and from the mountain and around town. There are lines to the Vail Golf Course, East Vail, and West Vail; the in-town black line circles between Vail and Lionshead Villages. Bus service is reduced outside of the main ski season (mid-Dec.-mid-Apr.).

Services

VISITOR INFORMATION

Vail operates two information centers. The **Vail Village Welcome Center** (241 S. Frontage Rd., 970/476-4790, www.vailgov.com, 8:30am-5:30pm daily in winter, 9am-8pm daily in summer, 9am-5pm daily spring and fall) is located on level 4 of the Vail Village parking garage. The **Lionshead Welcome Center** (395 E. Lionshead Cir., 970/476-4941, www.vailgov.com, 8:30am-7pm daily in winter, 9am-8pm daily in summer, 9am-5pm daily spring and fall) is in the southwest corner of the Lionshead parking garage's lower level. Either location can assist with restaurant and lodging reservations, booking seasonal activities, and maps. The town website (www.vail.com) is the best source of information for the ski resort (weather forecasts, snow conditions, grooming reports, lodging, activities), or call the Vail Resort (800/842-8062).

MEDIA AND COMMUNICATIONS

Vail Welcome Centers have free Wi-Fi. The **Vail Public Library** (Lionshead Village, 292 W. Meadow Dr., 970/479-2184, http://vaillibrary.com, 10am-8pm Mon.-Thurs., 11am-6pm Fri.-Sun.) has free public Internet workstations and wireless Internet access.

Vail's **post office** (1300 N. Frontage Rd. West, 970/476-1494, 8:30am-5pm Mon.-Fri., 8:30am-noon Sat.) is located on the north side of I-70 in the Cascade Village.

The *Vail Daily* (www.vaildaily.com) is the Vail Valley's daily paper, distributed for free in local coffee shops, restaurants, and stores. It focuses on local news, sports, and entertainment, and its website also features a calendar of upcoming events. The Zephyr radio station, KZYR (97.7 FM), "Ski Country" KSKE (101.7 FM), and Colorado Public Radio station KPRE (89.9 FM) all have a strong community-oriented focus.

MEDICAL

Based in Vail, the **Vail Valley Medical Center** (180 S. Frontage Rd. West, 970/476-2451, www.vvmc.com) serves the entire valley. Urgent care facilities include **Colorado Mountain Clinic** (970/926-6340, www.cmmhealth.com, 8am-5pm Mon.-Fri., 8am-2pm Sat.), which has three valley locations, including Vail (108 S. Frontage Rd. West #101), Edwards (322 Beard Creek Rd. #200), and Eagle (377 Sylvan Lake Rd. #210).

The Vail Valley

A few miles west of Vail, I-70 meets the Eagle River, a popular and beautiful fly-fishing stream that flows through a region commonly called the Vail Valley. Stretching about 40 miles from Vail to tiny Dotsero, where the Eagle joins the mighty Colorado River, this region has its own distinct character. Encircled by the 2.3-million-acre White River National Forest, the area feels more isolated, with smaller and more rural towns and an environment that blends the best of the central Rockies with a taste of western Colorado's drier, slickrock setting.

In addition to Vail Mountain, the area includes the affluent Beaver Creek ski area and the satellite towns of Arrowhead, Avon, and Edwards, as well as Red Cliff, Eagle County's oldest town, and Minturn, a former railroad crossroads that today hosts a thriving arts community and one of the state's most vibrant farmers markets.

BEAVER CREEK

Located just south of the interstate town of Avon, Beaver Creek Resort is synonymous with luxury. Its history is intertwined with that of the 1976 Winter Olympic games, which were originally awarded to the city of Denver. Some of the alpine events were planned for the still-to-be-built ski resort, but these plans were shelved after Colorado voters rejected a bond issue to finance the games and Denver became the only city to ever back out of hosting the Olympics.

In 1972, Vail Resorts purchased the land and began designing a European-style resort inspired by some of the Alps' top destinations. After a number of delays, Beaver Creek finally opened in 1980. Four years later, it expanded considerably after acquiring the neighboring Arrowhead Mountain. Today, Beaver Creek is celebrated for its abundance of well-appointed ski-in, ski-out accommodations, a diverse terrain accessible to skiers of all ability levels, annual World Cup races, and exceptional service.

Sports and Recreation
DOWNHILL SKIING AND SNOWBOARDING

No matter your ability level, you'll find plenty of runs to enjoy at **Beaver Creek**

Resort (26 Avondale Lane, Avon, 888/222-1878, www.beavercreek.com, $175 full-day lift ticket). The resort is well laid out across four mountains, which are separated by three base areas: Beaver Creek, Bachelor Gulch, and Arrowhead Villages. One of the resort's charms is skiing from village to village and back again. The Strawberry Park Express lift passes over some amazing houses (including one once owned by Tom Hanks). At the residential area's most uphill extent is the former residence of President and Mrs. Ford (an adjacent, flat-roofed building was used by their Secret Service detail). You can ski past these on the black-diamond President Ford's run.

Originally developed for beginner to intermediate skiers, **Arrowhead Mountain** is generally the quietest and best-suited area for families and those still learning to board and ski. Beginners in this part of the resort will especially enjoy the green **Little Brave** and **Sawbuck** trails. More fun green runs, including **Red Buffalo, Powell,** and **Solitude,** are located on the upper slopes of Beaver Creek Mountain, which is accessed by the painfully slow Drink of Water lift. These two areas also host most of the resort's seven Kids Adventure Zones.

With 42 percent of Beaver Creek's trails rated blue, intermediate skiers have plenty of great options. A good place to start is lower Beaver Creek Mountain's Centennial Express lift, which accesses **Gold Dust** and **Latigo.** Follow these with a run down **Harrier,** a steeper blue that leads to the Talons Restaurant. From here, you get a great view of the incredibly steep Birds of Prey area, where the World Cup races are held. If you're not up for trying those trails, take the Larkspur Express lift, which accesses the wide-open **Larkspur,** as well as **Primrose,** which leads back to the Strawberry Park area. At Arrowhead, **Golden Bear** and **Cresta** are two recommended blues.

Beaver Creek also offers several concentrations of advanced and expert runs, including the Rose Bowl, whose best run is **Ripsaw;** Grouse Mountain, where **Screech Owl** is known for holding powder long after most other runs; and the Birds of Prey area. This includes the **Kestrel** run, which is part of the women's Raptor World Cup race course, as well as the breathtakingly steep **Golden Eagle** trail, one segment of the men's Birds of Prey World Cup downhill course.

Beaver Creek Resort

ICE-SKATING AND SNOWSHOEING

The resort has **ice-skating** (60 Avondale La., Avon, 970/845-0438, www.beavercreek. com, noon-9pm daily in winter, 6pm-10pm daily in summer, $15 includes admission and skate rental) in the center of Beaver Creek Village. A **Nordic Sports Center** (1280 Village Rd., 970/754-5313, www.beavercreek. com, 8:45am-4pm daily mid-Dec.-early Apr., $36 lift ticket and $30-53 for gear rental) offers snowshoe as well as skate and telemark skiing rentals. Lessons are held in the resort's McCoy Park, where 32 kilometers of Nordic trails can be accessed via the Strawberry Park Express lift.

HIKING AND BIKING

During the summer, the resort offers a host of activities, including scenic chairlift rides, downhill mountain biking, horseback riding, and hiking. Of the designated hiking-only trails, four begin near the **Summer Adventure Center** (Starbucks Plaza, 970/754-5200, www.beavercreek.com, 9am-4pm daily mid-June-Sept.) in Beaver Creek Village. The **Creekside Family Walk** (1.5 miles) is an easy loop that meanders through Creekside Park, where there's a playground and picnic tables. The more challenging **Beaver Lake Trail** (6 miles) climbs past Beano's Cabin to Beaver Lake. The **Beaver Creek Hiking Center** (970/754-5373, www. beavercreek.com, 9am-4pm daily mid-June-early Sept.) offers guided hikes on Beaver Creek Mountain and other destinations, including fourteeners. **Beaver Creek Sports** (Beaver Creek Village, 970/754-6221, www. beavercreeksports.com, $50 for four hours) rents bikes at multiple area locations.

★ GOLF

Golf is Beaver Creek's biggest draw during the summer. The area boasts three championship courses, including the resort's Robert Trent Jones Jr.-designed **Beaver Creek Golf Club** (103 Offerson Rd., 970/754-5170, www. beavercreek.com, $205), known for its long, narrow fairways. The course has a dress code

and restricted public access; available dates and times are listed on the website. Guests staying in Vail Resorts lodging also have access to two nearby courses—one designed by Greg Norman and one by Tom Fazio—at the exclusive **Red Sky Golf Club** (1099 Red Sky Rd., 970/754-8425, www.redskygolfclub.com, $210-255).

FISHING

Fly-fishing in the Eagle River, Colorado River, and other nearby streams is a popular pastime in the Vail Valley. **Gore Creek Fly Fisherman** (1 Beaver Creek Pl., 970/754-5430, www.gorecreekflyfisherman.com, 10am-5pm Sat.-Sun.), the region's oldest fishing shop, provides gear, clinics, guided trips, and river reports at several area stores.

★ SPAS

Pure bliss awaits the visitors to Beaver Creek's many excellent spas. Top picks include the **Allegria Spa** (136 E. Thomas Pl., 970/949-1234, www.allegriaspa.com, treatments 9am-7pm daily during high season, $155 for 50-minute massage) in the Park Hyatt Beaver Creek Resort, where you can indulge in acupuncture and Ashiatsu treatments as well as lavender rose hot oil wraps, and the **Bachelor Gulch Spa** (130 Daybreak Ridge Rd., 970/343-1138, www.ritzcarlton.com, $195 for 60-minute massage) in The Ritz-Carlton Bachelor Gulch. The facility's 21,000-square-foot retreat has 19 treatment rooms, a mani-pedi salon, and men's, women's, and co-ed rock-lined grottos with sauna, steam, and hot and cold plunge areas.

Entertainment and Events

Beaver Creek is not as well known for its nightlife, but there are several fun places for après-ski deals. Within the resort, the **Dusty Boot Saloon** (210 Offerson Rd., 970/748-1146, http://dustybootbeavercreek.com, 11am-10pm daily) is known for its regular happy hour (3pm-5pm daily) as well as its thick, juicy steaks. In the Park Hyatt, the **8100 Mountainside Bar & Grill** (136 E. Thomas Pl., 970/949-1234, http://beavercreek.park.

hyatt.com, happy hour 2pm-5:30pm daily) has a good selection of local wines and microbrews. Outdoor fire pits keep you warm while drinking in the mountain scenery.

More (and cheaper) nightlife options are available in the nearby town of Avon, which is accessible by a free bus. One of the most popular spots is **Agave** (1060 W. Beaver Creek Blvd., 970/748-8666, 11:30am-10pm daily in high season), a Mexican restaurant known for live, late-night music and DJs, a large tequila selection, and its often-packed dance floor. **Loaded Joe's Coffeehouse and Lounge** (82 E. Beaver Creek Blvd., 970/748-1480, www. loadedjoes.com, 7am-2am daily in high season) is a more relaxed spot offering nearly round-the-clock beverages from gourmet espresso to beer and wine, as well as refreshingly simple sandwiches, salads, and burritos.

Known for its excellent acoustics, the 535-seat **Vilar Performing Arts Center** (68 Avondale La., 970/845-8497, www.vvf.org, box office 11am-5pm Mon.-Fri.) in the center of the Beaver Creek Resort hosts year-round concerts, musicals, and dance and classical music performances. Some of the recent headliners include K.D. Lang, Marc Cohn, the Dance Theatre of Harlem, and Boz Scaggs.

Signature summer events at the resort (www.beavercreek.com) include the **Blues, Brews, and BBQ** festival (late May), the **Independence Day Celebration** (July 4), the **Art Festival** (Aug.), and the **Wine & Spirits Festival** (mid-Aug.).

Food

Toscanini (Beaver Creek Village, 60 Avondale La., Avon, 970/754-5590, www.toscaninibeavercreek.com, 5pm-9pm daily, $12-38) is a surprisingly affordable, kid-friendly Italian restaurant known for its long list of exclusively Italian wine. The short menu includes delicious seafood and pasta dishes like porcini ravioli, as well as gourmet, Italian-style wood-fired pizzas. Consistently rated as one of Beaver Creek's top restaurants, the **Grouse Mountain Grill** (141 Scotthill Rd., 970/949-0600, www.grousemountaingrill.

com, 4pm-11pm daily, $35-39) is led by executive chef David Gutowski, who served as a featured chef at Manhattan's James Beard House. The menu varies seasonally, but everything is made in-house, including the garden-fresh salads, delectable lobster mascarpone, and mushroom agnolotti.

Beaver Creek's most adventurous dining option is **Beano's Cabin** (Beaver Creek Mtn., 970/754-3463, www.beanoscabinbeavercreek. com, 5:30pm-8:45pm daily early Dec.-early Apr., 5:30pm-8:45pm Thurs.-Sun. June-Sept., $129 for 5 courses). Part of the fun is simply getting here; in winter, the cozy cabin is accessible only by a 20-minute, open-air sleigh pulled by a snowcat. In summer, you can get here by van, wagon, or even horseback. The building's floor-to-ceiling windows highlight the spectacular setting beneath the steepest part of Grouse Mountain, and the food and wine list get rave reviews.

The winter sleigh rides and summer van shuttles both leave from the C Bar next to the Strawberry Express Lift. The wagon and horseback rides leave from the Beaver Creek Stables (Elk Track Rd.) just above the village.

For casual options, head to **Pho 20** (47 E. Beaver Creek Blvd., Avon, 970/748-3007, www. pho20avon.com, 11am-9pm daily, $8-14) for some Vietnamese noodle soup. **The Gashouse** (34185 U.S. 6, Edwards, 970/926-3613, www. gashouse-restaurant.com, 11am-10pm, $14-49) serves steak, duck, and seafood. Pub fare and foaming glasses of craft beer are at the **Gore Range Brewery** (105 Edwards Village Blvd., Edwards, 970/926-2739, www.gorerangebrewery.com, 11:30am-10pm daily, $12-28).

Accommodations

The accommodations at Beaver Creek are extremely expensive, especially during ski season. Cheaper options are available in nearby towns like Edwards and Eagle. There are also good deals to be had during the late spring and mid-fall mud seasons.

The Charter at Beaver Creek (120 Offerson Rd., 970/949-6660, www.wyndhamvacationrentals.com, $475-750) is a beautiful ski-in, ski-out property tucked between tall pine trees near the Elkhorn Lift in Beaver Creek Village. Guests can choose between cozy one- and two-bed lodge rooms with extra-thick mattresses and high-thread-count sheets or well-appointed condos with full kitchens, but you won't want to miss the lavish and surprisingly affordable breakfast buffet at **The Terrace Restaurant.** A full-service spa, on-site equipment rentals, hot tubs, indoor and outdoor pools, and a terrace fire pit—where s'more kits for the kiddos are sold—complete the European-style alpine village.

The **Park Hyatt Beaver Creek** (136 E. Thomas Pl., 970/949-1234, http://beaver-creek.park.hyatt.com, $397-522) has been consistently rated one of the top resorts in the western United States. Many of its 190 rooms have stunning mountain views, and the hotel allows dogs (with a post-pooch deep cleaning). **The Osprey at Beaver Creek** (10 Elk Track Rd., 888/605-3405, http://ospreyatbeavercreek.rockresorts.com, $909-1,079) is the closest hotel to a chairlift—just 26 feet separate it from the Strawberry Park Express lift. You don't even have to carry your skis; valets will do that for you. With only 45 guest rooms (plus one 2-bedroom penthouse), this boutique property has garnered accolades for its sophisticated mountain decor and intimate, cozy atmosphere.

Beaver Creek's most luxurious property, **The Ritz-Carlton Bachelor Gulch** (130 Daybreak Ridge Rd., 970/748-6200, www.ritzcarlton.com, $899-1,499) is designed to evoke "the great mountain lodges of the American West." Located in the middle of the resort, this luxe hotel is at the base of the Bachelor Gulch Express lift and has eyebrow-raising amenities like Bachelor, the property's "St. Bernard canine ambassador," fitness classes, whirlpools, a game room, The Bachelor Gulch Spa, and scenic views from all of its 180 rooms, which feature such perks as marble bathrooms with oversized soaking tubs and 400-thread count Frette linens.

Transportation and Services

CAR

Beaver Creek is located 13 miles west of Vail along I-70 at exit 163. At the town of Avon, turn left onto Avon Road and continue three miles south (Avon Road becomes Village Road south of I-70). From Denver the trip takes about 2.25 hours to drive, but can take substantially longer depending upon traffic and/or inclement weather.

Enterprise and Hertz have depots in Avon, the town closest to Beaver Creek Resort. In addition to numerous pay parking lots, Beaver Creek Resort offers convenient free parking and shuttle service to the mountain from the Elk and Bear lots, both located just west of the main welcome gate.

SHUTTLE AND BUS

Colorado Mountain Express (970/754-7433, www.coloradomountainexpress.com, $85-99 one-way from DIA, $39-49 one-way from EGE) offers frequent, year-round shuttles to hotels, condos, and other locations in the Vail Valley. **Fresh Tracks Transportation** (970/453-7433, www.fresh-trackstransportation.com, $50 Beaver Creek to Breckenridge) operates resort-to-resort shuttles between Beaver Creek and Copper Mountain, Keystone, and Breckenridge. **ECO Transit** (970/328-3520, www.eaglecounty.us, $7 one-way Beaver Creek to Vail) offers year-round service between Beaver Creek and the towns of Vail, Edwards, and Eagle. Catch the bus at Beaver Creek either by the Reception Center near the main gate or the Bear parking lot by the west entrance.

A free shuttle system operates within Beaver Creek and between Bachelor Gulch Villages (but not Arrowhead). Outside of the ski season, **Village Transportation** (970/949-1938, www.beavercreek.com, 7am-midnight daily) is available anywhere within the resort.

SERVICES

The closest hospital is the **Vail Valley Medical Center** (180 S. Frontage Rd. West,

970/476-2451, www.vvmc.com). The **Beaver Creek Medical Center** (1280 Village Rd., 970/949-0800, www.vvmc.com, 8am-5:30pm daily in winter), located in the Strawberry Park building across the skier bridge from Village Hall (near the base of the Strawberry Park lift), provides emergency and urgent medical care during the ski season.

MINTURN

Minturn is a small, sleepy community that feels like it's a world apart from the elegance and extravagance of Beaver Creek and Vail. An important mining and railroad hub in the late 1800s, Minturn today is a charming place to shop, hike, and enjoy a meal—or, if you enjoy serenity and nature, to base yourself out of while exploring the entire Vail Valley.

Five miles west of Vail, U.S. 24 heads south from the interstate to follow the Eagle River upstream. Minturn is located just a few miles up this route.

★ Minturn Farmers Market

Try to time your trip so that you can stop by the **Minturn Farmers Market** (downtown, www.minturnmarket.org, 9am-2pm Sat. July-early Sept.). Organized by the Town of Minturn (302 Pine St., 970/827-5645), the market is a microcosm of this vibrant community—a delightful combination of bright colors, fresh scents, happy chatter, and friendly smiles, all underlain by a strong sense of the town's creative independent spirit. Whether you're looking for fresh ingredients for a picnic lunch, a cup of fresh-brewed coffee, crunchy organic produce, or a handmade gift or souvenir to take back home, you'll love strolling through the colorful chaos of nearly 70 vendors' stalls, munching on locally made dishes and visiting with the locals.

Sports and Recreation

Minturn is almost surrounded by national forest, including the 122,800-acre **Holy Cross Wilderness,** named after its highest peak, Mount of the Holy Cross, a challenging fourteener. Named for a cross-shaped snowfield on the mountain's northeastern face, the peak was the centerpiece of a national monument designated by Herbert Hoover in 1933. After visitation declined and a rockfall obscured part of the cross, the National Park Service returned it to the White River National Forest in 1950. The Forest Service's **Holy Cross District** (24747 U.S. 24, 970/827-5715, www.fs.usda.gov) hosts 225 miles of trails and is now a hotbed of hiking, mountain biking,

Minturn Farmers Market

camping, backcountry skiing, and other recreation. The Downtown Minturn website (www.downtownminturn.com) lists a number of suggested hiking and biking trails and provides information about other popular local activities. Local resources include **Minturn Anglers** (102 Main St., 970/827-9500, www.minturnanglers.com, 10am-6pm daily in season) and **Mountain Pedaler** (161 Main St., 970/827-5522, www.mountainpedaler.com, noon-5pm Mon., 10am-6pm Tues.-Fri., 10am-4pm Sat. in summer).

Shopping

Explore some of the small indie shops downtown. **Eagle Valley Music & Comics** (211 Main St., 970/476-1713, 10am-8pm daily) has been in business since 1983. **Holy Toledo** (191 Main St., 970/827-4299, http://holytoledo.co, 10am-6pm Mon.-Fri., 10am-4pm Sat.-Sun.) is a fun and funky consignment shop housed in an old church (hence the tongue-in-cheek name).

Food

The **Sticky Fingers Café and Bakery** (132 Main St., 970/827-5353, 7:30am-5pm daily, $6) is the homey place where locals head for breakfast, lunch, and brunch, including flaky quiche, crunchy salads, and inspired drinks like lavender lattes and green goddess smoothies. For local color, head to the **Minturn Saloon** (146 Main St., 970/827-5954, www.minturnsaloon.com, 5pm-close in winter, 5:30pm-close in summer, $12-36), housed in a historic 1901 building whose wooden walls are plastered with more than 1,000 black-and-white photos and a stuffed buffalo head. This laid-back saloon serves up some of Colorado's best margaritas (try the Liquid Plummer), as well as large platters of Mexican food and some unique Old West dishes, like quail & enchilada and saloon steak.

Accommodations

Minturn's down-home lodging options are a welcome change from the sticker shock of the ski resort towns. The contemporary **Hotel Minturn** (167 Williams St., 970/331-5461, www.hotelminturn.com, $179-239) has heated floors, comfy beds, and a peaceful atmosphere ideal after a long day outdoors. The **Minturn Inn** (442 Main St., 970/827-9647, www.minturninn.com, $209-369) is a bed-and-breakfast that operates two properties: a beautifully renovated 1915 hewn-log cabin and a lodge located on the bank of the rushing Eagle River. The large rooms are spacious and bright; deluxe rooms have fireplaces and whirlpool tubs. The owners will greet you with warm cookies and a smile.

RED CLIFF

Blink and you might miss the tiny enclave of Red Cliff, named for the steep, reddish cliffs looming above the small cluster of old buildings and trailers along the upper Eagle River. The town was founded in 1879 as a mining camp during the state's silver boom. Today, it's best known for being the end point of a popular, year-round recreation trail.

Red Cliff is located nine miles south of Minturn on U.S. 24.

Shrine Pass

One of the central Colorado Rockies' most popular adventures is traversing **Shrine Pass Road,** which links Red Cliff with the top of Vail Pass on I-70. Thanks to the relatively gentle terrain, beautiful scenery, and easy access, the route is popular year-round with skiers, hikers, mountain bikers, and four-wheel drive and off-highway-vehicle drivers. The 11.2-mile (one-way) route customarily begins on the pass and ends in Red Cliff, the direction that minimizes the elevation gain (570 feet).

From the Vail Pass rest area on I-70, the route climbs steadily for 2.5 miles, then drops into a small bowl and crosses a saddle, where there are amazing views of the Gore and Ten Mile Ranges. After passing a clearing near several 10th Mountain Division huts, the road descends almost 2,500 vertical feet, roughly following the path of Turkey Creek. Along the way there are stunning views of the Mount of the Holy

Classic Ski Trails

Too much powder, too little time? Here are a dozen of the central Rockies' must-do ski runs, organized by difficulty:

- **Expert** (double-black diamond): Pallavicini (Arapahoe Basin), Golden Eagle (Beaver Creek)

- **Difficult** (black diamond): Riva Ridge (Vail), Peerless (Breckenridge), Starfire (Keystone), Rosi's Run (Copper)

- **Intermediate** (blue square): Cashier (Breckenridge), Flying Dutchman (Keystone), Dealer's Choice (Vail), Larkspur (Beaver Creek)

- **Beginner** (green circle): Schoolmarm (Keystone), High Point (Copper)

Cross, including from a large deck popular with wedding parties. The route ends in Red Cliff, where hungry explorers usually head straight to **Mango's Mountain Grill** (166.5 Eagle St., 970/827-9109, www.mangosmountaingrill.com, hours vary seasonally, $5-7) for tasty fish tacos, burgers, and frosty margaritas.

To avoid getting lost, bring a detailed route description, topographic map, and compass, and be sure to stay on the road. This route requires a shuttle; if you don't have access to two cars, local services like **Ski & Bike Valet** (970/476-5385, $75 including bike rental and shuttle) are available.

Breckenridge and Summit County

Although Vail is one of the state's best-known places, the resorts and towns in Summit County east of Vail are gems in their own right. Breckenridge Ski Resort is well visited; because it's at a higher elevation, the snow is consistently good. Another bonus is that the resort's five peaks offer plenty of interesting terrain that naturally separates into areas ideal for beginner, intermediate, and advanced skiers.

Located at the base of the resort, the town of Breckenridge has a charming appeal. The main street is lined with colorfully restored, mining-era buildings hosting dozens of excellent restaurants and charismatic shops, plus the West's oldest saloon. With the Keystone, Copper Mountain, and Arapahoe Basin resorts all within half an hour's drive, abundant opportunities for hiking, cycling, and other summer recreation, and several other interesting towns to discover, Summit County makes a great year-round base from which to explore Colorado's central Rocky Mountains.

BRECKENRIDGE

Of all the central Colorado ski towns, Breckenridge is the one with the most character. This is due in large part to its deep historic roots. Founded by gold prospectors in 1859 (more than a century before Vail), Breckenridge is packed with quaint reminders of its boom-and-bust past. This historic backdrop adds charm and vitality to this friendly, laid-back town, which feels like a real community rather than a tourist enclave. Add to this the stunning backdrop of the Ten Mile Range, almost 3,000 acres of world-class ski terrain in the adjacent resort, endless summer recreation, and its comfortable size and walkability, and it's no surprise that Breckenridge is one of Colorado's favorite destinations.

Sights
HISTORIC DISTRICT
Breckenridge's historic district is one of the oldest and largest in the state. More than 45

Breckenridge

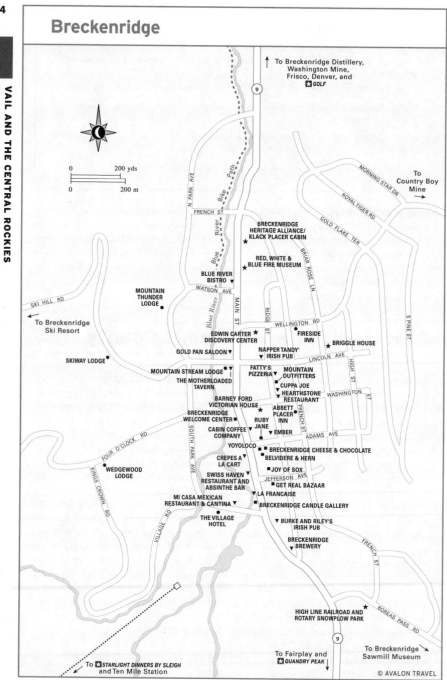

To Breckenridge Distillery, Washington Mine, Frisco, Denver, and ✚ *GOLF*

9

To Country Boy Mine

0   200 yds
0   200 m

N PARK AVE

Bike Path

MORNING STAR DR

ROYAL TIGER RD

FRENCH ST

Blue River

GOLD FLAKE TER

BRECKENRIDGE HERITAGE ALLIANCE/ KLACK PLACER CABIN ★

RED, WHITE & BLUE FIRE MUSEUM ★

BRIAR ROSE LN

BLUE RIVER BISTRO ▼

WATSON AVE

MOUNTAIN THUNDER LODGE ●

Blue River

MAIN ST

RIDGE ST

WELLINGTON RD

S PINE ST

SKI HILL RD

To Breckenridge Ski Resort

EDWIN CARTER ★ DISCOVERY CENTER

FIRESIDE INN

BRIGGLE HOUSE ★

GOLD PAN SALOON ▼

NAPPER TANDY' ▼ IRISH PUB

LINCOLN AVE

HIGH ST

SKIWAY LODGE ●

MOUNTAIN STREAM LODGE ●

THE MOTHERLOADED TAVERN

FATTY'S PIZZERIA ▼

MOUNTAIN OUTFITTERS ■

CUPPA JOE ▼

WASHINGTON ST

BARNEY FORD VICTORIAN HOUSE ★

HEARTHSTONE RESTAURANT ▼

BRECKENRIDGE WELCOME CENTER ■

ABBETT PLACER ● INN

RUBY JANE ▼

FRENCH ST

CABIN COFFEE COMPANY ▼

EMBER ▼

ADAMS AVE

YOYOLOCO ▼

BRECKENRIDGE CHEESE & CHOCOLATE ■

CREPES A ▼ LA CART

BELVIDERE & HERN ■

WEDGEWOOD LODGE ●

SWISS HAVEN ▼ RESTAURANT AND ABSINTHE BAR

JOY OF SOX ■

JEFFERSON AVE

GET REAL BAZAAR ■

MI CASA MEXICAN RESTAURANT & CANTINA ▼

LA FRANCAISE ▼

BRECKENRIDGE CANDLE GALLERY ■

THE VILLAGE HOTEL ●

FOUR O'CLOCK RD

SOUTH PARK AVE

KINGS CROWN RD

VILLAGE RD

BURKE AND RILEY'S ▼ IRISH PUB

BRECKENRIDGE ▼ BREWERY

FRENCH ST

HIGH LINE RAILROAD AND ★ ROTARY SNOWPLOW PARK

BOREAS PASS RD

9

To Fairplay and ✚ *QUANDRY PEAK*

To Breckenridge Sawmill Museum

To ✚ *STARLIGHT DINNERS BY SLEIGH* and Ten Mile Station

© AVALON TRAVEL

the Barney Ford Victorian House

blocks encompass the downtown, including both sides of Main Street and neighborhoods as far east as High Street. Within these boundaries are nearly 250 buildings listed on the National Register of Historic Places, including examples from all three of the town's main building phases. Many buildings host stylish boutiques, cozy coffee shops, and creative restaurants. Wandering through the district, exploring the local establishments in their historic venues, is one of the biggest delights of any visit to Breckenridge.

The town's first building phase began in 1859, when a prospecting company led by George Spencer established the town and named it Breckinridge after John Breckinridge, the current U.S. vice president. After Breckinridge joined the Confederate Army in 1860, however, the townspeople quietly changed the name to the current spelling, Breckenridge. Buildings constructed through the 1860s were mostly ramshackle cabins built of hand-hewn timber. One remaining example of this type of architecture

is the circa-1878 **Klack Placer Cabin** (just south of Washington Ave. between Ridge and French Sts.), one of Breckenridge's oldest residences. This rustic, two-room structure was restored by the **Breckenridge Heritage Alliance**, a local nonprofit that offers informative guided tours and hikes from the town's **Welcome Center and Museum** (203 S. Main St., 970/453-9767, http://breckheritage. com, tours 11am and 1:30pm Wed.-Sun. mid-Dec.-mid-Apr., 11am and 1:30pm Fri.-Sun. mid-Apr.-mid-June, $10).

The Welcome Center has an interesting story. During demolition of the previous building that stood on this lot, crews discovered a 19th-century log cabin sandwiched between two more recent additions. Now completely renovated, this cabin serves as an information center and interpretive museum with captivating displays narrating the town's evolution from Native American encampment to Victorian ski village.

One exhibit tells the story of Tom's Baby, one of the largest gold nuggets ever found in Colorado. After its discovery by miners Tom Groves and Harry Lytton in 1887, the 13.5-pound chunk of gold was shipped to Denver but mysteriously disappeared en route. Some 85 years later, it was rediscovered in a bank vault, though it had inexplicably lost five pounds. The skinnier, eight-pound nugget is now on display at the Denver Museum of Nature and Science.

BARNEY FORD VICTORIAN HOUSE

After Breckenridge's initial gold rush petered out, many miners left in search of other opportunities, and the camp's population plummeted. Then in 1879, the community experienced another boom when silver ore was found east of town. During this period, which continued through the 1880s, the railroad arrived and a new sawmill began operations, providing residents with milled boards that could be used to build more substantial structures.

By 1880, the downtown hosted dozens of buildings, including 18 saloons, a couple of dance halls, and a general store. Wealthier families built their homes east of Main Street, where the sun would reach them on winter afternoons. One of these is the **Barney Ford Victorian House** (111 Washington Ave., 970/453-9767, http://breckheritage.com, 11am-3pm Tues.-Sun. mid-Dec.-mid-Apr., 11am-3pm Fri.-Sun. mid-Apr.-mid-June, by donation), built in 1882 by Barney Ford, an escaped slave who first moved to Breckenridge during the silver boom. After being run off his mining claim, Ford spent some time in Denver, then returned in the early 1880s to establish a popular restaurant. After striking it rich following his investment in the Oro Mine, the town's first black business owner (and eventual member of the state legislature) built this beautiful Victorian-style home, complete with fussy curtains, intricate multicolored wallpaper, and period furnishings, for his family.

WILLIAM H. BRIGGLE HOUSE

Breckenridge's silver boom came to an end following the demonetization of silver and the Panic of 1893. By the start of the 20th century, miners turned to dredging, a technique that devastated the riverbeds and their vegetation but unearthed hundreds of thousands of dollars' worth of silver and gold. Built during this boom, the 1896 **Briggle House** (104 N. Harris St., 970/453-9767, http://breckheritage.com, tours by appointment, $10 adults) was one of the town's finest homes, where William, the town's mayor, and his wife, Kathleen, a musician, held concerts and entertained visitors amid plush Victorian decor, which has been carefully restored. Although the house isn't open regular hours, it is included in the Breckenridge Heritage Alliance's historic walking tours.

EDWIN CARTER
DISCOVERY CENTER

When Edwin Carter moved to Breckenridge in 1860, he worked as a miner. However, after observing the environmental destruction caused by hydraulic mining, whereby sand and gravel are dislodged with high-pressure hoses, Carter dedicated himself to collecting specimens of the birds and animals that were being decimated by these practices. In 1875, he built a log cabin to hold his growing collection of more than 3,000 specimens. This stout wooden cabin now hosts the **Edwin Carter Discovery Center** (111 N. Ridge St., 970/453-9767, http://breckheritage.com, 11am-3pm Tues.-Sun. mid-Dec.-mid-Apr., 11am-3pm Fri.-Sun. mid-Apr.-mid-June, by donation), whose displays include a hands-on taxidermy exhibit and an award-winning film about Carter's work and legacy.

BRECKENRIDGE
SAWMILL MUSEUM

Despite the importance of sawmills, which provided the lumber necessary to build many of the West's mining structures, commercial districts, and homes, there are few exhibits about this important facet of frontier history. The Breckenridge Heritage Alliance is currently building one at the old **Wakefield Sawmill** (Boreas Pass Rd., 1 mile east of S. Main St., 970/453-9767, http://breckheritage.com, 9am-5pm daily weather permitting, free), built in 1938 by Marion Wakefield, who operated the mill until the fall of 1959. A self-guided tour tells the story of how such mills operated, and the exhibits include a vintage Buckeye steam engine, which was used to power a similar sawmill in Leadville in the early 20th century.

RED, WHITE & BLUE FIRE MUSEUM

Although lumber was cheaper and easier to build with than stone, having wooden structures also meant that the town was very susceptible to fire. In response to a devastating fire in 1990, the town formed an all-volunteer fire department whose three companies—the Red, the White, and the Blue—were tasked with protecting the rapidly growing town. The **Red, White & Blue Fire Museum** (308 N. Main St., 970/453-2474, http://breckheritage.com, 9am-11am and 1:30pm-4pm Mon.-Fri., by donation) tells the story of these fire

Colorado's Kingdom

sunrise above Breckenridge

After gold was discovered on the Blue River in 1859, a mining camp was established in the isolated area now known as **Breckenridge.** The settlement has been a hub of activity, adventure, and lore ever since. Legend has it that the town was mistakenly left off an 1880s map of the United States and is thus considered its own kingdom.

Colorado's kingdom is home to a list of unique notable events. In 1883, a train carrying P. T. Barnum's circus couldn't make it over 11,493-foot **Boreas Pass**—at the time the world's highest railroad crossing. As trainers released their heavy circus elephants from their cars, the animals then purportedly helped push the cars up and over the Rockies.

In August of 1898, physician Joseph Condon shot dead saloonkeeper Johnny Dewers on Main Street. One week later, Pug Ryan and his henchmen robbed the Denver Hotel, where Breckenridge's elite gathered to gamble. The officers who managed to track Ryan down died in a fierce gun battle; Ryan escaped and stashed his loot.

In the winter of 1898, when Dr. Condon was to stand trial for his crime, proceedings were postponed due to the 'Big Snow'—so many flakes fell that Breckenridge residents had to dig tunnels to get around. With the supply train unable to get through and the town nearly starved for food, the citizens had to shovel out the wagon road over Boreas Pass, the same obstacle that had nearly stopped the circus in 1883.

After the gold ran out and the Wild West excitement died down, Breckenridge's population dipped below 300 souls and the few remaining residents feared they would soon be living in a ghost town. Fortunately, Colorado's ski industry was just beginning to take off and, in 1961, Rounds and Porter Lumber Company built a ski area next to town. In 1981, Breckenridge installed the world's first high-speed quad chairlift, ushering in a new era of adventure.

As for the kingdom's treasure, a group of shovel-toting schoolboys discovered Ryan's long-lost booty in 1908, buried close to town.

companies through displays of a restored hose cart and firefighting equipment from the original fire company, as well as tours led by modern-day firefighters.

HIGH LINE RAILROAD AND ROTARY SNOWPLOW PARK

Just east of Main Street on the south side of Boreas Pass Road, the **High Line Railroad and Rotary Snowplow Park** (189 Boreas Pass Rd., 970/453-9767, http://breckheritage. com, 11am-4pm Tues.-Sun. June-Sept., by donation) has an indoor museum and a year-round outdoor display featuring Engine No. 9, one of the narrow-gauge engines that provided crucial access to Colorado's isolated mining communities in the late 19th and early 20th centuries. The locomotive is located near the original High Line railroad track that ran between Breckenridge and Boreas Pass. A restored rotary, a replica caboose, and a 108-ton rotary snowplow, complete with its enormous, snow-blowing blades, are also on display. Machines like this were once used to clear snow from the tracks up to Boreas Pass, a feat that required the power from 4-6 locomotives. During the Big Snow of 1898, however, even this was insufficient to clear the tracks and get the supply train through, forcing the residents to shovel out the road by hand, a backbreaking effort that took 10 days to accomplish.

HISTORIC MINES

Following the discovery of gold and silver ore in this area, hundreds of underground mines sprouted up. One of the largest was the **Country Boy Mine** (542 French Gulch Rd., 970/453-4405, http://countryboymine.com, 9:30am-5:15pm daily late May-early Sept., reduced hours in fall, $29.95 adults). Located nine miles south of town, this restored site is a fun place to visit with the family, with gold panning in Eureka Creek, tours of original mine workings, displays of old mining equipment, a general store, burros to pet, and a slippery, 55-foot ore chute that you can rocket down.

A large silver and gold hard-rock operation, the **Washington Mine** (465 Illinois Gulch Rd., 970/453-9767, http://breckheritage.com, tours 11am and 1:30pm Tues.-Sun. mid-June-early Sept., $15) is a 20-minute drive southeast of downtown. Highly rated tours provide insight into what it must have been like for the more than 30 hardy miners who worked underground an average of 10 hours per day, six days a week, to earn about $3 per day. Following the mine's heyday around the turn of the 20th century, activity here waxed and waned until operations finally ceased in the early 1960s. In addition to touring a shaft and viewing old equipment, you can try your hand at panning for gold, or simply splash around in the creek. Access the site by following the Boreas Pass Road to the Illinois Gulch Road.

Sports and Recreation

While downhill skiing is the main draw during the winter, you can also strap on snowshoes or clip into cross-country skis to explore some of the vast wilderness surrounding the glitzy Summit County ski towns. In summer, visitors have their choice of many fun activities, including rafting, cycling, sailing, golf, and angling, as well as lacing up your boots and embarking on a quintessential Colorado experience: climbing a fourteener, one of the state's 54 peaks that top out above 14,000 feet in elevation.

DOWNHILL SKIING AND SNOWBOARDING

Breckenridge Ski Resort (1599 Ski Hill Rd., 800/789-7669, www.breckenridge.com, @BreckConditions on Twitter, $164 full-day lift ticket) is a wonderful area for downhill skiing and snowboarding. Typically open from mid-November through mid-to-late April, the resort has 2,908 skiable acres and up to 3,398 feet of vertical drop. With a high base area at 9,600 feet elevation and peaks topping out at nearly 13,000 feet, the resort is typically colder and often windier than other Colorado ski areas, but this also means that "Breckenfridge," as it's sometimes jokingly called, has stunning views and some of the fluffiest powder blanketing its slopes.

Five mountains, from north to south, are consecutively numbered Peak 6 to Peak 10. The village at the bottom of **Peak 8** is the resort's main base area. If you aren't staying in slope-side accommodations, try to arrive early (an hour before the lifts open) to park in the super-convenient **South Gondola Parking Lot** ($12 per day), from which you only need to walk a short distance to board the BreckConnect Gondola, which delivers you to either Peak 7 or 8. At the end of the day, you can follow the **4 O'Clock Run** back down to this parking lot. In addition to regular ski and board lessons, Breckenridge also offers specialty three-day packages ($705), including a three-day Women's Camp, Steeps Camp, and Kids' All-Mountain Camp.

About 11 percent of the mountain's 187 trails are classified as beginner, and these are grouped on the lower slopes of **Peak 8** and **Peak 9**. **Sawmill, Springmeier,** and lower **4 O'Clock Run** are all fun greens to try. With nearly one-third of the resort classified as blue, including most of the runs on Peaks 6, 7, and 9, Breckenridge is a great place for intermediate skiers. I enjoy warming up on the blue runs like **Claimjumper** on **Peak 7,** whose ratings feel a bit softer than the rest of the mountain, before heading to **Peak 6,** which was added to the resort in 2013. Since the **Kensho SuperChair** delivers you well above treeline, where the slopes are more exposed and windblown and the trails are less obvious, this part of the park always feels adventurous.

Black and double-black diamond skiers have their choice of runs on **Peak 10** and the higher portions of all five summits, including a number of expert runs off of North America's highest-elevation chairlift, the 12,840-foot **Imperial Express.** On Peak 7, **Ore Bucket** is known for retaining fresh powder. On Peak 10, **The Burn** is one of Breck's best-known tree-skiing runs, and **Cimmaron** is a steep and fast run with some really fun rollers. Breckenridge also has four terrain parks full of banks, boxes, jibs, jumps, and rails, and a 22-foot-tall superpipe, which

consistently attracts many of the country's top freestyle boarders and skiers.

CROSS-COUNTRY SKIING AND SNOWSHOEING

For those who prefer to ski under their own power through quiet, sunlit glades, Breckenridge has two Nordic centers. Based at the corner of Grandview Drive and Ski Hill Road (one mile west of its junction with Main St.), the **Breckenridge Nordic Center** (9 Grandview Dr., 970/453-6855, http://breckenridgenordic.com, $20) offers lessons, a variety of snowshoe tours, and gear rentals to explore the 25 miles of marked trails on your own.

The **Gold Run Nordic Center** (200 Clubhouse Dr., 970/547-7889, www.townofbreckenridge.com, $20) offers 18 miles of groomed trails and more than 8 miles of snowshoe trails along Gold Run Gulch, an open area on the northeast edge of town with forested, rolling terrain and some nice views of the Ten Mile Range. Lessons and gear rentals are available, and snow bikes ($15 per hour) are welcome on several of the trails each day. To get here from downtown, drive north on Main Street (Hwy. 9) to Tiger Road. Turn right here, then right again on Clubhouse Drive and follow it to its end at the center.

Backcountry skiers and snowshoers have almost unlimited terrain to choose from; the **Dillon Ranger District** (970/468-5400, www.fs.usda.gov or www.dillonrangerdistrict.com) has 25 snowshoeing and cross-country skiing trails plus 8 snowmobiling trails. Call ahead for the latest parking restrictions and avalanche and weather conditions. For hut-to-hut skiers, the nonprofit **Summit Huts Association** (524 Wellington Rd., 970/453-8583, http://summithuts.org, 9am-5pm Mon.-Fri., $25-38) operates four huts in Summit County; two are also available for summer use.

SLEIGH RIDES

A number of operators offer several types of sleigh rides in the Breckenridge area. For scenic daytime rides, including hot chocolate, try **Breckenridge Sleigh Rides** (pick up at Frisco Nordic Center, 616 Recreation Way, Frisco, 970/453-0222, http://dinner-sleighrides.com, $55-59), **Nordic Sleigh Rides** (6061 Tiger Rd., 970/453-2005, http://coloradosleighrides.com, $45), and **Breckenridge Stables** (200 Clubhouse Dr., 970/453-4438, www.breckstables.com, $59).

ICE-SKATING

Glide, spin, and twirl throughout the year at the **Stephen C. West Ice Arena** (189 Boreas Pass Rd., 970/547-9974, www.townofbrecken-ridge.com, schedule at http://breckenridgerec-reation.com, $12 including skates), which also has ice-skating lessons. Maggie Pond at the Village at Breckenridge also offers seasonal skating and rentals.

HIKING AND BIKING

With gorgeous alpine vistas, carpets of wildflowers, and hidden alpine lakes, the central Colorado Rockies are an ideal destination for hiking and biking in the summer. The **Dillon Ranger District** (680 Blue River Pkwy., Silverthorne, 970/468-5400, http://www.fs.usda.gov) has more than 200 miles of hiking trails, 100 miles of off-highway vehicle terrain, and 150 miles of mountain biking trails within its boundaries, which include the Frisco, Silverthorne, Green Mountain, and Keystone areas as well as Breckenridge. Maps and general trail information are available at the **Breckenridge Welcome Center** (203 S. Main St., 877/864-0868, www.gobreck.com, 9am-8pm daily). Many trailheads are accessed by dirt roads whose condition can vary dramatically depending upon the time of year.

A great place to stretch your legs is the popular **Boreas Pass Road,** a moderate hike or ride with a steady grade, abundant aspen, and wonderful views of the Ten Mile Range and the Blue River Valley. The road follows the old bed of the Denver, South Park, and Pacific Railroad from Breckenridge to South Park; from 1872 to 1938, this was the highest narrow-gauge railroad line in the country.

The trailhead is at Bakers Tank, an old water tank used to refill the always-thirsty steam engines that plied this route. From downtown Breckenridge, head south on Main Street, then turn left on Boreas Pass Road and follow it for 3.5 miles to the trailhead and parking lot on the left. From here, the road continues for 6.6 miles (one-way) to the top of 11,499-foot Boreas Pass, which is perched on the Continental Divide. You can turn around here or continue 10.4 more miles to the town of Como, which consists of a few homes and the state's last remaining stone, narrow-gauge roundhouse. The same trailhead accesses the steeper 2.7-mile **Bakers Tank Trail,** which has some nice views of Breckenridge Ski Resort and Quandary Peak.

About six miles farther up Boreas Pass Road is the 1.7-mile (one-way) **Black Powder Pass Trail,** which ends at a 12,159-foot saddle between Baldy and Boreas Mountains. At the top of the pass, park in the lot on the left-hand side. The trail begins northeast of the large building at the top; follow the track signed Boreas Ditch No. 2 and climb about 670 vertical feet to this spectacular perch with great views into both Park and Summit County.

The beautiful Blue Lakes are an ideal spot for a quick taste of high-altitude environment above timberline without a strenuous hike. From downtown Breckenridge, head south on Main Street, then right onto Blue Lakes Road (County Rd. 850). Continue straight at the fork and follow the road to its end just below the dam (about 2.2 miles) at 11,748 feet elevation. From the trailhead just above the northern end of the dam, the **North Monte Cristo Trail** (1.25 miles one-way) gains about 750 feet in elevation, passing historic mining relics and offering beautiful views of the Blue Lakes.

For a great outing, try the **Peaks Trail** (10 miles one-way), a hiking and mountain biking trail that climbs in and out of several drainages through shady lodgepole pine forest between Breckenridge and Frisco. To maximize the downhill, begin at Breckenridge. From the Highway 9 and Ski Hill Road junction in downtown Breckenridge, turn right on Ski Hill Road and continue past the Peak 8 base area. The trailhead is on the left just past the Grand Lodge at Peak 7. You can either shuttle a car to the second trailhead or ride the free Summit Stage back to the start.

★ QUANDARY PEAK

Experiencing the satisfaction of standing on the windswept summit of one of the state's highest mountains, craning your neck to take in the 360-degree views of craggy, snow-capped summits all around you, is a quintessential Colorado experience. One of the most popular and straightforward fourteener hikes is up **Quandary Peak** (7 miles round-trip, June-Sept.), whose summit stands an impressive 14,265 feet above sea level. Once you motivate for an early **6am start** (which is essential to beat potential afternoon thunderstorms), you'll find a good trail that follows the mountain's East Ridge through picturesque forest glades and open alpine meadows carpeted with wildflowers, where fuzzy, white mountain goats are frequently spotted. Closer to the top, where the trail winds around boulders as big as a car, you're likely to hear squeaking pikas and spot plump marmots darting between the moss-covered rocks. For acclimated and reasonably fit hikers, the round-trip should take **6-8 hours.**

For all its splendor, Quandary isn't that difficult of a mountain to climb if you're acclimated and well prepared; it's about 3,450 feet of elevation gain, and there is a good trail all the way to its rocky summit during the typical mid-June-early September climbing season. When you go, dress warmly and in layers, bring plenty of water, and keep a sharp eye out for lightning. To get to the trailhead from downtown Breckenridge, drive south on Main Street. Turn right on Blue Lakes Road (County Rd. 850), then right again onto Road 851, McCullough Gulch Road. Follow this 0.2 mile to the signed trailhead. The trail begins across the road from the parking area.

★ GOLF

Breckenridge is the only town that owns 27 holes designed by Jack Nicklaus. Nicklaus designed the original 18 holes in 1985 and added the "Elk Nine" in 2001. Thanks to its challenging play, awesome views, cool daytime temperatures, and high elevation, **Breckenridge Golf Club** (200 Clubhouse Dr., 970/453-9104, www.townofbreckenridge.com, $67-117 for 18

mountain goats on the slopes of Quandary Peak

holes) is consistently rated one of the top municipal courses in the country.

HORSEBACK RIDING

Breckenridge Stables (620 Village Rd., 970/453-4438, www.breckstables.com, $70 for a 1.5-hour ride) offers sleigh and horse-drawn carriage rides, lessons, and trail rides up into the Ten Mile Range.

FISHING

Breckenridge is a fantastic location for angling. The Blue River, a tributary of the Colorado, runs right through the center of town, offering many areas to cast a fly. The fishing after a snowy winter is particularly good, when the high waters are filled with rainbow, brown, and the occasional cutthroat trout. For guided trips, gear, and information on local conditions, stop by **Breckenridge Outfitters** (101 N. Main St., 970/453-4135, www.breckenridgeoutfitters.com, 7am-7pm daily in summer) or **Mountain Angler** (311 S. Main St., 800/453-4669, www.mountainangler.com, 7am-9pm daily June 15-Sept. 30).

WATER SPORTS

The central Rockies have plenty of frothing white-water on offer, including an intermediate, family-friendly, three-mile run on the Blue River that's just minutes from Breckenridge. This run depends on releases from Dillon Reservoir, so it has a short season. Contact **Breckenridge Whitewater Rafting** (877/723-8464, www.breckenridgewhitewater.com, $64) or **AVA** (800/370-0581, www.coloradorafting.net, $64) for conditions.

Stand up paddleboarding is popular on Maggie Pond (next to the Village at Breckenridge at the base of Peak 9). Rent gear from **Alpine Sports** (435 N. Park Ave., 970/453-9623, http://alpinesportsrental.com, 8am-8pm daily in winter, 9am-5:30pm daily in summer, $40 for 4 hours), which has three Breckenridge locations. For a unique combination, try one of **Meta Yoga Studios'** (970/547-9642, www.metayogastudios.com) stand up paddleboard yoga classes.

FUN PARK

During the summer, the base area for Peak 8 morphs into a hub of activities, including the **Breckenridge Fun Park** (Ski Resort Peak 8, 800/536-1890, www.breckenridge.com, 9:30am-5:30pm daily early June-early Sept., $77), where "kids" of all ages can fly down the Tenmile Flyer Zipline or alpine slide, putt on a mini golf course, ride the Gold Runner Coaster, and climb the towering Rockpile Climbing Wall. Other summer activities include lift-access mountain bike riding, guided hiking and segway tours, and scenic chairlift rides.

Entertainment and Events

NIGHTLIFE

Just two years after gold was discovered on the Blue River, the **Gold Pan Saloon** (103 N. Main St., 970/453-5499, www.thegoldpansaloon.com, 9am-2am Mon.-Thurs., 8:30am-2am Fri.-Sun.) opened its doors—a relative term, since at the time it was a canvas tent. It wasn't until 1879 that a permanent structure was built. More than 135 years later, "the Pan" is a legendary Main Street fixture, whose long history makes it the oldest continuously operating bar west of the Mississippi River, complete with swinging doors and a large mirror that reflects the mahogany Brunswick bar, which allows patrons who might be on the wrong side of the law to "watch their backs" while indulging in a drink or two. Be sure to check out the old safe, typical of Breck's early saloons, which allowed miners to secure their gold while hanging out in the saloon. The current owners revamped the menus, but it remains more of an après-ski spot and evening hangout with live music or DJs most weekends.

The **Blue River Bistro** (305 N. Main St., 970/453-6974, www.blueriverbistro.com, 11am-midnight Mon.-Sat., 10am-midnight Sun.) has a happy hour (3pm-6pm daily) at the bar and live music (5pm-10pm Sun.-Thurs. Jan.-Apr. and July-Aug., 5pm-10pm Fri.-Sat. May-June and Sept.-Dec.) featuring a variety of both local and Denver musicians.

For a more unique happy hour experience, head to the **Absinthe Bar** (Swiss Haven Restaurant, 325 S. Main St., 970/453-6969, www.swisshavenrestaurant.com, 4pm-11pm Sun.-Thurs., 4pm-1am Fri.-Sat.) to try the traditional green liqueur served with ice water and sugar. The **Breckenridge Distillery** (137 S. Main St., 970/547-9759, www.breckenridgedistillery.com, 11am-9pm daily) has a tasting room where you can sample bitters, spiced rum, and award-winning bourbon.

The **Breckenridge Brewery** (600 S. Main St., 970/453-1550, www.breckbrewpub.com, 11am-midnight daily summer and winter) was the town's first brewpub; it has beautiful views of the Ten Mile Range, an extensive late-night snack menu, and, of course, great beer. The **Motherloaded Tavern** (103 S. Main St., 970/453-2572, http://motherloadedtavern.com, 11:30am-2am daily) is known for its mason-jar cocktails and house-infused liquors like spiced Jack Daniels, and—for those late-night munchies—fried Twinkies and make-your-own s'mores. For Guinness on tap, martinis, and Irish Car Bombs, head to **Burkey and Riley's Irish Pub** (520 S. Main St., 970/547-2782, www.burkeandrileyspub.com, 11am-2am daily), located on the top floor of the La Cima Mall, and **Napper Tandy's Irish Pub** (110 Lincoln Ave., 970/453-4949, http://nappertandysbreck.com, 3pm-2am Mon.-Sat., 11am-2am Sun.), which features Thursday night beer pong and live music on Saturday.

FESTIVALS AND EVENTS

Breckenridge has a long list of fun-filled festivals. During **Kingdom Fest** (mid-June), the town celebrates its former status as a kingdom with outhouse races and gold-panning competitions. The **Breckenridge Music Festival** (www.breckenridgemusicfestival.com, mid-July-Aug.) is a series of more than 40 music performances, ranging from classical to blues and jazz. September brings the oddly timed **Oktoberfest** (www.gobreck.com) and the long-standing **Film Fest** (http://breckfilmfest.org).

Popular food and beverage festivals include the **Breckenridge Craft Spirits Festival** (www.breckenridgecraftspiritsfestival.com, Oct.), two **beer festivals** (http://breckenridgebeerfestival.com, Apr. and July), a **food and wine festival** (http://rockymtnevents.com, late July), and the **Breckenridge Wine Classic** (www.gobreck.com, mid-Sept.), which is held the same weekend as Palisade's **Colorado Mountain Winefest** (http://coloradowineexperience.com), the state's premier wine event.

In winter, check out the Budweiser-sponsored **International Snow Sculpture Championships** (www.gobreck.com, late Jan.), when four-person teams sculpt a 20-ton block of snow into a masterpiece—without power tools. At the zany **Ullr Fest** (www.gobreck.com, mid-Jan.), the town celebrates the Norse god of winter with a costume parade (complete with hot-tub and ski-jump floats), "Ullympic" competitions such as frying-pan flings, and plenty of horned headgear. **Mardi Gras in the Mountains** is February's biggest excuse to celebrate.

Shopping

More than 200 boutiques, galleries, and gift stores line Main Street and its adjacent streets. Prices here are a bit inflated, but still offer a great selection. Store hours vary during the shoulder seasons.

YoYo Loco (302 S. Main St., 970/368-2841, http://yoyoloco.com, noon-5pm Sun.-Mon. and Wed.-Thurs., 11am-6pm Fri.-Sat.) is the place to go for a huge assortment of yo-yos and specialty toys, while **Joy of Sox** (324 S. Main St., 970/453-4534, http://joyofsoxinbreck.com, 9am-9:30pm daily) has the area's best selection of cozy socks and fluffy slippers, as well as hats, toys, and sleepwear. **Ruby Jane** (232 S. Main St., 970/423-6947, www.valleygirlboutique.com, 10am-8pm Mon.-Sat., 10am-6pm Sun.) is a fun mix of stylish women's clothing from lace-trimmed tanks to loungewear and (of course) shoes.

If leather is more your style, check out **Belvidere & Hern** (308A S. Main St.,

970/409-2086, www.belviderehern.com, 10am-6pm daily), which sells scarves, soaps, and jewelry along with leather handbags and stitched purses. The **Breckenridge Candle Gallery** (326 S. Main St., 970/453-2389, www.globalcandlegallery.com, 10am-9pm daily) is a simple shop filled with beautiful, hand-carved candles and handmade soaps. The nearby **Breckenridge Cheese & Chocolate** (304 S. Main St., 970/453-7212, http://breckwineandcheese.blogspot.com, noon-8pm daily) is a great place to shop for specialty cheeses, meats, and small-batch chocolates.

East of Main Street, **Mountain Outfitters** (112 S. Ridge St., 970/453-2201, www.mtnoutfitters.com, 10am-6pm Mon.-Thurs., 9am-6pm Fri.-Sat., 10am-5pm Sun.) is an indie retailer with all the right gear for your next summer or winter adventure. The **Get Real Bazaaar** (105 Jefferson Ave., 720/934-5397, noon-5pm Sun.-Mon. and Wed., 10am-6pm Thurs.-Sat.) is a co-op featuring the work of more than 20 local small businesses.

Food

Breckenridge has an unusually good selection of restaurants. If you're in town during the peak ski season or a holiday, make a reservation. The town's overall vibe is laid-back and friendly, so there's no need to dress up, although most of the restaurants do ask that you not wear your ski boots inside!

BREAKFAST AND CAFÉS

A friend of mine who lives in Breckenridge starts each day by climbing the stairs up to **Cuppa Joe** (118 S. Ridge St. #7, 970/453-3938, 6am-3pm daily, $7-10), a casual, locally owned spot known for its great coffee, oatmeal lattes, and beautiful mountain views. The creative menu includes flaky scones, homemade granola (served with yogurt and fruit), and overstuffed breakfast burritos. The **Cabin Coffee Company** (222 S. Main St., 970/453-9336, http://cabincoffeecompany.com, 7am-5pm Sun.-Thurs., 7am-7pm Fri.-Sat., $5-9) is a cozy spot to sit and sip a steaming hot cocoa or single-origin coffee while curled up in front of the fireplace reading a book. The reasonably priced menu ranges from pastries, like enormous iced cinnamon rolls, to chicken pita sandwiches to unusual drinks like the Tumbleweed—a highly caffeinated concoction of white coffee, caramel sauce, and steamed milk topped with whipped cream and sea salt.

There's always a long line at ★ **Crepes**

Downtown Breckenridge has boutiques, gift shops, and galleries.

a la Cart (307 S. Main St., 970/453-0622, www.crepesalacarts.com, 9am-10pm Sun.-Wed., 9am-11pm, Thurs.-Sat.), a small stand with a few tables along Main Street that sells amazing sweet and savory crepes. Start with a basic crepe ($5.25) and choose your own toppings ($0.50-3), from meats and cheeses to savory sauces, Nutella, and even liqueurs. A few doors down, **La Française** (411 S. Main St., 970/547-7173, 8am-8pm daily, $6-13) is a French bakery and café whose handful of tables quickly fill up with customers sipping espresso drinks and enjoying thick sandwiches on fresh-baked baguettes, omelets, and a mouthwatering array of French pastries, tarts, and mousse (the three-chocolate mousse is divine!).

CASUAL

In an odd location tucked down the hallway of an industrial-looking building one block west of Main Street, ★ **Mi Casa Mexican Restaurant & Cantina** (600 S. Park Ave., 970/453-2071, http://micasamexicanrestaurant.com, 11:30am-9pm daily, $12-20) is definitely worth seeking out. Mi Casa has a comfortable atmosphere with several snug booths, Mexican-themed decor, and a large, decorative fireplace adorned with colorful chickens. Meals begin with a large basket of warm, homemade corn chips and three delicious fresh salsas—good sustenance while reading the extensive menu of traditional southwestern Mexican fare. A beverage menu includes a dozen margaritas, imported and micro-brewed beers, and more than 100 kinds of tequila.

For large portions of good Italian food, head to **Fatty's Pizzeria** (106 S. Ridge Rd., 970/453-9802, 11am-9pm daily, $8-22). Opened in 1981 in a 19th-century boarding house by Southside Johnny (a Chicago native), Fatty's serves hot meatball and sausage sandwiches, blue cheese and bacon burgers, and homemade chicken or eggplant Parmesan in addition to pizza. Happy hour includes $3 pizza slices, half-price appetizers, and daily drink specials. In summer, enjoy your meal out on the patio, which has great views and gorgeous displays of flowers grown by Johnny.

UPSCALE

Located in a historic home built in the early 1880s by a German immigrant, the **Hearthstone Restaurant** (130 S. Ridge St., 970/453-1148, www.hearthstonerestaurant. biz, 4pm-9:30pm daily, $25-44) is well known for its happy hour in the sumptuous Victorian Lounge. The mini menu ($5) features small plates of beef tenderloin tacos and brie and basil quesadillas, as well as beer, wine, and martini specials. Dinner is a more elegant affair, served in one of the numerous small dining rooms, featuring naturally raised game and beef, sustainably harvested seafood, and (in season) local produce.

Operated by an artist-turned-chef, **Ember** (106 E. Adams Ave., 970/547-9595, http://emberbreck.com, 4pm-9pm daily, $21-34) is as much about the experience as it is about the food. The warm decor, attentive service, and beautiful food presentation complement the meal. The mantra of owner Scotty B. is "uncommon food for the common man," a philosophy he clearly takes to heart when designing the seasonal menu, which features delicacies such as lamb cheeks, pig ear French fries, lobster biscuits and gravy, and lime-cured crickets!

★ STARLIGHT DINNERS BY SLEIGH

Life isn't measured by the number of breaths we take, but rather by the moments that take our breath away, according to a popular saying. One particularly breathtaking (and fun!) Rocky Mountain experience is a dinner sleigh ride. This family-friendly adventure begins in the early evening with a dash through the snow beneath (hopefully) starry skies, snuggled under piles of thick blankets, and ends with a delicious evening meal in cozy surroundings. In Breckenridge, starlight dinners are offered by **Breckenridge Ski Resort** (970/547-5740, www.breckstables.com, Wed., Thurs., and Sat. Dec. 3-Apr. 4, plus additional holiday hours, $90) at TenMile Station, an on-mountain restaurant located high on Peak 9. A snowcat helps pull the sleigh up the steep mountainside, and the experience focuses on the exceptional food, including your choice of entrées, such as blood orange-rubbed salmon or flame-broiled tenderloin of beef, along with decadent desserts like vanilla porter lava cake.

Accommodations

Accommodation prices are the highest during ski season and holidays, as well as during summer festivals and the all-too-short leaf-peeping season (early-Sept.). Early April, when the slopes are still open but the crowds have largely dissipated, is a good time to visit; Breckenridge's high elevation tends to preserve the snow here longer than at other resorts. October is a quieter (and cheaper) time to visit, when the weather tends to be very stable. For searchable lodging information and lift access, contact the resort (800/985-9842, ww.breckenridge.com). The town's tourism office (888/251-2417, www.gobreck.com) also has online lodging information.

$100-150

Given its great location three blocks east of downtown and 0.3 mile from the BreckConnect Gondola, the **Fireside Inn** (114 N. French St., 970/453-6456, www.firesideinn.com, $120-163) is a good value. Part bed-and-breakfast and part dorms, the rustic accommodations are far from luxurious, but the hot tub, ski storage, freshly baked cake for afternoon tea, and filling breakfasts make this a great alternative for those who can't fork out enough to stay lift-side.

$150-250

The **SkiWay Lodge** (275 Ski Hill Rd., 970/453-7573, www.skiwaylodge.com, $180-290) has 10 suites, several with fireplaces and private balconies, in an ideal ski-in, ski-out location one block from the BreckConnect Gondola and next to the Skyway Skiway at the end of the 4 O'Clock Run. The chalet-style accommodations are basic, without breakfast,

air-conditioning, and other luxury amenities, but the rooms are clean and comfortable, and there are two hot tubs sitting on the deck for an après-ski soak.

Located a few blocks east of Main Street, the **Abbett Placer Inn** (205 S. French St., 970/453-6489, www.abbettplacer.com, $149-259) is a cozy bed-and-breakfast housed in a renovated Victorian home listed on the National Register of Historic Places. Two suites and three guest rooms feature comfy, quilt-covered beds and private en suite bathrooms; all but one have private sitting areas. The inn also has outdoor seating, a Prodigy hot tub with massage jets, afternoon tea with homemade cake or cookies, and a warm, made-from-scratch breakfast served in the spacious dining room. Be sure to carefully review the policies before booking, as some guests have complained that they are overly restrictive (such as not being allowed to wear shoes in the house).

OVER $250

The **Mountain Stream Lodge** (303B N. Main St., 970/453-2975, www.mountain-streamlodge.com, $289) is a peaceful, timber-frame building built a decade ago along the beautiful Blue River. This combination vacation rental and bed-and-breakfast can accommodate parties of up to 22 people in its five guest rooms, six-person bunkroom, and townhouse that sleeps 2-6. The lodge boasts six gas fireplaces, a streamside hot tub with gorgeous views, immaculate kitchen, dining, and living rooms, and a location just steps from the gondola and downtown.

Located along the ski-out 4 O'Clock Run (three blocks from Main St.) and across the street from the Snowflake chairlift, the ★ **Wedgewood Lodge** (535 Four O'Clock Rd., 800/521-2458, www.tonti.com, $250-315) is a rare family-owned and operated facility. With many room options (all with full kitchens), reasonable high-season rates (for Breck), washers and dryers in the larger units, indoor and outdoor hot tubs, a dry sauna, and à la carte housekeeping services, this is a solid option for those willing to forgo some of the luxury to stay in an ideal location.

The Village at Breckenridge (535 S. Park Ave., 800/400-9590, www.breckresorts. com, $509-719) is a huge ski-in, ski-out condo complex in a great location at the toe of Peak 9's QuickSilver lift, which offers easy access to terrain of all ability levels. The accommodations, which are a quick 10-minute walk from town, range from studio to four-bedroom condos with full kitchens. The larger units have wood-burning fireplaces and balconies, and there is everything you need within the complex, including two restaurants (one in summer), a fitness center and spa, hot tubs, indoor and outdoor pools, an on-site ski/ bike shop, a winter childcare center, and a ski school. The complex also includes **The Village Hotel** ($439-479), whose rooms can accommodate up to four people.

Near the base of the BreckConnect Gondola, the ski-in, gondola-out **Mountain Thunder Lodge** (50 Mountain Thunder Dr., 970/547-5650, www.breckresorts.com, $605-799) is a resort-managed facility with condos ranging from studios to three bedrooms and multi-bedroom townhomes, all of which have an "elegant but rustic" decor— plenty of leather, wooden accents, and antler chandeliers. On-site amenities include private ski storage and two fitness centers, plus use of the bowling alley, billiard table, aquatics center, and spa at RockResorts' **One Ski Hill Place** (1521 Ski Hill Rd., 970/547-8900, www. breckresorts.com, $880-1,489), located about 1.5 miles away. Accommodations there range from studios to five-bedroom condos; all have moss rock fireplaces and sleeper sofas. If you don't feel up to cooking in the well-appointed kitchen, you can stop by the two on-site restaurants or the cleverly named T-Bar.

At the base of Peak 7 and the Independence SuperChair, the resort-run **Crystal Peak Lodge** (1891 Ski Hill Rd., 970/547-8900, www.breckresorts.com, $840) has 1-4-bedroom condos with kitchens and living rooms and all the deluxe amenities. There is one restaurant on-site, and you can quickly access

many more dining options by hopping on the gondola to get to town or to the base area at Peak 8.

Transportation and Services

CAR

Breckenridge is located 38 miles south of Vail. From Vail, follow I-70 East for 26 miles south to the junction with Highway 9. Take Exit 203 and follow Highway 9 south about 11 miles to Breckenridge, where it turns into Main Street. The ski resort is located west and south of town. During storms, Highway 9 is often more difficult to navigate than the interstate.

To reach Breckenridge from Denver, follow I-70 West for 77 miles to Highway 9 and head south. In ideal conditions, this 80-mile trip takes just under two hours to drive, but it can take substantially longer depending upon traffic and/or inclement weather.

PARKING

Parking downtown is limited, especially during the ski season. The most convenient access is from the **South Gondola Parking Lot** ($12 per day); as you enter the town, turn right onto Watson Street, cross the river, and take the next left into the lot.

Detailed information regarding free and pay parking lots is available online (www. townofbreckenridge.com and www.breckenridge.com).

SHUTTLE AND BUS

Two services operate shuttles between Breckenridge and Denver International Airport: **Summit Express** (855/686-8267, www.summitexpress.com, $44-60) and **Colorado Mountain Express** (970/754-7433, www.coloradomountainexpress.com, $66-77 one-way).

Fresh Tracks Transportation (970/453-7433, www.freshtrackstransportation.com, $63 one-way DIA to Breckenridge, $45 one-way Breckenridge to Vail) operates shuttles between DIA and Breckenridge as well as resort-to-resort shuttles between Breckenridge and Copper Mountain, Keystone, Arapahoe

Basin, Vail, and Beaver Creek. Summit County also offers the **Summit Stage** (970/668-0999, www.co.summit.co.us, phone inquiries 5am-2am daily), a free public bus service between Breckenridge and the towns of Frisco, Dillon, Silverthorne, and Blue River as well as the Arapahoe Basin, Keystone, and Copper Mountain resorts.

The **Breckenridge bus system** (970/547-3140, http://breckfreeride.com, year-round, free) shuttles people around town and to and from the mountain. There are eight separate lines, each designated by a color; the black line accesses lifts up to Peaks 7 and 8. Each line offers access to Breckenridge Station, where you can board the BreckConnect Gondola. Bus service is reduced outside of the ski season (mid-Nov.-mid-Apr.).

SERVICES

The **Breck Welcome Center** (203 S. Main. St., 877/864-0868, www.gobreck.com, 9am-8pm daily) offers information, maps, and brochures, and doubles as a free museum about the town's history. Contact **Breckenridge Ski Resort** (970/754-0015, www.breckenridge.com, 8am-6pm daily) for information about parking, ski school, and year-round activities and events.

The closest hospital is the **Vail Valley Medical Center** (180 S. Frontage Rd. West, 970/476-2451, www.vvmc.com). The **Breckenridge Community Clinic Emergency Center** (555 S. Park Ave., 970/453-1010, www.stanthonymountainclinics.org), located in the Village at Breckenridge at the base of Peak 9, provides emergency care during the ski season. Urgent care facilities include **Breckenridge Family Practice & Urgent Care** (400 N. Park Ave. #1A, 970/547-9200, www.highcountryhealth.com, 8am-6pm Mon.-Fri., 8am-1pm Sat., 10am-2pm Sun.).

FRISCO, DILLON, AND SILVERTHORNE

After you emerge from the western portal of the Eisenhower Tunnel on I-70, the highway drops rapidly into the valley of the Blue River. There, Lake Dillon, an important reservoir for the city of Denver, is nestled in a dramatic setting between the Front and Ten Mile Ranges. The small "service" towns of Frisco, Silverthorne, and Dillon grace its shores, and Keystone Resort, Summit County's largest ski area, is located just a few miles to the east. Although they lack the ritzy trappings of the nearby ski resorts, Frisco, Silverthorne, and Dillon are friendly, laid-back towns with deep historical roots, offering a great central location, a hub of year-round recreation, factory outlet shopping, and relatively affordable accommodations.

The recreation here is centered around Lake Dillon and the five ski resorts within half-an-hour's drive. There are also many hiking, biking, and backcountry ski trails, as well as alpine rivers and lakes, within the central Colorado high country.

★ Lake Dillon

In the late 1800s, today's Summit County consisted of a few, isolated outposts that sprang up along rivers in the high mountain valleys. At that time Dillon, which was incorporated in 1883, consisted of a few wooden cabins and a trading post built near the spot where three rivers—Ten Mile Creek and the Blue and Snake Rivers—merged, an ideal spot for stagecoaches and wagon freighters to break up their long journeys through the mountains. Once the railroads arrived, however, Dillon had to move not once, but twice, to remain along the main lines.

Those moves were trivial compared to Dillon's third move in the 1960s. For decades, the Denver Water Board had been eyeing the Blue River as a potential source of water for their growing city. The board slowly acquired the land and water rights it would need to build a reservoir, but it wasn't until the mid-1950s, after severe drought struck the region, that they notified all the residents that they needed to leave their property by September 1961. The board set aside acreage for a new town on the reservoir's northern shore, but the residents were responsible for the cost of moving their buildings. Many were abandoned, but several were moved to the town's current location, as well as to locations in Breckenridge, Frisco, and what would become Silverthorne. Completed in 1963, the massive earth-filled dam is more than a mile long and impounds more than 83 billion gallons of water.

During the winter, visitors and locals enjoy ice fishing and snowmobiling on the frozen lake, while during the summer, marinas in both Dillon and Frisco are hubs of summer recreation, especially the **Dillon Marina** (970/468-5100, www.townofdillon. com), which claims to be the world's highest deep-water marina. The **Frisco Bay Marina** (970/668-4334, www.townoffrisco.com) offers sailing lessons and boat rentals; canoe, kayak, fishing pole, and stand up paddleboard rentals; and boat tours, lakeside dining, and other services. Because the lake is a source of drinking water, swimming, water skiing, and other contact sports are not permitted.

If you want to ride the 18-mile paved path encircling the reservoir or the area's other fantastic bike paths, **Lake Dillon Bike Rentals** (149 Tenderfoot, Dillon, 970/468-8006, lake-dillonbikerentals.com, $28 per day) rents single and tandem bikes, as well as kids' bikes and Burley trailers.

Entertainment and Events

One of the area's most popular hangouts is the **Dillon Dam Brewery** (100 Little Dam St., Dillon, 970/262-7777, www.dambrewery. com, 11:30am-11:30pm Mon.-Thurs.,11am-midnight Fri.-Sat., 11am-11:30pm Sun., $11-23), a large and usually bustling brewpub along the lake's northern shore. A full range of seasonal and flagship beers include a golden Wildernest wheat and a dark McLuhr's Irish stout. The brewpub also has a long menu of food from burgers to Mountain Man mac and cheese, as well as daily dam deals.

The **Backcountry Brewery** (720 Main St., Frisco, 970/ 668-2337, http://backcountrybrewery.com, 11am-10pm Sun.-Thurs., 11am-11pm Fri.-Sat., $9-17) serves pub fare, including salads, pasta, and taco baskets, along with frosty pints of its Great American Beer Festival-winning craft beers. On the same street, the **Club House** (409 E. Main St., Frisco, 970/368-6624, www.clubhouse-frisco.com, 11am-12:20am Mon.-Fri., 8am-12:30am Sat.-Sun.) is Summit County's "first upscale cocktail lounge," with an indoor golf simulator, billiards, and plenty of screens to

Lake Dillon

watch the big game. A local establishment since 1973, **Moose Jaw** (208 Main St., Frisco, 970/668-3931, www.moosejawfrisco.com, 11am-2am daily) is a bar and hamburger joint with pool tables, foosball, and video games.

Shopping

It's easy to get your shopping fix at the **Outlets at Silverthorne** (246-V Rainbow Dr., Silverthorne, 866/746-7686, www.outletsatsilverthorne.com, 10am-8pm Mon.-Sat., 10am-6pm Sun.), a cluster of 50 stores in three shopping villages along I-70 with color-coded roofs (seriously!). The Green Village includes Levi's and OshKosh B'Gosh; the Blue Village has J.Crew, Nike, and the Loft; and the Red Village hosts Eddie Bauer and the Gap, among many others.

Stroll through central Frisco, where uniquely local shopping options include several studio-shops where you can watch products being made. Stop by the **Diane Hart Millinery** (120 Seventh Ave., Frisco, 970/390-7592, http://dianeharty.com, 11am-3pm Wed. and Sat. and by appointment) and **Gatherhouse** (110 Second Ave., Frisco, 970/485-2909, www.gatherhouse.com, demos 2pm-6pm Tues., Thurs., and Sat.), a glass-blowing workshop where you can watch owner John Hudnut transform molten glass into goblets, vases, and other fragile shapes. The eclectic **Frisco Emporium** (313 Main St., Frisco, 970/390-0774, 10am-6pm daily) is a fun place to poke around for fine art prints, jewelry, vintage clothing, trophy heads, and other random items.

Food

My family's favorite breakfast stop is the cozy **Log Cabin Café** (121 Main St., Frisco, 970/668-3947, www.logcabincafe.co, 7am-2:30pm daily, $5-12), which serves up stacks of "pancakes as big as your head," enormous cinnamon rolls, eggs Benedict, as well as satisfying lunch fare like wraps, burgers, salads, and chili for very reasonable prices. The **Butterhorn Bakery & Café** (408 Main St., Frisco, 970/668-3997, www.butterhornbakery.

com, 7:30am-2:30pm daily, $6-11) is a popular breakfast and lunch café, with a full range of coffee beverages, fresh-baked pastries, and a great sandwich selection, including chicken salad croissants and tuna melts. If you're in a rush to get to the slopes, they offer counter as well as table service.

When asked how a Cajun ended up in Summit County, Raymond Griffin, the Louisiana-born owner of the **Lost Cajun** (204 Main St., Frisco, 970/668-4352, www.thelostcajun.com, 11am-8pm Sun.-Wed., 11am-9pm Thurs.-Sat., $10-23), usually tells people that he got lost after getting drunk. Griff had long dreamed of living in the Rockies and finally made it a reality in 2010 after the Deepwater Horizon oil spill. The only complaint is that the restaurant is too small to hold everyone who wants to savor the bayou flavors of chicken and sausage gumbo (which takes up to six hours to cook), creamy lobster bisque, and crawfish étouffée—not to mention the excellent and authentic beignets.

The Historic Mint (347 Blue River Pkwy., Silverthorne, 970/468-5247, www.mintsteakhouse.com, 5pm-9pm daily, $16-33) is a steakhouse housed in Summit County's oldest building. Originally built as a saloon elsewhere in 1862, the structure moved to Frisco, then shifted again to the old town of Dillon in 1882. After the Denver Water Board decided to dam the Blue River, this building was one of the few deemed important enough to move; so in the early 1960s, it was relocated—for the third time—to its current spot in Silverthorne. The bar and the floorboards are original, so when you belly up to the bar, you can drink in all that history along with your frothy beer. The restaurant is known for its all-you-can-eat salad bar and prime cuts of steak, which you grill to perfection yourself on a seasoned lava rock grill.

★ STARLIGHT DINNERS BY SLEIGH

In Frisco, **Two Below Zero** (Frisco Nordic Center, 616 Recreation Way, Frisco,

970/453-1520, http://dinnersleighrides.com, $84-89) offers an old-fashioned experience, with a quiet, 20-minute horse-drawn sleigh ride through the forest to a heated tent, where a three-course meal of hot and hearty food awaits, including soup and artisanal rolls, grilled sirloin or marinated chicken breast, baked potatoes, warm apple pie, and cocoa (with a shot of peppermint schnapps). The meal is followed with entertainment by a professional musician who sang as part of a Kingston Trio reunion, then a peaceful glide back through the snow. Two Below Zero also offers summer chuck wagon dinner excursions. Book well in advance, especially during the holidays.

Accommodations

After touring the world as an alpine ski coach and competitive cyclist, Bruce Knoepfel decided to create an intimate bed-and-breakfast like those he enjoyed visiting in Europe. The result is the **Frisco Inn on Galena** (106 Galena St., Frisco, 970/668-3224, www.friscoinnongalena.com, $259-299), a mountain inn in a great location just off Frisco's main drag. It's known for its clean and cozy rooms, afternoon wine and cheese, made-from-scratch gourmet breakfasts, and attentive service. Originally a stagecoach stop in the late 1800s, the **Frisco Lodge** (321 Main St., Frisco, 800/279-6000, www.friscolodge.com, $129-224) is a bed-and-breakfast located in the heart of the Main Street action.

The no-frills **Silver Inn** (675 Blue River Pkwy., Silverthorne, 970/513-0104, http://silverinn.net, $165) is a family-run hotel in a good, central location near I-70, the outlet shopping, and Lake Dillon. The continental breakfast, however, is underwhelming. For 420-friendly accommodations, try **Bud & Breakfast at Mountain Vista** (385 Lagoon La., Silverthorne, 970/368-6757, www.budandbfast.com, $169-249), a Grateful Dead-themed mountain lodge whose rooms are named for the band members, including a plush purple Garcia suite.

Transportation and Services

CAR

The towns of Frisco, Dillon, and Silverthorne line I-70 along the north shore of Lake Dillon, approximately 35 miles east of Vail and 10 miles north of Breckenridge. From Vail, follow I-70 East about 25 miles to Frisco; Dillon is another 7 miles east. From Breckenridge, follow Highway 9 north for 10 miles to Frisco.

To reach the Lake Dillon area from Denver, take I-70 West to Exit 205 for Dillon and Silverthorne or Exit 203 for Frisco. In ideal conditions, this 71-mile trip takes 1.75 hours to drive, but it can take substantially longer depending upon traffic and/or inclement weather. Hertz has a car rental office in Frisco, and Enterprise has a location in Silverthorne.

SHUTTLE AND BUS

Two services operate shuttles between Denver International Airport and the towns surrounding Lake Dillon: **Summit Express** (855/686-8267, www.summitexpress.com, $49-65) and **Colorado Mountain Express** (970/754-7433, www.coloradomountainexpress.com, $66-77 one-way), which also offers shuttles from two downtown Denver locations.

Fresh Tracks Transportation (970/453-7433, www.freshtrackstransportation.com, $63 one-way DIA to Frisco, $40 one-way Frisco to Vail) operates shuttles between DIA and the Lake Dillon towns, as well as from Frisco to Vail and Beaver Creek. Summit County offers the **Summit Stage** (970/668-0999, www.co.summit.co.us, phone inquiries 5am-2am daily, free), a convenient bus service that links the towns of Frisco, Dillon, Silverthorne, and Leadville and the Breckenridge, Keystone, and Copper Mountain resorts. From Breckenridge, it's possible to take the Swan Mountain Flyer route to the Arapahoe Basin ski area.

SERVICES

For maps, brochures, travel advice, and Wi-Fi, head to the **Colorado Welcome Center** (246-V Rainbow Dr., Silverthorne, www.

colorado.com, 970/468-0353, 9am-5pm daily), tucked amid the outlet shopping stores. Frisco also has a very helpful **Information Center** (300 Main St., Frisco, 800/424-1554, www. townoffrisco.com, 9am-5pm early Sept.-mid-June, 9am-7pm mid-June-early Sept.).

For emergency medical care, head to the **St. Anthony Summit Medical Center** (340 Peak One Dr., Frisco, 970/668-3300, www. summitmedicalcenter.org), which is open 24 hours. Local urgent care facilities include **Silverthorne Family Practice & Urgent Care** (265 Tanglewood La. #E-1, Silverthorne, 970/468-1003, www.highcountryhealth.com, 8am-6pm Mon.-Fri., 8am-1pm Sat., 10am-2pm Sun.).

KEYSTONE

Keystone Resort (21996 U.S. 6, Dillon, 877/625-1556, www.keystoneresort.com, $135 full-day lift ticket) is one of four ski areas in Colorado managed by Vail Resorts. Thanks to its 3,148 acres of skiable terrain, Keystone is Summit County's largest resort, although a fair bit of this acreage is expert "hike-to" areas not used by most boarders or skiers. In addition to its size, several other characteristics set Keystone apart. One is its family-oriented focus, with such treats as the world's largest snow fort (complete with slides and mazes), a multi-lane tubing hill, half a dozen Kids' Adventure Zones on the mountain, and giant chess sets, checkerboards, and play structures scattered throughout the base areas. Other defining features include night skiing, the upper-mountain **Outpost Gondola,** a gorgeous mountain-to-mountain ride with amazing views that ends at an upscale restaurant, and **The Outback,** a remote mountain accessible to both intermediate and advanced skiers.

Keystone has a **Nordic Center** (River Course Clubhouse, 155 River Course Dr., 970/496-4275, www.keystoneresort.com, $13 one-day pass, $23-30 one-day gear rental), offering cross-country and skate skiing, snowshoeing, tubing, lessons, and rentals, as well as an all-you-can-eat soup buffet lunch (11:30am-2pm daily, $13).

Downhill Skiing

Keystone has two main base areas: **River Run** and **Mountain House,** located within less than a mile of each other along U.S. 6, the main road paralleling the resort. The **Lakeside/Conference Village** is a bit farther northwest but still within a short shuttle ride of the slopes. Both base areas access **Dercum Mountain,** named for Max Dercum, a forester who was one of Keystone's original owners and who also helped to develop Arapahoe Basin, Colorado's first ski area.

As the only portion of the resort that faces the base areas, Dercum Mountain is the most heavily used and the location of the night skiing (most weekends and holidays). On these evenings, one lift or gondola from each base area remains open until 8pm, allowing you to enjoy the thrill of boarding or skiing beneath the brilliant lights, an activity that's enhanced when fluffy flakes drift through the chilly night air.

The front side (Dercum Mountain) is where nearly all of the resort's 18 beginner (green) runs and kid-friendly adventure zones are located. Most of these are accessed by the **Peru Express** lift from the Mountain House base area, including the longest green, **Schoolmarm,** a fun run whose lower portions are a family-friendly slow ski zone. The **Kidtopia Snow Fort** and tubing hill can be accessed either by the River Run Gondola or the Summit Express lift, both in River Run Village. The **Keystone Ski & Snowboard School** (800/255-3715) offers group and private lessons at all ability levels beginning at age three, as well as special "Betty Fest" weekends for women.

Dercum Mountain has many excellent intermediate (blue) runs, which comprise 29 percent of Keystone's terrain. **Flying Dutchman, Spring Dipper,** and **Wild Irishman** are all classic "Let's do that again!" runs. Intermediate boarders and skiers comfortable on the front side will also enjoy exploring **North Peak** and **The Outback,** whose steeper and more remote runs are especially fun on crowded weekends, although the conditions can sometimes be icy. The Outback's flagship trail, **Elk Run,** is a nice cruiser, and runs like **Bighorn** and **Porcupine** are great for trying some easy bumps. The place for expert skiers is North Mountain, where bumps, glades, and steeps can all be found in abundance, along with a few steep blues to the sides. Be sure to try the groomed **Starfire,** one of Keystone's best runs; **Powder Cap,** known for its especially large bumps; and **Geronimo,** one of the resort's steepest runs.

★ Golf

Golf is one of the most popular activities on offer here during the summer. *Golf Digest* and *Golf Magazine* have both rated Keystone as one of America's best golf destinations thanks to its two 18-hole courses. In addition to **The River Course at Keystone** (155 River Course Dr., 970/496-1520, www.keystoneresort.com, $150), the **Keystone Ranch** (1239 Keystone Ranch Rd., 800/464-3494, www.keystoneresort.com, $130) is a par-72 course around a nine-acre lake designed by Robert Trent Jones Jr.

★ Spas

With so much recreation in the Colorado high country, it's sometimes easy to forget that you're on vacation. One of the best ways to schedule some down time for yourself is to visit one of the area's wonderful spas, which offer rejuvenating treatments ranging from caviar facials and wildflower body polishes to hot stone massages and Watsu (a warm saltwater therapy known for relaxing the spine and joints). In addition to all the standard services, the **Spa at Keystone** (22101 U.S. 6, 970/496-4118, www.keystoneresort.com, treatments 10am-6pm daily, $125 for 50-minute massage) offers such unusual luxuries as a 20-minute foot refresher, a coco-luscious body wrap and buff, and a 50-minute altitude massage, which is paired with oxygen to relieve discomfort brought on by the resort's high altitude. On the lower slopes of Peak 9, the **Spa** at **Beaver Run** (620 Village Rd., 970/453-8757, www.beaverrun.com, 9am-9pm daily during peak season, $100 for 60-minute massage) offers Watsu as well as facials and body treatments like the delicious organic Peruvian chocolate wrap.

Food

Keystone Resort (www.keystoneresort.com, 800/354-4386) operates three dining options high atop the resort's North Mountain, accessible only by gondola.

The **Alpenglow Stube** (5:30pm-8:30pm Wed., 11am-1:30pm and 5:30pm-8:30pm Thurs.-Sat., 10:30am-1:30pm Sun. in winter, $39-50) sits tucked into a small saddle with spectacular views. The restaurant is both cozy and classy (*stube* is German for a cozy, comfortable place), with rustic wooden decor, white linen tablecloths, and views of the alpenglow sunset. The short, meat-heavy menu includes choices such as cast-iron rendered duck breast and grilled tomahawk pork chop. Reservations are a must. The restaurant occasionally cannot be accessed due to inclement weather.

Next door, **Der Fondue Chessel** (5:30pm-8pm daily in summer and winter, $62 for 4 courses) specializes in cheese and chocolate fondue. The lower-budget **Outpost Lodge** (10am-6pm daily in winter, $8-14) is an open, log-cabin-like food court with noodles, cocoa, burgers, and standard ski fare. There's a large deck where you can soak up the sun and the views while munching.

River Run Village, Keystone's main base area, has a number of good dining options. Just steps from the River Run Gondola, the **New Moon Café** (140 Ida Belle Dr., 970/262-3772, http://newmooncafekeystone.com, 7:30am-5:30pm daily in winter, $7-13) bills itself as a "casual classic rock café." The simple but colorful establishment serves filling, all-day breakfasts like the Hawg burrito ("All the pork you can put on a fork!"), gooey paninis, and bacon spinach nachos, and features Keystone's only build-your-own Bloody Mary bar.

Named for the base area elevation, the **9280′ Tap House** (140 Ida Belle Dr., 970/496-4333, www.keystoneresort.com, 11am-9pm daily in winter, $12-14) has a long list of craft beers and custom cocktails (try the Montezuma mojito), as well as a large patio that's perfect for relaxing on sunny days. Enjoy the chicken wings or chili cheese fries and some of the village's best happy hour specials. The **Kickapoo Tavern** (129 River Run Rd., 970/468-0922, www.kickapootavern.com, 11am-10pm daily in winter, $12-27) has a great deck and serves up an unusual Tex-Mex menu, including Philly cheesesteak tacos, juicy steaks, and grilled chicken sandwiches.

As you walk through the village, the delicious scent of fresh-baked bread will guide your stomach straight to **Pizza on the Run** (140 Ida Belle Dr., 970/513-6636, www.pizzaontherunkeystone.com, 11am-9pm daily in winter, $9-14). This reasonably priced, family-owned restaurant serves up great braided-crust pizza with plenty of toppings as well as traditional Italian dishes like tortellini and homemade meat lasagna. If all that exercise has you craving something sweet, stop by **Mary's Mountain Cookies** (140 Ida Belle Dr., 970/262-3686, http://marysmountaincookies.com, 10am-9pm daily in winter, $3), where it's nearly impossible to decide between the 40 or so flavors of cookies (including gluten-free options) baked on the premises each day.

Keystone's 9280′ Tap House

Accommodations

Keystone Resort (855/603-0049, www.keystoneresort.com) manages essentially all of the resort's 1,200-plus lodging options. There is quite a range in quality, bedroom configurations, and, of course, price, which tends to drop the farther you get from the lifts and the links. Since the base areas are relatively compact and this is a purpose-built resort, it's not difficult to get around; there are convenient shuttles linking the lodging to all the major destinations.

Due to the lift configuration, Mountain Home Village—the original base area—is the best place for beginner skiers to stay, as well as families who prefer quiet evenings. Options here include **The Inn at Keystone** (21966 U.S. 6, $279-399), a dog-friendly inn within a short shuttle ride of the base area. This plain and (relatively) budget-friendly option includes a hot breakfast buffet, rooftop hot tubs with great views, and hotel rooms or one-bedroom suites.

Built in the early 1990s, River Run Village is the heart of the resort. The luxurious **Lone Eagle Condominiums** (23044 U.S. 6, $519-878) and **The Timbers** (21966 U.S. 6, $479-830) are closest to the slopes and the most upscale accommodations, but most of the other River Run lodging is within walking distance of the restaurants, shops, and gondola, including the **Jackpine & Black Bear Condominiums** (23110 U.S. 6, $385-425). The **Gateway Mountain Lodge** (21966 U.S. 6, $298-338) has condos with underground parking in a good, central location a short shuttle ride from the River Run

Village and steps from liquor and convenience stores.

The more residential West Keystone is the area to go for larger rentals that are still accessible by the frequent shuttles. Good options include the **Forest Condominiums** (21966 U.S. 6, $235-305), which have configurations that can sleep up to 10. Although it's farther from the lifts, the **Keystone Lodge and Spa** (22101 U.S. 6, $249-299) in Lakeside Village is less expensive in winter and comes with some upscale amenities and nice perks, including the spa and exercise room, private shuttles to the slopes and golf courses, free ski check-in at River Run (so you don't have to haul your gear back and forth), and even a Fast Pass, which allows you to skip the long gondola lines up until 10am.

Transportation and Services

CAR

Keystone Resort is located six miles west of Dillon along U.S. 6. From Denver, take I-70 West to Exit 205 for Dillon. After exiting, turn left onto the Blue River Parkway. After 0.2 mile, continue onto U.S. 6 East for six miles to the resort. In ideal conditions, this 77-mile trip takes about 1.75 hours to drive, but it can take substantially longer depending upon traffic and/or inclement weather.

Keystone is one of the only resorts with free parking that's actually close enough to walk to the slopes. The best spot is the River Run Free Lot, located about a five-minute walk from River Run Gondola.

SHUTTLE AND BUS

Shuttle services between Denver and Keystone include **Summit Express** (855/686-8267, www.summitexpress.com, $49-65) and **Colorado Mountain Express** (970/754-7433, www.coloradomountainexpress.com, $66-77 one-way), which also offers service from two Denver locations.

Fresh Tracks Transportation (970/453-7433, www.freshtrackstransportation.com, $63 one-way DIA to Keystone, $45 one-way Keystone to Vail) operates shuttles between

DIA and Keystone as well as from Keystone to Breckenridge, Copper Mountain, Vail, and Beaver Creek. Summit County offers the **Summit Stage** (970/668-0999, www.co.summit.co.us, phone inquiries 5am-2am daily, free), a convenient bus service linking the towns of Frisco, Dillon, Silverthorne, and Leadville and the Keystone, Breckenridge, and Copper Mountain resorts. From Keystone, it's possible to take the Swan Mountain Flyer route to the Arapahoe Basin ski area.

SERVICES

The closest hospital is the **Vail Valley Medical Center** (180 S. Frontage Rd. West, 970/476-2451, www.vvmc.com). In case of emergency, the **Keystone Medical Clinic** (1252 County Rd. 8, 970/468-6677, www.stanthonymountainclinics.org) is located in the Mountain House base area near the Argentine lift and is open daily during the ski season. The closest urgent care facilities are in Breckenridge and Silverthorne.

ARAPAHOE BASIN

Arapahoe Basin is known for its terrific and challenging skiing. Colorado's first ski area has an interesting history that began at the end of World War II, before downhill skiing had gained popularity as a fun pastime. In 1945, at the behest of Denver's forward-looking Chamber of Commerce, three men, including a veteran of the 10th Mountain Division ski troops and two U.S. Olympic Ski Team members, searched the state for terrain suitable for a ski resort. They chose the west side of Loveland Pass, a high-elevation area close to the Continental Divide and located just 60 miles from Denver, and named it Arapahoe Basin.

Although the U.S. Forest Service approved the developers' plan, the team couldn't find enough investors to fully finance it, so after cutting down enough trees to create the runs, the trio rigged up a single rope tow, which, for $1.25 a day, carried skiers just halfway up the mountain during the first 1946-1947 ski season. Following the installation of a single chairlift the following season, the number of visitors escalated from 1,200 to 13,000. Today, more than 425,000 skiers visit what may be North America's highest in-bounds terrain. The average 233-day season runs **mid-October to mid-June** (although there is occasionally enough snow to stay open for a 4th of July beach party).

Downhill Skiing and Snowboarding

Although it's quite a bit smaller than the nearby resorts, **Arapahoe Basin** (28194 U.S. 6, 888/272-7246, http://arapahoebasin.com, $89) attracts out-of-state visitors as well as many local die-hards. Of its 960 acres, 60 percent are classified as advanced or expert, so this is not the place to bring an inexperienced skier or boarder. The area is especially renowned for its Montezuma Bowl, a 400-acre, powder-filled basin added to the resort in 2007, as well as the famous **"Pali" lift** (pronounced "Polly"), which accesses the resort's signature trail, **Pallavicini,** a double-black diamond that is one of the state's steepest runs.

If once down those thigh-burning bumps feels like a warm-up, you should try the **Enduro Challenge** (mid-Apr.), when teams compete to ski the most runs off the Pali lift (which, except for the catwalks, only services black and double-black terrain). The current record is 72 in one day!

Food

Since "A Basin" is all about the skiing, there's little après-ski or luxury to speak of. The **Black Mountain Lodge** (888/272-7246, http://arapahoebasin.com, 10:30am-2:30pm daily, $10-18) is the only mid-mountain restaurant, serving fresh salads, slalom slope salmon, and smoked beef brisket.

The **6th Alley Bar & Grill** (in the A-Frame base lodge, 970/513-5705, http://arapahoebasin.com, 8:30am-5:30pm Mon.-Thurs., 8am-6:30pm Fri.-Sun. during ski season, $11-22) offers upscale options like rib-eye steak.

Copper Mountain's terrain

Getting There

Arapahoe Basin is located six miles west of Keystone along U.S. 6. From Denver, drive west on I-70 to Exit 216. Exit here and follow U.S. 6 west up the narrow, winding road, up and over 11,990-foot Loveland Pass to the ski area, which is located about eight miles from the interstate.

★ COPPER MOUNTAIN

My family's favorite ski area is **Copper Mountain** (209 10 Mile Circle, Frisco, 970/968-2318, www.coppercolorado.com, $78-100 for 1-day lift ticket), Colorado's "Goldilocks" resort. It's just the right distance from Denver, it's just the right size to have plenty of choice without getting lost, and it's the best laid-out area in the state, with terrain that naturally separates beginners from more advanced skiers and boarders. It also has a ski patrol that aggressively works to slow down any speed demons. Although Copper doesn't have the cachet of Vail and attracts fewer out-of-state visitors, it's a great mountain and a cheaper, more laid-back place to spend a fun day (or week) on the slopes.

Downhill Skiing and Snowboarding

The resort's three mountains increase in steepness from west to east, so unlike other resorts, where black, blue, and green trails overlap, at Copper it's easy to find a group of runs all at your ability level. For the same reason, it's a great place to learn how to ski. There are three villages, conveniently named East, Center, and West Villages, of which Center is the main base area.

Beginners should start either in **Center Village** on the **American Flyer** lift, which accesses **High Point**, a long and fun green, or in the **West Village** on the **Union Creek** lift. From here, you can ride three smaller lifts to access what my son calls "a beginner's paradise." There are two main clusters of intermediate (blue) runs. From **Center Village** take the **American Eagle** lift to **Main Vein,** one of the resort's flagship runs. From the top of American Eagle, you can also take the **Excelerator** to **Copperopolis,** a steep groomer that's frequently used as a training ground for the U.S. Ski Team. A handful of blues off the **Timberline Express** lift are also really enjoyable.

A good warm-up for advanced skiers is the short **CDL's** at the top of Excelerator. From there, you can head toward the **Super Bee** lift to try **Brennan's Grin** (if you like bumps) or **Rosi's Run** (if you prefer groomers). Many of Copper's best blacks are off some of its minor lifts, including **Matchless** and **Six Shooter,** which are both off the **Mountain Chief** lift in the Copper Bowl.

RENTALS AND LESSONS

The **Ski & Ride School** (866/464-4432, www.visitcoppermountain.com, $194-204 for a full-day lesson and gear rental) offers group and private board and ski lessons for youth and adults, including special teen classes and race training programs. The mountain's amenities include 13- and 22-foot half-pipes, five snow parks, and three learning terrains. You can rent gear at **Christy Sports** (104 Wheeler Pl., 970/968-2086, http://rental.christysports.com, $19-46 per package per day with advance reservation) or slopeside at **Copper Mountain Ski & Snowboard Rentals** (866/416-9876, www.coppercolorado.com, $36 per package per day).

Hiking and Biking

In summer, Copper Mountain offers scenic chairlift rides and downhill mountain biking as well as a host of family-friendly activities, including bungee jumping, bumper boats, go karts, a zip line, and mini golf.

A great summertime hike or mountain bike ride is the **Wheeler National Recreation Trail** (www.fs.usda.gov, 9 miles one-way), a beautiful path that climbs up and over the Ten Mile Range between Copper Mountain and McCullough Gulch south of Breckenridge. To minimize the elevation gain, start on the north side, at the edge of Copper Mountain's Far East Parking Lot (Hwy. 91) and finish at the southern trailhead on McCullough Gulch Road (Exit 203 on I-70 and drive south through Breckenridge to Blue River). After passing through the town, turn right onto Blue Lakes Road (Forest Road 850) for 0.1 mile, then turn right again onto McCullough Gulch Road (Forest Road 851). Half a mile past the Quandary Peak trailhead, turn right at the fork onto County Road 852. Proceed 0.5 mile to the trailhead at a sharp, left-hand bend.

Copper is also the starting point for the **I-25 Kia Copper Triangle** (http://copper-triangle.com, Aug., $140), one of the state's best road rides. This challenging, 78-mile loop climbs three major passes—Fremont (11,318 feet), Tennessee (10,424 feet), and Vail (10,666 feet)—for a total gain of 6,000 vertical feet. Like many of Colorado's organized rides, the Copper Triangle usually sells out in advance, so register early.

Food and Accommodations

Copper Mountain Resort (209 Ten Mile Cir., 888/219-2441, www.coppercolorado.com) manages all of the lodging in the base areas. The resort's "neighborhoods" offer a variety of accommodations ranging in quality, room configurations, and price—from hotel-style rooms to three-bedroom condos with kitchens, fireplaces, porches, and TVs. In Center Village, the **Burning Stones Neighborhood** ($357-559) has a great location just steps from both the American Eagle and the American Flyer lifts. The **Wheeler Neighborhood** ($288-392) in the East Village has quick access to the Super Bee lift and is a good spot for advanced skiers. Beginner-to-intermediate skiers should consider West Village options, including the **Telemark Neighborhood** ($303-392), a slightly longer (150-yard) walk to the slopes.

Most of Copper's dining options are in Center Village. Slopeside, the best bet is **Endo's Adrenaline Café** (base of American Eagle lift, 970/968-3070, 10:30am-10pm Mon.-Thurs., 10:30am-11pm Fri.-Sat. in winter, 11am-7pm daily in summer, $10-25), a relaxed establishment known for its mondo nachos, Colorado-raised Angus beef burgers, fish tacos, and long beer and cocktail lists. Thanks to the flaming fire pit, Endo's outdoor patio is a great place to relax and watch the action on the 22-foot-high half-pipe.

For cheaper eats, check out **Gustino's Lakeside Pizzeria** (near West Lake, 970/968-3222, 11am-9pm Sun.-Thurs., 11am-10pm Fri.-Sat., $6-24), a no-frills spot with some unusual flavor combos. Next door is **Mulligans Irish Pub** (231 Ten Mile Cir., 970/968-2084, www.mulligans.name, 5pm-2am daily, $9-14), Copper's best late-night bar. The motto at this casual indie establishment is "Come in. Have fun. Act Irish!" Greasy pub fare includes bangers and fries and fish and chips, as well as a long list of Colorado and Irish beers. If you still have some energy left, take advantage of their X-beer pong table, pool table, Jenga, and other late-night entertainment.

For more refined surroundings and upscale menus, try the **Storm King Lounge** (970/968-3083, 5pm-11pm daily, $15-80) for sushi or the **C.B. Grille** (910 Copper Rd., 970/968-3113, 5pm-9pm Tues.-Sat., $15-80) for locally sourced, pan-seared Colorado striped bass or maple rosemary roast chicken, as well as an extensive selection of domestic and international wines.

Transportation and Services

CAR

Copper Mountain is located 22 miles south of Vail and 20 miles northwest of Breckenridge on I-70. To reach Copper Mountain from Denver, take I-70 West to Exit 195. In ideal conditions, this 78-mile trip takes 1.5 hours to drive, but it can take substantially longer depending upon traffic and/or inclement weather.

Free daily parking and shuttle service to the mountain is available from the Alpine and Far East lots. All three villages have pay parking lots, although these can fill up quickly during the weekend.

SHUTTLE AND BUS

Shuttles between Denver and Copper Mountain include **Summit Express** (855/686-8267, www.summitexpress.com, $65) and **Colorado Mountain Express** (970/754-7433, www.coloradomountainexpress.com, $66-77 one-way).

Fresh Tracks Transportation (970/453-7433, www.freshtrackstransportation.com, $63 one-way DIA to Copper Mountain, $35 one-way Copper Mountain to Vail) operates shuttles between Denver airport and Copper Mountain, as well as from the mountain to Breckenridge, Keystone, Vail, and Beaver Creek. Summit County offers the **Summit Stage** (970/668-0999, www.co.summit.co.us, phone inquiries 5am-2am daily, free), a convenient bus service whose Copper Mountain route directly links the resort with a number of stops in Frisco.

SERVICES

The closest hospital is the **Vail Valley Medical Center** (180 S. Frontage Rd. West,

970/476-2451, www.vvmc.com). In case of emergency, the **Copper Mountain Clinic** (860 Copper Rd., 970/968-2330, www.stanthonymountainclinics.org) is located in Center Village and is open daily during the ski season. The closest urgent care facilities are in Vail and Silverthorne.

Aspen and the Roaring Fork Valley

O ne of Colorado's most beautiful areas, the Roaring Fork Valley is home to scenic fly-fishing, Wild West mining towns, and popular ski towns.

In 1879, intrepid miners searching for silver and gold high in the mountains of central Colorado braved the difficult and dangerous climb up and over the Continental Divide. As they descended the western slope, the men discovered the Roaring Fork Valley, a region of soaring, crimson-colored mountains surrounding a lush, green vale with a crystal-clear river flowing through its heart. The valley's beauty, along with its precious metals and steaming hot springs, quickly attracted thousands of people to the area. In just over a decade, the main town, renamed Aspen in 1892, surged to nearly 12,000 people and its silver production assumed global importance. Although Aspen's population dropped the following year after the price of silver crashed, the foundations had been laid for today's celebrated resort town.

The compact Roaring Fork Valley continues to have a disproportionate impact on the state's economy and culture. The swiftly flowing river stretches from its high-elevation headwaters near 12,095-foot Independence Pass to its confluence with the Colorado River in the bustling spa town of Glenwood Springs, about 60 miles downstream. In between lies the affluent community of Aspen, the region's unexpectedly laid-back cultural and tourism hub, as well as several small, close-knit communities stretching along the Roaring Fork's gorgeous tributaries. The Castle, Maroon, Fryingpan, and other descriptively named creeks feature world-class fly-fishing, plentiful hiking and cycling, and eerie ghost towns, as well as mile upon mile of incredible scenery, exemplified by the stunning Maroon Bells, whose twin, bell-shaped summits are the most photographed peaks in North America.

PLANNING YOUR TIME

Aspen has two high seasons: winter (late Nov.-mid-Apr), when skiers flock to the region, and summer (June-Sept.), when the quaking aspen leaves grace the valley. When the snow flies, Aspen is the region's major destination, and most visitors stay for at least

Previous: a mountain biker above Aspen; the slopes at Aspen Mountain. Above: downtown Aspen.

Look for ★ to find recommended sights, activities, dining, and lodging.

Highlights

★ **Wheeler Opera House:** This massive building, built in 1890 from locally quarried red stone, is one of Aspen's best-known landmarks (page 266).

★ **Smuggler Mountain Trail:** Hike with the locals up this short, steep climb that leads to large groves of rustling aspen trees, historic mining sites, and a viewing platform with bird's-eye vistas of Aspen (page 272).

★ **Art Galleries:** Wander through Aspen's many colorful art galleries, whose masterpieces range from striking photos of the Maroon Bells to more bizarre creations (page 276).

★ **Ice Age Discovery Center:** Learn about the recent discovery of a 150,000-year-old mammoth, ground sloth, and other well-preserved fossils during a reservoir expansion near Snowmass Mountain (page 282).

★ **Downhill Skiing and Snowboarding:** Burn out your thighs skiing **Snowmass Mountain,** which has a high proportion of intermediate trails (page 283).

★ **Independence Pass:** Steer around sweeping switchbacks as you climb past alpine wildflowers, a forsaken mining town, and snow-capped summits to the giddy heights of the highest paved crossing of the Continental Divide (page 286).

★ **Maroon Bells:** These crimson peaks are framed by white snow, blue sky, and golden aspen trees mirrored in the clear waters of a shimmering alpine lake (page 290).

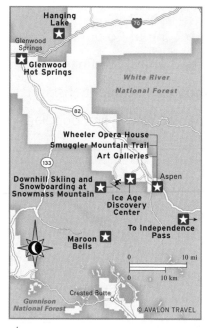

★ **Glenwood Hot Springs:** Soak away your sore muscles in the world's largest hot springs pool (page 291).

★ **Hanging Lake:** This trail begins near the banks of the frothing Colorado River and climbs the rugged walls of Glenwood Canyon to an impossibly blue lake fed by graceful waterfalls (page 294).

Aspen and the Roaring Fork Valley

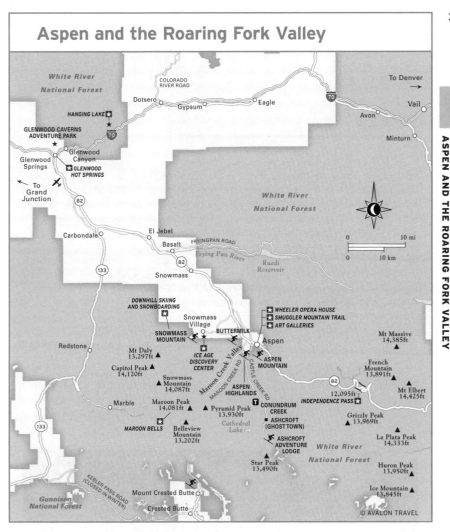

White River
National Forest

COLORADO
RIVER ROAD

To Denver →

Dotsero   Eagle   Vail
        Gypsum

HANGING LAKE   Avon

GLENWOOD CAVERNS
ADVENTURE PARK   Minturn

Glenwood
Canyon
Glenwood
Springs   GLENWOOD
             HOT SPRINGS

← To
Grand
Junction   82

White River

National Forest

El Jebel   0   10 mi
Carbondale
        Basalt   FRYINGPAN ROAD   0   10 km
               Frying Pan River
        82   Ruedi
                            Reservoir
       133
            Snowmass

DOWNHILL SKIING
AND SNOWBOARDING   WHEELER OPERA HOUSE
        Snowmass   SMUGGLER MOUNTAIN TRAIL
        Village   ART GALLERIES
    SNOWMASS   BUTTERMILK
    MOUNTAIN   Mt Massive
Redstone   Mt Daly   14,385ft
           13,297ft ICE AGE   Aspen
                     DISCOVERY ASPEN
Capitol Peak▲   CENTER   MOUNTAIN   French
14,120ft   Snowmass   Mountain
           ▲Mountain ASPEN   13,891ft
           14,087ft   HIGHLANDS
   Marble Maroon Peak   12,095ft   Mt Elbert
           14,081ft ▲Pyramid Peak INDEPENDENCE PASS 14,425ft
                     13,930ft CONUNDRUM
   133   MAROON BELLS   CREEK   Grizzly Peak
           Belleview   Cathedral ASHCROFT 13,969ft
           Mountain   Lake   (GHOST TOWN)
           13,202ft   La Plata Peak
                       ASHCROFT   14,333ft
                       ADVENTURE White River
                       LODGE   National Forest
                     Star Peak   Huron Peak
                     13,490ft   13,950ft

                                            Ice Mountain
   KEBLER PASS ROAD   13,845ft
   (CLOSED IN WINTER)
Gunnison   Mount Crested Butte
National Forest
            Crested Butte   © AVALON TRAVEL

a **few days,** and often a **week,** to enjoy all that the town and its four ski mountains offer.

Part of Aspen's allure is its isolation, especially in winter, when 12,095-foot **Independence Pass** is closed. Visitors must either pay to fly into the Aspen/Pitkin County Airport, conveniently located a few miles from downtown, or travel through Denver, about a five-hour drive away. If you fly into

the local airport and base yourself out of a posh hotel, you'll never need a car.

In summer, many travelers take advantage of the Denver airport's lower fares and rent a vehicle for the 3.5-4-hour drive over Independence Pass. With your own wheels, it's easy to explore the entire Roaring Fork Valley.

The town's already-high prices crest in

winter, particularly during the major holidays, though the snow is often better in the spring. Prices rise again in summer. In between, there are often good lodging and dining deals on offer.

Aspen is a year-round town, so it does not have a mud-season shutdown, although many establishments reduce their hours in late spring and fall.

Aspen

Aspen is relatively small and easy to navigate. With its stunning natural setting, charming and walkable downtown, vibrant cultural scene, extensive network of hiking and biking paths, and four ski mountains right outside the door, it's no wonder that this is one of the most appealing—and most expensive—towns in the Colorado Rockies. Along with its Who's Who cast of residential and visiting celebrities, the town's many fine dining options, boutique shops, luxury lodging, and reputation for superior customer service compound its enduring allure, making this golden town one of the most popular destinations in the country.

Aspen is located right at the base of Aspen Mountain (locally called Ajax), just a shuttle ride from the Buttermilk and Aspen Highlands ski areas. Snowmass, by far the region's largest resort and a winter destination in its own right, is located up a side canyon about 11 miles from downtown Aspen and is connected to the other mountains and the town by free, high-frequency shuttles.

SIGHTS

In Aspen, most of the sights are within the vibrant downtown, which lies south of Highway 82, locally called Main Street, and west of Original Street.

Aspen Art Museum

The striking, braided-pie-crust exterior of the **Aspen Art Museum** (590 N. Mill St., 970/925-8050, www.aspenartmuseum.org, 10am-6pm Tues.-Sun., free) is but a prelude of the thought-provoking programs, courses, and regularly rotating modern art exhibits

the chic Aspen Art Museum

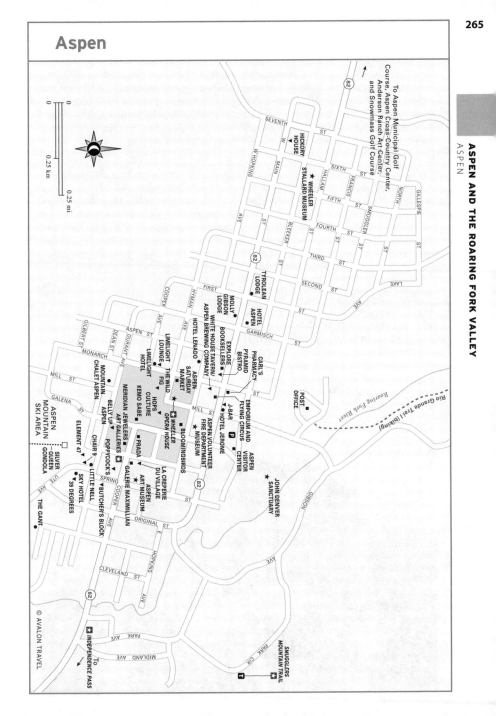

Aspen

0   0.25 km
0   0.25 mi

To Aspen Municipal Golf
Course, Aspen Cross-Country Center,
Anderson Ranch Art Center,
and Snowmass Golf Course

SEVENTH ST
HICKORY HOUSE
W HOPKINS AVE
MAIN ST
W
HALLAM ST
★ WHEELER STALLARD MUSEUM
SIXTH ST
FRANCIS ST
FIFTH ST
FOURTH ST
BLEEKER ST
THIRD ST
SECOND ST
NORTH ST
SMUGGLER ST
GILLESPIE ST

TYROLEAN LODGE
FIRST ST
COOPER AVE
HYMAN AVE
MOLLY GIBSON LODGE
HOTEL ASPEN
WHITE HOUSE TAVERN/ ASPEN BREWING COMPANY
ASPEN ST
EXPLORE BOOKSELLERS
CARL'S PHARMACY
EMPORIUM AND FLYING CIRCUS
GARMISCH ST
PYRAMID BISTRO
DEAN AVE
DURANT AVE
GILBERT ST
MONARCH
MILL ST
GALENA
HOTEL LENADO
LIMELIGHT LOUNGE
LIMELIGHT HOTEL
FIG
THE WILD
HOPS CULTURE
KEMO SABE
MERIDIAN JEWELERS
SATURDAY MARKET
ASPEN
BELLY UP ASPEN
ART GALLERIES
POPPYCOCK'S
PRADA
ELEMENT 47
CHAIR 9
LITTLE NELL
GALERIE MAXIMILIAN
SKY HOTEL
39 DEGREES
BUTCHER'S BLOCK
THE GANT
MOUNTAIN CHALET ASPEN
ASPEN MOUNTAIN SKI AREA
SILVER QUEEN GONDOLA
UTE AVE
SPRING ST
ORIGINAL ST
COOPER
HOPKINS AVE
CLEVELAND ST
GALENA
WHEELER OPERA HOUSE
BLOOMINGBIRDS
ASPEN VOLUNTEER FIRE DEPARTMENT
J-BAR
HOTEL JEROME
ASPEN VISITOR CENTER
MUSEUM
LA CREPERIE DU VILLAGE
ASPEN ART MUSEUM
POST OFFICE
JOHN DENVER SANCTUARY
Roaring Fork River
Rio Grande Trail (biking)
Rio Grande Trail (biking)
GIBSON
SMUGGLERS MOUNTAIN TRAIL
PARK CIR
MIDLAND AVE
PARK AVE
INDEPENDENCE PASS
To Smugglers Mountain Trail
INDEPENDENCE PASS

© AVALON TRAVEL

inside. The controversial aspects were highlighted within days of the museum's grand public opening in 2014, when 18,000 people quickly signed a petition opposing the Moving Ghost Town exhibit by Chinese artist Cai Guo-Qiang, which featured live, endangered tortoises wandering around the installation with iPads epoxied to their shells. Following the public outcry, the tortoises were moved to a sanctuary. The museum, whose woven exterior was designed by the Pritzker Prize-winning architect Shigeru Ban, is filled with sunny, open spaces that enhance the work of emerging international artists. Previous shows have ranged from the starkly simplistic work of Robert Breer to Haegue Yang's creations from mini-blinds and extension cords.

★ Wheeler Opera House

Aspen's best-known historical site, the **Wheeler Opera House** (320 E. Hyman St., 970/920-5770, www.wheeleroperahouse. com, box office open noon-5pm daily, $25-95), was built in 1889 by Jerome Wheeler, a partner in the Macy's department store chain. After a visit in 1883, Wheeler fell in love with Colorado and decided to invest in mines in the Aspen area, as well as a tramway and a smelter to transport and process their rich pockets of ore. After his efforts paid off handsomely, Wheeler constructed several of Aspen's prominent historical buildings, including the still-operating Hotel Jerome, the Wheeler Stallard House (now a museum), and the town's opera house, which opened to much fanfare in 1889. That night, the town's elite, lounging in plush Moroccan leather seats beneath a cobalt ceiling adorned with sparkling, silver stars, enjoyed a performance of *The King's Fool*.

Just four years later, the price of silver plummeted after Congress repealed an act that mandated federal purchases of the metal, and Wheeler entered bankruptcy proceedings. With little left to prop up the local economy, Aspen's grand buildings quickly fell into disrepair. Although the town acquired the opera house in 1918 for $1,155 in back taxes, it wasn't until 1979, when the town levied a new tax on real estate transfers, that funds became available for its restoration, which occurred in the mid-1980s. Restored to its position as the centerpiece of Aspen's cultural scene, the opera house today hosts about 300 events per year, ranging from opera performances to films, pop concerts, and dance recitals. The opera house is occasionally open for tours, but the

the historic Wheeler Opera House

dates and times vary; call the box office for more information.

which you can look down onto the town's modern fleet of shiny, red fire trucks.

Wheeler Stallard Museum

A few blocks northwest of the downtown, the **Wheeler Stallard Museum** (620 W. Bleeker St., 970/925-3721, http://aspenhistory.org, 10:30am-4:30pm daily mid-June to Labor Day, 1pm-5pm Tues.-Sat. Labor Day to mid-June, $10) is an 1888 Queen Anne-style Victorian brick home built (but never lived in) by Jerome Wheeler, the town's most prominent founding father. Guided tours focus on everyday life in the town's early days and include a rotating history exhibit.

Aspen Volunteer Fire Department Museum

Aspen's buildings are still protected by a volunteer fire department founded in 1881 during the town's heady mining boom. Today, the department's sparkling station houses a small **Fire Department Museum** (420 E. Hopkins Ave., 970/925-5532, http://aspenfire.com, 9am-5pm daily, free) that celebrates its heritage with displays of antique firefighting equipment, like circa-1886 hand-pulled hose carts as well as leather helmets and firefighting grenades. Plus, there are windows from

John Denver Sanctuary

Next to a walking path along the powerful Roaring Fork River, a simple **memorial** commemorates one of Aspen's most famous residents, singer-songwriter John Denver, who died in 1997 in a plane crash off the California coast. The poignant monument is a series of smooth stones in which lyrics from his best-known songs have been engraved, the most prominent of which is "Rocky Mountain High." The site is located along the recreation path on the south side of the Roaring Fork River a few blocks northeast of the intersection of East Main and North Mills Streets. There is no parking in the area, so it's best to use the parking garage at **Rio Grande Parking Plaza** (427 Rio Grand Pl., www.aspenpitkin.com, $1.50 per hour up to $15 per day) and walk the short distance to the river.

SPORTS AND RECREATION

Snowboarding and downhill skiing are Aspen's biggest draws, but the area has many other winter options, including snowshoeing, cross-country skiing, and snowmobiling, as

the John Denver Sanctuary

ASPEN

ASPEN AND THE ROARING FORK VALLEY

well as plentiful summer recreation, such as horseback riding, fishing, hiking, and cycling.

Downhill Skiing and Snowboarding

All four of the Aspen ski resorts are owned and operated by the **Aspen Skiing Company** (800/525-6200 or 970/923-1227, www.aspensnowmass.com, $149 full-day lift ticket, children under six ski free with a valid ticket). Tickets are valid at all four mountains, including Snowmass, located 11 miles west of downtown Aspen. Discount passes are available if you purchase your pass at least a week in advance and if you purchase multiple days at a time. (For example, in January through early April, a five-day adult ticket costs $495; a senior or child ticket is $290.) Discounts are also available with lodging packages.

All four of Aspen's mountains are linked by a free shuttle system; it's a good idea to take the shuttle instead of driving yourself to the ski area. The system is convenient enough that you can ski at one resort in the morning and a second in the afternoon. The **Ski & Snowboard School** (877/282-7736, www.aspensnowmass.com) offers riding and skiing instruction at all four resorts; beginner lessons are limited to just Buttermilk and Snowmass Mountains. If you crave powder off the beaten track, sign up for a guided backcountry **snowcat tour** through **Aspen Powder Tours** (970/920-0720, www.aspensnowmass.com).

Four Mountain Sports (970/920-2337, www.aspensnowmass.com, hours vary, $50 per day for beginning skier package, $63 per day beginning snowboard package) has nine locations, including at all four Aspen ski resorts. They'll deliver your gear to the resort of your choice, and you can even swap out for different skis if snow conditions change during your time there. Discounts are available if you book in advance.

ASPEN MOUNTAIN

Aspen Mountain (601 E. Dean. St., 9am-4pm daily), locally called **Ajax,** is the region's

Aspen Mountain in summer

oldest and best-known resort. In 1947 (the fledgling ski area's second season), the Aspen Skiing Company hired manager Dick Durrance, a 17-time national champion and Olympic ski racer. Durrance's successful bid to bring the 1950 World Championships to Aspen placed it firmly on the international ski map. The resort has been a renowned destination ever since. In 2017, Aspen will host the **Audi FIS World Cup Finals,** one of the most important events on the world tour.

Part of Ajax's appeal is that it rises 3,300 feet right behind town, so there's minimal hassle in getting here. The resort is known for its expert runs: 52 percent of its terrain is rated as expert (black) or extreme (double-black), and the remainder are intermediate. Ajax is not an area for beginner boarders or skiers. There is not a single green run and the ski school only offers lessons for intermediate to advanced adults.

Start your day on Ajax by heading to the edge of town to take the **Silver Queen Gondola** (included in winter lift ticket) to the top. Enjoy the gorgeous views, then head down the intermediate **Dipsy Doodle** to the **Ajax Express** lift, which accesses a number of other blue runs. Once you've warmed up, try some of Ajax's classic black runs, including **Face of Bell, Back of Bell, Ridge of Bell,** and **Blazing Star.**

ASPEN HIGHLANDS

The **Aspen Highlands** (199 Prospector Rd., 9am-3:30pm daily) ski resort is located just west of town, on the opposite side of Castle Valley from Aspen Mountain. The resort is known for its difficult terrain—52 percent of Aspen Highlands' runs are rated as expert or extreme—and varies from challenging steeps high on the mountain to long groomers on its lower slopes. Although the mountain has about 10 beginner (green) runs, its ski school only offers intermediate and advanced lessons.

Several attributes set Aspen Highlands apart. The scenic view from the top of Aspen Highlands is one of the best of any ski area in Colorado. You can see Pyramid Peak and both Maroon Bells, three of the state's most iconic peaks. The on-site **Cloud 9 Alpine Bistro** (76 Boomerang Rd., 970/923-8715, www.aspensnowmass.com, 11:30am-3:30pm daily, $47) is known for its excellent food. Best of all is the incredible **Highland Bowl,** whose lofty perch high on the ridge between Castle and Maroon Creeks translates into large moguls and 3,675 vertical feet of steep, open, hike-to terrain that is amazing on a fresh powder day.

Start with the Exhibition lift to **Exhibition** (green), or the Thunderbowl lift to wide-open **Golden Horn** (blue). Next, head toward some of the mountain's best blue runs, **Gunbarrel** on the Cloud 9 lift and **Broadway** off the Loge Peak lift, and then onto some of the classic blacks, like **South Castle, Moment of Truth,** and **Golden Horn Woods,** or the **Highland Bowl.**

BUTTERMILK

West of town, **Buttermilk** (38700 Hwy. 82, 9am-3:30pm daily) has a reputation that it's only good for beginners—but that's not the case (especially for snowboarders). The area is known for its many half-pipes and long terrain parks, where the electrifying Winter X-Games are held. Buttermilk is a great place to learn to ride or ski, and the ski school offers lessons for all ability levels. But with substantially less vertical feet (2,060 feet) than Aspen's other mountains, an easily manageable size, and 39 percent of the terrain rated intermediate, Buttermilk is also a great place to ski at an intermediate level.

Try taking the Summit Express lift from the base area to green classics like **Westward Ho** and **Larkspur;** both bring you back to the West Buttermilk Express lift. If you're ready to tackle something more challenging, head back toward The Cliffhouse, from which you can access two great blues: **Bear,** along the Summit Express lift, and **Buckskin,** near the Tiehack Express lift. If you're up for a black, give **Javelin** a try.

Cross-Country Skiing and Snowshoeing

With its many miles of groomed Nordic and pristine backcountry trails, the Roaring Fork Valley is an ideal place for cross-country and backcountry skiing and snowshoeing. If you have little or no experience, it's best to start with a lesson or a guided trip. Try one through the nonprofit **Aspen Nordic Council** (970/429-2039, www.aspennordic.com), which maintains the free, public **Aspen Snowmass Nordic Trail System** (www.aspensnowmass.com), a network of more than 60 miles of trails connecting Aspen, Snowmass, and Basalt. The trails range in difficulty level from beginner to expert.

A great place to begin your Nordic experience is at the **Aspen Cross Country Center** (39551 W. Hwy. 82, 970/925-2145, www.utemountaineer.com, 9am-5pm daily late Nov.-late Mar., $40 for a 45-min. lesson, $15-28 per day for rentals), a full-service ski center that offers lessons, tours, gear, and rentals, including classic and skate ski packages, chariots, and snowshoes. The same company operates another outlet in downtown Aspen, the Ute Mountaineer (210 S. Galena, 970/925-2849, www.utemountaineer.com, 9am-9pm Sun.-Thurs. and 9am-9:30pm Fri.-Sat.).

Another great area for ski touring is the Ashcroft Adventure Lodge (12500 Castle Creek Rd., 970/925-1044, http://pinecreek-cookhouse.com, Thanksgiving-early Apr., $25 full-day pass, $25 for Nordic ski or snowshoe rental), located 12 miles from Aspen at the end of the road up Castle Creek Valley. Here, 35 kilometers of groomed trails wind through 600 acres of national forest surrounding the ghost town of Ashcroft at about 9,500 feet in elevation. Group and individual lessons are available, as well as three-hour guided tours ($85-100), which include a hearty lunch at the Pine Creek Cookhouse (11399 Castle Creek Rd., 970/925-1044, http://pinecreekcook-house.com, 11:45am-1:45pm and 6:30pm-9pm daily in high season, $17-38 for lunch). A round-trip shuttle ($40) from Aspen is also available if you don't have your own wheels. To get here from downtown, head west on Main Street (Hwy. 82). At the large round-about west of town, take the last exit onto Castle Creek Road and follow it to its end at the seasonal closure gate.

If you decide to venture out on your own, the Aspen-Sopris Ranger District (970/963-2266, www.fs.usda.gov) has information regarding backcountry trails. Before you go, be sure to obtain a detailed route description and check on the conditions with the ranger district and the Colorado Avalanche Information Center (http://avalanche.state.co.us), which has an important Know Before You Go section and a sign-up for Twitter updates. One of the region's most popular year-round backcountry destinations is Conundrum Creek (http://www.fs.usda.gov), a moderately difficult, 8.5-mile-long trail that climbs about 2,500 feet from the trailhead to a series of hot springs. Although it's free, you must register at the trailhead, carry a copy of the paperwork with you, and obey all regulations. Camping around the hot springs is only allowed at designated sites,

most of which are about 0.25 mile before you reach the springs. Because the route crosses three creeks, it may be inaccessible during spring runoff. To get to the trailhead from downtown, drive west on Main Street (Hwy. 82) to the large roundabout west of town. Exit onto Castle Creek Road and follow this for five miles, then turn right onto narrow Conundrum Road. Continue straight for 1.1 miles to the trailhead. Overflow parking is on Castle Creek Road.

10TH MOUNTAIN DIVISION HUTS

Part of the nonprofit 10th Mountain Division Hut Association, the Alfred A. Braun Hut System (1280 Ute Ave., Aspen, 970/925-5775, www.huts.org, $28 per person, per night) is composed of seven public huts, all located near treeline, scattered throughout the extensive White River National Forest south of Aspen. This system allows you to do both out-and-back as well as hut-to-hut backcountry trips while spending the night in rustic but comfortable accommodations, usually equipped with bunks, propane burners, and sometimes basic cookware. You must have an advance reservation. Members are allowed to book cabins first either online, by phone, or by visiting the reservations office (8am-4pm Mon.-Fri. mid-Mar.-Nov., 8am-5pm Mon.-Fri. Dec.-mid-Mar.). Some of the bunks can be booked individually, whereas some cabins require that you reserve and pay for all of the beds. After members register, the remaining spots, if any, are typically allocated through a lottery system. Non-members can begin booking for the following winter on June 1. Since the huts in this system are in areas of known avalanche terrain, it's imperative to check with the Colorado Avalanche Information Center before you go. The routes are neither marked nor maintained. The website has detailed registration information and trailhead directions.

Snowmobiling

Snowmobiling is another popular winter recreation activity in this area. The area's most scenic tours are offered by **T Lazy 7** (2139 Maroon Creek Rd., 970/925-4614, www.tlazy7.com), a fifth-generation ranch in an incredible location partway up the Maroon Creek Road. They offer four different guided tours, the most popular of which is the two-hour **Maroon Bells Tour** (9am, 11:30am, and 2:30pm Tues.-Sat., $250 for one rider, $370 for two riders) from the ranch to Maroon Lake, where, weather permitting, you'll have great views of the peaks and (unlike in summer) the vista all to yourself. No experience is necessary, and the minimum age is just four years. The ranch also offers several other tours, including a 3.5-hour lunch ride up Independence Pass.

If you'd like to roar out on your own, an option close to downtown Aspen is **Smuggler Mountain Road.** A popular hiking trail in summer, this four-wheel drive road leaves from the east edge of town, winding its way up for 1.5 miles to a viewing platform with fantastic vistas of the town and three of the ski resorts. From here, it's another 4.5 miles to the **Warren Lakes,** another popular destination. For more information, contact the **Aspen-Sopris Ranger District** (970/963-2266, www.fs.usda.gov). To get to the trailhead from downtown, head east on Main Street (Hwy. 82), turn left (north) onto Mill Street, then right onto Gibson Avenue. After 0.2 mile, veer onto South Avenue, which turns into Park Circle. Smuggler Mountain Road is on the left. **Western Adventures** (555 Allen Way, Woody Creek, 970/923-3337, www.westernadventuresinc.com, $380-500 per day for a snowmobile) rents snowmobiles and related gear and also leads several tours ranging 2-4 hours.

Hiking and Biking

There is fantastic hiking and cycling in and around Aspen and throughout the surrounding 2.3 million acres of **White River National Forest** (900 Grand Ave., Glenwood Springs, 970/945-2521, www.fs.usda.gov, @WhiteRiverNews). The websites www.aspentrailfinder.com and www.aspenchamber.

org are good resources for finding the hike best suited for your group. You can rent both road and mountain bikes (and even stand up paddleboards) from **Aspen Bike Tours & Rentals** (430 S. Spring St., 970/925-9169, http://aspenbikerentals.com, $45 for a half-day full-suspension mountain bike), which also has tandems, scooters, and electric bikes.

A good place to begin is the slopes of **Aspen Mountain** just south of the downtown. Here, you have the option of combining a ride on the **Silver Queen Gondola** (www.aspensnowmass.com, 10am-4pm daily mid-June-early Sept. and 10am-4pm weekends late May-mid-June, $19-22) with a hike up or on the 3,300-foot mountain, where there are great views of town. There's a short and easy 0.9-mile **Nature Trail** at the top of the gondola, several "blue" intermediate trails, including the 4.9-mile **Aspen Mountain Summer Road,** and the challenging, steep, 2.5-mile **Ute Trail** on the mountain's east side. The moderate 1.5-mile (one-way) **Ajax Trail** also parallels the base.

The **Rio Grande Trail** is a nearly flat hiking and biking trail that follows the old railroad bed along the Roaring Fork River for 42 miles to Glenwood Springs. If you need an intermediate target, it's 18 miles (one-way) to the town of Basalt from the trailhead behind the Aspen post office on Puppy Smith Road. Only the first two miles are paved. For a great one-way outing, ride the trail in one direction and then take a bus back; see the RFTA website (www.rfta.com) for more details.

The **East of Aspen Trail** (www.aspenrecreation.com) is a three-mile dirt path that parallels the Roaring Fork southeast of town. Both hikers and mountain bikers will also enjoy the moderate **Hunter Creek Trail,** a 6.5-mile (one-way) walk along the creek through the Hunter Valley and up to wildflower-filled meadows and several abandoned homesteads. The trailhead is just east of a set of apartments on Lone Pine Road.

In addition to the Smuggler Mountain Trail, mountain bikers will enjoy the **Government Trail** (www.fs.usda.gov), an advanced 10-mile single-track ride that connects Aspen with Snowmass Village. To get to the southern trailhead, drive west on Highway 82 to the large roundabout and exit onto Maroon Creek Road. Continue one mile to the recreation center, where the trail begins behind the baseball fields.

★ SMUGGLER MOUNTAIN TRAIL

This 3.5-mile loop hike or mountain bike ride on the eastern edge of town is a favorite outing for both locals and visitors. The short but steep trail provides a great workout and gives you an enticing taste of the area's great hiking and beautiful scenery. The trail begins at a small parking area at the bottom of the steep, four-wheel drive Smuggler Road. At the first switchback, there's a good view of the old structures marking the **Smuggler Mine.** Discovered in 1879, it's one of Aspen's oldest claims and the site where the world's largest nugget of silver was found in 1894—an enormous rock that weighed 1,840 pounds!

From here, the route simply continues up the road. The higher you climb, the better the views become. After 1.4 miles, you reach a group of signs and branching trails. Take the narrow path to your right to a bench and a large wooden deck from which there are amazing views of Aspen, tucked into the emerald-green Roaring Fork Valley, far below.

Make your outing into a loop by heading up the **B.T.S. Trail,** which winds through a series of beautiful aspen groves. Near the end of this trail, there are signs directing you to two more historic mine sites, the **Park Regent** and the **Bushwacker,** which both have interpretive signs. Continue to the end of the B.T.S., which rejoins the **Smuggler Mountain Road.** If you have time, you can follow the road all the way up to the Warren Lakes (6 miles one-way from the trailhead), or you can return to the viewing platform, enjoy the panoramic vista again, and then retrace your steps back to your car.

To get here from downtown, head east on Main Street (Hwy. 82), turn left (north) onto Mill Street, then right onto Gibson Avenue. After 0.2 mile, veer onto South Avenue, which turns into Park Circle. Smuggler Mountain Road is on the left. There is limited parking at the trailhead.

Fishing

The Aspen area is well known for its excellent fly-fishing, including the Roaring Fork River and its many tributaries like the sparkling **Fryingpan River,** which is legendary

Aspen from Smuggler Mountain Trail

for its large trout. Access the Roaring Fork in downtown Aspen near Mill Street, or drive a short distance out of town in either direction on Highway 82. To reach the Fryingpan River, drive north on Highway 82 to its junction with the Fryingpan Road (Rd. 105) near the town of Basalt. Follow this upstream to discover the many beautiful holes where cutthroat, brown, speckled, and rainbow trout loiter, along with the occasional whitefish. All of the Roaring Fork is catch-and-release, and special regulations (www.recreation.gov) apply along the Fryingpan, which the Colorado Wildlife Commission has designated as Gold Medal waters. About 14 miles upstream of Basalt, the **Ruedi Reservoir** is another great fishing spot.

If you've never tried fly-fishing or prefer to go with a guide, **Aspen Flyfishing** (601 E. Dean St., 970/920-6886, www.aspenflyfishing.com, $275 for half-day wading trip) in the Gorsuch Ski Shop leads year-round guided wading trips on the Roaring Fork and Fryingpan Rivers, as well as float-fishing trips on the Roaring Fork and Colorado Rivers. They also sell fishing licenses. **Aspen Trout Guides** (520 E. Durant Ave., 970/925-1200, www.aspentroutguides.com, $250 for half-day trip) has similar offerings, plus kids' half-day fishing trips and custom overnight trips.

Rafting and Kayaking

Aspen Whitewater Rafting (866/377-4837, www.aspenwhitewater.com, $86-94 for half-day Roaring Fork trip) offers half-day rafting trips on the Roaring Fork and Arkansas Rivers ranging in difficulty from beginner to advanced. They also offer self-propelled trips in inflatable kayaks known as duckies. **Blazing Adventures** (800/282-7238, www.blazingadventures.com, $83-98 for half-day Roaring Fork trip) has comparable offerings.

Horseback Riding

In combination with the **T Lazy 7 Ranch** (2139 Maroon Creek Rd., 970/925-4614, www.tlazy7.com), located partway up Maroon Creek Road, **Maroon Bells Outfitters**

(970/920-4677, http://maroonbellsaspen.com, $75 for one hour) offers hour-long and half-day summer horseback rides through the national forest surrounding the beautiful Maroon Creek Valley. They also offer overnight pack trips.

Golf

In this town of superlatives, it's no surprise that there are several well-known golf courses on which to test your mettle. These include the challenging, public 18-hole course at the **Aspen Golf & Tennis Club** (39551 Hwy. 82, 970/429-1949, www.aspengolf.com, $99-160 peak season, including cart), which *Golfweek* magazine ranked as Colorado's best municipal course. Known for its length as well as its numerous water features, the course has great views of the peaks along the Continental Divide and is also Audubon-certified.

Located at the base of steep Mount Sopris, the **River Valley Ranch Golf Club** (303 River Valley Ranch Dr., Carbondale, 970/963-3625, www.rvrgolf.com, $50-99) is also open to the public. *Golf* magazine dubbed it "the new jewel of the Rockies."

ENTERTAINMENT AND EVENTS

Nightlife

After a full day of skiing, relax at the popular **J-Bar** (330 E. Main St., 970/429-7674, https://hoteljerome.aubergeresorts.com, 11:30am-1am daily) in the Hotel Jerome, which has an upscale saloon-style ambiance and a diverse menu of filling foods (including their "locally world famous" burgers) to pair with pitchers or frosty pints of local and imported beers. If it's not too cold, the outdoor bar stools and tables at **HOPS Culture** (414 E. Hyman Ave., 970/925-4677, www.hopsculture.com, 11:30am-11pm daily) are great places to sip one of the restaurant's 200 craft beers or seasonal cocktails (try the Kalamazoo Shake-aroo!). The modern brick-and-wood interior features another large bar and cozy tables filled with chattering patrons enjoying seasonally inspired comfort food like bacon cheddar tater tots, beer brats, and a chicken 'n' waffles platter.

One of the locals' (and my) favorite hangouts is the **Aspen Brewing Company** (304 E. Hopkins Ave., 970/920-2739, http://aspenbrewingcompany.com, noon-midnight daily, off-site brewery tours $20), whose deck has great views of Aspen Mountain. The beers are brewed just outside of town and include the year-round Independence Pass ale and Pyramid Peak porter, as well as a rotating selection of seasonal and barrel-aged brews like the Bourbon Barrel Imperial Red. Try a tasting flight if you can't pick just one. The brewery features live music on most Fridays and Saturdays during the winter and the summer, as well as great happy hour specials (5pm-7pm daily).

At the bottom of Aspen Mountain in the Sky Hotel, **39 Degrees** (709 E. Durant Ave., 970/925-6760, www.theskyhotel.com, 11:30am-midnight Sun.-Wed., 11:30am-2am Thurs.-Sat.) is a lively après-ski lounge that *USA Today* named as one of the "top nine snug hotel bars to warm you up in winter." It's also a great place to hang out by the pool in the summer. Each evening from 5pm to 6pm, the lounge hosts an Altitude Adjustment wine hour. A slightly longer walk from the slopes brings you to the spacious **Limelight Lounge** (355 S. Monarch St., 970/925-3025, www.limelighthotel.com, 3pm-10pm daily), which has happy hour specials (3pm-7pm daily), a great wine list, and hand-tossed, wood-fired pizzas, fresh salads, and savory small plates, like baked spinach artichoke dip, if you want to roll straight into dinner. The lounge has live music Thursday-Monday nights during the ski season and also offers special beer pairing dinners twice a month.

About eight miles north of town, the laid-back **Woody Creek Tavern** (2 Woody Creek Plaza, Woody Creek, 970/923-4585, www.woodycreektavern.com, 11am-10pm daily) is worth the trip just to see its interior, where the walls are plastered with hundreds of photos, newspaper clippings, artwork, license plates, and just about anything else you can imagine. Once the favorite haunt of gonzo journalist Hunter S. Thompson, the tavern is known for its fresh-squeezed lime margaritas but also has a decent beer and wine selection, as well as a Mexican-inspired menu with staples like cheese enchiladas and fish tacos.

Downtown Aspen's best place to catch live music is **Belly Up Aspen** (450 S. Galena St., 970/544-9800, http://bellyupaspen.com, hours vary, $25-95 for general admission), which

HOPS Culture

hosts more than 300 events each year, including occasional headliners like Stephen Marley, Chris Isaak, Jane's Addiction, and Seal. During ski season, **Chair 9** (675 E. Durant Ave., 970/920-4600, www.thelittlenell.com, 3:30pm-7:30pm daily in winter) in the Little Nell features DJs or live music.

Festivals and Events

Festivals are a big part of the Aspen scene. The town's year-round calendar of events (970/925-1940, www.aspenchamber.org) begins with the four-day **Wintersköl** (downtown, Jan., prices vary, but many events are free), a zany mid-winter celebration that dates back to 1951. Events include a snow-carving competition, a snow-biking challenge, a canine fashion show, and "Soupsköl." For Christmas, the town hosts the **12 Days of Aspen** (downtown, Dec., prices vary), which features plenty of vintage holiday fun, such as Victorian caroling, visits from Santa and his reindeer, and fireworks, as well as film screenings, ugly sweater après-ski, and events like the Little Nell Hotel's famous New Year's **Dom Pérignon Party** ($600 a head). The biggest cold-weather event is the **Winter X Games** (http://xgames.espn.go.com, late Jan.), an extreme sport competition held at the Buttermilk resort, where athletes complete incredible feats like a "double backside alley-oop rodeo" on the half-pipe and mid-air flips on snowmobiles. Spectators flood the town to watch contests like the signature Ski Big Air and Snowboard Big Air.

Summer brings a new event almost every week. The best known is the **Aspen Music Festival** (www.aspenmusicfestival.com, June-Aug., prices vary), one of the nation's top classical music celebrations. The eight-week calendar is packed with orchestra, chamber symphony, and opera performances that take place at a variety of venues around town, including the historic Wheeler Opera House, the Joan and Irving Harris Concert Hall, and the enormous Benedict Music Tent near the banks of the Roaring Fork River. The visual arts are featured during the smaller **Aspen Arts Festival** (350

E. Durant Ave., www.artfestival.com, end of July), when Wagner Park overflows with stalls where you can meet the artists and shop for that perfect painting or vase.

Aspen hosts the renowned **Food & Wine Classic** (www.foodandwine.com, mid-June, $1,350 for a 3-day pass), one of the nation's largest culinary events. Celebrity chefs, winemakers, and culinary connoisseurs from around the globe offer a series of grand tastings, cooking classes, lectures, and other events. The **Aspen Ideas Festival** (www.aspenideas.org, late June, $10-150 for single events) features eight days of nonpartisan lectures, debates, and panel discussions that tackle societally critical topics ranging from the environment to politics to the economy.

SHOPPING

Most of Aspen's shops are centered around the downtown pedestrian mall, a zone that stretches east-west from Hunter to Monarch Streets and north-south from Hopkins to Durant Avenues. The district includes the fun **Aspen Dancing Fountain** (www.aspendancingfountain.com), the brainchild of a computer wizard and a local sculptor, the grassy **Wagner Park** (350 E. Durant Ave.), and the bricked Cooper Avenue and Hyman Avenue Malls.

Shopping is an important part of the Aspen experience for many visitors. While there are plenty of high-priced downtown designer stores like **Prada** (312 S. Galena St., 970/925-7001, www.prada.com, 11am-6pm Mon.-Sat., noon-5pm Sun.) and **Louis Vuitton** (205 S. Mill St., 970/544-8200, http://us.louisvuitton.com, 10am-6pm Mon.-Sat., noon-6pm Sun.) that draw in the celebrities, there are also some great boutique clothing stores, outdoor gear shops, and quirky indie establishments.

The family-owned **Pitkin County Dry Goods** (520 E. Cooper Ave., 970/925-1681, www.pitkincountydrygoods.com, 11am-7pm daily), one of Aspen's oldest retail stores, sells women's and men's contemporary casual clothing, including sportswear and denim, as well as shoes, jewelry, and other accessories.

For Western wear, mosey on over to **Kemo Sabe** (434 E. Cooper St., 970/925-7878, www. kemosabe.com, 10am-7:30pm daily), which sells pricey, American-made Grit leather bags, cowboy boots, one-of-a-kind "dress" cowboy hats, and handmade leather belts and buckles (or you can also design your own).

If you're a shoe fanatic, **Bloomingbirds** (461 E. Hopkins St., 970/925-2241, 10am-6pm Mon.-Sat., 11am-5pm Sun.) is the place to pick up high-end stilettos, boots, and handbags. Aspen's premier jewelry store is **Meridian Jewelers** (525 E. Cooper Ave., 970/925-3833, www.meridianjewelers.com, 11am-5:30pm daily), whose showcases are filled with sparkling gems (if you need to ask the price, you probably can't afford it).

For books and maps, head to **Explore Booksellers** (9221 E. Main St., 970/925-5338, www.explorebooksellers.com, 10am-9pm daily), located in a small, brown Victorian building whose nooks and crannies are bursting with books. In addition to an emphasis on kids' books, the store has a good selection of most other genres and a good selection of regional titles. The small café upstairs is Aspen's first "nutritarian" restaurant and serves good coffee in addition to its nutrient-dense foods.

In summer, dozens of stalls at the **Aspen Saturday Market** (Hyman and Hopkins Aves., www.aspenpitkin.com, 8:30am-3pm Sat. mid-June-early Sept., 9am-3pm Sat. mid-Sept.-mid-Oct.) overflow the blocks of the downtown's eastern edge. Local rules dictate that only items made, grown, and produced in Colorado can be sold. If you forgot your toothbrush, need a prescription filled, or want to buy a bottle of wine, stop by **Carl's Pharmacy** (306 E. Main St., 970/925-3273, www.carlspharmacy.com, 9am-9pm daily), Aspen's iconic drug store, a local institution since 1965.

★ Art Galleries

One of Aspen's great pleasures is wandering through the downtown, browsing Aspen's diverse assortment of art galleries. Sure, the prices are exorbitant, but most proprietors will welcome you even if you're just browsing, and it's fun to dream about how you'll decorate your next $10 million mountain-front home. A great shop to begin at is one of Aspen's most unique establishments, the fun and funky **Emporium and Flying Circus** (315 E. Main St., 970/544-2499, www.emporiumandflyingcircus.com, 10am-6pm daily), a co-op that features a constantly rotating selection of arts and crafts from 70 artists. Before

one of Aspen's colorful art galleries

you even step in the door, you walk through an eclectic "garden," and the shop is "overflowing with fun and frippery," from scarves to house signs to locally thrown pottery.

The **Forré & Co. Fine Art Gallery** (426 E. Hyman Ave., 970/544-1607, forrefineart. com, 11am-8pm Sun.-Thurs., 11am-9pm Fri.-Sat.) is best known for its intriguing exhibits, which change every few months. Previous shows have included the works of H. Claude Pissarro, Ashley Collins, and Moshé Y, along with many others. The family-owned **Isberian Rug Company** (516 E. Hyman Ave., 970/925-8062, www.isberianrugs.com, 9am-5pm Mon.-Fri., 10am-5pm Sat.) has a bewildering assortment of beautiful Oriental, antique, and modern rugs, as well as handmade Turkish kilims and Navajo weavings.

Serious collectors will not want to miss the spacious, open interior of **Galerie Maximillian** (602 E. Cooper Ave., 970/925-6100, http://galeriemax.com, 10am-8pm Mon.-Sat., 11am-7pm Sun.), which displays just a fraction of its museum-quality collection, including artwork from 19th- and 20th-century masters like Picasso, Renoir, and Chagall, as well as contemporary artists such as Damien Hurst and Takashi Murakami. Tucked into a courtyard just off of Cooper Avenue, **Aspen Grove Fine Arts** (525 E. Cooper Ave., 970/925-5151, https://aspengrovefineart.com, 10am-9pm Mon.-Sat., 10am-5pm Sun.) features traditional and contemporary works in a variety of mediums, from Western and landscape paintings to modernistic, free-form bronze sculptures.

FOOD

For a town that's famous for its haute cuisine, Aspen can still be surprisingly affordable if you stick to large breakfasts, snacks, and bar food. Of course, you can easily drop hundreds of dollars on a fancy dinner with wine. Restaurant hours frequently change, especially during the quieter spring and fall seasons. Call ahead to ensure your choice is open. Reservations are highly recommended during the bustling summer and ski seasons.

Breakfast and Cafés

A great locals' pick for breakfast and lunch, especially in summer when you can take advantage of the outdoor seating, is **Aspen Over Easy** (304 E. Hopkins Ave., 970/429-8693, www.aspenovereasy.com, 9am-4pm daily, $8-14). Started by a group of friends whose idea was to provide sustainable (and affordable) dining in Aspen, this casual restaurant serves up great food, from croissant breakfast sandwiches to barbecue ranch burgers with tangy onion rings.

Located not far from the Silver Queen Gondola, **Poppycock's** (665 E. Cooper Ave., 970/925-1245, http://poppycockscafe.com, 7am-2:30pm Mon.-Sat., 7am-2pm Sun., $6-13) is best known for its old-fashioned oatmeal buttermilk pancakes and French toast, as well as delicious herb, ham, and chile crepes.

Casual

For a quick grab-and-go sandwich, head to **The Butcher's Block** (424 S. Spring St., 970/925-7554, www.butchersblockaspen.com, 8am-6pm daily, $4-14). You can call ahead or stop by to order one of their thick chicken or seafood salad sandwiches, homemade soups, or meaty Italian subs. They also sell gourmet food items, in case you run out of caviar.

For family-friendly Italian food, head to **Brunelleschi's** (205 S. Mill St., 970/544-4644, www.zgpizza.com, 11am-10:30pm daily, $12-27). The name, which the kids' menu simplifies to Brun-o-let's-ski, comes from a dome covering Italy's Florence Cathedral. The restaurant is best known for its tasty, thin-crust pizzas, which are on the small side. If you've worked up a good appetite, try the traditional spaghetti, linguini, and lasagna entrées.

The **Meat & Cheese Restaurant** (317 E. Hopkins Ave., 970/710-7120, http://meatandcheeseaspen.com, 11am-10pm daily, $13-32) is an interesting concept; founded by the local Avalanche Cheese Company, the starkly modern interior features a farm shop as well as a simple restaurant that sells creamy artisan cheeses, freshly baked bread, cured meats, and fresh salads as part of entrées or European-style meat-and-cheese boards.

The healthiest choice in town is undoubtedly **Pyramid Bistro** (221 E. Main St., 970/925-5338, www.pyramidbistro.com, 11:30am-9pm daily, $19-29), a stylish spot with walls of windows, a pleasant outdoor deck, and a simple menu of fresh salads and innovative vegetarian and meat dishes such as sweet potato gnocchi or coriander-dusted duck breast. If instead you find yourself craving some classic barbecue, head on over to the much more casual **Aspen Hickory House** (730 W. Main St., 970/925-2313, www.hickoryhouseribs.com, 8am-2:30pm and 5pm-9pm daily, $13-26) for large portions of saucy baby back ribs, pulled pork, and deep-fried catfish.

One of Aspen's most popular establishments, the ★ **White House Tavern** (302 E. Hopkins Ave., 970/925-1007, http://aspenwhitehouse.com, 11am-10pm Sun.-Thurs., 11am-11pm Fri.-Sat., $16-23) is housed in a beautifully restored 1883 miner's cottage, one of Aspen's oldest buildings. The cozy, wooden interior, which can get noisy when the place is packed, has a number of comfortable booths along one wall and a curved, wooden bar lining the other, as well as a great outdoor seating area. The short food menu focuses mostly on meat and fish sandwiches and small bites like deviled eggs, but also includes roasted chicken and Thai steak salads. The drink menus feature a good selection of red and white wines, Colorado craft beer, and creative cocktails.

Upscale

Operated by a wife-and-husband team, **La Creperie du Village** (400 E. Hopkins Ave., 970/925-1566, www.lacreperieduvillage.com, 11:30am-close daily, $26-42) is an upscale French bistro where chef Andreas Neufeld dishes up culinary highlights from the Alps, such as charcuterie boards, sweet and savory crepes, traditional Swiss raclette, and a divine black truffle cheese fondue. The restaurant has an open kitchen overlooked by a set of bar stools, a community table, and a sunny outdoor patio with European-style sidewalk tables.

Aspen's top sushi restaurant is the highly acclaimed ★ **Matsuhisa** (303 E. Main St., 970/544-6628, www.matsuhisarestaurants.com, open seating 5:30pm-11pm daily, $29-42 entrées), named for renowned chef Nobu Matsuhisa. Housed in a 120-year-old Victorian, the restaurant has been a downtown institution since its opening in 1998. Make reservations weeks in advance for a seat in the main downstairs dining room, or simply drop by to see if there's room at the more casual sushi bar. The dinner menu features sushi and sashimi, as well as specialties like squid pasta with light garlic sauce.

For an intimate, candlelight dinner, try **The Wild Fig** (315 E. Hyman Ave., 970/925-5160, www.thewildfig.com, 11:30am-3pm and 5:30pm-10pm daily, $24-45), a Mediterranean-inspired brasserie with a mouthwatering menu of fresh starters, like the fig salad or Spanish gazpacho, and delicious entrées, such as house-made fettuccine and fig and honey-glazed duck breast. The extensive cocktail menu includes unusual concoctions like ginger margaritas.

Jimmy's (205 S. Mill St. #2, 970/925-6020, www.jimmysaspen.com, 5:30pm-11pm daily, $15-59) serves upscale American fare, including its excellent rib eye and other steaks, crab cakes, and an award-winning, ultra-decadent volcano cake. In addition to the delicious food, the restaurant is famous for its potent house cocktails and for hosting one of the nation's largest selections of agave-based spirits.

The Little Nell's signature restaurant, ★ **Element 47** (675 E. Durant Ave., 970/920-4600, www.thelittlenell.com, breakfast 7am-10:30am, lunch 11:30am-2pm, dinner 6pm-9pm daily, $27-65), is considered Aspen's finest dining establishment. Its name is a tribute to silver, the 47th chemical element on the periodic table. Eating at this rare five-star, five-diamond ranked restaurant is a one-of-a-kind experience, supervised by a whole team of culinary professionals, including executive chef Matt Zubrod and master sommelier Carlton

McCoy, who oversees a 20,000-bottle wine cellar and recertification of the coveted Wine Spectator Grand Award. The menu features seasonally inspired dishes like grilled cauliflower steak, dry-aged duck breast, and butter-poached Maine lobster, as well as royal Kaluga caviar, which is sold by the ounce. Complete your dining experience with one of the delectable desserts, like white chocolate popcorn or a traditional crème brûlée.

ACCOMMODATIONS

Aspen's accommodations are spread throughout the downtown. Many of the priciest digs are clustered at the base of the mountain, but there are more choices scattered throughout downtown. Prices tend to be quite expensive in both winter and summer; there are few deals to be had outside of these seasons. Cheaper accommodations can be found in outlying areas stretching north from Aspen, including Basalt, El Jebel, Carbondale, and even in Glenwood Springs, an hour's drive north.

$150-250

One of the least expensive places to stay in Aspen is the family-owned **Tyrolean Lodge** (220 W. Main St., 970/925-4595, www.tyroleanlodge.com, $220-245). Although it's located right on the busy main street, it's also just a few blocks from downtown, and the free ski shuttle stops right outside the door. Its 16 rooms are basic (think 1970s decor) but spacious, have kitchenettes, and accommodate up to five people apiece. Be aware that the lodge has no elevator, so if you book a room on the third floor, be prepared to climb up and down the stairs.

$250-350

Although the 53 rooms are basic and it's located right on Main Street, the **Molly Gibson Lodge** (101 W. Main St., 970/925-3434, www.mollygibson.com, $295-370) has a wonderful pool that's heated year-round, free daily après-ski wine-and-cheese parties, a free buffet breakfast, fireplace and

whirlpool tub suites, and free guest parking just three blocks from the downtown. One of Aspen's few surviving, Old World-style ski lodges, the **Mountain Chalet Aspen** (333 E. Durant Ave., 970/925-7797, www.mountainchaletaspen.com, $219-334) has a family-friendly atmosphere, with a cozy living room where you can warm up next to a roaring fire, group breakfast tables, and a fantastic location near the base of Aspen Mountain. The no-frills rooms and suites are clean and comfortable and come in a variety of configurations, from economy rooms with original 1950s furniture to remodeled two-bed, two-bath apartments with full kitchens and living rooms. With a heated outdoor pool, hot tub, and fitness center, as well as free parking, the chalet represents one of Aspen's best values.

Over $350

With a fantastic location facing Wagner Park and within walking distance of the Silver Queen Gondola and the downtown, the contemporary ★ **Limelight Hotel** (355 S. Monarch St., 970/925-3025, www.limelighthotel.com, $405-1,120) is one of Aspen's top lodging options. From king rooms to spacious suites, the hotel has 10 different types of rooms to choose from. All have very comfortable beds and a simple, inviting decor. The enormous, open lounge with leather couches and lime-green accents is a great après-ski spot, as well as the location of the impressive (and complimentary) Continental Divide breakfast buffet. The Limelight also goes well beyond the usual pool-and-hot tub amenities. They offer free bikes to cruise around town and both a ski concierge and an adventure concierge to help you plan your next hike, bike ride, tennis match, or mogul run. The concierge can even set up a one-way, 11-mile hike to Crested Butte, during which you're equipped with a SpotSatellite GPS device so that your private transport is waiting for you when you reach the end of the trail.

Located steps from Aspen Mountain's Silver Queen Gondola, the stylish 90-room **Sky Hotel** (709 E. Durant Ave., 970/925-6760, www.theskyhotel.com, $160-799) has a unique decor, with captivating black-and-white photos on the walls, headboards designed to resemble cable-knit sweaters, and racing stripes on the curtains and walls. Sky offers deluxe, premier, and superior rooms with one or two beds, plus spacious suites, pet-friendly rooms, an evening wine reception, and a late check-out time (noon).

The chic, glass-fronted **Hotel Aspen** (110 W. Main St., 970/925-3441, www.hotelaspen.com, $323-584) has 45 luxurious rooms and suites with comfy beds draped with 300-thread-count sheets and fluffy down duvets. Room options range from traditional king rooms to more lavish fireplace or private whirlpool tub suites. The hotel has free guest parking, a heated outdoor pool and steaming hot tub, and a popular (and free) après-ski wine-and-cheese reception each afternoon in addition to a complimentary hot breakfast.

A stout brick building built by Jerome Wheeler (of the Wheeler Opera House fame) in 1889, the **Hotel Jerome** (330 E. Main St., 970/920-1000, https://hoteljerome.aubergeresorts.com, $689-855) has a distinctive Western ambiance—antlers, moose heads, and photos of Native Americans adorn the walls. The striking lobby features comfortable sofas and chairs next to a roaring fireplace, above which hangs an enormous portrait of Jerome Wheeler, one of Aspen's most prominent founding fathers. Rooms include loveseats or a lounge chair and feature cozy king-size beds; several suites are also available. In addition to a spa, the hotel has two bars and an upscale restaurant.

Set on five lush acres three blocks east of Aspen Mountain, **The Gant** (610 S. West End, 970/925-5000, www.gantaspen.com, $591-799) is a gorgeous property that offers condominiums (1-4 bedrooms). All rooms include romantic wood-burning fireplaces, full kitchens, and a balcony or patio. Valet parking, bell and concierge service, and free in-town and airport transport round out the amenities.

In a park-like setting about 1.5 miles north of downtown, the beautiful 40-acre **Aspen Meadows Resort** (845 Meadows Rd., 800/452-4240, www.aspenmeadows.com, $288-499) has 98 bright Bauhaus-design suites with floor-to-ceiling windows, functional work spaces, and comfortable sitting areas. The resort is the home of the Aspen Institute, an influential nonpartisan think tank that hosts intellectual gatherings to tackle some of our nation's most critical challenges, from improving homeland security to combating economic inequality.

The ★ **Little Nell** (675 E. Durant Ave., 970/920-4600, www.thelittlenell.com, $1,232-1,532) has the reputation of being Aspen's most luxurious hotel, as well as the best hotel between the Atlantic and Pacific Coasts. It's a beautiful facility located steps from the Silver Queen Gondola and the vibrant downtown. The 78 rooms and 14 suites are gorgeous, comfortable, and have unique floor plans that include gas fireplaces. Most also have private balconies, many with fantastic views of Aspen Mountain. The hotel's adventure concierge can set you up with private stargazing tours (with champagne), bike rides with former pro cyclists, shotgun rides in working snowcats, and just about any ski adventure you can imagine.

CAMPING

Two miles northwest of Basalt on Highway 82, the year-round **Aspen-Basalt Campground** (20640 Hwy. 82, Basalt, 970/927-3405, www.coloradodirectory.com, $47) has 43 shaded, level RV sites, most of which are pull-through. There are also a number of campgrounds in the White River National Forest. The closest one to Aspen is **Difficult Campground** (5 miles south of Aspen on Hwy. 82, 877/444-6777, www.recreation.gov, late May-Sept., $24 per site), whose 47 sites along the Roaring Fork River can accommodate trailers up to 40 feet long. About two-thirds of these can be reserved in advance; the rest are first-come, first-served.

TRANSPORTATION AND SERVICES

Air

Denver International Airport (DEN, 8500 Peña Blvd., 303/342-2000, http://www.flydenver.com) is the closest major airport to Aspen. The smaller **Aspen/Pitkin County Airport** (ASE, 233 E. Airport Rd., 970/920-5384, http://aspenairport.com), located just a few miles northwest of Aspen on Highway 82, has direct, year-round flights from Denver, nonstop summer flights from Houston, Chicago, San Francisco, and Los Angeles, and direct flights from all of these cities, plus Minneapolis/St. Paul, Atlanta, and Dallas/Fort Worth, during ski season.

Most major car rental companies, including Avis, Budget, and Hertz, have depots at the Aspen/Pitkin County Airport.

Car

Aspen is located along Highway 82, an upgraded road that branches off from I-70 to run southeast along the Roaring Fork River. In summer, Highway 82 continues up and over Independence Pass to its end at the junction with U.S. 24, the north-south road along the Arkansas River Valley that provides access to Denver via both I-70 (to the north) and U.S. 285 (to the south).

How long it takes to drive between Denver and Aspen/Snowmass depends upon the time of year. In summer, when spectacular **Independence Pass is open** (usually Memorial Day-early Nov.), it takes roughly four hours to drive this 159-mile route. To reach Aspen from Denver, take I-70 West for 74 miles to Exit 195 for Copper Mountain. Exit and follow Highway 91 south over Fremont Pass for 22 miles to its junction with U.S. 24. Continue south on U.S. 24 for about 16 miles to the junction with Highway 82. Turn right here to climb up and over Independence Pass, which in 43 miles arrives in Aspen.

When **Independence Pass is closed** (Nov.-May), take I-70 west to Glenwood Springs and head south on Highway 82 to

Aspen. Although it's possible to drive this 198-mile route in as few as 3.5 hours, it typically takes 4-5 hours or more, depending upon traffic, road conditions, and construction, especially in Glenwood Springs.

Either way, you'll need to cross at least one major mountain pass. In winter, check on road conditions and chain laws with the Colorado Department of Transportation (in-state 511, www.cotrip.org).

Parking

Parking in Aspen is an issue in both summer and winter. Ask your hotel if they have space available. If they don't, you can either try to find a spot on the street (although most of the roads surrounding the downtown have 2-hour limits) or use the **Rio Grande Parking Garage** (427 Rio Grande Pl., just off Mill St., $15 per day). In both summer and winter, free **Galena Street Shuttle** continuously shuttles visitors from this garage to the Silver Queen Gondola.

In Aspen, leave your car parked and use the **4 Mountain Connector** bus (www.rfta.com, free) to get around town and between the ski resorts. Aspen Mountain is so close to Aspen that you must take a shuttle or park in town. Aspen Highlands has limited pay parking (www.aspensnowmass.com). Buttermilk has free, year-round parking in all of its lots along Highway 82 (except during the Winter X Games).

Shuttle, Bus, and Train

Most accommodations provide free shuttle service to and from the Aspen/Pitkin County Airport. The **Roaring Fork Transit Authority** (970/925-8484, www.rfta.com, free) rides into town via its frequent VelociRFTA bus line. Information is available at the Guest Services booth near the baggage claim.

Colorado Mountain Express (970/754-7433, www.coloradomountainexpress.com, $120-135 one-way) provides shuttle service between DIA and the Aspen/Snowmass area;

the trip typically takes 5.5 hours. The company also serves Glenwood Springs and several smaller towns along the Roaring Fork Valley.

From downtown Denver, both **Greyhound** (www.greyhound.com, $35-40 one-way) and **Amtrak** (www.amtrak.com, $84 one-way) provide bus and train service to Glenwood Springs, from which you can take the local RFTA bus to Aspen. Both options take longer than a shuttle.

Services

VISITOR INFORMATION

The **Aspen Chamber Resort Association** (www.aspenchamber.org) has information on tourism-related topics. The downtown **visitor center** (425 Rio Grande Pl., 970/925-1940, 8:30am-5pm Mon.-Fri.) is next to the Rio Grande Parking Garage; a **Guest Pavilion** (Cooper Ave. and Galena St., 10am-7pm daily in summer, 10am-6pm daily in winter, shorter hours in shoulder seasons) is stocked with brochures on the Cooper Avenue Mall.

The best source of information related to the ski resorts is the **Aspen Skiing Company** (800/525-6200, www.aspensnowmass.com), which has information about the mountains, lodging, snow and grooming reports, and year-round activities.

MEDIA AND COMMUNICATIONS

The *Aspen Times* (www.aspentimes.com), the town's weekly paper, features local news, sports, and events. **KAJX** (91.5 FM) is the local public radio station, and **Thunder** (93.5 FM) features classic hits. Aspen's remodeled **library** (590 N. Mill St., 970/429-1900, http://pitcolib.org, 9am-8pm Mon.-Thurs., 9am-6pm Fri.-Sat., noon-6pm Sun.) has free public Internet access.

Aspen's **post office** (235 Puppy Smith St., 970/925-7523, 8:30am-5pm Mon.-Fri., 9am-noon Sat.) is located north of the downtown. From East Main Street, follow Mill Street north. Turn onto the second left; the post office will be on your left.

MEDICAL

Located on Castle Creek Road south of the roundabout on the west edge of town, the **Aspen Valley Hospital** (401 Castle Creek Rd., 970/925-1120, www.aspenvalleyhospital.org) is the regional medical care center and also offers after-hours medical care. The resorts all have ski patrols for slopeside emergencies.

SNOWMASS VILLAGE

Compared to Aspen, Snowmass Village has always been a sleepier spot. Unlike Aspen, it lacks historical roots; it was a relaxed ranching area until the Snowmass Mountain ski resort opened in 1967. Thanks to multiple expansions and renovations since then, the resort has blossomed into one of Colorado's best ski destinations, as well as the location of a recent—and unexpected—archaeological discovery.

★ Ice Age Discovery Center

Located in the heart of Snowmass Village, the small **Ice Age Discovery Center** (54B Snowmass Village Mall, 970/922-2277, www.gosnowmass.com, 10am-5pm daily June-Sept., free) lets visitors share in some of the excitement of the groundbreaking discoveries at the nearby **Snowmastodon Site.** The informative displays include background information, a half-sized wooden mammoth skeleton, fun kid activities, and a video about the excavations. There are also fossil casts of mastodon and mammoth teeth that you can touch.

Snowmass Mountain

In addition to excellent skiing and snowboarding in winter, **Snowmass Mountain** (97 Lower Mall, Snowmass Village, 9am-4pm daily) offers tubing ($33) near the top of the **Elk Camp Gondola.** Visitors can also take a guided **snowshoe or ski tour** (970/925-5756, $38-58) to learn about alpine ecology from an **Aspen Center for Environmental Studies** (www.aspennature.org) naturalist.

The Snowmastodon Site

In mid-October of 2010, a bulldozer operator working on the expansion of the Ziegler Reservoir, which supplies water to Snowmass Village, accidentally uncovered some very large bones. Jesse Steele, the operator, immediately informed his supervisor, and the two of them plied the Internet, searching for information. After correctly identifying the remains as mammoth bones, they notified the Denver Museum of Nature and Science, which negotiated a construction delay with the Snowmass Water and Sanitation District and then quickly began excavations.

All told, the team had just seven weeks to uncover and document as many remains as possible before the site was flooded by the expanded reservoir. Despite unpleasant weather conditions and knee-deep mud, the crew did a fantastic job of uncovering nearly 5,000 bones that belonged to megafauna, including mammoths, mastodons, bison, American camels, and a giant ground sloth—the first ever found in Colorado. The finds also included about 26,000 bones from at least 30 species of small Ice Age animals, such as muskrats, beavers, frogs, lizards, and snakes, as well as the remains of 60 plant species.

Now considered one of the world's most significant Ice Age fossil locales, the **Snowmastodon Site** provides a rare glimpse into what the environment was like on Snowmass Mountain from about 140,000 to 55,000 years ago, when a small glacial lake and wetlands existed here.

★ DOWNHILL SKIING
AND SNOWBOARDING

Snowmass Mountain is one of the best ski mountains in Colorado, with 4,406 feet of vertical rise and 3,332 skiable acres (1.5 times larger than Aspen's three other areas combined!). Snowmass also has the largest base resort, which is known for its many ski-in, ski-out accommodations, which help spread

visitors out and reduce the hassle of getting to and from the lifts.

The widely varied terrain makes it a family-friendly resort; riders and skiers of all ability levels have plenty to entertain them. Snowmass is best known for its excellent intermediate terrain, with half of the resort's 94 trails rated blue. Three terrain parks include more than 100 features—a triple line of jumps

Snowmass is one of the world's most important Ice Age fossil sites.

and variously shaped boxes and rails at the **Makaha Park,** as well as the 22-foot Zaugg-cut **Snowmass Superpipe** at **Snowmass Park.** The ski school offers lessons for all ability levels.

Start by heading from the transit center to the Village Express lift. From the top, ski down the intermediate **Sunnyside** or **Banzai Ridge** trails to the Big Burn lift, which leads to some beautiful blues like **Dallas Freeway** and **Sheer Bliss.** There's another great concentration of blue runs off the Elk Camp Gondola and Elk Camp lifts. If you're up for more advanced runs, head to Sam's Knob lift on the opposite side of the mountain for some great black trails like **Slot** and **Wildcat.** Two of the best double-blacks are **Grinder** and **Sunkissed.**

HIKING AND BIKING

Naturalists from **Aspen Center for Environmental Studies** (www.aspennature.org, mid-June-Labor Day, free) lead two daily nature hikes at Snowmass Mountain. The first one begins at 10am and focuses on wildflowers; the second begins at 1pm and teaches about the Ice Age discovery site. Both hikes depart from the Ice Age Discovery Center (54B Snowmass Village Mall).

Snowmass Mountain has more than 75 miles of mountain biking trails that vary from moderate single-track to gonzo downhill trails. From late June to Labor Day, cyclists can take the Elk Camp Gondola or Elk Camp lift to access the **Snowmass Bike Park** ($42 per day), a network of about 25 miles of trails, including the beginner 3.5-mile **Verde** and several intermediate to advanced routes.

Snowmass Mountain hosts about 50 miles of single-track, including the **Tom Blake,** which begins near the Snowmass Village Mall. **Government Trail** (www.fs.usda.gov) is an advanced 10-mile single-track ride that connects Snowmass Village with Aspen. The trailhead is located at the end of Wood Run Road. A gated dirt road on the far side leads to trailhead parking.

Entertainment and Events

Snowmass Village's after-hours entertainment centers around après-ski activities; to go bar-hopping or hear live music, head into Aspen, a free, 20-minute shuttle ride away. One of the most popular spots in Snowmass is **Nest Public House** (130 Wood Rd., 970/923-8000, www.viceroyhotelsandresorts.com, 11am-7pm daily) in the luxurious Viceroy Snowmass. The gastropub has a relaxed ambiance with both indoor and poolside seating. Along with a good selection of beer, the bar has a diverse menu ranging from brats to Korean short rib tacos. On the Snowmass Mall, the **New Belgium Ranger Station** (100 Elbert La., 970/236-6277, www.rangerstation.org, 11am-10pm daily) is a pub with a happy hour (2pm-6pm daily), 12 New Belgium craft beers on tap, and great bar food like bison chili nachos.

Snowmass Village hosts a number of festivals and events, including the boot-stompin' fun at the **Snowmass Rodeo** (www.snowmassrodeo.org, Wed. nights early June-mid-Aug., $20) and the **Craft Beer Rendezvous** (www.gosnowmass.com, mid-June, $30 for a 3-hour tasting). The **Jazz Aspen Snowmass** (http://jazzaspensnowmass.org, May, $200-650 for 3 days) is held over Labor Day weekend. The **Snowmass Balloon Festival** (www.gosnowmass.com, mid-Sept., free) is one of the highest-altitude events of its kind in the country. Pilots compete in races across the Roaring Fork Valley and line up for the beautiful Saturday Evening Glow. The uplifting event is held in conjunction with the **Snowmass Wine Festival** (www.snowmasswinefestival.com, mid-Sept., $85-95 grand tasting), which features a Ferrari Showcase and tastings of 300 wines from around the globe.

Food

For a quick cup of coffee or tea, a freshly blended smoothie, or a bagel on the way to the lifts, stop by **Fuel Café** (45 Village Run Cir., 970/923-0091, 7am-5pm daily in winter, 7am-3:30pm daily in summer, $3-8) in the

Snowmass Village Mall. In the same location, ★ **The Stew Pot** (62 Elbert La., 970/923-2263, www.eatsnowmass.com, 11am-9pm daily, $6-11) is the village's most popular lunch stop, known for its hearty, simmering soups made fresh each morning, plus a large selection of warming stews, chili, sandwiches, and crispy salads. They also serve beer and wine.

At the large **Venga Venga Cantina** (105 Daly La., 970/923-7777, www.richardsandoval.com, 3pm-9pm Mon.-Wed., noon-10pm Thurs.-Fri., 11am-10pm Sat., 11am-9pm Sun., $15-23), Mexican-born chef Richard Sandoval serves up a delicious menu of updated Mexican classics like pulled-chicken burritos, cheese-draped chile rellenos, and sizzling iron skillet fajitas, as well as a bewildering selection of 75 different tequilas and mescals. It's in a great ski-in, ski-out location at the base of the Fanny Hill trail, with an outdoor patio and fire pits.

One of the village's most popular restaurants is ★ **Il Poggio** (57 Elbert La., 970/923-4292, http://ilpoggio.webs.com, 5:30pm-10pm daily, $13-37), an Italian restaurant that specializes in rich pasta dishes like gnocchi and sweet potato ravioli, fragrant pizzas fired in a stone pizza oven, and meaty *secondi* dishes like Colorado lamb *spiedini* (skewers). Top it off with dark chocolate mousse cake or housemade biscotti.

Accommodations

Lodging options at Snowmass range from hotel rooms to fully equipped condos or a swanky resort. Located just steps from the Elk Camp Gondola, the beautiful ski-in, ski-out **Crestwood Condominiums** (400 Wood Rd., 800/356-5949, www.thecrestwood.com, $643-870 for 1-bedroom condo) have fully equipped kitchens, gas fireplaces, and private balconies, as well as a slopeside skier service center, where you can store your gear. A bit farther from the slopes (but still within walking distance of restaurants), the **Laurelwood Condominiums** (640 Carriage Way, 800/356-7893, http://laurelwoodcondominiums.com, $214-300) accommodate up to four people comfortably; condos have kitchens, wood-burning fireplaces, and a private balcony or patio, as well as access to tiered stone hot tubs for soaking.

Located about 100 yards from the slopes, the **Pokolodi Lodge** (25 Daly La., 800/666-4556, www.pokolodi.com, $229-399) bills itself as one of Snowmass' most affordable lodging options. Nonsmoking rooms are basic but comfortable, and the lodge has a complimentary continental breakfast and outdoor heated pool and hot tub. There is no private parking for guests. The lodge has substantial discounts during the shoulder seasons.

The most luxurious accommodations in the village are at the ★ **Viceroy Snowmass** (130 Wood Rd., 877/235-7577, www.viceroyhotelsandresorts.com, $467-780), a gorgeous ski-in, ski-out property located at the base of the mountain next to the Assay Hill lift and within a short walk of the Elk Camp Gondola. The ecofriendly property features a 7,000-square-foot spa, a heated outdoor saline pool, and several dining options—from a relaxed lobby cocktail bar to an upscale restaurant. Room configurations include studios and one- to four-bedroom suites, all with kitchens.

Camping

There are four basic **White River National Forest** campgrounds (Aspen-Sopris Ranger District, Hwy. 82, 970/925-3445, www.fs.usda.gov/whiteriver) on Highway 82 between Aspen and the summit of Independence Pass. Some of the sites can be reserved online (877/444-6777, www.recreation.gov); the rest are first-come, first-served. Amenities include drinking water and vault toilets.

Difficult Campground ($24) has 47 sites five miles east of Aspen. **Weller Campground** (opens in May, $21) has 11 sites nine miles east of Aspen. **Lincoln Gulch Campground** (opens mid-June, $20) has seven sites 11 miles east of Aspen. **Lost Man**

Campground (opens in June, $20) has 10 sites 14 miles east of Aspen.

Transportation and Services

CAR

To get to Snowmass Village from Aspen, follow Main Street west to its junction with 7th Street. Turn left onto 7th Street; in 500 feet turn left again onto West Hallam Street, which turns into Highway 82. Follow Highway 82 west for about two miles to the junction with Owl Creek Road. Turn left onto Owl Creek Road and continue 5.5 miles to the village.

PARKING

There is free parking at the **Town Park Station** (2909 Brush Creek Rd., Snowmass Village), where you can take a free shuttle to the Snowmass Center. There are a number of pay lots closer to the base area, including the **Base Village Parking Garage** ($30 per day). The prime spots near the mall all require a parking permit, which you can purchase on a weekly basis from your lodging company.

SHUTTLE

It's easy to get around the village using the free **Village Shuttle system**

(970/923-3500, http://snowmasstransit.com). Eight color-coded routes operate regularly during the ski season, with reduced hours in the summer. The system accesses nearly every lodging option around the village and efficiently delivers skiers to the large, central **Snowmass Transportation Center** at the base of the **Elk Camp Gondola** and **Village Express lift.**

The village shuttle also provides a connection to the Roaring Fork Valley's **RFTA** (www.rfta.com), the regional bus service with year-round transportation between Snowmass Village and Aspen. During the ski season, RFTA also operates the **4 Mountain Connector** between Aspen's four ski resorts. This stops at several locations in Snowmass, including the mall, the base village, and the Snowmass Center.

SERVICES

Snowmass Tourism (www.gosnowmass. com) has a helpful website covering all things Snowmass as well as a **Guest Services and Information Office** (970/922-2233, 9am-3pm daily mid-Nov.-mid-Apr.) at the entrance to the village, where you can gather information about transportation, activities, snow conditions, lodging, and restaurants.

The Roaring Fork Valley

The Roaring Fork Valley is one of the most beautiful parts of one of the most beautiful states. In addition to Snowmass Mountain, Aspen Skiing Company's fourth and largest resort, the area around Aspen includes an important archaeological site, one of Colorado's highest mountain passes, eerie ghost towns, scenic valleys, and myriad recreational opportunities. Best of all, these sights and activities are spread across a very compact area, so you can easily explore it all from a single base in Aspen, Snowmass Village, or Glenwood Springs.

★ INDEPENDENCE PASS

One of the highest passes in the state and the highest paved crossing of the Continental Divide, 12,095-foot-high **Independence Pass** was spotted by Zebulon Pike in 1806 but not surveyed until 1873. As part of the Continental Divide, the pass was originally designated as the limit of Caucasian settlement in the late 1800s. But in 1879, mining prospectors defied the government's orders and crossed the pass on the Fourth of July, the patriotic holiday that gave the pass its name. Energetic entrepreneurs quickly built a toll road, which they cleared of snow by hand, but this route was abandoned after the Colorado Midland Railroad reached Aspen. It wasn't until the 1920s that a new road was built over the pass on a route very similar to todays. With its snaking switchbacks, narrow pavement, and slow-moving vehicles, Independence Pass is an adventure to drive (or cycle), but the spectacular scenery is well worth the effort.

From Aspen, follow Highway 82 (Main St.) southeast out of town. The steep road climbs more than 4,000 feet in 20 miles, following the clear Roaring Fork River most of the way. As you climb, you'll pass a number of campgrounds and trailheads before arriving at the **Grottos,** a popular picnic area where you can take a short walk to look down on an **ice cave,** a photogenic slot canyon whose shady interior harbors ice long into summer.

About 15 miles from Aspen, you arrive at the ghost town of **Independence,** where you can stroll past more than a dozen wooden buildings built by miners trying to eke out a living in the harsh environment at almost 10,100 feet. During the winter of 1899, the worst storm in the state's history cut off all supply routes to the town. Before they ran out

of food, the miners dismantled their houses to make skis, which they used to flee to Aspen.

From Independence, it's another four miles up the impressively steep and winding road to the pass, where you can easily pull over to snap photos and enjoy close-up views of the hardy alpine tundra and fantastic 360-degree vistas of the Sawatch and Elk mountain ranges.

CASTLE CREEK VALLEY

Southwest of Aspen, two clear, sparkling creeks, both tributaries of the mighty Roaring Fork River, have carved deep and beautiful valleys through the heart of the rugged Elk Mountains. Their slanting red layers offer a colorful contrast to the dark evergreen forest, quaking aspen trees, lingering snow patches, and Colorado-blue skies. Both Castle Creek and Maroon Creek Valleys are located within the public lands of the **White River National Forest** (www.fs.usda.gov). Easily accessible from both Aspen and Snowmass, the valleys are popular day-trip destinations for scenic drives, biking, hiking, fishing, and horseback riding, as well as exploring the dilapidated structures in the abandoned mining town of Ashcroft.

the Continental Divide near 12,095-foot Independence Pass

Castle Creek Road

Castle Creek Valley separates downtown Aspen from the Aspen Highlands resort. From Aspen, Castle Creek Road climbs 13 miles south through the valley to the ghost town of Ashcroft. Along the way, several trailheads line the road and lead to many tempting hikes. At five miles from Aspen, Conundrum Road is a short spur that leads to the start of the very popular **Conundrum Creek Trail** (8.5 miles one-way), a moderately difficult route that climbs about 2,500 feet to a series of hot springs.

At about 9.5 miles from Aspen, the trailhead for the **American Lake Trail** branches off to the right. For the first 1.5 miles, the trail climbs steeply up a series of switchbacks, then levels out until it reaches a pretty lake about 3.2 miles from the start. The total elevation gain is about 2,000 feet.

From the American Lake Trailhead, Castle Creek Valley Road continues to climb uphill, passing many excellent fishing and picnic spots before reaching the fascinating ghost town of Ashcroft.

Ashcroft

The small town of **Ashcroft** (Castle Creek Rd., 13 miles south of Aspen, 970/925-3721, http://aspenhistory.org, tours 9am-5pm daily mid-June-Labor Day, 9am-5pm Tues.-Sat. Labor Day-early Oct.) was built over two weeks in 1880 by a group of intrepid prospectors led by "Crazy" Charles Culver and W. F. Coxhead. By 1883, the camp had a population of close to 2,000 with a school, sawmills, and 20 saloons. Although its initial silver production was fantastic, the deposits were shallow, and big strikes in Aspen soon lured away most of the inhabitants. By the turn of the 20th century, only a handful of single men remained; they reportedly spent most of their days in the local bar rather than working their claims. By 1939, all of the original inhabitants had passed away. Soon thereafter, a group of sportsmen built a European-style ski resort with a tramway up nearby Mount Hayden. The Army's **10th Mountain Division** trained at this facility during the summer of 1942. After World War II ended, the ski development moved downstream to Aspen, and Ashcroft became a ghost town that was later listed on the National Register of Historic Places.

Today, visitors can stroll past the buildings or take an Aspen Historical Society-sponsored **tour** ($5) to learn more about Ashcroft's fascinating history. One of the best-preserved

the ghost town of Ashcroft

buildings is the **Blue Mirror Saloon,** which still has a roof and a small sign hanging over the door. Although the **post office** is an original building, it's not the original post office, which was once a much larger building. (As the population shrank, the town downsized to this smaller establishment.) The false fronts on some of the buildings were added in the 1950s, when the TV series *Preston of the Yukon* was filmed here.

Cathedral Lake and Pine Creek

From Ashcroft, Castle Creek Road climbs past the groomed cross-country ski trails operated by the Ashcroft Adventure Lodge. In 1.5 miles, a trailhead on the right leads to the **Cathedral Lake Trail** (2.8 miles one-way), a beautiful but steep hike up 2,400 vertical feet to one of the area's prettiest alpine lakes. A series of switchbacks climbs to a fork and turns left toward the lake. From Cathedral Lake, prepared hikers can continue another 2.5 miles to 13,500-foot **Electric Pass,** with amazing views of the Elk Mountains. Complete the hike early in the day before afternoon thunderstorms begin.

From the Cathedral Lake Trailhead, Castle Creek Valley Road continues one mile uphill before reaching the end of the pavement at a junction with two rough four-wheel drive roads: one road leads to Cooper Creek; the other heads to Pearl Pass. Hiking and dispersed camping are allowed in the area.

About 0.5 mile before the end of the road is the spiffy **Pine Creek Cookhouse** (11399 Castle Creek Rd., 970/925-1044, http://pinecreekcookhouse.com, 11:45am-1:45pm and 6:30pm-9pm daily in high season, $17-38), where you can stop for a gourmet lunch or dinner in either the summer or the winter.

Getting There

From Aspen, follow Main Street west to its junction with 7th Street. Turn left onto 7th Street; in 500 feet turn left again onto West Hallam Street and continue west for 0.5 mile to a large roundabout. Take the last exit, Castle Creek Road (County 15), and head south. Castle Creek Road parallels Castle Creek for about 13 miles to the end of the pavement at a junction with two four-wheel drive Forest Service roads.

MAROON CREEK VALLEY

The Maroon Creek Valley separates the Aspen Highlands and Buttermilk ski resorts and leads to the gorgeous twin peaks known as

the beautiful Maroon Bells

the Maroon Bells. A trip up this valley to see the peaks of the Maroon Bells is a highlight.

★ Maroon Bells

The gorgeous **Maroon Bells** are twin bell-shaped peaks whose vibrant yellow and orange aspen displays, white snow fields, and striped maroon rocks are reportedly the most photographed peaks in North America. The most popular times to visit are summer and early autumn, when the quaking leaves in the surrounding aspen groves slowly turn to gold, adding yet another vibrant color to the valley's brilliant hues of blue, red, and green.

Access is via Maroon Creek Road, a paved, windy road that is easy to follow. The road passes a couple of idyllic ranches and campgrounds on the way to a series of small parking lots scattered around the loop at the end of the road. From the parking areas, a short, flat, and gravel trail traces the shoreline of **Maroon Lake,** where you can snap the iconic image of the crimson, bell-shaped peaks reflected in the lake's shimmering waters.

Hiking and Biking

There are many great hikes with phenomenal views of the jagged red peaks in the **Maroon Bells-Snowmass Wilderness** (Maroon Lake area, www.fs.usda.gov), as well as the Forest Service's East and West Maroon Portal parking areas near the end of Maroon Creek Road. The moderate hike to Crater Lake is along the **Maroon-Snowmass Trail** (1.8 miles one-way), which leaves from the Maroon Lake parking area. From the East Maroon Portal trailhead, the moderate (but long) hike on the **East Maroon Trail** (10.5 miles one-way) gains about 3,100 vertical feet en route to **East Maroon Pass.** The difficult **West Maroon Trail** (6.5 miles one-way) departs from the Maroon Lake parking area. This route climbs about 3,000 feet

to the top of **West Maroon Pass.** Descend the other side to join the Frigid Air Pass Trail to Crested Butte via Schofield Park, an additional 11 miles.

One popular way to get to the bells is by biking. Sure, the 10-mile route climbs about 2,000 vertical feet, but it's a fairly steady gradient with great scenery. Zipping back down to town is a lot of fun, especially without many cars on the road.

Getting There

Due to the Maroon Bells' popularity, visitors can only drive their own vehicles up Maroon Creek Road during the **shoulder seasons** (mid-May-mid-June and early Oct.-mid-Nov., $10 per vehicle). In high season, visitors must use the **Castle/Maroon RFTA bus** (runs every 20 minutes, 8:05am-5pm daily mid-June-early Oct., www.rfta.com, $8), which departs from the Aspen Highlands ski area (199 Prospector Rd., Aspen). From mid-June through early October, visitors can only drive private vehicles to the lake before 8am or after 5pm.

From Aspen, follow Main Street west to its junction with 7th Street. Turn left onto 7th Street; in 500 feet turn left again onto West Hallam Street and continue west for 0.5 mile to a large roundabout. Take the second exit onto Maroon Creek Road, which parallels Maroon Creek, and drive about 9.5 miles to a large Forest Service parking area.

Maroon Creek Road is typically closed from about mid-November to mid-May. In winter, access is by cross-country skiing or a snowmobile tour from the **T-Lazy 7 Ranch** (2139 Maroon Creek Rd., 970/925-4614, www.tlazy7.com, $250 for 2 hours), located partway up the valley. Although getting to the Maroon Bells in winter requires more effort, seeing the snow-covered peaks without the crowds is a rich reward.

Glenwood Springs

The small, vibrant town of Glenwood Springs is located in a spectacular setting at the "T" junction of two major rivers, the Roaring Fork and the Colorado. With flat space mostly confined to the two narrow valley bottoms, the town has never had much room to grow; this is why the downtown area is divided, with the hot springs and most of the other attractions stretching along the north bank of the Colorado River, while the downtown shopping-dining district is situated along the opposite bank. Fortunately for visitors, there is a pedestrian bridge linking the two areas across the Colorado, so it's very easy to walk between them.

SIGHTS

The gushing hot springs along the banks of the Colorado River have long been known to members of the Ute tribe, who considered them sacred. Once miners established a camp in the area in 1883, however, the Ute were quickly displaced by rowdy gunslingers and prostitutes. In 1887, after a fierce competition between railroad companies, the Denver & Rio Grande Railroad became the first line to reach Glenwood Springs. With its arrival, the town's population boomed from 1,200 in 1887 to 2,500 the following year, which also saw the completion of the enormous Glenwood Hot Springs Pool.

Hot Springs

Located along the Colorado River just upstream of the hot springs pool, the historic **Yampah Spa & Salon** (709 E. 6th St., 970/945-0667, www.yampahspa.com, 9am-9pm daily, $15 for an all-day pass) consists of three underground caves whose increasingly hotter temperatures amount to a natural sweat bath. There is also an on-site salon and spa.

On the opposite side of town, the **Iron Mountain Hot Springs** (281 Centennial St., 970/945-4766, www.ironmountainhotsprings.

com, 9am-10pm daily, $25 for an all-day pass) is an attractive complex of 16 small soaking pools with sparkling gem names like Ruby, Jade, and Topaz. Their iron-rich waters range 99-108°F. During the summer, it's best to come early or late in the day because only a few pools have shade and the combination of hot sun and hot water can be overwhelming. There is also a cooler (and larger) family pool with a hot tub alongside, as well as a clean and modern bathhouse and a small café with fresh food at surprisingly reasonable prices.

★ **GLENWOOD HOT SPRINGS**
In the early 1880s, Walter Devereux, a mining engineer who had made a fortune investing in Aspen's silver mines, paid $125,000 for 160 acres of land and a series of hot springs along the Colorado River—which, he envisioned, could be transformed into a world-class resort. To develop the springs, Devereux had to build a massive stone wall to divert the river's flow, an enormous undertaking that took years to complete, according to the book *Glenwood Hot Springs: Celebrating 125 Years.* But Devereux persevered, and on July 4, 1888, he opened the world's largest hot springs pool. Once the pool opened, Devereux immediately began constructing an elegant bathhouse and the high-brow **Hotel Colorado,** which opened to much acclaim in 1893. Since then, it has hosted prominent guests from around the globe, including Presidents Teddy Roosevelt, Taft, and Hoover.

Today, the **Glenwood Hot Springs** (401 N. River St., 970/947-2955, www.hotspring-spool.com, 7:30am-10pm daily in peak season, 9am-10pm daily in off-season, $16-21 per pass) remains one of Colorado's top attractions. The complex consists of two enormous pools, the 104°F therapy pool and the 90°F swimming pool, where, for an extra charge, daredevils can slip down two tall waterslides. Other amenities include the

Glenwood Springs

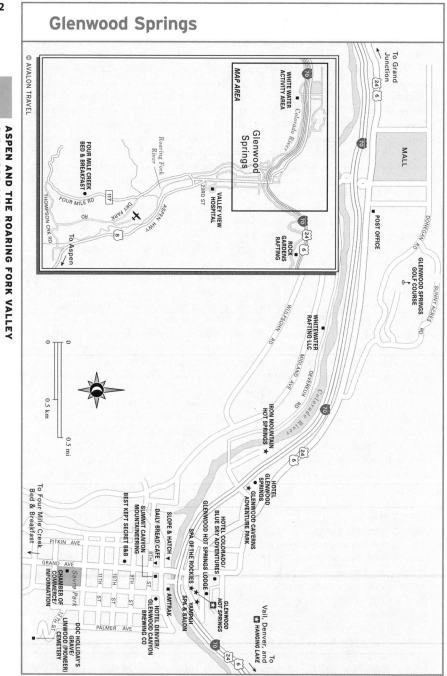

© AVALON TRAVEL

MAP AREA

WHITE WATER
ACTIVITY AREA

Colorado River

Glenwood
Springs

Roaring Fork
River

FOUR MILE CREEK
BED & BREAKFAST

FOUR MILE RD

THOMPSON CRK RD

DRY PARK

ASPEN HWY

To Aspen

23RD ST

VALLEY VIEW
HOSPITAL

ROCK
GARDENS
RAFTING

To Grand
Junction

MALL

POST OFFICE

GLENWOOD SPRINGS
GOLF COURSE

DONEGAN RD

SUNNY ACRES RD

0   0.5 km
0   0.5 mi

WULFSOHN RD

MIDLAND AVE

DEVEREUX RD

Colorado River

WHITEWATER
RAFTING LLC

IRON MOUNTAIN
HOT SPRINGS

HOTEL
GLENWOOD
SPRINGS

GLENWOOD CAVERNS
ADVENTURE PARK

HOTEL COLORADO/
BLUE SKY ADVENTURES

GLENWOOD HOT SPRINGS LODGE

SPA OF THE ROCKIES

GLENWOOD
HOT SPRINGS

YAMPAH
SPA & SALON

AMTRAK

HOTEL DENVER/
GLENWOOD CANYON
BREWING CO

To
Vail, Denver, and
HANGING LAKE

To Four Mile Creek
Bed & Breakfast

BEST KEPT SECRET B&B

SUMMIT CANYON
MOUNTAINEERING

DAILY BREAD CAFE

SLOPE & HATCH

PITKIN AVE

GRAND AVE

CHAMBER OF
COMMERCE/
INFORMATION

Sayre Park

DOC HOLLIDAY'S
GRAVE/
LINWOOD (PIONEER)
CEMETERY

PALMER AVE

11TH ST
10TH ST
9TH ST
8TH ST
12TH ST

Glenwood Springs

The small, vibrant town of Glenwood Springs is located in a spectacular setting at the "T" junction of two major rivers, the Roaring Fork and the Colorado. With flat space mostly confined to the two narrow valley bottoms, the town has never had much room to grow; this is why the downtown area is divided, with the hot springs and most of the other attractions stretching along the north bank of the Colorado River, while the downtown shopping-dining district is situated along the opposite bank. Fortunately for visitors, there is a pedestrian bridge linking the two areas across the Colorado, so it's very easy to walk between them.

SIGHTS

The gushing hot springs along the banks of the Colorado River have long been known to members of the Ute tribe, who considered them sacred. Once miners established a camp in the area in 1883, however, the Ute were quickly displaced by rowdy gunslingers and prostitutes. In 1887, after a fierce competition between railroad companies, the Denver & Rio Grande Railroad became the first line to reach Glenwood Springs. With its arrival, the town's population boomed from 1,200 in 1887 to 2,500 the following year, which also saw the completion of the enormous Glenwood Hot Springs Pool.

Hot Springs

Located along the Colorado River just upstream of the hot springs pool, the historic **Yampah Spa & Salon** (709 E. 6th St., 970/945-0667, www.yampahspa.com, 9am-9pm daily, $15 for an all-day pass) consists of three underground caves whose increasingly hotter temperatures amount to a natural sweat bath. There is also an on-site salon and spa.

On the opposite side of town, the **Iron Mountain Hot Springs** (281 Centennial St., 970/945-4766, www.ironmountainhotsprings.

com, 9am-10pm daily, $25 for an all-day pass) is an attractive complex of 16 small soaking pools with sparkling gem names like Ruby, Jade, and Topaz. Their iron-rich waters range 99-108°F. During the summer, it's best to come early or late in the day because only a few pools have shade and the combination of hot sun and hot water can be overwhelming. There is also a cooler (and larger) family pool with a hot tub alongside, as well as a clean and modern bathhouse and a small café with fresh food at surprisingly reasonable prices.

★ GLENWOOD HOT SPRINGS

In the early 1880s, Walter Devereux, a mining engineer who had made a fortune investing in Aspen's silver mines, paid $125,000 for 160 acres of land and a series of hot springs along the Colorado River—which, he envisioned, could be transformed into a world-class resort. To develop the springs, Devereux had to build a massive stone wall to divert the river's flow, an enormous undertaking that took years to complete, according to the book *Glenwood Hot Springs: Celebrating 125 Years.* But Devereux persevered, and on July 4, 1888, he opened the world's largest hot springs pool. Once the pool opened, Devereux immediately began constructing an elegant bathhouse and the high-brow **Hotel Colorado,** which opened to much acclaim in 1893. Since then, it has hosted prominent guests from around the globe, including Presidents Teddy Roosevelt, Taft, and Hoover.

Today, the **Glenwood Hot Springs** (401 N. River St., 970/947-2955, www.hotspringspool.com, 7:30am-10pm daily in peak season, 9am-10pm daily in off-season, $16-21 per pass) remains one of Colorado's top attractions. The complex consists of two enormous pools, the 104°F therapy pool and the 90°F swimming pool, where, for an extra charge, daredevils can slip down two tall waterslides. Other amenities include the

Glenwood Springs

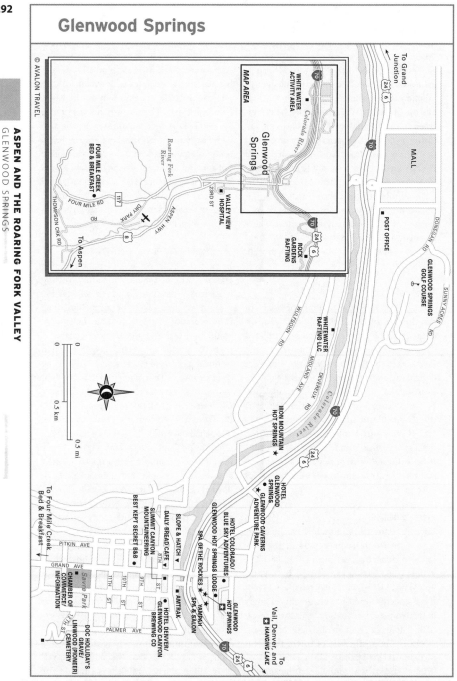

© AVALON TRAVEL

To Grand
Junction

MAP AREA

WHITE WATER
ACTIVITY AREA

Colorado River

MALL

Glenwood
Springs

Roaring Fork
River

FOUR MILE CREEK
BED & BREAKFAST

THOMPSON CRK RD

FOUR MILE RD

DRY PARK RD

23RD ST

VALLEY VIEW
HOSPITAL

ASPEN HWY

RD

To Aspen

POST OFFICE

ROCK
GARDENS
RAFTING

DONEGAN RD

GLENWOOD SPRINGS
GOLF COURSE

SUNNY ACRES RD

WULFSOHN RD

WHITEWATER
RAFTING LLC

MIDLAND AVE

DEVEREUX RD

Colorado River

IRON MOUNTAIN
HOT SPRINGS ★

0

0

0.5 km

0.5 mi

To Four Mile Creek
Bed & Breakfast

BEST KEPT SECRET B&B

SUMMIT CANYON
MOUNTAINEERING

DAILY BREAD CAFE ▼

SLOPE & HATCH ▼

GLENWOOD HOT SPRINGS LODGE

HOTEL COLORADO/
BLUE SKY ADVENTURES

GLENWOOD CAVERNS
ADVENTURE PARK

HOTEL
GLENWOOD
SPRINGS

PITKIN AVE

GRAND AVE

Sayre Park

CHAMBER OF
COMMERCE/
INFORMATION

11TH ST

10TH ST

9TH ST

8TH ST

SPA OF THE ROCKIES

AMTRAK

HOTEL DENVER/
GLENWOOD CANYON
BREWING CO

YAMPAH
SPA & SALON

GLENWOOD
HOT SPRINGS

DOC HOLLIDAY'S
GRAVE/
LINWOOD (PIONEER)
CEMETERY

12TH ST

PALMER AVE

Vail, Denver, and
To
★ HANGING LAKE

restored original bathhouse, a small kiddie pool, and a cafeteria-style dining room. The pool is open year-round, and one of the most enjoyable times to submerge yourself in the mineral-rich waters is during a frigid winter evening while fluffy snowflakes drift down from the jet-black sky.

Next to the pools is a bright and modern fitness center. At the beautifully decorated, full-service **Spa of the Rockies** (877/947-3331, www.spaoftherockies.com), you can pamper yourself with services ranging from a signature mineral mud ritual ($199 for 90 minutes) to a Colorado River stone massage ($169 for 90 minutes). Check online for parking information due to major construction in the area.

Glenwood Caverns Adventure Park

The **Glenwood Caverns Adventure Park** (51000 Two Rivers Plaza Rd., 800/530-1635, http://glenwoodcaverns.com, 9am-9pm daily in summer, 10am-9pm Fri.-Sun. mid-Nov.-Feb., $27 for tour, $50 for all-day pass) is not your typical theme park. Its history dates back to the late 1800s, when Charles Darrow discovered an extensive cave system riddling a mountain high above Glenwood Springs. He

opened the caves up to the public in 1895 and introduced some of the country's first electric lights there two years later. After World War I began, the caves were closed. It wasn't until 1999 that owners Steve Beckley and his wife, Jeanne, reopened them to the public.

In 2003, the duo added a gondola up to the caves, the nation's first alpine coaster, and a number of other thrill rides. It's an interesting combination that makes a fun outing, especially for families. Ride the tram up the mountain to tour the historic **Fairy Cave** or the **Kings Row Cave,** where the ceiling drips with stalactites and other cave decorations like popcorn and rippling bacon (cavers are hungry people), then whiz down the mountain on the fun alpine coaster. There are several other nail-biting rides, including a giant swing that flings you out over the canyon's yawning chasm.

SPORTS AND RECREATION

Glenwood Springs' largest draw has always been its fabulous recreation. In addition to soaking in the area's thermal springs, visitors can enjoy many other fun outdoor activities, most notably white-water rafting, hiking, and biking.

Glenwood Springs lies at the junction of the Roaring Fork and Colorado Rivers.

Hiking

The out-and-back **Grizzly Creek Trail** (3.4 miles one-way) follows a beautiful side canyon from the Grizzly Creek rest area along I-70 (exit 121) five miles east of Glenwood Springs. The trail leaves from the upper parking lot. In a verdant side canyon to the west, the **Jess Weaver Trail** (3.6 miles one-way) follows No Name Creek on a pretty out-and-back hike. To reach the trailhead, drive 0.5 mile north of the Grizzly Creek rest area.

By far the area's most beautiful hike, however, is the one up to Hanging Lake.

★ HANGING LAKE

Hanging Lake is a shimmering, blue-green lake tucked into the rugged limestone walls high above the raging Colorado River. This National Natural Landmark is unique in the southern Rockies—the lake formed by the deposition of travertine, a type of limestone. The lake also supports one of the region's largest and best examples of a hanging plant community.

Glenwood Hot Springs

The steep **Hanging Lake Trail** (1.2 miles one-way) begins from the parking area at Hanging Lake and climbs about 1,000 vertical feet from the bottom of Glenwood Canyon to the lake. This fragile environment is visited by up to 100,000 people per year, so it's critical to follow all regulations to preserve it. Swimming and dogs are not allowed. If the parking lot is full, the Forest Service asks that you drive back at a different time or return via bicycle.

The trail is located 10 miles east of Glenwood Springs. From Glenwood Springs, take I-70 to Grizzly Creek (exit 121), then get back on I-70 eastbound to the Hanging Lake exit. The trail begins on the left (just before the bridge), about 0.25 mile east of the rest area.

Biking

The popular **Glenwood Canyon Recreation Trail** leads through scenic Glenwood Canyon along I-70 east of town. Access the trail next to Yampah Caves at the east end of 6th Avenue. From the hot springs pool, the paved 14.5-mile trail follows the Colorado River to the end of the canyon near Dotsero. Although it's an uphill ride out of Glenwood, it's a steady gradient; water is available at the rest stops along the way. If the uphill ride is too much, the **Glenwood Adventure Company** (723 Cooper Ave., 970/340-8396, http://glenwoodadventure.com, $39 rental and shuttle) will shuttle you and a rental bike to the top of the canyon—all you need to do is coast back to town! **Canyon Bikes** (9319 6th St., 970/945-8904, http://canyonbikes.com) offers the same package, as well as hourly ($8) and daily ($40) rentals.

Glenwood Springs is one end of the **Rio Grande Trail,** a nearly flat 40-mile recreation trail that follows an old railroad bed along the Roaring Fork River for 42 miles to Aspen. For a great one-way outing, ride the trail in one direction and then take a bus (www.rfta.com) back.

Rafting and Kayaking

Thanks to the convergence of two of Colorado's largest rivers in downtown Glenwood Springs, the town's most popular summer recreational activities are white-water rafting and kayaking. The Roaring Fork River is a relaxing float trip with just a few, small rapids. The Colorado River provides an assortment of difficulty levels, depending upon the flows and where you put in on the river. Several companies offer guided rafting and kayaking trips.

Rock Gardens Rafting (1308 County Rd. 129, 800/970-6737, www.rockgardens.com, $52 for half-day trip) offers both family-friendly floats and adrenaline-pounding adventures, both of which can be combined with a zip-line experience. Both **Whitewater Rafting LLC** (2000 Devereux Rd., 970/945-8477, www.coloradowhitewaterrafting.com, $52 for half-day trip) and **Blue Sky Adventures** (319 6th St., 970/945-6605, www.blueskyadventure.com, $55 for half-day trip) have comparable offerings. Blue Sky also has inflatable kayaks that you can paddle yourself. Kayakers and stand up paddleboarders can practice their skills at the town's **White Water Activity Area** (2302 Midland Ave., www.glenwoodrec.com/whitewater-park) on the Colorado River. If you don't have your own boat or stand up paddleboard, rent one at **Summit Canyon Mountaineering** (732 Grand Ave., 970/945-6994, $60 per day for a kayak package).

FOOD

Grand Avenue is lined with great dining options. **Daily Bread Café** (729 Grand Ave., 970/945-6253, 7am-2pm Tues.-Fri., 8am-2pm Sat., 8am-noon Sun., $7-12) serves up the best breakfast in Glenwood. Choose from a long list of options, such as smoked salmon-stuffed Scandinavian omelets, Spinbacado Benedict, and Polish sausage and eggs. The huge portions will fill you up before heading out on a rafting or cycling adventure.

The dark **Italian Underground Ristorante** (715 Grand Ave., 970/945-6422, 5pm-10pm daily, $12-16) has red-and-white checkered tablecloths, empty Chianti bottle decor, and great Italian classics such as spaghetti and meatballs, meaty lasagna, and linguine with spinach and shrimp. Facing the Colorado River, **Slope & Hatch** (208 7th St., 970/230-9652, http://slopeandhatchgws.com, 11am-9pm daily, $7-12) is a casual eatery with a simple menu focused on "Taps, Tacos, and Dogs." Their loyal following swears by the

Hanging Lake in Glenwood Canyon

creative taco options like margarita grilled shrimp and Thai veggie stir-fry, as well as the local, natural-casing hot dogs served with salty, fresh-cut fries.

Facing the river on the east side of Grand Avenue, the **Glenwood Canyon Brewing Company** (402 7th St., 970/945-1276, http://glenwoodcanyonbrewpub.com, 11am-10pm daily, $10-23) is an enormous restaurant-brewery whose menu includes pub favorites like burgers and fish and chips, as well as some less-common dishes like the tangy Jamaican jerk mahi and mustard-glazed bourbon salmon. Pair any of the meals with a pint of one of the house-brewed beers, like the Hanging Lake Honey Ale, a silver-medal winner at the 2013 Great American Beer Festival, or my favorite, the Grizzly Creek Raspberry Wheat.

ACCOMMODATIONS

My favorite place to stay in town is the ★ **Glenwood Hot Springs Lodge** (415 E. 6th St., 970/945-6571, www.hotspringspool.com, $250). Located just steps from the hot springs pools, this renovated hotel has well-appointed rooms with comfortable beds, free Wi-Fi, and plenty of free parking. Best of all, the price includes unlimited use of the hot springs pools, free pool towels, and breakfast at the poolside grill. It's in an excellent downtown location close to the pedestrian bridge across the river.

In a great location near the hot springs, the venerable **Hotel Colorado** (526 Pine St., 970/945-6511, www.hotelcolorado.com, $119-179) has 17 different styles of rooms and suites that can accommodate up to eight guests. Classic rooms come with king, queen, and double queen configurations. Amenities include a coffee and juice bar, a spa, seasonal recreation shops, an upscale restaurant, and even hypnotic meditation.

On the west side of town, the **Hotel Glenwood Springs** (52000 Two Rivers Plaza Rd., 888/411-8188, http://thehotel-glenwoodsprings.com, $139-249) is a great

cycling through Glenwood Canyon

family-friendly place to stay, located at the base of the gondola and just a short walk from both Two Rivers Park and the Iron Mountain Hot Springs. The rooms are large and quiet (some come with whirlpool tubs) and pets are welcome (for an additional fee). Plus, it has its own indoor waterpark!

Glenwood has a couple of nice bed-and-breakfasts, including the **Best Kept Secret B&B** (915 Colorado Ave., 970/945-8586, www.bestkeptsecretbb.com, $124 per night, two-night stay during peak season), just one block off of Grand Avenue. Five miles south of town is the more rustic **Four Mile Creek Bed & Breakfast** (6471 County Rd. 117, 970/945-4004, www.fourmilecreek.com, $95-165) with two classic rooms, two log cabins (which sleep up to four), and a suite in a historic red barn on a beautiful property homesteaded in 1885. There's even a small Bunkhouse Museum that recreates cowboys' living quarters from the early 20th century.

Glenwood Canyon

The 12-mile stretch of I-70 between Glenwood Springs and tiny Dotsero (about 33 miles west of Beaver Creek) is one of the most rugged and beautiful stretches of the entire interstate highway system. With vertical limestone walls rising up to 2,000 feet above the frothing Colorado River and several shady tributaries, it's a beautiful area for hiking, cycling, and white-water rafting. Although the Denver & Rio Grande Railroad followed the canyon in the late 19th century and a gravel road was built here in 1902, it wasn't until 90 years later, in 1992, that the "final link" of I-70 was completed through it. At the time, the new winding, raised viaducts and bridges were considered an engineering marvel, and the Colorado Department of Transportation won a special award for keeping much of the canyon's environment intact. The $490 million price tag for the 12-mile stretch still makes it one of the most expensive sections of the interstate highway system.

Although the canyon's spectacular scenery can be enjoyed while just driving through its depths, it's far better to stop at one of the three rest facilities: No Name, Grizzly Creek, or Hanging Lake, where you can walk along the river, spread out a picnic, watch kayakers dodge white-water rapids, hike up one of the beautiful tributaries, or cycle along the paved bike path that parallels the river.

TRANSPORTATION AND SERVICES

Car

To get to Glenwood Springs from Aspen, head west on Highway 82 for 40 miles. To reach Glenwood Springs from Denver, take I-70 west to Exit 116. This 157-mile route typically takes 3.5 hours to drive, depending upon traffic and road conditions. Along the way, you need to cross 10,662-foot Vail Pass; in winter, check conditions and chain laws at Colorado Department of Transportation (511, ww.cotrip.org).

Parking is always a challenge in Glenwood, a situation that's exacerbated by the ongoing replacement of the main bridge across the Colorado River. Check with your lodging to find out what parking options are available.

Shuttle, Bus, and Train

Colorado Mountain Express (970/754-7433, www.coloradomountainexpress.com, $120-135 one-way) provides transport between

DIA and hotels and homes in Glenwood Springs. The trip typically takes 4-4.5 hours.

From downtown Denver, both Greyhound (www.greyhound.com, $35-40 one-way) and Amtrak (www.amtrak.com, $84 one-way) provide service to Glenwood Springs. Amtrak follows a beautiful route through the otherwise inaccessible Gore Canyon and makes a convenient overnight outing from Denver.

Services

Visit Glenwood Springs (www.visitglenwood.com) and the visitor center (802 Grand Ave., 970/945-6580, 8am-6pm Mon.-Fri., 10am-4pm Sat.-Sun.) are the best sources of visitor information. The local Chamber of Commerce (www.glenwoodchamber.com) also has information on lodging, dining, shopping, and local events. The town's primary medical care facility is the Valley View Hospital (1906 Blake Ave., 970/945-6535, www.vvh.org), which has both emergency and acute care departments.

Mesa Verde and the Southwest

The southwestern corner of Colorado is a beautiful and isolated region that encompasses a startling amount of diversity.

Here the state's most rugged peaks loom above verdant, wildflower-filled valleys and sheer gorges; old mining head frames cling to steep, scarlet hillsides; earthy plateaus and pink sandstone towers rise above crumbling cliff dwellings and high-altitude slickrock desert; and tall mesas covered with aspen groves burst into glorious color each autumn.

The region's centerpiece is the range known as the San Juan Mountains, a breathtaking, 12,000-square-mile knot of craggy peaks so rugged and high that only a few, twisting roads dare to cross their steep slopes. Like the mountains, rivers have played an important role in shaping and defining this distinctive landscape. Their importance is especially evident in the town of Grand Junction, which is named for its location at the confluence of the Gunnison and the Colorado Rivers. Here, high-elevation vineyards and orchards blossom on stony terraces lining the powerful Colorado River, whose frothing waters beckon white-water rafters, kayakers, and anglers. Higher on the Gunnison River, a national park showcases a gorge with walls so precipitous and dark that it's called the Black Canyon.

Thanks to the rugged and secluded terrain, this region does not have a single anchor; where you decide to visit is determined by your focus. In winter, snowboarders and skiers travel to the mining-turned-tourist towns of Crested Butte and Telluride to enjoy the legendary slopes and the lively historic districts at their bases, or visit Ouray to test their mettle at the ice-climbing park and recover from their efforts in the town's steaming hot springs. In summer, the energetic college town of Durango makes a great base to jump aboard the historic narrow-gauge railroad that penetrates some of the San Juans' most striking scenery; to enjoy locally grown food, a frosty mug of craft beer, and live, toe-tapping music; and to contemplate Mesa Verde National Park's internationally renowned cliff dwellings, whose geometric stone-and-mortar structures echo the area's long and fascinating human history.

Previous: the view from Lizard Head Pass in the San Juan Mountains; sunset near Grand Junction.
Above: downtown Silverton.

Look for ★ to find recommended
sights, activities, dining, and lodging.

Highlights

★ **Kokopelli's Trail:** Pedal through some of the Southwest's most stunning high-desert scenery along this 142-mile "bikepacking" route (page 303).

★ **Colorado National Monument:** This stunning national monument protects one of Colorado's most dramatic landscapes (page 309).

★ **Palisade Wineries:** Swirl, sniff, and savor the fruits of Colorado's award-winning wineries at the many family-owned operations (page 311).

★ **Grand Mesa Scenic and Historic Byway:** Explore the heights of Grand Mesa, the world's largest flat-topped mountain (page 314).

★ **Crested Butte Mountain Resort:** This marvelous mountain boasts great terrain near one of the state's most historic districts (page 320).

★ **Yankee Boy Basin:** Drive, bike, or hike to this enchanting alpine basin (page 335).

★ **Durango & Silverton Narrow Gauge Railroad:** Board a historic narrow-gauge railroad for an unforgettable trip through the San Juan Mountains (page 338).

★ **Mesa Verde National Park:** Visit North America's largest cliff dwelling, whose preserved walls offer a spectacular glimpse into the lives of the Ancestral Puebloans (page 340).

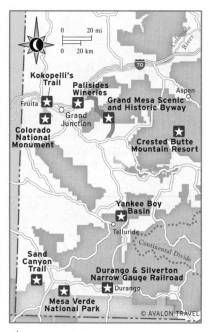

★ **Sand Canyon Trail:** Bike or hike this beautiful slickrock trail through Canyons of the Ancients National Monument (page 344).

Mesa Verde and the Southwest

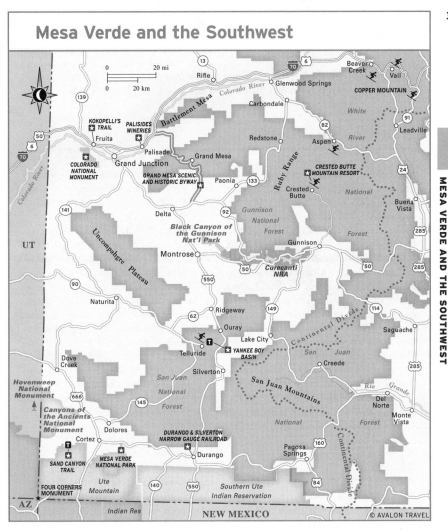

PLANNING YOUR TIME

In winter, Crested Butte, Telluride, and Ouray are the region's primary destinations. Given the distances to get here, most visitors stay for one week to enjoy the many ski runs and other attractions. These ski towns are of manageable size, so it's no problem to base out of a local hotel without renting a car.

In summer, you'll want to explore farther afield; rent a vehicle so that you can easily loop between the main towns. Plan to tour the San Juans' incredibly scenic byways; explore the extensive wild horse range near Grand Junction, where bands of mustangs still roam free; and visit outlying highlights such as Paonia, Colorado's farm-to-table capital.

The southwestern region is the most isolated in the state. While several regional airports, including the Durango-La Plata, Telluride, Montrose, Gunnison-Crested

Butte, and Grand Junction airfields, offer commercial service from Denver and a few other cities, none is a major hub. If you take advantage of the better connections and cheaper fares into Denver International Airport, be aware that routes to these southwest destinations involve driving over multiple mountain passes, which sometimes close in inclement weather. In ideal circumstances, Crested Butte is about a 4.5-hour drive from Denver, whereas Telluride and Durango are both about 6.5 hours away.

Grand Junction

Situated just 25 miles from the Utah state line, the relaxed town of Grand Junction straddles two worlds: the quintessential Colorado Rockies and the spectacular, slick-rock scenery of the American Southwest. Grand Junction is named for its location at the junction of Colorado's two most important rivers, the Gunnison and the Colorado, which was once called the Grand River. Above these fertile valleys, colorful mesas capped with aspen loom large, and the vast canyon-carved plateau of Colorado National Monument soars just west of town. Over the last few decades, Grand Junction has successfully morphed from a lonely interstate outpost into a boom-and-bust energy and agricultural center. The thriving, fun-loving community of about 60,000 boasts a flourishing arts scene, up-and-coming wineries, and fabulous recreation.

SIGHTS
Art on the Corner
The blocks around downtown Grand Junction feature an unusual, year-round outdoor art exhibit. The first of its type in the state, and one of the earliest in the nation, **Art on the Corner** (Main St. between 3rd and 4th Sts., https://downtowngj.org/aotc, free) features about 100 whimsical sculptures, from a biking dinosaur and a glittering chrome bison to *Breakfast,* a giant ant eating an oversized apple core. The exhibit includes several rotating installations. You can pick up a map of the sculpture locations at the **Grand Junction Visitor & Convention Bureau** (740 Horizon Dr., 970/244-1480, www.visitgrandjunction.

com, 8:30am-6pm Mon.-Fri., 9am-6pm Sat.-Sun. late May-late Sept.; 8:30am-5pm Mon.-Fri., 10am-4pm Sat.-Sun. late Sept.-late May).

Museum of the West
The **Museum of the West** (462 Ute Ave., 970/242-0971, www.museumofwesternco. com, 9am-5pm Mon.-Sat., noon-4pm Sun. May-Sept.; 10am-5pm Mon.-Sat Oct.-Apr., $7) packs 1,000 years of western Colorado history into a compact space, including a large display of prehistoric Anasazi, Hohokam, and Mimbres pottery and a second Native American art exhibit featuring prehistoric rock art panels, Hopi kachinas, and woven Navajo rugs. The museum also has a large firearms collection and a re-creation of Grand Junction from the early 1900s.

Western Colorado Botanical Gardens
Located on 15 acres along the Colorado River, the **Western Colorado Botanical Gardens** (641 Struthers Ave., 970/245-3288, http:// wcbotanic.org, 10am-5pm Wed.-Sun., $5) features a butterfly house, a tropical greenhouse, and a series of small, verdant gardens, including a fragrant rose garden, a kids' secret garden, and a gorgeous orchid display.

Western Colorado Center for the Arts
The **Western Colorado Center for the Arts** (1803 N St., 970/243-7337, http://gjart-center.org, 9am-4pm Mon.-Sat., $3, free on Tues.) offers art classes and field trips as well as exhibits featuring the work of both local

Grand Junction

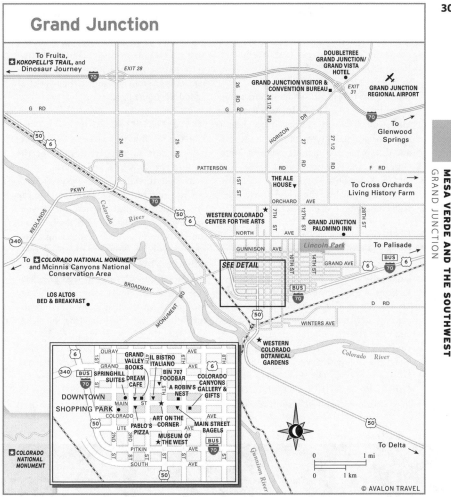

and national artists. Most of the center's 300 permanent works feature Native American artifacts.

SPORTS AND RECREATION
Biking
★ KOKOPELLI'S TRAIL

Named for the spirited Hopi flute-playing muse, the 142-mile **Kokopelli's Trail** (www. blm.gov) traverses some of the American Southwest's most stunning scenery between the two mountain-biking meccas of Grand Junction and Moab, Utah. Due to its length and the complete lack of water along the way, the trail is primarily used by mountain bikers who ride it as a day trip, or as an extended, multi-day through-route—a great adventure that requires extensive advanced planning.

The trail ranges in difficulty from flat, paved roads to steep, narrow single-track and is marked at intersections by brown fiberglass posts. The route is divided into nine sections; the eastern trailhead is located in

Loma, about 15 miles west of Grand Junction (Exit 15 off I-70).

Grand Junction has several great bike shops, including **Bicycle Outfitters** (537 N. 1st St., 970/245-2699, www.gjbikes.com, 9am-6pm Mon.-Fri., 9am-5pm Sat.-Sun.), which rents bikes and also has information about local trails. The **Colorado Plateau Mountain Bike Trail Association** (http:// copmoba.org) has information about the trail and the six popular mountain-biking loops close to Grand Junction that utilize its first section. *Kokopelli's Trail & Loops Map* is also available at local bike shops and provides detailed descriptions of each section.

Fishing

Given all the rivers and reservoirs in the area, it's no surprise that fishing is also a popular activity around Grand Junction. The five sections of the **James M. Robb Colorado River State Park** (www.cpw.state.co.us, $7 per day) stretch from Fruita to Island Acres and offer assorted angling experiences. Try your luck in the powerful Connected Lakes along the Colorado River or fish the quiet lakes at the **Fruita** (off Hwy. 340 in Fruita), **Corn Lake** (accessed via 32 Rd. in Grand Junction), and **Island Acres** (off I-70 east of

Grand Junction) sections, which are stocked throughout the year.

The area's only local fly shop, **Western Anglers** (413 Main St., 970/244-8658, http:// westernanglers.com, 9:30am-5:30pm Mon.-Sat.), offers lessons and guided trips as well as a good selection of gear.

White-Water Rafting

The Grand Junction area is a popular boating destination best known for the 17-mile **Westwater Canyon** run, an intermediate-to-expert (Class III-IV) stretch of the Colorado River with challenging white water, beautiful beaches, side canyons adorned with prehistoric petroglyphs, crimson cliffs up to 1,200 feet towering above your head, and a series of 11 boiling rapids with names like "Bowling Alley" and "Sock it to Me." **Rimrock Adventures** (970/858-9555, http://rradventures.com) offers full-day trips for $170, as well as many other experiences, including a full-day float on **Ruby and Horsethief Canyons,** a stretch of the Colorado River that's closer to Grand Junction and has just as beautiful scenery, but essentially no white water. **Adventure Bound River Expeditions** (800/423-4668, www.adventureboundusa.com) offers both one- and

a cyclist pedals through Colorado's amazing scenery

two-day floats through Ruby in addition to a number of longer trips.

Golf

The Golf Club at Redlands Mesa (2325 W. Ridges Blvd., 970/263-9270, www.redlandsmesa.com, $55-65) is an award-winning, Jim Engh-designed championship course with 11 elevated tees, 41 bunkers, and stunning views of the Colorado National Monument.

ENTERTAINMENT AND EVENTS

Nightlife

Part of the Breckenridge-Wynkoop Brewery chain, the **Ale House** (2531 N. 12th St., 970/242-7253, www.alehousegj.com, 11am-midnight daily, $10-24) is Grand Junction's primary nightlife spot. The brewery serves a great selection of handcrafted Colorado beer along with hand-tossed pizzas, bison and beef burgers, and larger plates like fish and chips and smoked pork and grits.

Performing Arts

Built in 1923, the renovated, 1,090-seat **Avalon Theatre** (645 Main St., 970/263-5700, www.tworiversconvention.com, $6-175) is western Colorado's premier performing arts center. The theater has served as a venue for many traveling performers, including John Philip Sousa, Pat Benatar, and Lyle Lovett. In addition to live music, dance, and theatrical performances, the theater hosts a foreign and indie film series.

On Main Street, the **Mesa Theater** (588 Main St., 970/773-1775, http://mesatheater.com, $10-30) attracts primarily young crowds for musical acts with unusual names like Kirko Bangz, Sister Sparrow and the Dirty Birds, and Yelawolf. Older audiences generally tend to prefer the **Grand Junction Symphony Orchestra** (414 Main St., 970/243-6787, www.gjso.org), which plays at a variety of local venues.

Festivals and Events

The region's largest country music festival is

Country Jam (Jam Ranch off U.S. 6, Mack, http://countryjam.com, $99), a four-day event with more than 30 performances across three stages. The event is held at the Jam Ranch in Mack, five miles west of Grand Junction. Weekend ticket holders can even camp onsite, so you don't miss a single tune from headliners like Kenny Chesney, Tyler Farr, and Brad Paisley. (Note that campsites do not include admission to the festival, which must be purchased separately; rates vary.)

To reach the site from Grand Junction, drive 21 miles west on I-70 to the town of Mack. The **Rally Bus** (http://rallybus.net, rates vary) offers shuttle service during festival days.

SHOPPING

Centered on Main Street between 3rd and 7th Streets, downtown Grand Junction is a compact, pedestrian-friendly district lined with historic buildings filled with charming galleries and quaint shops, a retro theater, and a nice selection of restaurants. On the district's southeast side, locally owned **Enstrom Candies** (701 Colorado Ave., 970/683-1000, www.enstrom.com, 7am-8pm Mon.-Fri., 8am-8pm Sat., 10am-4pm Sun.) was founded in Grand Junction in 1929 by Chet Enstrom, whose delectable almond toffee soon gained worldwide recognition. In 1965, Chet sold the business to his son and daughter-in-law so that he could launch a political career. The business continued to expand under their leadership and is now run by the fourth generation of Enstroms. Each batch of toffee is still made by hand; you can watch the process and sample the efforts, as well as shop for truffles, toffee popcorn, and other mouthwatering confections, in their cheerful retail store.

A Robin's Nest (602 Main St., 970/245-0109, www.arobinsnestgj.com, 10am-5pm Mon.-Sat., 11am-3pm Sun.) is the largest antique and collectibles store between Denver, Las Vegas, and Salt Lake City. Owners Robin and Shane Allerheiligen, both Grand Junction natives, offer everything from tube radios to steampunk jewelry to paintings by local artists. Other local art stores include the Silver Leaf Gallery (438 Main St., 970/314-7632, 10am-5pm Tues.-Fri., 10am-4pm Sat.-Sun.), the Working Artists Gallery (520 Main St., 970/256-9952, 10am-5pm Tues.-Sat.), and Colorado Canyons Gallery & Gifts (623 Main St., 970/314-2054, www.ccgal.com, 10am-5:30pm Mon.-Sat.).

Colorado's oldest operating footwear store is Benge's Shoes (514 Main St., 970/242-3843, www.benges.com, 10am-5pm Mon.-Sat.), which is known for its great service as well as an extensive selection of practical and stylish footwear from brands ranging the entire alphabet from Alegria to Ziera.

Grand Junction has several bookstores, including the downtown indie Grand Valley Books (350 Main St., 970/424-5437, 10am-7pm daily) and Barnes & Noble (2451 Patterson Rd., 970/243-5113, https://stores.barnesandnoble.com, 9am-9pm Mon.-Thurs., 9am-10pm Fri.-Sat., 10am-8pm Sun.).

FOOD

For breakfast or lunch, join the crowd of locals at ★ Main Street Bagels (559 Main St., 970/241-2740, http://gjmainstreetbagels.com, 6:30am-6pm Mon.-Sat., 7am-3:30pm Sun., $5-10), a fabulous family-owned bakery housed in a historic bank building, where you can sit at the community tables or in the old room-sized safe and sip the excellent coffee or house-brewed chai and munch on thick sandwiches heaped on artisan bread, crunchy salads, or one of the delicious and gooey cinnamon rolls or pecan sticky buns. Just three blocks west, the spacious Dream Café (314 Main St., 970/424-5353, www.dreamcafegj.com, 7am-2pm daily, $7-12), which has a divine, cloud-and-sky-themed decor, also serves hearty breakfasts and lunches from savory crepes and Dream burgers with herb garlic fries to banana split pancakes.

Inspired by the unconventional creations of legendary artist Pablo Picasso, Pablo's Pizza (319 Main St., 970/255-8879, www.pablospizza.com, 11am-8:30pm Sun.-Thurs., 11am-9pm Fri.-Sat., $7-11) serves up uncommon pizza combos with great names like the meat-heavy Italian Stallion, the barbecue sauce-and-chicken-laden Cowboy, and the cheesy Let It Brie.

For a more upscale meal, try Il Bistro Italiano (400 Main St., 970/243-8622, www.ilbistroitaliano.com, 11am-2pm and 4:30pm-9pm Mon.-Fri., 4pm-8:30pm Sat.-Sun., $13-23), which has separate lunch and dinner menus that feature an extensive selection of

Main Street Bagels

traditional and modern Italian dishes ranging from antibiotic-free pesto chicken to veal medallions sautéed with garlic, white wine, prosciutto, asiago, and sage. The tasty, individual, stone-fired pizzas are a great value, and the restaurant also has an extensive wine list and a rotating assortment of delectable desserts like chocolate cherry almond tart to linger over.

For fresh farm-to-table fare, stop by **Bin 707 Foodbar** (225 N. 5th St., 970/243-4543, www.bin707.com, 10am-10pm daily, $8-29), which serves dinner much later than most Grand Junction restaurants. Their made-from-scratch menu uses predominantly locally sourced ingredients to create flavorful combos like heirloom carrot gazpacho, pan-seared Skuna Bay salmon, and their signature dish, Colorado lamb tenderloin.

ACCOMMODATIONS

Accommodations in Grand Junction are mostly limited to chains. If you prefer to stay downtown, there are several hotels within steps of both the convention center and the main cluster of shops and restaurants, including the **SpringHill Suites Grand Junction** (236 Main St., 970/424-5777, www.marriott.com, $179) and the **Hampton Inn Grand Junction** (205 Main St., 970/243-3222, http://hamptoninn3.hilton.com, $189).

For local color, albeit with fewer amenities, try the **Grand Junction Palomino Inn** (2400 North Ave., 970/242-1826, www.elpalominomotel.com, $100), a comfortable, classic motor inn on historic U.S. 6, whose excellent rates include a decent continental breakfast. The boxy rooms include two full or one king-size bed with colorful accents and artwork, as well as small microwaves and fridges. Guests must be at least 12 years old.

Grand Junction's most distinctive accommodations are located outside of town. Located four miles west, the ★ **Los Altos Bed and Breakfast** (375 Hillview Dr., 970/256-0964, www.losaltosgrandjunction.com, $139-215) is a meticulously maintained bed-and-breakfast on a hilltop

perch with stunning views of Colorado National Monument's deep canyons. The modern building's five cozy rooms and two suites are carefully decorated with European-style furniture, such as cherry queen-sized sleigh beds and overstuffed wingback chairs. French doors access the wraparound decks, an ideal place to relax and watch the sun set.

Six miles west of downtown, **The Chateau at Two Rivers Winery** (2087 Broadway, 970/255-1471, www.tworiverswinery.com, $92-155) is a modern, upscale "country French" inn tucked between vineyards near the base of the Colorado National Monument. Each of the 10 spacious rooms is bright and cheerful, with country decor, a large private bathroom, and one or two king- or queen-sized beds. A large, upstairs deck is an ideal spot for watching the sun set while enjoying a glass of wine and some of the gourmet cheese sold on-site.

Thirteen miles east in the small community of Palisade, the Victorian-style **Wine Country Inn** (777 Grande River Dr., 970/464-5777, www.coloradowinecountryinn.com, $169-199) sits amid 21 acres of grapevines near the base of the beautiful Book Cliffs. The 80 contemporary guest rooms have a retro ambiance with thick drapes, plush bedding, upholstered chairs, and restored historic photographs on the walls. Double queen and king rooms are available, including some with a private patio. The inn offers free afternoon tastings of local wines as well as a deluxe hot breakfast.

CAMPING

Two sections of the **James M. Robb Colorado River State Park** (800/678-2267 or 303/470-114, www.cpw.state.co.us, $24-28) offer camping. **Island Acres** (1055 I-70, Palisade) has 80 sites, half of which have full hook-ups. The **Fruita** section (595 Colo. 340, Fruita) has 57 sites available, 22 of which have full hookups; another 22 have only electricity. Sites at both locations can be reserved up to six months in advance. Although year-round camping is permitted, there is no running water November-March, when the toilet and shower block is also closed.

RV Parks near Grand Junction include **Junction West RV Park** (793 22 Rd., 970/245-8531, www.junctionwestrvpark. com, $38-42) and **Mobile City RV Park** (2322 U.S. 6 and U.S. 50, 970/242-9291, www.mo-bilecityrv.com, $28), both of which are open year-round.

TRANSPORTATION AND SERVICES
Air

The closest major airport to Grand Junction is **Denver International Airport** (DEN, 8500 Peña Blvd., 303/342-2000, www.flydenver. com), but the **Salt Lake City International Airport** (SLC, 776 N. Terminal Dr., Salt Lake City, 801/575-2400, www.slcairport.com) is just 40 miles farther away. The smaller **Grand Junction Regional Airport** (GJT, 2828 Walker Field Dr., 970/244-9100, www. gjairport.com), located three miles northeast of town, offers nonstop, year-round service to Denver, Dallas, Houston, Phoenix, Las Vegas, and Salt Lake City, as well as seasonal service to Los Angeles.

Sunshine Taxi (970/245-8294, www.sun-shinetaxigj.com) offers local transportation, including to and from the Grand Junction airport.

Train and Bus

From downtown Denver, both **Greyhound** (www.greyhound.com, $45-67 one-way) and **Amtrak** (www.amtrak.com, $100 one-way) provide service to Grand Junction. Several buses travel daily between Denver's Union Station and the Grand Junction bus station (230 S. 5th St., 970/242-6012, 1am-6:30am and noon-6:30pm daily). Amtrak's California Zephyr route stops at the Grand Junction train station (339 S. 1st St.).

In addition, **Road Runner** (970/553-0389, http://roadrunnerstagelines.com, $40 one-way to Durango) offers once-daily service

to Telluride and Durango from the Grand Junction bus station.

Car

Grand Junction is located along I-70 about 240 miles west of Denver and 25 miles east of the Utah border. To reach Grand Junction from Denver, it's best to follow I-70 west over Vail Pass. The drive takes 4-4.5 hours, although it can take substantially longer during rush hour and/or inclement weather.

To reach downtown Grand Junction from the regional airport, take Sunstrand Way to H Road. Continue to the junction with 27 Road. Turn left at the junction and follow 27 Road south to a traffic circle. Take the first exit onto Horizon Drive and follow this street for 0.7 mile to 16½ Road. Turn left onto 16½ Road and follow it south, continuing straight onto North 7th Street for an additional 1.7 miles. At the traffic circle, take the second exit onto South 7th Street, then immediately turn right onto Colorado Avenue, which leads into the downtown.

Avis (2828 Walker Field Dr., 800/352-7900, http://locations.avis.com), **Enterprise** (406 S. 5th St., 855/266-9565, www.enterprise.com), and **Thrifty** (750 Horizon Dr., 877/283-0898, www.enterprise.com) are among the many car rental companies with depots in Grand Junction.

Services

The **Grand Junction Visitor Center** (740 Horizon Dr., 970/244-1480, www.vis-itgrandjunction.com, 8:30am-6pm Mon.-Fri., 9am-6pm Sat.-Sun. late May-late Sept., 8:30am-5pm Mon.-Fri., 10am-4pm Sat.-Sun. late Sept.-late May) is located south of I-70 at Exit 31, one mile west of the airport and about four miles northeast of downtown. Stop by for friendly help with reservations and reams of information about local and regional attractions. The Grand Junction Visitor Center has free Wi-Fi.

The Daily Sentinel (www.gjsentinel. com) is the town's longstanding daily paper.

It features local and statewide news, sports, and events. KAFM (88.1 FM), the town's public radio station, KOOL (107.9 FM), and KEKB (99.9 FM) country radio all have a strong, local focus.

Grand Junction's **post office** (241 N. 4th St., 970/244-3407, 9am-5:15pm Mon.-Fri., 10am-1:30pm Sat.) is located two blocks north of Main Street in the downtown.

The **Mesa County Central Library** (443 N. 6th St., 970/243-4442, http://mesacountylibraries.org, 9am-8pm Mon.-Thurs., 9am-6pm Fri., 9am-5pm Sat., 1pm-5pm Sun. mid-Sept.-mid-May) has free public Internet workstations and wireless Internet access.

Local hospitals include **St. Mary's Medical Center** (2635 N. 7th St., 970/298-2273, www.stmarygj.org) and the **Community Hospital** (2351 G Rd., 970/242-0920, https://secure.yourcommunityhospital.com), both of which offer 24/7 emergency care. **Community Care of the Grand Valley** (1060 Orchard St., 970/644-3740, https://secure.yourcommunityhospital.com, 8am-8pm Mon.-Sat., noon-4pm Sun.) and **Mountain Peaks Urgent Care** (http://mountainpeaksurgentcare.com) in Fruita, Montrose, and Cedaredge offer urgent care services seven days a week.

FRUITA
★ Colorado National Monument

Colorado National Monument (Fruita, 970/858-3617, www.nps.gov, $10 per vehicle) is a 20,500-acre wonderland of quintessential Western high-desert scenery that looms above the west side of Grand Junction. This tableland is located at the very edge of the Colorado Plateau, the high and rocky upland that stretches across the Four Corners region all the way to the Grand Canyon. Although the plateau's red-and-white sandstone layers usually lie flat, here by Grand Junction they have been warped into a single, giant staircase-like fold that geologists call a monocline. Thanks to this folding, Mother Nature has been able to more easily chip away at the relatively soft rock, ultimately carving 11 deep canyons through the colorful sandstone, deposited during the time that the dinosaurs wandered the area, as well as the darker and much older rocks below.

In some places so much sandstone has been removed that only towering monoliths remain. Each tower was evocatively named by early explorers like John Otto, a self-described trail builder who settled in Grand Junction in 1906. He quickly fell in love with

Colorado National Monument

this landscape and began to construct a network of trails through the canyons and up on the plateau. The local chamber of commerce soon took notice and began to advocate for setting the land aside as a national park. After a Congressional slowdown threatened to derail the process in 1911, President Howard Taft used his authority to instead protect it as a national monument. Otto was appointed as the park's first ranger for the whopping salary of $1 per month.

The main source of information about the park and current conditions is the **Saddlehorn Visitor Center** (1750 Rim Rock Dr., Fruita, 970/858-3617, 8am-6pm daily in summer), located about four miles south of the Fruita entrance along Rim Rock Drive.

SCENIC DRIVE

The monument's main attraction is the incredibly scenic **Rim Rock Drive,** which runs for 23 miles along the series of canyon rims between the **West Entrance** near Fruita and the **East Entrance** just west of Grand Junction. Along the way, 19 overlooks with interpretive signs allow you to photograph and enjoy sweeping views of the impressive canyons, search for soaring raptors and light-footed desert bighorn sheep, and wander through the plateau's extensive pinyon-juniper woodlands.

HIKING

The monument also offers superb recreation, from hiking and biking to technical rock climbing. The easy **Canyon Rim Trail** (0.5 mile one-way) starts behind the Saddlehorn Visitor Center and follows the cliff edge above Wedding Canyon, where there are great views of several colorful monoliths, including the Kissing Couple, Praying Hands, and the park's largest and most famous tower, Independence Monument. More than a century ago, Otto carved a long, steep stairway into this tower so that he could place an American flag on its summit after Taft's declaration. The **Coke Ovens Trail** (0.5 mile one-way) leaves from a trailhead on Rim Rock Drive, 3.8 miles east of the Saddlehorn Visitor Center. The trail descends to an overlook of a group of bulbous sandstone rocks named for their resemblance to old coking ovens.

One of my favorite hikes is the evocatively named **Devils Kitchen Trail** (0.75 mile one-way), a mostly flat path that leads from a trailhead 0.2 mile west of the monument's East Entrance to an open circle of impressive standing rocks. Instead of looking down on

a desert bighorn

the canyons, here you get to wander through the beautiful, sweeping sandstone layers, an experience that gives you a fresh perspective on the canyons' impressive scale. The same trailhead accesses the **No Thoroughfare Canyon Trail** (6.5 miles one-way) and the **Old Gordon Trail** (4 miles one-way). Just across the road, the historic **Serpents Trail** (1.75 miles one-way) begins its winding route up the 16 crooked switchbacks that comprised the monument's main road until 1950.

BIKING

The two main cycling options include the route from the visitor center to **Artists Point** (7 miles one-way), which climbs 500 feet and has great views of Monument Canyon. The much more difficult 33-mile **Grand Loop** includes Rim Rock Drive's entire 23-mile length (and 2,200-foot vertical climb) plus the flatter South Broadway and South Camp Roads that connect the monument's two entrances.

CAMPING

The only established campground within the national monument, ★ **Saddlehorn Campground** (4 miles south of the west entrance, 877/444-6777, www.recreation.gov, year-round, $20) has 80 sites spread among three loops. Loops A and C are all first-come, first-served sites, but spots in Loop B can be reserved up to six months in advance for dates in March-October.

GETTING THERE

To get to the **East Entrance** from downtown Grand Junction, drive north on 1st Street, then west on Grand Avenue, which turns into Broadway/Road 340. Follow this for 0.75 mile, then turn left onto Monument Road and drive southwest for 3.5 miles to the entrance booth.

To get to the **West Entrance** from downtown Grand Junction, drive north on 5th Street to the junction with Grand Avenue. Turn left on Grand and follow this 0.3 mile to the junction with I-70 Business Loop. Turn right here and follow this north for five miles to its junction with U.S. 50. Follow U.S. 50 east

for 5.5 miles to the town of Fruita. At the junction with Highway 340 East, exit and follow Highway 340 south about 2.5 miles to the national monument entrance.

Dinosaur Journey Museum

The **Dinosaur Journey Museum** (550 Jurassic Ct., Fruita, 970/858-7282, www. museumofwesternco.com, 9am-5pm daily May-Sept., 10am-4pm Mon.-Sat., noon-4pm Sun. Oct.-Apr., $9) takes you on a journey through time to learn more about the dinosaurs that roamed this area about 175 million years ago. The highlight of this fun and family-friendly museum is the robotic replicas of dilophosaurus, triceratops, and stegosaurus, which are controlled by a series of levers and buttons, plus a glassed-in paleontology lab where you can watch paleontologists preparing some of the region's best fossil discoveries. The museum also houses plenty of tracks, artwork, replica bones, and a few real fossils. Kids love the spitting dinosaur, the earthquake simulator, and making their own tracks in a large sandbox.

To get here from I-70, take Exit 19 for Highway 340 East. Turn left and drive 0.5 mile south to Jurassic Court.

PALISADE
★ **Wineries**
The **Grand Valley American Viticultural Area** (www.coloradowine.com) includes more than 20 wineries, most of which are small, family-owned operations, as well as a couple dozen fruit growers best known for their scrumptious peaches. The majority of the Grand Valley AVA wineries are clustered around the small town of Palisade, sandwiched between I-70 and the Colorado River. Most are open year-round and offer brief tours of their winemaking facilities. Some offer free tastings, while others charge a modest fee that is usually waived with a purchase.

Of all the state's wineries, **Plum Creek Winery** (3708 G Rd., Palisade, 970/464-7586, www.plumcreekwinery.com, 10am-5pm daily) has garnered the most awards,

Mike the Headless Chicken Days

One of Colorado's most bizarre festivals, Mike the Headless Chicken Days (www.miketh-eheadlesschicken.org, cost varies) occurs during the first weekend in June in the small town of Fruita, located just a few miles west of Grand Junction. For two days, the 12,000-odd locals gather in Civic Center Park (325 E. Aspen Ave.) to celebrate "la dolce vita" with a free car show, a 5K run, and live music, as well as more unusual activities like poultry shows, a wing-eating contest, a rooster-calling contest, and Chicken Poop Bingo.

The poultry-themed festivities commemorate an unusual hero: Mike the Headless Chicken, a local rooster who in 1945 not only survived a beheading by farmer Lloyd Olsen (whose wife, Clara, had decided to serve him for dinner that night), but thrived for 18 months afterward. The explanation for his survival was that the axe had missed the jugular vein, and a clot had prevented his bleeding to death. Although Lloyd had to give him water and grain through an eyedropper, Mike grew from 2.5 to 8 pounds, went on tour, and was featured in *Life* and *Time* magazines. Although Mike died about 18 months after his beheading, his indomitable spirit and will to live endures in this fun-filled festival, whose motto is, "It is a great comfort to know you can live a normal life, even after you have lost your mind." If you miss the festival, you can pay homage to his headless statue on the corner of Aspen and Mulberry in downtown Fruita.

including several Wine of the Year awards for two of their white varietals, the riesling and the chardonnay. **Carlson Vineyards** (461 35 Rd., Palisade, 970/464-5554, www.carlsonvineyards.com, 10am-5:45pm daily) is a relaxed, down-to-earth spot that enjoys making wine accessible to everyone. If you've never experienced wine-tasting, it's a great place to head to sample Tyrannosaurus Red (named for a T. rex dinosaur skeleton found in the Grand Valley), which is made from dry German Lemberger grapes, as well as peppery Cougar Run Shiraz and the sweeter Laughing Cat Riesling.

St. Kathryn Cellars and **Talon Winery** (785 Elberta Ave., Palisade, 970/464-9288, www.talonwinebrands.com, 10am-5pm daily) share a bright and spacious tasting room that has a small exhibit covering the history of Colorado winemaking as well as a long granite bar for tasting. Most of the St. Kathryn wines are made from fruit other than grapes, including the Golden Pear and the Peach Passion. The Sweet Scarlet, which won a gold medal in the 2015 Colorado Governor's Cup Competition, is a 50/50 blend of blackberry wine and merlot grapes. The adjacent Talon Winery has more traditional offerings,

including cabernet sauvignon, merlot, pinot grigio, and The Falconer, a premium blend of several "black" European grapes. They also sell fudge.

The **Fruit and Wine Trail** (http://visit-palisade.com) is a scenic driving (or cycling) route that winds past bountiful orchards, fragrant lavender fields, colorful fruit stands, and some of Colorado's best wineries. Along the way, enjoy the play of light and shadow on the stunning sandstone scenery. **American Spirit Shuttle** (970/523-7662, www.americanspiritshuttle.com, noon-4pm Sat., $35-40) offers scheduled tours of four wineries as well as private tours.

Festivals and Events

Festivals in the small town of Palisade, just east of Grand Junction, revolve around its agricultural heritage. These include the **Colorado Lavender Festival** (www.coloradolavender.org, free) in early July, the **Palisade Peach Festival** (http://palisadepeachfest.com, $7) in mid-August, and the area's most popular event, the **Colorado Mountain Winefest** (http://coloradowine-experience.com, Sept., $25-190), the state's largest and oldest wine festival, which features

Colorado Wine

Swirl, sniff, and savor the fruits of some of Colorado's best wineries

Colorado is increasingly gaining national recognition for its wine production. The **Grand Valley American Viticultural Area** (www.coloradowine.com) includes more than 20 wineries, whose grapes are grown on well-drained, stony Colorado River terraces that resemble the more renowned terraces along the Rhône River in southern France. Fortunately, the prices here are much more reasonable than in Châteauneuf-du-Pape, and the winemakers less bound by tradition and strict agricultural controls. This gives both the growers and the wineries the freedom to flirt with new combinations of fruit, honey, and herb-infused wines, as well as both classic and less-common grapes, including cabernet franc, petit verdot, riesling, and viognier. The valley's long, warm days allow the grapes to fully ripen, which increases their natural sugars, while the cool nighttime temperatures preserve their acidity. Colorado's wineries are some of the highest in the world, and the combination of this elevation, the dry, sunny climate, fertile soils, and distinct microclimates fosters flavorful grapes that ultimately make great wine.

Most of Colorado's wineries are small, family-owned operations that produce just a few thousand cases per year. The winemakers' stories are fascinating and encompass many diverse backgrounds, but a unifying theme is their passion for their products. Although the industry is centered in the Grand Valley, there are more concentrations of vineyards in the Four Corners area, Delta and Montrose Counties, and the West Elks AVA, as well as a number of wineries along the Front Range.

tastings from 50 Colorado wineries, live music, great food, and winery tours.

LITTLE BOOK CLIFFS WILD HORSE AREA

Eight miles northeast of Grand Junction, the 36,000-acre **Little Book Cliffs Wild Horse Area** (2815 H Rd., 970/244-3000, www.blm.

gov, free) is a gently sloping mesa dissected by several steep canyons. Although it's not far from the interstate, this area has a wild and remote feeling that's accentuated by its main attraction: a herd of wild horses protected by the 1971 Wild and Free-Roaming Horse and Burro Act, which manages unclaimed burros and horses on public lands throughout the western United States.

The herd is always on the move, so there's no guarantee of seeing any if you venture up here. But those who do are treated to the breathtaking sight of stallions galloping freely across this seemingly untouched land. Several primitive hiking and horseback trails crisscross the area, accessible via two entrances.

Getting There

In winter, wild horses are most often spotted closer to the **Coal Canyon** entrance. From Grand Junction, take I-70 East to Cameo (Exit 45). Drive over the Colorado River and continue northwest for 1.5 miles to the Coal Canyon trailhead (closed to motorized traffic Dec. 1-May 30).

In summer, it's best to enter the area from the higher **De Beque/Winter Park Road** entrance. From Grand Junction, take I-70 East for 35 miles to De Beque. Turn left to cross the Colorado River and follow Roan Creek Road into the town of De Beque. Turn left onto 4th Street, then left onto Curtis Avenue, which ends at 2nd Street. Follow 2nd Street west to Winter Flats Road (four-wheel drive only) and turn right. You'll drive 20 miles down Winter Flats Road to a fork. The right branch leads to the North Soda area, while the left branch leads to Indian Park.

★ GRAND MESA SCENIC AND HISTORIC BYWAY

About 30 miles east of Grand Junction, I-70 meets Highway 65 east, which climbs the 63-mile **Grand Mesa Scenic and Historic Byway** (Hwy. 65, www.grandmesabyway. com) to **Grand Mesa,** a flat-topped mountain that rises 6,000 feet above the adjacent river valleys. A gorgeous drive loops around the mesa, past huge, old-growth evergreen trees, large groves of quaking aspen, and more than 300 turquoise lakes. This scenic plateau is a destination for panoramic views, cool forests, and plentiful year-round recreation. In summer, camping, angling, boating, biking, and hiking are the main activities. In winter, folks come for snowmobiling, snowshoeing, cross-country skiing, and downhill skiing at the **Powderhorn Mountain Resort** (48338 Powderhorn Rd., Mesa, 970/268-5700, www. powderhorn.com, 2pm-6pm Fri., 10am-5pm Sat.-Sun.) on the mesa's western edge.

The **Grand Mesa Visitor Center** (Hwy. 65, 970/856-7554, www.grandmesabyway. com, 9am-5pm daily late May-late Sept., free) is 22.5 miles south of Mesa. From there, Highway 65 continues south for 30 miles, connecting to U.S. 50 and Highway 92 in the town of Delta.

Grand Mesa

Black Canyon of the Gunnison National Park

Although the spectacular Black Canyon of the Gunnison is not the longest or deepest gorge in the American West, "no other canyon in North America combines the depth, narrowness, sheerness, and somber countenance of the Black Canyon of the Gunnison," wrote noted geologist Wallace Hansen. The gorge was carved by the powerful Gunnison River, which initially set its course in softer volcanic rocks. Like a saw blade in a wooden groove, once the river had carved this initial channel, it was easiest for it to remain there, even after it encountered the incredibly hard metamorphic rocks below. Over millions of years, the river—which once had larger flows than it does today—gradually excavated this incredible gorge, whose walls are so tough that, unlike the Grand Canyon, they barely retreated from the river. This geological "perfect storm" created a canyon so deep and sheer that its walls are higher than Chicago's Willis Tower, and its inner gorge so narrow that it receives only minutes of sunlight each day. These deep shadows, plus the rocks' dark hue, gave rise to its unusual name.

SIGHTS

The gorge's 12 most spectacular miles are preserved within the **Black Canyon of the Gunnison National Park** (Hwy. 347, 970/641-2337, www.nps.gov, $15 per vehicle per day). The main recreational activities are hiking and cycling (or cross-country skiing in winter) along the rim roads and trails and peering over the edge of the abyss to search for the river far below. Because the river is so swift and dangerous, rafting is heavily discouraged in the park, and there are no maintained trails into the inner canyon. This relative lack of activities is a blessing; Black Canyon of the Gunnison is far quieter than most western

national parks, making it a great place to camp, search for great-horned owls and other birds, and enjoy the spectacular scenery without the crowds.

It is a three-hour drive between the canyon's South and North Rims, each of which has a campground. The North Rim is the quieter of the two and closes in winter. The most popular way to experience the Black Canyon's stunning scenery is by driving the paved **South Rim Road**, which has a dozen overlooks between the **South Rim Visitor Center** (Hwy. 347, 7 miles north of intersection with U.S. 50, 8am-6pm daily late May-early Sept., reduced hours in off-season) and the end of the road at **High Point.** The views from the visitor center, Chasm View, and Painted Wall View are especially good, as is the end of the day from Sunset View. In winter, the South Rim Road is only open to the visitor center.

The last seven miles of the **North Rim Road** (closed in winter) are unpaved, and it has a number of excellent viewpoints, including The Narrows View, which overlooks the canyon's narrowest point (a mere 40 feet wide at river level).

HIKING

The South Rim has four short, maintained trails from which you can explore the canyon's ecology. These include the sunny **Rim Rock Nature Trail** (1 mile round-trip) and the **Oak Flat Loop Trail** (2 miles round-trip), both of which leave from the South Rim Visitor Center. The Oak Flat Loop Trail is a great option for people who want to explore below the rim without committing to hiking all the way to the river.

At the end of the South Rim Road, the **Warner Point Nature Trail** (1.5 miles

Black Canyon of the Gunnison National Park

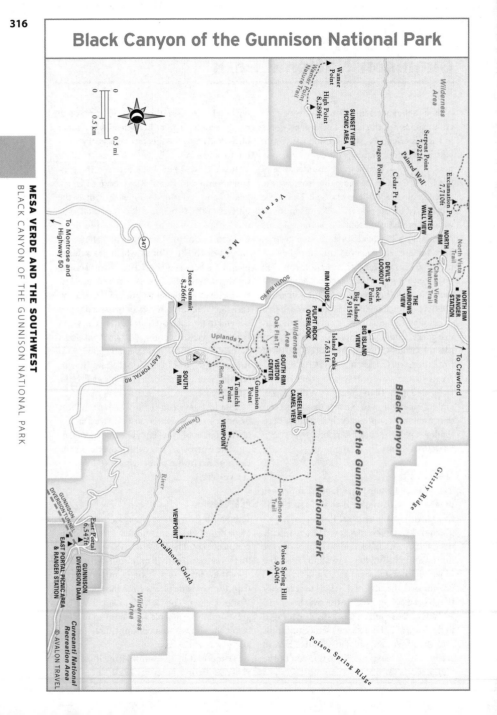

Wilderness Area

Warner Point

High Point
8,289ft

SUNSET VIEW PICNIC AREA

Warner Point Nature Trail

Serpent Point
7,922ft
Painted Wall

Dragon Point

Cedar Pt.

Exclamation Pt.
7,710ft

PAINTED WALL VIEW

NORTH RIM

North Vista Trail

Chasm View Nature Trail

NORTH RIM RANGER STATION

DEVIL'S LOOKOUT Rock

Big Island
7,915ft

Point

THE NARROWS VIEW

BIG ISLAND VIEW

RIM HOUSE

SOUTH RIM RD

PULPIT ROCK OVERLOOK

Island Peaks
7,631ft

To Crawford

Jones Summit
8,266ft

Uplands Tr.

Oak Flat Tr.

Wilderness Area

SOUTH RIM VISITOR CENTER

Rim Rock Tr.

EAST PORTAL RD

SOUTH RIM

Tomichi Point

Gunnison Point

KNEELING CAMEL VIEW

VIEWPOINT

Gunnison River

Deadhorse Trail

Black Canyon

of the Gunnison

National Park

Grizzly Ridge

VIEWPOINT

Deadhorse Gulch

Poison Spring Hill
9,040ft

GUNNISON DIVERSION TUNNEL

East Portal
6,547ft

EAST PORTAL PICNIC AREA & RANGER STATION

GUNNISON DIVERSION DAM

Wilderness Area

Poison Spring Ridge

Curecanti National Recreation Area

© AVALON TRAVEL

To Montrose and Highway 50

347

Vernal Mesa

0   0.5 mi
0   0.5 km

Black Canyon of the Gunnison National Park

down into the Black Canyon. The trailhead is located next to the parking area adjacent to the small **North Rim Ranger Station** (North Rim Rd.).

CAMPING

Camping is available year-round in the **South Rim Campground** (South Rim Rd., 970/641-2337, www.nps.gov, water late May-mid-Sept., $16-22 per site), whose 88 sites are divided into three loops, one of which has electrical hookups and two of which can be reserved in advance. Amenities are limited to vault toilets and trucked-in drinking water in summer.

The smaller **North Rim Campground** (North Rim Rd., 970/641-2337, Apr.-mid-Nov., www.nps.gov, $16 per site) has just 13 sites. There is no electricity, and amenities are limited to vault toilets and seasonally trucked-in water.

GETTING THERE

To get to the South Rim from Gunnison, follow U.S. 50 West for about 57 miles to the junction with Highway 347. Turn right onto Highway 347 and follow this road for about five miles, where it turns into the South Rim Road. To access the North Rim from Grand Junction, follow U.S. 50 East to its junction with Highway 92 in the town of Delta. Turn left and follow Highway 92 east for about 31 miles to the town of Crawford. At the junction with Fruitland Mesa Road, turn right and follow this road for 3.3 miles, then continue straight on Road 7745 for 1.2 miles until the junction with Black Canyon Road. Turn right to follow Black Canyon Road for about five miles to the national park.

round-trip) wanders through the local pinyon-juniper forest with great views of the San Juan Mountains and a fabulous look down into the sheer Black Canyon. Pick up a guide to the flora along this trail at the visitor center.

On the North Rim, my favorite hike is the walk along the **North Vista Trail** (3 miles round-trip) to Exclamation Point, a fitting name for the excitement inspired by the fabulous inner-canyon views. For a more strenuous hike, follow this trail an additional two miles (one-way) to Green Mountain for 360-degree views of Grand Mesa, the Uncompahgre Plateau, and a different perspective peering

Curecanti National Recreation Area

Curecanti National Recreation Area

Upstream of the Black Canyon of the Gunnison National Park, the **Curecanti Recreation Area** (www.nps.gov) is a series of three reservoirs constructed along the course of the tamed Gunnison River. Farthest east and closest to the town of Gunnison, **Blue Mesa Reservoir** is Colorado's largest body of water as well as the nation's largest kokanee salmon fishery. Downstream, the **Morrow Point Dam** and its namesake reservoir were primarily built to generate hydropower, whereas the function of the **Crystal Reservoir** is to maintain steady flows through the Black Canyon.

Because it's the largest and easiest to access, Blue Mesa Reservoir is the main destination for anglers and boaters, as well as hikers, campers, and bird-watchers. U.S. 50 parallels the reservoir's northern shore for about 16 miles before crossing the reservoir on **Middle Bridge** to follow its southern shoreline, passing many campgrounds, picnic areas, and boat launches en route. **Boating** and year-round **angling,** especially for trout and salmon, are the most popular activities on Blue Mesa Reservoir, but there is also great wade- and float-fishing on the Gunnison and several nearby rivers. If you're interested in a guided trip, **Gunnison River Guides** (970/596-3054, http://gunnisonriverguides.com) is one of the most experienced services in the area, and the **Gunnison River Fly Shop** (300 N. Main St., 970/641-2930, http://gunnisonflyshop.com, 9am-5pm Thurs.-Tues.) has all the gear you'll need.

If you're more of a landlubber, the two-mile (one-way) **Dillon Pinnacles Trail,** which leaves from the trailhead by U.S. 50 just north of Middle Bridge, has great views of the reservoir, the San Juan Mountains, and the series of small volcanic pinnacles for which it's named.

I also highly recommend a **Morrow Point Boat Tour** (970/641-2337, www.nps.gov, 10am and 12:30pm Wed.-Mon. early June-early Sept., $24), a ranger-led excursion on the recreation area's long, narrow middle reservoir. This 1.5-hour trip, which begins at the Pine Creek boat dock by milepost 130 on U.S. 50, explores the upper reaches of the Black Canyon and provides a great introduction to its fascinating geology, ecology, and history. Prepaid reservations are required.

For more information, stop by the **Elk Creek Visitor Center** (102 Elk Creek, Gunnison, 970/641-2337, www.nps.gov, 8am-6pm daily in summer, reduced hours in fall-spring), located 16 miles west of Gunnison on the south side of U.S. 50.

Crested Butte and Gunnison

Once a grimy gold-turned-coal-mining town, Crested Butte, perched high in a pretty mountain valley at nearly 8,900 feet in elevation, now boasts the state's largest and one of its best-preserved National Historic Districts. Elk Avenue, the town's main street, is lined with brightly colored, Victorian-era buildings packed with boutique shops and a great assortment of restaurants and brewpubs. Just three miles to the north along Gothic Road, Crested Butte Mountain Resort has fantastic boarding and skiing. Thanks to this charismatic combination, along with the area's relaxed and friendly vibe, locals often refer to it as "the last great Colorado ski town."

Adding to the area's appeal is its small size (just 1,500 permanent residents) and its isolation. Crested Butte is a solid five-hour drive from Denver in good conditions; in winter, the only road in or out is Highway 135 from Gunnison. But the commitment that it takes to get here is well worth the effort; the air is fresh, the mountain views are fabulous, the skiing and mountain biking are world-class, and the laid-back town is the perfect size for strolling.

SIGHTS
Crested Butte National Historic District

The town's colorful Victorian buildings are centered on Elk Avenue and comprise a registered National Historic District. Many of these historic buildings have been converted into shops and cozy restaurants where you can sip chai or cocktails and admire the buildings' intricate architectural details. The former general store, constructed in 1883, has been converted into the **Crested Butte Mountain Heritage Museum** (331 Elk Ave., 970/349-1880, http://crestedbuttemuseum.com, 10am-6pm daily in high season, $5), where you can see the original coal stove and a model railroad, as well as learn about the town's coal mining history. In summer, the museum staff offer guided **walking tours** (9am Tues. and Thurs., $10) through the district; winter tours are only available by appointment.

Crested Butte's downtown historic district

Crested Butte

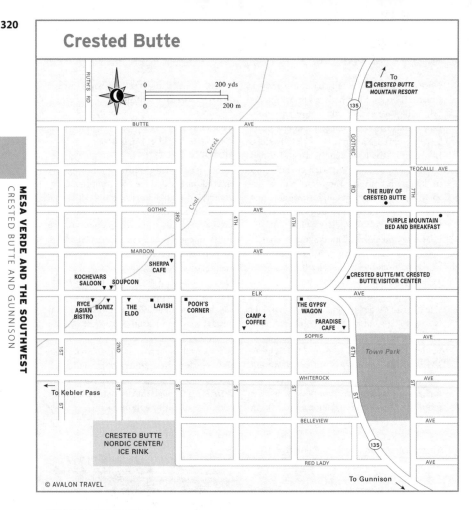

SPORTS AND RECREATION

Downhill Skiing and Snowboarding

★ CRESTED BUTTE MOUNTAIN RESORT

Despite its formidable reputation, **Crested Butte Mountain Resort** (12 Snowmass Rd., 970/349-2222, www.skicb.com, 9am-4pm daily, $108) is a great mountain for boarders and skiers of every ability level. Best known for its extreme terrain—including Rambo, whose 55-degree pitch is North America's steepest "in-bounds" ski run, other infamously steep double-black diamonds like Banana, Sock-It-to-Me, and Staircase, and the extreme terrain in Teocalli Bowl—the mountain also has significantly more beginner (green) runs than many purportedly "easier" areas like Steamboat and Telluride. The only downside to Crested Butte is the snow. Although it officially gets 300 inches per year, these seem to come in just a few, large storms, so the quality is not always as good as at some of the state's other resorts.

The densest concentration of green trails,

including the fun Roller Coaster, is located off of the Red Lady Express lift. Intermediate boarders and skiers flock to the Paradise Bowl, where Forest Queen and the wide-open, partially groomed runs are some of the best in the state. The many single black diamond runs like International off the Silver Queen Express lift are fun cruisers for advanced skiers.

The mountain has one main base area that's accessed by four lifts, so it's a very easy resort to navigate. Crested Butte's **Ski & Ride School** (Gothic Center, 877/547-5143, www.skicb.com, $118-129 for a half-day adult group lesson) offers group and private board and ski lessons for every ability level. Several sport shops, including **Christy Sports** (32 Crested Mtn. La., 970/349-6601, http://rental.christysports.com, 8am-6pm daily in winter, $22-40 package per day), located just a few steps north of the Red Lady Express lift, rent snowboard and ski packages.

Cross-Country Skiing and Snowshoeing

The area around Crested Butte also has superb backcountry and Nordic skiing and snowshoeing. A great place to start is at the nonprofit **Crested Butte Nordic Center** (620 2nd St., 970/349-1707, http://cbnordic.org, 8am-5pm daily in winter, $18 per day), which grooms 55 kilometers of trails in the area, making the town the self-declared "Nordic Ski Capital" of Colorado. The center also offers rental packages ($20 per day for classic or skate ski package), tours, private lessons, and clinics, as well as a fun backcountry dining adventure to the **Magic Meadows Yurt** (970/349-1707, https://cbnordic.org, $135 for a five-course dinner), located about a mile from a trailhead about five minutes' drive from the center.

For a backcountry experience, **Crested Butte Mountain Guides** (202 Elk Ave., 970/349-5430, http://crestedbutteguides.com, 8:30am-5pm Mon.-Sat., 9am-4pm Sun.) offers mountaineering, backcountry splitboard, and snowshoeing clinics, among many others, as well as guided tours. In summer, they offer local rock climbing and mountain biking trips.

Hiking

Crested Butte and its environs offer a tremendous amount of hiking. You can take advantage of the **Silver Queen Express** lift (9:30am-2:30pm daily mid-June-early Sept., reduced hours Fri.-Sun. early Sept.-early Oct., $21 single ride) to haul yourself partway up the steep climb up 12,162-foot Crested Butte Mountain. The resort offers daily **guided hikes** (www.skicb.com, 10am daily, $48) to the summit. You can also take the lift up and then walk down the 4.3-mile (one-way) Silver Queen Road.

Beyond the ski resort, there is a fantastic network of trails crisscrossing the beautiful Elk Range. A few highlights include the easy stroll past fields of wildflowers and aspen groves to pretty Judd Falls along the **Copper Creek Trail** (1.5 miles one-way), which begins near Gothic at the end of Highway 135. To get here from downtown, head north on Gothic Road past Mt. Crested Butte. Veer right after the Snodgrass Trailhead parking lot and descend into the river valley past the town of Gothic. Park in the signed Copper Creek lot on the right side.

The moderate **Green Lake Trail** (3.5 miles one-way) begins at the Crested Butte Nordic Center (620 2nd St.) and ends at a beautiful picnic area. The trail rises south, then turns right onto Wildcat Road and continues on a trail after the road dead-ends. At the junction with Trapper's Crossing Road, turn right and watch for a sign for the Green Lake Trail on the left.

Biking

Crested Butte Mountain Resort's **Evolution Bike Park** (877/547-5143, http://bike.skicb.com, hours vary, $30 for an all-day pass) has 20 routes, about half of which are also open to hikers. The difficulty of each route is rated by the same system as the ski trails, ranging from beginner (green) to expert (double-black diamond). All are accessed via the **Red**

Lady Express lift (http://bike.skicb.com, 9:30am-5pm daily mid-June-early Sept., reduced hours Fri.-Sun. early Sept.-early Oct., $43 one-day pass).

Outside the resort are dozens more excellent rides, including the most famous, **Pearl Pass,** a 38-mile ride to Aspen over the namesake 12,700-foot-high pass. The route follows Road 738, a rough four-wheel drive road that leaves Highway 135 a few miles south of Crested Butte. At the pass, riders follow Road 129 down to Castle Creek Road, which intersects with Highway 82 just west of Aspen. Obtain detailed directions and maps from a local shop before setting out.

A less demanding trail is the 2.5-mile **Lower Loop,** which is close to town and has a moderate grade suitable for beginners. To reach it, pedal north on 1st Street, then west on Butte Avenue, which turns into Peanut Lake Road. The trailhead is across the street from the old Peanut Mine. At the end of Gothic Road (north of the resort), access the popular 14-mile **401 Trail,** an advanced trail with wonderful views of the Maroon Bells and plenty of aspen and blossoming wildflowers. From town, pedal up Highway 135 past the ski area to Schofield Pass, where you turn right onto the signed single track. You can ride it as an out-and-back or as a loop.

Golf

The semi-private course at **The Club at Crested Butte** (385 Country Club Dr., 970/349-6127, www.theclubatcrestedbutte. com, $75-149 for 18 holes includes cart and practice balls) allows the public to play (noon-2pm or 4pm, depending upon the day). The course is spread across 160 acres of meticulously maintained fairways, aspen groves, and trout-filled lakes. Men must wear shirts with collars, tailored slacks or long shorts, tucked-in shirts, and ball caps with the bills pointing forward. Women are required to wear blouses and tailored slacks, long skirts, or shorts. It's worth putting up with their rules to play the Robert Trent Jones II-designed championship course just

for its tremendous views of the surrounding Elk Mountain Range.

ENTERTAINMENT AND EVENTS
Nightlife

Mt. Crested Butte ski resort tends to be family oriented, so its nightlife is pretty much limited to après-ski drinks at hot spots like the **Avalanche Bar & Grill** (15 Emmons Rd., 970/349-7195, www.avalanchebarandgrill. com, 11am-9pm daily in season) and the large deck at **Butte 66** (11 Snowmass Rd., 970/349-2999, www.skicb.com, 11am-close daily in season), known for its spiked milkshakes.

Downtown, the most popular hangout is **The Eldo** (215 Elk Ave., 970/349-6125, www. eldobrewpub.com, 3pm-2am daily), which bills itself as "a sunny place for shady people." This microbrewery serves up a large menu of appetizers, wraps, sandwiches, and "dank ass burgers," plus plenty of cold beer. They also have live bands several nights a week. Established in 1886, laid-back **Kochevars Saloon** (127 Elk Ave., 970/349-7117, www. kochevarscb.com, 2pm-2am Mon.-Fri., 11am-2am Sat.-Sun.) is Crested Butte's oldest tavern and gaming hall. It's best known for its drink specials and long happy hour (2pm-7pm daily).

Festivals and Events

During summer, the area hosts a number of festivals, including the **Crested Butte Music Festival** (http://crestedbuttemusic-festival.org, $30-250), a series of musical concerts held each July, and the **Tour de Forks,** a series of summer culinary events that culminates with the **Wine & Food Festival** (late July, $10-90). Both series are organized by the **Crested Butte Center for the Arts** (606 6th St., 970/349-7487, www.crestedbut-tearts.org). The **Crested Butte Mountain Theatre** (403 2nd St., 970/349-7487, www. cbmountaintheatre.org, $25-30), established in 1972, produces several shows each year, ranging in style from cabaret theater to comedies to musicals.

SHOPPING

The historic district is a great place to shop, with diverse, locally owned boutiques, friendly shopkeepers, and cheaper prices than glitzy Aspen or Vail. **Lavish** (234 Elk Ave., 970/349-1077, www.lavishcb.com, 10am-6pm daily) is a small accessory store that specializes in unique, limited-edition hats, jewelry, and other accessories. **Rhapsody** (327 Elk Ave., 970/349-3427, 11am-7pm daily) is a "Bohemian inspired mountain town trendy clothing boutique" that also sells jewelry and dream catchers.

The Gypsy Wagon (506 Elk Ave., 970/349-7261, www.the-gypsy-wagon.com, noon-5pm daily) is a small, local chain that sells free-spirited clothing (Twiggy dresses, off-the-shoulder blouses, and muscle T-shirts), trendy sandals, and other cool stuff like cactus candle sets. If you're shopping for a little one, visit **Pooh's Corner** (302 Elk Ave., 970/349-6539, 10am-6pm daily) for Legos, soft stuffies, balloons, games, and other toys galore.

At the Crested Butte Mountain Resort, **CB Mountain Outfitters** (Treasury Ctr., 970/349-4117, www.skicb.com, 8am-5pm daily in winter) and **Thin Air** (Mountaineer Square, 970/349-4045, www.skicb.com, 9am-5pm daily in winter) rent and sell outdoor equipment. Downtown, **The Alpineer** (419 6th St., 970/349-5210, http://alpineer.com, 9am-6pm daily) sells and rents bikes, skis, snowboards, and other outdoor apparel.

FOOD

Downtown Crested Butte has a larger selection of restaurants, and more enticing options, than the standard slopeside fare served at most of the resort restaurants. If you're staying at the resort, it's well worth taking the free, 10-minute shuttle into town.

Downtown

You'll know you're in heaven when the scent of freshly baked pastries greets you as you walk in the door of **Paradise Café** (435 6th St., 970/349-5622, 7am-2pm Mon.-Sat., 7am-1pm Sun., $5-11). This longstanding locals' hangout has a great outdoor patio, strong Bloody Marys, and large plates of delicious sugar-dusted French toast, build-your-own omelets, and Paradise cheesesteak sandwiches. If you're only after a quick dose of caffeine, head to the colorful cabin that houses the funky **Camp 4 Coffee** (402½ Elk Ave., 970/349-2500, www.camp4coffee.com, 6:30am-5:30pm daily), which serves coffee made from small-batch, hand-roasted beans.

For casual dining, try **Bonez** (130 Elk Ave., 970/349-5118, www.bonez.co, 11:30am-10pm daily, $15-26), a tequila bar/Mexican grill with unusual skull-themed decor, lots of ceramic plates hanging on the walls, and an enormous list of tequilas to choose from. The menu features creative combinations like West Elk chile rellenos and lobster tacos, as well as more traditional dishes like steak or shrimp fajitas. In a quieter location a block off the main drag, **Sherpa Café** (313 3rd St., 970/349-0443, 11am-9:30pm, $11-14) serves up hearty servings of *thukpa* (Tibetan noodle soup), curries, and Tibetan *momo* dumplings beneath Buddha print-covered walls. **Ryce Asian Bistro**'s (120 Elk Ave., 970/349-9888, www.ryceasianbistro.com, 11:30am-10pm Mon.-Sat., 4pm-10pm Sun., $12-20) simple, chic interior is usually packed with patrons happily munching on delicious Chinese and Thai entrées like teriyaki chicken, basil duck, and Yunnan eggplant. A summer bonus is the row of garage doors that open up to let in the fresh mountain breeze.

A decidedly more upscale option is ★ **Soupçon Bistro** (127 Elk Ave., 970/349-5448, www.soupcon-cb.com, 6pm-8pm daily, $39-47), a small, romantic restaurant housed in a historic mining cabin tucked into an alley just off of the main street. Chef Jason Vernon oversees a large wine cellar and a small but carefully selected menu of beautifully presented dishes like crispy skin-on striped bass and slow-braised beef short ribs. Try to leave enough room for the divine Grand Marnier soufflé.

Crested Butte Mountain Resort

Most resort restaurants are only open in winter, so call in advance outside of the bustling ski season. In the resort base area, **Spellbound Pizza** (Treasury Ctr., 970/349-2998, www.skicb.com, 11am-3pm daily, $7) is a casual spot to warm up and enjoy cheesy slices of pizza as well as the pasta and salad bars. Located in the Mountaineer Square breezeway, **Jefe's** (970/349-4450, www.skicb.com, 11am-4pm daily, $9-11) features classic Tex-Mex dishes like meat- or bean-topped nachos and spicy pork green chili.

Dinner options include the Grand Lodge's **Woodstone Grille** (6 Emmons Rd., 970/349-8030, www.skicb.com, 7am-10am and 5pm-10pm daily, $10-20), known for its fire-baked pizzas, steaming pasta dishes, and jalapeño peanut popper appetizers. It's also a great place to grab breakfast or hang out in the afternoon and enjoy a round of billiards. Inside the slopeside Elevation Hotel and Spa, **9380'** (500 Gothic Rd., 970/251-3030, www.9380prime.com, 7am-9pm daily, $14-34) serves up classic favorites like BLTs, as well as dinner entrées such as a half rack of lamb and a fish of the day. The interior is relatively upscale; the outdoor patio has several cozy fire pits and is a more relaxed spot (pets are also allowed).

ACCOMMODATIONS

The bulk of the slopeside accommodations are owned by the resort, and prices increase the closer to the lifts you get. Condominiums are often a better value than standard hotel rooms, especially for larger groups.

Downtown

★ **The Ruby of Crested Butte** (624 Gothic Ave., 800/390-1338, www.therubyofcrestedbutte.com, $149-299) is a highly lauded guesthouse whose six bright and comfortable rooms are tastefully furnished with antiques. There are beautiful views of Mt. Crested Butte from the rooms, a luxurious six-person hot tub,

and a generous organic morning spread that *Colorado Scenic Byways* has rated "Crested Butte's best breakfast." A block away, the **Purple Mountain Bed and Breakfast** (714 Gothic Ave., 970/349-5888, www.purplemountainlodge.com, $119-249) has six rooms, each with a private bath and within easy walking distance of the historic district. The gourmet multi-course breakfast includes locally roasted coffee, and the lodge also has a Ghirardelli hot chocolate bar, Colorado craft beer on tap, and delicious desserts to finish off your perfect day. Guests must be 16 years or older.

Crested Butte Mountain Resort

The family-owned **Nordic Inn** (14 Treasury Rd., 970/349-5542, http://nordicinncb.com, $85-255) is located in the only remaining original hotel that opened in 1963, along with the resort. Although it lacks frills, it's a great value with large rooms, plus a free, hearty continental breakfast served in the spacious dining room and an electric shuttle to drive you to and from the base area.

Much higher on the luxury (and price) scale, the 226-room **Grand Lodge Resort & Suites** (6 Emmons Rd., 970/349-8000, www.skicb.com, $239) is a large, less-personal hotel. Given its location just 200 yards from the slopes and the comfortable, oversized rooms, the prices are surprisingly affordable (for a ski resort), especially for the suites. Amenities include a spa, indoor-outdoor pool, and a steaming outdoor hot tub.

An excellent ski-in, ski-out property, the **Elevation Hotel and Spa** (500 Gothic Rd., 970/251-3000, www.elevationresort.com, $153-199) is located steps from both the Silver Queen Express and Red Lady Express lifts. It offers nine different configurations of rooms and suites, many of which have balconies with views of the slopes and beautiful Mt. Crested Butte, as well as small kitchenettes. The hotel also has an indoor heated pool, a town shuttle, and a free ski valet so you don't have to lug your gear up to your room.

TRANSPORTATION AND SERVICES

Air

Denver International Airport (DEN, 8500 Peña Blvd., 303/342-2000, http://www.flydenver.com) is the closest major airport to Crested Butte. The smaller **Gunnison-Crested Butte Airport** (GUC, 711 Rio Grande Ave., 970/641-2304, www.gunnisoncounty.org), located 28 miles south of Crested Butte, has direct, year-round flights from Denver, non-stop summer flights from Houston, and direct flights from both of these cities, plus Dallas, Chicago, and Los Angeles, during the ski season. **Alpine Express** (800/822-4844, http://alpineexpressshuttle.com, $38 one-way) offers shuttle service between the Gunnison airport and the town and ski resort.

Telluride Express (970/728-6000, www.tellurideexpress.com, $53 one-way) offers shared shuttles from the Montrose-Telluride Regional Airport to the town of Crested Butte.

To reach Crested Butte from the Gunnison airport, head east on West Rio Grande Avenue. After half a mile, West Rio Grande Avenue veers left and becomes Main Street. Continue straight (north) on Main Street (Hwy. 135) for 27 miles to Crested Butte.

Car

Crested Butte is one of the most isolated resorts in Colorado. In winter, the only available route is Highway 135 from Gunnison. From Grand Junction, U.S. 50 follows the Gunnison River south for 120 miles to the town of Gunnison. From Gunnison, Highway 135 heads north for 27 miles to Crested Butte. In summer, when **Kebler Pass** is open (usually late May-early Nov.), you can reach Crested Butte via Road 12, a good dirt road that connects with the North Fork Valley near Paonia.

Parking is an issue. During ski season, no parking is allowed on any street within Mt. Crested Butte. Ask your hotel if they have space available; if not, there is limited free parking on the north side of the Grand Lodge Resort & Suites. The town of Crested Butte has strict winter parking regulations, so be sure to pay attention to the signs.

Parking is allowed on Elk Avenue for up to two hours (8am-5pm daily). You can park in the public lots (8am-2:30am) east of the 6th Street/Elk Avenue intersection. Once you find a spot, it's most convenient to leave your car there and take the free Mountain Express shuttle to get around.

Bus and Shuttle

Express Arrow (877/779-2999, http://expressarrow.com, $37 one-way) offers once-daily bus service from both the Denver Greyhound and Amtrak stations to Gunnison. From Gunnison, take the Gunnison Valley RTA bus (www.gunnisonvalleyrta.com, free) to Mountaineer Square in Mt. Crested Butte.

The **Mountain Express** (970/349-7318, www.mtnexp.org) operates a free, year-round bus system that transports visitors between Crested Butte Mountain Resort, downtown Crested Butte, and most lodgings. Five color-coded lines circulate about every 15 minutes during winter (early Dec.-mid-Apr.). The green Town Shuttle operates between downtown Crested Butte and the ski resort. Service is reduced outside of the main ski season.

Services

The **Crested Butte/Mt. Crested Butte Chamber of Commerce and Visitor Center** (601 Elk Ave., 970/349-6438, www.cbchamber.com, 9am-5pm daily) has a welcome center at the intersection of Highway 135 and Elk Avenue. The website www.visitcrestedbutte.com is packed with information about local recreation, upcoming events, and lodging. The best source of information for trail conditions, snow reports, and year-round activities is **Crested Butte Mountain Resort** (877/547-5143 and 970/349-2222, www.skicb.com).

The closest hospital for emergency care is the **Gunnison Valley Hospital** (711 N. Taylor St., Gunnison, 970/641-1456), which also has a **family medicine clinic** (970/642-8413). In Crested Butte, the small

Paonia and the North Fork Valley

Paonia, Colorado's farm-to-table capital

One of my favorite small towns in Colorado is petite Paonia, located in the beautiful North Fork Valley, where the Gunnison River's clear water lazily winds through a fertile vale ringed by high mesas and forested peaks. With one national and two state parks nearby, as well as more than three million acres of national forest, this region is a great place for cycling, hiking, fishing, boating, and hunting. Paonia also hosts the state's greatest concentration of sustainable and organic growers, making it a center of fresh farm-to-table food and some great Colorado wine.

WINERIES

Paonia is the core of the West Elks American Viticultural Area, and most of the local wineries offer free tastings from late May through the end of October. Two of my favorites are **Stone Cottage Cellars** (41746 Red Rd., 970/527-3444, www.stonecottagecellars.com, 11am-6pm daily), where you can taste a peppery, full-bodied syrah and a crisp pinot gris in their quaint, stone tasting room located next to grape-studded vines, and **Azura Cellars** (16764 Farmers Rd., 970/390-4251, www.azuracellars.com, 11am-6pm daily), where the artist-owners showcase their artwork as well as their wine in a stunning setting on the steep slopes high above the valley. **Alfred Eames Cellars,** Paonia's best-known winery, offers tastings at **Delicious Orchards** (39126 Hwy. 133, Hotckhiss, 970/527-1110, www.bigbs.com, 9am-7pm daily), a great local fruit stand that also sells half a dozen flavors of local **Big B's** organic hard cider.

FOOD AND ACCOMMODATIONS

Paonia's can't-miss restaurant is the **Living Farm Café** (120 Grand Ave., 970/527-3779, http://thelivingfarmcafe.com, 8am-9pm Wed.-Mon., 8am-2pm Tues., $14-24), where chef Mike Gillespie incorporates locally harvested ingredients into delicious combinations like his signature dish, elk osso buco. There is a small inn ($90-115) right above the restaurant, or you can stay in one of the town's outlying bed-and-breakfasts, like the beautiful **Agape Farm and Retreat** (12123 Slate Point Rd., 970/527-3385, www.agapefarmandretreat.com, $145-155), where you can sleep in a surprisingly cozy yurt tucked into a fragrant flower garden.

Town Clinic of Crested Butte (214 6th St., 970/349-6749, www.towncliniccb.com, 9am-noon and 1pm-6pm Mon. and Fri., 1pm-9pm Thurs. and Sat., 1pm-5pm Sun.) offers care during limited hours. During the ski season, the **Crested Butte Medical Center** (12 Snowmass Rd., Mt. Crested Butte, 970/349-0321, www.cbmedicalcenter.com, 9am-4:30pm daily Nov.-Apr.), at the base of the Silver Queen Express lift, offers urgent and injury care. The resort also has a ski patrol for slopeside emergencies.

Telluride

Nestled in the bottom of a glacial valley so steep that it's called a box canyon, Telluride is stunningly beautiful and offers exceptional year-round recreation. Once a relaxed hippie hangout far off the beaten path, the town has turned into an increasingly expensive festival and skiing destination for the rich and famous, such as Jerry Seinfeld, Nicolas Cage, Oprah Winfrey, and Tom Cruise.

The Ute were the first known people to inhabit the Telluride Valley, where they hunted deer, elk, and sheep on forays from summer base camps established along the beautiful San Miguel River. The town of Telluride was founded as a mining community in the late 1800s to take advantage of the gold discovered in the region's highly mineralized volcanic rocks. The Ute name for the area, which translates to "the valley of the hanging waterfalls," was too tongue-twisting for Caucasians to repeat, so the miners called it Columbia.

However, the U.S. Post Office rejected this moniker (it duplicated the name of a mining camp in California), so the locals had to come up with something new. There are two prevailing theories: the name either comes from the mineral tellurium, which is commonly found in association with gold (although it is not found here); or it stems from the infamous send-off reputedly given to departing fortune-seekers heading to the San Juans, "To hell you ride."

SIGHTS
Telluride National Historic Landmark District
Telluride is considered one of the most important locations associated with American mining history and received a special National Historic Landmark designation in 1961. Hall's Hospital, one of the town's oldest buildings, was built in 1896 and is now the home of the **Telluride Historical Museum** (201 W. Gregory Ave., 970/728-3344, www.telluridemuseum.org, 11am-5pm Mon.-Sat., 1pm-5pm Sun. in summer, 11am-5pm Tues.-Sat. in winter, $5). Exhibits focus on Telluride's geological past and the uplift of the San Juan Mountains; others describe the native Nuchu people, and the inspiring story of the Telluride Blanket. The museum sponsors occasional guided **walking tours** ($10-15) of the town's historic sites, including the Lone Tree Cemetery. Download the self-guided walking tour (www.telluride.toursphere.com) and visit the old red light district or the spot where Butch Cassidy's first bank robbery took place.

SPORTS AND RECREATION
The main draws to Telluride are the nearly endless recreation and stunningly scenic backdrops of steep-walled valleys with gushing waterfalls and colorful meadows. The region is especially well known for intermediate to advanced downhill skiing at the Telluride Ski Resort.

Downhill Skiing and Snowboarding
TELLURIDE SKI RESORT
Ranked as one of the nation's top places to ski, the **Telluride Ski Resort** (565 Mountain Village Blvd., 970/728-7517, www.

Telluride

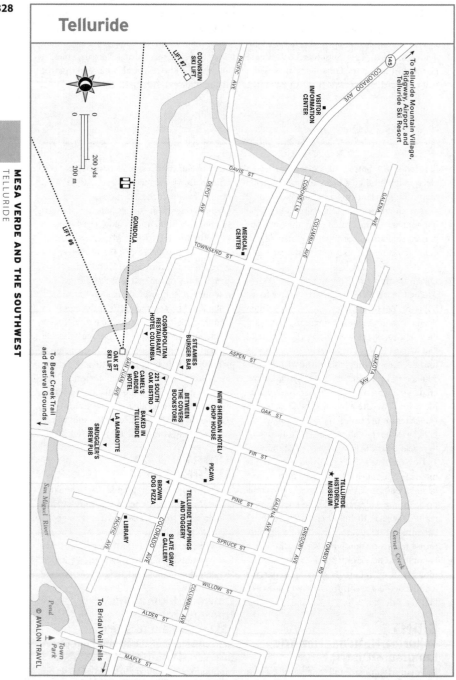

COONSKIN SKI LIFT

LIFT #7

PACIFIC AVE

COLORADO AVE

145

To Telluride Mountain Village,
Ridgway Airport, and
Telluride Ski Resort

VISITOR
INFORMATION
CENTER

0

0

200 yds

200 m

GONDOLA

LIFT #8

DAVIS ST

DEPOT AVE

CORONET LN

COLUMBIA AVE

GALENA AVE

MEDICAL
CENTER

TOWNSEND ST

COSMOPOLITAN
RESTAURANT/
HOTEL COLUMBIA

STEAMIES
BURGER BAR

ASPEN ST

DAKOTA AVE

OAK ST
SKI LIFT

SAN JUAN AVE

221 SOUTH
OAK BISTRO

CAMEL'S
GARDEN
HOTEL

BAKED IN
TELLURIDE

BETWEEN
THE COVERS
BOOKSTORE

NEW SHERIDAN HOTEL/
CHOP HOUSE

OAK ST

LA MARMOTTE

SMUGGLER'S
BREW PUB

FIR ST

PICAYA

TELLURIDE
HISTORICAL
MUSEUM

BROWN
DOG PIZZA

TELLURIDE TRAPPINGS
AND TOGGERY

PINE ST

GALENA AVE

GREGORY AVE

TOMBOY RD

Comet Creek

Sun Miguel River

LIBRARY

PACIFIC AVE

COLORADO AVE

SLATE GRAY
GALLERY

SPRUCE ST

WILLOW ST

COLUMBIA AVE

To Bear Creek Trail
and Festival Grounds

ALDER ST

Pond

Town
Park

To Bridal Veil Falls

© AVALON TRAVEL

MAPLE ST

Telluride Ski Resort's gondola in summer

Plunge and **Bushwacker** and big mogul runs like **Mammoth.** Snowboarders enjoy the mountain's four terrain parks, especially **Misty Maiden**, whose jumps, rails, and boxes are designed for advanced-to-expert riders. A series of intermediate and advanced runs also leads directly to the edge of the downtown on the mountain's steep northeastern slopes.

Telluride's **Ski School** (565 Mountain Village Blvd., 970/728-7414, www.tellurideskiresort.com, $125 for a half-day adult group lesson) offers group and private board and ski lessons for every ability level. With five area locations, **Telluride Sports** (www.telluridesports.com, $27-47 per day) is a convenient place to rent snowboard and ski packages as well as bikes in summer.

The resort's **Mountain Village Center** is separate from downtown Telluride, but the two are linked via a **gondola** (7am-midnight daily year-round, free). The 13-minute gondola ride travels from Oak Street Plaza to Mountain Village Center, passing the intermediate loading area Station St. Sophia, which has some of the best views in the state.

Hiking

Telluride's best-known hike is in the **Uncompahgre National Forest** (Norwood Ranger District, 1150 Forest St., Norwood, 970/327-4261, www.fs.usda.gov). Beautiful **Bridal Veil Falls** (1.8 miles one-way), the state's tallest free-falling waterfall at 365 feet, is clearly visible on the steep canyon wall as you drive into town. This pretty cataract is a beacon for hikers, bikers, and four-wheel drivers. Although it's a steep trail, the reasonably fit shouldn't have much trouble making it up the 1,650 vertical feet. In good weather, it's possible to continue to beautiful **Blue Lake,** located above treeline at 12,400 feet; the trail passes wildflowers and old mining cabins. To get to the trailhead from downtown Telluride, head east on Colorado Avenue past the Pandora Mill site. Shortly after the road turns to dirt, park at the Valley View Area lot and walk up the rough dirt road to the waterfall.

tellurideskiresort.com, $114 for a one-day pass) has some of the most stunning scenery and best terrain in the state, if not the country, especially following three recent expansions that added world-class areas like Prospect Bowl, Palmyra Peak, and Revelation Bowl to its acreage.

Of the resort's more than 2,000 skiable acres, the majority are for intermediate and advanced skiers. Its 16 lifts and two gondolas access 125 trails, the longest of which is about 4.5 miles long. The greatest concentration of beginner (green) trails is the half dozen runs just above the Mountain Village, accessed by the hybrid Chondola lift. Intermediate boarders and skiers should head up the Prospect Express lift for open cruisers and the Polar Queen Express lift for forgiving bump runs like **Polar Queen** and **Dew Drop.** Experienced skiers will enjoy the many steep advanced (black diamond) and expert (double-black diamond) runs accessed by the Plunge lift, including steep groomers like **The**

FESTIVALS AND EVENTS

Telluride has more than a dozen festivals during the summer; the biggest and best known is the **Telluride Bluegrass Festival** (www.bluegrass.com, mid-June, $230 for 4-day pass), encompassing four days of musical festivities and concerts by big names like Sam Bush, Mumford & Sons, and the Counting Crows. Other popular events include the **Mountainfilm Festival** (www.mountainfilm.org, late May, prices vary), which features more than 100 flicks, the **Telluride Film Festival** (www.telluridefilmfestival.org, Labor Day weekend, $390 per pass), and the winning combination of **Blues & Brews** (www.tellurideblues.com, mid-Sept., $190 for 3-day pass).

SHOPPING

Downtown has a beautifully restored historic district that houses many charming shops and excellent restaurants, although prices tend to be high.

A local establishment since 1974, **Between the Covers Bookstore** (224 W. Colorado Ave., 970/728-4504, www.between-the-covers.com, 9am-7pm Mon.-Sat., 9am-5pm Sun.) is a fantastic bookstore crammed with an impressive selection of more than 10,000 maps, books, and cards, including local history and natural history guides. Its cozy atmosphere is only enhanced by the smell of freshly roasted coffee served up at the interior coffee bar.

Picaya (101 W. Colorado Ave., 970/728-0954, http://picaya.com, 10am-9pm daily) is a bright and cheerful store that sells sustainably sourced jewelry, housewares, vintage framed photographs and Born to Ski signs, and lots of Buddhist prayer flags. It's named for a volcano near Guatemala City, where owner-traveler Lisa Horlick sources some of the store's exotic and ecofriendly wares.

A local fixture since 1972, family-owned **Telluride Trappings and Toggery** (109 E. Colorado Ave., 970/728-3338, http://thetelluridetoggery.com, 9am-9pm daily) is the town's longest-operating retail store. The Toggery sells everything from modern Southwestern jewelry to recycled rugs and has a good selection of both men's and women's clothing and shoes from labels like Tommy Bahama, Gramicci, and Ugg.

If you're searching for art, look for the cast-bronze pooch and water bowl outside **Slate Gray Gallery** (209 E. Colorado Ave., 970/728-3777, www.slategraygallery.com, 10am-6pm Tues.-Sat.). This main street addition sells "home embellishment, personal adornment, and general finery," including a nice selection of Colorado- and Native American-inspired paintings.

FOOD
Downtown

Telluride's primo breakfast spot is a big red barn called **Baked in Telluride** (127 S. Fir St., 970/728-4775, www.bakedintel.com, 5:30am-10pm daily, $4-15). Located between the gondola and the downtown, this bakery has a great selection of soups, salads, sandwiches, filling sourdough crust pizzas, evening dinner specials, and a variety of egg-and-cheese-filled croissants, plus a delectable case of baked goods to grab on your way to the slopes.

The contemporary **Steamies Burger Bar** (300 W. Colorado Ave., 844/843-2867, www.steamiesburgers.com, 8am-10pm daily, $5-10) steams its burgers and veggies and uses organic, whole-grain ingredients to create healthy alternatives to greasy fast food. They also have hot dogs, salads, and plenty of vegetarian choices as well as a gravy and kibble sundae for your dog. Another casual local fave is **Brown Dog Pizza** (110 E. Colorado Ave., 970/728-8046, www.browndogpizza.com, 11am-10pm daily, $10-18), whose chef, Jeff Smokevitch, won first place at the 2015 Pizza World Championships in Parma, Italy, for his (locally) famous Parma Italia square, Detroit-style, deep-crust pizza. The Dog also serves up steaming plates of house-made pasta with rich sauces like Bolognese, made from a 125-year-old recipe registered with the Italian government.

Smuggler's Brew Pub (225 S. Pine St., 970/728-5620, www.smugglersbrewpub.com, 11am-9:30pm daily, $12-38) serves an extensive menu of sandwiches, pasta, salads, and entrées made in-house from fresh, local ingredients. In addition to the Infamous Crispy Chic-Filet sandwich, the pub serves up grass-fed pork chops and steaks, colorful salads, and its notable elk Bolognese pasta. It also has a lively happy hour (3pm-5:30pm daily).

Housed in a 19th-century mining cabin, La Marmotte (150 W. San Juan Ave., 970/728-6232, www.lamarmotte.com, noon-2pm and 5pm-10pm Fri., 5pm-10pm Sat.-Thurs., $31-50) serves a rotating menu of upscale French bistro fare, such as coq au vin, plus unusual desserts like chocolate and sour cherry mousse terrine. Bargain hunters will want to try the bar bistro menu (5pm-6pm daily), which features half-price appetizers and $8 glasses of wine. A few blocks away in the Hotel Columbia, chef-owner Chad Scothorn oversees the acclaimed Cosmopolitan Restaurant (301 W. San Juan Ave., 970/728-1292, http://cosmotelluride.com, 5pm-close daily, $28-49), where each dish on the small menu is artistically presented to patrons seated in the contemporary dining room. In addition to meat-based and vegetarian entrées such as vegetable ramen or barbequed sustainable salmon, the restaurant offers several sushi options along with an extensive wine list.

Located in a historic home just a few steps from the gondola, 221 South Oak Bistro (221 S. Oak St., 970/728-9507, www.221southoak.com, 5:30pm-close daily, $29-50) is owned and operated by Eliza Gavin, an award-winning chef who garnered a top-10 spot on Bravo's *Top Chef* competition. The bistro has a beautiful garden patio for dining outdoors in summer, as well as window nooks in which to huddle during the winter. With an extensive and carefully selected wine list and a great selection of vegetarian and meat dishes and scrumptious desserts, 221 is a great choice for celebrating a special occasion.

Mountain Village

Located at the top of the gondola, Alfred's (Mountain Village, 970/728-7474, www.tellurideskiresort.com, 5:30pm-9:30pm daily, $27-52) is Telluride's flagship restaurant. Beneath a gleaming wood-beam ceiling adorned with antler chandeliers, a wall of floor-to-ceiling windows instantly draws your attention to the stunning mountain backdrop and the Victorian mining-era town far below. The restaurant features one of the largest wine lists in the state and a rotating menu of chef Mike Regrut's impeccably presented entrées, such as Day Boat Alaskan halibut and veal scaloppine.

ACCOMMODATIONS
Downtown

The Camel's Garden Hotel (250 W. San Juan Ave., 970/728-9300, www.camelsgarden.com, $425-600) bills itself as the planet's closest hotel to a ski lift. You can't argue with the location at the bottom of both the free gondola and Chair 9, nor the luxurious rooms, suites, and condos, which feature fireplaces and balconies as well as custom-crafted furnishings and Italian marble bathrooms. Just across the street from the gondola is the Hotel Columbia (301 W. San Juan Ave., 800/201-9505, www.columbiatelluride.com, $195-505), a modern, multi-story brick building constructed in 1994 and renovated in 2009. Some of its chic, studio-style rooms and suites include hot tubs, kitchenettes, balconies, and gas fireplaces. In addition to the upscale Cosmopolitan Restaurant (970/728-1292, http://cosmotelluride.com, 5pm-9:30pm daily, $28-49), the hotel also boasts a cozy lounge and a private wine vault that can be rented out.

For a historic location on the main thoroughfare, book into the 26-room New Sheridan Hotel (231 W. Colorado Ave., 970/728-4351, www.newsheridan.com, $203-278), housed in a fully renovated 1895 red brick building. Located just a few blocks from the gondola, the highly lauded hotel has a rooftop bar with amazing views, an excellent restaurant, the Chop House (233 W.

Colorado Ave., 970/728-9100, www.newsher-idan.com, 5:30pm-9pm daily, $24-56), and cozy rooms, each with a beautifully tiled en-suite bathroom.

Mountain Village

In the heart of the Mountain Village, the **Madeline Hotel** (568 Mountain Village Blvd., 970/239-0119, www.madelinetelluride. com, $439-549) has the reputation of being Telluride's choicest accommodations. Ideally located in the center of the village near the gondola, the hotel features a full-service ski valet, a sky terrace with an outdoor pool, hot tubs, fire pits, and amazing mountain views, a tranquil spa, and in-room bath baristas. The luxurious rooms range from spacious guest rooms with large, soaking tub-equipped bath-rooms to stunning 1-4-bedroom suites and residences with full gourmet kitchens and floor-to-ceiling windows.

Situated on a spectacular perch next to the Mountain Village, **The Peaks Resort & Spa** (136 Country Club Dr., 970/728-6800, www.thepeaksresort.com, $350) has incred-ible views in every direction. The resort has luxurious rooms, suites, and penthouses, plus cabin or condo rentals in its See Forever Village. The rooms are impeccable, and the

amenities top-notch, but the steep resort fees have taken some guests by surprise.

CAMPING

The town of Telluride operates the **Town Park Campground** (500 E. Colorado Ave., 970/728-2173, www.telluride-co.gov, mid-May-mid-Oct., $17-23), the only spot in Telluride where you're allowed to park over-night or sleep in your RV. The length is lim-ited to 30 feet. The first-come, first-served facility does not have any hookups.

TRANSPORTATION AND SERVICES
Air

Denver International Airport (DEN, 8500 Peña Blvd., 303/342-2000, http://www.flyden-ver.com) is the closest major airport.

The smaller **Montrose Regional Airport** (MTJ, 2100 Airport Rd., Montrose, 970/249-3203, www.montrosecounty.net), located about 65 miles north of Telluride, has multi-ple daily flights year-round from Denver, non-stop summer flights from Dallas, Houston, Chicago, and Los Angeles, and direct flights from all of these cities, plus Phoenix, Atlanta, New York, Las Vegas, and San Francisco during the ski season. Avis, Budget, Hertz,

Camel's Garden Hotel

and National have depots at the Montrose-Telluride Regional Airport. **Tellurides** (970/275-9604, http://tellurides.com, $150 round-trip) provides private cars from the Montrose-Telluride airport to town.

From the Montrose-Telluride airport, head southwest on South 1st Street. At the first cross street, turn right onto South Townsend Avenue. After 0.1 mile, turn left onto West Main Street and continue straight on this for about half a mile. At the junction with Chipeta Road, turn left and follow it for three miles to U.S. 550 South.

Car

Telluride is located 65 miles south of Montrose. From Montrose and U.S. 50, head south on U.S. 550 for about 25 miles to the town of Ridgway. Turn right onto Road 62 and continue west for 23 miles to Placerville. Turn left onto Road 145 and drive southeast for about 16 miles to Telluride. If you're heading to the ski resort's Mountain Village, drive to the first traffic circle on Road 145. The first exit leads to Mountain Village Boulevard and the resort.

Driving to Telluride can involve navigating multiple mountain passes. In winter, check road conditions and chain laws by contacting the Colorado Department of Transportation (dial 511, www.cotrip.org).

Parking is an issue during summer and the winter ski season. Downtown parking is limited to three hours. To stay longer, use the free Carhenge Lot (just off West Pacific Ave.) near the base of Lift 7 on the west side of town. In the resort's Mountain Village, paid parking is available at the Heritage Parking Garage (below the Madeline Hotel). Free day parking is available in the Meadows Run Parking Lot at the end of Adams Ranch Road.

Bus and Shuttle

Telluride Express (970/728-6000, www.tellurideexpress.com, $53 one-way) offers shared shuttles from the Montrose-Telluride Regional Airport to downtown Telluride, Mountain Village, and the town of Crested Butte.

In Telluride, the easiest (and most scenic) way to get between downtown and the Mountain Village is the **gondola** (7am-midnight daily year-round, free). The gondola picks up from downtown's Oak Street Plaza (W. San Juan Ave.). The **Galloping Goose** shuttle (www.telluride-co.gov, 7am-9pm daily, free) loops through downtown, picking up at various stops along Colorado Avenue and stopping at the gondola. Free shuttles circulate throughout Mountain Village Center during ski season.

Services

The **Telluride Visitor's Center** (236 W. Colorado Ave., 888/605-2578, www.visittelluride.com, 10am-7pm daily) is also located along Road 145, the main route into town. For trail conditions, snow reports, and year-round activities, contact **Telluride Ski Resort** (970/728-6900, www.tellurideskiresort.com). The closest hospital for emergency care is the **Telluride Regional Medical Center** (500 W. Pacific Ave., Telluride, 970/728-3848, https://tellmed.org). The Telluride Ski Resort also has a ski patrol for slopeside emergencies.

Ouray

Ouray, with its encircling wall of high, snow-capped peaks, bills itself as the Switzerland of America. The attractions here include the challenging ice-climbing park, beautiful summer hikes, and lazy, year-round soaks in Ouray's historic hot springs.

The town's captivating history is reflected in its unusual name. Ouray is christened for the famous chief of the Ute tribe who tried but failed to secure a treaty with the U.S. government to allow the Ute to remain in western Colorado. Because he believed that war against the government would result in the tribe's demise, Ouray pursued a path of peace through negotiation, a decision for which some members of his tribe considered him a traitor. Ouray once lived in a cabin on the outskirts of town, conducted meetings and rituals here, and soaked in the town's sacred hot springs.

OURAY HOT SPRINGS

No trip to the area would be complete without a rejuvenating soak in the large pool at **Ouray Hot Springs** (1220 Main St., 970/325-7073, http://ourayhotsprings.com, 10am-10pm daily, $12 for an all-day pass). Used since at least the 14th century, the springs originate as 150°F water from the box canyon on the west side of town. The water, which is rich in magnesium, boron, and lithium, among other minerals, is then piped to the pool. Built in the 1920s, the pool is divided into three sections that range in temperature from 67°F to 104°F. The cooler sections host some fun play areas with floating volleyball nets and waterslides for the kiddos. It's the perfect place to warm up on a cold winter day while fluffy snowflakes drift through the air, or relax on a balmy summer evening as yet another spectacular sunset bathes the box canyon in rich, golden light.

OURAY ICE PARK

Ouray Ice Park (280 County Rd. 361, 970/325-4288, http://ourayicepark.com, 8am-4pm Mon.-Fri., 7:30am-4pm Sat.-Sun. weather permitting, free) is the brainchild of a California beach bum-turned-ice climber and the manager of the Ouray Hydroelectric

Ouray Hot Springs

Hike to Cascade Falls along the Perimeter Trail.

$60 for all-access pass), held in mid-January each year.

HIKING

For a great overview of Ouray and its many scenic attractions, hike the five-mile **Perimeter Trail** (www.ouraytrails.org), which climbs steeply up the box canyon wall from a trailhead across the street from the visitor center. Once the trail flattens out, it begins to circle around the entire valley and soon meets up with spectacular **Cascade Falls,** which pours down from a slot carved into the canyon's eastern wall. The trail then crosses a Gambel oak-covered stretch, where it crosses the 5th Avenue Trail, one of several intermediate access points. After crossing a side creek, the route briefly follows the road that leads up to the Amphitheater Campground before wandering past the **Baby Bathtubs Trail.** The route then bends west to cross the old miners' Potato Patch and U.S. 550, before entering the ice-climbing park along the **Ice Park Trail** and passing an old water pipeline. The Perimeter Trail then crosses County Road 361 before climbing again to the Box Canyon Bridge, perched high above the spectacular Canon Creek slot canyon. The trail then descends through a tunnel into a series of neighborhoods, where you can wander the final mile back to the visitor center, located next to the hot springs pool on the west side of Main Street as you enter town.

★ Yankee Boy Basin

One of the most scenic spots in the San Juan Mountains, **Yankee Boy Basin** (Uncompahgre National Forest, 970/327-4261, www.fs.fed.us) is a gorgeous alpine basin that is especially spectacular in midsummer, when incredible displays of wildflowers carpet the steep slopes beneath its crown of craggy peaks. The basin is known for its incredible concentrations of columbine, Colorado's state flower; its challenging access; and for being the start of the ascent of one of Colorado's most beautiful fourteeners, the 14,150-foot Mt. Sneffels, named for the

Plant, who owns an easement through the beautiful Uncompahgre Gorge just south of town. Together, the two experimented with various ways of "farming" ice to create a series of 200 routes along the gorge's steep walls. At first, the townspeople thought they were nuts; after pipes froze solid, they would cart them into town to defrost them in a hot tub. But their perseverance eventually paid off, and the park is now one of the country's best-known ice-climbing destinations. Located just a short walk from the downtown, the routes are accessed from a flat trail that parallels the gorge's upper wall, which is divided into 14 sections with endearing names like Shithouse Wall. Each route is assigned a difficulty grade, and there's even a section for kids to climb.

Unless you're an experienced ice climber, it's best to hire a local guide such as **Peak Mountain Guides** (280 7th Ave., 970/325-7342, www.peakmountainguides.com) to show you the ropes.

Ouray's signature event is its three-day **Ice Festival** (http://ourayicepark.com,

Icelandic mountain that rose above the great fissure in Jules Verne's classic novel *Journey to the Center of the Earth*. From the lower trailhead, the three-mile (one-way) hike up Mt. Sneffels gains 2,900 feet in elevation.

Yankee Boy Basin is accessed by a rough dirt road whose upper portions are only navigable by a four-wheel drive vehicle. It's best to take a jeep tour, such as the three-hour outing offered by **Switzerland of America** (226 7th Ave., 970/325-4484, https://soajeep.com, $58).

SHOPPING

Ouray's best gallery is **Ouray Glassworks** (619 Main St., 800/748-9421, www.ourayglassworks.com, 9am-7pm daily in summer, 9am-4pm daily in winter), where local artist Sam Rushing, a former chemist, creates exquisite handblown glass right before your eyes. In addition to dainty bud vases and colorful globe ornaments, the store sells beautiful beadwork and pottery. Funky **Wildflower Boutique** (9735 Main St., 970/325-4089, www.ouraywildflower.com, 9:30am-9pm daily in summer, 10am-5:30pm daily in winter) sells quirky creations ranging from zesty moose seasoning to colorful metal animal outlines and local cookbooks.

FOOD

For frosty pomegranate margaritas, crunchy corn chips, and large plates of traditional Mexican favorites, check out **Buen Tiempo** (515 Main St., 970/325-4544, www.buentiemporestaurant.com, 11:30am-9:30pm daily in summer, 11:30am-close Sat.-Sun. in winter, $11-16). **BrickHouse 737** (737 Main St., 970/325-7236, http://brickhouse737.com, 5pm-9:30pm daily, $19-34) is located in a cozy, two-story brick building where executive chef and climber Cory Sargent (who trained under Bryan Moscatello from Aspen's Little Nell) creates delicious plates, like elk Bolognese and seared scallops, that incorporate as many fresh, locally produced ingredients as possible. **Mouse's Chocolates** (520 Main St., 970/325-7285, https://mouseschocolates.com, 7am-10pm daily) serves up the winning

wildflower-filled meadows in the San Juans

combination of chocolate and coffee. You may have to go twice to get both the hand-roasted coffee and some dreamy chocolate pecan fudge. Don't miss the mocha milkshake with espresso whipped cream.

ACCOMMODATIONS

Ouray's best value is probably the **Matterhorn Inn** (201 6th Ave., 970/325-4938, http://matterhorninnouray.com, $129), whose traditional motor inn-style rooms one block off of Main Street have been renovated to include laminate floors, granite countertops, and comfy pillow-top mattresses. The price includes a simple complimentary breakfast at a nearby deli. If you'd rather stay within walking distance of the hot springs, the **Hot Springs Inn** (1400 Main St., 970/325-7277, www.hotspringsinn.com, $175) has spacious rooms with private balconies overlooking the gurgling Uncompahgre River, as well as a microwave and fridge in each room. Amenities include on-site hot tubs, grills, laundry, free Wi-Fi, and a free complimentary breakfast.

The historic **Beaumont Hotel & Spa** (505 Main St., 970/325-7000, www.beaumonthotel. com, $139-199) has hosted guests for more than 130 years. Each of the 12 rooms and suites is uniquely decorated with antique furniture, some of which is original to the hotel, and has a beautiful view of the surrounding box canyon. Rooms have either a queen- or king-size bed and can accommodate two people. The larger Presidential Suite, where President Roosevelt once stayed, still retains its original windows and can sleep up to six people. Amenities include a heated, off-street parking lot, large desks, free Wi-Fi, and a continental breakfast.

CAMPING

In a pretty setting along the Uncompahgre River in northern Ouray, the **4J+1+1 RV Park** (790 Oak St., 970/325-4418, www.ouraycolorado.com, May-Oct., $26-36) is close to the hot springs pool and within walking distance of downtown. Located along the river a little farther north, the **Ouray RV Park & Cabins** (1700 Main St., 970/325-4523, www.ourayrvpark.com, year-round, $20-199) has tent and RV sites as well as deluxe and "camping" cabins.

TRANSPORTATION AND SERVICES

Air

The **Montrose-Telluride Regional Airport** (MTJ, 2100 Airport Rd., Montrose, 970/249-3203, www.montrosecounty.net), located 38 miles north of Ouray, has multiple daily flights year-round from Denver as well as nonstop summer flights and direct flights during the ski season. Car rental depots are at the airport. **Tellurides** (970/275-9604, http://tellurides.com, $150 round-trip) provides private cars from the Montrose-Telluride airport to Ouray.

Car

To get to Ouray from the town of Montrose, turn left onto U.S. 550 and head south for 35 miles to Ouray. From Ouray, U.S. 550 continues 70 miles south, following the stunning **Million Dollar Highway** to Silverton and Durango. Part of the All-American San Juan Scenic Byway (www.colorado.com), the narrow, winding road travels 25 miles through the spectacular mountain scenery separating Ouray from the old mining town of Silverton. The road has steep drop-offs not protected by guardrails; check current conditions and chain laws in effect at the Colorado Department of Transportation (dial 511, www.cotrip.org).

Services

The Ouray **visitor center** (1230 Main St., 970/325-4746, www.ouraycolorado.com, 9am-6pm Mon.-Sat., 10am-4pm Sun. in summer, reduced hours fall-spring) is conveniently located on the west side of Main Street just as you enter town. The **Ouray County Emergency Medical Services** (541 4th St., 970/325-7275, http://ouraycountyco.gov, 8am-4:30pm Mon.-Thurs.) provides emergency medical service during limited hours.

OURAY

MESA VERDE AND THE SOUTHWEST

Mesa Verde and the Four Corners

Colorado's far southwestern corner has a look and feel unlike any other part of the state. It is a land of light and shadow, where a single, puffy cloud darting across the sun's face can dramatically change the lighting on the twisted trunk of a gnarled pinyon tree or a dainty petroglyph pecked into a rough canyon wall. It's also an area of intense aridity and, in summer, searing heat, conditions that have not only helped to shaped the rugged landscape of high sandstone plateaus carved by deep canyons, but also the hundreds of generations of people who have thrived in their shadows.

The region's undisputed highlight is Mesa Verde National Park. Here, intricate, multistory cliff dwellings tucked into enormous sandstone alcoves offer keen insight into the lives of the ancient people who once farmed the mesa tops and lived in the tiny mud-brick rooms. Several other nearby national monuments protect many impressive ruins, as well as acre upon acre of gorgeous slickrock scenery, where crimson and white sandstone monoliths tower above sparse vegetation and secluded archaeological sites.

In between the area's many monuments, the small, spread-out town of Cortez offers basic services. Farther east, the lively college town of Durango straddles the very different worlds of sandstone and the rugged San Juan Mountains. Durango is the start of one of the region's top attractions, an unforgettable, historic, narrow-gauge train ride through otherwise inaccessible wilderness to the mining town of Silverton, which clings to the steep mountainsides, as well as its Victorian-era roots.

The Four Corners area is beautiful any time of year, although it can be extremely hot in summer. Spring and autumn are both ideal times to visit. In spring, the cottonwoods along the sparse creeks begin to leaf out. In autumn, the leaves turn gold and the distant mountaintops are dusted with fresh snow. Winter nights are chilly, but the daytime temperatures are usually quite pleasant. Winter also brings Mesa Verde's signature event. For one magical night in early December, Cliff Palace, the park's largest dwelling, glows with the dancing light cast by thousands of luminaria lanterns.

DURANGO
★ Durango & Silverton Narrow Gauge Railroad

While in Colorado's southwestern corner, try to set aside a day for an unforgettable trip on the **Durango & Silverton Narrow Gauge Railroad** (479 Main Ave., 970/247-2733, www.durangotrain.com, early May-mid-Oct., $89-199 round-trip). The train follows the historic 45-mile-long, three-foot-wide narrow gauge track originally laid along the sparkling Animas River in 1882. The track connected the railroad hub of Durango with the rich mines in Silverton, a picturesque Victorian mining town in the heart of the rugged San Juan Mountains.

From the painstakingly restored depot on the south side of Durango's bustling downtown, the coal-fired steam locomotive pulls a series of vintage railroad cars through a roadless wilderness of soaring peaks and steep river valleys. After 3.5 hours of chugging through some of the San Juans' incredible scenery, the train reaches tiny **Silverton,** where (on most trips) you have a couple of hours to stretch your legs, grab a bite to eat, and explore the quaint shops along the main street before re-boarding for the return trip. The round-trip journey takes about nine hours, so it's a full-day adventure.

If that sounds like too much, you can also ride the train in one direction and take a bus back in the other ($18 per person), which typically saves 1.5 hours. Or combine a ride with a half-day raft trip or other outing. Several classes of cars are available, from outdoor seats, where you're dusted with flakes of ash, to the splendid Presidential Class car with built-in Pullman berths.

Food and Accommodations

Durango is a fun college town with a great selection of brewpubs, restaurants, and comfortable accommodations. The always-packed **Steamworks Brewing Company** (801 E. 2nd Ave., 970/259-9200, http://steamworksbrewing.com, 11am-midnight Mon.-Thurs., 11am-1:30am Fri., 9am-1:30am Sat., 9am-midnight Sun., $12-29) is a warehouse-restaurant with an extensive pub-style menu of soups, salads, pizzas, and burgers, plus some chicer options like Alaskan Dungeness crab and cajun boil.

The more upscale **Ken & Sue's** (636 Main St., 970/385-1810, www.kenandsues.com, 5pm-9pm Sun.-Thurs., 5pm-10pm Fri.-Sat., $11-30) serves flavorful pasta dishes and Asian-inspired entrées like spicy stir-fry shrimp and a veggie rice bowl, as well as several fresh salads. Ken & Sue's is also well known for its specialty martinis and mouthwatering desserts.

Within walking distance of the train depot, the **Rochester Hotel** and the **Leland House**

(726 E. 2nd Ave., 970/385-1920, www.rochesterhotel.com, $199-259) are family-owned historic bed-and-breakfasts located across the street from each other. Each rooms in the Leland House is named for an historic Durangoan and is decorated with photos and memorabilia. Rooms range from standard queens to apartment-style suites with comfy living rooms with gas fireplaces. A former boarding house, the Rochester Hotel now has 15 modern suites with one king or two queen beds and private bathrooms.

Transportation and Services

From Ouray, U.S. 550 travels 70 miles south to Durango. The road has steep drop-offs not protected by guardrails; check current conditions (dial 511, www.cotrip.org).The east-west U.S. 160 connects Durango with the entrance to Mesa Verde National Park (35 miles west) and to Cortez (45 miles west).

Durango-La Plata County Airport (DRO, 1000 Airport Rd., Durango, 970/382-6050, www.flydurango.com) offers daily service by United Airlines and American Airlines, including nonstop service to Denver. Alamo, Avis, Enterprise, Hertz, and National have car rental depots at the Durango-La Plata County Airport.

the Durango & Silverton Narrow Gauge Railroad

Durango has a large **Welcome Center** (802 Main Ave., 800/525-8855, www.durango.org, 9am-7pm Sun.-Thurs., 9am-8pm Fri.-Sat.) with friendly and knowledgeable staff. The **Mercy Regional Medical Center** (1010 Three Springs Blvd., 970/247-4311, www.mercydurango.org) is Durango's main medical center.

★ MESA VERDE NATIONAL PARK

Beautiful **Mesa Verde National Park** (U.S. 160, 970/529-4465, www.nps.gov, $20 May-Oct., $15 Nov.-May) protects nearly 5,000 archaeological sites spread across a large and beautiful mesa whose higher elevations receive more precipitation than the surrounding valleys. Thanks to this increased moisture, cooler temperatures, and better soils, more pinyon and juniper trees are able to thrive here, hence the origin of the Spanish phrase, translated as green table, for which the park is named.

History

Capped by a thick layer of buff-colored sandstone, this large tableland is dissected by a series of north-south canyons that, from the air, give it a wavy appearance. About 1,400 years ago, a group of people now called the Ancestral Puebloans made their way into this region and began to farm the mesa tops and construct crude buildings. Over time, they built more elaborate structures, culminating in the spectacular cliff dwellings for which the park is known. The Puebloans built these "first neighborhoods" inside giant sandstone alcoves to protect themselves from intruders and the elements, and also to live next to springs that served as vital sources of water (and originally helped to create the alcoves). The Ancestral Puebloans flourished at Mesa Verde for about 700 years, until the late AD 1200s. Within the span of one or two generations they deserted their homes. Thanks to the natural protection in the alcoves and the arid environment, the remains of many

mesa-top sites, as well as the spectacular cliff dwellings, have been remarkably preserved, providing visitors from around the world with an evocative glimpse into the lives of the ancient people who lived here.

All of the dwellings are built of sandstone and mortar, with wooden beams for support. The Ancestral Puebloans shaped each block of sandstone using even harder stones collected from the river beds, then cemented these together with thick mortar made from a combination of soil, ash, and water. To fill in the larger gaps, the villagers used small stones, called chinks, that provided additional support. Some of the dwellings were later decorated with earth-toned plasters. The Ancestral Puebloans were constantly remodeling the tiny rooms and adding new ones.

Sights

The park's main draw is its remarkable cliff dwellings. The most spectacular of these are **Balcony House, Cliff Palace,** and **Long House,** which can only be visited on ranger-guided tours ($4). Sadly, Spruce Tree House, the park's best-preserved dwelling, remains closed due to danger from rock falls.

Tickets for each tour can be purchased in person up to two days in advance. Ticket locations include the Welcome Center (928 E. Main St., Cortez, 970/565-4048, www.colorado.com, 9am-5pm daily), the park's Morefield Ranger Station (Morefield Campground, 5pm-8:30pm daily late May-early Sept.), the park's Chapin Mesa Archeological Museum (20 miles south of park entrance, 8am-6:30pm daily early Apr.-mid-Oct.), and the **Mesa Verde Visitor and Research Center** (btw. U.S. 160 and the entrance, 7:30am-7pm daily late May-early Sept., shorter hours in winter). In addition to exhibits on the Ancestral Puebloan people, the visitor center includes a bookstore, restrooms, and free Wi-Fi.

Due to high demand during the summer, it's not always possible to visit both Balcony House and Cliff Palace on the same day. Consider staying longer, or visiting **Long**

House, the park's second-largest dwelling, instead.

If you only have half a day, I recommend driving the park road south to the Chapin Mesa area, where you can see some of the mesa-top sites at **Far View** and visit either Cliff Palace or Balcony House.

CLIFF PALACE

After living on the mesa top for nearly 600 years, the Ancestral Puebloans began building pueblos beneath the area's impressive overhanging cliffs. The structures range greatly in size, from one-room storage areas to entire villages. The largest of these is **Cliff Palace** (tours late May-mid-Sept., $4), with more than 150 rooms and 20 circular kivas, distinctive circular pits likely used for performing cultural rituals. Considering that three-quarters of the park's 600 cliff dwellings contain just 1-5 rooms, Cliff Palace is exceptionally big, a true neighborhood where an estimated 100 people once lived.

BALCONY HOUSE

With just 40 rooms, nearby **Balcony House** (tours late Apr.-Oct., $4) is an intermediate-size complex. One of the first things that you'll notice on either tour is how cramped the rooms are; the average Ancestral Puebloan male stood 5-feet 4-inches tall, and the average female about 5 feet.

To access their mesa-top gardens, the villagers used hand- and footholds carved into the sandstone, as well as tall, wooden ladders. You'll climb a 32-foot modern version of this during the Balcony House tour. This adventurous outing also involves climbing a 100-foot staircase into the canyon and clambering through a 12-foot-long, 18-inch-wide tunnel. I highly recommend it!

CHAPIN MESA
ARCHEOLOGICAL MUSEUM

The **Chapin Mesa Archeological Museum** (20 miles south of park entrance, 8am-6:30pm daily May-mid Oct., reduced hours in Oct.) makes a great first stop to view an orientation film and explore a series of educational exhibits. You can also register at the museum to hike the **Petroglyph Point Trail** (2.4 miles round-trip), which accesses close-up views of ancient rock art, including hunting scenes, spirals, and dainty handprints.

From the museum, the park road continues southwest along the six-mile **Mesa Top Loop Road** (8am-sunset daily). The scenic drive tours several overlooks and

Cliff Palace

structures, including the Sun Temple and several pithouses.

FAR VIEW SITES

A stroll to **Far View House** (1.5 miles round-trip) visits several nearby sites, including eye-catching spiral petroglyphs at the **Pipe Shrine House.** The unnamed trail is open sunrise-sunset year-round and is located four miles north of the Chapin Mesa Archeological Museum. This area also includes **Far View Lodge,** the park's only accommodations.

WETHERILL MESA

Located on the west side of the park, Wetherill Mesa is a long, protruding peninsula of land bordered by impressive canyons whose sandstone cliffs host many natural alcoves. Ancestral Puebloans took advantage of many of these landmarks to build storage buildings and homes in their protective shadows.

Long House is the park's second-largest cliff dwelling. It can only be visited as part of a two-hour, ranger-guided **tour** (purchase tickets in advance of driving out here). The tour begins at the **Wetherill Mesa Kiosk** (9am-6:30pm daily May-Sept., reduced hours Sept.-Oct.) and ends at the Long House trailhead. Excavated between 1959 and 1961, the site includes about 150 rooms and 21 kivas whose beams date as far back as AD 1145. Archaeologists believe that 150-175 people once lived beneath the shadow of its 300-foot-long alcove. Of special note is a well-preserved, triangular tower rising four stories from floor-to-ceiling at the western end of the alcove. The tour involves walking 2.5 miles and climbing two 15-foot ladders.

If you have time, take a self-guided tour to **Step House** (1 mile round-trip, 9am-4pm daily mid-May-mid-Oct.). The hike begins near Wetherill Mesa Kiosk and descends to a pithouse and some petroglyphs. Accessible from the same kiosk is the **Badger House Trail** (2.5 miles round-trip, early May-late Oct.), which visits four mesa-top sites.

Wetherill Mesa is accessed via a 27-mile drive (1.5 hours) south from the visitor center. The road is open 8am-7pm daily May-September and closes by October 31.

Food

In addition to the **Mesa Verde Metate Room Restaurant** (970/529-4422, 5pm-9:30pm daily in season, $20-32) in the Far View Lodge, there are several seasonal dining options. The casual, self-service **Far View Terrace Café** (0.25 mile south of the visitor center, 970/529-4444, 7am-8pm daily, $6) has reasonably priced food, including Navajo tacos and fresh coffee. Farther up the road, near the Chapin Mesa Archeological Museum, the **Spruce Tree Terrace Café** (970/529-4465, 9am-6:30pm daily, $6) is a convenient place to grab a bite to eat before or after your cliff dwelling tour. There's a nice outdoor patio, or you can get a picnic lunch to go. Near the Morefield Campground, the **Knife Edge Café** (800/449-2288, 7am-10am, 11am-2pm, and 4:30pm-7pm daily, $5) is best known for its pancake-and-sausage breakfasts, which are popular among campers.

Accommodations and Camping

The only lodging available in Mesa Verde National Park is the **Far View Lodge** (mile marker 15, 970/529-4421, www.visitmesaverde.com, mid-Apr.-mid-Oct., $130-202), located 15 miles up the park's only road. Of the lodge's 150 Southwestern-styled rooms, 60 include either one king or two double beds as well as a small fridge. While they lack TVs, the rooms have free Wi-Fi and sweeping views. The rates include a full breakfast, and dinner is available on-site at the contemporary Mesa Verde Metate Room Restaurant; reservations are strongly recommended.

If you prefer to sleep out under the amazingly bright stars, the 267-site **Morefield Campground** (800/449-2288, www.nps.gov, late Apr.-mid-Oct., $31) is located four miles south of the park entrance. Some sites can be reserved in advance. Amenities include flush toilets, showers, a camp store, laundry, and a dump station.

Getting There

The national park is accessed via one clearly signed road that branches south from U.S. 160 about 10 miles east of Cortez and 35 miles west of Durango. The park road travels south past the visitor center and campground, where gas is available. About 15 miles south of U.S. 160, the road splits; one branch turns west toward Wetherill Mesa, while the main road continues south to Chapin Mesa, the location of Balcony House and Cliff Palace.

Animas Transportation (2023 Main Ave., Durango, 970/259-1315, www.animas-transportation.com) will shuttle a carload to the park on a per-mile basis, which works out to about $150 one-way.

CORTEZ AND VICINITY
Anasazi Heritage Center

Located 10 miles north of Cortez, the **Anasazi Heritage Center** (27501 Hwy. 184, Dolores, 970/882-5600, www.blm.gov, 9am-5pm daily Mar.-Oct., 10am-4pm daily Nov.-Feb., $3) is a great starting point for visits to the region's many archaeological attractions. This museum tells the story of the Ancestral Puebloans, whose ancient artifacts, including sandals, baskets, pottery, tools, and art, were beautifully preserved in the region's arid climate. In addition to two 12th-century archaeological sites, the museum has exhibits on local history, more recent Native American cultures, and area attractions, as well as a half-mile nature trail and picnic area. The museum serves as the information center for **Canyons of the Ancients National Monument.**

Canyons of the Ancients National Monument

Established by presidential proclamation in 2000, **Canyons of the Ancients National Monument** (27501 Hwy. 184, Dolores, 970/882-5600, www.blm.gov, 9am-5pm daily Mar.-Oct., 10am-4pm daily Nov.-Feb., free), southwest of Cortez, is a relatively untouched wilderness of flat-topped mesas and twisting canyons whose colorful sandstone walls harbor the largest concentration of archaeological sites in the country. Most of these are Ancestral Puebloan ruins built between the 10th and 12th centuries, but the monument also includes more recent Ute and Navajo sites. The only developed area within the monument is the **Lowry Pueblo National Historic Landmark,** an intricate stone complex that includes 40 rooms and nine kivas, including the so-called Great Kiva, a round, underground chamber believed to have been

Canyons of the Ancients National Monument

Canyons of the Ancients National Monument

used by Ancestral Puebloans for spiritual rites. The monument's other main attraction is the gorgeous Sand Canyon Trail.

★ SAND CANYON TRAIL

A great way to see some of the smaller ruins and experience the beauty of the stark southwestern Colorado landscape is to hike the **Sand Canyon Trail** (6.5 miles one-way), which connects Roads N and G in the sparsely populated region southwest of Cortez. Logistically, it's easiest to drive to one of the trailheads and hike out and back, but if you have access to two vehicles, you can enjoy hiking the entire trail as a one-way route. Although the trail is relatively flat, there is one steep section of switchbacks along the trail's northern half that descends about 700 feet (from north to south) in just 0.5 mile.

From the southern trailhead in beautiful McElmo Canyon, it's just a one-mile walk to the **Saddlehorn Pueblo,** a two-room cliff dwelling tucked into a natural alcove in a large rock that looks like the horn of a saddle. This walk begins by ascending a steep slickrock slope to the left of the national monument sign. From the top, the trail bends left around a large block of rock and follows a trail marked by large cairns across the slickrock.

After a series of spur trails, you'll see the distinctive saddlehorn rock on the left, about a mile from the start. From the beams of a kiva ruin excavated here in the late 1980s (and later backfilled), archaeologists have dated its occupation to about AD 1250-1285.

To reach the southern trailhead from Cortez, drive south on Road 491. At the signs for the airport, turn right (west) on County Road G and follow it 12 miles west to the trailhead parking on a rough, slickrock surface on the north (right) side of the road directly across the street from a sign for Sutcliffe Vineyards. Regardless of how far you hike, be sure to carry plenty of water, obtain a detailed route description, and follow all BLM hiking tips and regulations.

Ute Mountain Indian Trading Company and Museum

The options for shopping are limited in this sparsely populated region, but one place worth stopping is the **Ute Mountain Indian Trading Company and Museum** (27601 E. U.S. 160, Cortez, 970/565-4492, http://ute-mountaintrading.com, 9am-6pm Mon.-Fri., 10am-5pm Sat., 10am-4pm Sun.). Owned by the Ute Mountain Ute Tribe, this large store located about a mile east of downtown

the Sand Canyon Trail

Colorado's Early Inhabitants

Saddlehorn Pueblo in Canyons of the Ancients Monument

Southwest Colorado's impressive cliff dwellings and other archaeological sites were largely built by the **Ancestral Puebloans,** the group of people who moved into and farmed in the Four Corners region prior to AD 1300. Formerly called the Anasazi, the Navajo term for ancient enemy, this culture is now more appropriately called Ancestral Puebloan, and their descendants, the Pueblo people, still live in about 20 communities in Arizona and New Mexico. The earliest traces of the cliff dwellers date to at least AD 1, and possibly as early as 1500 BC. After arriving in the Four Corners region, the Ancestral Puebloans successfully farmed the mesa tops for more than a thousand years, but completely abandoned the region around AD 1280. Once treated as a grand mystery, their departure is now believed to be the result of long-term climate change, which significantly reduced crop yields. Tree-ring records and other data indicate that several persistent drought cycles affected the region, with peaks occurring in the early 900s, early 1100s, and the late 1200s, the period that coincides with the Ancestral Puebloans' emigration from the Four Corners region.

Cortez sells contemporary handcrafted Native American pottery, jewelry, kachinas, and other knickknacks, many of which are made by tribal members. Each piece of pottery is signed and stamped with the tribal seal, and the collection includes some beautiful pieces of traditional hand-coiled pottery. As a bonus, Guy Drew Vineyards, one of Colorado's best wineries, operates a small tasting room here (2pm-6pm Tues.-Sat., free). If you prefer to see the gorgeous location where Guy Drew makes his wine, you can also visit the 155-acre vineyard and winery in McElmo Canyon, **Guy Drew Vineyards** (19891 Road G, Cortez, 970/565-9211, www.guydrewvineyards.com, noon-5pm daily, free).

Food

Cortez has a number of surprisingly good places to eat; most are in the intimate downtown area centered on U.S. 160. For excellent Mexican food, head to **Pepperhead Restaurant** (44 W. Main St., 970/565-3303, www.pepperheadcortez.com, 11:30am-8:30pm Tues.-Sat., $8-13). The moniker comes from a person who, like the father-daughter team that owns the place, is obsessed with chile peppers. The house specialties include mole chicken, Pepperhead steak, and flavorful chile rellenos bursting with cheese. Just across the street, the Main Street Brewery (21 E. Main St., 970/564-9112, www.mainstreetbrewerycortez.com, 3:30pm-close Mon.-Thurs., 11:30am-close Fri.-Sun., $6-26) serves up juicy, hand-cut steaks, fresh salads, and thick cheeseburgers in a historic building with a tin ceiling and colorful wall murals.

A mile to the east, Thai Cortez (1430 E. Main St., 970/564-3151, 11:30am-2:30pm and 4:30pm-9pm Mon.-Sat., $12-18) has a long list of lunch specials plus pad Thai and savory seafood and meat dishes like *gang peth ped yang,* roasted duck and veggies in a Thai red curry sauce.

Accommodations

In downtown Cortez, the best lodging options are all chain hotels, particularly the Hampton Inn (2244 E. Hawkins St., 970/564-5924, http://hamptoninn3.hilton.com, $169) and the Holiday Inn Express (2121 E. Main St., 970/565-6000, www.ihg.com, $143-168), both located next to U.S. 160, the main road through town.

Although they're located farther afield, there are some more distinctive accommodations in the area that are worth seeking out. These include the unique Kelly Place Bed and Breakfast (14537 Road G, Cortez, 970/565-3125, www.kellyplace.com, $125-160), a 38-acre estate of peaceful gardens and fruit orchards planted among 25 carefully documented prehistoric archaeological sites, including a nicely preserved kiva. You can stay in a basic, comfortable lodge room, rent a cabin, or pitch your tent on the grounds, and there is hiking and guided horseback rides into beautiful Canyons of the Ancients National Monument right out the back door.

The area's most luxurious accommodations can be found at Canyons of the Ancients Guest Ranch (7950 Road G, Cortez, 970/565-4288, http://canyonoftheancients.com, $190-365 per night, plus a surcharge for one-night stays), which has four beautifully appointed houses ranging from a cowboy log cabin to a Pueblo-style adobe abode. Decorated with Southwestern flair, the units house 2-5 people and can be rented by the weekend, week, or even longer stays.

Transportation and Services

To reach Cortez from the Durango-La Plata Airport, head north on Airport Road. After 0.75 mile, turn left onto Road 172 and follow this north for 5.5 miles to U.S. 160. Turn left onto U.S. 160 and follow it west about 52 miles through Durango to Cortez. The 60-mile trip takes about an hour to drive.

From Telluride, Road 145 leads to Cortez and the Four Corners area in about 80 miles (1.5 hours).

There is a large Colorado Welcome Center (928 E. Main St., Cortez, 970/565-4048, www.colorado.com, 9am-5pm daily) staffed by a cadre of friendly volunteers.

The closest hospital for emergency care is Southwest Memorial Hospital (1311 N. Mildred Rd., Cortez, 970/565-6666, http://swhealth.org), which also offers walk-in care (8am-8pm Mon.-Fri., 8am-4pm Sat.).

HOVENWEEP NATIONAL MONUMENT

Stretching along the Colorado-Utah border, Hovenweep National Monument (970/562-4282, www.nps.gov, free) encompasses six prehistoric villages built between AD 1200 and 1300 that collectively housed more than 2,500 people. Located in the beautiful canyon country accessed via the western side of McElmo Canyon, southwest of Cortez, the monument includes several separate park service units. The monument's name comes from the Ute word for deserted valley and is best known for its impressive and unusual towers, which the ancients built in a variety of square, circular, oval, and D shapes. Archaeologists speculate that these may have been used as celestial observatories, or perhaps defensive structures, homes, or more mundane storage facilities. Discovered in 1854 by a Mormon explorer, the ruins weren't protected until President

Warren G. Harding declared them a national monument in 1923.

Sights

The ruins are spread out, so it's a good idea to stop by the **visitor center** (8am-6pm daily May-Sept., reduced hours in off-season) in Utah for maps and information. The visitor center is located within the Square Tower Unit, which consists of a group of structures built on the rim of a beautiful sandstone canyon. A great way to explore this unit is by walking the **Rim Trail Loop** (1.5 miles). The route circles the head of Little Ruin Canyon, passing a number of interesting structures. The **Stronghold House** is named for its imposing, fortress-like appearance. The Ancestral Puebloans climbed up to the house via tiny hand- and footholds chipped into the rock. The carefully constructed **Twin Towers** once hosted 16 rooms in two towers, one of which was horseshoe-shaped. The most impressive site is **Hovenweep Castle,** located a short walk from the visitor center. The structure has two distinctive, D-shaped towers made of carefully hewn stones that required considerable skill to make. The tree rings on a wooden beam found in one of the towers has been dated to AD 1277, making this one of the last structures built in the region before the people left.

Camping

A small, year-round **campground** ($10 per site) is located near the visitor center. Only a few of the 31 sites can accommodate RVs, and there are no hookups. All sites are assigned on a first-come, first-served basis. Amenities are limited to tent pads, picnic tables with shade structures, and fire rings, plus flush toilets and running water. Limited amounts of drinking water are only available during summer.

Getting There

To reach the Hovenweep visitor center from Cortez, head west on Main Street to the junction with Broadway (U.S. 491). Turn right and follow U.S. 491 North for about 19 miles. Turn left onto BB Road and follow it west for six miles to its junction with County Road 10. Turn left to head southwest on County Road 10 for about 20 miles, crossing into Utah en route. At the junction with Road 268A, turn left and follow 268A for half a mile to the visitor center.

FOUR CORNERS MONUMENT

The official **Four Corners Monument** (U.S. 160 about 38 miles south of Cortez, 928/206-2540, www.navajonationparks.org, 8am-8pm daily late May-mid-Sept., reduced hours in off-season, $5) marks the only spot in the United States where four states—Colorado, New Mexico, Arizona, and Utah—come together. It's a neat geographic site surrounded by a large circle of stalls where members of the Navajo tribe, to whom this land belongs, hawk turquoise jewelry and other Native American-style wares.

To get to the monument from Cortez, head west on Main Street to the junction with Broadway (U.S. 160/U.S. 491). Turn left and follow U.S. 160 south for about 39 miles, veering west to remain on U.S. 160 where U.S. 491 branches off. At the junction with Highway 597 in New Mexico, turn right and follow Highway 597 north for about half a mile to the tribal park entrance.

Colorado Springs and the Southeast

C olorado's extensive southeastern corner is home to Colorado Springs, the state's second-largest city, and its most prominent and best-known landmark— Pikes Peak.

Named for the intrepid explorer Zebulon Montgomery Pike, one of the first Caucasians to explore this region, the peak is also called America's Mountain due to the inspiration it gave Katharine Lee Bates, an English professor from Wellesley College who composed the stirring lyrics of "America the Beautiful" while gazing at the breathtaking views from its lofty summit. From spacious skies and purple mountain majesty to the endless, fruitful plains, this region exemplifies the splendor that she so poetically described in this patriotic song.

Perhaps as a reflection of this dramatic landscape, many notable historic events have unfolded across southeastern Colorado, from the westward migration of pioneers along the legendary Santa Fe Trail to the discovery of gold in the region's cold, clear streams, an event that sparked the Pikes Peak Gold Rush, one of the most significant migrations in our continent's history. From frontiersmen like Kit Carson to dauntless entrepreneurs, the people who arrived in Colorado during this time laid the foundations for most of our towns and cities and sparked our evolution from wilderness to statehood.

Today, a tangible trace of the Wild West lives on across this region, blended with an irresistible infusion of the Centennial State's warm hospitality, first-rate amenities, and vibrant recreational activities. Within half a day's drive, you can visit a historic fort or the restored brick buildings in the old territorial capital; you can ascend Pikes Peak or paddle a rubber raft through some of the nation's best-known white-water rapids; and you can marvel at ancient petrified redwood stumps or gaze into the depths of the Royal Gorge from one of the world's highest suspension bridges. No matter what you do or where you go, you'll relish the stunning natural beauty that inspired Bates and so many other people.

Previous: Pikes Peak as seen from Garden of the Gods; hiking above the Arkansas Valley.
Above: Old Colorado City.

Look for ★ to find recommended
sights, activities, dining, and lodging.

Highlights

★ **The Broadmoor:** This Italian Renaissance-style resort boasts three golf courses, its own lake, an award-winning spa, 18 restaurants, 25 shops, and nearly 800 well-appointed rooms (page 355).

★ **Red Rock Canyon Open Space:** Explore a series of red rock canyons below Pikes Peak (page 357).

★ **Garden of the Gods:** The park's dramatically tilted rock fins are accessible via horseback, hiking, climbing, or a gorgeous scenic drive (page 364).

★ **Pikes Peak:** Ascend the breathtaking summit of North America's most-visited mountain (page 369).

★ **National Mining Hall of Fame and Museum:** This captivating museum highlights mining's important societal role across the country (page 373).

★ **Hot Springs:** Soak to your heart's content in one of the Arkansas River Valley's rejuvenating hot springs (page 375).

★ **White-Water Rafting and Kayaking:** The Arkansas River has a wide variety of white-water runs through spectacular scenery (page 377).

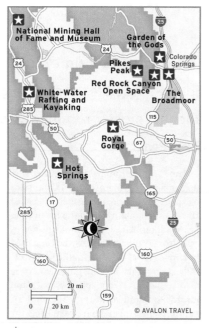

★ **Royal Gorge:** The sheer walls of this breathtaking gorge rise 1,250 feet above the Arkansas River (page 381).

Colorado Springs and the Southeast

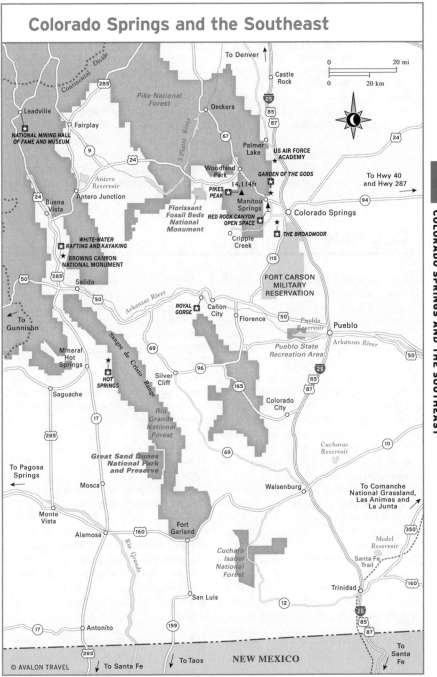

To Denver

Castle Rock

0   20 mi
0   20 km

Continental Divide

Pike National Forest

Deckers

Leadville

NATIONAL MINING HALL OF FAME AND MUSEUM

Fairplay

Palmer Lake

US AIR FORCE ACADEMY

GARDEN OF THE GODS

To Hwy 40 and Hwy 287

Woodland Park

Antero Reservoir

PIKES PEAK
14,114ft

Manitou Springs

Colorado Springs

Buena Vista

Antero Junction

Florissant Fossil Beds National Monument

RED ROCK CANYON OPEN SPACE

THE BROADMOOR

Cripple Creek

WHITE-WATER RAFTING AND KAYAKING

BROWNS CANYON NATIONAL MONUMENT

Salida

FORT CARSON MILITARY RESERVATION

To Gunnison

Arkansas River

ROYAL GORGE

Cañon City

Florence

Pueblo Reservoir

Pueblo

Mineral Hot Springs

HOT SPRINGS

Silver Cliff

Pueblo State Recreation Area

Arkansas River

Saguache

Rio Grande National Forest

Colorado City

Sangre de Cristo Range

Cucharas Reservoir

Great Sand Dunes National Park and Preserve

To Pagosa Springs

Mosca

Walsenburg

To Comanche National Grassland, Las Animas and La Junta

Monte Vista

Model Reservoir

Alamosa

Fort Garland

Cuchara Isabel National Forest

Santa Fe Trail

Trinidad

Rio Grande

San Luis

To Taos

Antonito

To Santa Fe

To Santa Fe

NEW MEXICO

To Santa Fe

© AVALON TRAVEL

PLANNING YOUR TIME

A **couple of days** will be enough to enjoy a few of the highlights in and around Colorado Springs, including Pikes Peak and Garden of the Gods, although you'll surely wish you had longer to linger. To go white-water rafting, hiking, or to visit some of the region's rich historic sites, you'll want at least **four days**—two to explore Colorado Springs and two to venture farther afield.

During the **summer**, the hot days are ideal for white-water rafting, hiking, cycling, and ascending the summit of Pikes Peak or one of the region's other high peaks.

In **winter**, the weather is cold and sometimes stormy, but you may also be treated to gorgeous sights like freshly fallen snow glistening on the brick-red rocks in Red Rock Canyon Open Space, or the stunning fireworks display set off from the top of Pikes Peak each New Year's Eve.

The months of **September** and **October** are ideal times to visit; there are fewer crowds at the major attractions, colorful fall displays, and seemingly endless comfortable, sunny days. However, an occasional blizzard can disrupt transportation any time from late fall until early May.

Colorado Springs

Located about an hour south of Denver, the Springs, as Colorado's second-largest city is often called, is a rapidly growing metropolis of about 650,000 people. Since its founding in 1871 by General William Jackson Palmer, co-owner of the predecessor to the Union Pacific Railroad, Colorado Springs has maintained strong military ties. Following the attack on Pearl Harbor, the city donated 137,000 acres along its southern border to the federal government to build Fort Carson, which remains an important military facility. More installations soon opened. In 1954, the U.S. Air Force Academy opened northwest of town followed a dozen years later by the North American Aerospace Defense Command (NORAD), whose early-warning system tracks flights within U.S. and Canadian airspace—including Santa Claus every Christmas Eve.

A regionally important economic engine and a great source of local pride, this heavy military presence gives Colorado Springs a generally more conservative outlook than Denver and other Front Range communities. It also offers unique attractions, such as the U.S. Olympic Training Center, a converted Air Force base that serves as an important preparation facility for rising athletes.

Downtown Colorado Springs is centered around a square east of I-25 between Monument Creek and the Platte, Colorado, and Wahsatch Avenues. This includes Acacia Park, which was established in 1871 on land donated by General William Jackson Palmer. Colorado College, a private liberal arts school, is located less than one mile north of the park. The Garden of the Gods and The Broadmoor are scattered along the west side of the interstate and along U.S. 24.

SIGHTS

Colorado Springs Fine Arts Center

The centerpiece of the **Colorado Springs Fine Arts Center** (30 W. Dale St., 719/634-5581, www.csfineartscenter.org, 10am-5pm Tues.-Sun., $10) is an excellent art museum that features exhibits by nationally and internationally renowned artists like Salvador Dalí and rock musician photographer Larry Hulst. A permanent collection showcases works by luminaries like Ansel Adams and Georgia O'Keeffe.

U.S. Olympic Training Center

This large 35-acre complex in the heart of Colorado Springs is the flagship training

Colorado Springs

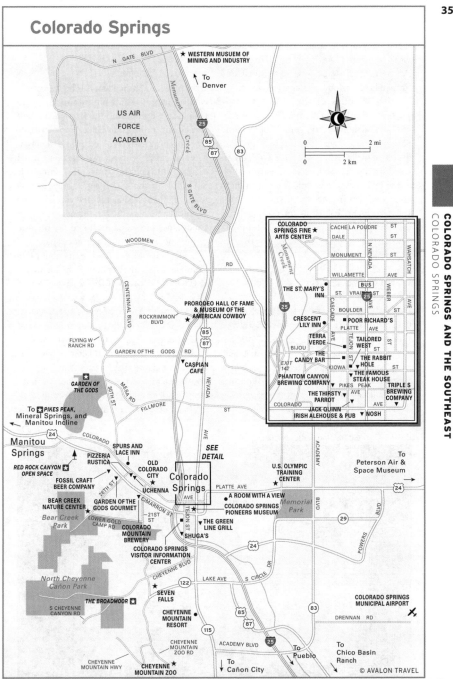

★ WESTERN MUSUEM OF MINING AND INDUSTRY

N GATE BLVD

↑ To Denver

US AIR FORCE ACADEMY

25

85

87

83

0   2 mi

0   2 km

Monument Creek

S GATE BLVD

WOODMEN RD

CENTENNIAL BLVD

PRORODEO HALL OF FAME & MUSEUM OF THE AMERICAN COWBOY ★

ROCKRIMMON BLVD

FLYING W RANCH RD

GARDEN OF THE GODS RD

CASPIAN CAFE ▼

★ GARDEN OF THE GODS

To ★ PIKES PEAK, Mineral Springs, and Manitou Incline ←

30TH ST

MESA RD

NEVADA AVE

FILLMORE ST

85 87

DETAIL INSET:

COLORADO SPRINGS FINE ★ ARTS CENTER

CACHE LA POUDRE ST

DALE ST

Monument Creek

MONUMENT ST

N NEVADA

WAHSATCH

WILLAMETTE AVE

THE ST. MARY'S INN ★

BUS 25

VRAIN ST

WEBER

AVE

CASCADE

25

BOULDER ST

CRESCENT LILY INN ■

■ POOR RICHARD'S

PLATTE AVE

TERRA VERDE ▼

AVE

TEJON

TAILORED WEST ■ ST

BIJOU

EXIT 142

THE CANDY BAR ▼

■ ST

KIOWA

■ THE RABBIT HOLE

THE FAMOUS STEAK HOUSE ▼

ST

PHANTOM CANYON BREWING COMPANY ▼

PIKES PEAK

TRIPLE S BREWING COMPANY ▼

THE THIRSTY PARROT ▼

AVE

COLORADO

AVE

JACK QUINN IRISH ALEHOUSE & PUB ▼

▼ NOSH

SEE DETAIL

Manitou Springs

24

COLORADO

RED ROCK CANYON OPEN SPACE ■

SPURS AND LACE INN ■

PIZZERIA RUSTICA ▼

OLD COLORADO CITY ★

26TH ST

FOSSIL CRAFT BEER COMPANY

BEAR CREEK NATURE CENTER ★

GARDEN OF THE GODS GOURMET ★

UCHENNA ▼

Colorado Springs

CIMARRON ST

LOWER GOLD CAMP RD

21ST ST

COLORADO MOUNTAIN BREWERY ▼

COLORADO SPRINGS VISITOR INFORMATION CENTER ★

Bear Creek Park

ACADEMY

U.S. OLYMPIC TRAINING CENTER

PLATTE AVE

AVE

● A ROOM WITH A VIEW

● COLORADO SPRINGS PIONEERS MUSEUM

TEJON ST

▼ THE GREEN LINE GRILL

SHUGA'S ▼

Memorial Park

BLVD

24

To Peterson Air & Space Museum →

24

29

POWERS BLVD

North Cheyenne Cañon Park

CHEYENNE BLVD

LAKE AVE

S CIRCLE DR

122

SEVEN FALLS ▼

THE BROADMOOR ■

S CHEYENNE CANYON RD

CHEYENNE MOUNTAIN RESORT

115

85 87

COLORADO SPRINGS MUNICIPAL AIRPORT

DRENNAN RD

✈

CHEYENNE MOUNTAIN HWY

CHEYENNE MOUNTAIN ZOO RD

CHEYENNE MOUNTAIN ZOO ★

ACADEMY BLVD

25

To ↓ Cañon City

To Pueblo →

To Chico Basin Ranch

© AVALON TRAVEL

center of the U.S. Olympic Committee. A visitor center features a rotunda with large screens that display an inspiring "Olympic Moments" video and rotating exhibits on Olympic and Paralympic athletes who have lived and trained here, including Michael Phelps.

Official tours of the **U.S. Olympic Training Center** (1 Olympic Plaza, 719/866-4618, www.teamusa.org, 9am-4:30pm Mon.-Sat. June-mid-Aug., 9am-4pm Mon.-Sat. mid-Aug.-May, $12) begin with a video narrated by NBC's Bob Costas. The film is followed by a visit to the center's main strength and conditioning area and several of the sports centers. Facilities on the tour may include the wrestling, shooting, and men's gymnastics areas, as well as one of the two enormous pools.

Colorado Springs Pioneers Museum

Housed in the former El Paso County Courthouse, the **Colorado Springs Pioneers Museum** (215 S. Tejon St., 719/385-5990, www.cspm.org, 10am-5pm Tues.-Sat., free) has a number of interesting exhibits. Learn about the "rich" history of the Pikes Peak region—from the mining and pioneer days to more recent events like the devastating

2012 Waldo Canyon Fire and the grueling Pikes Peak Marathon.

Old Colorado City History Center

Originally established as a mining camp just east of an important mountain pass, Old Colorado City became the first permanent settlement in the Pikes Peak region in 1859. The town quickly evolved into a regional economic hub, with a glass works, railroad offices, four gold ore mills, and numerous bars and brothels. During its heyday, the town briefly served as the first capital of the Territory of Colorado, but the nearby city of Colorado Springs soon eclipsed the historic center and, in 1917, finally annexed it.

Today, visitors can learn more about Old Colorado City's most famous faces and places at the **Old Colorado City History Center** (1 S. 24th St., 719/636-1225, www.occhs.org, 11am-4pm Tues.-Sat. May-Sept., 11am-4pm Thurs.-Sat. Oct.-Dec., 11am-2pm Thurs.-Sat. Jan.-Apr., free), which also offers a free tour of this National Historical District. The four blocks of narrow alleyways, quaint galleries, boutiques, and restaurants are located in attractive brick buildings centered around inviting Bancroft Park. Community events include

the U.S. Olympic Training Center visitor center

Today, the large complex of multi-storied, red-roofed buildings surrounds manicured lawns and an artificial lake. Hour-long **tours** (10:30am Tues., Thurs., and Sat., free) are open to guests and non-guests and meet at the concierge office next to the hotel bar.

The Broadmoor is located south of Colorado Springs off Cheyenne Boulevard.

The Broadmoor

Seven Falls

Seven Falls (6 Lake Ave., 719/476-6700, www.broadmoor.com, 9am-8pm daily, $14) refers to a series of cascading waterfalls located at the back of a narrow, 1,250-foot deep canyon. After parking in the complimentary lot, visitors are shuttled to the entrance. From there, it's just a short tram ride ($1) or a 0.8-mile uphill walk to the base of the tiered, 181-foot-high fall located beneath twin rock formations called the Pillars of Hercules. Even better views, and several other hikes, are available from the top of a series of 224 stairs.

Cheyenne Mountain Zoo

The **Cheyenne Mountain Zoo** (4250 Cheyenne Mountain Zoo Rd., 719/633-9925, www.cmzoo.org, 9am-5pm daily, $19.75) houses some 750 animals, including 30 endangered species. Exhibits range from the African Rift Valley—home to giraffes, meerkats, zebras, and African lions—to Rocky Mountain Wild, where moose, mountain lions, and gray wolves are on display. Other attractions include a 1937 carousel and the Mountaineer Sky Ride ($5), an open-air chairlift that offers aerial views of the zoo, the city, and the plains to the east. Also on-site is the **Will Rogers Shrine of the Sun,** an 80-foot-high stone observation tower built of native stone and crowned with a turret.

The zoo is located seven miles south of downtown Colorado Springs on the slopes of Cheyenne Mountain.

seasonal festivities, the free Old West-themed **Territory Days** (Memorial Day weekend), and **First Friday ArtWalks** (5pm-8pm Fri. Aug.-early Dec.).

★ The Broadmoor

Known as "the Grand Dame of the Rockies," **The Broadmoor** (1 Lake Ave., 719/634-7711, www.broadmoor.com) is more of an experience than a luxury hotel. Built by Spencer Rose (an entrepreneur who made a fortune in the rich gold fields of nearby Cripple Creek), the original 1918 Italian Renaissance-style building cost $2 million—a fortune at the time. Rose's goal was to design the finest hotel in the United States and he spared no expense, hiring the nation's top architects, landscapers, and golf course designers. He even dismantled and relocated an English pub to the hotel's interior. In order to create an entire guest experience, he also incorporated one of the nation's first full-service spas, a shooting school, a polo field and riding arena, and even an airport hangar into the facilities.

ProRodeo Hall of Fame and Museum of the American Cowboy

The world's only museum dedicated solely

to the sport of rodeo is the **ProRodeo Hall of Fame and Museum of the American Cowboy** (101 Pro Rodeo Dr., 719/528-4764, www.prorodeohalloffame.com, 9am-5pm daily May-Aug., 9am-5pm Wed.-Sun. Sept.-Apr., $7). The Hall of Champions features more than 275 bareback riders, calf ropers, and steer wrestlers, as well as famous stock contractors, rodeo clowns, and 28 legendary animals, including Necktie. (The notorious bucking bronc was immortalized near the museum's entrance in a bronze statue on whose back Casey Tibbs, the "Babe Ruth of Rodeo," is valiantly trying to remain seated.) Museum exhibits on cowboy gear change annually. Live roping events occur May-October.

Western Museum of Mining and Industry

The exhibits at the award-winning **Western Museum of Mining and Industry** (225 N. Gate Blvd., 719/488-0880, www.wmmi.org, 9am-4pm Mon.-Sat., $9) will transport you back to the 19th century, when mining underpinned much of the western U.S. economy. Twice-daily tours are included with admission and detail how various minerals are produced. Exhibits include a jaw

crusher, a 35-ton Corliss steam engine, and an old stamp mill. Also on-site are Nugget and Chism, two burros whose ancestors once helped prospectors haul valuable gold ore.

U.S. Air Force Academy

The **U.S. Air Force Academy** (www.usafa. af.mil) is the youngest of the military's five academic institutions. The gorgeous campus spans 18,500 acres; currently, only a small portion is open to visitors.

The **Barry Goldwater Air Force Academy Visitor Center** (2346 Academy Dr., 719/333-2025, 9am-5pm daily, free) features historical exhibits on the academy's former and current superintendents, a movie showcasing the cadet experience, and a snack bar and gift shop. From the visitor center, walk along a short nature trail to view the academy's iconic **Cadet Chapel** (719/333-4515, 9am-5pm Mon.-Sat., 1pm-5pm Sun.), a striking aluminum and glass triangular structure supported by 17 tall spires. The building houses four chapels, each with separate entrances, plus an all-faiths room to accommodate cadets of different religions. The Field House and Falcon Athletic Center, the Arnold Hall

the U.S. Air Force Academy's Cadet Chapel

student center, and the Honor Court (between Arnold Hall and the chapel) are usually open to visitors. Weather permitting, you can also view the **Cadet Lunch Formation** (11:30am-noon Mon.-Fri. mid-Aug.-mid-May).

The academy is located eight miles northwest of Colorado Springs on I-25. Visitors may only enter the campus via the North Gate (follow the signs on I-25). If you'd rather not drive, **Gray Line of Denver** (800/472-9546, www.grayline.com, $140) offers all-day tours to the academy, Garden of the Gods, and the top of Pikes Peak from Denver.

SPORTS AND RECREATION

An extensive network of local parks, Pike National Forest (www.fs.usda.gov), and private attractions offer ample opportunities for hiking, biking, horseback riding, and rock climbing.

Hiking and Biking

To rent a mountain or road bike, stop by **Ted's Bicycles** (3016 N. Hancock Ave., 719/473-6915, www.tedsbicycles.com, 9am-6pm Mon.-Sat., $20-45 for 6 hours).

★ RED ROCK CANYON OPEN SPACE

Red Rock Canyon Open Space (3550 W. High St., http://redrockcanyonopenspace.org, dawn-dusk daily, free) preserves a network of easy trails that explore a series of beautiful red rock canyons nestled below Pikes Peak. The nearly-1,500-acre parcel is popular with hikers, bikers, rock climbers, and runners for its serene Southwestern slickrock and wonderful views.

A fantastic three-mile loop begins at the Ridge Road/U.S. 24 parking area. Start on the **Contemplative Trail**, which climbs gradually between two sandstone ridges. At the trail junction after 1.1 miles, turn east onto the **Quarry Pass Trail.** Near the end of the trail, you will walk through an old quarry, where blocks of 250-million-year-old sandstone were cut to erect many of the historic buildings in Old Colorado City. After descending steps carved into the red rock, turn left to follow the **Red Rock Canyon Trail** to the parking lot. Head left (west) around the Lower Dog Loop and the mountain bike area to return to the trailhead.

To reach the trailhead from Colorado Springs, take I-25 to Exit 145 and head west on Fillmore Street (which turns into Fontmore

an old quarry in Red Rock Canyon Open Space

Road, and then West Fontanero Street). In 2.5 miles, turn left onto North 31st Street and continue 0.7 mile. Turn right onto U.S. 24 and drive west for 0.6 mile. Turn left onto Ridge Road and continue to the parking area on the left.

BEAR CREEK REGIONAL PARK
Stretching along its namesake creek, the **Bear Creek Regional Park** (245 Bear Creek Rd., 719/520-6387, http://adm.elpasoco.com, 5am-11pm daily, free) has picnic pavilions, playgrounds, and horseshoe and volleyball courts, as well as 10 miles of family-friendly hiking and biking trails. The on-site **Bear Creek Nature Center** (9am-4pm Tues.-Sat.) hosts displays about the short grass prairie, streamside riparian, and scrub oak woodland ecosystems and the diversity of animals who live here.

To get here, take U.S. 24 west to 21st Street. Turn south on 21st Street and continue to the nature center.

NORTH CHEYENNE CAÑON PARK
Known for its evergreen forest and graceful waterfalls, the 1,600-acre **North Cheyenne Cañon Park** (2120 S. Cheyenne Cañon Rd., 719/385-6086, http://cheyennecanon.org, free) is home to half a dozen trails. From the **Helen Hunt Falls Visitor Center** (9am-5pm daily June-Aug., 5am-11pm daily May-Oct., 5am-9pm daily Nov.-Apr., free), follow the short 0.3-mile (one-way) trail to Helen Hunt and Silver Cascade Falls. Longer routes include the **Columbine Trail** (4 miles one-way), which climbs 1,000 feet from the **Starsmore Discovery Center** (9am-5pm daily June-Aug., 9am-3pm Tues.-Sat. Apr.-May and Sept.-Oct., free) near the park entrance.

To get to the park from downtown Colorado Springs, head south on Nevada Avenue to Cheyenne Boulevard. Turn west onto Cheyenne Boulevard and follow it until it becomes North Cheyenne Cañon Road at the discovery center.

Golf
The Broadmoor Golf Club (1 Lake Ave., 719/577-5790, www.broadmoor.com, $140-280) offers its club members and guests three championship courses designed by the likes of Arnold Palmer and Robert Trent Jones Sr. All courses feature gorgeous views and challenging greens that are notoriously difficult to read. Players are required to hire a caddie or rent a cart when playing before 2pm (May-Oct.).

Local public courses include the **Antler Creek Golf Course** (9650 Antler Creek Dr., 719/494-1900, www.antlercreekgolf.com, $42-52), Colorado's longest course; the city's par-72 **Patty Jewett Golf Course** (900 E. Espanola St., 719/385-6950, https://parks.coloradosprings.gov, $29-31); and the nine-hole **Cherokee Ridge Golf Course** (1850 Tuskegee Pl., 719/597-2637, www.cherokeeridgegolfcourse.com, $29).

Horseback Riding
Colorado Springs is surrounded by a number of ranches, many of which offer trail rides and other adventures. Family-owned **Old Stage Riding Stables** (6620 Old Stage Rd., 719/448-0371, www.comtnadventure.com, $49 for 1 hour) offers children's pony rides, 1-2-hour trail rides, and biking packages. The working **Chico Basin Ranch** (22500 Peyton Hwy. S., 719/683-7960, www.chicobasinranch.com) has a "ranch experience" program in which people with prior riding experience can participate in daily ranch activities.

ENTERTAINMENT AND EVENTS
Bars and Clubs
Owned by four Air Force Academy graduates, **Jack Quinn Irish Alehouse & Pub** (21 S. Tejon St., 719/385-0766, www.jackquinnspub.com, 11am-close daily) is a favorite spot for military personnel and is a hangout for the local running club. The pub serves up foaming glasses of Guinness and English Young's double chocolate stout, as well as a long list

of European and American beers. The requisite fish and chips and other pub grub fills the menu. **The Thirsty Parrot** (32 S. Tejon St., 719/360-3333, https://thirstyparrotcos.com, 4pm-2am Tues.-Sat.) is known for its extralong happy hour (4pm-7pm Tues.-Sat.) and a Caribbean-themed menu that includes hot wings, volcano nachos, and parrot fries.

For an upscale option, disappear down **The Rabbit Hole** (101 N. Tejon St., 719/203-5072, www.rabbitholedinner.com, 4pm-1:30am daily), a chic underground bar that once served as the county morgue. It is now a cozy red-brick and gleaming wood establishment known for craft cocktails and an *Alice-in-Wonderland* Eat Me menu.

Breweries

Colorado Springs is home to two dozen breweries, many of which offer occasional tours and tastings. **Triple S Brewing Company** (318 E. Colorado Ave., 719/344-5477, http://triplesbrewing.com, 11am-10pm Tues.-Sat., noon-8pm Sun.) is owned by an Army special forces officer-turned-brewer. The Triple S stands for sip, savor, and stay, which you'll surely do after tasting one (or more) of the American-style ales served by friendly "beeristas."

Phantom Canyon Brewing Company (2 E. Pikes Peak Ave., 719/635-2800, www.phantomcanyon.com, 11am-2am Mon.-Sat., 10am-2am Sun.) is known for its creative craft concoctions. **Fossil Craft Beer Company** (2845 Ore Mill Rd. #1, 719/375-8298, www.fossilbrewing.com, 2pm-10pm Mon. and Wed.-Fri., noon-10pm Sat., noon-7pm Sun.) is a taproom in Old Colorado City known for its three flagship beers: Evolution Ale, Mammoth India Pale Ale, and Stone Age Stout.

Live Music

The **Zodiac Venue** (230 Pueblo Ave., 719/632-5059, http://zodiacvenue.com, hours and prices vary) is an eclectic downtown bar that features open mic nights and a diverse lineup of live entertainment—from comedy to punk to jazz. Considered Colorado Springs'

best live music venue, **Black Sheep** (2106 E. Platte Ave., 719/227-7625, hours and prices vary) has a loyal following for what it describes as a "cutting-edge punk & indie-rock vibe & graffiti art" atmosphere.

For those interested in the performing arts, **The Mezzanine** (20 N. Tejon St., 719/577-4556, www.themezzcos.com, hours and prices vary) features artists from around the world performing classical music, full-length musicals, jazz, and operas, as well as dramas.

Festivals and Events

In keeping with its Wild West history and ranching roots, Colorado Springs sponsors a **Summer Rodeo Series** (1045 Lower Gold Camp Rd., 800/755-0935, www.cosrodeo.com, mid-June-mid-Aug., $22) at the Norris-Penrose Event Center. The **Pikes Peak or Bust Rodeo Days** (1045 Lower Gold Camp Rd., www.pikespeakorbust.org, July, $34-46) starts with a parade followed by four days of rodeo performances. The last day features evening championship competitions in bareback riding, barrel racing, and bronc and bull riding.

Held on the twisting Pikes Peak Highway, the **Pikes Peak International Hill Climb** (1631 Mesa Ave., Suite E, 719/685-4400, www.ppihc.com, June, $60-70) is the nation's second-oldest motor sports race. The **Pikes Peak Ascent and Marathon** (441 Manitou Ave., Ste. 100, Manitou Springs, 719/473-2625, www.pikespeakmarathon.org, Aug.) is the taxing foot race up (and back down) the mountain.

SHOPPING

Colorado Springs' best shopping districts are the bustling downtown and a cluster of galleries and indie stores in the quaintly restored Old Colorado City.

Art Galleries

Old Colorado City hosts the city's highest concentration of art galleries. A great place to browse their tremendous diversity is along Colorado Avenue between 27th and 23rd Streets. You'll find the **Hunter-Wolff**

Gallery (2510 W. Colorado Ave., 719/520-9494, www.hunterwolffgallery.com, 11am-5pm Sun.-Thurs., 11am-7pm Fri.-Sat.), which features American-made, museum-quality fine arts in 20 mediums—from oil and watercolor paintings to raku. One block away, **The Michael Garman Museum and Gallery** (2418 W. Colorado Ave., 719/471-9391, www.michaelgarman.com, 10am-5:30pm daily) is a Western-themed gallery featuring Garman's striking sculptures. It's worth stopping by just to see his Magic Town, a miniature "everyday city neighborhood" whose 18 buildings are filled with detailed sculptures.

The **Laura Reilly Fine Art Gallery** (2522A W. Colorado Ave., 719/650-1427, www.laurareilly.com, 11:30am-5:30pm Thurs.-Sat. and by appointment) features beautiful landscapes from one of the city's best-known painters. Just a few blocks east, the **Cucuru Gallery Café** (2332 W. Colorado Ave., 719/520-9900, www.cucurucafe.net, 11am-8pm Mon.-Wed., 11am-9pm Thurs. and Sun., 11am-11pm Fri.-Sat.) bills itself as the place "where people meet the arts." Part restaurant and part gallery, this family-owned and -operated business features five art-filled rooms, plus a large patio ideal for summer happy hours (3pm-6pm Mon.-Fri.).

Books

For a good selection of locally oriented reading materials, visit **Poor Richard's** (320 N. Tejon St., 719/578-5549, http://poorrichards.biz, 9am-9pm daily) in downtown Colorado Springs. The bookstore also features a restaurant, wine bar, and toy store. On the western edge of Old Colorado City, **The Bookman** (3163 W. Colorado Ave., 719/636-0055, 10am-7pm Mon.-Sat., 10am-5pm Sun.) is crammed with a huge selection of books ranging from science and philosophy to New Age.

Clothing

Tailored West (103 N. Tejon St., 719/371-2244, www.tailoredwest.com, 10am-6pm Mon.-Wed., 10am-8pm Thurs.-Sat.) focuses on American-made, Western-inspired

clothing for both women and men. The downtown store has an extensive selection of footwear, especially cowboy boots, and American-made silk blouses, lace tunics, and designer jeans from Scully, Elietian, Tin Haul, and their in-house brand, Ver'e'ne. A fun downtown boutique is **Terra Verde** (208 N. Tejon St., 719/444-8621, http://terraverdestyle.com, 10am-6pm Mon.-Sat., 11pm-4pm Sun.), which specializes in contemporary women's clothing and beautiful jewelry, including sparkling Adesso copper earrings and elaborate necklaces from Ayalabar.

Gourmet Goodies

Kids will love **The Candy Bar** (124 N. Tejon St., 719/434-7325, 10am-9pm Mon.-Sat., 11am-7pm Sun.), a colorful downtown shop bursting with bottles of old-fashioned soda pop, hand-dipped chocolates, and bins of bulk candy in every shape and flavor.

FOOD
Breakfast and Cafés

For breakfast, stop by the top-rated **Garden of the Gods Gourmet** (410 S. 26th St., 719/471-2799, www.godsgourmet.com, 8am-2pm and 5:30pm-8:30pm Mon.-Sat., 8am-3pm Sun., $6-24), a bright and homey café committed to using locally and sustainably sourced ingredients. You can taste the freshness in breakfast classics like Mountain Man hash and banana bread French toast. Lunch and dinner entrées range from classic curry chicken salad to Colorado buffalo pastrami sliders. The companion **Garden of the Gods Gourmet Market** (8am-7:30pm Mon.-Sat., 8am-5pm Sun.) sells equally fresh soups, salads, and entrées—the perfect fixings for a delicious picnic lunch.

American

Shuga's (702 S. Cascade Ave., 719/328-1412, http://shugas.com, 11am-midnight daily, $9-12) is a funky restaurant and bar whose menu of salads, soups, sandwiches, and starters—including their signature jalapeño, bacon, and gouda mac and cheese—is popular with the city's budget-minded college students. Wash it all down with a frosty glass of lavender lemonade.

The Green Line Grill (230½ Pueblo Ave., 719/964-1461, http://greenlinegrill.com, 11am-1am Mon. and Thurs., 11am-midnight Tues.-Wed., 11am-3am Fri.-Sat., $5-8) is a retro burger joint where you can grab a famous El Reno-style onion fried burger (and sweet-mustard El Reno slaw) for lunch, dinner, or a late-night snack. Top it off with a basket of chef Bobby Couch's hand-cut fries and a cold fountain drink.

Brewpub

Colorado Springs' most unique restaurant location is the ★ **Colorado Mountain Brewery** (600 S. 21st St. #180, 719/466-8240, www.cmbrew.com, 11am-9:30pm Sun.-Thurs., 11am-10:30pm Fri.-Sat., $10-27), housed in a beautifully restored, 14-stall railroad roundhouse built by the Colorado Midland Railroad in 1887-1888. This upscale brewery is one of my family's favorite places to dine; the kids can order heaping platters of mountain nachos or individual-size pizzas, while the adults can enjoy more varied options like beer cheese soup and quinoa salad with shrimp. Frosted mugs of Monumental Stout, Roller Coaster Red, and other Old World-style beers round out the drink offerings.

Ethiopian

Colorado Springs' only Ethiopian restaurant sits tucked into the back of a strip mall. The award-winning **Uchenna** (2501 W. Colorado Ave., 719/634-5070, 11:30am-2pm and 5pm-8pm Tues.-Fri., noon-2pm and 5pm-8pm Sat.-Sun., $10-15) has a casual and friendly ambiance, soothing background music, and great food whose spice level can be adjusted. Don't miss smiling chef Maya's *yebeg tibs* (lamb cubes sautéed with garlic, ginger, and spices), seafood plate, or numerous vegan and veggie options. Even skeptical kids will have fun eating with the traditional *injera* bread.

Italian

Old Colorado City has excellent Italian food; two standouts are housed in cozy, historic brick buildings. **Paravicini's Italian Bistro** (2802 W. Colorado Ave., 719/471-8200, http://paravicinis.com, 11am-9pm Sun.-Thurs., 11am-10pm Fri.-Sat., $11-26) offers an upscale menu of veal piccata, eggplant parmesan, and other classic entrées; seafood pastas and steaks; and a long wine and cocktail list. The casual **Pizzeria Rustica** (2527 W. Colorado Ave., 719/632-8121, http://pizzeriarustica.com, 5pm-9pm Mon.-Thurs., noon-9pm Sat.-Sun., $11-15) has been nationally recognized for both its freshly baked, Neapolitan-style artisanal pizzas and the groundbreaking sustainability efforts of its chef-owner Dave Brackett, a retired Air Force veteran. This winning combination has resulted in the pizzeria's designation as Colorado's "greenest" restaurant.

Mediterranean and Tapas

For an intimate atmosphere, try **Nosh** (121 S. Tejon St., 719/635-6674, www.nosh121.com, 11am-9pm Mon.-Thurs., 11am-10pm Fri., 5pm-10pm Sat., $9-18), a modern tapas bar whose koi pond wall murals are as colorful and distinctive as the wide-ranging menu. Choose from small plates, like beet caprese, wonton nachos, a variety of Asian-inspired noodle bowls, and the popular Korean crispy Asian wings. Nosh also has a long list of wines, beers, and cocktails as well as some good happy hour specials (3pm-close Mon., 3pm-6pm Tues.-Fri.).

Located five miles north of downtown, the **Caspian Café** (4375 Sinton Rd., 719/528-1155, www.caspiancafe.com, 11am-9pm Mon.-Sat., 4pm-8pm Sun., $10-27) is worth seeking out for its flavorful Mediterranean entrées, like gyros and Moroccan roast chicken, falafel-filled pitas, and an extensive list of starters, including smoky baba ghanouj and tangy shrimp pesto. Try to leave room for a piece of the flaky house baklava.

Steak

An upscale option downtown is **The Famous Steakhouse** (31 N. Tejon St., 719/227-7333, www.thefamoussteakhouse.net, 11am-10pm Mon.-Fri., 4pm-10pm Sat.-Sun., $29-59), a self-described "swanky Chicago-style steak joint with big portions." In addition to filet mignon and other prime cuts of beef, the menu includes fresh Hawaiian ahi tuna steak and Colorado lamb rack, along with salads and sides like baked potatoes smothered with butter and sour cream.

ACCOMMODATIONS

Although Colorado Springs has a huge supply of chain hotels, there are a number of hidden gems near downtown and Old Colorado City. And there's The Broadmoor, one of the state's most distinctive properties.

$100-150

The ★ **Spurs and Lace Inn** (2829 W. Pikes Peak Ave., 719/227-7662, http://colorado-bnb.com, $115-150) is a popular bed-and-breakfast located in a late-1800s home that was later relocated to Old Colorado City. Each of the five cozy rooms (double occupancy only) has queen-size, four-poster beds and private baths—but no TVs. With a garden gazebo and a large front porch with comfy chairs, the inn is a great place to relax and enjoy the peaceful ambiance and gourmet, three-course breakfast (8am daily).

A Room with a View (528 E. Bijou St., 719/633-3683, www.arwav.biz, $75-125) is a cyclist-friendly bed-and-breakfast in the downtown area with three rooms in a lovely Victorian. The bright and cozy rooms have colorful accents and rocking chairs. Guests share a covered porch, an airy common room, and washer/dryer facilities.

The **Crescent Lily Inn** (6 Boulder Crescent St., 719/442-2331, www.crescentlily-inn.com, $95-140) has five rooms in a beautifully restored Victorian home. Room decor includes an assortment of period-style furniture, unique accents, embroidered bedspreads, and lace curtains. All rooms have

private baths and amenities include a gourmet breakfast.

$150-250

Just around the corner from Old Colorado City, the homey **Old Town Guesthouse** (115 S. 26th St., 719/632-9194, www.oldtownguesthouse.com, $175-275) has eight rooms with private baths, waveless floatation mattresses, high-speed Wi-Fi, and in-room fridges. Half of the rooms feature a private hot tub, while three rooms have steam showers. With the exception of the Colorado Columbine room (which has a king-size bed), all rooms include queen beds. Book a room with a cozy fireplace for a romantic weekend or rejuvenating getaway. The hospitable innkeepers provide afternoon snacks, complimentary drinks, and a hearty breakfast to power you through your day.

A few blocks east of Old Colorado City, and close to the interstate, the **1902 Holden House** (1102 W. Pikes Peak Ave., 719/471-3980, www.holdenhouse.com, $155-175) is actually three buildings that host six Victorian-style guest suites. Rooms are decorated with antiques, fireplaces, and hand-painted murals. Each suite is named for a mining region and has a queen- or king-size bed, private bath, and fireplace; most have large soaking tubs and marble showers. A gourmet breakfast is served in the restored 1898 dining room (or in your suite) and includes fresh-baked muffins, an egg dish, and fruit, along with coffee, juice, and tea.

West of downtown Colorado Springs, the **Cheyenne Mountain Resort** (3225 Broadmoor Valley Rd., 719/538-4000, www.cheyennemountain.com, $179-229) is a pint-sized Broadmoor. The 200-acre complex has 316 rooms and suites plus three dining options, an on-site spa, an 18-hole golf course, 17 indoor and outdoor tennis courts, five pools, an impressive 9,000-square-foot fitness center, and its own lake. Located across eight different lodges, the tastefully decorated rooms are cozy and colorful and have beautiful views. The resort fee ($24 per night) includes parking, fitness classes, outdoor tennis and boating, Wi-Fi, and access to the fitness and aquatic centers.

Over $250

Situated just a few blocks from Colorado College, **The St. Mary's Inn** (530 N. Nevada Ave., 719/540-2222, www.thestmarysinn.com, $230-450) is a popular bed-and-breakfast that has won the coveted "Best of the West and Rockies" award every year since 2008—and for good reason. The historic 1895 house oozes charm with eight bright and cheerful suites featuring private, granite-tiled baths and queen- or king-size beds draped with luxurious linens. Several of the suites also have jetted whirlpool tubs. Guests must be 16 years or older.

★ **The Broadmoor** (1 Lake Ave., 719/634-7711, www.broadmoor.com, $265-385, $32 resort fee) is more of an experience than a luxury hotel. The longest-running consecutive winner of both the *Forbes* Five-Star and the AAA Five-Diamond Awards, The Broadmoor is known for its luxurious facilities and superior service.

The resort hosts nearly 800 guest rooms and suites, as well as cottages, brownstones, and an Estate House, in addition to several seasonal "wilderness" properties (the luxuriously rustic Cloud Camp, The Ranch at Emerald Valley, and an upscale Fishing Camp). Rooms in the Main complex feature vintage decor with rich brocade bed canopies, while those in the South complex feature more modern furnishings. All rooms contain either a single king bed or two doubles, upscale bathrooms, and a cozy seating area or spacious desk. Suites, cottages, and brownstones are the height of luxury. Most rooms offer views of the mountains or the lake. Guests enjoy access to Wi-Fi, a first-rate fitness center, local shuttles, a movie theater, and use of the resort's paddleboats. Also on-site is a luxurious 38-room spa with dozens of massage, nail, and body therapies, three pools, indoor and outdoor tennis courts, and 26 specialty stores.

TRANSPORTATION AND SERVICES
Air
There are two good options for flying into Colorado Springs: **Denver International Airport** (DEN, 8500 Peña Blvd., 303/342-2000, http://www.flydenver.com) and the smaller **Colorado Springs Airport** (COS, 7770 Milton E. Proby Pkwy., 719/550-1900, www.flycos.com), located about 11 miles southeast of the downtown. There are non-stop flights to Colorado Springs from a dozen major cities, including Seattle, Los Angeles, Phoenix, Dallas, Houston, Orlando, Atlanta, and Chicago.

Avis, Budget, and Enterprise have depots at the Colorado Springs Airport. Budget also has a location near the Garden of the Gods.

To reach downtown from the Colorado Springs Airport, head west on U.S. 24 then north on I-25 to Exit 142 (Bijou St.).

Car
Colorado Springs is located 70 miles south of downtown Denver on I-25. Because the city stretches north-south along the interstate, travel during rush hour and in bad weather can result in long delays. To avoid backups, try to drive through Colorado Springs midday, when there are fewer cars on the road.

To reach Colorado Springs from Denver, follow I-25 South toward Colorado Springs. Take Exit 142 (Bijou St.) to reach the downtown area a couple of blocks east of the interstate.

Shuttle and Bus
Colorado Springs Shuttle (719/687-3456, www.coloradoshuttle.com, $40-50 one-way DIA to COS) provides daily transport to several locations in Colorado Springs every two hours starting at 5am. **Greyhound** (120 S. Weber St., 719/635-1505, www.greyhound.com, $11-14 one-way) provides service from downtown Denver to the Colorado Springs bus station. **Springs Cab** (719/444-8989, www.springscabllc.com) offers local transport around town.

Services

VISITOR INFORMATION

The **Colorado Springs Visitor Information Center** (515 S. Cascade Ave., 719/635-7506, www.visitcos.com, 8:30am-5pm Mon.-Fri., 10am-2pm Sat.-Sun., reduced hours in winter) is located at the southern end of the downtown. Stop by for help with reservations, information on local and regional attractions, access to their free Wi-Fi, and piles of maps and brochures. The visitor bureau also has an online app that can be downloaded from their website. Obtain more information about Old Colorado City in the district's small **Welcome Center** (2324 W. Colorado Ave., 719/577-4112, http://shopoldcoloradocity.com).

The Gazette (http://gazette.com) is Colorado Springs' Pulitzer Prize-winning daily newspaper; it features mostly local news and posts dining reviews and other visitor information online. The weekly *Independent* (www.csindy.com) is another good traveler resource. KRCC (91.5) is the local NPR station, KVOR (740 AM) is the top local news-talk station, and Blazin' 98.5 plays R & B and hip-hop.

MEDIA AND COMMUNICATION

Colorado Springs' main **post office** (201 E. Pikes Peak Ave., 719/570-5336, 9am-5:30pm Mon.-Fri., 8am-1pm Sat.) is located in downtown, east of I-25 and one block north of Colorado Avenue.

The downtown **Penrose Library** (20 N. Cascade Ave., 719/531-6333, http://ppld.org, 9am-9pm Mon.-Thurs., 10am-6pm Fri.-Sat., 1pm-5pm Sun.) has free public Internet workstations and wireless Internet access.

MEDICAL

Memorial Health has two 24/7 locations: **Memorial Hospital Central** (1400 E. Boulder St., 719/365-5000, www.uchealth. org) and **Memorial Hospital North** (4050 Briargate Pkwy., 719/364-5000, www. uchealth.org).

Vicinity of Colorado Springs

A series of small towns and noteworthy attractions are scattered around the northern and western sides of the enormous Pikes Peak massif. The community of Manitou Springs has been a destination for tourists since General William Jackson Palmer founded a "scenic health resort" there in 1872. Florissant Fossil Beds National Monument is one of the world's richest fossil deposits. Cripple Creek is a mining-turned-gambling town where the excitement of the world's greatest gold rush still lingers.

★ GARDEN OF THE GODS

Garden of the Gods (1805 N. 30th St., Colorado Springs, 719/634-6666, www.gardenofgods.com, 5am-11pm daily May-Oct., 5am-9pm daily Nov.-Apr., free) is a 1,300-acre park with rows of radically tilted, 300-foot-high red and white rock fins that form a stunning foreground for Pikes Peak's dramatic slopes and lofty summit. The park's name comes from surveyor Rufus Cable, who excitedly declared the area "a fit place for the gods to assemble."

Begin your exploration at the park's **Visitor & Nature Center** (8am-7pm daily late May-early Sept., 9am-5pm early Sept.-late May, free), where you can time travel a billion years in 15 minutes in the on-site movie theater ($6) and view state-of-the art exhibits about the park's geology and ecology. (Don't miss the one about Campi, a dinosaur skull found in 1878 and stored at Yale University ever since.)

Sights and Activities

Popular stops within the park include Balanced Rock, the Siamese Twins, and the two-hour rides for all levels. A special 2.5-hour ride (Labor Day-Memorial Days) circles the park's entire perimeter.

The **Garden of the Gods Trading Post** (324 Beckers La., 719/685-9045, www.gardenofthegodstradingpost.com, 8:30am-8:30pm daily in summer, 9am-5pm daily in winter) claims to be the state's largest and oldest gift shop. It boasts more than 90,000 items ranging from Native American artwork to tacky shot glasses and T-shirts. The adobe complex also houses the Balanced Rock Cafe and sells Colorado City Creamery ice cream.

Getting There

From downtown Colorado Springs, take U.S. 24 north to Exit 146 (Garden of the Gods). Drive west for 2.5 miles, then turn left on 30th Street. Continue one mile to the visitor center.

MANITOU SPRINGS

one of Manitou Springs' celebrated springs

famous Kissing Camels rock formations. The park offers free, guided **nature walks** (30 minutes, 10am and 2pm daily, weather permitting) that depart from the North Main parking lot. Walks explore the rock formations near Tower of Babel and the Kissing Camels. Alternatively, **Adventures Out West** (719/219-0118, www.advoutwest.com, $17) offers jeep, Segway, or 1909 bus tours through the park.

The 15 miles of scenic hiking trails include the popular **Perkins Central Garden Trail** (1.5 miles round-trip), a flat walk through the park's tallest spires. The quiet **Chambers-Bretag-Palmer Trail** (3 miles round-trip) loops around much of the park. Garden of the Gods also allows mountain biking on designated trails as well as rock climbing.

One of the most fun ways to tour the stunning Garden of the Gods is via horseback, just as the area's first explorers did. **Academy Riding Stables** (4 El Paso Blvd., 888/700-0410, www.academyridingstables.com, year-round, $49 for 1 hour) offers one- and

Just six miles west of Colorado Springs, Manitou Springs is a distinct community built around the naturally carbonated mineral springs that are scattered across the quaint and historic downtown. Before it became a tourist town in the 1870s, Manitou was a sacred spot for Cheyenne, Ute, and other native tribes who believed the springs' natural carbonation was the breath of a great spirit. (Manitou is a Native American word for "spirit.") The compact town is easy to explore on foot; browse more than a dozen colorful art galleries, dine in idiosyncratic restaurants, and play in a vintage arcade.

Sights

MINERAL SPRINGS

Manitou's historic springs were renovated following a revival of the spa culture in the late 20th century. Today, each spring is marked with a plaque summarizing its history and dissolved mineral content. One of the great delights of visiting town is grabbing a cup and sampling the water from the various springs; each has its own distinct taste and degree of effervescence. For a map of the springs, stop by the **Manitou Springs Visitor Center**

Around Manitou Springs

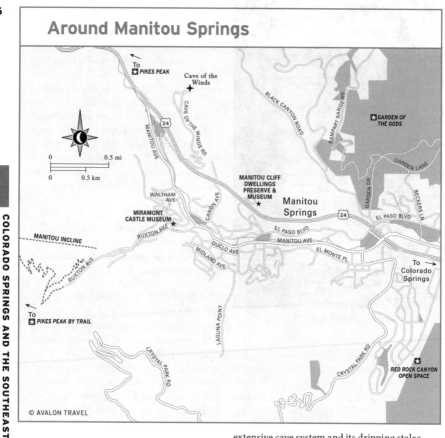

To ✦ PIKES PEAK

Cave of the Winds

BLACK CANYON ROAD

RAMPART RANGE RD

✦ GARDEN OF THE GODS

CAVE OF THE WINDS RD

24

MANITOU AVE

GARDEN LANE

0   0.5 mi

0   0.5 km

GARDEN DR

BECKERS LN

MANITOU CLIFF DWELLINGS PRESERVE & MUSEUM ★

WALTHAM AVE

CANYON AVE

Manitou Springs

24

EL PASO BLVD

MIRAMONT CASTLE MUSEUM ★

RUXTON AVE

EL PASO BLVD

MANITOU INCLINE

DUCLO AVE

MANITOU AVE

RUXTON AVE

MIDLAND AVE

EL MONTE PL

To → Colorado Springs

To ✦ PIKES PEAK BY TRAIL

LAGUNA POINT

✦ RED ROCK CANYON OPEN SPACE

CRYSTAL PARK RD

CRYSTAL PARK RD

© AVALON TRAVEL

(354 Manitou Ave., 719/685-5089, http://manitousprings.org, 8:30am-5pm Mon.-Fri., 9am-4pm Sat.-Sun.) or download one online (http://manitoumineralsprings.org). In summer, the **Manitou Springs Foundation** (http://manitoumineralsprings.org) offers guided walking tours each Saturday.

CAVE OF THE WINDS

High on the rim of Williams Canyon, **Cave of the Winds** (100 Cave of the Winds Rd., 719/685-5444, http://caveofthewinds.com, 10am-5pm daily year-round, tours $20-30) combines cave tours with several daredevil rides ($20-50), including the heart-stopping TERROR-Dactyl free fall. If you prefer to keep your feet firmly on the ground, explore the extensive cave system and its dripping stalactite, stalagmite, and "soda straw" decorations on a 45-minute discovery tour or a 1.5-hour lantern-light tour.

MANITOU CLIFF DWELLINGS

The **Manitou Cliff Dwellings** (10 Cliff Rd., 719/685-5242, www.cliffdwellingsmuseum.com, 9am-6pm daily May-Aug., 9am-5pm daily Mar.-Apr. and Sept.-Oct., 9am-4pm daily Nov., 10am-4pm daily Dec.-Feb., $9.50) museum and preserve features a cliff dwelling that was relocated here from a canyon near Mesa Verde in the early 1900s in order to protect it from looters. Dwellings were disassembled block-by-block, packed on oxen, then shipped by railroad, and eventually carried to this site by horse and wagon.

Workers carefully reassembled the 700-year-old dwellings.

Today, visitors can walk through the 40-room complex sheltered beneath a large sandstone overhang. The site also includes a three-story, Taos-style Pueblo that was expanded into a pottery museum and gift shop.

MIRAMONT CASTLE MUSEUM

Built in 1895 as a home for Father Francolon, a French-born Catholic priest, the stately 14,000-square-foot **Miramont Castle Museum** (9 Capitol Hill Ave., 719/685-1011, www.miramontcastle.org, 10am-4pm Tues.-Sun. early Sept.-late May, 9am-5pm daily late May-early Sept., $9) is known for its bizarre combination of architectural styles ranging from Moorish and Elizabethan to half-timber chateau. Since it was built at a time of unrest in France, the Father reportedly incorporated hidden compartments, tunnels, and other escape routes into the building's design.

After being used as a sanitarium, the castle became a tourist sight. Visitors can enjoy a self-guided tour or a twice-daily docent-led tour in summer. The castle's **Queen's Parlour Tearoom** (719/884-4109, 11am-3pm daily Memorial Day-Labor Day) offers an additional—and delicious—opportunity to explore the region's history, with a tea and lunch menu developed from authentic Victorian-era recipes. Reservations are recommended.

Hiking

Built for a cable car to carry equipment up Pikes Peak, this steep track was later converted into the **Manitou Incline** (www.visitcos.com, 6am-8pm daily Apr.-Oct., 6am-6pm Nov.-Mar.), a popular hiking trail whose 2,000-vertical-foot climb over one mile makes it one of the most challenging treks in the state. From the trailhead on Ruxton Avenue, the route climbs steeply the entire way, intersecting the **Barr Trail** (www.barrtrail.net) about 0.75 mile from the start. From the Barr Trail junction, the Incline crests a false summit before climbing another 300 stairs to the top of the incline. On the descent, it's safest to follow the Barr Trail four miles back down to a trailhead on Hydro Street. This trailhead is located just past the parking lot for the Cog Railway, a short distance west of where the Incline starts.

The Incline trailhead is located on Ruxton Avenue, where there is very little parking. Hikers should instead park in the lots along Manitou Avenue, then walk up Ruxton

the Cave of the Winds

Avenue to the Incline's start (or take a free summer shuttle).

Shopping

Manitou Springs is the perfect place for holiday shopping. At **Christmas in Manitou** (726 Manitou Ave., 719/685-4290, www.christmasinmanitou.com, 10am-5pm Mon.-Fri., 10am-6pm Sat.-Sun.), floor-to-ceiling trees and shelving sparkle with holiday decor—Christmas collectibles, candles, and lights. Ornaments can even be personalized while you wait.

The many galleries include the **Commonwealth Artists Co-Op** (102 Canon Ave., 719/685-1008, www.commonwheel.com, 10am-6pm daily), which features glassware, jewelry, paintings, pottery, and sculpture made by Colorado artists.

Food

For great coffee and delicious food with a cozy ambiance, head to **Good Karma Coffee Lounge & Deli** (110 Canon Ave., 719/685-2325, www.goodkarmacoffeelounge.com, 7am-3pm Sun.-Thurs., 7am-9pm Fri.-Sat., $6-11), a counter-service restaurant that serves tasty breakfast options such as omelets, Benedicts, and biscuits and peppered country gravy. A smaller lunch menu includes pork green chili and tasty sandwiches like maple-roasted butternut served on a pumpkin roll.

For a casual dining option try the community-oriented **Adam's Mountain Café** (26 Manitou Ave., 719/685-1430, www.adamsmountain.com, 8am-3pm Sun.-Mon., 8am-3pm and 5pm-9pm Tues.-Sat., $10.50-18.50), known for their fluffy, three-egg omelets. Adam's also serves an extensive dinner menu with plenty of veggie and vegan options like spicy *chana masala* and "slow food" barbecue tofu, as well as meaty choices like red curry *panang* chicken.

If you're starving after hiking the Manitou Incline, head straight to local fave ★ **Savelli's** (301 Manitou Ave., 719/685-3755, www.savellispizzapastasubs.com, 11am-8:30pm daily, $9-15) for a few slices of their

bacon cheeseburger pizza, a provolone-draped meatball sub, or a heaping bowl of creamy fettuccine Alfredo. If you still have room, order the delish chocolate lava cake.

Accommodations

A former boarding house and stagecoach stop, **The Cliff House** (306 Canon Ave., 719/785-1000, www.thecliffhouse.com, $110-365) has hosted hunters, trappers, and distinguished guests like President Theodore Roosevelt, Thomas Edison, and P. T. Barnum. The 54 comfortable rooms and suites blend historic appeal with modern amenities, such as premium bedding, fireplaces, towel warmers, and heated toilet seats. The on-site, award-winning **Cliff House Hotel Dining Room** (6am-10:30am, 11:30am-2:30pm, and 5:30pm-9pm daily, $21-38) is a modern, Victorian, fine-dining establishment specializing in new American cuisine, like Atlantic lobster bisque, Rocky Mountain trout, and bacon-wrapped elk rib eye.

The **Avenue Hotel Bed and Breakfast** (711 Manitou Ave., 719/685-1277, www.avenuehotelbandb.com, $130-185) is a restored turn-of-the-20th-century boarding house with seven large rooms and suites. Rooms include one king- or queen-size bed and private baths, most of which still have old claw-foot tubs. The property includes a Carriage House, featuring two units with private entrances and full kitchens.

Blue Skies Inn (402 Manitou Ave., 719/685-3899, www.blueskiesinn.com, $145-240) is a colorful bed-and-breakfast with 10 large suites featuring vibrant decor designed by the artist-owner. Many rooms have a daybed in addition to a king- or queen-size bed; all have fireplaces and either a large two-person shower or a soaking or jetted tub. The peaceful 2.5-acre grounds feature a small stream and tall trees interspersed with bright flower beds.

Transportation

Manitou Springs is located along U.S. 24 about six miles west of Colorado Springs.

From Colorado Springs, take Exit 141 off I-25 and head west on U.S. 24 for four miles to the Manitou Avenue/Business exit. Drive west on Manitou Avenue for one mile to reach the small downtown. It's also possible to take the **Mountain Metro** bus (https://coloradosprings.gov, $1.75 one-way) from the **Downtown Terminal** (127 E. Kiowa St.) to Manitou Springs.

★ PIKES PEAK

Pikes Peak (www.pikespeak.us.com) is a magnificent mountain that soars 8,000 feet above the Great Plains. Unlike most of Colorado's Front Range peaks, Pikes has no shroud of foothills to obscure it.

In 1806, Lieutenant Zebulon Pike became the first Euro-American to lay eyes upon the peak. He made plans to climb it, which he presumed would be its first ascent. But after waist-deep snow and a lack of proper clothing defeated him, Pike declared the mountain unscalable—a prediction that was disproved 14 years later when Dr. Edwin James, a naturalist on another exploration party, successfully ascended it. James brought down samples of hitherto unknown plants, including what is now Colorado's state flower: the beautiful blue columbine. While the peak was originally named in James' honor, the mountain's name was changed 20 years later to instead honor Pike. (Fortunately, another peak west of Boulder was named for James.)

The fame of Pikes Peak exploded again in 1859, when sparkling flakes of gold were discovered along the banks of Clear Creek near what is today the town of Golden, triggering the state's gold rush. Fortune seekers used Pikes Peak as their landmark, and "Pikes Peak or Bust!" became their collective cry (despite the fact that the gold had been discovered more than 100 miles north of the mountain).

Today, more than 600,000 people ascend Pikes Peak each year, making it the most-ascended mountain in the United States.

Pikes Peak Highway

Visitors have several options for getting to the top of Pikes Peak, all of which are an adventure. One option is to drive to the summit along the spectacular switchbacks of the 19-mile **Pikes Peak Highway** (http://pikespeak.us.com, 7:30am-6pm daily late May-early Sept., 7:30am-5pm daily Sept., 9am-3pm daily Oct.-late May, $14 per person or $40 per vehicle). This toll road is open year-round, weather permitting. Be sure to bring plenty of warm and windproof clothes, water, and

The cog railway ascends Pikes Peak.

food, and verify that your gas tank is full before you start the drive.

The famous highway starts about 0.5 mile west of U.S. 24 and bends 162 times, passing numerous roadside vista points, trailheads, and attractions en route. One of the first stops is the **North Pole** (5050 Pikes Peak Hwy., 719/684-9432, http://northpolecolorado.com, opening dates and hours vary, $22), an amusement park geared toward elementary-age kids. The tollgates appear at **mile marker 1.**

Beyond the tollgates, the highway passes the **Crowe Gulch Picnic Grounds** before entering **Pike National Forest** (www.fs.usda.gov). Just past **mile marker 3,** look for the infamous Bigfoot Crossing sign, placed to mark the location where a visitor purportedly saw a Big Foot in 2001. At **mile marker 6,** sparkling **Crystal Creek Reservoir,** a popular fishing spot, appears. A **visitor center** with stunning views and a nature trail is located just past the dam.

About one mile beyond the visitor center is a sign for the North Slope Recreation Area, where an unpaved road leads to two more reservoirs for fishing, hiking, biking, and picnicking.

Just after this turnoff is the starting line for the **Pikes Peak International Hill Climb**

(www.ppihc.com). Past **mile marker 12** is the **Glen Cove Inn,** a cabin-turned-inn that settler Frank Tweed developed in the late 1800s for people traveling the original carriage road. It still serves today's travelers with a restaurant, gift shop, and restrooms.

At **mile marker 14,** the highway finally reaches treeline and truly incredible views. Here the road snakes up several switchbacks so sharp that they're called the "Ws." The pullout near **mile marker 18** is one of the best spots on the mountain to see bighorn sheep, the state mammal. The last mile wraps around the peak's south side, where you can see Cripple Creek and the Sangre de Cristo Range.

Upon arrival at the 14,110-foot summit **(mile marker 19),** towering nearly three miles above sea level, snag one of the parking spots and enjoy the 360° views. Enter the **Summit House** (hours vary year-round, $1-8) to escape the wind and enjoy one of the famous high-elevation donuts, as well as sandwiches, salads, and hot drinks, before heading back down the highway.

Cog Railway

An alternative way to reach the top is by riding the historic, 125-year-old **Broadmoor**

Pikes Peak Highway

A Rockin' New Year's Eve

One of Colorado's most colorful traditions is watching the gorgeous fireworks display launched from the summit of Pikes Peak each New Year's Eve. An annual event since 1922, the display is fired by a group of about 30 robust mountaineers known as the **AdAmAn Club** (www.adaman.org) due to the fact that they only increase their membership—"add a man"—by one person each year. The members begin their adventure on December 30, climbing the Barr Trail up to **Barr Camp** (www.barrcamp.com), where they spend the night. On the last day of the year, they flash mirrors from timberline to let their families know they're safe before completing the ascent in the early afternoon. Above treeline, the climb is particularly difficult due to the windswept, icy slopes and the numbing cold, with wind chills often hovering around -50°F. After reaching the summit, the group unloads the fireworks (which are transported there earlier in the year) and wait for the stroke of midnight. In clear weather, the display can be seen for hundreds of miles along the Front Range and to the east across the Great Plains.

Pikes Peak Cog Railway (515 Ruxton Ave., 719/685-5401, www.cograilway.com, hours vary seasonally, $32-38 per person, $5 parking). The railway was built by Zalmon Simmons (inventor of the Simmons Beautyrest Mattress Company) after he rode to the top of Pikes Peak in the late 1880s on a mule. Determined that visitors should be able to reach the top more comfortably, Simmons raised the required capital to start building the railway in 1889. The first steam train reached the summit on the last day of June in 1891 and service has continued ever since.

The train operates year-round, but hours and frequency vary. During the high season (mid-Mar.-late Oct.), there are up to 12 trips per day (3 hours round-trip, including 30 minutes at the summit to enjoy the views). In winter, the train makes just two trips per week and only ascends to 11,500-foot Inspiration Point (2 hours, 15 minutes round-trip). These trains fill up quickly, so it's best to make reservations in advance.

Pikes Peak Mountain Bike Tours (www.bikepikespeak.com, $140) and **Challenge Unlimited** (www.bikithikit.com, $135) offer a Ride-N-Rail package tour, whereby visitors can ascend Pikes Peak via the Cog Railway and then bike back down.

Barr Trail

Fit hikers can ascend Pikes Peak via the **Barr Trail** (www.barrtrail.net), the route used for the annual Pikes Peak Ascent and Marathon (www.pikespeakmarathon.org, Aug.). One of the most challenging trails in the state, the Barr Trail climbs 7,900 feet in 11.8 miles (one-way). The trailhead is located at 515 Ruxton Avenue, just west of the Cog Railway parking lot.

Getting There

To reach the Cog Railway parking area from I-25 in Colorado Springs, take Exit 141 west onto U.S. 24 for four miles to the Manitou Avenue exit. Turn right onto Manitou Avenue and proceed west three miles to a traffic circle. Exit the circle onto Ruxton Avenue and drive 0.75 mile to the top of the street. After passing the cog railway parking area, take a right onto Hydro Street and park in the small pay lot at the top. If this lot is full, retrace your route to search for a legal spot on Ruxton Avenue or park in one of the Manitou Springs lots. Due to the high volume of traffic, there is a free **summer shuttle** (daily in high season, hours vary) from the downtown Manitou Springs parking lot (10 Old Man's Trail) to the trailhead.

FLORISSANT FOSSIL BEDS NATIONAL MONUMENT

Beneath a series of grassy meadows and forested hills, **Florissant Fossil Beds National Monument** (15807 County Rd. 1, Florissant, 719/748-3253, www.nps.gov, 8am-6pm daily June-early Sept., 9am-5pm daily mid-Mar.-May and early Sept.-Nov., 9am-4:30pm daily Dec.-mid-Mar., $5) preserves one of the world's richest fossil beds—from large petrified redwood tree stumps to the individual lenses in a fly's compound eye. An entire ecosystem flourished here about 34 million years ago and has been fortuitously preserved.

At that time, a lush forest carpeted this valley, where redwoods thrived alongside hardwood trees, ferns, and palms. Just 15 miles to the southwest, however, a large volcano loomed above the land, and flows of ash periodically disgorged down its flanks, which sometimes collapsed to send torrents of mud roaring down the valley at speeds of up to 100 miles per hour. One of these torrents dammed a local creek, forming a long, narrow lake where creatures that slowly sank to the bottom were entombed in mud and preserved for posterity.

Sights and Recreation

Some of the more than 50,000 specimens that have been unearthed here can be viewed in the fantastic **visitor center.** Peer at flying ants, beetles, spiders, and the first-known fossil tsetse fly, as well as catfish, suckers, and other fish and even a small opossum. The park's best-known attractions are the ancient redwood stumps, whose bases were buried 16 feet deep in a gooey mud that helped to preserve them. A trio of impressive stumps is located just behind the visitor center; or walk the one-mile **Petrified Forest Loop** to see the Big Stump, whose 40-foot girth supported a 500-1,000-year-old tree that towered 200 feet above the forest floor. The park has 13 additional miles of trails, including the 3.8-mile **Hornbek Wildlife Loop,** which visits an old homestead.

Getting There

The monument is located about 30 miles west of Manitou Springs. To get here from I-25, take Exit 141 and follow U.S. 24 West for 35 miles to the tiny town of Florissant. In town, turn left on Teller County 1 and follow this road south for two miles to the national monument.

the petrified Big Stump at Florissant Fossil Beds National Monument

CRIPPLE CREEK

Cripple Creek's (www.visitcripplecreek. com) most interesting attraction is the gold rush-era **Mollie Kathleen Gold Mine** (9388 County Rd. 67, 719/689-2466, www.goldminetours.com, 9am-5pm daily Apr.-Sept., $20). Visitors can don a hard hat, step into an old-fashioned open elevator, and descend a 1,000-vertical-foot shaft to an old tunnel to view mining equipment and gaze at one of the region's sparkling gold deposits.

The **Cripple Creek Jail Museum** (136 W. Bennett Ave., 719/689-6556, www.visit-cripplecreek.com, 10am-5pm daily in summer, 9am-4pm Thurs.-Sun. in winter, $2) is located in a building that served as the county jail for almost a century. The original cells have been preserved, making this the self-declared "hottest selfie spot" west of the Mississippi River.

A ride on the **Cripple Creek & Victor Narrow Gauge Railroad** (520 E. Carr Ave., 719/689-2640, http://cripplecreekrailroad. com, 9:30am-5pm daily late May-early Oct., $15) cruises four miles past old mines to an abandoned mining camp before returning to the 1894 depot. The 45-minute tours aboard the steam locomotive offer a scenic introduction to Cripple Creek.

Getting There

Cripple Creek lies about 40 miles west of Manitou Springs. From Manitou Springs, follow U.S. 24 West for 20 miles to the town of Divide. Take Highway 67 South for 19 miles to the town of Cripple Creek.

The Arkansas River Valley

Thanks to abundant sunshine, clear mountain air, and gorgeous scenery, the Arkansas Valley is a magnet for locals and visitors alike.

From its first trickle high in the snow-capped peaks surrounding the old silver-mining town of Leadville, the Arkansas River flows south through a high-elevation valley walled on both sides by impressively steep mountains.

En route to the Royal Gorge, the Arkansas River flows south past Buena Vista and Salida, two fun-loving outdoor recreation hubs. Between these towns, the river rushes through a pretty canyon comprising the heart of Browns Canyon, a national monument and a focal point for white-water rafters from across the country.

LEADVILLE

Located at 10,152 feet above sea level, Leadville is the highest incorporated city in the United States. Although its population today hovers around 2,500, the so-called Two-Mile-High City was the state's second-largest community during its heyday in the late 19th century. The small town is packed with historic sites, including a national mining museum.

Sights

★ NATIONAL MINING HALL OF FAME AND MUSEUM

With three levels of exhibits, the **National Mining Hall of Fame and Museum** (120 W. 9th St., 719/486-1229, www.mininghalloff-ame.org, 9am-5pm daily, $12), which is housed in a century-old Victorian schoolhouse, tells the story of mining from the Bronze Age to the present. One highlight is the walk-through replica of an 1880s-era hard rock mine, complete with a blacksmith shop and hoist room, designed by a former mine electrician. Still blinking from the dark, you emerge into the Gold Rush Room, where samples of gleaming gold from 17 U.S. states are on display, including a brilliant, 23-ounce golden nugget unearthed nearby in the legendary **Little Johnny Mine,** where J. J. Brown, the husband of *Titanic* survivor Margaret "Molly" Brown, hit a vein of gold so pure that at the time it was heralded as the world's richest strike.

MATCHLESS MINE

The National Mining Hall of Fame and Museum organizes hour-long guided tours to the **Matchless Mine** (E. 7th St., 719/486-1229, www.mininghalloffame.org, 1pm and 3pm daily in summer, $12), the silver mine that enriched Silver King (and U.S. Senator) Horace Tabor and his wife, Elizabeth "Baby Doe" Tabor. Today, the underground mine is marked by a wooden headframe, piles of rubble, outbuildings, and a dilapidated cabin where Baby Doe lived following Horace Tabor's death. Tours include the opportunity to try your hand at gold panning.

HEALY HOUSE MUSEUM & DEXTER CABIN

Two of Leadville's earliest homes have been preserved in the **Healy House Museum & Dexter Cabin** (912 Harrison Ave., 719/486-0487, www.historycolorado.org, 10am-4:30pm daily late May-mid-Oct., $6). Built in 1878, the clapboard Greek Revival Healy House was the home of one of Leadville's earliest founders, mining engineer August Meyer. Next door sits a log cabin built in 1879 by businessman James Dexter, one of the state's first millionaires and a mean poker player. It was later relocated to this site.

The house and cabin offer a fascinating glimpse into mountain life in the late 19th century. In addition to sumptuous Victorian furnishings, the Healy House hosts artifacts belonging to Augusta and Horace Tabor and other pioneering Leadville families. The cabin contains some of the painting, coin, and gem collections that Dexter assembled during his lifetime.

Hiking

Bordered on both sides by high alpine ranges, the Arkansas Valley is one of the state's best places for hiking, particularly if you like going uphill. One of the most rewarding hikes is the one to the summit of 14,439-foot **Mount Elbert** (www.14ers.com), the highest point in Colorado. The standard route climbs the straightforward Northeast Ridge Route, which gains 4,700 vertical feet over 4.5 miles (one-way). Even though the route is fairly straightforward, it's important to get a dawn start in order to avoid afternoon thunderstorms. Plan to hike this peak in summer (mid-June-early Sept.) after the route is clear of snow.

The Northeast Ridge Route trailhead is accessed from U.S. 24 south of Leadville. Follow U.S. 24 west to County Road 300. Turn right

the National Mining Hall of Fame and Museum

atop Mount Elbert

Rd. 306, Buena Vista, 719/395-6434, http://cottonwood-hot-springs.com, 8am-10pm daily, $18-20) is a low-key facility with half a dozen pools tucked beneath the trees along the edge of Cottonwood Creek. Each pool is a different temperature and some are shaded by canopies, so it's easy to find one that's just right for you. A variety of spa services are also available on-site.

The springs are located about 5.5 miles east of Buena Vista, at the start of County Road 306, which leads up to the top of beautiful Cottonwood Pass.

A decidedly more upscale option is the **Mount Princeton Hot Springs Resort** (15870 County Rd. 162, Nathrop, 719/395-2447, http://mtprinceton.com, 9am-10pm Mon.-Thurs., 9am-11pm Fri.-Sun., $18-22), a great place to soak your stress away. This large complex includes two separate areas: the **Upper Pools and Water Slide** (9am-6pm daily late May-early Sept.) and the **Creekside Hot Springs and Historic Bath House** (open year-round). Built in the mid-1800s, the bathhouse has a soaking pool and an exercise pool along with showers and lockers. Alternatively, enjoy relaxing in one of the 20 stone pools along the edge of Chalk Creek—a great place to soak while gazing at the stars or catching fluffy snowflakes on your tongue!

Mount Princeton is located south of Buena Vista along County Road 162. From Buena Vista, drive eight miles south on U.S. 285. Past the town of Nathrop, turn west onto Country Road 162 and continue 4.5 miles to the resort.

St. Elmo

Tucked below the dramatic slopes of Mount Princeton is the creaking ghost town of **St. Elmo,** a tribute to the hardy miners who lived and worked their claims in this remote and windswept valley. Founded in 1880 along Chalk Creek, the town boasted 2,000 people until the early 1920s, when mining declined and the railroad discontinued its service there.

Today, people visit the site to enjoy the scenery, view the scattered remnants of the town's many hotels, saloons, and dance halls,

and drive west for 0.7 mile to the junction with County Road 1. Turn south to follow County Road 11 toward Halfmoon Creek. After 1.2 miles, turn right onto the dirt road to Halfmoon Creek. Continue about five miles to the trailhead on the left, where there is a large parking area and outhouses.

Transportation and Services

Leadville is 130 miles west of Colorado Springs and 24 miles north of Buena Vista. From Colorado Springs, follow U.S. 24 west for 95 miles to Buena Vista, then turn north and continue to the small downtown of Leadville.

For more information, visit the **Leadville and Twin Lakes Visitor Center** (809 Harrison Ave., 719/486-3900, www.leadvilletwinlakes.com, 9am-4pm Thurs.-Sun., 10am-4pm Mon.).

BUENA VISTA AND VICINITY
★ Hot Springs
Cottonwood Hot Springs (18999 County

and visit the restored **St. Elmo General Store** (719/395-2117, www.st-elmo.com, 9am-5pm daily mid-May-Sept., 10am-4pm daily Oct.), which sells souvenirs, snacks, and antiques. The store also rents all-terrain vehicles and has a rustic three-person cabin ($79, minimum 2-night stay) for overnight stays.

St. Elmo is located 11 miles west of Mount Princeton Hot Springs along County Road 162.

Hiking

The 14,196-foot **Mount Yale** (www.14ers.com) is one of the only fourteeners accessible via a paved road. The standard route climbs Mount Yale's southwest slopes along an easy-to-follow trail that gains 4,300 vertical feet over 4.75 miles (one-way). There are excellent views from the summit. Plan to hike this peak in summer (mid-June-early Sept.) after the routes are clear of snow.

From the junction of U.S. 24 and West Main Street/County Road 306 in Buena Vista, drive west on County Road 306 toward Cottonwood Pass for 12 miles to the Denny Creek Trailhead parking lot on the right.

Accommodations and Camping

The **Mount Princeton Hot Springs Resort** (15870 County Rd. 162, Nathrop, 719/395-2447, http://mtprinceton.com, cabins $400-550, lodge rooms $175-200) complex contains a spa and dining facilities, as well as several lodging options with access to the on-site hot springs, sauna, steam rooms, and fitness center. Choose from rustic 1-2-bedroom cabins (sleeps 2-8 people) with fireplaces and convenience kitchens to lodge rooms with two beds, a private bath, in-room mini-fridge, and a small flat-screen TV.

Cottonwood Hot Springs (18999 County Rd. 306, Buena Vista, 719/395-6434, http://cottonwood-hot-springs.com, lodge rooms $119-169, dorms $55-95, cabins $195-315, camping $35-45) also has on-site lodging options, ranging from lodge rooms and dorms to cabins and tent camping.

Located one mile east of the trailhead to Mount Yale is the basic **Collegiate Peaks Campground** (County Rd. 306, 877/444-6777, www.recreation.gov, $20). The 56 sites are a convenient place to camp the night prior to climbing Mt. Yale in order to acclimate to the high elevation and get an early start. The campground and trailhead are less than a 15-minute drive from the Cottonwood Hot Springs, a great place to soak your sore muscles at the end of your descent.

Transportation and Services

Buena Vista is located about 95 miles west of Colorado Springs and 25 miles north of Salida. From Colorado Springs, follow U.S. 24 west for 78 miles to the junction with U.S. 285. Turn south onto U.S. 285 and drive 13 miles to another junction with U.S. 24; turn right (north) and continue to the town of Buena Vista. The main downtown is located east of the highway along Main Street.

To continue on to Salida, take U.S. 285

Cottonwood Hot Springs

rafting the mighty Arkansas River

South for 16 miles to County Road 291. Turn southeast onto County Road 291 and drive another eight miles to Salida.

Stop by Buena Vista's **Visitor Center** (343 U.S. 24, 719/395-6612, www.buenavista-colorado.org, 9am-5pm Mon.-Sat.) for more information.

BROWNS CANYON

The centerpiece of the 21,500-acre **Browns Canyon National Monument** (www.fs.fed.us or http://brownscanyon.org) is the Arkansas River, which flows through a series of beautiful canyons between Buena Vista and Salida. Activities here focus on the river: fishing, white-water rafting, and kayaking.

Jointly administered by the U.S. Forest Service and the Bureau of Land Management, this relatively new national monument does not have a visitor center or centralized facilities. While it is free to enter, several sites within the monument may charge parking fees.

★ White-Water Rafting and Kayaking

People travel from all over to kayak and raft the Arkansas River's frothing rapids. Unless you're an experienced boater with your own gear, it's best to go on an organized trip with a guide. The state's first (and longest) licensed outfitter is family-owned **Dvorak Expeditions** (17921 U.S. 285, Nathrop, 800/824-3795, https://dvorakexpeditions.com, $60 for a half-day trip). They offer everything from half- and full-day trips through Browns Canyon to superb four-day trips. If the river is running low, they can offer adventures on eight other rivers.

Browns Canyon Rafting (30375 U.S. 24, Buena Vista, 719/275-2890, http://raftbrownscanyon.com, $63 for a half-day trip) also offers full- and half-day Arkansas River trips.

Fishing

The section of the Arkansas River between Buena Vista and Salida is part of the state's longest stretch of Gold Medal waters. A good access point is **Hecla Junction State Park** (10142 County Rd. 194, Salida, 719/539-7289, http://cpw.state.co.us). There are nearly eight miles of public water where anglers can fish for rainbow and brown trout (Apr.-Oct.).

For information about guided trips, river conditions, and gear, stop by **Arkanglers Fly Shop** (www.arkanglers.com), which has storefronts in Buena Vista (517 S. U.S. 24, 719/395-1796, 8am-6pm Mon.-Sat., 8am-5pm Sun.) and in Salida (7500 U.S. 50, 719/539-3474, 8am-6pm Mon.-Sat., 8am-5pm Sun.).

SALIDA

The largest town in the Arkansas Valley, Salida has the best selection of restaurants and places to crash. The compact downtown is easy to explore on foot. Along the town's eastern edge, part of the Arkansas River has been sculpted into a kayaking playpark, making it a fun place to stroll by.

Food

For a quick snack or breakfast on the go,

stop by the **Little Red Hen Bakery** (302 G St., 719/539-2401, 6am-6pm Mon.-Sat., 7am-2pm Sun., $2-8) for a mouthwatering selection of freshly baked breads, muffins, and breakfast sammies. After a fun day outdoors, **Moonlight Pizza & Brewpub** (242 F St., 719/539-4277, www.moonlightpizza. biz, 11am-9pm Mon.-Sat., 11am-8pm Sun., $8-14) is a great place to sip a foaming mug of amber beer or old ale and chow down on a Fullzone calzone, a cosmic Hawaiian pizza, or a Texas barbecue chicken sandwich. **Amica's** (127 F St., 719/539-5219, www.amicassalida.com, 11:30am-9pm daily, $10-15) is a popular Italian joint serving paninis, salads, and crispy, wood-fired pizzas loaded with toppings. Top it all off with a selection from their award-winning microbrews.

In keeping with the river-running theme, **Currents** (122 N. F St., 719/539-9514, http:// salidacurrents.com, 11am-10pm daily, $14-16) is a fine-dining establishment with a menu focused on fresh seafood and thick, juicy steaks. The restaurant also has a good selection of wine, spirits, and beers; live music is performed several nights each week.

Accommodations

Salida has a couple of unique properties, including the **Tudor Rose** (6720 Paradise Acre Rd., 719/539-2002, www.thetudorrose.com, $95-185), which sits on a secluded ridge with top-of-the-world views. Converted into a bed-and-breakfast in 1995, the manor has six large guest rooms with private baths, mini fridges, and large satellite TVs. There are also two comfortably furnished chalets ($180-200 for 2 people, breakfast not included) with full kitchens and spacious great rooms that can sleep up to six guests. The Tudor Rose is located 1.5 miles from downtown Salida off U.S. 50.

The **Mountain Goat Lodge** (9582 U.S. 285, 719/539-7173, http://mountaingoatlodge.com, $133-159) is a pet-friendly bed-and-breakfast set on a 20-acre goat farm. The lodge's six cheerful rooms all come with private baths, themed decor, and private balconies with beautiful views. Two main-floor suites can accommodate up to four guests. Hosts Gina and D'Arcy Marcell offer cheese-making, chicken-raising, and goat-care classes; the lodge's small herd of goats provides the milk for the delicious breakfast chèvre and thick yogurt. The lodge also rents a retro camper ($88, mid-May-mid-Oct.). The lodge is located 6.5 miles west of Salida off U.S. 285.

Transportation and Services

Salida is located approximately 100 miles west of Colorado Springs and 60 miles west of Cañon City. To reach Salida from Colorado Springs, drive to Cañon City by taking Exit 140 off I-25 and driving south on County Road 115 for about 34 miles to the junction with U.S. 50. Turn right onto U.S. 50 and continue west for about 68 miles. Downtown Salida is located north of U.S. 50; turn right on G Street, which leads to the town center at 1st Street.

Salida's **Chamber of Commerce** (http:// salidachamber.org) has a helpful website and operates a downtown **visitor center** (406 W. U.S. 50, 719/539-2068, 9am-5pm Mon.-Fri.).

Cañon City and the Royal Gorge

Nestled in a mountain embayment, the pretty community of Cañon City makes a great base from which to visit the region's top attraction: the Royal Gorge, a scenic canyon on the Arkansas River whose depths you can explore via train or a soaring suspension bridge.

SIGHTS

The Winery at Holy Cross Abbey

The Winery at Holy Cross Abbey (3011 E. U.S. 50, 719/276-5191, http://abbeywinery.com, 10am-6pm Mon.-Sat. and noon-5pm Sun. in summer, 10am-5pm Mon.-Sat. and noon-5pm Sun. Jan.-Mar., free) is a "divine" place to taste some Colorado-made wine. Established by an order of Benedictine monks on the grounds of a historic abbey, the Front Range's largest winery offers a large selection of traditional varietals like chardonnay, syrah, and merlot, as well as its well-known Apple Blossom, a slightly tart beverage made from locally grown apples. Tastings are free except for reserve wines ($1 each).

Skyline Drive

A short but spectacular scenic detour, **Skyline Drive** follows the crest of a narrow, 800-foot-high hogback where, in addition to stellar views, you can also see a fabulous series of 107-million-year-old dinosaur tracks (look for an interpretive sign adjacent to the road). Some of the 50 bulges still sport toe-like protrusions, identifying their makers as a group of ankylosaurs, low club-tailed dinosaurs that looked like overgrown armadillos. Amazingly, these tracks weren't discovered until 1999.

To reach Skyline Drive from Cañon City, head west on U.S. 50 for 3.4 miles to the marked right turn onto Skyline Drive. Though paved, this narrow, winding road lacks guardrails and is not suitable for RVs; it should not be driven in bad weather.

Royal Gorge Regional Museum and History Center

On the west side of downtown Cañon City, the **Royal Gorge Regional Museum and History Center** (612 Royal Gorge Blvd., 719/269-9036, http://rgmhc.org, 10am-4pm

ancient ankylosaur tracks along Skyline Drive

Wed.-Sat., free) hosts a variety of interesting exhibits, including Dinosaur Migration, which features a cast of the planet's most complete stegosaurus skeleton, as well as other fossils found in the famous **Garden Park Fossil Area** (6 miles north on the Garden Park-Shelf Rd., 719/269-8500, www.blm.gov, free).

Museum of Colorado Prisons

The first jail was built here in 1871 while Colorado was still a territory. Since then, Cañon City and the surrounding unincorporated portions of Fremont County have become the self-declared Corrections Capital of the World. The area currently hosts 11 state and federal prisons. With some 3,500 high-paying jobs, the prisons are a very important part of the local economy, as is tourism.

The **Museum of Colorado Prisons** (201 1st St., 719/269-3015, http://prisonmuseum. org, 10am-6pm daily in summer, 10am-5pm Wed.-Sun. in winter, $7) aims to educate visitors about the history of prisons in the state. Located in a former state-run women's facility, the museum unlocks the mysteries of life behind bars, from the inmates' and guards' everyday routines to the state's notorious prison riots in the early 1900s.

SHOPPING

Cañon City's historic downtown buildings host a number of indie shops. Fresh-scented **Aspen Meadows Handcrafted Soaps** (432 Main St., 719/276-0311, www.aspenmeadowssoaps.com, 10am-4:30pm Tues.-Sat.) sells body scrubs, creams, candles, and lotions, as well as beautiful handmade soaps. Northwest of town, **The Gold Mine Rock Shop** (44864 U.S. 50, 719/276-9353, http://thegoldminerockshop.com, 10am-6pm daily) has a large selection of semiprecious stones such as amethyst, sapphire, and quartz, along with other treasures.

FOOD AND ACCOMMODATIONS

The **Jewel of the Canyons Bed and Breakfast** (429 Greenwood Ave.,

719/275-0378, www.jewelofthecanyons.com, $139) is a restored 1890s Victorian with four cozy guest rooms featuring queen beds and private baths located nearby. Breakfast includes farm-fresh eggs and produce, local meat, and fresh-ground coffee. A covered front porch overlooks the verdant gardens and is a lovely place to enjoy your meal.

Pizza Madness (509 Main St., 719/276-3088, www.mypizzamadness.com, 11am-9pm Sun.-Thurs., 11am-9:30pm Fri.-Sat., $5-13) is a spacious yet frequently packed parlor serving fresh salads and delicious pizzas made from thick, hand-tossed dough. Choose from a variety of sauces and toppings.

Hungry hikers will enjoy the juicy hamburgers at **Bunkhouse Burgers** (2147 Fremont Dr., 719/315-4174, www.bhburgers. com, 10:30am-8pm Mon.-Thurs., 10:30am-9pm Fri.-Sat., 11am-8pm Sun., $4-10), made from locally raised and grass-fed beef.

For an upscale meal, try Cañon City's top-rated restaurant ★ **Le Petit Chablis** (512 Royal Gorge Blvd., 719/269-3333, http://lepetitchablis.com, 11:30am-1:30pm and 5:30pm-8:30pm Tues.-Thurs., 11:30am-1:30pm and 5:30pm-9:30pm Fri., 5:30pm-9:30pm Sat., $15-30). The popular bakery and dining establishment features authentic French dishes like French onion soup, red snapper cordon bleu, and even escargot.

TRANSPORTATION AND SERVICES

Cañon City is located 45 miles south of Colorado Springs. From Colorado Springs, take I-25 to Exit 140 and head south on County Road 115 for about 34 miles to the junction with U.S. 50. Turn right onto U.S. 50 and continue west for 10.5 miles. Turn right onto 15th Street, then head north for one block; follow a traffic circle around to the third exit onto Main Street to access the small downtown. The best source of information about the city and its attractions is the local **Chamber of Commerce** (403 Royal Gorge Blvd., 719/275-2331, www. canoncity.com).

Great Sand Dunes National Park

North America's tallest sand dunes

Along the eastern edge of Colorado's San Luis Valley is a vast, high-elevation basin almost as large as the state of New Jersey. The **Great Sand Dunes National Park and Preserve** (11999 Hwy. 150, Mosca, 719/378-6300, www.nps.gov, $15) hosts a remarkable dune field with mounds of sand up to 750 feet high. While these are the tallest dunes in North America, they are utterly dwarfed by their incredible backdrop—the long line of the jagged Sangre de Cristo mountain range. The dunes are tucked up against an embayment in the Sangre de Cristos, which bound the valley's eastern edge. The western side is marked by the San Juan Mountains, where much of the dunes' sand originates.

No trails cross the ever-shifting dune field, but visitors can explore via sandboard or sand sled, equipment specifically made for sliding down sand; the closest hills are accessible from Dunes parking area. The nearby **Oasis Restaurant and Store** (7800 Hwy. 150 N., Mosca, 719/378-2222, www.greatdunes.com, Apr.-Oct., $20) rents sandboards and sand sleds, and provides food and accommodation options near the park.

A **visitor center** (8:30am-6pm daily in summer, 9am-4:30pm daily fall-spring) has natural history exhibits and park information. Some of the 88 tent and RV sites at the **Piñon Flats Campground** (877/444-6777, www.recreation.gov, Apr.-Oct., $20) can be reserved up to six months in advance.

Great Sand Dunes National Park is located 150 miles south of Cañon City and 90 miles south of Salida via U.S. 285. From Colorado Springs, it is a 175-mile drive south via I-25 and U.S. 160.

★ ROYAL GORGE
Royal Gorge Bridge & Park

The deepest river canyon through the Front Range, the 10-mile-long Royal Gorge is the centerpiece of the **Royal Gorge Bridge & Park** (4218 County Rd. 3A, 888/333-5597, http://royalgorgebridge.com, park open 7am-dusk daily, rides 10am-dusk daily, $20).

The **Visitor Center** (10am-dusk daily) is located on the north rim of the gorge and offers natural history displays, a gift shop, a children's playground, and a restaurant. The on-site theater shows films that delve into the gorge's human history, including the legendary Royal Gorge Railroad War.

From the visitor center, ride the **Aerial**

Gondola across the gorge. It's nearly vertical walls soar up to 1,200 feet above the Arkansas River and are just 50 feet apart at the canyon's narrowest point. While magnificent from either rim, the views become even more breathtaking when gazing into the abyss from North America's highest **Suspension Bridge.** The bridge's deck dangles a dizzying 955 feet above what some call the Grand Canyon of the Arkansas.

For thrill-seekers, the cross-gorge **Cloudscraper zipline** ($50) offers an exciting perspective. Or, you can ride the stomach-lurching **Royal Rush Skycoaster** ($30), which sweeps you through the air in a 50-mph free fall before dangling you over the gorge, 1,200 feet above the river.

Royal Gorge Route Railroad

For those who prefer to keep their feet firmly planted on solid ground, the **Royal Gorge Route Railroad** (330 Royal Gorge Blvd., 719/276-4000, http://royalgorgeroute.com, hours vary, $44-60) explores the gorge from the bottom. Service classes range from basic coach (purchase food and drinks) to dinner trains (three-course meal included). Special seasonal events include an Oktoberfest lunch

train, a Mother's Day brunch ride, and the heartwarming Santa Express trains (Nov.-Dec.) that transport excited kids to meet Santa at the North Pole.

White-Water Rafting

One popular way to see the gorge is via a challenging white-water rafting run. A number of local outfits offer half- and full-day trips, including **Royal Gorge Rafting** (45045 W. U.S. 50, Cañon City, 719/275-7238, www.royalgorgerafting.net, Apr.-Sept., $79-139) and **Echo Canyon River Expeditions** (45000 W. U.S. 50, Cañon City, 800/755-3246, www.raftecho.com, Apr.-Sept., $79-135).

Getting There

The gorge is located 13.5 miles northwest of Cañon City, 58 miles south of Colorado Springs, and 54 miles east of Salida. From Cañon City, follow U.S. 50 northwest for eight miles, then turn left onto County Road 3A. From Colorado Springs, follow Highway 115 South for 54 miles to U.S. 50 and turn west. Continue west on U.S. 50 to County Road 3A and turn left.

From Salida, drive 54 miles east on U.S. 50 and turn right onto County Road 3A.

the suspension bridge spanning Royal Gorge

The Santa Fe Trail

There is still plenty of adventure to be had along the Colorado portion of the 1,200-mile-long Santa Fe Trail, the historic 19th-century trade route that stretched from western Missouri to Santa Fe, New Mexico. For nearly 60 years, this route was a vital military and commercial path along which thousands of emigrants also journeyed.

The trail's western portion had several branches. The more northerly Mountain Route followed the Arkansas River across western Kansas and eastern Colorado to present-day La Junta, where it left the river to strike southwest across the parched plains toward the trading center of Trinidad and Raton Pass (the border between Colorado and New Mexico). In the late 1800s, this was a steep and grueling obstacle for heavy wagons, which crawled up the pass single-file at speeds as slow as 0.5 mile per hour.

LA JUNTA
Bent's Old Fort National Historic Site

A sense of exploration lives on in this southeastern region, where small communities boast markers, museums, and other sites celebrating this historic path. The most noteworthy is **Bent's Old Fort National Historic Site** (35110 Hwy. 194, 719/383-5010, www.nps.gov, 8am-5:30pm daily June-Aug., 9am-4pm daily Sept.-May, $3), an impressive, reconstructed, 1840s fur-trading post where emigrants, trappers, soldiers, and the Arapaho and Cheyenne tribes peacefully traded furs, purchased supplies, and rested from their arduous journeys.

LAS ANIMAS
Boggsville Historic Site

About 12 miles east of Bent's Old Fort in the small town of Las Animas, **Boggsville Historic Site** (Hwy. 101, 10am-4pm daily late May-early Sept., 10am-4pm Wed.-Sun. late Apr.-late May and early Sept.-late Oct., free) is home to a few dilapidated buildings—all that remains from this crucial 19th-century settlement where Kit Carson once lived.

Bent's Old Fort National Historic Site

COMANCHE NATIONAL GRASSLAND

The 443,000-acre **Comanche National Grassland** (1420 E. 3rd St., La Junta, 719/384-2181 or 877/444-6777, www.fs.usda.gov) is a beautiful and surprisingly varied landscape that ranges from short grass prairie to rocky canyons surrounded by pinyon-juniper forest. This rugged region is home to 300 species of animals and birds, and it once sheltered Native Americans who left behind stone shelters and rock art still visible today.

The **Picketwire Canyonlands** site is home to North America's largest dinosaur trackway, where more than 1,000 footprints of allosaurus and apatosaurus have been preserved. The site is only accessible via an 11.3-mile round-trip hike or bike ride or on a **guided auto tour** (719/384-2181, www.recreation.gov, 8am Sat. May-June and Sept.-Oct., $15). A high-clearance four-wheel drive vehicle (and a good spare tire) is needed and reservations are required. The eight-hour tours begin at the **Comanche National Grassland Office** (1420 E. 3rd St., La Junta, 719/384-2181).

GETTING THERE

La Junta is located about 100 miles southeast of Colorado Springs and Cañon City. From Colorado Springs, follow I-25 south for 40 miles to the town of Pueblo. Turn east on U.S. 50 for 65 miles to the town of La Junta. Las Animas is located 20 miles farther east on U.S. 50.

Comanche National Grassland

Background

The Landscape

Encompassing a little more than 104,000 square miles, Colorado is the nation's eighth-largest state and the highest, with an average elevation of 6,800 feet. However, this is simply an average; as visitors will quickly discover, Colorado's dramatic terrain varies more than two vertical miles from the towering 14,439-foot summit of Mount Elbert, the highest peak in the Mississippi River drainage, to the 3,315-foot depth of a river canyon crossing the state's eastern border.

Exploring Colorado involves many ups and downs: from mile-high Denver up to the aptly named "high country" to the drop along the Colorado River through spectacular Glenwood Canyon en route to Aspen and Grand Junction. These remarkable changes in elevation contribute to the state's famously variable weather, which can wreak havoc on transportation plans but also blesses ski resorts with an average of 300 inches of fresh, fluffy powder each year. While the thin, dry air and copious sunshine can cause nuisances like nosebleeds and shortness of breath, it also means that the stars are brighter, the spectacular scenery is more vivid, and there are dozens of legendary "Colorado Blue Bird" days—local slang for perfect, sunny ski days following an overnight snowfall.

GEOLOGY AND GEOGRAPHY

Colorado is divided into three general physiographic provinces: the relatively flat eastern plains; the rugged Rocky Mountains, where prominent ranges are separated by deep valleys; and the western mesa country, a relatively untouched wilderness of flat-topped, juniper-dotted mesas sliced by deep and winding river canyons.

Colorado's stunning scenery is the result of billions of years of geological events. Some events, like volcanic flare-ups, were short and dramatic, exceeding any eruptions that human beings have ever witnessed. However, the rise and fall of mountain ranges took hundreds of millions of years to accomplish. The state's oldest exposed rocks are about 1.8 billion years old, whereas the youngest rocks are still actively forming. This long and tumultuous geologic history has not only created Colorado's unsurpassed beauty—enjoyed daily by the millions of people who live here—but also underpins much of its history and economy, from mining to tourism and recreation.

The Plains

The western edge of the vast Great Plains stretches across eastern Colorado to the toe of the Rocky Mountains, creating one of the most abrupt physiographic changes on the continent. This region is covered by a thick blanket of sedimentary rocks left behind by a series of shallow seas that inundated this region between about 550 and 70 million years ago; these include volcanic rocks from major eruptions farther west, including Yellowstone; and sediment shed off the Rocky Mountains.

The resulting layers of sand, gravel, and ash formed important aquifers, sponge-like units of rock that store and transmit large quantities of freshwater to farms across the Midwest. During the last five million years, the region's streams have carved into the thick sedimentary blanket of the plains, gradually lowering this landscape.

The Front Range

Much of Colorado's population—including

---

the cities of Fort Collins, Boulder, Denver, Colorado Springs, and Pueblo—lives east of the Rockies along the mountain front, which is called the Front Range. Colorado's Front Range communities are some of the highest in the Great Plains region; Denver's famous "Mile High City" nickname comes from the fact that one of the steps up to the Capitol Building is situated exactly one mile above sea level.

Geologists have determined that no fewer than three mountain ranges have risen in this region. Beginning about 65 million years ago, tremendous earth forces driven by compression off the coast of California initially raised the Colorado Rockies. Another range rose earlier in roughly the same spot. Geologists call this the Ancestral Rockies, which formed here about 300 million years ago. Once uplifted, these ancestral mountains slowly wore away. Grain by grain, powerful rivers carted off the remnants of the range's craggy peaks and deposited them in a thick apron of sediment at the toe of the former mountains. Nearly 200 million years later, the uplift of the modern Rockies dramatically tilted this thick sediment pile, creating some of the Front Range's beautiful scenery, such as the rocks in the Garden of the Gods, Boulder's Flatirons, Eldorado Canyon, and Denver's Red Rocks Amphitheatre.

In Eldorado Canyon, there is evidence that an even older mountain range once existed here. A few scraps of a bullet-hard metamorphic rock known as quartzite sits exposed in a narrow, 10-mile band running south from Eldorado Canyon State Park. This quartzite is a mind-blowing 1.7 billion years old! Its original sand grains indicate this rock formed from sediment shed off an even older mountain range that lay a few dozen miles to the west, a range that was probably raised at Colorado's very birth.

The Mountains

Central Colorado's impressive mountain ranges are collectively known as the Colorado Rockies, part of the great chain of mountains that stretches more than 3,000 miles from British Columbia in Canada to southern New Mexico. The Colorado Rockies initially formed during the massive mountain-building event that roiled this region about 75 million years ago. The volcanic activity and mineral-rich fluids associated with this event created a long line of rich gold, silver, and other precious metal deposits, collectively known as the Colorado Mineral Belt. This mining belt stretches from Boulder in the northeast to Durango in the southwest; the opulent ore sparked Colorado's greatest gold rush and laid many of the foundations for our modern state.

While the linear Sawatch, Ten Mile, Mosquito, Park, and Sangre de Cristo ranges run north-south through the center of the state, the San Juans in southwestern Colorado have a distinctly different feel. Unlike other ranges, the San Juans are primarily volcanic, the result of a massive series of eruptions that swept across the western United States about 37 million years ago. This volcanic activity created a knot of high mountains with different mineral deposits and soils than those found elsewhere in the state.

Around the time of those eruptions, extension in the Earth's crust began to stretch part of Colorado, creating a series of deep, north-south valleys, including the San Luis and Arkansas River Valleys, which split the state's highest mountain ranges right down the middle. The San Luis later filled with sediment shed off the bordering mountains, creating the distinctive, wide, flat, and high-elevation valley that today hosts North America's tallest sand dunes.

Colorado's mountains were sculpted into modern masterpieces by powerful glaciers. About 2.5 million years ago, the global climate cooled enough to allow the growth of large mountain glaciers in the northern hemisphere for the first time in hundreds of millions of years. Since then, periodic changes in the Earth's orbit have repeatedly warmed and cooled the planet enough that the glaciers have alternately grown and shrunk

Cripple Creek

historic mining structures along the Gold Belt Byway

Most of Colorado's gold and silver deposits are located in an elongated mineral belt stretching from Boulder to the San Juans. The gold at Cripple Creek, however, is found in a small and isolated deposit associated with an ancient volcano that erupted about 32.5 million years ago. This was not an average, run-of-the-mill volcano; its magma was unusually rich in the element sodium, a trait shared by almost all of the world's enormous gold districts. This volcano also experienced particularly violent eruptions caused by the hot magma's interactions with groundwater. Whenever they met, the water instantly flashed into steam, causing the volcano to explode so forcefully that the eruption shattered the surrounding rock, which tumbled back into the empty magma chamber, leaving behind a thick mound of rubble.

Later in the volcano's life, hot water charged with dissolved gold and other valuable minerals repeatedly welled up and bathed this rubble, changing its composition and enriching it beyond any miner's wildest dreams. This perfect storm of geologic events left behind small but incredibly valuable concentrations of minerals, including two-inch-wide veins filled with up to 43 percent gold. One of these sparkling veins caught the eye of a Cripple Creek area rancher in 1891. After he promptly filed a claim, word spread like wildfire, and the area's population boomed from 500 to 10,000 residents.

Since then, the district has produced an enormous amount of wealth. More than 23 million ounces of gold—more than the Alaska and California gold rushes combined—have been extracted from just seven square miles. Worth more than $33 billion in today's prices, this fortune is not just historical; an open-pit mine in the area still extracts more than $1 million worth of metal daily from the region's unusual volcanic rocks.

during the so-called Ice Ages. The waxing and waning of glaciers up to 25 miles long and 2,000 feet thick put the finishing touches on the Colorado Rockies, including the fabulous scenery on display in Rocky Mountain National Park.

As a result of these "uplifting" geologic events, Colorado hosts many of the highest peaks in the Lower 48 and some of North America's highest-elevation communities, including Alma at 10,578 feet, the highest incorporated town in the United States, as well as two-mile-high Leadville, America's highest city.

The Western Slope

The only major community located west of the Colorado Rockies, Grand Junction is named for the intersection of two major rivers, the Gunnison and the Colorado. (Initially called the Grand, the Colorado was named by early Spanish explorers who used the Spanish word for "ruddy" because its waters were so silty they sometimes appeared red.) These rivers are important sources of water in western Colorado and throughout the Southwest, nourishing dozens of orchards and vineyards on well-drained river terraces.

The Western Slope's high mesas are part of the Colorado Plateau, a physiographic region characterized by deep canyons carved into high-elevation plateaus formed from colorful and mostly flat sedimentary rocks. In several parts of this plateau, faults associated with the uplift of the Rocky Mountains have created monoclines: enormous, one-sided folds in otherwise horizontal rocks that look like giant risers between the treads of a staircase. Western Colorado has two such monoclines: Colorado National Monument near Grand Junction and Dinosaur National Monument in the state's far northwestern corner.

CLIMATE

Elevation determines the climate in Colorado. The Royal Gorge can be sweltering at the same time that the top of Pikes Peak, less than a 75-mile drive away, is experiencing a severe blizzard. Nowhere in Colorado is there a particularly gentle climate; sudden changes in weather, hurricane-force winds, and temperature fluctuations of 30°F in a single hour are all relatively common and make it an exciting place to visit.

Winter

Although winter is typically cold across the state, the air's low humidity means that winter days can be surprisingly mild. Denver's average daytime temperatures hover around 47°F in January and 49°F in February. For many Coloradoans, this is warm enough to wear shorts when it's sunny—which it usually is.

Spring

Spring begins in March, when the mountains usually receive their highest snowfalls and the skiing is awesome. At this time, the plains, Western Slope, and Front Range seem to experience all four seasons at once, with gentle rains and the occasional blizzard rapidly alternating between warm snaps. By late April, the state's lower elevations are usually emerald green and dotted with wildflowers. May and June are wonderful months, with daytime temperatures climbing into the 80s; although it can still drop below freezing at night, especially in the mountains.

Summer

By early July, the high country bursts into bloom and the daytime temperatures at lower elevations rise into the 90s, while nights remain pleasantly cool. By mid-to-late July, the monsoon season usually kicks in, bringing refreshing heavy downpours and thunderstorms each afternoon and, if it's strong enough, a second wildflower bloom. If you're in the high country during this season, hit the trail at dawn in order to avoid afternoon thunderstorms and steer clear of narrow canyons that can fill with deadly water in a matter of minutes—even if it's not raining where you are.

Fall

In September, the monsoon ceases, bringing a seemingly never-ending string of crisp, sunny days and colorful leaf displays in September and October. As the sun sinks and the temperatures dip, attention turns back to the high country, where the highest ski resorts begin to make snow in order to battle for the honor of being the first to open that season. By Thanksgiving, all resorts are open and snow returns across the state, beginning the cycle anew.

ENVIRONMENTAL ISSUES

Colorado struggles with a number of environmental issues, including energy and water development, limited water resources, and the state's mining legacy.

Fracking

One hot-button issue is hydraulic fracturing, a process that entails injecting fluids underground at pressures high enough to fracture the surrounding rock in order to form cracks through which previously rockbound fossil fuels can flow. Colloquially called fracking, this process permanently changes the rocks and produces wastewater laced with proprietary chemicals that, according to opponents, can contaminate important underground sources of drinking water. While this process has been used for more than 60 years, it has become controversial due to increased use and the expansion into suburban areas. There is also an increased risk of earthquakes from injecting the salty wastewater (produced later in the process), along with the gas or oil, into deep waste-fluid injection wells. Small earthquakes have occurred near wastewater injection wells around Greeley and in southern Colorado; more powerful tremors associated with wastewater injection in other states have brought this issue to prominence across the country. Many Colorado communities have responded by passing or trying to enact anti-fracking legislation, which most energy companies have opposed. Governor Hickenlooper (who initially worked as a geologist) has organized a commission to address fracking-related issues, but that hasn't stopped anti-fracking groups from putting stringent measures before voters.

Water

The rivers draining the Rockies provide life-sustaining water to the parched plains, the western mesa country, and six other states in the American Southwest. Recent drought and wildfires have brought the issue of water conservation into public consciousness. Denver and other communities have decreased their per-resident water usage by ripping out water-guzzling lawns and switching to low-flow toilets and showerheads. These changes, however, are not enough. Due to the state's growing population, as well as the effects of climate change, state officials are predicting a water shortage of 560,000 acre feet—roughly the volume of Lake Granby, the state's fourth-largest reservoir—by 2050. To counter this looming shortage, Colorado officials have developed a new state water plan, which encourages conservation while increasing water storage, possibly by building controversial

Old mine tailings are found across the state.

new dams or other diversions. With a price tag that's expected to run $100 million per year for 30 years, both the funding and the ensuing controversy make the plan's fate very uncertain.

Mining's Environmental Legacy

The environmental destruction wrought by mining was brought to the public's attention in dramatic fashion. In August 2015, workers accidentally destroyed a plug holding back wastewater draining from southwestern Colorado's historic Gold King Mine. This breach caused several million gallons of yellow water tainted with toxic chemicals to pour into the Animas River near Durango and eventually into the Colorado River, an important source of drinking water for about 40 million people. The area around the mine had long been contaminated due to the drainage of acidic water from the Gold King Mine, but the area had never been remediated; local officials feared that the stigma of a Superfund site would limit tourism. Following the spill, the local board of trustees and county commissioners approved a resolution seeking Superfund status—a long, complex, and expensive process. Remediation is likely years away. Many other, smaller mines across the West may never be cleaned up.

391

BACKGROUND
PLANTS AND ANIMALS

Plants and Animals

Thanks to its huge range in elevation, variable climate, and diverse environments, Colorado hosts an impressive array of flora and fauna, including 750 species of invertebrates, 460 species of birds, and nearly 100 species of fish, as well as several thousand native plants. Large protected areas like Rocky Mountain National Park—home to more than 275 types of birds, 60 species of mammals, and about 900 plant species—are crucial for protecting the state's ecological diversity. Colorado's flora and fauna are organized into half a dozen life zones, ecological communities whose characteristic plants and animals are determined by elevation, the availability of water, soil type, and the direction that a slopes faces.

SHORTGRASS PRAIRIE

The state's lowest elevations are dominated by shortgrass prairie, which begins at the toe of the Front Range and extends eastward across the plains. Because the prairie receives too little precipitation to support many trees, blue grama and other grasses, as well as rabbitbrush, dominate this ecosystem, which coyote, black-tailed prairie dogs, and black-tailed rabbits characteristically roam. Many birds, including golden eagles, red-tailed hawks, and Western meadowlarks, are frequently spotted overhead.

RIPARIAN

Along the river corridors, riparian ecosystems thrive. The moister soils encourage the growth of shrubs and trees, particularly cottonwoods, whose leaves turn golden yellow in autumn. The riparian zones are crucial for wildlife; nearly every plains mammal and many birds use the riparian corridors for habitat at some point during their life or migration cycles.

FOOTHILLS SCRUB

In the dry foothills scrub, neither grasses nor trees can thrive. Deciduous bushes like Gambel oak and mountain mahogany populate this ecosystem. Mule deer, with their long ears, are frequently seen here, as are coyotes and birds, including black-billed magpies and scrub jays.

PINYON-JUNIPER WOODLANDS

At elevations ranging 5,000-8,000 feet, Colorado hosts roughly five million acres of pinyon-juniper ("pj") woodlands. Colorado pinyon pines and the Utah or one-seed junipers have developed resistance to both cold and drought, which is handy given that winter temperatures can drop well below freezing and the average annual precipitation usually hovers between 10 and 15 inches. These woodlands are most extensive on the Western Slope, including the Mesa Verde area, with smaller areas in south-central Colorado and on the state's southeastern plains. Characteristic wildlife includes mule deer, mountain lions, pinyon jays, and ash-throated flycatchers.

As you move higher into the mountains, the cooler temperatures and higher precipitation allow taller trees to grow. These are evident in the montane and sub-alpine ecosystems, which, along with the highest-elevation tundra life zone, are present in Rocky Mountain National Park and many of the state's other alpine areas.

MONTANE

The montane life zone ranges 6,500-9,500 feet and is dominated by tall conifer trees, which reproduce via cones instead of flowers. Trees here include ponderosa pine, whose bark often smells like butterscotch, and Douglas fir, whose cones look like they have dozens of little tails sticking out of them. Drier, south-facing slopes tend to host more ponderosa pines, whereas the wetter, north-facing slopes usually have more Douglas firs and beautiful Colorado blue spruce. In addition to mule deer, elk, black bears, and black Abert's squirrels are frequent montane visitors, along with Steller's jays and Western tanagers flying overhead. In Rocky Mountain National Park, most large mammals, including elk, bighorn sheep, mule deer, and moose, spend at least part of the year in this life zone.

SUB-ALPINE

Above about 9,500 feet, the longer, colder winters are too harsh for the montane trees to survive. Instead, the sub-alpine life zone is characterized by spruce-fir forests with brushy undergrowth and, at higher elevations, stunted trees. Many birds, including ravens, downy and hairy woodpeckers, and Steller's jays, can be seen here, along with long-eared snowshoe hares and black bears, bobcats, and mountain lions.

a meadow of blooming alpine wildflowers

The World's Largest Living Organism

Many biologists believe that Earth's largest living organism is an aspen grove. These distinctive, white-barked trees are naturally found in the montane and sub-alpine zones, but are also frequently planted at lower elevations. Aspens *(Populus tremuloides)* reproduce through their roots (called suckers), which send up new chutes that eventually grow into trees. Their root systems are interconnected; entire hillsides can be covered by a single organism whose leaves all appear at the same time in spring and simultaneously turn yellow in the fall, creating gorgeous foliage displays.

These clonal colonies can be enormous; scientists have estimated that the Pando Grove in southern Utah's Fishlake National Forest hosts about 47,000 trunks and weighs more than 13 million pounds. Other (Colorado-based) scientists argue that groves on Kebler Pass in Colorado, northwest of Crested Butte, may be even larger, but they haven't been fully studied yet.

Aspens turn gold in the high country.

Regardless of who wins this contest, the aspen are in trouble. Since the mid-1990s, scientists have noticed that an increasing number of aspen have died, but they have been at a loss to explain why. Some argue this dieback is due to grazing animals, which can eat the young chutes, or suppression of wildfire, which these iconic trees need to successfully compete with conifers. While research continues, forest managers have fenced off part of Utah's Pando Grove in hopes of protecting one of the world's largest living organisms.

BACKGROUND
HISTORY

ALPINE

Colorado's highest-elevation life zone is the alpine ecosystem, a wild and windy place that is too cold for trees to grow. Here, tiny wildflowers like baby-blue alpine forget-me-nots cling close to the ground. Where temperatures are higher, bighorn sheep, camouflaged ptarmigans, squeaky picas, and yellow-bellied marmots scurry around.

History

ANCIENT AND ARCHAIC CIVILIZATIONS

Colorado was one of the first places to harbor people near the end of the last Ice Age. Archaeological excavations of ancient stone tools and bones indicate that as early as 14,000 years ago, Paleoindians were hunting in what is now Denver's southeastern suburbs as well as the far-eastern edge of the state. By about 11,000 years ago, the development of more sophisticated tools (including the first fluted arrowheads) led to the start of what is known as the Clovis culture. The Dent Site along the South Platte River east of present-day Loveland was the first site to show that people co-existed with, and hunted, mammoth.

Over time, as megafauna like the mammoth slowly became extinct, the Paleoindians adapted by hunting smaller animals with smaller, Folsom-style arrowheads. The Lindenmeier Archaeological Site, now part of the City of Fort Collins' Soapstone Prairie

Natural Area, is recognized as the most extensive campsite ever found from the Folsom tradition. Excavations there have uncovered bone and stone tools, scrapers, arrowheads, and spear points, as well as tiny decorative beads and etched disks—some of the most ancient and best evidence that the earliest North Americans used symbolic decoration.

For thousands of years during the Archaic Period, early Coloradoans became semi-nomadic hunter-gatherers who continued to hunt while also harvesting nuts and seeds. As the millennia passed, people became increasingly dependent upon agriculture and began to live in semi-permanent groups and farm in river valleys.

By the end of this period (about 1,000 BC), people had become completely dependent upon agriculture, especially corn, which was likely introduced to the region by the Mogollon (a culture based in southern New Mexico and Arizona that interacted with the Ancestral Puebloans in the Four Corners region). As they became increasingly dependent upon corn and other crops, the Ancestral Puebloans built permanent structures, including pithouses, pueblos, and circular ceremonial rooms called kivas. Over time, they constructed increasingly elaborate structures, culminating in the spectacular cliff dwellings for which Mesa Verde National Park is best known.

The Ancestral Puebloans flourished at Mesa Verde and many other Four Corners locations for about 700 years, until the late AD 1200s. Within the span of one or two generations, however, they deserted their homes, possibly due to a series of devastating droughts. In their place came the Ute, who gradually pushed into Colorado from Utah and Nevada, as well as many other Native American tribes, including the Navajo, Cheyenne, Sioux, Shoshone, and Arapaho.

EUROPEAN SETTLEMENT
Spanish Arrival

The first nonnative settlers to visit the region were the Spanish, who traveled north from Mexico in the 16th century searching for gold and other precious metals. When reports of pretty villages along the Rio Grande River reached Spanish leaders, they dispatched explorer Juan de Oñate to colonize the area. Intent on spreading Christianity to the native people, the Spanish took over New Mexico and claimed the territory of Colorado. After a settlement near present-day Pueblo failed, the Spanish did not establish any further settlements north of the Arkansas River.

Instead, the Spanish made several exploratory trips into Colorado's mountain ranges, including a 1765 foray led by explorer Juan Rivera. In 1776, Escalante and Dominguez, two Franciscan priests, led another expedition across southwestern Colorado while forging a trade route from Santa Fe to California that became known as the Old Spanish Trail. During that trip, the party visited the San Juan Mountains and was the first to find and describe Ancestral Puebloan ruins.

The Louisiana Purchase

Throughout the second half of the 18th century, control of the region west of the Mississippi River switched between France and Spain. By the dawn of the 19th century, Napoleon regained control of the vast Louisiana Territory, which stretched from New Orleans to Canada's southern Alberta and Saskatchewan Provinces. Faced with renewed conflict with England, Napoleon decided to sell the territory; in 1803, the United States quickly accepted the deal. For Colorado, the purchase was especially significant because it led to negotiations with Spain to define the territory's borders. In the end, the United States received part of the plains and the Front Range while the Spanish maintained their hold on the rest of the Rockies and the western plateaus.

Unsure exactly what he had purchased, President Thomas Jefferson dispatched explorers to visit this vast region. American explorations in Colorado began in earnest in 1806, when U.S. Army officer Zebulon

Pike visited the area on a mission to follow the Arkansas River to its source. During this trip, Pike explored central Colorado and spotted the mountain behind Colorado Springs that would later bear his name. From there, Pike journeyed into southern Colorado, where the Spanish arrested him and part of his party for crossing their border. After taking them to Santa Fe for questioning, the Spanish released the men the following year.

Fur Traders and Emigrant Trails

After Mexico gained its independence in 1821, the United States and Mexico put aside their differences and began a lucrative trade relationship based in large part on beaver pelts and other furs. Traders from Missouri to Santa Fe established small posts along the Arkansas and other rivers. This process resulted in the creation of the Santa Fe Trail, which for 60 years served as a vital military and commercial path.

Of the many trading posts founded along the route, the most famous was Colorado's Bent's Fort. Established in 1833 near Las Animas, the fort was where trappers, soldiers, and Native Americans could trade and buy supplies. In 1846, the United States went to war with Mexico and Bent's Fort was absorbed into the United States and transformed into a training area for soldiers. After two years of war, Mexico relinquished its northern territories, paving the way for American settlement in that area.

THE GOLD RUSH

In the summer of 1858, a party of prospectors from Oklahoma discovered a small amount of gold near Denver's Confluence Park. Word of the strike spread like wildfire, sparking the Pikes Peak Gold Rush, which brought an estimated 100,000 fortune seekers to the region over the next several years. Although the gold deposits along the rivers and streams were quickly depleted, the miners soon discovered much more valuable deposits in the nearby mountains, which helped attract more people,

including farmers, ranchers, and businesspeople, to the area.

In the wake of the gold rush, Colorado became an official U.S. territory in 1861, but as the gold played out, the region's population dropped dramatically. To counter this decline, boosters like William Gilpin, the territory's first governor, encouraged railroads to extend their lines to the territory. This helped modernize the mines and coaxed farmers and ranchers into settling on the fertile eastern plains.

THE INDIAN WARS

The encroaching Caucasian settlements caused conflict with Native Americans, including the Comanche, Kiowa, Cheyenne, and Arapaho tribes who had longstanding cultural and legal claims in Colorado. After forming a loose alliance, the Native Americans battled federal troops during a bloody and tragic period known as the Colorado War (1863-1865).

In 1864, Cheyenne and Arapaho warriors murdered the Hungate family on their ranch some 30 miles from Denver. American troops, led by Colonel John Chivington, responded by slaughtering hundreds of Arapaho and Cheyenne, including many women and children, in the Sand Creek Massacre. The hostilities continued for many years until another skirmish, known as the Meeker Massacre, occurred in 1879. Nathan Meeker, the founder of the city of Greeley, was killed along with 10 other whites after attempting to "reform" Native Americans according to Christian traditions. As hostilities spread, Congress passed legislation that removed the Ute from Colorado and took away some of the land the United States had formerly granted to them. Ultimately, these events took away the leverage of Ute leaders such as Chief Ouray and allowed settlers to assume control of the state for good.

BOOM AND BUST

As fears of Native American attacks dissipated and railroads spread across the land, homesteaders began flocking to Colorado

Territory. Statehood arrived in 1876, just 23 days after the nation's centennial, giving rise to Colorado's official nickname: The Centennial State.

Colorado's population continued to grow; the state's silver mines flourished in Leadville, Aspen, and parts of the San Juans. Thanks to this prosperity, fancy hotels and opera houses sprang up across the state. Colorado's economy boomed until 1893, when Congress' repeal of the Sherman Silver Purchase Act caused the price of silver to collapse overnight. As the mines closed, the displaced workers flooded Denver in hopes of finding other jobs, leaving ghost towns and economic depression in their wake.

For the next few decades, Colorado was on an economic roller coaster ride. Bloody strikes in mining towns like Cripple Creek and Telluride led to confrontations between management and labor. At its peak in 1914, an altercation near Trinidad resulted in a number of deaths. The state's economy recovered briefly during a World War I-era silver boom, but was quickly followed by the Great Depression, when many of the state's farmers and ranchers went bankrupt.

TOURISM

The cycle of despair was finally broken in the 1930s, when President Franklin D. Roosevelt's New Deal revitalization programs pulled Colorado out of its long economic slump. The New Deal programs employed more than 40,000 Coloradoans who built hundreds of schools, courthouses, roads, and bridges, along with major irrigation projects. Roosevelt's Civilian Conservation Corps (CCC) also built a number of structures that remain today, including Rim Rock Drive in Colorado National Monument and Morrison's Red Rocks Amphitheatre.

In the 1950s, the construction of major roads such as I-70 sped up access to the Rocky Mountains, and Colorado began to market its scenic splendor and abundant recreation. By the 1960s, tourism had become the state's third-largest industry.

Thanks to pioneers such as Norwegian immigrant Carl Howelsen (who built Colorado's first ski jump in Steamboat Springs in 1914), the sport of skiing slowly developed a reputation in the early 20th century. Visionary entrepreneurs platted resorts in former mining towns like Breckenridge and unheard-of areas like Vail. By the 1960s, Steamboat Springs, Aspen, Breckenridge, and Vail were all competing for tourist dollars—especially after President Gerald Ford brought two Alpine World Ski Championships (along with international press coverage) to Vail. Since then, skiing in Colorado, and tourism in general, has evolved into a multi-billion-dollar industry.

COLORADO TODAY

Colorado is known for its large aerospace and science- and math-based industries, its high concentration of high-tech workers, and for hosting many start-up companies. These more stable industries have helped to balance out Colorado's original focus on natural resources, including oil, gas, and minerals, and brought many high-paying jobs to the state.

The state's central location has also played an important role in its economic and social development. The state-of-the-art Denver International Airport, one of the largest and busiest in the nation, opened in 1995 and the final stretch of I-70 through Glenwood Canyon was completed in 1992, finally giving Denver and the rest of the state easy driving access to Vail, Aspen, Grand Junction, and points west. In the 1990s, Denver began to overhaul its metropolitan area, revitalizing its downtown, completing several major transportation projects, and building Coors Field, to re-establish its leadership role embodied in its historic nickname, Queen City of the Plains.

As Colorado continues to expand and flourish, residents are enjoying economic prosperity and mountain lifestyles while grappling with both historic and novel challenges.

Government and Economy

GOVERNMENT

For years, Colorado was a politically conservative "red" state in elections, overwhelmingly voting for George W. Bush in 2000 and 2004 and generally electing Republican representatives and senators. While many of the state's residents, including ranchers and farmers on the plains and military personnel and families around Colorado Springs, remain staunchly conservative, Denver has grown increasingly liberal, due in part to the influx of people from states like California. Boulder, home of the state's flagship university, is one of the more liberal cities in the country and a frequent stop for liberal political candidates; Colorado Springs is a popular stop for conservatives.

As a result of these mixed demographics, Colorado elections have often had seemingly contradictory results. In 2004, an overwhelming Bush victory was paired with Democrat Ken Salazar's election to the U.S. Senate and state Democrats took over the legislature for the first time in decades. However, Colorado is now more of a swing state, with more than 50 percent of residents voting for President Obama in 2008 and 2012; the election of Denver's mayor, Democrat John Hickenlooper, as governor in 2010; and the re-election of Democrat Senator Michael Bennet the same year, despite the Tea Party revolution. In 2014, Hickenlooper narrowly won re-election, but will step down from the position in 2019 due to term limits.

Colorado's split personality persists in its U.S. Congressional delegation. As of 2016, Colorado had one Republican and one Democratic senator, and the House of Representatives delegation is split 4-3 in favor of Republicans. Of the 100 state General Assembly members, 51 are Democrats.

ECONOMY

Colorado was founded on fur trading, mining, and livestock. With the advent of irrigation, agriculture became an important contributor to the economy, particularly crops of hay, alfalfa, wheat, sugar beets, and fruit. Following World War II, the state's resource-based economy diversified as federal defense spending, energy production, and tourism all grew.

Although this diversification has helped stabilize Colorado's economy, the state has experienced many boom-and-bust cycles. A large slump in the late 1960s was followed by unprecedented economic growth fueled by the baby boomers' prosperity, high oil and gas prices, and a shift toward advanced technology. But the good times can't last forever; the prosperity ended in the mid-1980s with an economic downturn the likes of which had not been seen since the 1890s silver bust. The recession was due in large part to the collapse of oil prices, as well as the state's declining real estate markets.

The economy again rebounded in the 1990s, when the state added almost 700,000 new jobs, including in telecommunications, new technologies, and the service sector. At the turn of the millennium, the state's economy again declined, due in large part to the collapse of the high-tech industry. Fortunately, this didn't last as long as the previous downturn. The state's economy is once again booming, with a $315 billion total GDP in 2015, according to the Federal Reserve Bank of St. Louis. The state's very low unemployment rate hovers at about 3 percent.

Colorado is known for its concentration of high-tech industries and scientific research facilities, including a large number of federal research agencies. Other top business sectors include manufacturing, food processing, and federal services, including numerous military installations, the U.S. Mint in Denver, and prisons. Colorado, and particularly Boulder and Denver, are hotbeds for high-tech start-ups. The Front Range is also widely recognized for its leading role in the craft beer and natural foods industries. Agriculture remains an important part of the economy, with farm receipts totaling about $7.5 billion in 2015.

Tourism is a crucial and growing part of the modern economy. The number of visitors to Colorado has increased steadily; in 2016, more than 77 million people visited the state, collectively spending an all-time high of $19 billion.

People and Culture

DEMOGRAPHICS

Colorado is one of the fastest-growing states in the nation; since the official 2010 U.S. Census, the Bureau estimates that the state's population has expanded 8.5 percent to a total of 5.4 million people. Many out-of-state newcomers are attracted by the state's booming economy, low unemployment rate, pleasant climate, and abundant outdoor recreation. This rapid increase has also brought problems: crowded schools and congested roads, which the state and local governments struggle to keep up with.

Coloradoans are physically active and relatively young; about two-thirds of the population is under age 49, with about 40 percent under age 30. Colorado is also largely Caucasian, with 87.5 percent of the population self-identifying as white in 2015. The African American population is 4.5 percent, significantly less than the nationwide average of 13.3 percent. About 21 percent of the state's population identifies as being Hispanic or Latino, up from 17 percent in 2000. Denver is by far the state's most diverse area.

Coloradoans tend to be wealthier and more highly educated than the national average; 90.4 percent have a high school degree, and 37.5 percent hold at least a bachelor's degree, more than the nationwide average of 30.4 percent. The median household income (2010-2014) in Colorado is about $59,500, more than $7,500 higher than the national average.

One thing that unites Coloradoans is our love for nature and the outdoors. As a whole, Colorado is a genuinely friendly and laid-back state that many people have chosen to move to for the economic advantages and the mountain lifestyle. These attributes also make it a great place to visit.

THE ARTS

Colorado has a vibrant arts and cultural scene, particularly in the larger cities and ski towns, including Denver, Colorado Springs, Boulder, Aspen, and Vail.

Music

Colorado has a strong musical tradition. In the 1960s and 1970s, the state's tourism industry grew and some of the people who visited Colorado were musicians, including Elton John and members of Chicago and Earth, Wind & Fire. Chicago recorded three albums at Caribou Ranch near Nederland; Elton John even named an album after the ranch.

For decades, Colorado had the reputation of being a summer stopover for rising rock stars, including Dan Fogelberg, the Rolling Stones, the Eagles, and the Grateful Dead, whose reincarnation (Dead & Company) returned to play at Boulder's Folsom Field in 2016 for the first time in 15 years.

No history of music in Colorado would be complete without mention of Denver's Red Rocks Amphitheatre, one of the most stunning outdoor concert venues. The amphitheater has hosted regular concert seasons every year since 1947 and has witnessed many notable performances, including concerts by The Beatles, Jimi Hendrix, U2's 1983 "Under a Blood Red Sky" concert, and the infamous 1971 Jethro Tull performance that led to the so-called Riot at Red Rocks, after which rock concerts were banned for five years.

Today, the Colorado music scene continues

to thrive; many local artists and groups use Red Rocks, as well as other local venues, to launch and further their careers. A few notables include The Fray, The String Cheese Incident, and Big Head Todd and the Monsters. In addition, the Front Range hosts many smaller live music venues, including The Fillmore, Ogden Theatre, and the Fox Theatre, along with dozens of clubs.

Augmenting the music scene are Colorado's many music festivals, most of which are held in summer; these include RockyGrass in Lyons, Telluride Bluegrass Festival, Bravo! Vail classical music festival, and Jazz Aspen Snowmass festival. The Colorado Symphony Orchestra also offers regular classical, opera, and chamber music performances in Denver.

Theater

Denver and Boulder are anchors for the state's vibrant theater scene. Denver's theatrical centerpiece is the Denver Performing Arts Complex, one of the nation's largest performing arts centers with 10 separate performance spaces, including an opera house, the Boettcher Concert Hall, and the Buell Theatre. Denver's Shadow Theatre Company

features African American theater, while the Su Teatro Cultural and Performing Arts Center highlights Latino culture.

Boulder's largest indoor venue is the Dairy Arts Center, where both Boulder Ballet and the Boulder Ensemble Theater Company perform regularly. The University of Colorado is best known for its outstanding summer Shakespeare Festival. Colorado Springs hosts theatrical productions at the Colorado Springs Fine Arts Center.

Despite the town's tiny population, Grand Lake (on the west side of Rocky Mountain National Park) has what the *Denver Post* called one of the state's "premier summer musical companies." The Rocky Mountain Repertory Theatre performs popular Broadway musicals here in a state-of-the-art venue.

Visual Arts

Denver is home to a number of renowned visual arts collections and museums, including the Denver Art Museum; the Denver Public Library's Central Library; and the unique Clyfford Still Museum, which houses about 95 percent of this important 20th-cenury painter's works. Both Denver and Boulder also have contemporary art museums, while Colorado

a summer concert in Vail

Springs has the excellent Fine Arts Center museum, with works by renowned artists such as Ansel Adams and Georgia O'Keeffe.

Art galleries abound across the state, including around Larimer Square in Denver; along the bustling Pearl Street Mall in Boulder; in Old Colorado City near Colorado Springs; and in many of the mountain towns, especially Aspen, Vail, and Estes Park. Everyone from window-shoppers to serious collectors enjoys browsing the diverse assortment of mediums and styles on offer. Aspen's art museum hosts a striking exterior and thought-provoking exhibits that befit this affluent and intellectual town.

SPORTS

Colorado has a plethora of year-round sporting events ranging from traditional spectator sports like the Denver Broncos to amateur competitions and events. These vary from family-friendly 5K runs and Ironman 70.3 triathlons to ski jumping at Steamboat's Winter Carnival to Ride the Rockies, a seven-day bike tour through some of the state's most spectacular scenery.

Essentials

Transportation

GETTING THERE

Air

Denver International Airport (DEN, 8500 Peña Blvd., Denver, 303/342-2000, www.flydenver.com) and **Colorado Springs Airport** (COS, 7770 Milton E. Proby Pkwy., Colorado Springs, 719/550-1900, www.flycos.com) are the state's largest airports serviced by major carriers. DIA is conveniently located with services such as rental cars, buses, light rail, and taxis all easily accessible. While fares fluctuate, they are usually highest during the summer and the winter holidays. To connect en route to Denver during the winter, it's best to choose a hub in a more temperate climate such as Dallas/Fort Worth (DFW).

Colorado has a number of regional airports that are typically serviced by a few major carriers, including United Airlines, American Airlines, and/or Delta Airlines. These include the **Durango-LaPlata County Airport** (DRO, 1000 Airport Rd., Durango, 970/382-6050, www.durangogov.org), which serves the Four Corners area, and **Grand Junction Regional Airport** (GJT, 2828 Walker Field Dr., Grand Junction, 970/244-9100, www.gjairport.com) in west-central Colorado.

Several ski towns are located near airports whose service expands in winter. Aspen is located near the **Aspen/Pitkin County Airport** (ASE, 233 E. Airport Rd., Aspen, 970/920-5384, www.aspenairport.com). Vail and Beaver Creek are served by the **Eagle County Regional Airport** (EGE, 219 Eldon Wilson Rd., Gypsum, 970/328-2680, www.eaglecounty.us). Crested Butte is served by the **Gunnison-Crested Butte Airport** (GUC, 711 Rio Grande Ave., 970/641-2304, www.gunnisoncounty.org). Telluride is served by the **Montrose Regional Airport** (MTJ, 2100

Airport Rd., 970/249-3203, www.montrosecounty.net).

Car

Colorado is crisscrossed by two major interstates that intersect near downtown Denver: **I-25** cuts north-south along the Front Range and **I-70** runs east-west. North of Denver, **I-76** crosses both I-70 and I-25 before running diagonal across the state's northeastern corner to meet **I-80** just across the Nebraskan border.

Train

Amtrak (800/872-7245, www.amtrak.com) has two major routes that pass through Colorado. The beautiful California Zephyr route runs daily between Chicago and San Francisco with stops in Fort Morgan, Denver, Fraser-Winter Park, Granby (near Rocky Mountain National Park), Glenwood Springs, and Grand Junction. The daily Southwest Chief runs between Chicago and Los Angeles with stops in Lamar, La Junta, and Trinidad in the state's southeastern corner.

Bus

Greyhound (800/231-2222, www.greyhound.com) is most easily accessed from Denver's Union Station (1701 Wynkoop St.). From Union Station, bus routes continue on to Colorado Springs, Pueblo, Alamosa, Fort Collins, Gunnison, Vail, Grand Junction, and Durango, among other cities.

GETTING AROUND

The most efficient way to travel around the state is by car. Within the cities of Denver, Boulder, and Fort Collins, as well as the destination ski towns, it's usually possible to get around by walking, cycling, or via public

Driving Distances

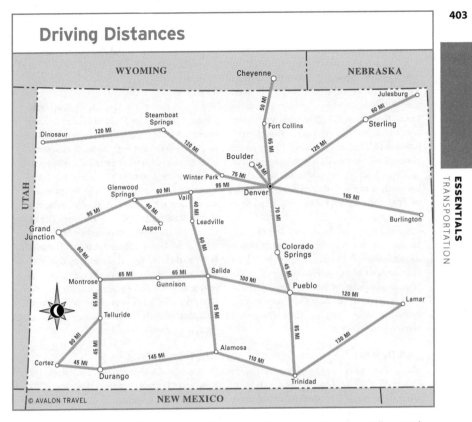

transport. Getting to smaller towns usually requires having your own vehicle.

Air

Flying between cities is only recommended if you're traveling from Denver or Colorado Springs to Grand Junction or one of the more remote skiing destinations like Crested Butte or Telluride. Within Colorado, **United Airlines** (800/864-8331, www.united.com), **Great Lakes Airlines** (800/554-5111, www.flygreatlakes.com), and **Allegiant Air** (702/505-8888, www.allegiantair.com) are among the carriers offering regional service.

Car

Interstate highways (I-70, I-25, and I-76) are the fastest and most convenient roads across the state. However, these roads are frequently congested during rush hour, especially around Denver and Colorado Springs.

During adverse weather conditions and peak traffic, stretches of I-70 west of Denver—particularly the 25-mile section between the Eisenhower Memorial Tunnel and the town of Idaho—can be frustratingly slow, especially on Friday (west-bound) and Sunday (east-bound) afternoons in both summer and winter. If you don't need to be anywhere by a certain hour, it's best to pull off and grab a bite to eat; the worst of the traffic usually clears up within a couple of hours unless there's a blizzard raging. When possible, try to time your trips in and out of the mountains on a Saturday or during the middle of the week.

Many of the state's minor roads cross higher elevations and mountain passes, which can be potentially dangerous when the weather turns bad. Many Coloradoans own all-wheel drive or four-wheel drive vehicles for navigating snow-packed roads and icy neighborhood streets, which are typically left unplowed. Consider renting a four-wheel drive vehicle if visiting during the winter. If you don't have four-wheel drive, know that passenger vehicles are sometimes required to have tire chains to navigate passes, even on interstates. Other passes close in winter and don't reopen until late spring. Check road conditions and chain laws online at the **Colorado Department of Transportation** (511, ww.cotrip.org or www.codot.gov).

Colorado's amazing scenery and rich history are highlighted along the state's 26 scenic and historic byways, 11 of which have been designated national scenic byways. The 26 routes include the Peak-to-Peak Highway west of Boulder, the San Juan Skyway near Telluride, and the Flat Tops Trail near Steamboat Springs.

CAR RENTAL

Major car rental agencies operating in Colorado include **Alamo** (844/351-8646, www.alamo.com), **Avis** (800/633-3469, www.avis.com), **Dollar** (800/800-4000, www.

dollar.com), and **Hertz** (800/654-3131, www.hertz.com), all of which have outlets at Denver International Airport and additional locations throughout the state.

Train

For a fun overnight trip along **Amtrak**'s (www.amtrak.com) California Zephyr route, ride the stretch between Denver and Glenwood Springs. In addition, some of Colorado's historic railroads still operate along scenic routes that are particularly beautiful in autumn when the aspen leaves are changing. These include the **Royal Gorge Route Railroad** (U.S. 50 and 3rd St., Cañon City, 719/276-4000, www.royalgorgeroute. com), the **Georgetown Loop Historic Railroad** (Loop Dr., Georgetown, 888/456-6777, http://georgetownlooprr.com), and the state's most famous narrow-gauge route, the **Durango & Silverton Narrow Gauge Railroad** (479 Main Ave., Durango, 888/872-4607, www.durangotrain.com).

Shuttle or Bus

Most major cities have local bus services. The **Regional Transportation District** (RTD, 303/299-6000, www.rtd-denver.com) serves the Denver-Boulder area. The **Mountain**

Driving offers flexibility for exploring Colorado.

Metropolitan Transit (719/385-7433, http://parks.coloradosprings.gov) is in Colorado Springs. The **Roaring Fork Transportation Authority** (970/925-8484, www.rfta.com) operates local buses and rapid transit in and around Aspen, Glenwood Springs, and Rifle.

The Colorado Department of Transportation oversees the inter-regional **Bustang** (800/900-3011, www.ridebustang.

com), which offers express bus service during commute hours. Most ski towns also have shuttle systems that operate during peak times, including Aspen, Steamboat Springs, Crested Butte, and Summit County.

A number of companies offer bus tours in Colorado, including **Gray Line** (800/472-9546, www.grayline.com), which serves Rocky Mountain National Park as well as Colorado Springs and Denver locations.

Recreation

Colorado's prime attraction is the great outdoors: breathtaking places, from the deepest canyon to the highest summit, where locals and visitors can relax in unspoiled nature. Just as diverse is the variety of activities on offer. Whether you enjoy swishing through waist-deep powder on downhill skis, fishing by a crystal-clear lake, or hiking through vibrant alpine tundra bursting with colorful blooms, Colorado is the place to immerse your senses in nature's scenic splendor.

PUBLIC LANDS

A large proportion (about 43 percent) of Colorado's land is publicly owned. About 7 percent is owned by the state itself, whereas 36 percent (roughly 24 million acres) is owned by the federal government, which manages these rich resources through several agencies, including the National Park Service, the U.S. Forest Service, and the Bureau of Land Management.

National Parks

The **National Park Service** (303/969-2500, www.nps.gov) oversees 16 parks, monuments, and trails across Colorado. Sites vary widely, from North America's tallest sand dunes and Mesa Verde's fabulous Ancestral Puebloan cliff dwellings to enormous petrified redwood stumps in Florissant Fossil Beds National Monument.

Wilderness Areas

Since the passage of the Wilderness Act of 1964, Congress has protected more than 40 parcels in Colorado as wilderness areas: untrammeled natural areas that help preserve a great diversity of plant and animal life. This designation also provides opportunities for visitors to experience solitude and participate in primitive (undeveloped) recreation. Colorado's wilderness areas are managed both by the U.S. Forest Service (www.fs.usda.gov) and the BLM (www.blm.gov). One of the state's most popular sites is the **Maroon Bells-Snowmass Wilderness** near Aspen (the location of the iconic twin Maroon Bells peaks), which some conservationists argue is in danger of losing many of the qualities for which it was preserved.

State Parks

Colorado Parks and Wildlife (1313 Sherman St., Denver, 303/297-1192, www.cpw.state.co.us) maintains 42 state parks covering more than 220,000 acres. Most sites are reservoirs, and all offer excellent recreational opportunities ranging from snowmobiling and ice fishing to boating, hiking, and camping. Entrance fees typically run $7-9 per day.

HIKING

Scenic hiking trails abound throughout Colorado. After acclimating to the elevation,

Leave No Trace

Whether you're enjoying a picnic lunch, white-water rafting, or backpacking along a long-distance trail, it's important to practice Leave No Trace principles so that the beautiful area you came to enjoy will remain so in the future. Embodied in the phrase, "Take only pictures; leave only footprints," this outdoor ethic covers every part of your experience outdoors.

· Plan thoughtfully using appropriate maps and other navigation tools.

· Pack carefully to minimize the amount of waste you'll need to carry out.

· Follow regulations regarding pets, group size, and where activities like camping and campfires are allowed; make absolutely certain that you completely extinguish any fire.

· Minimize land disturbance by cycling or walking through, rather than around, muddy trails; avoid off-trail shortcuts.

· Fill your memory cards instead of your pockets.

· Pack out all trash, including toilet paper, and properly dispose of human waste in cat holes dug at least 70 steps from camps, trails, and sources of water.

· Avoid disturbing wildlife. If you extend your arm in front of you and hold up your thumb, it should completely cover the animal; if your thumb doesn't, you're too close.

This philosophy applies equally to overnight visitors and day-trippers. No matter how long we stay outdoors, each and every one of us is responsible for preserving the natural beauty of Colorado's, and all other states', natural areas. For more information, visit the Center for Outdoor Ethics' **Leave No Trace** (https://lnt.org).

there are a number of appropriate hikes for a range of ages and fitness levels. Stroll to see ancient rock art on the Petroglyph Point Trail (2.4 miles round-trip) in Mesa Verde National Park. Follow the moderate Mesa Trail (7.3 miles one-way), the crown jewel of Boulder's extensive open space system. Challenge yourself by hiking up one of Colorado's 54 fourteeners or tackling the distinctive Twin Sisters Peak in Rocky Mountain National

Rock climbers scale the walls in Eldorado Canyon State Park.

RECREATION

popular biking tours and events. The challenging **Triple Bypass Bicycle Ride** (http://triplebypass.org, July) climbs three major passes, gaining more than 10,000 vertical feet over about 120 miles. A more moderate but equally scenic option is the **Tour of the Moon** (http://tourofthemoon.com, Sept.-Oct.) through Colorado National Monument.

Mountain Biking

Colorado features outstanding mountain bike trails that range in difficulty from smooth forest roads to white-knuckle single-track with killer views. Mountain-bike friendly towns include Crested Butte, home to excellent rides such as Pearl Pass, a challenging 38-mile ride to Aspen via a 12,700-foot pass. Grand Junction serves as the eastern base for many classic single track routes, including the stunningly beautiful 142-mile Kokopelli's Trail to Moab. **Singletracks** (www.singletracks.com) provides a list of other popular trails in Colorado.

In summer, most of the ski areas allow cyclists to pedal down their slopes, then haul their bikes back uphill on a gondola or ski lift. Winter Park bills itself as **Mountain Bike Capital USA** (www.mtbcapitalusa.com). Fat bikes (extra-wide tires) allow cyclists to ride through deep snow and have become extremely popular at many of the state's resorts.

Several advocacy groups build trails and educate the public, including the **Colorado Mountain Bike Association** (www.comba.org) along the Front Range and the **Colorado Plateau Mountain Bike Trail Association** (www.copmoba.org) in western Colorado.

ROCK CLIMBING

Rock climbing is a popular sport in Colorado, particularly the sandstone walls in Eldorado Canyon State Park near Boulder and Garden of the Gods near Colorado Springs, as well as the sheer granite cliffs of Lumpy Ridge in Rocky Mountain National Park. Two companies offer beginner-through-advanced instruction, as well as guided climbs (including equipment rental): **Colorado**

Park. If you're interested in backpacking but don't have much experience, consider hiring a backcountry outfitter to guide you up some of Colorado's more strenuous trails.

BIKING

Colorado is a well-known cycling destination. There are numerous local clubs, informal meet-ups, and tours across the state. With more than 300 miles of dedicated bikeways, Boulder is an extremely bike-friendly town with many excellent flat and foothills rides. On Denver's western fringe, the town of Golden makes a great cycling base, with great access to the 20-mile-long Clear Creek Trail as well as the classic climb up Lookout Mountain. **Bicycle Colorado** (http://bicyclecolorado.org) has bicycling maps, tips, and ride information online.

Tours

The **Bicycle Tour of Colorado** (www.bicycletourcolorado.com, June) is an annual seven-day tour and one of the state's many

Mountain School (2829 Mapleton Ave., Boulder, 800/836-4008, www.coloradomountainschool.com) and The Colorado Climbing Company (1031 Mt. Werner Circle, Colorado Springs, 719/209-6649, www.coclimbing.com).

RAFTING AND KAYAKING

Colorado boasts more than a dozen frothing rivers ideal for white-water rafting and kayaking. Top destinations include the Colorado, Roaring Fork, Arkansas, South Platte, Gunnison, Green, and Yampa Rivers, as well as Clear Creek just west of Denver. While the season generally lasts May-September, the rivers typically run highest mid-May-June. The state's classic runs include: the Numbers, Browns Canyon, and Royal Gorge stretches on the Arkansas River; the Split Mountain and overnight Gates of the Lodore runs through the gorgeous canyons in Dinosaur National Monument; the Gunnison Gorge on the Gunnison River; and the De Beque Canyon and Ruby-Horsethief flat-water stretches of the Colorado River.

Colorado Parks & Wildlife (www.cpw.state.co.us) provides a list of outfitters for the Arkansas Headwaters Recreation Area. Whitewater Rafting in Colorado (www.raftinfo.com), Colorado Tourism (www.colorado.com), and Colorado Whitewater (www.coloradowhitewater.org) websites include links to outfitters as well as other whitewater resources.

FISHING

With 6,000 miles of rivers and 2,000 lakes hosting 35 species of fish, Colorado is a great place for angling. Top rivers include the Cache La Poudre River near Fort Collins; the Yampa River in and near Steamboat Springs; the Arkansas River in southeastern Colorado; and the Roaring Fork River near Aspen. Fishing opportunities abound in the state's many sparkling lakes, including Trappers Lake, Lake Dillon (near the Breckenridge and Keystone ski resorts), and the many beautiful lakes in Rocky Mountain National Park. Colorado Parks & Wildlife (www.cpw.state.co.us) is your go-to source for the state's fishing brochure, maps, and regulations, as well as for non-resident fishing passes ($9-21).

FOUR-WHEEL DRIVES

A great way to explore Colorado's plentiful public lands is by four-wheel drive. Prime destinations include Pearl Pass, a rough road between Crested Butte and Aspen, and the Yankee Boy Basin, a gorgeous, wildflower-filled basin high in the San Juan Mountains near Ouray.

Guided tours can cost $50-300, depending on length. If you prefer to explore the state's roughest roads yourself, rent a Jeep ($150-250 per day). When venturing into state and national parks and forests, check with the rangers for guidelines and obey all posted regulations. Good resources for finding outfitters and guides include Colorado Tourism (www.colorado.com), DuranGO Outdoors (www.durangoutdoors.com), Best of Salida (www.salida.com), and www.centralcolorado.com. For an off-road trail map, visit www.coloradodirectory.com.

GOLF

Thanks to the high, thin air, balls fly about 10 percent farther at a mile-high elevation. Lower your handicap at one of Colorado's more than 300 public and private courses, which encompass everything from desert to alpine environments. The state's most famous links are located in the mountains, particularly the championship courses in Beaver Creek and Vail. Denver also has a number of reputable courses, including the unique Fossil Trace Golf Club (www.fossiltrace.com) in Golden, where you can putt next to prehistoric fossils. Green fees range widely ($24-250 for 18 holes); most courses also offer equipment and cart rentals.

HORSEBACK RIDING

From kids' pony rides to multi-day trail rides, many options exist for experiencing

Colorado by horseback. Popular rides include the spectacular **Garden of the Gods** (www.academyridingstables.com) near Colorado Springs and **Rocky Mountain National Park** (www.sombrero.com). In Colorado's "cowboy corner" near Steamboat Springs, a number of local ranches offer guided trail rides and overnight adventures. For more information, visit the **Colorado Dude and Guest Ranch Association** (www.coloradoranch.com).

WINTER SPORTS
Skiing and Snowboarding
Skiing and snowboarding are the quintessential Colorado winter activities and a major portion of its multi-billion-dollar tourism industry. Visitors travel from all over the world to enjoy Colorado's renowned combination of 300 days of sunshine, 300 inches of snow, and the 2,435 feet of vertical rise that the resorts average each year.

Each of the state's 25 resorts sports its own personality. The **Colorado Ski Country USA** (http://coloradoski.com) and **Colorado Tourism** (www.colorado.com) websites offer detailed, up-to-date information. Skis, boots, poles, and helmets can be rented from sporting goods stores at or near all the resorts. Snowboarding can be found at all the major ski resorts, both on the slopes and in terrain parks. Most ski shops also rent boards.

Nordic (cross-country) and backcountry skiing immerses you in the state's peaceful beauty along both groomed and ungroomed trails. Most resorts offer Nordic trails. Rocky Mountain National Park is a popular backcountry destination. Colorado's system of 34 **ski huts** (https://olb.huts.org) connects 350 miles of backcountry trails.

Before you head out, check the avalanche risk at pertinent ranger districts or online at **Colorado Avalanche Information Center** (http://avalanche.state.co.us), which also has an important Know Before You Go section and a sign-up for Twitter updates. The **Cross Country Ski Association** (www.coloradocrosscountry.com) has

additional statewide information on its website.

Snowmobiling
Colorado boasts more than 3,000 miles of snowmobile trails, many of which are located near Grand Lake, the self-proclaimed Snowmobiling Capital of Colorado. Whether you're looking for guided tours or a vehicle rental, the **Colorado Snowmobile Association** (www.snowmobilecolo.com) and **Colorado Tourism** (www.colorado.com) websites provide information to get you started. Check avalanche risks at pertinent ranger districts and online at the **Colorado Avalanche Information Center** (http://avalanche.state.co.us).

SPECTATOR SPORTS
Denver is a football town, but people across the state tend to wear orange and blue whenever the **Denver Broncos** (www.denverbroncos.com) play. Denver has six other professional sports teams, including the **Colorado Rockies** (www.colorado.rockies.mlb.com) baseball team. Opening day is celebrated by the painting of a purple stripe down the center of Blake Street near Coors Field.

Denver hosts the **Colorado Avalanche** (National Hockey League, www.coloradoavalanche.com), the **Denver Nuggets** (National Basketball Association, www.nba.com/nuggets), the **Colorado Rapids** (Major League Soccer, www.coloradorapids.com), as well as two lacrosse teams, the **Colorado Mammoth** (www.coloradomammoth.com) and the **Denver Outlaws** (www.denveroutlaws.com).

The state's largest colleges, including the University of Colorado, Colorado State University, and the Air Force Academy, all have Division I football teams.

Denver is home to the **National Western Stock Show** (www.nationalwestern.com, Jan.), as well as other professional rodeo events, including the **Steamboat Springs Cowboys' Roundup Days** (www.steamboatchamber.com, July).

Accommodations and Food

ACCOMMODATIONS

Whether you prefer to snooze in a peaceful camping spot tucked beneath the trees, a posh resort, or a historic Victorian bed-and-breakfast, you will find many great options in Colorado.

Hotels and motels abound, with prices and amenities that run the full gamut, particularly in ski areas. Bed-and-breakfasts are cozy and more personalized options that sometimes come with unexpected perks such as learning how to milk goats. The **Bed and Breakfast Innkeepers of Colorado** (www.innsofcolorado.org) and **Bed and Breakfast Inns ONLINE** (www.BBonline.com) provide listings. Since the 1880s, dude ranches have dotted the Colorado landscape, catering to those who want to truly "experience" the West. The **Colorado Dude and Guest Ranch Association** (www.coloradoranch.com) has more information.

High season rates vary depending upon location. At the ski resorts, high season typically runs late December-late March, with the highest demand during the weeks of Christmas and New Year's, as well as the Martin Luther King Jr. and Presidents' Day weekends. For the rest of the state, high season is June-August. It's often possible to score lower rates, especially during the "mud" seasons in the mountains (typically mid-Apr.-late May and mid-Oct.-mid-Nov.).

CAMPING

Camping is very popular in Colorado and is a great way to immerse yourself in the state's gorgeous scenery. Most campgrounds are open Memorial Day-Labor Day, but many have extended seasons. Generally, lower-elevation sites such as those in the Grand Junction area are open March-October; sites in the mountains, such as those in Rocky Mountain National Park, have seasons that vary according to snowfall. Facilities in the state and national parks as well as U.S. Forest Service campgrounds are usually primitive and typically include vault toilets and a spigot for water. Online reservations are possible at **State of Colorado** (http://parks.state.co.us) and **Recreation.gov** (www.reserveamerica.com).

Sports Authority Field at Mile High, home of the Denver Broncos

Colorado has many excellent private campgrounds, which generally have spiffier amenities, including restrooms with running water and hot showers, and kid-friendly attractions like playgrounds and swimming pools. Many of these facilities also rent cabins.

FOOD

Colorado boasts a large number of award-winning chefs and renowned restaurants as well as a number of unique, quintessential dining experiences. Dining options range from high-end restaurants in Aspen and fresh farm-to-table bistros in Boulder to colorful food trucks and gastropubs in Denver.

Gourmands will want to sample Denver establishments, such as tiny Mizuna and Elway's famous steakhouse. In Boulder, stop in at Frasca Food and Wine and the Flagstaff House before heading to the mountain towns of Aspen, Vail, Beaver Creek, and Telluride for more highly lauded options.

Some of Colorado's hidden dining gems include the Gold Hill Inn, a historic log cabin in a quaint foothills gold-mining town. The delicious, six-course meal has been called one of the nation's best restaurant deals. At Summit County's colorful Minturn Farmers Market you can sample mouthwatering fresh produce, homemade tamales, and grilled chicken pitas.

Colorado Cuisine

The state's variety of microclimates, abundant sunshine, fertile soils, and a commitment to sustainable farming practices create a uniquely Colorado cuisine.

Specialties include juicy Western Slope peaches, Southwestern green chilis, the state's famous trout, and grass-fed beef, bison, and lamb. In summer, Boulder, Fort Collins, Colorado Springs, and Denver host regular farmers markets—ideal places to shop for local produce and handmade products.

Colorado's several wilderness restaurants combine a love of outdoor recreation with great food. Accessible only by foot, skis, gondola, or sleigh, these quintessential experiences handsomely reward the extra effort to get there. Many are based in Summit County and include Starlight Dinners by Sleigh in Breckenridge and Frisco; the Alpenglow Stube at Keystone Resort; and Beano's Cabin, a cozy hut at Beaver Creek that's only accessible via horseback or a snowcat-pulled open sleigh.

Festivals and Events

Colorado hosts a number of excellent food and beverage festivals each year, including the **Blues, Brews, and BBQ** festival in Beaver Creek (May); Aspen's **Food & Wine Classic** (www.foodandwine.com, June), one of the nation's largest culinary events; Palisade's **Colorado Mountain Winefest** (http://coloradowineexperience.com, Sept.), the state's premier wine event; and Denver's **Great American Beer Festival** (www.greatamericanbeerfestival.com, Oct.).

Vegetarian and Vegan

It's easy to find vegetarian food in Colorado, and possible to eat vegan in most of the state's college towns, especially Denver, Boulder, and Fort Collins. Gluten-free is becoming an increasingly popular option, available in grocery and natural food stores as well as college town restaurants.

Beer, Wine, and Spirits

Colorado is one of the nation's hottest spots for craft brews. With 125 breweries and taprooms in Denver (and more scattered along the Front Range), this region is called the Napa Valley of beer. Start by visiting **Wynkoop Brewing Company** (www.wynkoop.com) is LoDo's original brewery, started in the 1980s by Governor John Hickenlooper.

Fort Collins was dry until 1969. Today, it has 20 breweries, including the industry-leading **New Belgium Brewery** (www.newbelgium.com) and **Odell Brewing Company** (www.odellbrewing.com), the state's second-oldest brewery. Colorado Springs, Boulder, Breckenridge, and Aspen all host excellent brewpubs and craft breweries.

Farm-to-Table

Enjoy locally grown and raised food.

Colorado is a growing center for the farm-to-table movement, which is based on the concept of cooking with locally grown and sourced foods and beverages as much as possible. When the ingredients are organically grown and directly distributed, the food is incredibly fresh and flavorful, even if the menus are more limited. In the Gunnison River's beautiful North Fork Valley, the tiny town of **Paonia** has the greatest concentration of sustainable organic growers and is a center of fresh farm-to-table food and drink, including the fabulous **Living Farm Café** and wineries such as Stone Cottage Cellars and Azura Cellars.

The Kitchen Denver is a delicious farm-to-table option in downtown Denver. Environmentally conscious Boulder is a great spot for farm-to-table cuisine. Many establishments near the pedestrian Pearl Street Mall utilize local produce, dairy, and meat in their kitchens, including **SALT,** and the stunning **Dushanbe Teahouse,** a handcrafted Persian teahouse from one of Boulder's sister cities.

Travel Tips

WHAT TO PACK

Traveling in Colorado will likely take you from the plains to the high peaks, so it's essential to pack layered clothing to help you stay warm (or cool) as the elevation changes and nighttime temperatures fall. Rain gear is important, especially when planning excursions into the mountains; afternoon thunderstorms frequently roll in during the summer. Be sure to pack sunscreen, which you'll almost immediately need, as well as a first-aid kit and a water filter for exploring outdoors.

TOURIST INFORMATION
Area Codes

Colorado has four area codes. Denver and central Colorado (including Boulder) use the 303 and 720 area codes. Southeastern Colorado, which includes Colorado Springs and Pueblo, use area code 719. Northern and western Colorado, including Grand Junction, Durango, Aspen, and Fort Collins, use 970.

Internet and Cell Service

Most cell phone networks have good reception along the Front Range; however, cell phones often won't work in the mountains and in remote corners of the state. Do not depend upon your cell phone in case of an emergency. For those hiking Colorado's fourteeners, online (www.14ers.com) trip reports include the quality of cell phone coverage on each summit.

Maps

The **Colorado Tourism** website (www.colorado.com) has a downloadable map and statewide vacation guide. Most local chambers of commerce, visitor bureaus, and ski resorts produce additional tourism literature.

I highly recommend purchasing the **Colorado Road & Recreation Atlas,** published by Benchmark Maps. The detailed scale is very useful for navigating and finding your way to the state's more remote sites.

If you plan to do a lot of hiking or back-country adventures, purchase the relevant topographical maps from the online **USGS Store** (https://store.usgs.gov), **National Forest Map Store** (www.fs.fed.us), or one of the U.S. Forest Service offices. Almost every town in Colorado has at least one outdoor store, where you can usually find maps relevant to that area.

Time Zone

Colorado is in the **Mountain Time Zone;** it is one hour ahead of the Pacific Standard Time Zone on the West Coast and two hours behind the Eastern Central Time Zone on the East Coast. It's -7 GMT during the winter and -6 GMT late March-early November, when daylight saving time is followed statewide.

INTERNATIONAL TRAVELERS

Visiting from another country, you must have a **valid passport** and a **visa** to enter

the United States. Some countries may qualify for the **Visa Waiver Program;** check the **U.S. Department of State** online (http://travel.state.gov) to determine whether you'll need a visa; most European nationals do not.

The U.S. dollar is the currency. Currency exchanges are generally available at banks, hotels, and larger airports like Denver International. The most convenient way to access cash is via automatic teller machines. Most Colorado establishments accept travelers checks, particularly those from Visa and MasterCard, as well as credit cards.

Tip 15 percent to taxi drivers and 15-20 percent on restaurant bills. For larger groups, restaurants will often tack an additional 18 percent onto the bill; check before you pay. At bars and clubs, tip about $1 per drink when ordering at the bar. At hotels, tip $1-2 per bag for delivering luggage to your room and $1-2 per day for housekeeping. Tip $2-5 for a valet-parking attendant.

Electricity across the U.S. is 120 volts, with a two-prong, flat-headed plug.

ACCESS FOR TRAVELERS WITH DISABILITIES

Most public buses are wheelchair accessible; wheelchair ramps and accessible elevators are available at most venues. Access can be more difficult outdoors; contact the **National Park Service** (www.nps.gov), the **Colorado Parks & Wildlife** (www.cpw.state.co.us), and the **Breckenridge Outdoor Education Center** (www.boec.org) for accessible sights and activities.

Several Colorado organizations offer outdoor adventures specifically for those with physical disabilities, including **Ignite Adaptive Sports** (Eldora Mountain Resort, 2861 Eldora Ski Rd., Nederland, 303/258-1166, www.igniteadaptivesports.org) and the **National Sports Center for the Disabled** (Winter Park Resort, 85 Parsenn Rd., Winter Park, 970/726-1518 or 303/316-1518, www.nscd.org).

Wilderness on Wheels (U.S. 285, Grant, 303/403-1110, www.wildernessonwheels. org, 9am-6pm daily late May-mid-Oct.) and Adaptive Adventures (1315 Nelson St., Lakewood, 877/679-2770, www.adaptiveadventures.org), both based in the greater Denver area, organize hiking, alpine sports, camping, and rock climbing adventures for people with disabilities.

Colorado residents with disabilities, including veterans, can receive the special Access Pass to state parks by applying through Colorado Parks & Wildlife (www.cpw.state.co.us). The National Park Service (www.nps.gov) also provides a free lifetime Access Pass for U.S. citizens and permanent residents with disabilities; apply in person or by mail.

TRAVELING WITH CHILDREN

Most cities offer plenty of kid-friendly activities and many ski resorts offer lessons to kids and teens and may even provide childcare. Many major attractions offer discounted admission for children. Some bed-and-breakfasts and fine-dining establishments will not allow children; ask before making a reservation.

SENIOR TRAVELERS

Many museums, attractions, and ski resorts, as well as restaurants, retail stores, and hotels, offer senior discounts. AARP members (www. aarp.org) have access to a number of discounts through their membership; Savvy Seniors Colorado (www.coloradosavvyseniors.com) provides a list of some of these companies and their discount offers.

Colorado seniors can receive a discounted annual pass to state parks through Colorado Parks & Wildlife (www.cpw.state.co.us). The National Park Service (www.nps.gov, $10) offers a lifetime America the Beautiful National Parks and Federal Recreational Lands Senior Pass for U.S. citizens and permanent residents aged 62 or older; apply in person or by mail.

Road Scholar (www.roadscholar.org) offers a number of educational trips across the state. Although trips vary in length, most last 6-9 days and cover a wide range of attractions, interests, and activity levels—from historic railroads and scenic byways to fall photography and hiking some of Colorado's famous fourteeners.

GAY AND LESBIAN TRAVELERS

Same-sex marriages have been legally recognized in Colorado since 2014. Portions of the state are more open to the LGBT community, including Denver, Boulder, and many of the mountain resort towns. Boulder and Denver are both known for their gay clubs (www.glbtcolorado.org). However, some parts of the state, including rural areas and Colorado Springs, tend to be more conservative; members of the LGBT community may find a less welcome reception.

Health and Safety

WEATHER CONCERNS

Visitors should be prepared for rapid weather changes. In summer, lightning is a danger when outdoors and even during occasional spring skiing "thundersnows." Hikers should check the weather beforehand, leave at dawn in order to avoid afternoon thunderstorm build-up, and descend from high and exposed places such as summits, ledges, and ridges if a storm arrives. Rapid temperature changes of 30 or more degrees are common; be prepared with layered clothing, hats, gloves, and rain gear that can be added or removed as needed.

At a high altitude, sunburn can occur in less than 10 minutes. When outdoors, apply a broad-spectrum sunscreen with SPF 15 or higher every couple of hours. If skiing, most resorts have sunscreen available at their ski patrol huts.

Dehydration and Heatstroke

Dehydration is an issue in our arid climate, especially in summer when the sun is intense and the temperatures high. Symptoms of dehydration include excessive thirst, dry lips, and dizziness. Carry plenty of water (at least one gallon per person) in order to counteract Colorado's extremely low humidity. If you feel dizzy, cranky, or thirsty, sit down in some shade and slowly sip water or drink an electrolyte replacement. If symptoms worsen or are left untreated, heatstroke can occur, a life-threatening condition.

Hypothermia and Frostbite

Be aware of hypothermia and frostbite symptoms when outdoors in cold conditions. Hypothermia is a dangerous drop in body temperature for which immediate medical attention is necessary. Symptoms often include lethargy, confusion, and a drop in both heart rate and breathing. Frostbite occurs when body tissues freeze from reduced blood and oxygen flow because blood vessels have contracted during a prolonged exposure to cold. Symptoms often include skin that feels numb or turns blue. If frostbite occurs, soak the affected area in warm water or cover it with warm clothing and seek medical attention.

Prevent these conditions by wearing several dry layers of warm wool or synthetic polypropylene clothing, carrying hand and toe warmers, drinking plenty of hot fluids, and eating regularly. When possible, take frequent indoor breaks to warm up.

ALTITUDE SICKNESS

Most visitors will not be acclimated to Colorado's high elevations. Air at higher elevations contains less oxygen, thus people at higher altitudes receive less oxygen in their body. Stay hydrated to help stave off the effects of altitude sickness. Mild reactions include lightheadedness and headaches, but

some people experience more severe reactions, such as nausea and intense headaches, especially while engaging in strenuous activities. If you feel severe symptoms, seek medical attention. Altitude sickness is usually treated by descending in elevation and resting, but there are also medications that your doctor can prescribe beforehand.

There's no way to judge how your body will react, so take it slow and give yourself several days to adjust to changes in altitude and elevation. Get plenty of sleep and avoid alcohol and other dehydrating beverages.

WILDLIFE

Colorado is home to many wild animals, the vast majority of which are shy and avoid human contact. (While hiking up Mount Yale in central Colorado, I once came across an absolutely enormous moose who simply kept chewing while I slowly backed away.) When outdoors or on the trail, always be on the lookout for wild animals, especially mountain lions, black bears, and rattlesnakes. Colorado Parks & Wildlife offers the following guidelines for interacting with wildlife:

- Observe wildlife from a safe distance.
- Move slowly, and don't surprise the animals.
- Do not chase wildlife.
- Do not feed wild animals.
- Leave young wildlife alone.

If you accidently encounter a mountain lion, bear, or other large animal, stay calm and back away slowly. Try to appear larger by raising your arms over your head. While backing away, stay aware of your surroundings; you don't want to place yourself between a mother bear and her cub. Give all creatures plenty of space and pack out any garbage or unprotected food.

Rattlesnakes are the only venomous snakes in Colorado. They are present in many areas of the state below about 9,000 feet, particularly along the Front Range, the plains, and western Colorado. Rattlesnakes blend in with their surroundings and like to hide. When exploring these regions, keep any pets close or on a leash and never place hands or feet in a spot that you can't see.

Insects, Spiders, and Parasites

Ticks are small black bugs that can transmit Rocky Mountain spotted fever and other diseases to humans and other animals. Tick habitat includes grassy areas, the edges of woodlands, and brushy areas alongside fields. Ticks are most active from spring through early summer. To avoid ticks, wear layers over your skin, use bug repellent with DEET, and tuck in your clothes. After hiking, immediately check your skin and scalp for ticks and remove any before they have time to imbed.

If a tick does attach itself to your skin, remove it. The **Centers for Disease Control & Prevention** (www.cdc.gov) provides instructions for tick removal; use tweezers to grab the tick near the mouth and pull it straight up so that the entire tick is pulled out. After pulling the tick off, clean the spot and sanitize it with rubbing alcohol. Save the tick in a sealed container and bring the specimen in for testing of Lyme disease.

Colorado has several species of spiders that can be harmful to humans. The most common is the western black widow, which is very timid and easy to recognize thanks to its shiny black color and a red hourglass on the belly. Black widows like to hang out in woodpiles and abandoned rodent holes. If bitten, head directly to the nearest hospital to receive antivenin.

Giardia is an intestinal infection caused by the parasite *Giardia lamblia.* Symptoms include cramps, diarrhea, and nausea. Giardia can be contracted by contact with fecal matter, drinking untreated water that has been infected, or eating infected food. While in the backcountry, boil or filter any drinking water and sanitize your hands prior to eating or drinking.

POISONOUS PLANTS

Poisonous, even deadly, plants grow in certain regions of Colorado. Avoid eating berries and mushrooms from plants that you are unfamiliar with. Water hemlock should be left alone, since even a very small dose can be fatal. It is identifiable by its tiny white flowers and the yellow liquid contained in its long, hollow, green stems.

EMERGENCY AND MEDICAL SERVICES

Colorado's cities offer a range of highly regarded hospitals, urgent care centers, and doctors. Many ski towns also have clinics, and the resorts have ski patrols to assist with injuries or altitude-related issues. Rural areas and small mountain towns may be farther from hospitals or urgent care centers.

CRIME

Always remain aware of your surroundings and guard any personal property. When traveling by car, lock your vehicle. In hotels, especially in larger cities, store valuables in on-site safes. Standard precautions include avoiding walking alone at night or visiting crime-plagued areas.

Resources

Suggested Reading

ART AND CULTURE

Brown, G. *Colorado Rocks! A Half-Century of Music in Colorado.* Boulder, CO: Pruett Publishing, 2004. Interviews and colorful anecdotes about the adventures of many famous musicians in Colorado, including The Beatles, Billy Joel, John Denver, and U2.

Collier, Grant. *Colorado: Moments in Time.* Lakewood, CO: Collier Publishing, 2004. One of eight Colorado nature photography books published by this professional photographer, this book focuses on many of the state's landmark attractions.

Fielder, John. *John Fielder's Best of Colorado (4th Ed.).* Denver, CO: John Fielder Publishing, 2015. One of nationally acclaimed nature photographer and conservationist John Fielder's many books on Colorado, this guide shares his insider knowledge and inspiring photographs of 165 Colorado locations gained from his two million miles of travel around the state.

Welsh, Johnny. *Weedgalized in Colorado: True Tales from the High Country.* Frisco, CO: Peak 1 Publishing LLC, 2015. An entertaining and informative read about the evolution of Colorado's cannabis culture written by a professional bartender.

FOOD

Bone, Eugenia. *At Mesa's Edge: Cooking and Ranching in Colorado's North Fork Valley.* Boston, MA: Houghton Mifflin Harcourt, 2004. Part memoir and part cookbook, this is the story of a New York City food writer whose husband convinces her to move to a ranch in tiny Crawford, Colorado, where—after struggling with loneliness, insolent skunks, and barbed wire—she slowly adjusts to a rural lifestyle and its bounty.

Castaneda, Eliza C. *Food Lovers' Guide to Colorado: Best Local Specialties, Shops, Recipes, Restaurants, Events, Lore, and More!* Guilford, CT: Globe Pequot, 2002. Part of a state-by-state series, this book is the perfect companion for traveling foodies, with good coverage of lesser-known shops, restaurants, and events.

Counihan, Carole. *A Tortilla is Like Life: Food and Culture in the San Luis Valley of Colorado.* Austin, TX: University of Texas Press, 2010. Written by an anthropology professor, this book is a collection of the food-centric histories of 19 Hispanic American women with deep roots in Colorado's San Luis Valley.

Morris, Michele. *Tasting Colorado: Favorite Recipes from the Centennial State.* Helena, MT: Farcountry Press, 2013. From Grilled Palisade Peaches and Chili-Chocolate Bourbon Cake to Buffalo Redeye Stew, this compendium of mouthwatering recipes from Colorado's guest ranches, restaurants, and bed-and-breakfasts highlights some of the best food in the state.

HISTORY

Abbott, Carl, Stephen Leonard, and David McComb. *Colorado: A History of the Centennial State (5th Ed.).* Niwot, CO: University Press of Colorado, 2013. A lengthy and exhaustively researched chronology of the entire state, with a new chapter on sports history.

Byrd, Isabella. *A Lady's Life in the Rocky Mountains.* Norman, OK: University of Oklahoma Press, 1975. The captivating story of an Englishwoman who explored the Rocky Mountains on her own one winter in the late 1800s.

Danilov, Victor J. *Colorado Museums and Historic Sites: A Colorado Guide Book.* Boulder, CO: University Press of Colorado, 2000. A comprehensive list of the state's historic sites, without much narrative.

Fay, Abbott. *A History of Skiing in Colorado.* Lake City, CO: Western Reflections, 2000. The fascinating 100-year history of Colorado's signature sport.

Fay, Abbott. *I Never Knew That About Colorado: A Quaint Volume of Forgotten Lore.* Lake City, CO: Western Reflections, 1997. Little-known anecdotes about "the fringe of Colorado history," like the time it snowed ducks on I-70.

Hafnor, John. *Strange but True, Colorado: Weird Tales of the Wild West.* Vancouver, Canada: Lone Pine Publishing, 2005. Seventy stories of little-known oddities in Colorado's history.

Iverson, Kristen. *Molly Brown: Unraveling the Myth.* Boulder, CO: Johnson Books, 1999. A fascinating and well-researched account of the *Titanic*'s best-known survivor, who struck it rich in Leadville and lived in Denver for many years.

Maclean, John N. *Fire on the Mountain: The True Story of the South Canyon Fire.* New York, NY: Harper Perennial, 2009. A critically acclaimed account of a 1994 forest fire in Colorado whose effects, through a long string of mistakes, were compounded into one of the greatest firefighting tragedies in our nation's history.

Nolte Temple, Judy. *Baby Doe Tabor: The Madwoman in the Cabin.* Norman, OK: University of Oklahoma Press, 2009. A modern retelling of the sad mining-era tale of Leadville's Baby Doe Tabor based on a record of her own writings.

Ubbelohde, Carl, Maxine Benson, and Duane Smith. *A Colorado History (10th Ed.).* Portland, OR: WestWinds Press, 2015. From the Ancestral Puebloans and Louisiana Purchase explorers to the 21st century, this is the preeminent book on the Centennial State's fascinating history.

NATURE AND ENVIRONMENT

Abbott, Lon and Terri Cook. *Geology Underfoot Along Colorado's Front Range.* Missoula, MT: Mountain Press Publishing Company, 2012. Of course I'm biased, but I believe that my husband's and my book is the best guide on Front Range geology for a lay audience.

Cassells, E. *The Archaeology of Colorado.* Boulder, CO: Johnson Books, 1997. Still the most comprehensive guide to the state's archaeological treasures, this book covers everything from Paleoindian bison and mammoth hunters to the historic Ute and Plains Native American tribes.

DeLella Benedict, Audrey. *The Naturalist's Guide to the Southern Rockies.* Ward, CO: Cloud Ridge Publishing, 2014. A guide to the natural history of the Southern Rocky Mountain landscape and the remarkable flora and fauna that have adapted to it.

Irwin, Pamela and David Irwin. *Colorado's Newest and Best Wildflower Hikes: Boulder, Breckenridge, Colorado Springs, Denver, Fort Collins, Rocky Mountain National Park, Vail.* Boulder, CO: Westcliffe Publishers, 2008. A great wildflower hiking guide for most of the places you'll want to visit, written by a dynamic author-photographer team. Other titles in this series cover the rest of the state.

Mills, Enos. *The Adventures of a Nature Guide.* London, United Kingdom: Forgotten Books, 2015. A reprint of the adventurous accounts of the founder of Rocky Mountain National Park, who widely rambled around the wild Estes Park region alone and unarmed.

Philpott, William. *Vacationland: Tourism and Environment in the Colorado High Country.* Seattle, WA: University of Washington Press, 2014. This lively book describes the post-World War II transition of the I-70 corridor and the Colorado high country from a little-visited region to a prime destination and the changing environmental attitudes accompanying it.

Tekiela, Stan. *Birds of Colorado Field Guide.* Cambridge, MN: Adventure Publications, 2011. Learn to identify more than 140 bird species that visit Colorado in this informative field guide by an award-winning naturalist.

Tekiela, Stan. *Trees of Colorado.* Cambridge, MN: Adventure Publications, 2007. Learn to identify more than 70 Colorado trees in this informative field guide by an award-winning naturalist.

Young, Mary. *Colorado Wildlife Viewing Guide (2nd Ed.).* Guilford, CT: Falcon-Guides, 2000. Maps, descriptions, and directions to the best wildlife viewing areas, along with safe-viewing tips.

RECREATION

Berman, Joshua. *Moon Colorado Camping: The Complete Guide to Tent and RV Camping.* Berkeley, CA: Avalon Travel, 2016. The most up-to-date and comprehensive guide on camping in the Centennial State is written by a *Denver Post* columnist who has been camping since the age of four months.

Foster, Lisa. *Rocky Mountain National Park: The Complete Hiking Guide.* Estes Park, CO: Renaissance Mountaineering, 2013. The most in-depth guide to exploring Rocky Mountain National Park both on and off the trail.

Lipker, Kim. *60 Hikes Within 60 Miles: Denver and Boulder Guide Book.* Birmingham, AL: Menasha Ridge Press, 2010. One of the state's best-selling hiking guides, this book covers 60 hikes within an hour of Denver and Boulder.

Mayer, Landon. *Colorado's Best Fly Fishing: Flies, Access, and Guide's Advice for the State's Premier Rivers.* Boiling Springs, PA: Headwater Books, 2011. Tips on tackle, techniques, and the best places and times to fish in Colorado.

Pearson, Mark and John Fielder. *The Complete Guide to Colorado's Wilderness Areas.* Denver, CO: John Fielder Publishing, 2002. This remains the only comprehensive guide to Colorado's 41 Wilderness Areas.

Roach, Gerry. *Colorado's Fourteeners: From Hikes to Climbs (3rd Ed.).* Golden, CO: Fulcrum Publishing, 2011. The best and most comprehensive guidebook for ascending Colorado's famous fourteeners.

Sink, Mindy. *Walking Denver: 30 Tours of the Mile-High City's Best Urban Trails, Historic Architecture, River and Creekside Paths, and Cultural Highlights.* Birmingham, AL: Wilderness Press, 2011. Explores the best paths, parks, and cultural attractions in the Mile High City through the eyes of a former *New York Times* journalist.

Warren, Scott. *100 Classic Hikes in Colorado (3rd Ed.)*. Seattle, WA: The Mountaineers Books, 2008. An inspiring list of 100 regionally organized hikes to put on your must-do list.

ATLASES

Benchmark Maps. *Colorado Road & Recreation Atlas (5th Ed.)*. Medford, OR: Benchmark Maps, 2015. The must-have collection of recreation, landscape, and metro-area maps for the entire state.

Freed, Doug. *Colorado by the Numbers: A Reference, Almanac, and Guide to the Highest State*. Grand Junction, CO: Virga, 2003. Fascinating demographics about the Centennial State, with a foreword by Governor John Hickenlooper.

Noel, Thomas and Carol Zuber-Mallison. *Colorado: A Historical Atlas*. Norman, OK: University of Oklahoma Press, 2015. This updated atlas features more than 200 color maps and photos that highlight Colorado's natural areas and little-known facts about the state.

Internet Resources

TRAVEL INFORMATION

American Southwest
www.americansouthwest.net
This website includes information on major tourist stops in southwestern Colorado, along with maps and links to hotel searches.

Bureau of Land Management Colorado
www.blm.gov
Information about BLM conservation programs, national recreation areas, and range and wild horse management areas.

Colorado Department of Transportation
www.cotrip.org
The state's best resource for up-to-date traffic conditions, travel alerts, and road closures as well as the state's 26 scenic and historic byways.

Colorado Springs Convention & Visitors Bureau
www.visitcos.com
A thorough directory of the activities, events, shops, attractions, accommodations, and restaurants in and around Colorado's second-largest city.

Colorado Tourism
www.colorado.com
The most comprehensive travel website about Colorado, with information on historic sites, ski resorts, visitor centers, and recreation areas.

Colorado Vacation Directory
www.coloradodirectory.com
Although primarily an advertising site, this directory provides information about visitor activities and amenities that can be searched by location, name, and features.

National Park Service
www.nps.gov
Detailed information on the location, natural and human history, and activities in all of Colorado's National Park Service sites, from the historic Santa Fe Trail to Trail Ridge Road in Rocky Mountain National Park.

Santa Fe Trail Association
www.santafetrail.org

Maps, sightseeing information, and other useful resources for travelers visiting all or part of the historic, 1,200-mile Santa Fe Trail.

State of Colorado
www.colorado.gov

The official State of Colorado website, with links to state parks and information on hunting and fishing licenses.

U.S. Forest Service
www.fs.usda.gov

Camping, recreation, and natural history information for the more than 13 million acres in Colorado managed by the U.S. Forest Service.

Visit Denver
www.denver.org

The official guide to Colorado's largest city and surrounding regions.

NEWS, CULTURE, AND RECREATION

14ers.com
www.14ers.com

This volunteer-run website is a resource for those who enjoying hiking the state's many fabulous 13,000- and 14,000-thousand foot-high peaks.

5280 Magazine
www.5280.com

An informative website for the greater Denver area describing everything from sports and food to bars, outdoor recreation, and local culture.

Colorado Brewers Guild
http://coloradobeer.org

Stories, photos, and videos tell the stories of the members of this craft beer-brewing guild, a nonprofit association representing more than half of the state's 300 licensed breweries.

Colorado Public Radio
www.cpr.org

The online source of information for Colorado Public Radio's news, information, and music programming.

Colorado Ski Country USA
www.coloradoski.com

Everything you need to know for planning a Colorado ski vacation.

Colorado Wine
www.coloradowine.com

Run by the Colorado Wine Industry Development Board, this site describes Colorado's winemaking tradition and has the most comprehensive information on the state's more than 120 wineries.

The Denver Post
www.denverpost.com

Colorado's largest newspaper has coverage of news, sports, and entertainment that is available free online.

ProTrails Colorado
www.protrails.com

A searchable collection of brief hiking trail descriptions throughout the state organized by location.

Index

List of Maps

Photo Credits

Also Available

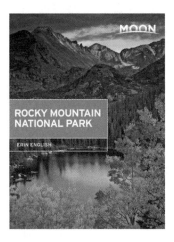

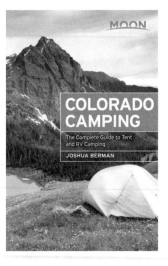

MAP SYMBOLS

═════ Expressway	○ City/Town	✈ Airport	⛳ Golf Course
──── Primary Road	◉ State Capital	✈ Airfield	P Parking Area
──── Secondary Road	⊛ National Capital	▲ Mountain	▲ Archaeological Site
┄┄┄ Unpaved Road	★ Point of Interest	✛ Unique Natural Feature	⛪ Church
──── Feature Trail	• Accommodation		⛽ Gas Station
----- Other Trail	▼ Restaurant/Bar	☇ Waterfall	Glacier
·········· Ferry	■ Other Location	▲ Park	Mangrove
═══ Pedestrian Walkway	Λ Campground	⊡ Trailhead	Reef
▥▥▥ Stairs		⛷ Skiing Area	Swamp

CONVERSION TABLES

°C = (°F - 32) / 1.8
°F = (°C x 1.8) + 32
1 inch = 2.54 centimeters (cm)
1 foot = 0.304 meters (m)
1 yard = 0.914 meters
1 mile = 1.6093 kilometers (km)
1 km = 0.6214 miles
1 fathom = 1.8288 m
1 chain = 20.1168 m
1 furlong = 201.168 m
1 acre = 0.4047 hectares
1 sq km = 100 hectares
1 sq mile = 2.59 square km
1 ounce = 28.35 grams
1 pound = 0.4536 kilograms
1 short ton = 0.90718 metric ton
1 short ton = 2,000 pounds
1 long ton = 1.016 metric tons
1 long ton = 2,240 pounds
1 metric ton = 1,000 kilograms
1 quart = 0.94635 liters
1 US gallon = 3.7854 liters
1 Imperial gallon = 4.5459 liters
1 nautical mile = 1.852 km

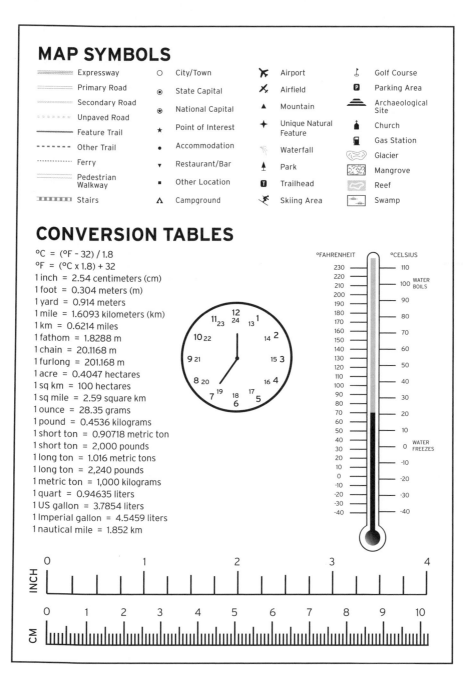

MOON COLORADO

Avalon Travel
An imprint of Perseus Books
A Hachette Book Group company
1700 Fourth Street
Berkeley, CA 94710, USA
www.moon.com

Editor: Sabrina Young
Series Manager: Kathryn Ettinger
Copy Editor: Naomi Adler Dancis
Production and Graphics Coordinator:
  Lucie Ericksen
Cover Design: Faceout Studios, Charles Brock
Interior Design: Domini Dragoone
Moon Logo: Tim McGrath
Map Editor: Kat Bennett
Cartographers: Brian Shotwell, Kat Bennett
Proofreader: Alissa Cyphers
Indexer: Greg Jewett

ISBN-13: 978-1-63121-506-3
ISSN: 1085-2697

Printing History
1st Edition — 1992
9th Edition — May 2017
5 4 3 2 1

Text © 2017 by Terri Cook.
Maps © 2017 by Avalon Travel.
All rights reserved.